His Way

A BIOGRAPHY OF **Robert Muldoon**

BARRY GUSTAFSON

AUCKLAND UNIVERSITY PRESS

First published 2000
This edition 2001

Auckland University Press
University of Auckland
Private Bag 92019
Auckland
New Zealand
http://www.auckland.ac.nz/aup

© Barry Gustafson, 2000

ISBN 1 86940 243 X

Cover design by Christine Hansen
Printed by Printlink, Wellington

HIS WAY

Dedicated to

Thea and Margaret,

the long-suffering wives of the

subject and the author.

Contents

Acknowledgements

Authors invariably accumulate numerous debts. My first and deepest thanks go to my wife, Margaret, who often found me preoccupied by this project throughout the 1990s and whose comments on various parts of the text were very helpful.

Sir Robert and Dame Thea Muldoon and their daughter Barbara Williams discussed fully and frankly with me various matters and Dame Thea made me very welcome in her home while I was researching the papers stored there. Without their input and the papers Sir Robert made so freely available to me the biography would have been far less rich in detail and insight than I believe it is.

Numerous other people made their time, recollections and opinions available to me, as listed in the Bibliography. All those interviews contributed to my account though I take full responsibility for my final analysis which often synthesises many other inputs and interpretations.

Officials of the National Party in both Head Office and the Auckland Division, notably Roger Gill, Margaret Skews and John Tremewan; members of the National Party's Parliamentary Research Unit; and staff of the National Archives and National Library, especially the Alexander Turnbull Library, assisted in locating and making available information. The Noeline and Robert Chapman Audio-visual Archive at the University of Auckland also was a major resource.

Among the papers in the Alexander Turnbull Library are those collected by Denis Wederell during the 1960s for the biography he hoped to write but did not. I was especially grateful to Mr Wederell for his permission to use this major source of information, including letters from and interviews with people who had died before I commenced my research.

During the time the book evolved a number of secretaries typed drafts of various chapters. Kay Eady, Gillian Volp, Katrina Ward, Peta Bamber, Carmel Conlan, Julia Hung, Maria Jacob and Heidi Kubler all assisted in transforming an often amended manuscript into the final typescript.

To the newspapers, photographers, cartoonists and photo archives, all acknowledged individually throughout the book, who gave me permission to produce illustrations, my thanks are also recorded.

Further improvements resulted from the comments of Brian Easton, Sir Robert Jones, and Rt Hon David Lange, who read parts of the typescript, and an anonymous reader who read the entire text. Jenny Chapman helped check a number of facts and footnotes during the copy-editing stage.

The professional expertise of the Auckland University Press, notably Elizabeth Caffin, the publisher, Simon Cauchi, the editor who also compiled the index, Katrina Duncan who designed and typeset the book, Christine Hansen, who created the cover, and Christine O'Brien and Catriona Robertson, who organised the publicity, turned the typescript into a book which I hope many will enjoy reading as much as I did researching and writing it.

Introduction

TOWARDS THE END OF 1988 SIR ROBERT MULDOON INVITED me, in my capacity as chairman of the Auckland College of Education, to come on to his Radio Pacific talkback programme on a Sunday afternoon and discuss bicultural and bilingual education. During a news break he mentioned that he had just read for the second time my biography of Michael Joseph Savage, and had enjoyed it again. I replied that one day somebody would try to write a well-researched biography of him and I hoped that person would not have the same trouble as I had experienced in getting material on Savage's life. Muldoon said that was no problem as he had kept almost everything in his archives. Almost as an afterthought I added that if he was prepared to be interviewed by me and to make his papers available I would not mind attempting the task myself. His reply was to invite me to come round and talk with him at home the following morning.

I was not confident he would agree to co-operate with me in the researching and writing of his biography because in 1984 he had been the one member of the National Party's Executive who had spoken and voted against my being authorised to write the National Party's history for the fiftieth anniversary of its foundation. He had argued that someone with my long Labour background could not possibly write a history sympathetic to the National Party. After its publication in 1986 he had telephoned to tell me he had been mistaken. He added, however, that although he could find no errors of fact and thought I had been fair, even when criticising him, nevertheless I had missed some nuances because I had not been involved personally in the events.

When I arrived at Muldoon's home the day after the broadcast, he met me at the door, ushered me into his lounge and after we had sat down said without any preamble, 'Where do you wish to start?' I replied that I thought we were going to discuss whether I would write the biography or not, but he had clearly made up his mind and simply enquired, 'Do you want to start interviewing me or do you want to know about my papers?' Over the next few years I interviewed Sir Robert eighteen times for up to four hours on some occasions. While working chronologically through the interviews we sometimes spent a whole session on a particular aspect of his philosophy, personality, policies or actions. These interviews usually took place in the lounge of his Auckland home, and each session was invariably interrupted on a number of occasions by people phoning and asking for his advice on a bewilderingly wide range of matters: for example, how to arrange a welfare benefit; could he help the caller get a state house; was their pension safe if it was paid into the ASB. Muldoon always listened carefully, responded courteously, and either suggested a remedy, offered assurance or promised to look into the matter and get back to the caller as soon as possible. He never appeared annoyed, impatient or frustrated by the interruptions.

Sir Robert gave me the combination of his office safe and the keys to two large strongrooms in which he had deposited all his public and personal papers. The collection in quantity rivalled, and in quality probably surpassed, the fabled Nash papers. He also made available to me his parliamentary office, when he was not present, and the papers there, and gave me free access to both his library and the papers stored in his garage at home. I started work on the material early in 1989 and was able almost to complete my work on the papers located in Wellington during a leave in early 1990. In 1991 and 1992 I worked on the papers in his home and also re-examined the papers of the National Party, which I had first researched in 1984 and 1985, and those in the National Research Unit and in various collections of the Alexander Turnbull Library.

I prepared a list of about 140 people whom I intended to interview and gave this list to Sir Robert for additions. He suggested another 40 people, most of whom were connected with his early or private life. Nearly all those people were interviewed although for varying reasons five declined: Bill Rowling, Colin Moyle, Bob Tizard, Ruth Richardson and Simon Upton. The last three did, however, discuss their general assessments of Muldoon in brief conversations with me. Richardson replied that she had 'total contempt for Muldoon. I dislike him and have no desire to contribute anything to his biography. He was a disaster for the party and the country.'[1] Upton and Tizard wanted to keep their stories for books they planned to write themselves. Tizard's was tentatively entitled, he told me, *Bastards I Have Met* and was to be in two volumes, the second devoted entirely to Muldoon. I also had the advantage of having frequently discussed Muldoon with Rowling, Moyle and Tizard, as well as other Labour politicians such as Norman Kirk, Arthur Faulkner and Martyn Finlay, during the 1960s and 1970s.

In the four years I worked on Muldoon's biography while he was still alive, he only three times, either in private or public, queried or commented specifically on what I was doing. On the first occasion in 1989, when at a National Party gathering he was attacking academics in general and political scientists in particular, I interjected, 'You should watch what you say, Sir Robert, because I'm going to have the last word on you.' He paused, fixed me with a steely gaze and retorted, 'I'm disappointed in you, Dr Gustafson. I didn't think it was going to be that kind of biography.'

On the second occasion he introduced me in early 1990 to some visitors to his office as the author of a biography of Michael Joseph Savage, which they should read. I commented that I was also writing one on him. When the visitors asked when it would be published, before I could reply, Muldoon stated, 'It will be a few years yet. This is not a once-over-lightly book but a carefully researched, warts-and-all biography, and I won't live to see it.'

The third occasion was a fortnight before his death when, as he farewelled me from his home, he told me to remember that 'the best thing I've ever done was to marry Tam'.

The writing of biography is very difficult; information is always only partial and both the writer and the writer's sources see things often from subjective, value-laden perspectives. There is always the danger that the subject may be lost in the context if too much material is available, as in the case of Muldoon, or that there may be considerable gaps in an author's knowledge of the subject's life, motives and relationships – gaps which either leave question marks or tempt one to speculate. There is also a danger as well as an advantage in hindsight, and any author needs to consider how their subject saw things at the time and not only how they have come to be seen in the light of subsequent outcomes or knowledge not available when a particular decision was made. Mistakes or bad decisions are often more obvious in retrospect, but even then what is judged to be a 'mistake' or a 'bad decision' may depend heavily on one's point of view. The writer of a biography must also attempt an assessment of a public figure's private life and inner personality. A good biography needs to be more that just an account of achievements, failures, virtues and vices. People are complex and often contradictory. One should go beyond a descriptive narrative into some kind of analytical assessment of the whole person without necessarily trying to force the material to fit some preconceived psycho- or socio-biographical model.

In political journalism and political biography a politician is sometimes compared to other politicians with similar characteristics. Thus Muldoon, because of some perceived similarities, has been compared variously with Winston Churchill, Richard John Seddon, Keith Holyoake, John A. Lee, Nikita Khrushchev, Benito Mussolini, Adolf Hitler, Huey Long and Richard Nixon. Such comparisons are usually misleading because of the tendency to go beyond one or two common features to attribute other characteristics consciously or subconsciously, but unfairly and inaccurately. Nevertheless, Muldoon and Nixon were similar in many ways.[2]

Both were essentially shy men, self-conscious from childhood about their height (or rather their lack of it), their appearance (each had a distinctive facial characteristic), and their relatively humble origins. Both were little influenced by their fathers but greatly influenced by strong-willed mothers and by church upbringings that emphasised individual effort, diligence, responsibility and sobriety. Driven by insecurity and a need for achievement and recognition, each man immersed himself in matters at hand and worked hard for everything he got. They believed that one should never be discouraged and should never stop fighting, no matter what the odds. In their political lives both Muldoon and Nixon made their reputations by talking tough, using scare tactics, exploiting bogus and peripheral issues as well as real and central ones, and assuming that people are motivated more by fear than by love. Each man became the public defender of individualism and capitalism but was prepared to work with socialists and communists, had a soft spot for the underdog, and was contemptuous of the establishment. They did not seek simply to defeat rivals and political foes but to destroy them, sometimes personally as well as politically. Although they became the leaders of their respective parties, they were never really accepted by many in the party hierarchies, who barely tolerated or actively disliked or even hated leaders 'from the wrong side of the tracks'. In turn Muldoon and Nixon, who were both somewhat cocooned in sycophancy at the peak of their power, had few real friends, trusted almost no one, and when their usefulness to their parties ended were left finally to face their enemies alone, unrepentant and unbowed.

Two questions need to be considered when writing or reading political biography: what is political leadership and power, and what should such a study include and possibly exclude?

Those of you who have read my biography of Michael Joseph Savage will recollect my debt to James McGregor Burns's book *Leadership*, in which a distinction is made between the moral leader and the transactional leader.[3] The moral leader is one who seeks to inspire change; the transactional leader manages the status quo. Moral leadership appeals to less selfish values and seeks to redefine people's legitimate personal aspirations and needs in such a way that the consciences of people are aroused and they are moved to righteous action. Needs become rights, rights become hopes, hopes become aspirations, and aspirations become expectations. A transactional leader, on the other hand, bargains for votes by offering jobs, houses, pensions, and the satisfaction of the voters' short-term needs, wants and emotions. The transactional leader is not a dictator, for a dictator does not lead in the sense of having to persuade and seek assent from those who are governed. But the transactional leader does tend to ignore long-term strategy in favour of short-term tactics. The immediate goal and detailed management become more important than any vision. Such a leader seeks not to turn a minority crusade into reality but to identify and cultivate a majority of voters in order to achieve, and remain in, power.

It would be easy to say that Sir Robert Muldoon was simply and clearly a transactional leader, a political manager and manipulator of public opinion, but I am not prepared to do so. He has proved somewhat more difficult for me to categorise than Savage, but I do not believe, as most of his critics argue, that he was interested solely in office and power for its own sake. He did seek to serve a higher end, even if that end was only to achieve what his detractors ridicule, leaving New Zealand no worse than he found it and striving to defend Keynesian economic management and the welfare state, which he believed had served New Zealand well throughout much of his lifetime.

Muldoon was certainly not a radical reformer. He believed in, and indeed excelled in, operating the levers of power but took time to get used to new ideas. Many he could not accept because of what he judged to be the human cost. Despite his sometimes fiery rhetoric, he was a careful, cautious, and moderate man when it came to policy. In many ways his intimidating manner was a defensive mask behind which he hid his innate shyness and insecurity. Even when uncertain he did not prevaricate but projected himself as positive, confident and firmly one way or the other. As one of his critics in caucus observed, as a result of his early life Muldoon constantly sought respect and

> built up a rhinoceros skin around a very vulnerable inner self. Totally contrary to public opinion which saw him as a shafting bastard he was really a sensitive, caring man who couldn't pursue policies that hurt people. That paralysed him in the later years of his premiership . . . His humanity was one of the major directing forces and constraints on him. He worried like hell trying to find policies to shelter people from pain and that led to his ad hoc intervention.[4]

The laissez-faire free market as an economic mechanism was always something he distrusted. It needed to be regulated in the interests of ordinary people. He found it increasingly difficult, however, to find a middle way between too much intervention and too much emphasis on fair distribution, on the one hand, and efficiency of production and rational market signals on the other.

He also distrusted theories based on ideology, whether from the extreme Left or the extreme Right. He opposed egalitarianism but he also opposed elitism. His goal was always a fair society characterised by equality of opportunity. In explaining in 1984 why he rejected New Right economic advice from the International Monetary Fund, the Treasury, the Reserve Bank, and some National Party colleagues, he commented: 'Politicians put the social content into Treasury advice. Treasury advice is hard, it's cold and very narrow. It is correct if you want to achieve a result rapidly.'[5] As he remarked to another interviewer, 'the excessively simplistic attitude of those people . . . the rigid adherence to what they espouse would be disastrous, and would cause massive increases in unemployment and business failure.'[6]

True leadership, Muldoon believed, involved going with one's instincts, not just with one's informed intellect. There had to be a balance between any leader's ability to absorb, understand and utilise knowledge and their intuitive common sense and feel for public opinion. Politicians had to feel for people as well as think about policies and processes. He was relentlessly sceptical of those who advocated Utopian ideological solutions which involved sacrificing the welfare of many individual people in the present for the sake of advancing some dubious collective good in the future.

Like Seddon, Massey and Holyoake before him, Muldoon was anti-elitist and anti-intellectual and exalted 'ordinary people' and their wishes and interests.[7] Those leaders fostered and represented a popular conservatism which reflected the reality of New Zealand's social make-up, refashioning and blending radical and conservative themes. Populists, such as Muldoon undoubtedly was, also tend to oppose both the class systems and also the estrangement of individuals from society. They stress conformity rather than pluralism and attack equally the left-wing 'stirrers' or the right-wing 'greedies' who threaten the unity or prosperity of the 'ordinary people'. They see the role of the government as being to manage an economy and a society in which individuals can enjoy the opportunities of capitalism while being protected from its excesses. Populists value stability and strongly oppose intellectuals whose ideas may cause systemic instability and resulting insecurity for many individual men and women. Muldoon, like most populists, had a clear idea of the type of society he wanted, and in retrospect he argued that from 1975 until 1984 'I spent nearly nine years keeping the farmers on their farms, the small businessmen in business, the workers in their jobs and the families in their homes.'[8]

As a top-down force that meets, manipulates and mobilises but does not initially create the bottom-up force of collective discontent, populist leaders are strong personalities with an obsessive will to be leader, the ego to believe that they have more ability and integrity than their rivals, and are ready to run personal risks, endure contempt and ridicule, and rise to conflict. Such politicians articulate discontent, usually appeal to some nostalgic and over-romanticised virtues of the past, promise hope for the future, and ask voters for their trust. Their charisma is enhanced by the situation and by what they have come to symbolise. In the eyes of a significant section of the community such a leader becomes the defender of the people's cause, promising protection from the upheavals that threaten or disadvantage them and promising justice, or revenge, against those who exploit or oppress them or are seen as a danger. The more a populist leader is attacked by the political, commercial, intellectual and social establishment, the more they are perceived as a hero with a moral agenda and the courage of their convictions. And in the television age an electronic populist is able to appeal directly to their constituency above and beyond the confines or intermediacy of press or party.

Muldoon was the last prime minister of New Zealand who grew up in hard times and experienced personally the consequences of two world wars. Like Holland and Holyoake, his predecessors as party leader, he was, as one journalist observed, 'pragmatic, non-doctrinaire, materialistic and reflected the upwardly mobile in a country which knew affluence without extremes of wealth, and where those whose industry matched their aspirations could build a good life for themselves.'[9] But by 1985 Muldoon was the representative of a bygone era battling against a new generation which was coming to dominate both the Labour and National parties.

Although a statist and a centralist, Muldoon was not a Marxist socialist, as some right-wing critics suggested. Nevertheless, although Labour saw Muldoon as the symbol of everything that was wrong, he was in political conviction and concern for the majority of ordinary people the most sympathetic of all National's leaders towards Labour's traditional aims. Despite his fervent denials, he was influenced by broader socialist ideals as well as populism when he intervened in the economy to prevent or minimise unemployment, or to establish social policies such as national superannuation, or to defend strong, universally accessible, public health and education systems – all of which were paid for by direct taxation and thus brought about a redistribution of wealth from the more fortunate to the less fortunate members of society. As the editor of the *Dominion* perceptively commented when Muldoon retired from Parliament, Muldoon had 'a healthy regard for community values, and that shaped his style of government and economic management. His background dictated that . . . His was the socialism of middle New Zealand, and . . . there is widespread support for his philosophy that poverty is intolerable, and affection for the old man in his battle to preserve it.'[10]

Unlike most socialists, however, Muldoon was also a pragmatic stabiliser. His values, outlook and objectives were rooted firmly in his own experiences and not in the realm of his imagination. He was not an innovator or even a leader able to adapt easily to organic systemic change. He sought to make the New Zealand system more efficient and more humane, not to change it fundamentally. In the end it can be argued that his vision became too restricted to the present and too narrow in considering alternatives, and he became paralysed and discredited by his own pragmatism. He made stability his highest, indeed overriding, goal and ironically, in doing so, he made it more likely that his departure would be followed by radical change.

Muldoon had the potential to go down in New Zealand's history as a great prime minister but fell short of realising that potential because of two flaws in his personality. The less important of the two, though the one most people remember, was his abrasive and sometimes savage reaction to opposition and criticism. He could be, and often was, impatient, intimidating, scary even, and easily moved to contempt or cold anger. More important, however, was his innate conservatism which prevented his taking advantage of his majority after 1975 to restructure and deregulate New Zealand's economy more gradually, more rationally and more humanely than Roger Douglas and the Fourth Labour Government were partly forced and partly chose to do after 1984. Muldoon's concern for the ordinary person would have tempered the social consequences of the economic reforms, and his common sense would have softened the harsh ideological dogmatism of the extreme proponents of the New Right.

Certainly Muldoon was neither blind to the problems facing New Zealand nor deaf to the various solutions the IMF and younger and more radical economists in the Reserve Bank and Treasury were proposing. But either because he thought the social costs were too great, or because he believed he could still make the old system work, or because he thought that the voters would punish his party too much, or perhaps for all three reasons, he missed the opportunity to save by more pragmatic reform the mixed economy and the welfare state to which he was so genuinely attached. He forgot or perhaps chose to ignore the adage that those who wish to avoid eventual revolutionary change must manage evolutionary change. There are dangers in being too conservative. Like his mentor Holyoake, Muldoon chose to postpone radical reform, buy off the interest groups, and marginalise and denigrate his opponents. It was not enough and both he and the system he sought to defend were swept away after 1984. Following any revolution the old regime rarely gets a fair deal. History is written by victors and by survivors. Muldoon became nearly everyone's scapegoat.

The 'great person' approach to history or politics often ignores or minimises the supporting cast around the leader and the symbiotic relationship between the two. As one writer has observed, power is essentially the ability to get things done and that invariably requires the co-operation of others, usually through a complex and extensive organisation.[11] Power is not found in isolation but in relationships, especially with one's colleagues, allies, subordinates and constituents. As Gardner has noted, 'Leaders cannot maintain authority . . . unless followers are prepared to believe in that authority. In a sense leadership is conferred by followers.'[12] Nothing Muldoon achieved could have occurred without the (often enthusiastic) support or at the very least the acquiescence of others. Muldoon may have been the most influential member of the third National Government but he was not solely responsible either for all the successes or for all the mistakes of the administration he led and personified.

People whose power is perceived as growing attract followers and authority, as Muldoon did in the mid-1970s. Leaders perceived as losing power find their support dwindling and their views increasingly challenged by those seeking to distance themselves from them or to replace them. Formal authority, position and power are granted by others and are withdrawn when a leader's reputation for being effective erodes. This is especially so when many of those supporters in cabinet, caucus and the party organisation have a 'love–hate' relationship with the leader. Leaders who become too self-centred, arrogant and uncaring about the sensitivities and egos of others may well lose essential allies and even create active opposition among those on whom their continued leadership depends. In his earlier years Muldoon assiduously cultivated many of his colleagues and built coalitions of support in both caucus and the National Party organisation. In later years he became almost contemptuous of their opinions and feelings, and even those who still respected him no longer particularly liked him. Nevertheless, until 1984 few criticised or opposed him openly, and after 1984 the attempt by many of his former allies and sycophants to make him the sole scapegoat for the 1975–84 National Government's failures infuriated him and his remaining admirers and defenders, not least his erstwhile friend and critic, Sir Robert Jones. As another of Muldoon's long-time critics within the Wellington Division of the National Party observed shortly before Muldoon was deposed as leader, he felt sorry for him because for years Muldoon had been 'the victim of a gutless caucus . . . the victim of a gutless cabinet' and of a Dominion Council which also had not held the leader accountable.[13]

To recognise the complicity of others is not to diminish the impact of leadership. A powerful leader is one who, by the strength of their personality, self-confidence and drive, ideas, knowledge and competence, can inspire and mobilise others and influence the decisions and direction of an organisation in order to achieve results the leader desires. Gaining, exercising and retaining power is demanding and exhausting work and requires focus, a capacity to keep learning, adaptability and survival. To be able to do all that requires physical, mental and emotional strength, energy, perseverance, on occasions ruthlessness, and not a little luck. Power is achieved and maintained one transaction at a time and demands continuous success if it is not to be challenged.

Muldoon believed that people wanted a strong, competent leader and sought to cultivate that image. His early reputation, however, was built not only on his firm, direct even abrasive image but more on his projection of ability, reliability, sense of direction and achievement. A very effective performer on television, he might not have been so successful in gaining or retaining power in an earlier era when television was less important and the party caucus and organisation more important. Television enabled him to appeal directly to the broader electorate and project himself not as an equivocator or vacillator but as a decisive, predictable and persistent politician. He was seen as a competent manager with a strong agenda. His power became much more fragile as that image came under increasing pressure in the early 1980s, as his competence was called into question and as both colleagues and voters came to dwell more on his arrogance.

Power is won by being in the right place at the right time and seizing the opportunity as Muldoon did both in 1967, when he first became Minister of Finance, and in 1974 when he replaced Jack Marshall. His willingness between those dates to work hard, to be loyal to Holyoake, and to get things done also won him Holyoake's support, first as a mentor and eventually as an indispensable ally in the leadership contest with Marshall. Once in power, as Muldoon again showed, a leader has enhanced opportunities to control information and agendas, allocate resources, cultivate and reward allies and subordinates, sideline or punish critics and rivals, appeal directly to the party organisation or to the electorate, and continue to build formal authority and personal reputation. Leaders also can advance their own goals and programmes and thwart alternatives. However, Muldoon also exemplified the fact that if power becomes too much invested in a single leader and that person's insight, judgement or communication skills begin to fail, then the organisation, party or government the person leads may be gravely damaged.

With his devastating personality and fearsome intellect, and holding as he did the two most important posts of prime minister and minister of finance with their superior access to and command of information, Muldoon had too much power. Because power is exercised nearly always in situations of conflict and confrontation, he came to be seen as a dogmatic dictator. His power became too centralised and too arbitrary, and in many ways his government became presidential rather than parliamentary in both style and substance. He appeared to be the type of leader who believed that team dynamics and processes and devolved management inhibited his individual decisiveness and control. Over time not only most of his cabinet and caucus colleagues but also party officials, government advisers and interest group leaders all became disenchanted with his personality, policies and leadership style because they believed he did not respect them, consult them, trust them or listen to them sufficiently.

As both New Zealand and the world changed markedly during the 1970s and 1980s, new approaches, relationships and policies were required. Muldoon was reluctant to innovate and to a large extent was trapped by past habits, previous policy choices and traditional loyalties. He failed even to recognise the need for dramatic change, let alone accomplish it. Because Muldoon's style of government was pitched to a previous era and to older values, it appealed less and less to younger New Zealanders who wanted to remove the restrictions on them that had originated in and been justified by the depression and war in the 1930s and 1940s. As Pfeffer has commented, 'Power is lost . . . because circumstances are often more changeable than we are'.[14]

Muldoon did not totally lose his power after he lost the position of prime minister or even the position of National Party leader in 1984. Certainly he lost his major platform with its accompanying status and rewards but, following a short period of assessment, he reasserted himself and advocated his views directly through the Sunday Club, in weekly broadcasts on Radio Pacific, and internationally through his chairmanship of the Global Economic Action Institute. For any person the loss of power and position can be painful, indeed devastating, even though rationally one must accept that nothing is surer than that those who acquire power will in time lose it. Political parties constantly rejuvenate themselves by bringing in new people, new ideas and new skills to cope with new problems, demands and constituencies. There is an organic process of continuing transformation. But knowing when to let go, and being able to do so with grace, is comparatively rare among politicians. Quite apart from enjoying the intrinsic satisfactions and perquisites of a position of power, leaders such as Muldoon, who continue to regard themselves as more able and more popular than their rivals and potential successors, find it very hard to give up the leadership and go quickly and quietly.

Another question concerning leadership is whether leaders are born or made, whether genetics or socialisation are the determining factors. Intelligence and physical energy are clearly characteristics of most successful politicians but on their own are not enough. What distinguishes a successful politician is not intelligence or physical energy, characteristics shared by many others, but the compulsive, sometimes obsessive, ambition and personal desire to lead which, coupled with the luck of being in the right place at the right time, allows a few to emerge from the many.

Some leading politicians, because of their childhood or adolescent experiences, exhibit a greater need for self-esteem, authority over their life, and willingness to take risks than others. Some political analysts and historians make much of the connection between early childhood socialisation and later adult attitudes, personality and behaviour. John Henderson, for example, in 1982 used the work of James Barber on the character of US presidents to make a tentative assessment of New Zealand prime ministers.[15] Henderson categorised New Zealand prime ministers into active and passive, positive and negative personalities. Muldoon, like Kirk, Seddon, Massey, Savage and Fraser, was clearly an active rather than a passive politician. He was very energetic, enjoyed rather than endured political life and had few other satisfactions apart from politics. According to Henderson's analysis, however, Muldoon exhibited active-negative characteristics in that he tended to distrust colleagues, was consumed by compulsive ambition, sought power almost to the exclusion of other objectives and hid his insecurity beneath a very aggressive front. He was certainly not an example of two of Henderson's and Barber's other categories, the passive-negative category of reluctant politician or the passive-positive category of non-aggressive consensus seekers. The fourth category, active-positive, are often the achievers who are free from self-centred inner demands that prevent rational decisions and who make choices that can be altruistic and not limited by personal needs. While no doubt a case might be made for putting Muldoon in this category, he does appear on the surface to fit more clearly with most of New Zealand's great politicians in the active-negative category.

This brings me to my second question of what is biography, particularly political biography. In July 1984 the Stout Research Centre for the Study of New Zealand Society, History and Culture held its inaugural conference. The conference theme was 'Biography in New Zealand' and the papers were subsequently published.[16] At that conference Colin Davis questioned whether biography was important at all, arguing that 'politics is essentially a social activity; to individualise from one perspective is to distort and misunderstand it'.[17] I cannot agree. Certainly, as one political historian has observed, politicians' personalities 'merge into the organic life of their office, and their stories become hard to distinguish from the history of the nation itself'.[18] A Lenin or a Stalin, a Gorbachev or a Yeltsin, a Hitler or a Mussolini, a Churchill or a Thatcher, a Savage or a Muldoon, a Roger Douglas or a Ruth Richardson may be to a large extent the product of 'social activity', but it is a symbiotic relationship and individuals do react to and influence their social and political environments to varying extents. I am not a Marxist determinist who believes that individuals have no significant impact on their own life, their environment and history, although it would be foolish to deny that factors outside one's own control provide opportunities and limitations to what any individual or indeed group of people can achieve. Individuals do make a difference. They cannot be separated from their context but neither should they be regarded as passive irrelevancies in a detailed analysis of that context or buried in some collective mass.

Jock Phillips asked a slightly different question in 1984 though it was related to Davis's assertion. Phillips, who unlike Davis accepted a relationship but was not certain exactly what it was or whether it could ever be accurately defined, asked, 'Can a biographer ever penetrate to the inner reality of another person's life?'[19] My response is that a biography is one person's version of another person's life. Of course it is a presumption to write about someone else for no one completely understands their own complex motivations and inconsistencies, let alone another person's. But that should not prevent the attempt being made.

In the preface to my biography of Savage I argued that as a biographer I see a person as essentially what he or she does, and when and where and, in so far as I can ascertain, why. My biography of Savage was, and my biography of Muldoon will be, basically a historical narrative with only passing attention to psycho-biography or psycho-history. Readers will discern in my attempt to analyse Sir Robert Muldoon elements of psychology, sociology, political science, public administration, economics and philosophy as well as history, but all are incidental to my prime purpose of following Muldoon as I tried to follow Savage through his life and describe it as accurately as I can. Contemporary events which do not directly concern that life I largely ignore but many other incidents are selected, described and analysed in some detail, not only because of their importance as events in the life of Muldoon but also because of the light they throw on his character, motivation and achievements.

No biographer can be completely sure that he or she has captured the whole truth. Indeed I believe no one can. But without descending to either hagiography or a desire to sensationalise or discredit it is possible to tell a story presenting, as accurately and as honestly as one can, the public and private life, relationships, successes and failures, joys and sorrows, the process of socialisation (particularly in the critical early years) that formulated character, personality, perspectives, expectations, goals, inhibitions, identity, the stock of ideas, values, influences and where they came from – and, most tentatively of all, inner motivation and self-image. Where possible, I let the events and the person speak for themselves without embellishing them with superfluous interpretation.

Keith Sinclair in his address to the 1984 conference strongly attacked a 'life and times' approach to biography.[20] He argued that a writer should be very selective so that the person does not disappear behind masses of detail about the politics, society or economy in which the person lived and operated. 'In a biography, events revolve around the person, and not vice-versa.' The revelation and exploration of character must be accorded the highest priority, and indeed Sinclair went as far as to argue that there is no such thing as 'political biography'. He asserted that 'Biography is biography . . . Its ultimate aim is to present a personality, to reveal the inner man, "the dialogue of self with soul."'[21]

As I have suggested earlier, I tend to agree with Sinclair's warning that a biography should not also be the history of a nation or of a government or of a political party. But it seems to me to be impossible to ignore the times – the environment – with which the subject of the biography interacted and which provided that individual with socialisation, opportunities, challenges, limits, tasks, alliances, and opponents. There is clearly an inextricable interrelationship between a politician such as Muldoon and the world about him. One must discuss the social, economic, cultural, political, intellectual and administrative context that helped make him what he was and to which he responded. Only by examining many episodes, many layers, many relationships, many incidents, many aspects of a person's life, some better documented than others, can one approach the essential core of one's subject and see patterns emerge.

Muldoon had the misfortune to be prime minister during one of the most difficult periods in New Zealand's history. The country's high living standards could not be maintained by its traditional agricultural production and exports, no matter how technically efficient. The entry of Britain to the European Economic Community and the ending of imperial preference, the collapse of the Bretton Woods agreement which had underpinned the international monetary system, the two oil shocks of the 1970s, long-term out-of-control international inflation, a collapse of agricultural commodity prices, and the start of the electronic information age – all made obsolete the assumptions and arrangements which both Labour and National politicians had taken for granted and relied on for almost half a century. Muldoon was a product of that earlier era. He understandably found it difficult to accept that the changes which were taking place both locally and globally were irreversible and required imaginative new policies, not simply more careful management and more detailed intervention along traditional lines.

By the mid-1970s the Keynesian assumption that full employment, an expanding economy and a stable currency could be achieved by central government management, deficit financing and high public expenditure was being seriously questioned. Economic stagnation, rising unemployment, high interest rates and crippling rates of inflation forced governments throughout the Western world to question the economic orthodoxy that had prevailed since the Great Depression of the 1930s. Also challenged was the high level of taxation required to maintain the welfare state, to subsidise farmers, big businesses and militant unionists, and to support a pervasive bureaucracy. Muldoon found it very difficult intellectually and psychologically to abandon the values and methods of Keynesian orthodoxy; indeed, he never did.

I certainly agree with another of Sinclair's assertions that 'while history aspires to be a social science, biography aspires to be literature. In many ways the biography resembles the novel.' Indeed, I would take it further. In research I am very much a historian and social scientist leaving no stone unturned, examining evidence, seeking insights from models and paradigms, and suspending judgement until all the evidence is in – or as much as I am able to find. One of the reasons why my biography of Savage took six years to research and write was that I had to search assiduously both in New Zealand and Australia for little-known, fragmentary, long-lost snippets of evidence. In the case of Muldoon it has taken me ten years, partly because I kept being distracted by other duties and projects, and partly because the evidence and material and the number of people with insights and information and opinions provided such a vast resource that I was worried about overlooking a major piece of evidence or not properly considering someone else's informed judgement about some incident or detail. But when I came to compress and generalise from the mountain of evidence, when I started to make judgements and sought to tie together my research into what I hoped would become a sophisticated whole, then I did resemble a novelist developing the structure of the book, the plot, the context, the interrelationship among characters and above all the characterisation of my central figure to portray the essence of that person's life.

In his contribution in 1984, Katherine Mansfield's biographer Antony Alpers referred to 'primary biography' – a process which presents information and a viewpoint but from which later analytical works will follow, drawing on the basic facts established in the primary biography but often arguing a revisionist interpretation.[22] Muldoon wrote half a dozen books on his life, views and achievements.[23] Others, such as Spiro Zavos, have attempted biographies.[24] Hugh Templeton and Sir Robert Jones have written their reminiscences of Muldoon.[25] A two-part television documentary, *Muldoon: The Grim Face of Power*, 1994, was a very negative, one-dimensional attempt at revisionist interpretation after Muldoon's death by Neil Roberts, who had been responsible in 1989 for an obsequious *Magic Kiwi* television programme on Muldoon while he was still alive. My biography of Muldoon is different from all of these but it will not be, I suspect, the last word and may well be used as a primary biography by subsequent analysts. The detailed research that I have summarised in the biography will provide many pegs on which differing interpretations of Muldoon may be hung in the future.

As one political scientist who knew him well has observed, 'No one is neutral about Sir Robert. He provoked in the electorate almost equal measures of blind rage and unquestioning adoration. Rob's Mob was no figment of his imagination, but a considerable slice of the electorate for whom he embodied an assurance that it was all right to feel as they did, and that he would keep the world the way they wanted it.'[26] I doubt whether many people, either those who uncritically supported him such as Rob's Mob or those who totally denounced and condemned him, will agree completely with my overall assessment, which sets out neither to praise nor condemn but seeks to portray and understand a man of many strengths and certainly some equally great weaknesses.

Erik Olssen, in a commentary on Sinclair's paper in 1984, noted that politicians have a vested interest in projecting a public persona.[27] Certainly this is true of Muldoon, who carefully cultivated his public image, an image incidentally which his opponents in the Labour Party were prepared to accept and to see consolidated. But was the public image the real person and did it truly reflect his self-view, his philosophy of life, his conscious and subconscious motivation? Nearly everyone thinks they know the real Muldoon. My research suggests that few if any knew the whole man. People saw one aspect of his life over a particular finite time and generalised from that. Many of those I interviewed had a narrow or partial relationship with him. Some were strongly subjective, sometimes understandably so, in their assessment of him. Nearly all agreed that he was very intelligent, had an astonishing memory, was able quickly and accurately to comprehend briefings, was decisive in making decisions though if time permitted he could defer them for further consideration, was willing to listen to other opinions even if he didn't accept them, was impeccably formal with his professional advisers, was totally loyal (indeed, to a fault) to those who loyally supported him, was sympathetic and patient with the underdog, and was able to speak clearly, effectively and with authority. Most also commented on his commitment to an independent public service, the long hours of intense work he put in year after year, and his independence and toughness in resisting pressure from powerful interest groups. There was also general agreement that he could be extremely brutal verbally when dealing with other politicians (National as well as Labour) and that he became increasingly preoccupied with the detailed management of government and short-term political tactics, neglecting broader and long-term interests to the detriment of both his party and the country. The general picture of the public Muldoon, therefore, is reasonably well known and was not too difficult to portray in the biography, although the details of numerous incidents did make writing it a technically difficult task.

More difficult, however, was determining the extent to which one discusses the private person in political biography. Olssen argued that 'it is the person as a politician you are interested in', not unconnected aspects of the person's life. Certainly as biographer I have no problem with discussing some aspects of the private Muldoon, a man shy and sensitive in some ways, brutal and insensitive in others. One has to point out the mischievous sense of humour and dry wit evident in the private man which sometimes misfired in public, and one cannot ignore assessing the possible influence of alcohol as a factor in several major political incidents such as the calling of the 1984 election or the attack on Colin Moyle. Beyond that, the biographer may well be inhibited by sensitivity to the feelings of surviving relatives and may have to make decisions on whether or not to include or to explore certain material such as rumours and allegations of extramarital sexual liaisons. Indeed, the overall picture of the man may not be accurately reflected if undue attention is paid to one or two incidents of interest to muckrakers or sensation-seekers. Whether a politician has an affair with someone may be of general interest or of use in assessing him as a person but it may also be very peripheral to political biography.[28]

Olssen argued that a biographer had to like someone before spending five or six years or more studying and reliving their life; I'm not certain that is necessarily true. Sinclair, I believe, was somewhat bored by and contemptuous of Nash but wrote an excellent biography of him. I liked Savage and enjoyed every moment I spent on that biography. Muldoon I found fascinating, and the hours I spent interviewing him were among the most stimulating of my professional career. Although I spent much of my earlier life as one of his political opponents, I believe I have been fair in recreating his life and have been able to see his point of view, though not always agreeing with it. Certainly, had I been someone whom in the past he had demolished personally, I would have found it very difficult to be objective or to want to spend my time thinking or writing about him. Indeed, I was somewhat disconcerted when I opened his files on Labour Party MPs and members to find at the top of the first folder notes and newspaper clippings on me dating back twenty years.

Muldoon certainly did not cultivate a 'nice guy' image. When he was 'absolutely livid those present actually felt the electricity in the air to the point where people were almost afraid to breathe. Muldoon could inject that amount of fear and drama.'[29] His reputation for brutal counterpunching made opponents reluctant to get into a verbal fight with him for fear of being mauled in retaliation. There are those who came into conflict with Muldoon, some of whom I have interviewed, who are scarred emotionally for life. Many others became almost totally dominated by him. Some respected him. Others disliked him as much as he despised them.

Suffice it to say in conclusion that, in my opinion and taking into account the length of time and the extent to which they personally dominated the political agenda, there are eight great political figures in New Zealand history over the past hundred years: Seddon, Massey, Savage, Fraser, Sidney Holland, Holyoake, Muldoon and Roger Douglas, the last the only one in my list not to become prime minister. Only two of those men were really radicals who changed the shape and nature of our economy and our society: Savage and Douglas. Muldoon was a populist conservative who sought, by and large, to defend by centralised and interventionist regulation the political, economic and social values and systems that the Liberals and the Savage Labour Government established. In the end he failed and the ultra-conservative Muldoon was replaced as minister of finance by a radical Labour politician who quickly, systematically and probably irreversibly demolished the first Labour Government's heritage. Towards the end of his life Muldoon fulminated impotently from the sidelines against the destruction of a Labour-created New Zealand way of life that he as National's leader had devoted his life to preserving. That I see as one of the great ironies of New Zealand political history.

CHAPTER I

Family and Childhood

ALMOST HALF NEW ZEALAND'S MALE POPULATION OF MILITARY age served in the armed forces during the 1914–18 war. Half of those became casualties and one in seven died on the slopes of Gallipoli or the fields of Flanders. Among those who returned to New Zealand many were old before their time, traumatised by the ghastly experiences they had endured. They returned to a country in which war profiteers and speculators had flourished but where returned soldiers had to struggle to find a job or a home and re-establish themselves into civilian life. Many of those who did start a business or break in a farm found their dreams and achievements subsequently smashed by the Great Depression which started in the later years of the 1920s.

Staff Sergeant James Henry (Jim) Muldoon, a clerk at Kempthorne and Prosser Ltd, Auckland, who had been born at West Derby near Liverpool on 21 April 1882, and his younger brother Corporal John Wesley (Wes) Muldoon, a salesman with the NZ Farmers Co-operative in Ashburton, were two such survivors.[1] The sons of James Henry Muldoon (senior) and Jane Ellen Muldoon (née Griffith), they had enjoyed a stable, religious, family-centred upbringing which had ill equipped them for the horrors of trench warfare.

Their father, born in Enniskillen, Ulster, and their mother, born in Dwygy-fyllchi, Wales, were evangelical Methodists. In 1892 James senior decided to leave his job as manager of a grocery shop in West Derby, Lancashire, and emigrate to New Zealand as an unordained missionary of the Methodist Church. The family settled first in Collingwood Street and later in Seymour Street in Auckland where James became an evangelist and social worker in charge of the Helping Hand Mission in Freeman's Bay, for many years one of the poorest working-class areas in New Zealand. A strongly evangelical and fundamentalist lay preacher, opposed (in his grandson's words) to 'Satan, the Pope, and the Demon Rum', James Muldoon during 1893 conducted evangelical meetings in eighteen North Island towns and 'upwards of 350 persons professed conversion during the tour, and about the same number of christians and backsliders were restored'.[2] James, who later became a land agent and Justice of the Peace, was a prominent member of the Pitt Street

Methodist Church, where he formed and led the Wesleyan Young Men's Institute and coached the Pitt Street Methodist Association Football Club. The church's successful soccer team included not only the two Muldoon boys but also the Gunson brothers, the sons of Auckland's 1915–25 mayor, and the Winstone brothers, one of whom, Frank, captained the team.

Before the war, Jim and Wes Muldoon were healthy, happy, rather 'proper' young men. Jim, although short and stocky, was a fine sportsman who switched from soccer to rugby, playing while working as an accounts clerk in a produce merchants in Oamaru for a team which won the North Otago Rugby Football Union tournament. Later he became an Auckland senior rugby referee, 'who gave his decisions in no uncertain manner. Players both large and small accepted his decisions with respect.'[3] Wes shifted to Wellington to work. Gregarious and popular he became engaged to a Wellington girl. Then came the war. When Wes's fiancée's brother joined him overseas, he found that his future brother-in-law, a teetotaller before the war, was in custody for creating disorder in the YMCA, disobeying an officer and allowing a prisoner to escape. Wes returned from the war a 'larrikin' and an alcoholic and the engagement broke up.[4]

Some indication of what the two brothers and many other young men experienced in the trenches overseas is given in Wes's diary. On the day he landed at Gallipoli, for example, he wrote that 'Old mates of mine from all over NZ have been killed and wounded and it was a pitiful sight to pass the lonely graves on the beach.'[5] Two months later he described how 'On Sunday evening it was murder here. The Turks came in hundreds hurling themselves into our trenches . . . It was just a shambles. The place ran with blood . . . sick of all this fighting.'[6] In September, weak with dysentery, Wes was evacuated but recovered physically to fight on in France.

His brother Jim, who had earlier spent three years with the North Otago Mounted Rifles, at the age of 33 sailed to Europe with the 4th Battalion of the New Zealand Rifle Brigade and served in Egypt and France for three years and twenty-four days from 1915 to 1918.

Returning to New Zealand in January 1919, Jim Muldoon started his own grain and seed business at Whangarei, where two of his sisters lived and where his mother retired to after her husband's death. Unfortunately, the business, which was inadequately insured, burnt down shortly after Jim had married Amie Rusha Browne at the Kingsland Methodist Church on 29 October 1919. Jim returned to Auckland and got a job as a meter reader at the Auckland Electric Power Board and also did some part-time bookkeeping work. On 25 September 1921, when Jim was 39 and Amie 32, a son, Robert David Muldoon, was born at 'Willesden' hospital in Gillies Avenue, Auckland. He was named Robert after a friend of his parents, Frank Robinson, who had been killed at Passchendaele. Jim Muldoon was described on his son's birth certificate as a 'Government Inspector'. At the time of Rob's birth his parents were living at 8 Bellwood Avenue, Mount Eden. In 1922 the family moved into a house they built with a state loan at 34 (later renumbered 20) Western Springs Road. Amie was to live there until she died in her sleep in

October 1968, a few weeks before her eightieth birthday, and her only son Rob lived there apart from his war service until his marriage at the age of 29 in 1951.

Amie had been born at Napier on 29 November 1888 and was the eldest child of Jerusha (also known as Rusha) Browne (née Smith), whose father had owned a brickworks at Badingham in Suffolk, and Walter Clayton Browne, who was the display manager of the Auckland Department store Smith and Caugheys. The couple, who had married in England in 1885 but migrated to New Zealand the following year, had two other children, Walter (Wally) and Florence (Flossie), but Jerusha's 'no-hoper husband' walked out on her and the children about 1905 and reportedly went to Australia. He was never again mentioned in the family and Jerusha developed a strong dislike for male 'rotters'.[7]

None of Jerusha's children went to secondary school, although Wally was top of English at Newton East Primary School. The family, though respectable, was very poor and Jerusha and Amie both worked as seamstresses. Wally from the age of 9 or 10 collected firewood in a trolley and sold it door to door. On leaving school at 14 he was offered a job as office-boy by Frank Winstone, his Sunday School teacher at Pitt Street Methodist, and after subsequently qualifying as an accountant he went on to become managing director of Frank M. Winstone Ltd, the Auckland seed merchants.

One of Jerusha's grandchildren remembered her as 'a hard old bird', who in her sixties and seventies before she went blind walked miles every Wednesday from Western Springs to Mount Albert to visit her son's family. She carried an umbrella which she used as a walking stick, the *thump, thump* on the path warning of her arrival.[8] The same umbrella was often waved as she made an interjection at the many political meetings she frequented.

'Old Jerusha', as she was called by younger family members, was politically quite radical. She detested the Reform Party, worked for the Liberal Party, supported the 'Red Feds' during the 1913 strike, later became an active member of the Morningside branch of the Labour Party, admired Richard John Seddon and Michael Joseph Savage, about whom she talked constantly and whose photo she had on the wall, and became an ardent radio listener to 'Uncle Scrim' and 'Uncle Tom' and the 'Friendly Road' on 1ZB. Muldoon later claimed that his grandmother's 'hero worship of Seddon' influenced him into regarding 'King Dick' Seddon as 'New Zealand's greatest ever politician', while he was also 'brought up to regard Bill Massey as a devil incarnate.'[9]

In the later years of her life, Jerusha, whom some of her grandchildren also remembered as a dogmatic, critical woman of whom they were somewhat afraid, lived with her younger daughter Flossie Stone at 40 Finch Street, some two hundred yards downhill from Rob's home. Although Rob had little to do with his paternal grandparents, he was closer to his maternal grandmother than any of his cousins, who remembered Rob visiting her almost every day after school.[10] Particularly after she became blind in the early 1930s, she spent a great deal of her time listening to radio and talking with visitors. Rob Muldoon remembered that as a child and young man, 'I admired the old lady tremendously and enjoyed being with her . . . I used to go and spend hours with her, arguing politics and current affairs, and in later years hearing of the latest of her friends who had died. She died in 1951, in her ninetieth year.'[11] Discussing his grandparents in later years, he observed that they were 'Irish, English and Welsh' who came to New Zealand 'to get away from a class-conscious society' and like other New Zealanders 'very quickly fashioned for themselves an egalitarian tradition' and 'learned to live with each other and live with our Maori people on a basis of mutual acceptance and understanding. That is why I and many others who were born and bred in this country deeply resent and bitterly oppose those who misguidedly try to foment class hatred or racial antagonism in New Zealand.'[12] Muldoon believed that many of his own political ideas and attitudes came from his grandmother's influence on him in those formative years. Certainly, if a cousin's recollection is correct, Jerusha also imparted to Rob at an early age a great ambition. Sliding down the grassy slopes of Onetangi on nikau palms during a holiday at Waiheke, the 12-year-old Rob told 10-year-old Lawrie, 'One day I'm going to be Prime Minister.' Muldoon was not amused when his cousin replied, 'What's a prime minister?'[13]

The day after the 1935 election the extended Browne family met for their regular monthly Sunday lunch, always a roast cooked on a coal range, at the home of Flossie and her railway worker husband, Will Stone, who later became a storeman at Alfred Bucklands. Jerusha and Flossie were jubilant at Labour's landslide victory and the victory of their 'great Saviour', Michael Joseph Savage. They believed tough times required tough leaders with answers. As far as Jerusha was concerned, the only salvation for New Zealand in the 1930s was the Labour Party and she kept her two oldest grandsons, Rob and Lawrie, 'well-informed from a one-eyed point of view'. Lawrie in retrospect expressed some surprise that Rob, who was 'relatively underprivileged' and 'brought up in an atmosphere of socialism' was not converted by his forceful and intelligent grandmother, who exercised such 'a strong force on Rob's views and personality'.[14] But although not converted to socialism or the Labour Party, Rob from a very young age became a supporter of the welfare state and developed a strong belief that society should not throw the aged, widows, deserted wives, invalids or the unemployed into the gutter.

The 1920s were difficult years with economic slumps in 1921–22 and 1925–26 before in 1929 New Zealand collapsed into the Great Depression of the 1930s. The financial pressures on Rob's parents, however, were not their sole or even their primary cause for concern. Jim's health progressively declined during the decade, until by 1928 he had lost the use of his right arm and left leg, the power of speech, and most of his memory. Amie had the primary task of coping with the tragedy, becoming the family's sole source of income, and explaining the situation to her young son. Rob was told that his father had had a stroke resulting from an old war injury. It was not the truth, though one understands why Amie concealed that from her son. Years later Rob discovered that, like many returned soldiers, his father was suffering the effects of syphilis, which as it advanced caused strokes, fits and partial paralysis which left him forgetful, deluded and anti-social, degenerating from an intelligent man to a pitiful wreck. However, because tertiary syphilis and the onset of mental degeneration usually takes about twenty years, it is unlikely to have appeared as early as the late 1920s. It is possible that Jim Muldoon was initially hospitalised because of a mental breakdown or stroke caused by continual stress resulting from a combination of post-war psychosis and the collapse of his business, although academic studies of venereal disease have found that men from very religious backgrounds are also often much more deeply disturbed psychologically than non-religious men by syphilitic affliction. He may well have simply withdrawn into himself and only later in the hospital exhibited the symptoms of the venereal disease that was eventually to kill him. Certainly there were many other ex-servicemen at Wolfe's Home at the Psychiatric Hospital at Point Chevalier where Jim Muldoon spent almost twenty years until his death in 1946.[15]

After he entered hospital, Jim was rarely spoken of at family gatherings, or at least not when the children were present. Everyone knew where he was, but it was generally regarded as shameful if someone was in an asylum, and Jim was only mentioned briefly when Amie after a visit said she had taken him some apples or baking or that he was better or worse.

It was rare for children or teenagers to visit relatives, even parents, in the asylum and as late as the 1970s it was discouraged by the hospital authorities. Rob's cousin, Lawrence Browne, remembers at about the age of 12, when Rob was about 14, going to visit his Uncle Jim in hospital. At the time Lawrence was attending Gladstone Road School, near the asylum, and the children often used to 'give cheek to the loonies'. His Uncle Jim, however, would come and speak to the children and at that time, about 1935, his condition did not seem too bad.[16] Amie visited her husband regularly until his death, as did her brother Wally and some neighbours, but Rob went less frequently as his father's condition deteriorated over the years, and most if not all the family saw his eventual death as a relief.

A neighbour recalled Rob's mother as 'one of the hardest-working women I ever knew' and one of Rob's cousins described his Aunt Amie as a marvellous person for whom he had 'more admiration . . . than any other woman I knew, and not only because she was such a great cook'. She was 'tall (about 5 foot 10), handsome and well turned out'.[17] She always wore big hats and carried an umbrella, and whenever she met Lawrence in Queen Street, or as she often did went to the races at Ellerslie or Alexander Park 'to meet friends and imbibe the atmosphere', she was always so well-dressed and well-groomed that 'no one would have guessed her circumstances.' She was a 'very strong personality, very hospitable, very hardworking.'[18] Amie had many friends and neighbours, whom she entertained at home and who kept an eye on her and her son's welfare. The children were usually kept out of the front room of her cosy little house, which was reserved for special occasions and visitors, but from time to time the children were allowed to sit in the immaculately clean and tidy front room and listen to records of Gracie Fields, Flanagan and Allen, and 'Bye Bye Blackbird' on Amie's large old gramophone while their mothers played cards.

Muldoon was spoilt by his mother, who thought her only son was wonderful. The whole world revolved round her son, and Muldoon and his mother developed a mutually intense and defensive maternal-filial relationship, especially during the many long years her husband was in hospital. Muldoon was not house-trained as a boy because his mother did everything for him. Even after he was married, when his mother came to visit Rob and his wife, Thea, she would take his shoes out of the closet and clean them.[19]

A very capable and self-sufficient woman who, despite being of average build, gave an impression of great strength, Amie could be very determined in insisting that her son do his homework, thus inculcating her own work ethic. She was also meticulously tidy, and as soon as meals were finished the dishes had to be done and everything tidied up. Muldoon later credited his mother's example and influence for his own obsession to do things immediately, like answering mail. His mother always told him, 'If you've got to do it sometime, do it now.'[20]

One of Muldoon's other lifelong habits was less beneficial. Although not completely poverty-stricken by any means, the family was certainly not wealthy either and there was a strong belief in 'waste not, want not'. Amie served her son large helpings of food and encouraged him to eat everything put in front of him. In later years as the family's fortunes improved, a favourite meal was a mountain of steak and kidney pie and vegetables followed by home-made apple-pie with both custard and cream. Muldoon for the rest of his life ate the wrong foods, in large quantities, and always cleaned his plate.[21]

Although Muldoon sometimes admitted that 'we did not have an easy time' during the Depression,[22] he was annoyed years later when a biographer suggested that he was traumatised by poverty and was not well fed as a child, having to eat broken biscuits and rotten fruit. Many children tended to buy or beg broken biscuits and older fruit from the grocer or greengrocer on the way home from school but they were not forced to do it and there was always adequate good food in the Muldoon household. Many young children living frugally did not realise they were poor until someone told them or they compared their circumstances with others more fortunate as they grew older. It was not a sin to be poor but sometimes it felt like it was. Rob and the other children in the neighbourhood ate pies and stews made from rabbits sold to their parents by the itinerant 'rabbit man'.[23] Rabbits were also stocked by the local fish shop, and fish was cheap. But there were also large quantities and a wide variety of vegetables from their own gardens and home-baked scones, cakes, biscuits and rice puddings. At weekends they sometimes had mutton or sausages from Barnaby's butcher shop in Morningside and occasionally a welcome gift of a joint of meat from Ted Sandall. Sandall, a retired butcher who lived below the Muldoons, kept a stable of trotting horses, and during the Depression also gave the Muldoons a daily billy of milk from his house-cow.[24] Lumpy rolled oats were cheaper and more common for breakfast than the smoother but dearer Creamoata brand of porridge. Most families also made their own peanut butter by mashing up cheap peanuts in the mincer.

Because of her circumstances Amie was very cautious with money, buying only small presents at Christmas or for birthdays. She carefully hid one-pound notes under the carpet in the lounge for a rainy day, and some were still there when the carpet was taken up after her death. Her son also adopted a relatively frugal approach to money throughout both his private and public life.

Muldoon's dogmatism, stubbornness and even fierceness may have reflected the personalities of both his grandmother Jerusha and his mother Amie. Both, from necessity, had to be very strong women and younger family members remembered them as busy women with plenty to say, much of it controversial. Amie not only had to earn a living for herself and her son and pay off the mortgage on the house by working as an upholstress and occasionally taking in boarders. She also mowed her steep lawns with a hand mower, kept with the help of her son a large vegetable garden, made all her own jams and preserves, and sewed her own and some of her son's clothes. Every Saturday for many years, occasionally accompanied by Rob, she walked the two miles from Western Springs to the mental asylum at Point Chevalier to visit her husband. She worked long hours, and not only her son but her neighbours would hear her treadle sewing machine going late at night, and even on occasions 'right though the night',²⁵ as she made loose covers for furniture, many sold through Smith and Caugheys. She also made large curtains for the Regent and St James Theatres, dust covers for the furnishings in Government House, and had a large clientele in Remuera. Without a car she had to travel everywhere by tram, carrying material to measure or covers to fit.

Muldoon's discussion of his family background in *The Rise and Fall of a Young Turk* is interesting not only for what he reveals but also for what he ignores or conceals. His grandparents, only one of whom he really knew, receive 125 lines, more than half of them on Jerusha Browne. His mother and father get 75 lines, two-thirds on his mother and the remainder largely some non-specific comments about his father's sporting achievements and war service. One uncle, his father's brother, who had little influence on Muldoon's life, receives 71 lines, half extracted from a war diary, but his mother's brother, whom he knew well and who had a considerable influence on his life, is mentioned only in one line. In short, Muldoon concentrates on the two key women in his early life, his grand-mother Jerusha and mother Amie, and largely ignores the two most important men, his father Jim and less understandably his uncle Wally. Perhaps Muldoon (consciously or subconsciously) almost concealed the existence and influence of these two men on his life because he felt that his successful, popular and respected uncle was what he wished his unfortunate father had been.

Wally Browne, whose business career was starting to prosper and who was generous in sharing his increasing new-found wealth, did what he could to help his sister and became a surrogate father-figure for his nephew after his brother-in-law was hospitalised. Declared unfit for war service because of a heart condition caused by rheumatic fever as a child, Wally had married Gwendoline Kemp, the daughter of a prominent Baptist family, and their eldest son Lawrence (Lawrie) was born two years after Rob in 1923. The cousins were to become close friends. Before World

War II the Browne family, which had three sons and a daughter, regularly rented holiday baches at Oneroa and Onetangi on Waiheke Island or at Browns Bay or Milford, and Rob always went with them. Wally Browne had a good mind and a wide range of interests and shared these with his inquisitive young nephew.

Wally was a deacon and Bible Class teacher at Mount Albert Baptist Church and from 1912 had been one of the leaders of the Young Men's Christian Association, helping to develop the boys' camp at Hunua. He remained actively involved with the YMCA until his death in 1963. Although Amie was not a churchgoer, Rob's uncle encouraged his nephew from about the age of 6 to become involved in the Mount Albert Baptist Sunday School and later the YMCA, especially its soccer club of which Browne was the first and long-time secretary.[26]

If his grandmother Jerusha Browne was a left-wing political influence on the young Muldoon, his uncle was a counterbalancing right-wing influence. Wally did not follow his mother's left-wing loyalties though he did not risk her ire by arguing with her. Indeed, after she went blind, her son always collected Jerusha and took her to vote. The first time Jerusha asked if he had put ribbons on the car and felt them just to be sure. She took it for granted that they would be red and never found out that her son was driving her to the polling booth in a car with blue ribbons.[27]

Browne moved in Auckland's top business circles, became so rich that he bought a home in Paritai Drive and cruised first-class on the *Queen Mary*, and served as a member of the National Party's Auckland Divisional Finance Committee. He was widely read and a great admirer of the Reform Party's very conservative William Downie Stewart, who resigned as Minister of Finance rather than devalue the New Zealand currency. In his younger days Browne had topped New Zealand in his accountancy exams and as his nephew grew older he introduced Rob to economics and accountancy also. After Muldoon returned from the war, he often stayed with the Brownes at their new bach at Manly, where his cousins became somewhat frustrated when Rob refused to go fishing or do the dishes because he was constantly engrossed in reading books on hard-core economics, the titles of which his cousins, themselves on the way to becoming prominent Auckland businessmen, could not even understand.[28]

One neighbour, who knew both Rob and his father, recalled Rob as a boy having 'intelligence, ambition, a sense of humour, last but not least, agility'. He settled differences of opinion with other boys himself, was 'not possessed of a superior complex', and was a 'good mixer'.[29] It was a description with which his two closest childhood friends, Jack Ryder and Dick Fickling concurred.[30]

Jack, who was two years older than Rob, lived eight houses away in Western Springs Road and Dick, who was one year older, lived next door to the Muldoons. All three went to Mount Albert Primary and Kowhai Intermediate Schools, where they were in different classes. The primary school was about a quarter of a mile walk from where they lived and the intermediate about a mile. Jack lost contact with Rob and Dick when they went to Mount Albert Grammar where, by jumping form two at Kowhai, Rob ended up in the same third form as

Dick. Jack became a coachbuilder, freezing worker and finally a watersider who was for a time blacklisted by employers after the 1951 strike. He also during his lifetime collected an amazing museum of antiques and memorabilia. Dick, who was the youngest of seven children, moved from Western Springs when he was about 15, became a clerk, subsequently administration manager of UEB Industries, and was elected mayor of Mount Roskill. None of the three families had much money. Jack's father was a railway shunter who spent much of the Depression on relief work. Dick's father worked at Kent's Bakery in Newmarket.

The three boys, Rob, Jack and Dick, collected shellfish from Point Chevalier beach, blackberries from round the derelict Stone Jug Pub opposite Western Springs, and watercress from Western Springs. They sold the watercress for fowl food at a penny a bag. They ran messages for their parents, buying kumara from tattooed Maori women who came by train from Helensville to Morningside to sell their produce. They rode on the back of Buchanan's bakery cart and shovelled up the horse shit from the carriers' horses and from the racing stables over the back fence to be used as manure for their parents' large and productive vegetable gardens. They regularly collected rags, bones and bottles to sell to hawkers. Bottles could earn as much as a shilling a sack. Eden Park was a particularly productive hunting ground for cigarette cards and beer bottles. The boys carried sugarsacks of bottles home along the railway track and large water pipe that ran between Sandringham and Morningside. They walked everywhere because there was rarely money to pay the penny tram fare, and if they had a penny there were always better ways to spend it.

The trio had a lot of fun after school or at weekends. Occasionally they went to the Western Springs speedway to watch the bikes racing around the track. Afterwards Rob and his barefooted playmates pretended they were speedway riders. They wrote 'Norton' or 'Douglas' on hats and chased each other on foot or on homemade scooters around the lawn or raced toy cars down inclines. One of his friends recalled that Rob, the youngest and smallest of the three, was very competitive and could become sulky if beaten. They also made sleds and after greasing the runners with dripping careered down the grassy slopes at Western Springs or Fowlds Park. They built tree huts in the back garden, had a secret hideaway under the Morningside railway bridge, played in a nearby quarry, and on Sundays frolicked in the sawdust heaps in the yard of the local box factory. They made canvas canoes which they carried to Point Chevalier beach where they pretended to be Indians. They fished for piper and spotties around the Point Chevalier reef with bamboo rods and dead maggots for bait. For bigger fish the lines were baited with rotten meat. On the ten acres of open farmland opposite their homes they played cricket, soccer, rugby and league. Some Saturday afternoons, if they could find the threepence entry cost, they went to the matinée films at the Royal picture theatre in Kingsland.

As a child Muldoon was adventuresome and somewhat accident-prone. When he was five years old, for example, he slipped while playing on the front gate. A pointed dowling upright pierced his cheek, breaking the muscle and leaving him

with a distinctive scar and lopsided smile. On another occasion the three boys were
digging out an underground hut in the back garden. They often dug a hole, exca-
vated side rooms, and covered the top of the hole with wood and soil to form a
roof. This time Rob, energetically wielding a spade, hit Dick Fickling on the
forehead, resulting in copious bleeding and another lifelong scar.

Other local boys were less friendly to Muldoon. One, the son of the local grocer,
recalled how he and other *Auckland Star* delivery boys used to wait daily for
Muldoon under the Morningside railway bridge as he returned home from school.
They would pelt him with lumps of clay and stones and tease him as a 'namby
pamby mommy's boy' or a 'loony like your father in the madhouse'.[31] They
recognised that he was very bright but a loner, different in many ways, and teased
him in school and out of it. Muldoon learnt during the daytime to protect himself
from shame, to hide his hurt feelings, to retaliate both verbally and (insofar as a
small boy can) physically against his tormenters, and to strive for success and
respect. At night the lonely only child lay awake in the dark, listening to the
sounds of the animals from the nearby zoo and crying quietly about the loss of his
father.

Unlike many Labour politicians, Rob Muldoon did not in later life talk much
about the effect of illness, poverty, insecurity and the Depression of the 1930s on
his early life, but those things undoubtedly influenced his outlook, values and
aspirations as much as they did those of many politicians on the Left. His often
frightening political personality and aggressive leadership style as an adult may
well have been rooted also in that somewhat lonely, insecure and resentful
childhood. Muldoon never forgot his own personal experiences or the sights he saw
as an impressionable and vulnerable little boy and adolescent, and in one of his
autobiographical books he noted: 'I saw too much real poverty and degradation
during the Depression to have anything but a burning compassion for those who
have been deprived of the most important possession of all, their human dignity.'[32]
He remembered the relief workers constructing the playing fields at Mount Albert
Grammar School, the golf course, the many stone walls. On Saturdays he sometimes watched the relief workers' cricket team, in which some of his friends'
unemployed fathers played. He listened to stories about his friends' older brothers
in isolated camps planting trees. The parents of one of his best friends had the
mortgage on their home foreclosed by the Government, which then rented the
house back to them. Reflecting on the unemployed, Muldoon told a journalist
years later: 'It was apparent that most, I imagine through no fault of their own, had
no secondary education and no careers behind them. I resolved, at about 13 or
something, to get my head down and never be in that position.'[33] Muldoon
developed a tremendous, single-minded drive and was determined never to let
anything or anyone get on top of him.

CHAPTER 2

School and Church

MULDOON'S EARLY SCHOOLING WAS AT MOUNT ALBERT Primary in School Road and at Kowhai Junior High School (later called Kowhai Intermediate). He commenced in August 1925, one month before his fifth birthday, and he recalled that 'I was involved in a fight on my first day.'[1] Although he was naturally clever, his handwriting was very untidy, he could not draw, and his desk was usually a mess. Muldoon believed that this lack of artistic ability and neatness cost him the top place in his primary and intermediate classes, lamenting years afterwards that 'I seldom topped the class . . . because in writing, art, and handwork I was always near the bottom. "Good work but untidy" was my standard report, to the constant distress of my mother. In aggregate however my other subjects kept me in the top three, usually beaten by some bright girl who was also good at art.'[2]

The Depression was reflected very much in the education sector in 1932. In that year the Teachers' Training Colleges at Wellington and Dunedin closed, the number of pupils in secondary schools dropped over 10 per cent, many classes had over fifty pupils, and only half the children leaving primary schools went on to post-primary education.[3] Rob's teacher in Form 1A at Kowhai described him as 'a boy of outstanding ability and industry' and suggested in 1932 that he should sit the Humphrey Rawlings Scholarship.[4] This scholarship, established from the estate of an Auckland businessman who died in 1884, was usually attempted by Form 2 pupils and was open to any child under the age of 12 attending a public school in the Auckland province. The winner, who had to establish that his father was poor, received free tuition and textbooks for three years at Auckland or Mount Albert Grammar School or King's College, together with an annual maintenance allowance of £10. The books were subsequently handed on to the Rawlings Scholar from the next year. The exam consisted of English, Arithmetic, English History and Geography. There had to be at least twenty entrants from a minimum of five schools before the exam was held. Muldoon won the scholarship in 1932, becoming the forty-ninth recipient of the award. He and his mother never seriously considered his taking up the scholarship at King's College, because (in Muldoon's words) it would have been 'inappropriate and too costly for travelling'. Travel was also a factor in excluding Auckland Grammar, so Muldoon in 1933, at 11 years old and having skipped Form 2 at Kowhai, enrolled at Mount Albert Grammar School, where he remained for four years.

Mount Albert Grammar, which was started in 1922 and staffed largely by teachers drawn from Auckland Grammar, was one of only about half-a-dozen secondary schools in Auckland in the 1930s and drew its pupils from a large geographic area covering most of West Auckland. It was a strict and very formal school with a limited choice of mainly academic subjects and quickly developed a good academic and sporting record.

Muldoon believed erroneously that for the first two years he was at the school he was its youngest pupil. He was the first year but in 1934 he was not because a third-former, Ronald Barker, who had been born in February 1922, was about six months younger. Muldoon was also one of its smallest pupils and had the reputation of being very bright. Almost inevitably he was 'looked on as a curiosity' and was nicknamed 'Pussy'. To Barker, who became his school friend, 'He always seemed to be a bit of a cat that walked by himself.'[5] Because he was 'bullied a bit', he 'became defensive'. With no older, larger brother to defend him, Muldoon decided to become verbally and, on occasions, physically belligerent, working on the assumption that 'If you can't knock 'em off, try and scare 'em off.'[6] An old school friend noted that 'he didn't duck anything. He would get stuck in. He was never afraid.'[7]

Frequently, Muldoon found himself in trouble for what were usually minor infringements such as not wearing a cap or fooling in class. Although caned only three times during his time at MAGS, Muldoon was often put on detention. On one occasion he was called before the headmaster, Fred Gamble, who told Muldoon that he was down for so many detentions that it would take him the rest of the year to complete them and that he was in fact receiving more detentions than he was working off. Gamble suggested that Muldoon attend every detention the school held over the following month and if he did not get any more he would be pardoned the outstanding detentions. At the next detention Muldoon attended, the pupils were told to jog repeatedly round the quadrangle. Muldoon got bored and ankle-tapped the boy in front, who fell into a rubbish bin. Muldoon lost the chance to reduce his list of detentions.[8]

Mount Albert Grammar School had a school farm and a boarding hostel which accommodated pupils who wanted to learn about agriculture. The farm was out of bounds to other pupils but fascinated many city children. On one occasion, in 1934, when he was in the fourth form, Muldoon went exploring and while hanging by his legs from a branch fell out of a macrocarpa tree, breaking his arm. He recalled that his friends thought it was a huge joke. Before being transferred to hospital, Muldoon was treated in the medical room by a fellow pupil, Laurie Salas, who later became a doctor and boasted that Rob had been his first serious patient.[9] Muldoon was subsequently absent from school for four weeks.

Muldoon played in the Mount Albert Grammar School's Junior B soccer team in 1933, 1934 and 1935 before captaining the Intermediate B team in 1936. Mount Albert Grammar was very strong at soccer in 1936, its Intermediate A team, which included Muldoon's YMCA friend Bill Adair, winning the championship by beating Auckland Grammar 16–0. Muldoon's Intermediate B team won only two of its ten games, but held the unbeaten MAGS A team to a five-goal margin and the AGS team to a 4–1 win.[10] Saturday afternoons, Muldoon played a second game of soccer for the YMCA Club, on one occasion winning a special medal for all-round play and sportsmanship.[11]

One of Muldoon's friends who played with him at both Mount Albert Grammar and the YMCA remembered Rob as a player without finesse or a sense of positional play but who was totally committed, charging around the field after the ball 'like a bull at a gate' and giving everything a go.[12] Another friend, an Auckland Secondary School representative and MAGS A team player, also did not rate his friend highly as a skilful player though not questioning his determination.[13]

Muldoon dabbled unsuccessfully at school with boxing in 1935, joined the chess club the same year, and was runner-up in the school draughts contest in 1936. Muldoon admitted that he lacked the patience to play chess and quickly lost concentration.

From about the age of 10, at the YMCA in Wellesley Street every Friday night, Muldoon enjoyed playing indoor basketball, billiards, snooker and table tennis, and he also attended YMCA boys camps at the Hunua Falls. He often went with friends to watch major rugby, soccer and league games at Eden, Blandford and Carlaw Parks.

In the first term of 1933 Gamble recorded on Muldoon's school record card that Muldoon had done 'very well under the circumstances'.[14] It was not quite clear what the circumstances were, though possibly the reference was a recognition that Muldoon was the youngest pupil in that school and had entered Form 3A without passing through Form 2 at Kowhai Intermediate. It may also have indicated that the headmaster was aware of Muldoon's home situation. No doubt Gamble hoped that the situation would improve as the boy matured.

Muldoon's academic record at Mount Albert Grammar over the entire four years, however, was not particularly distinguished. He appears to have relied on his lively intelligence and good memory rather than the drudgery of concentrated and persistent study. Apart from English, where he was usually near to if not at the top of the class, he was rarely in the top third in any subject, and this was reflected in the headmaster's overall comment each term, usually a 'satisfactory'.

His English teacher for the four years he was at MAGS was J. H. Harvey. At different times he also was taught by other well-known teachers such as J. R. Caradus (Science), H. Towers (Maths), G. R. Coldham (French) and H. R. Brock (Latin). Harvey was the only teacher at MAGS Muldoon remembered with affection. The other teachers 'considered that my attitude to school work was rather less than was desirable.'[15] Muldoon loathed the discipline and tedium of learning foreign languages and did not do well at French or Latin. Indeed, Latin was the one subject he was taught for four years but did not sit for School Certificate.

In 1936 C. T. ('Sticky') Harris, a teacher at Mount Albert Grammar, carried out an American-devised intelligence test on all fifth-form pupils. They were doubled on bicycles to the Training College where students conducted the tests, which consisted of mental arithmetic, tiny sketches with errors, and psychological profile questions. Harris subsequently told a pupil called Harvey Blanks that he and Muldoon had scored the highest marks and received 'genius' ratings on the IQ tests. Interestingly, Blanks and Muldoon disliked each other, although they did not know each other well. Muldoon remembered Blanks as a 'deviously humorous individual', whose initials, H.R.L., he usually expanded to 'His Royal Lowness', while Blanks recalled Muldoon as 'a singularly colourless boy', wearing 'enormous pantaloon-like shorts' and 'totally lacking in any sense of humour'.[16]

Muldoon claimed that, because he was too young, his headmaster did not let him sit matriculation in his third year, 1935, but his marks suggest that the head may have been more concerned about the adequacy of Muldoon's academic preparation than about his age. He sat the exam the following year. Although a fourth-year pupil, Muldoon was not a sixth-former in 1936 and only sixth-formers could use fountain pens. Muldoon was incensed and wrote in *The Albertian* a piece called 'Villains'.

> Now I have heard of pirates
> In China and Malay,
> Of robbers bold in days of old,
> Who rode the King's highway,
> The Bedouins of the desert,
> The rustlers in 'the States',
> Bushrangers of Australia,
> Ned Kelly and his mates;
> But though these purple villains,
> Have thrilled us now and then,
> They're angels all, compared to him
> Who barred my fountain pen.[17]

Although students had to sit only five subjects, including a foreign language, it was common for brighter students to sit six. Muldoon dropped Latin but still sat six subjects. He passed only two of them: History (69 per cent) and English (64 per cent). Even these marks probably disappointed him, particularly English in that he had been first out of thirty-five pupils in his class in the two previous school English exams and had received the class certificate for English at the prize-giving. His other marks were Mathematics 47, Chemistry 47, Physics 46 and French 32. Because of the compulsory foreign language requirement, his low mark for French had to be included in his total of 259 for his top five subjects and his overall average of 51.8 per cent. His 32 for French was only two above the minimum mark for a subject to count.[18] In retrospect, Muldoon freely admitted that he did not really concentrate on his academic studies at school, especially in subjects that did not interest him.[19]

In a testimonial written for Muldoon on leaving school, the headmaster, Gamble, gave a reasonably positive assessment of Muldoon's achievements and potential: 'His results are highly creditable to him, for to his natural ability he has added a strong degree of diligence and perseverance. The combination of innate talents and the faculty to concentrate should take him far in future life.'[20] Muldoon 'never thought of going to university because I needed to get out to work to earn some money. My mother was virtually the sole support of the family from about 1928 on. Although I could have stayed another year at MAGS and gone for university scholarship, getting a job was more important and most accounting students at that time studied part-time.'[21]

On leaving school at the end of 1936, shortly after he turned 15, Muldoon went to work as an office-boy at Fletcher Construction Company. He was paid 10 shillings a week, a wage he doubled by changing jobs and taking a similar post at the Auckland Electric Power Board on 29 April 1937. At the beginning of 1938 he enrolled by correspondence in Hemingways accountancy courses, working on his studies in the evenings and at weekends.[22] He recalled: 'I went to Hemingways because I wanted to study at home rather than going out to evening classes. This type of study was less formal and appealed more to me as I could do the work when I felt like it and make my own pace through the course. I took the whole of my professional accountancy examinations through Hemingways.'[23]

Muldoon worked for the AEPB as an office junior in the Cash Analysis Department until August 1940 when he was promoted to arrears clerk. He worked five-and-a-half-day weeks, including Saturdays from 8.30 to 11.30.[24] His untidiness, lack of discipline and mischievous sense of humour did not endear him to older managers at the AEPB. It was expected that everyone in the office would be neat, diligent and serious the whole time, and there was little toleration of a teenager who played the fool and appeared to be less than one hundred per cent committed to the job. Muldoon was not regarded highly for his cluttered desk, or for knocking over a bottle of ink, or for organising a contest to see which of the office boys could race fastest to the post office with the mail, weaving their way through Queen Street crowds.[25]

On 8 December 1937, after an interview with N. M. Speer, Secretary of the AEPB, Muldoon received a written warning about his conduct. In the letter to 'Master R. D. Muldoon', Speer recorded that the Board was 'not entirely satisfied with Robert's work in the office up to that date' and would 'place him on probation for a further period of six months'. Speer added: 'I feel quite certain, however, that you have the ability, and it is only a matter of applying yourself diligently to your work in the future. In the meantime we are prepared to increase your salary by half the normal amount, that is by two shillings and six pence per week, and I am arranging for this to take effect as from the termination of your [first] six months employment with us.'²⁶ Muldoon clearly respected the warning and his employment was subsequently confirmed.

Although he took leave from the Power Board to commence his military service in January 1941, Muldoon kept returning to the AEPB throughout that year, working for several weeks, then doing more army training and courses and then again returning to work. In October he was transferred to the meter room, where he remained until he left finally on 9 January 1942 for camp and then New Caledonia.²⁷

During his school years and while he worked for the AEPB prior to the war, much of Muldoon's social activity revolved round the Mount Albert Baptist Church and the YMCA. Shortly after his father was admitted to hospital, his uncle Wally Browne had started collecting his nephew, then about 6 years old, and taking him with his cousins to the Sunday School at the Mount Albert Baptist Church. Muldoon was to attend regularly and became very much involved in the church's youth activities until he went overseas in the army fourteen years later. He returned to the church in 1947, remaining a church member until he married in 1951 and became an Anglican like his wife Thea.

The Mount Albert Baptist Church, established in 1915, was at the time Muldoon attended a thriving, vigorous and evangelical church centred around a number of large families. It was also a close-knit community, almost tribal in its intermarriages and the willingness of its members to help each other not only spiritually but practically in business or when misfortune struck. By today's standards it was theologically fundamentalist, morally very puritanical, and sectarianly quite anti-Catholic.²⁸

The church had a large Sunday School and Bible Class and its youth work centred round the Christian Endeavour Society, which although partly social also taught its members, and gave them frequent opportunities, to conduct services and prepare and deliver sermonettes. Among the most prominent deacons concerned with youth work were Wally Browne, who taught in both the Sunday School and Bible Class at various times, Harvey Turner, the Sunday School superintendent, and Turner's brother-in-law Roy Thompson, a Bible Class leader who also captained the Boys' Brigade. Thompson, an electrician and a returned soldier, was remembered as 'the straightest fellow you could meet and a great influence on all the young people'.²⁹

The Bible Class when Muldoon was a member numbered about seventy, with young men and young women meeting separately. Muldoon became a particularly close friend of Colin Busfield, who was later to be the best man at his wedding and general manager of the Auckland Savings Bank. Colin's father, Rev. Leonard Busfield, was a radical Baptist minister, who headed the Auckland Sunday School Union for many years. A pacifist and Fabian socialist, Rev. Busfield stood as a Labour candidate for the Auckland City Council. During the depression of the 1930s, Colin's father, who had 'fallen on hard times', died. Colin, then aged 13, remembered Wally Browne becoming to the Busfield boys a father-figure in much the same way as he had done for his nephew Rob. Rob's mother, Amie, also became a close friend and strong support of Hilda Busfield after the death of her husband.[30]

Rob and Colin as teenagers not only went to Bible Class and church together but also regularly played snooker at the YMCA, watched speedway at Western Springs or football at Eden Park, or played tennis at the Mount Albert Baptist Tennis Club. Muldoon was secretary-treasurer of the tennis club which played on courts at the back of a large home owned by the prominent Baptist layman J. A. Penman, who built a number of churches and other buildings such as St Cuthbert's College.

Two ministers had some influence on Rob, his cousins and his friends. Rev. John Laird, who always wore a frock coat, was a somewhat dour, scholarly and controversial pastor of Mount Albert Baptist during the 1930s.[31] An Irishman, he was very anti-Catholic. He offended many of the businessmen in his congregation, including Wally Browne, by preaching that it was sinful to speculate in shares. When he returned from a visit to Germany, he spoke publicly of the good that Hitler was doing for the German people – an opinion he shared incidentally at the time with the controversial local Labour Member of Parliament, John A. Lee. Laird may well have influenced the young Muldoon in his lifelong moral dislike of usury. The Baptist emphasis on individual work and responsibility and a tendency to see all ethical choices in stark black and white, right and wrong, were also evident in Muldoon's character. Muldoon's favourite verse of Scripture learnt as a child and often quoted in later life was 'For if the trumpet give an uncertain sound, who shall prepare himself to the battle?' (1 Corinthians 14:8).

The second minister, who was at Mount Albert Baptist from 1940 to 1948, was a complete contrast to his predecessor. Only 28 years old when he arrived, Rev. Hayes Lloyd was a fiery, emotional, evangelical preacher. Hayes Lloyd and Muldoon remembered each other with respect and some affection. The minister recalled 'a happy and popular young man active in the Bible Class, the Christian Endeavour Society and the tennis club'.[32] Muldoon said that Hayes Lloyd had 'tremendous charisma' and that his 'sermons held one spellbound'.[33]

Baptists do not practise infant christening but believe that a person should only be baptised by complete immersion after they have reached an age when they can make an informed decision on whether or not they wish to be spiritually 'born again' and become a Christian. The baptism is simply a public affirmation and declaration of that decision to accept Christ and be converted to a future life directed and empowered by God's Holy Spirit. It is not a step that either the church or an individual takes lightly. Baptist churches regard conversion as a prerequisite for baptism and, in most cases, baptism as a prerequisite for full church membership, although most Baptist congregations include significant numbers of non-baptised adherents.

Most of Rob's cousins and friends were baptised in their teens before the outbreak of war in 1939. Muldoon at about 18 years of age had remained unconvinced that baptism was either 'necessary or appropriate', and told Laird so.[34] With the exception of Wally Browne's family, most of Muldoon's relations were Methodist or, like his mother and maternal grandmother, non-practising Anglicans. Neither Methodists nor Anglicans saw believers' baptism or baptism by immersion as necessary. Even with the expectation and support of a Baptist family, the public profession of faith by total immersion is a very emotional and daunting event for most people, and Muldoon did not enjoy such support from his immediate family, although his aunt, Gwendoline Browne, a very devout and determined Baptist, tried hard to talk him into it.[35]

While overseas during the war, however, and possibly as a result of his experiences in Italy, Muldoon changed his mind and wrote a letter to Hayes Lloyd telling him that he had decided to be baptised on his return to New Zealand. When Muldoon did return, Hayes Lloyd reminded him of his pledge and after preaching a 'hellfire sermon' made an appeal for those who wished to repent and be baptised to come forward and signify their intention. Muldoon did not immediately respond, but 'the appeal went on and on until Rob responded'.[36] Following his baptism Muldoon became a full member of the church on 1 June 1947.[37] It is perhaps worth noting that during Hayes Lloyd's ministry 186 new members joined the Mount Albert Baptist Church, 59 of them from the youth group.[38]

Although he joined the church, Muldoon found himself distracted after 1947 by his membership of the Junior National Party, which provided an alternative location for social activities, and by his growing friendship with Thea Flyger, a young Anglican woman, who lived at Belmont on Auckland's North Shore. Not only Muldoon but also his cousin Lawrence and his close friend Colin felt that older church members tended to treat the young returned servicemen as if they were still Bible Class boys and they stopped going to church regularly and became involved in more family-centred or secular activities and the advancement of their business or professional careers. Their Baptist upbringing continued to influence their values and outlook, however, and forty years later Muldoon was still able to assert that he believed in the existence of God the Creator, that he viewed the Bible as the word of God, that he accepted by faith that there was life after death, and that he felt he could in this life communicate with and receive guidance directly from God. Nevertheless, he no longer went to church, partly because he thought that the churches which were theologically convincing were no longer dynamic and those such as the charismatic Pentecostal churches which were dynamic were not theologically convincing.[39]

CHAPTER 3

War and Work

MULDOON ENLISTED IN THE ARMY ON 28 NOVEMBER 1940, shortly after his nineteenth birthday. He was posted to the 3rd Battalion of the Auckland Regiment, a territorial infantry regiment.[1] He entered Waiouru Camp for his basic training on 6 January 1941, completing it three months later in a somewhat unusual way. At the conclusion of the training the young soldiers were dropped by truck at night in the backblocks of the Volcanic Plateau. It was snowing and very dark. Muldoon tripped and fell into an open latrine. He ended up in Waiouru Camp hospital suffering seriously infected abrasions.[2]

Holding no illusions about war, Muldoon saw his military service as an undesirable and hopefully temporary disruption to his life. He did not want to be a soldier and was determined that when the war ended he would not be left like his father and uncle had been left after the previous war. As a result, while he somewhat calculatingly and cynically wanted sufficient non-commissioned rank 'to avoid fatigues and other menial tasks', he frankly admitted that he 'refused the occasional opportunity to sit for a commission as I did not want added responsibility' and 'kept my attention on the world after the war and took what joy there was in the meantime. I studied for my final accountancy subjects.'[3]

Nor did Muldoon ever try to present his war service or himself in a heroic light. Indeed he tended to portray himself as not only a reluctant but a bumbling and somewhat ineffective soldier. His friend from school and YMCA days, Bill Adair, was in the same battalion as Muldoon and remembered him as a quiet corporal who unlike most did not throw his weight around or appear to like or fit well into military life.[4] Muldoon was quite prepared to admit that at times he was frightened, that he kept his head well down when less cautious people around him were being shot,[5] and that on one occasion soldiers advancing and noticing that he was being left behind at the bottom of trench checked to see where he had been hit and to their disgust found he was asleep.[6] On another occasion, while cleaning his tommy gun in Italy, he shot himself through his trousers, scarring his hip. As he recognised himself, had the wound been more serious, 'no one would have believed it was not a self-inflicted wound.'[7]

After completing his basic training and having been promoted to lance-corporal on 20 August 1941, Muldoon was posted as an instructor to the Northern Military District's school at Narrow Neck on Auckland's North Shore. There he remained, training recruits, until November 1942, except that for part of the time he was at Matakana near Warkworth or at Glenbervie near Whangarei. He was promoted to corporal in January 1942 and to sergeant in June of the same year. On 27 November 1942, shortly after his twenty-first birthday, Muldoon, according to his official record of service, 'reverted to Private at his own request', and was posted to 37 Battalion of the 3rd Division. Four weeks later he sailed for New Caledonia.

Before leaving New Zealand Muldoon and his comrades were told that they would be fighting their way ashore when they reached their destination.[8] Instead, they found Noumea ablaze with lights on New Year's Eve. The New Zealand soldiers, however, were not allowed to go ashore and had to go round the coast where they set up their headquarters. Although a few Japanese snipers had to be cleaned out of nearby islands, there was little fighting. Shortly after his arrival Muldoon was again promoted in January 1943 to the rank of lance-corporal.

Muldoon preferred to be in intelligence rather than fighting units and was delighted to become part of the garrison headquarters intelligence unit. It consisted of Captain Frank Foster, Sergeant Vic Stace, Corporal Neil Instone, Lance-Corporal Muldoon and about eight privates. Muldoon was known to the others as Bob, not Rob. Foster, Stace and Instone had been in the Wellington Battalion and knew each other quite well. Muldoon was odd man out.

The New Zealanders, who after being based at Nemera moved north to Bourail, spent much of their time training other soldiers in surveillance, reconnaissance and map-reading at an intelligence school run by Muldoon. The unit also often mapped trails on the island, with Muldoon and his colleagues dressed in shorts or muslin loincloths slashing their way through thick undergrowth.

Stace recalled Muldoon as an excellent instructor both in the classroom and out in the field. He was also very considerate of his colleagues. On one occasion, for example, while out on manoeuvres, Stace burnt his shoulder while boiling water. Muldoon insisted on carrying Stace's rifle the rest of the way as well as his own.

Muldoon and Instone disagreed on almost everything, frequently arguing with considerable heat. Both men had very definite views on a wide range of controversial subjects and neither was willing to make concessions. Stace, who later became assistant general manager of Prudential Insurance and who had known Instone since 1932, at first shared a tent with Instone and Muldoon and sometimes had to use his rank to end late-night debates that were preventing him getting to sleep.

In his spare time, Muldoon continued working on accounting and secretarial studies, but he also extended his grasp of the colonial French language with the help of Thérèse Magnier, the daughter of an elderly French settler. Previously a teetotaller who had taken the temperance pledge in Sunday School, he also developed a taste for wine and learnt to trade with American soldiers who always seemed to have lots of everything. On one occasion Muldoon found himself in trouble with his colleagues for going absent without leave in order to spend some time with a Women's Army Corps girlfriend in Divisional Signals.

Because Stace had completed five years of French at college and was somewhat more proficient in speaking the language than Muldoon, he got the task of living with a French family on the other side of the island in order to liaise with the local people and purchase fresh provisions for the troops. Muldoon was quite envious and determined to have a similar posting. In August 1943 he returned to New Zealand for five weeks to attend an NCO intelligence course at Trentham and then returned to the Pacific, where he remained for a further eleven months. He was promoted to corporal and spent six of those months at Houailou on the east coast of New Caledonia, purchasing fruit and other produce for the army. He stayed with the Voison family, who were descended from French settlers who had married into the local community. Muldoon recalled that 'At that time it was a good war. The river ran by with deep pools for swimming . . . The farmer's daughter was attractive and friendly. What more could a young soldier want?'[9]

Returning to New Zealand at the end of August 1944, Muldoon found that those soldiers with specific trades and skills were offered the opportunity of returning to civilian life. He recalled that the rest, 'the useless ones, including accountants, were after a month at Papakura shipped off to Italy.'[10] In actual fact it was not a month but over four months before Muldoon, having reverted to the rank of lance-corporal, embarked with the 14th 2nd NZEF Reinforcements for the Middle East, and not until 13 March 1945 after a short time in Egypt that he joined the Divisional Cavalry Battalion in Italy. The Battalion was formed towards the end of the war by converting the cavalry from scout cars to an infantry regiment. C Squadron was commanded by Major Duncan MacIntyre and D Squadron by Major John Marshall. Lance-Corporal Muldoon was posted to D Squadron. Many of the soldiers were inexperienced infantry, either recent reinforcements from New Zealand or soldiers drawn from armoured, machine gun or motorised units. As a result they suffered relatively heavy casualties in the following weeks.[11]

Once again Muldoon sought to attach himself to an intelligence unit and applied for a vacancy. He was interviewed and apparently accepted because of his experience and because most of the others in the unit also seemed to be Irish New Zealanders such as himself. However, when the rest said that they were going to Mass and Muldoon declined on the grounds that he was a Baptist, he missed out on the posting. Muldoon always believed that he was the victim of religious discrimination.[12]

On 9 and 10 April the Division took part in an assault across the Senio River and on 18 and 19 April defeated German paratroopers at the Gaiana River. The fighting was quite heavy and Muldoon was glad that during the advance they had had the Maori Battalion on their left flank. He remembered resting on a river bank in the Po Valley watching Maori soldiers coming back from the front with their captured draught horses, chickens and German flags. Of the thirty-two soldiers who started in his troop in Italy only five went through the whole month-long campaign; the others, including the troop's officer, Gilbert Murray, were killed, wounded or became ill. Muldoon later wrote, 'Of my service in Italy I can only say that I was lucky.'[13]

The Senio and Gaiana River crossings were accomplished at night and in fog under heavy German and Allied gunfire. Muldoon suspected that some of the Allied barrage was closer to him than to the Germans. As the shells came in, he realised that he could be dead at any moment and that there was absolutely nothing he could do about it except drop to the ground if one sounded too close. He was frightened and desperate to keep in touch with the men to his left and right. He decided that if he ever got out of the nightmare alive he would never again be frightened of anything.[14]

On one occasion the New Zealand troops dug in on a stopbank with the enemy dug in only a hundred yards away across the river. Muldoon and the other soldiers had to dash with their mess tins back into a paddock behind their trenches to get their meals and thus risk exposing themselves to German snipers. Muldoon seriously considered going hungry.[15]

On 2 May the Division entered Trieste, where the remnants of German units were resisting the attack of Yugoslav Communist partisan forces. Seven days later Germany surrendered and the war in Europe ended. Muldoon was delighted, and the end of the war coincided with his sitting his cost accountancy exams. The squadron was camped five miles outside Trieste, and Muldoon claimed that as Marshall's tent was the only one with a table and chair, he sat the exam there with the orderly officer as supervisor. Marshall, however, claimed that he supervised the exam, recalling that 'I lay on my camp bed and read a book while he sat his exam. It was a warm, sunny afternoon, the tent flaps had been rolled up and were open to the view of a green field and shady trees.'[16]

The Division was preparing to move from Italy to the Pacific to take part in the planned invasion of Japan when, in August 1945 following the dropping of the atomic bombs on Hiroshima and Nagasaki, Japan surrendered. Muldoon had no desire to go to Japan and his length of time in the army made him eligible for discharge. Although part of the Division under MacIntyre did join J-force and take part in the Allied occupation of Japan, Muldoon remained in Italy for a short time before being discharged.

During that time Muldoon worked briefly in Trieste as a liaison clerk attached to the Scots Guards before moving to an army school just outside Florence, where for several months he instructed soldiers wishing to pursue further education in accountancy prior to their rehabilitation. On 19 October, shortly after being promoted to corporal for the third time in September 1945, he was posted to the 18th New Zealand Armoured Regiment and reverted again to the rank of lance-corporal. In December he sailed to London where he took up an armed services educational bursary, which gave him about £2 a week. He was discharged from the army in February 1946.

Muldoon arrived in England shortly before Christmas 1945 and spent it with relatives in Suffolk. Rationing was very tight and there were shortages of everything. The war-shocked British were also worried that the Soviet Union was emerging as a potential enemy as great as Nazi Germany, and Muldoon found the combined war damage, scarcity and insecurity very depressing.[17] He claimed, 'That year in Britain was one of the hardest that I have spent.'[18]

Although homesick, Muldoon had come to England for a purpose and obtained employment at Robson, Morrow and Co., Moorgate, London, a large cost accounting firm at the forefront of modern management accounting. Lawrence Robson, the senior partner and, at the time Muldoon joined the firm, past president of the Institute of Cost and Works Accountants, recalled that Muldoon

> was principally engaged during that time on the audits of a series of large engineering groups and was particularly interested in standard costs and budgetary control, inventory control and the auditor's involvement with valuation of stocks and work-in-progress. His colleagues here remember him for his personality and his dry sense of humour. He proved himself to be a capable and persistent investigator of the financial and audit problems with which he was confronted.[19]

Muldoon became part of a team auditing industrial companies throughout Britain, but mainly in the industrial Midlands. Many of his evenings were spent in dreary hotel rooms studying for his cost accounting exams.

When he was in London, Muldoon boarded with a family called Bates at Reigate. When not working or studying he watched soccer matches and cricket, went to a few shows, and roamed around London sightseeing. Most of his spare time went to preparing for exams administered by the Institute of Cost and Works Accountants. After six months he passed the intermediate cost accounting exam and after twelve months in December 1946 the final exam. Others expressed some surprise when he came top of the final exam and was the first overseas student to win the Leverhulme Prize. The Leverhulme Prize had been founded in 1933 to honour Lord Leverhulme's presidency of the Institute of Cost and Works Accountants from 1919, when it was founded, until 1925 and was awarded to the best paper in Costing in the Institute's final exam.[20]

During his stay in Britain Muldoon located and stayed with relatives of his mother near Ipswich and was attracted to the Suffolk countryside. He found tremendous ignorance of New Zealand in England and was astonished when some workmates believed his tall stories, for example that New Zealanders used different-sized shells and stones for money. He had little time or inclination, however, to make friends or extend his visit. He arrived back in New Zealand on the *Rimutaka* in February 1947.

The Auckland Electric Power Board had held Muldoon's job for him during the war, and on his return to New Zealand he went back to work for them. Although he had been admitted to the New Zealand Society of Accountants as an Associate Registered Accountant on 18 November 1942,[21] had subsequently qualified as a cost accountant by the examinations he had completed in the army and in England, and had been formally congratulated by resolution of the AEPB Board for the award of the Leverhulme Prize,[22] he was given back his old job of arrears clerk. He complained and was transferred to the AEPB's stores office where he spent the next three months filling in stock cards and resenting very much a hierarchical system in which he was still very near the bottom.[23] On 27 June 1947 he left the Board's employment. In a reference for Muldoon the Power Board's Secretary noted, 'I regret that at the present time this Board has no suitable position available which we could offer him, and it is for this reason only that he is leaving the Board's employ. We are very sorry to lose his services, but he carries with him our best wishes for his future success.'[24]

Wally Browne was still taking a close interest in his nephew's welfare. Browne served with Charles Mills on a number of Baptist committees and was president of the Ludhiana Mission in India. Mills, another prominent Baptist layman who went to the Baptist Tabernacle in Queen Street, was a partner in the accountancy firm of Kendon Mills, which had been established by William Kendon in 1907 and whose offices were on the sixth floor of The Tower, Chancery Chambers, in O'Connell Street. Browne used his contact with Mills and with Kendon, who also was a member of the Baptist Tabernacle and president of the Auckland Sunday School Union, to arrange jobs first for his nephew Rob and later for his son Graham.[25] It was perhaps no coincidence that about that time the firm also became the auditors of Frank M. Winstone Ltd, of which Browne was managing director.

Muldoon commenced working for Kendon and Mills as chief clerk. Within three years in March 1950 he became a partner in the firm. The firm was relatively small and its fees were not exorbitant, but it had a large turnover. In the year Muldoon became a partner, gross fees totalled £4,280. Rent cost £160, general expenses £353, other expenses £52. Salaries for employees totalled £905. Of the three partners, Mills received £1,579, Kendon £600 and Muldoon £609 16s 1d, which was about twice what he had received as an employee during the previous year.[26]

Muldoon also taught auditing to adult students in evening classes at Seddon Memorial Technical College as a means of augmenting his income, and throughout the ten years he taught there he became known to many younger budding accountants, including Brian Tyler, who was later to become Auditor-General.

By 1947 when Muldoon joined Kendon Mills, 'Willie' Kendon was old and not really carrying a full load as a partner. In 1953 'Charlie' Mills became ill. This put Muldoon under considerable pressure. Mills's son, Fred, had qualified as an accountant in 1949 but was working for another firm. In 1953 he took up a partnership in his father's firm. Two years later, in October 1955, Graham Browne, who had earlier been in partnership with Clive Haszard, fell out with Haszard and shifted with some of his clients, accepting a partnership with Mills and Muldoon so that the firm became Kendon Mills Muldoon and Browne.[27]

The key person in the office apart from the partners was Mrs Edith Heath, a widow who preferred to be known in the office by her maiden name as Miss Simmonds. Miss Simmonds had joined the office when Kendon established the firm in 1907 and remained for fifty years. She was confident and competent but 'found Robbie hard to take'. In personality Muldoon was quite different from Kendon, who was 'the stereotype of the Victorian bookkeeper crouched on a high stool over a sloping desk writing slowly all day in beautiful copperplate', or Charles Mills, who was 'brisk and positive' and still very much the Royal Flying Corps officer that he had been in World War I.[28]

At the time there were about ten reasonably well-known accounting firms in Auckland, of which Kendon Mills Muldoon and Browne was one. Most accountants in Auckland knew each other quite well and often met informally, chatting over a leisurely afternoon tea at the Mayfair Tearooms on the corner of Vulcan Lane and O'Connell Street. Muldoon also lunched most days between 1947 and 1960 with his friend Colin Busfield at the RSA cafeteria opposite his accounting office. Many accountants and lawyers also had church, political or social interests and no one worried if a partner vanished from the office for a few hours to do something unconnected with business.

Fred Mills spent much of the 1950s in awe of his partner, who as an accountant could be 'really quite brilliant' and could recall lists of figures forward and backward and rarely be wrong.[29] He was also often mischievous. Muldoon constantly joked with or played jokes on the staff. When a new office-girl, for example, brought him a cup of tea on her first day, Muldoon in a gruff voice barked, 'What's the meaning of this? You've brought me a left-handed cup of tea. I'm right-handed.' The girl was so startled she jumped and tipped the cup of hot tea right down his front. On another occasion he convinced a naive young office-worker that corned mutton came from Waiheke because the sheep on the island drank salt water. Most of the time Muldoon was friendly and without pretension, happy to talk and joke not just with the 'upper echelon' of clients but with the lowliest of employees. Quite a few of the staff would babysit for Muldoon, not because they had to but because they liked him.

On occasion, however, Muldoon could be 'abrasive and dogmatic'. Although patient with and prepared to help someone who wanted to learn, he was impatient with fools and know-alls. He disliked incompetence, and as a busy man who hated wasting time he could appear intolerant and rude. Particularly when he was canvassing as a candidate in 1954, 1957 and 1960 he often came back into the office 'tired, uptight and snappy', and his colleagues learnt to avoid him even to the extent, as Fred Mills did, of 'walking past his office door at below desk height.'[30]

The firm, which in addition to the partners at first employed about four office staff, had a mixed bag of clients. The most prominent were the Foodstuffs–Four Square grocery chain (whose books Kendon had audited since the Baptist Heaton Barker started it as a co-operative buying group in 1922), the department store Kirkpatrick and Stevens, the law firm Russell McVeagh, and Christopher Bede Studio. Muldoon's first major task on joining Kendon Mills was to devise a general costing and accounting system for Christopher Bede, whose owner, Bill Doherty, was in the process of turning the business from a one-man photographer's business to a New Zealand-wide and very large and profitable enterprise. Doherty needed an accounting system that gave him weekly up-to-date accounts and had a stand-up fight with Muldoon at their first meeting, finally shouting at him, 'You're the accountant. Put in the system and I'll run the business.' Muldoon provided the expertise and set up the system.[31]

Will Kendon also off-loaded on to Muldoon the All Golds Rugby League Association, whose accounts Kendon had been keeping. Muldoon immediately realised what Kendon apparently had not noticed. Much of the All Golds' income came from the illegal sale of liquor through a locker system run in conjunction with the billiard room. Baptist accountants were the bookkeepers for one of Auckland's major after-hours 'sly-grog' outlets.[32]

Muldoon also had as clients a Yugoslav fisherman, John Rouse, and Bob Rope and Bert Hyde who ran the Hauraki Towboat Company, which consisted of a single tug and barge shifting sand and shingle in the Hauraki Gulf. The waterfront was a tough and colourful place and Muldoon made friends as well as clients out of some of the very interesting people he found there, such as Marie George who ran the Blue Boats. One of the Hauraki Towboat Company's and Blue Boats' competitors was Lance Julian who ran the Auckland Water Transport Company. Julian's offices were at the end of Princes Wharf in Quay Street. When Julian's old bookkeeper retired, Julian asked Muldoon to take over the accounts. Muldoon did so and because Julian operated largely on a cash basis Muldoon was frequently down on the wharves meeting the boats and paying wages and expenses. Julian did not use waterside workers to load and unload his barges, which carted logs from Warkworth, sand and shingle from Takatu, and loads down the Gulf and up river to Paeroa. Particularly during the 1951 wharf strike things were very tense because Julian's boats were the only ones operating. Julian was always hard up, and Muldoon had to devise means of servicing unpaid and unpayable bills by each month arranging to pay off a percentage of each one.[33]

Julian was thrilled with Muldoon's handling of his affairs, particularly the way he dealt with an unproductive two-year tax investigation of Julian's accounts by Inland Revenue, and when about 1954 Julian and Winstones created a joint company, Gulf Freighters, Muldoon became a director. He was also made a co-trustee with Julian's son Harry of Lance Julian's will. When Julian died in 1957, the company was in serious trouble. There were mortgages on all the boats; death duties, because of the high assessed value of the boats, were an impossible liability; and there was no money in the bank. Muldoon and Harry Julian met Inland Revenue, told them that the boats were overvalued on the current market, and requested three years to pay the death duties by quarterly instalments at the bank rate of interest. Inland Revenue argued that the proposal was 'very unorthodox', but were eventually persuaded by Muldoon's figures and arguments and agreed to the arrangement.[34]

Foodstuffs, which Barker's son Phil was starting to expand dramatically after the war into the biggest grocery wholesaler in New Zealand, was another client Muldoon valued. As a co-operative wholesaler, Foodstuffs did not pay tax but distributed its profits to the individual grocers, who then paid tax on their total net profits. Muldoon took over the audit of Foodstuffs shortly after he joined Kendon

Mills and devised systems to make sure that the pre-signed cheques that each grocer gave to Foodstuffs were adequately protected. There were no monthly statements or invoices but every week when the orders came in the delivery was costed and a cheque filled in with the amount and banked. If a grocer on checking the delivery note found a discrepancy, an adjustment was made without question the following week. The system meant there was very little clerical work and no cash flow problems for the co-operative wholesaler.[35]

With his very conservative approach to accounting, Muldoon throughout his life was opposed to 'creative accounting', which he believed was designed to avoid legitimate tax or mislead investors and shareholders. He believed as an auditor that there was always some tension between satisfying the directors of a company, who decided which auditor to employ, and the shareholders, whose interests needed to be protected even if that involved criticising the company's management or directors. As a cost accountant, he looked carefully at the cost factors in production or at ways of defining those costs and improving the methods of production or the management and accounting systems in order to increase efficiency, productivity, profitability and accountability.

In 1956 Muldoon became a fellow of the New Zealand Society of Accountants and was also elected president of the New Zealand Institute of Cost Accountants. In that latter position he was responsible for negotiations which integrated the Institute with the Society. A Cost and Management Accounting Division was then created within the Society of Accountants. In 1956 he also organised the first joint cost and management seminar with the New Zealand Institute of Management. This work won him in 1957 the Society's Maxwell Award for the member who did the most in any particular year to further knowledge of cost and management accounting in the community.[36]

When Charles Mills had become ill in 1953, one of the jobs he gave up was electorate secretary of the Rodney National Party. Mills had encouraged Muldoon's activity in the National Party and was happy to see his junior partner stand as National's candidate in Mount Albert in 1954 and also take over the secretaryship in Rodney and subsequently in the new electorate of Waitemata.

After Muldoon entered Parliament in 1960, he still visited the office from time to time, but as Mills and Browne became busier they took on more senior staff to cover their partner's absence. For a time he paid his parliamentary salary into the firm and the three partners split the firm's profits including the salary three ways. Muldoon became Under-Secretary for Finance in 1963 and became a partner in name only, though he still kept in touch with what was happening in the firm. When he became Minister of Finance in 1967 and especially as he became more controversial, his association with the firm, even as a non-active partner, became somewhat of a mixed blessing as the clients covered a wide range of political viewpoints.[37]

Even after National's loss in 1972, when Muldoon did visit the office a little more, it was usually only to chat to a few older clients or drop off parts of the manuscript of *The Rise and Fall of a Young Turk* to be typed. From 1975 he attended only a few functions at Kendon Mills Muldoon and Browne and in 1984 was paid out as a partner when it amalgamated with the international firm of Klynveldt Main Goedler, which subsequently became KMG Peat Marwick. Some of Kendon's partners chose to go instead to Coopers Lybrand or Price Waterhouse. Long before then Muldoon had effectively ceased to be an accountant and had become a full-time professional politician.

CHAPTER 4

The Junior Nationals
and Marriage

IN 1944 THE CHAIRMAN OF THE AUCKLAND DIVISION OF THE National Party, Alex McKenzie, asked Dr James Rutherford, professor of history at Auckland University College, if he would establish a Junior National Party organisation in Auckland as part of a general campaign to revitalise the party and provide 'the training ground for our future candidates and members of Parliament'.[1] The 18–30 age range and particularly young returned servicemen were targeted for membership. One of the first functions was a picnic for 150 returned sailors. The first formal meeting was held on 21 September 1944 when Rutherford was elected as president and Marjorie Gadsby as secretary. Dr Roy McElroy spoke to the inaugural meeting on 'The Place of Youth in the Politics of the Postwar World'. Two committees, one for social activities and the other for educational and political activities, were set up. By March 1946 there were 416 members in Auckland and by March 1947, 950.[2]

Colin Busfield heard about the Junior Nationals shortly after he returned from overseas. He and other returned servicemen had come out of regimented armed service and were dismayed to find New Zealand a restrictive and regulated society. They wanted to get on with their lives after wasted years at war and resented and protested against the restraints imposed on them by the Labour Government. The National Party was seen by many returned servicemen as radical liberators opposed to an authoritarian and paternalistic government. Busfield joined the Junior Nationals and in March 1947 accepted an invitation to form a branch in the Mount Albert electorate. Among those whose help he sought was his old friend Rob Muldoon, who had just returned from overseas to his home in Western Springs and who had already attended a couple of Junior National dances at Colin's invitation. Colin became branch chairman at the inaugural meeting and Rob one of the five men and five women on the committee.

Shortly afterwards, in August 1947 the Labour member of Parliament for Mount Albert, Arthur Richards, died. A by-election was held in September. Muldoon became very active in the campaign, a report in *Junior News* commenting

that 'with Robbie Muldoon as organiser of Junior activity, Juniors have helped
with the roll purge, distribution of electoral numbers cards, and have been ready
for any tasks they are able to do.'[3] Twenty-six local Junior 'Nats' were involved,
helped by about thirty from elsewhere in Auckland. The activity was in vain and a
young journalist, Warren Freer, won the seat for Labour and was to hold it for the
next thirty-four years.

In March 1948 Muldoon succeeded Busfield as chairman of the Mount Albert
Junior Nationals, heading a committee that included at least nine of his Mount
Albert Baptist Bible Class friends, notably Colin and Alan Busfield, Alan Jenkin
and Graham Browne. Muldoon also became, at the April annual meeting of the
Divisional Junior Nationals, deputy chairman of the Division's Education and
Political Committee and the committee's representative on the Divisional Executive. The Education and Political Committee was chaired by Peter Dempsey,
who had completed a Master of Arts in history under Rutherford and who replaced
Rutherford as the Auckland Junior Nationals' president at the Juniors' third
annual general meeting on 11 March 1947. Dempsey at the age of 22 had also
been the National candidate for the Ponsonby seat at the 1946 elections.[4]

The Education and Political Committee organised meetings addressed by MPs.
It also sponsored debating teams and competitions, and Muldoon became a keen
debater. Debating, not only for entertainment but also to train young political
activists in public speaking, researching material, organising arguments and
chairing meetings, was a popular activity among a minority of Junior Nationals,
particularly those who were politically ambitious. Heckling was allowed during
the debates. Muldoon rarely became flustered by it. If he could not immediately
think of a telling response, he simply ignored the interjection, raised his voice a
little, and carried on with his argument. The debaters were also often rowdy and
cheeky interjectors at Labour Party public meetings, and sometimes went to Myers
Park on a Sunday afternoon to heckle the Communist Party's soapbox speakers.

Junior National teams debated among themselves and also competed against
other debating societies in Auckland. The electorate secretary of Mount Albert was
Bill Allingham, an accountant who was some five years older than Muldoon.
Allingham suggested that the Mount Albert Junior 'Nats' should have their own
debating team and one was formed consisting of Allingham, Colin Busfield and
Muldoon. Later Muldoon teamed with Barry Purdy and Dan Kerruish. Purdy was a
particularly effective debater with an attractive platform manner. Muldoon was
more serious and very detailed in preparing an argument and planning tactics.

The Mount Albert team was quite successful, competing against teams from
the Junior Chamber of Commerce, the University, the Waterside Workers' Union,
Mount Eden Prison, and various debating societies. It won, for example, three of its
first four competitive debates, and tied on the fourth. One of those debates, which
they were able to argue with conviction, was against University. Taking the
negative on the proposition 'That protection of secondary industry is in the best
interest of New Zealand', they won by 286 to 260 points.[5]

Muldoon's team never won the prestigious Athenaeum Cup for the best debating team in Auckland or the Westminster shield for the best Junior National team in New Zealand, but they were twice runners-up for the Athenaeum Cup. The first time they lost to the prison team, which included a murderer and a safe-breaker, and Muldoon suggested his opponents had more time than his team to prepare their case. The second time they lost the final to the wharfies' team, led by the well-known communist Bill McAra. Indeed, all three members of the wharfies' team at that time, Muldoon thought, were members of the Communist Party, and they used to farewell the Junior Nats after a debate with the cheery salutation, 'Goodnight, comrades, we'll meet again over the barricades.'[6]

The Fabian Society wrote to the Auckland Debating Association noting that it was a pity that the final debate in 1949 was on the topic, 'That divorce should be made easier', and suggested that a political topic would have been better. The Fabians then invited the Junior Nats and the wharfies to hold a second debate on the proposal, 'That the young people of New Zealand prefer economic security to personal freedom.' Muldoon and his colleagues agreed to debate provided that the teams argued against their personal political inclinations. The wharfies agreed, but the Fabian Society insisted that they wanted a debate reflecting convictions. The Junior Nats were required by the party's president, Alex McKenzie, to use material prepared by three senior members of the National Party, Will Fortune, Ronald Algie and Martin Nestor, and the event turned into a humourless, partisan slanging match.[7]

Muldoon and the Junior Nats complained that pressure from the senior party officials had taken all the pleasure out of debating. Fortune and Algie then met all the young debaters and asked them bluntly if they were prepared to comply with party discipline and seriously prepare themselves for political careers. Some, including Colin Busfield and Gainor Jackson, refused but Muldoon and Dempsey agreed to accept senior direction.[8]

Alan Busfield, who also debated on occasions in Muldoon's team, recalled that on one occasion Muldoon claimed he had gone into a church in New Plymouth for some peace and contemplation before a debate. He said during the summing-up that he had found the minister's notes on the pulpit. Towards the end the minister had written a comment in the margin: 'Argument weak, increase volume.' Muldoon suggested that summed up the other debating team's performance.[9]

In October 1948, at a special meeting, Muldoon was elected chairman of the Auckland Divisional Junior Nationals, replacing Dempsey, who had left for England on a Rotary scholarship. He defeated Bill Twentyman, who had been a foundation Junior Nat in 1944 and chairman of the Social Committee since 1945, in a secret ballot after both nominees had spoken for ten minutes. The deputy chairman, Marjorie Gadsby, who had acted after Dempsey's departure, did not seek the chair. *Junior News*, reporting the election, concluded: 'In Mr Muldoon the Junior Section has a chairman who will encourage and assist the political aims of the Party, at the same time fully realising the importance and work of its social-activities.'[10] Muldoon had also attended his first meeting of the Auckland Divisional Executive of the National Party on 10 August 1948 and, except for a couple of years at the beginning of the 1950s, was to remain a member until a few months before his death almost forty-four years later.

Over the following eighteen months, Muldoon, who was re-elected chairman in March 1949, presided over the peak of Junior National membership and activity in the Auckland Division and earned the praise of McKenzie, who commented on the 'good progress' and considerable increase in membership under 'the able chairmanship of Rob Muldoon'.[11] Membership rose to 2900 members in eleven branches, which often combined for social activities on Friday nights at the National Party rooms on the corner of Queen and Customs Street, only yards away from both the central city tram terminus and the ferry buildings. At a time when few young people had cars the National Party rooms were one of the most accessible places to young people from any part of Auckland. As chairman, Muldoon was out almost every night at committee meetings, dances, debates, and, as the 1949 election drew near, campaign activities.

In March 1949 'Muldoon presented a paper on "The Production Problem" which was his recent survey of the practical application and advantages of the profit sharing scheme' and in the same month the Junior Nationals had a seminar on communism 'with particular reference to freedom of speech and freedom of assembly'.[12] Six speakers stressed that communist means should not be used to defeat communism. Communists 'must have absolute freedom' in New Zealand. Muldoon, however, took a much tougher line. In his first lengthy political opinion recorded for posterity, he argued in these terms:

> The British Empire dropped the cricket attitude during the War with Germany and retaliated in kind with indiscriminate bombing and commando tactics. Let us apply the same ideas to Communism. In particular follow their methods: they wish to use the weapons of democracy to destroy it – deny them these weapons. Liquidate them by deporting any person who refuses to swear allegiance to the British Crown or breaks this oath by word or deed. In my opinion their allegiance to a foreign power should forfeit their rights as British citizens.[13]

Even at the start of the Cold War these were fairly extreme views, though not uncommon at that time in the Western World.

Subsequently, although he always remained strongly anti-communist, Muldoon moderated his views on communists somewhat, admitting that

> Most of them of course start from a burning sense of injustice based on their own experience and this is a valid and legitimate emotion. Where they go wrong I believe is in fastening on an outmoded theory that you can remedy these injustices by pulling down the people at the top, the successful companies, and by redistributing inherited wealth.[14]

This sympathy for the poor and the powerless was to remain a constant feature of his outlook and policies throughout his political life, as was his dislike of those who tried to pull everyone down to the lowest common denominator. So also was his willingness to retaliate overwhelmingly and without worrying too much about showing a gentlemanly 'cricket attitude' to his opponents.

Politics was not the most important reason why Junior Nationals joined the organisation. Most were interested primarily, and some exclusively, in having fun. There was a simplicity and lack of sophistication about Junior National occasions at that time. No liquor was allowed at any Junior function, despite the fact that many of the men were returned servicemen in their mid and late twenties. Functions were usually chaperoned by even older National Party members, who frowned on 'necking', let alone anything sexually more serious.[15] Everything was rather proper and morally harmless. Dances, socials, teas, picture theatre groups, barbecues, picnics, indoor games evenings, tennis tournaments, harbour cruises, weekend trips to Rotorua, Wairakei, Piha, Mount Maunganui, Ruapehu and Egmont, and, in conjunction with the National Party's women's sections, debutante balls were all used to attract and retain Junior members.

Social activities were not neglected during Muldoon's tenure as Junior chairman, even though he himself did not particularly like dancing. In the three months of October, November and December 1949, for example, there were thirty-four social activities, three or four a week, including Hallowe'en, a vice-versa evening, a carnival, a Guy Fawkes party at the Mount Albert Tennis Pavilion with fireworks on the tennis courts, a pre-election party, a Mad Hatters dance, six Christmas parties, and picnic trips to Cowes Bay, Kawau Island, Pakatoa Island and the Waitakeres.[16] The Junior Nats even had rather childish games evenings. Muldoon's favourite game was one in which everyone sat in a circle on the floor and in turns threw dice. Whoever got an agreed score had to put on a hat, belt, tie and gloves and then with a knife and fork eat a frozen block of chocolate. They had to stop when the next person threw the correct number and pass everything over to them. Muldoon loved it, and his friends suspected that he sometimes cheated so that he could eat the whole block.[17] Muldoon headed a very talented and active organisation, many of whose leading figures were returned servicemen who were to become prominent in the Auckland business community.[18] There were also a large number of young women active in Junior Nationals. Many parents were reluctant to let their well-brought-up 'nice girls' attend public dances at the Orange Hall or Peter Pan but were happy to allow their daughters to attend well-supervised dances and outings organised by the Junior Nats. One of the women recalled the organisation as a 'matrimonial agency' and a male Junior said it was a 'marriage bureau', a meeting place for future husbands and wives.[19] Most of the men mentioned above married young women they met at the Junior National functions.[20] Many of those couples remained friends and admirers, though not always uncritical ones, of Muldoon for the rest of their lives. For forty years they had an annual reunion over Anniversary Weekend.

Muldoon's contemporaries in the Junior Nationals in the 1947–50 period almost all remembered him at that time as a pleasant, fun-loving young man, whose mischievous humour lacked the corrosive quality which later marked the wit of the older politician.[21] Thea Frogley, for example, recalled the younger Rob as 'a bright, happy bloke, who laughed a lot and stood out in a crowd'. He was the jovial master of ceremonies at her wedding, but in later years 'the person who stood up and made public statements didn't seem too familiar'. Dempsey noted his sense of humour and fun, his obvious concern for ordinary people, and the fact that Muldoon was not devious or given to 'simulating an opinion or a stand. He said things as he saw them and said what he meant . . . He didn't suffer fools gladly, especially those with pretensions.' But Dempsey also regretted that in his later years Muldoon seemed to be 'unnecessarily abrasive . . . obsessed with the idea that he had to be blunt to the point of being rude. The reputation for calling a spade a spade perhaps took possession of his personality.'[22]

One person who was not an unqualified Muldoon admirer was Marjorie Gadsby, who later married Ferguson Prince. She regarded the Junior National organisation, with some justification, as 'her baby' and in the eyes of some Junior Nats 'mothered them'.[23] Muldoon as chairman tried to formalise the Junior Nationals' organisation, which had grown swiftly and somewhat haphazardly around the person of its hard-working foundation secretary, whom Muldoon recalled as 'the rock on which the Junior Nats were founded.'[24] The 1950 annual report made reference to new by-laws originated by Muldoon, 'who has been the force behind so much that has been achieved this year . . . Committees have their existence, relationships and authorities clearly defined and are able to work smoothly and speedily' – as a result of the by-laws.[25] Gadsby, who was some twelve years older than Muldoon, resented and resisted his organisational reforms and had a number of heated arguments with him. On at least one occasion she stormed out of a meeting in tears and Colin Busfield, who was the treasurer and supported Gadsby in that dispute, later observed: 'Marjorie and Rob never saw eye to eye and never will.'[26]

Although Muldoon was for the rest of his life to clash with some women on various committees and in the National Party caucus, he did manage to work reasonably well with others. Thea McKinstry represented the Herne Bay Junior Nats on the Divisional Executive and recalled that almost the whole committee was male. As chairman, Muldoon was 'always so nice and asked me for my opinion and respected my views'.[27]

Another young woman who was impressed was Thea Flyger, whom Muldoon first met when he attended a seminar on voluntary unionism in 1947.[28] She was one of the few young women present and looked much younger than she was. Muldoon was astonished to find that not only was she 20 but that, like himself, she was an accountant. Both became members of the Divisional Junior Education and Political Committee during 1947, Muldoon representing the Mount Albert and Thea the North Shore Junior Nationals. Interestingly, the Education and Political Committee had nine members, only three of whom were women. The Social Committee in contrast had twenty-eight members, fourteen of whom were women.

Muldoon did not seek re-election as Junior chairman in 1950, and although he served until 1957 on the Division's Junior Advisory Committee, he played a less prominent role in the Junior Nationals and for several years concentrated more on marriage and establishing a home and business.

Thea Flyger's father, Stanley, was an Auckland builder who had earlier trained as an engineer and worked as a surveyor at the Glen Afton mine, west of Huntly. He and his wife, Annie, had three children, of whom Thea was the second after an older sister and before a younger brother. Born at Pukemiro, Thea was educated at Belmont Primary and Takapuna Grammar Schools. An Anglican, she taught Sunday School at St Michael's Church, Bayswater. When she left school she worked for the public accounting firm of Battley and Johnson and was one of only three women enrolled in accountancy night classes at Seddon Memorial Technical College. Later she worked in the costing office of Holeproof Ltd.

Stanley Flyger took his daughter with him to both National and Labour Party meetings and she had helped her uncle and aunty at functions organised by the Belmont National Party. Thea, however, joined the Young Nationals largely for social rather than political reasons. With her friend Geraldine (Gerry) Byrne, Thea regularly caught the ferry to attend Young National functions in the city. She revelled in the tennis on floodlit courts, the dances, debates and weekends away at Waiheke or Waitomo.

Thea, or Tam as Rob called her, was a tiny, neat, gentle, quietly spoken person. She was also intelligent and even as a young woman self-assured and emotionally strong. In physical build and personality she was almost the opposite of Rob's mother Amie Muldoon. Thea started going out with Rob shortly before her twenty-first birthday in March 1948. Rob's friend, Alan Jenkin, concurrently started dating Thea's friend Geraldine. Both men in later life recalled how smitten they must have been with their future wives. The men regularly took Thea and Gerry home to Devonport on the last ferry from town, then walked them to their homes, then walked back to Devonport and caught the night launch to Auckland, and finally, having missed the last tram, walked back to Mount Albert.[29]

Colin Busfield, who was best man at Rob and Thea's wedding, recalled that Rob and Thea did not formally announce their engagement. The Junior Nats were on a launch heading off to Waiheke for a weekend when someone noticed and announced the fact that Thea was wearing an engagement ring.[30] They were married at Holy Trinity Church, Devonport, on 17 March 1951. Rob was 29 and Thea had turned 24 just four days before the wedding.

Thea wanted flowers in church for her wedding but Canon R. J. Stanton, who officiated at the wedding, would not allow them because.it was Lent. Thea suggested delaying the wedding so that she could have flowers, but the less romantic of the two accountants argued that they had to be married by 31 March so that he could claim the married couple's tax rebate for the previous year.

Thea stopped working after her marriage. Although her mother was not enthusiastic about her daughter marrying an older man so clearly committed to a political career, and indeed one who was to seek a nomination within months of the wedding, Thea's parents after the marriage proved very supportive of the young couple.[31] Rob and Thea lived with her parents while Thea's father and brother, with Rob's help as a labourer at weekends, built them a new home nearby at 48 Lake Road, Devonport. The house was financed and furnished with a serviceman's rehabilitation loan.

Within a short time three children were born: Barbara in December 1951, Jennifer in 1953 and Gavin in 1956. Because their parents had a rare blood incompatibility, all three pregnancies and deliveries caused concern but were successfully accomplished.

The first ten years of marriage were happy days for Rob and Thea and their children. They were just like many other ordinary young families living in Devonport. The children went to the Vauxhall kindergarten and then the girls went to the nearby local primary school and the local Methodist Sunday School. Thea's mother and father lived only five minutes' walk away, and Thea had friends around her with children of similar age. Until Jennifer was born, the family did not have a car but relied on public transport. Thea, an excellent dressmaker, made most of her own and the girls' dresses and knitted all their jumpers. Rob created a huge vegetable garden and built a glasshouse at the back of the house. He involved the girls as helpers in his garden working with him on Saturdays before he took them to Takapuna, Devonport or Eden Park to watch a rugby game and give Thea a break from the children. Most nights when he came home from work in summer the family strolled down for an evening swim at Narrow Neck Beach.

The family enjoyed an annual holiday at a beach: first in rented baches at Matapouri, Buffalo Beach or Taupo. One friend also recalled happy picnics at Pakiri, Sandspit and Hatfields, where during 1959 Thea's father, again with Rob's help, built over numerous weekends a small bach on a half-acre right-of-way section for the Muldoons.[32] Almost every school holiday and holiday weekend thereafter Thea was to retreat with the children to the beach, where they swam, read, walked, fished and enjoyed picnics. Rob joined them when he could at weekends. Even after Muldoon entered Parliament and after the family moved to Wellington, the children knew that every school holiday they would be together as a family at the beach and while in Auckland would be able to spend time with their grandparents. In retrospect, Thea believed that if the first ten years of marriage had not been so happy and had not provided such a strong base, the marriage and the family might not have survived some of the more stressful and nasty later years.[33]

Following his marriage in 1951 Muldoon joined the Takapuna Horticultural Society in order to get packets of seeds and information about gardening.[34] He subsequently started growing and showing pansies and lilies and revealed an 'inherent love of horticultural pursuits . . . and persevered with the growing of the difficult and unusual.'[35] He won various awards. Muldoon also belonged to the Auckland Lily Society and became a delegate to the Auckland Horticultural Council, the co-ordinating body of over seventy societies in and around Auckland. As the council's treasurer Muldoon led a small subcommittee which raised the money to purchase and alter 'The Chimes' boarding house as a headquarters for the council. He also was prominent in constructing floral displays at Western Springs and lecturing to horticultural societies all over Auckland. He was elected president of both the Auckland Lily Society and the Auckland Horticultural Council. Those who worked with him recalled his 'wonderful sense of humour'[36] and the fact that he was 'steadfast, reliable and ever willing to correct when necessary, and to advise, always without fear or favour.'[37] In recognition of both his expertise and his leadership of the council, Muldoon became a Fellow of the Royal Institute of Horticulture. Although gardening remained a lifelong interest and he did the gardening at first, after he entered Parliament and particularly in later life gardening was left largely to Thea as her husband devoted himself more and more exclusively to politics.[38]

CHAPTER 5

Three Times Lucky:
The Mount Albert (1954),
Waitemata (1957)
and Tamaki (1960) Campaigns

A S WELL AS BEING ACTIVE IN THE JUNIOR NATIONALS, PRIOR to the 1949 election Muldoon was also secretary of the St Luke's senior branch in Mount Albert. There he became closely associated with others who saw party membership as involving more than the collection of subscriptions and work at election times. L. E. Adams, who was later principal of Glendowie College and president of the Post Primary Teachers' Association, was a branch chairman in Mount Albert in the late 1940s and 'admired his efforts to get cracking on policy matters in the party when I as an older member had become disillusioned with the party's neglect of the political ideas of its workers . . . I saw in Rob Muldoon someone who took a dim view of this.'[1]

Within months of his marriage, Muldoon in 1951 sought National's nomination for the Mount Albert seat but lost to Reg Judson, the mayor of Manurewa, who had stood for the seat in 1949 and had more than halved the Labour majority. Muldoon came runner-up and after the selection meeting was told by McKenzie, the party president, that he had done well and would make a good MP one day.[2]

During the early 1950s the National Party's Mount Albert electorate organisation slumped. By December 1952 only three of its six branches were functioning and membership was down to 1000, well below the 2030 in 1941.[3] In 1953 a report to the Division lamented that in Mount Albert there was 'Great apathy to be contended with'.[4] Freer had held the Mount Albert seat at the 1951 election by 604 votes, but boundary changes prior to the 1954 election considerably strengthened Labour's hold by adding the Wesley state housing area from Roskill and a Labour-voting area in the west from Waitakere. The seat hardly looked National's best bet for a win from Labour at the forthcoming 1954 election.

Muldoon 1970. *Dominion*.

Above: Jerusha and Walter Clayton Browne, Muldoon's maternal grandparents. LAWRENCE BROWNE.

Top right: Jerusha Browne, Muldoon's formidable left-wing grandmother. LAWRENCE BROWNE.

Bottom right: Amie Muldoon (née Browne), Muldoon's mother. MULDOON PAPERS.

Above left: Amie Muldoon in Queen Street, Auckland, May 1946. CANDID CAMERA STUDIES/MULDOON PAPERS.

Above right: Walter Browne, Muldoon's uncle, had a considerable influence on his nephew's career and upbringing. LAWRENCE BROWNE.

Left: James Henry (Jim) Muldoon, Muldoon's father. MULDOON PAPERS.

Above: Robert David Muldoon, aged 1.
MULDOON PAPERS.

Right: Muldoon, aged 6, and Richard Fickling,
aged 8, and snapper they caught at Point
Chevalier beach in 1928. RICHARD FICKLING.

Above: Muldoon, second from left, front row, in Form 1A Kowhai Intermediate School, 1932. MULDOON PAPERS.

Left: Muldoon, aged 11, at Mount Albert Grammar School, 1933. MULDOON PAPERS.

Above: The Intelligence Section,
15 Brigade, New Caledonia 1943.
From left Corporal Neil Instone, Driver
Lance Borreson, Captain Frank Foster,
Sergeant Vic Stace, and Lance Corporal
Robert Muldoon. MULDOON PAPERS.

Right: Lance-Corporal Robert
Muldoon in Italy, 13 May 1945.
MULDOON PAPERS.

Above: Muldoon (bottom right), as chairman of the Auckland Junior Nationals, looks at the camera while all other eyes are on National Prime Minister Sidney Holland as he leaves the Civic Theatre, Auckland, during the November 1949 election campaign. *NZ HERALD.*

Left: The Junior Nationals 1950. From left: Fred Brittain, Muldoon holding Thea Flyger's hand, Ann Turnbull, Alan Jenkin, ?, Valerie Nilson, Ferguson Prince with his arm round Marjorie Gadsby, ?, Colin Busfield, ?, Peter Dempsey. COLIN BUSFIELD.

Above: The bride and groom, 1951.
SUTCLIFFE PHOTOGRAPHY/MULDOON PAPERS.

Top left: Muldoon's father-in-law, Stanley Flyger, built his daughter and son-in-law this house in Devonport in 1951. MULDOON PAPERS.

Bottom left: Rob and Thea at a Junior National Ball in July 1952. MULDOON PAPERS.

A more likely win was the new seat of Waitemata, which Muldoon started to represent on the Divisional Executive from its meeting of 4 March 1954. Shortly before, he had replaced his partner Charles Mills as electorate secretary of the Rodney electorate. When Waitemata was formed, Muldoon became its secretary. Under the leadership of Jim Holdaway old branches were reorganised, new branches formed, and there was considerable activity across the electorate. The electorate also criticised the National Government's 1954 Budget, Muldoon, on behalf of Waitemata, telling the Divisional Executive 'that the Budget proposals were not satisfactory to Superannuitants'. He requested that the matter be taken up with the Dominion Council of the party.[5]

National believed that, with the right candidate and a concerted campaign, it would win the new marginal seat of Waitemata stretching up the east coast of Auckland's North Shore. There was some concern, however, that none of the three initial nominees was suitable, though in retrospect it is difficult to see why. Harold Barry owned a chain of butcher shops; Leonard Bradley, a former Lieutenant Commander in the Navy, was an insurance manager; and Peter Dempsey, though only 29, had an excellent academic and party record and had started a commercial career. More importantly, Dempsey had contested the old Ponsonby seat, which had included Birkenhead and Northcote, in 1946 and had made personal friends with some of those who were now key figures in the new electorate. Throughout April and May 1954, however, pressure was put on Sir John Allum and W. J. Scott to be nominated but both declined.[6]

By early April the Labour candidate, Norman King, had been door-to-door canvassing full-time for several months, and the National Party officials in the electorate were becoming worried.[7] The selection was finally scheduled for 31 May but the withdrawal of Bradley led to the reopening of nominations. Two further nominations were forthcoming: Muldoon and another accountant Clive Haszard, who was eight years older than Muldoon and who, after a fine academic and sporting career, had served during the war as an officer in the Royal Navy. The selection was not held until late June when Dempsey became the candidate. In mid-October, however, Dempsey withdrew and a further selection was held, when Dr Hubert Morrison, a prominent doctor and sheep farmer of Wellsford, defeated a much stronger field of nine other nominees. Muldoon this time was not among them because, partly by stressing his Mount Albert connections, he had won the Mount Albert nomination in a two-way contest with Haszard, who lived in Kohimarama, after they had both been unsuccessful in the first Waitemata section.[8]

The campaign in Mount Albert was launched by Hon. John Marshall, who spoke in Muldoon's support at the Mayfair Theatre in Sandringham on 1 November. In his various speeches and newspaper articles during the 1954 campaign, Muldoon attacked socialists and Social Crediters who, he argued, believed in a simple, single solution to the world's complex problems. 'Today's problems have to be solved as they arise, although certainly by looking ahead. However, today, more than ever before, you cannot afford to be dogmatic . . . a complex answer is needed for a complex question.'[9] He also attracted a storm of interjections at one meeting by saying that the main difference between communists and socialists was that the former hoped to achieve the shared goal by revolution and the latter by education.[10] His fourteen public meetings were not particularly well attended, ranging from seven at Waikowhai to thirty at Balmoral.

Even discounting the low attendances, Muldoon's meetings were not unqualified successes. At one rowdy but good-humoured meeting in St Giles' Church all thirty members of the audience were Labour, as the vote of thanks but no confidence at the end revealed. At another meeting at St Luke's Church the lights went out and Muldoon had to stop speaking until someone found a shilling for the power meter. At a third in a school hall a small, elderly man in the front row kept asking Muldoon detailed questions about monetary theory. Muldoon found out later that his interrogator was Frank Langstone, the former Labour cabinet minister who later stood as a Social Credit candidate. Muldoon's evening, street-corner meetings also were not without incident, one irate man threatening to knock his block off for waking his baby. There were other irritations during the campaign. Muldoon's new Morris Minor car was defaced by children polishing it with scoria while he was away canvassing and his major billboards were demolished by opponents within about twenty-four hours of their erection.[11]

In his major election pamphlet, Muldoon listed eight major political beliefs which by and large he sought to adhere to for the rest of his political career. He told the voters,

I BELIEVE
That human values are more important than material values.
That the individual does not exist for the State – rather the State for the individual.
That class consciousness and the class war have no place in New Zealand.
That our people will never accept ultimate Socialism or its ally Communism.
That the National Government's record in maintaining industrial peace entitles it to the gratitude of every decent citizen.
That Social Security is the right of every New Zealander, young and old.
That the family must be retained as the basis of our national life.
That a Member of Parliament must make himself freely available in the interests of the people of his Electorate.[12]

He elaborated on some of these principles in a candidate's statement printed in the *Mt Albert Enterprise* in which he declared that 'Politicians must never forget that they are not dealing with statistics but with people. Any politician who forgets that his actions impinge directly on the daily lives of two million human beings is already on the way out . . . Our policy is designed to encourage every man to work to improve his position while ensuring that those in need are adequately provided for.' After noting that energetic, large-scale planning by the government was necessary to safeguard full employment in the future and that 'family life is . . . the rock on which our civilisation is built', Muldoon admitted that he had 'no simple solution for this country's problems' but offered 'my energy, my goodwill and a sincere desire to assist'.[13]

The National Party organisation in Mount Albert in 1954 was very weak and most of the work fell on Muldoon, on the electorate chairman, Jim Freeman, who was the general manager of Universal Business Directories, and on a very small team of helpers. Together they put up the billboards, organised the meetings, delivered the pamphlets, and canvassed door to door. Muldoon concentrated his canvassing on the Mount Albert and Mount Roskill state housing areas but to no avail, though his dogged work won him the admiration and gratitude of those who were involved in his campaign.

Muldoon not only impressed the Mount Albert organisation. During the campaign he found time to address the Auckland Women's Division of the party, its long-time and formidable leader, Mrs Doreen Bray, reporting that 'he was splendid'.[14] Despite such compliments and despite National winning the election overall, Muldoon lost to Freer by 3226 votes. Following the 1954 election Muldoon resumed his role as secretary of the Waitemata electorate and one of its representatives on the National Party's Divisional Executive. There he expressed continued concern at the damage done to the party by the change of candidate in Waitemata prior to the election.[15]

During 1955 and 1956 Muldoon became more prominent in discussions at the divisional level. He pressed for a simple pamphlet pointing out the fallacies in Social Credit and warned of the danger to National which the new Social Credit League posed in farming communities.[16] He served on a subcommittee on the cost and future of the party's paper *Freedom*,[17] was convener of an 'advisory committee to investigate problems and act as guide and liaison' for the Junior Nationals,[18] advocated the appointment of additional paid canvassers in and more visits by MPs to marginal seats,[19] was appointed to a small committee to organise assistance to the Grey Lynn and Waitakere electorates,[20] and was added to a special subcommittee of the Dominion Publicity Committee established to counter Social Credit.[21]

Although the organisation of the Waitemata electorate was 'patchy' and some of its branches were not functioning, the electorate committee pressed for an early selection of their candidate in 1957 and challenged the Dominion Council's decision not to allow it.[22] As a result of the challenge, permission was granted. The selection meeting was held in Albany on Monday 27 May.[23] There were 116 voting delegates representing 2285 members in thirteen branches, the largest of which were Birkenhead, Browns Bay and Northcote. The electorate also included all the East Coast Bays from Castor Bay north to Orewa and Whangaparaoa. There were five nominees: Muldoon, Leonard Bradley, Richard Pilling, Cliff Utting and James Watson. Although Utting, the mayor of Birkenhead, was the most prominent local candidate, the selection became a two-candidate race between Muldoon and Bradley, a 51-year-old field manager for Colonial Mutual Assurance who had stood four times over the previous eight years for National in the Labour strongholds of Auckland Central, Onehunga and Otahuhu. Muldoon with 59 votes, one more than half the total, won the selection on the first ballot from Bradley, who was supported by 39 delegates.[24]

The National Party was very nervous about the local work and reputation of King, the Labour MP, who according to Muldoon 'had made representation a full time job. Visits all parts of electorate weekly at advertised times. Gives handouts to daily papers on electorate affairs 2–3 times a week. Gets more newspaper publicity than all the other local MPs together.'[25] Muldoon decided he had to match King's canvassing, meetings and publicity. By August Holdaway was able to report that all the branches were now working and 'Mr Muldoon was doing a lot of personal canvassing.'[26] During November alone Muldoon held thirty public meetings, three at 10.30 a.m., seven at 2 p.m. and twenty at 8 p.m. Every population centre in the widespread electorate was covered. Senior National MPs such as the Prime Minister Keith Holyoake, Tom Shand and Dame Hilda Ross appeared in support. In all, 500 posters were put up during the campaign but Muldoon's campaign secretary W. J. A. Stewart lamented that 'hooligans and ill-wishers are carrying out wholesale destruction of those posters which have been erected.'[27]

When canvassing houses and shops Muldoon developed a brisk style. He tried not to spend more than a couple of minutes with each voter, introducing himself, telling them he did not wish to waste their time, and then moving on. He tried not to discuss policy because the voters often disagreed and it wasted time. Many of the homes in Waitemata, especially in the Birkenhead area, were down long drives which Muldoon found very frustrating, particularly when there was no one home or he found the voter unsympathetic.

Sometimes he wondered if his canvassing was counterproductive. On one occasion, for example, on a wet, cold afternoon, with a bruised heel, he limped down a long steep drive and knocked on a door. Finally a woman appeared and told Muldoon she had just got to bed after having her teeth out. Muldoon apologised and decided to call it a day and start again next door the next morning. The drives, however, looked the same and early the next morning he got the same woman out of bed. On another occasion he spent a considerable time shouting at a deaf voter who finally agreed to vote for him. Some months after the election Muldoon was told by a party activist who had accompanied him that day that the old chap and his wife had proudly told the activist, 'we voted for that nice Mr King you brought to see us'.[28]

Muldoon developed an affection for many of the active National Party workers in the electorate though they could occasionally frustrate him. On one occasion, for example, he drove to the Upper Waiwera Hall for a lunchtime meeting. The ramshackle building was locked and there was no sign of life. Muldoon drove over to the home of the local branch chairman. His sister told Muldoon that her brother was on his tractor up the top of a steep hill. When Muldoon got there he was told that the chairman knew no one would turn up to hear him so had not bothered coming down to open up the hall.[29]

For several years Muldoon had been studying and talking about the flaws in Social Credit and found many in the Waitemata electorate who were willing to debate the subject with him. Although opponents, Muldoon developed a liking and a respect for many of the old Social Crediters and recalled that he had 'never found one who was a ratbag'.[30] He sympathised with their conclusion that they were doing a worthwhile job which they were good at, that they were hard-working and conscientious, but that because they could barely scratch out a living there had to be something wrong with the system. Clearly, they believed, high interest rates, speculation, the money supply, and unearned income were all part of the problem.

Muldoon concluded that the basic fallacy of Social Credit's A + B theory, that the supply of money was significantly less than the supply of goods and services, was that it ignored the velocity of currency circulation. £1 was not worth £1 of goods. If moved around quickly enough it would buy much more, leading to a considerably higher turnover of goods and services. Increasing consumer demand, not an artificially increased supply of currency, Muldoon argued, was the critical factor in stimulating growth in an economy.

Muldoon addressed thirty-seven meetings during the Waitemata campaign and usually travelled to his evening meetings with a core of about a dozen supporters. The largest meeting at the Kiwi Cinema in Birkenhead attracted 250 people, many of whom came not to listen to Muldoon but to heckle Shand, who was speaking in his support.

Muldoon covered a wide range of topics at his public meetings, suggesting caning for juvenile delinquents, reduced bridge tolls, no means test for superannuitants, and targeted assistance to the poorest rather than a £100 tax rebate to the richest income earners, which Labour was proposing.[31] As he did later in his career, he usually spoke from headings and brief notes for about twenty minutes before answering questions for an hour or an hour and a half.

In a message to voters in Waitemata, Muldoon wrote: 'I am somewhat independent in outlook, and thus I find my political home in the National Party. I could never submit to the rigid party discipline of the Labour Party, nor to the depressing doctrine of socialism and class consciousness. New Zealanders came here to get away from all that . . . Every act of a politician has an impact on the lives of the two million people in New Zealand and it is the humanitarian aspect of politics with which I am most concerned.'[32] In its election summary, the *New Zealand Herald* concluded that in Waitemata 'the campaigning has been gentlemanly . . . The worst thing Mr Muldoon has said of Mr King to date is: "He has done a good job for the electorate".'[33]

The Waitemata electorate in 1957 was one of the fastest-growing in New Zealand and was to grow even faster following the building of the harbour bridge. Many young families responded positively to Labour's promises of a £100 tax rebate, 3 per cent housing loans, and capitalisation of the family benefit to provide the deposit on a home. King's majority rose from 387 over Morrison in 1954 to 2191 over Muldoon in 1957. Although the party failed to win the seat, the electorate chairman, Holdaway, told the Divisional Executive that 'An excellent effort had been made by the candidate and the electorate could not have been better served.'[34]

One of the Auckland seats National lost by 589 votes at the 1957 election was Tamaki, where Eric Halstead, the Minister of Industries and Commerce and Customs, had been defeated by Labour's Bob Tizard. The campaign in Tamaki had been very personal and bitter and there was a perception that Halstead had contributed to his own defeat. Although he may well have been reselected as National's candidate in 1960, and although National's potential vote in the electorate had been augmented by considerable private house building in Kohimarama, Beverley Hills and Glendowie, Halstead chose, partly because of his nasty experience in 1957 and partly because his accountancy partners were unhappy with his return to politics, not to seek the nomination again.[35]

Muldoon decided that King could not be defeated in Waitemata in 1960 but did believe that Tamaki could be won back from Labour.[36] Mrs May Hill, the chairwoman of the Tamaki Women's Section, invited Muldoon to speak to the women at their May meeting and he subsequently visited the various branches. Muldoon exuded confidence and convinced many key activists that he could win the seat.

The Tamaki Electorate Committee requested permission to hold an early selection because they had by April 1960 over 2000 members and were anxious to get a candidate 'for whom some 200 meetings in private homes will be arranged.'[37] Permission was granted and eight candidates faced the 218 voting delegates representing 4347 financial members from seven branches at the selection meeting in the RSA Memorial Hall, St Heliers, on 5 July 1960.[38] The *Glen Innes Gazette*, in its 'Tis Said' column, noted, 'That among the eight nominations for the national [sic] candidate for Tamaki are W. H. Fortune, former MP and cabinet minister, and C. Haszard, who contested Otahuhu last election. Others are said to be "lesser lights".'[39]

That somewhat lukewarm opinion of the nominees was shared by Holyoake, who told McKenzie twice that he was concerned that 'you haven't got an outstanding candidate in Tamaki, and if we don't win Tamaki we won't become the Government'.[40] McKenzie assured the leader that 'he need not worry because Robert Muldoon was amongst the candidates, that I was sure he would be the people's choice' and that 'he would find he had in his team a very able member who would go places.'[41] Muldoon not only had the support of the very influential McKenzie; Halstead also put his weight behind him.[42]

Halstead had not only known Muldoon through the National Party but also had been head of the Commerce Department at Seddon Memorial Technical College where Muldoon had taught accounting. Indeed, he had tried unsuccessfully to convince Muldoon that he should further his education by taking a university degree in either economics or liberal arts. In Halstead's view, although Muldoon had 'a very good brain' and 'was an extremely good accountant', he lacked 'the discipline of a university degree' and 'if there's one quality that he is missing, that was the breadth of thinking.'[43] Nevertheless, in 1960, having decided that he would not seek the nomination for Tamaki again, Halstead supported Muldoon: 'He looked the best of the bunch and I told my people to support him.'[44]

Much of the early attention in the selection was focused on Fortune. Fortune was at the time the chairman of the Auckland Division, having failed to be returned to Parliament in 1954 after having represented the Eden seat from 1946 to 1954 and been Minister of Police. He had not contested the 1957 election but had re-entered active politics following an apparently successful heart operation in England in 1958. In 1960 Fortune was 62 years of age and had he been selected for Tamaki would not have represented it for long. He entered hospital on 8 November and died three months after the election. The concerns about his age, vigour and health expressed at the time of the selection may well help explain why even though seen as the front runner he did not get the nomination.

A more formidable older nominee would have been Sir Leslie Munro. Munro was a lawyer, former editor of the *New Zealand Herald*, and one-time representative of New Zealand at the United Nations where he had presided over the General Assembly. Munro, who was still in the United States, wanted the Tamaki nomination but only if he did not have to contest the selection ballot. A week before the selection meeting, McKenzie, the president of the party, called the nominees for Tamaki together. He explained the situation and asked if they would all withdraw in Munro's favour.[45] If anyone refused then there would have to be a selection, which Munro had made plain he was not prepared to contest. Fortune agreed to withdraw in Munro's favour.

Muldoon had met Munro years before when, as editor of the *Herald*, he had addressed a luncheon meeting of Junior Nationals, chaired by Muldoon. Munro had asked Muldoon, 'What do you do for a living, young man?' When Muldoon replied that he was an accountant, the somewhat pompous older man had responded, 'Hmm, an inferior profession.'[46] Muldoon now made it plain that he, for one, was not withdrawing in anyone's favour. Munro knew the rules for candidate selection and was welcome to contest the Tamaki nomination but he would have to beat Muldoon to get it. The other nominees concurred with Muldoon and the selection proceeded without Munro.

The eight nominees were 'imprisoned in the basement billiard room attached to the R.S.A. Hall in Tamaki.'[47] The only lighting in the room was a light over the billiard table, which was kept going by Fortune, who was the chairman of the Auckland Electric Power Board at the time, feeding a meter with coins. During the course of the evening, Muldoon mentioned to the other candidates that 'his income was getting to the stage where he wondered whether he could afford to go into politics'.[48]

When Muldoon spoke to the meeting, he spent time talking about his children and the problems he had with them, and entertained the audience with his dry humour. Other candidates took themselves much more seriously and dealt with less down-to-earth and personal matters. Muldoon won the nomination on the first ballot.

Muldoon found that the Labour Government's 1958 'Black Budget' had 'knocked the stuffing out of the Labour Party' in the electorate.[49] It was never really strong again in Tamaki. The National Party organisation, on the other hand, had revitalised itself after its humiliation in 1957 and was well on its way to becoming the strongest electorate organisation in the party's Auckland Division over the following thirty years. While Labour's total branch membership in the Auckland region covering 22 seats fell from 6889 in 1957 to 3828 in 1960, National's membership in the Auckland Division was a record 48,783 and in Tamaki alone reached 5025, the largest National membership of any electorate in New Zealand that year.[50]

With the help of this formidable party organisation, Muldoon canvassed about 3000 houses, held house meetings nearly every night, and spoke at nineteen public meetings over the twenty-two days before the election. The public meetings were rowdy but not as unruly or as nasty as those faced by Halstead three years before.

Again Muldoon found canvassing at times amusing or embarrassing. On one occasion he held on to the door handle while pressing the bell and when the door opened the handle came off in his hand. He handed it to the bemused voter. Another time he took a step backward as the door opened, knocked a cactus plant from a rack of pot plants on the porch, caught it in mid-air, and for days afterwards pulled cactus spines from his hands and tried not to shake hands with voters.[51] Even as a candidate Muldoon found that some people expected him to act as an MP and to pursue inquiries on their behalf with the State Advances Corporation, or to see the Council about the neighbour's dog, or to make representations to the Post Office about the need for a telephone box in the street.

On the cover of his election pamphlet for Tamaki in 1960 Muldoon introduced himself as 'Bob Muldoon' who 'does not promise you the moon'. He went on to stress that 'I will work for all the residents of Tamaki electorate irrespective of their political views'. He also highlighted the fact that 'The National Party gives its Members in the House the right of a free vote on matters of conscience and I believe there is a need . . . to take a firm stand on moral issues.' This and his speeches against the failure of education and the effect of pornography in the decline of moral standards among young people may well have convinced some religious voters to switch from the more secular and libertarian Tizard.

Both Muldoon and Tizard believed Muldoon won a large proportion of the Catholic vote in Tamaki at the 1960 election. Muldoon argued that he had not specifically targeted that vote or compromised his principles by supporting state aid to Catholic schools.[52] He did, however, concentrate his canvassing on Labour rather than National voting areas in the electorate and knocked on every door in Glen Innes, a strong Labour-voting state house suburb whose parish priest was a Father O'Reilly. Muldoon and O'Reilly had a number of meetings at which Muldoon listened carefully to what O'Reilly had to say, not only about education but also about other problems his parishioners faced. Tizard proved less sympathetic and (as Muldoon later suggested) there was a streak in Tizard's personality which led him to offend unnecessarily rather than be seen to be 'sucking-up' to pressure groups.[53] As a result, Tizard aggressively declared that he would have nothing to do with state aid, and his antagonistic attitude rather than his policy position may well have offended Catholic voters. When O'Reilly told them that

Muldoon was more sympathetic than Tizard, Tizard was very upset. Allegations were made that O'Reilly had given parish records to Muldoon to help him in his canvassing, but this was subsequently categorically denied by the priest.[54] O'Reilly continued to support Muldoon in 1963 and even in 1966 against the Labour candidate Kevin Ryan, a prominent Catholic lawyer.

Muldoon won thirteen polling booths in 1960, sweeping Glendowie, Kohimarama, Mission Bay and St Heliers and winning one of the two booths in Orakei. Tizard took the other Orakei booth and all the booths in the state house areas of Point England, Glen Innes, Glen Taylor and Glen Brae. The overall Labour vote, however, dropped 6.81 per cent and a political scientist observed that 'In Tamaki, there was considerable movement against Labour in Mr Tizard's best booths.'[55] Polling 8728 votes to Tizard's 7580, Muldoon with a majority of 1148 votes became the Member of Parliament for Tamaki. He was to hold the seat with comfortable and sometimes very large majorities for the next thirty-one years.

CHAPTER 6

The MP for Tamaki 1960–63

MULDOON'S VICTORY IN TAMAKI MEANT AN UPHEAVAL for his family. Although euphoric at the victory, Rob and Thea recognised that the shift from their home in Devonport to Tamaki might be difficult for the children. Barbara was 9 years old, Jenny 8 and Gavin 4. The girls, who after the shift were enrolled in St Thomas's School, were bewildered but seemed to adjust quickly. Gavin was more disturbed both by the move and the frequent absences of his father in Wellington.[1] All three children had lived relatively sheltered lives before 1960. They had not travelled widely and did not have television. Indeed, the major reason for getting television after the family moved to Tamaki was to attract babysitters to look after the children when Thea accompanied her husband to functions at night. As a result Barbara, Jennifer and Gavin did not understand what their father's becoming an MP really meant or where the Wellington he started to spend so much time at was. Even though Muldoon took the children to St Thomas's Anglican church and Sunday School most weekends and also tried to maintain the summer evening family swims, now at Kohimarama Beach, Thea, like many other MPs' wives, became after 1960 virtually a solo parent, having to cope with the children largely on her own and do many things for the children that a father could normally do. In time she even taught them all to drive.

MPs were also not particularly well paid at that time and had many demands made on them. Muldoon worried about the financial sacrifice he and his family would be making by his going into Parliament. The family also came under other pressures. As a section of the public became very anti-Muldoon, so the pressure on the family grew. People wanting to annoy Muldoon and knowing he was in Wellington would ring his Kohimarama home and wake or abuse Thea and the children at 2 or 3 o'clock in the morning night after night.

Nor was the lifestyle of a backbench MP in Wellington particularly attractive. From 1960 until 1963, when in Wellington, Muldoon rented a room from a public servant who lived on his own in a small house in Glenside Terrace a short walk from Parliament. He later boarded with Duncan MacIntyre, Peter Gordon and Venn Young in Hawkestone Street, also close to Parliament. Muldoon, whose breakfast consisted of a glass of water, half a grapefruit and occasionally a piece of toast, partly because of his constant battle to hold his weight, had lunch and dinner at Bellamy's.

Like all young backbench MPs, Muldoon found he only saw his children at weekends and then he was often out at functions or working in the electorate. At the end of 1963, with his appointment as an under-secretary, he moved into a ministerial house in Beauchamp Street and the family moved to Wellington so that he could see his wife and family at least each morning and usually at tea-time. One drawback was that Thea no longer had the close parental support she had enjoyed from her mother and father, and they in turn during the last years of their lives had to depend largely on her sister.

The house in Beauchamp Street had a big back lawn, was next to tennis courts, and was near to Karori Primary School, which all three children initially attended. Subsequently Barbara and Jennifer went as day pupils to nearby Marsden College, while Gavin for four years boarded at Rathkeale College north of Masterton. Muldoon believed in retrospect that it was a mistake to have sent the very sensitive and vulnerable Gavin to boarding school.[2] Gavin, who subsequently completed a BCom and became a financial controller, found himself continually judged not as himself but as a reflection of what people thought of his father.

All three of the children suffered because of their father's reputation and got into squabbles at school over things they were not responsible for and about which they knew nothing. The children of politicians, Muldoon believed, have a very tough time and inevitably feel a sense of neglect when both parents are out all the time at functions. Although the parents are often conscious of the effect on their children they cannot really make up the time lost because of the seven-day-a-week pressure that politicians and their spouses face.

The children eventually developed strategies to cope. Barbara, a nurse, for example, deliberately used to lose her name badge and when asked by patients in her ward if she was related to Muldoon used to reply, 'No, my father is an accountant.' Jennifer, who became a clothing designer, as a teenager called herself Jenny Roberts in an attempt to avoid having to listen to others' opinions about or having to discuss or defend her father. In time Muldoon as Prime Minister felt that he was becoming isolated from his family, which grew to include six grandchildren, although Thea remained close to them. When one grandchild was two years old, for example, Muldoon saw him only twice in that year. The child used to kiss the television and say 'Poppa' when Muldoon appeared on it.

Muldoon claimed with justification in his 1963 election publicity that he was 'particularly noted' for his 'totally unbiased service and attention to all members of his constituency regardless of their political affiliations . . . and is willing to assist anyone with problems.'[3] This was not mere puffery and his opponents as well as his supporters acknowledged the truth of the assertion.

The Tamaki electorate had all the problems associated with rapid recent housing development and as its MP Muldoon found himself faced with many complaints about lack of amenities, inadequate public transport services, drainage problems, and social welfare situations. About one-third of the electorate were low income tenants in cheap homes. Many private house-owners were upset at the continued development of state housing alongside them. Muldoon found himself frequently visiting the offices of the State Housing Department and the Auckland City Council. He irritated his own ministers and the Council by constantly protesting against what he regarded as unjustifiably high state and council housing rentals. He became involved in settling neighbourhood fights, such as the case of a woman who hit her neighbour with a length of timber every night when the neighbour came home until Muldoon arranged to have the victim transferred to another state house. He was called out frequently to inspect and advise on flooding from poor drainage or leaking roofs. In one block of about fifty houses there were thirteen families with serious criminal records, and increasingly families being allocated state houses were those with problems. In later years, as the ethnic make-up of Glen Innes and other state housing areas in the Tamaki electorate changed, Muldoon became more concerned with immigration as well as housing problems.

By the 1980s the proportion of elderly people in the electorate had increased dramatically compared to the 1960s, but in these earlier years the large number of young families in the electorate resulted in a large number of school pupils. Muldoon frequently visited schools, particularly the new ones such as St Thomas, Glendowie, Churchill Park and Selwyn College, talking with parents and teachers and trying to obtain prefabricated temporary classrooms or to accelerate the building of permanent classrooms.

His interest in horticulture made Muldoon a natural ally of Miss Winifred Huggins and the St Heliers Beautifying Society, which planted trees on Achilles Point and elsewhere and fought a campaign to save and develop as a bush reserve an area known as Dingle Dell, which was subsequently in 1982 renamed the Vellenoweth Reserve after a Mrs Anna Vellenoweth who had been responsible for keeping it in public ownership in 1904.

The president of the Glen Innes Residents and Ratepayers Association noted that, except for a licensing trust hotel in Glen Innes, 'In every other matter . . . Bob Muldoon has done all in his power with the greatest expedition to assist' the local community.[4] Muldoon opposed the Licensing Commission's proposal to put a number of new hotels in the Eastern suburbs because he believed that they were residential areas which did not need additional alcohol outlets. Praise for their local MP also came from teachers, for example, the principal of Glendowie College, who wrote that, Muldoon 'has done quite a lot for the college . . . [and] has been meticulous in answering any request',[5] and from the Eastern Districts Solo Parents 'who are fans too'.[6] The president of the Glen Innes Senior Citizens' Club was particularly fulsome in his assessment of Muldoon as MP for Tamaki, recording that

Nothing ever seems too much or too trivial for him to do for our members . . .
Without him we would not have the finest Senior Citizens' Club in New Zealand . . .

In spite of heavy responsibilities he makes time to meet me or communicate with us every month . . . From his election as the Member for Tamaki, Mr Muldoon has taken a keen interest in pensioners' housing . . . visiting occupants, helping them with their problems, and encouraging them in the new surroundings at their advanced age. He has earned the love and support of the aged of Tamaki. To us he has no equal.[7]

Muldoon not only worked hard to get rooms for the Senior Citizens' Club but also lobbied the Council to build more pensioner flats. He pressed for an underpass under the Glen Innes Railway station and for grants to build the Glen Innes swimming pool and grounds for the local athletics club.

As a local MP, Muldoon even found himself involved in one of New Zealand's most sensational murder investigations, the Bassett Road machine-gun killings.[8] A constituent rang one night while Muldoon was having dinner to say he needed to see Muldoon urgently. Muldoon drove to an address in the electorate where he was told by a very worried man that an acquaintance, Frederick Gillies, whom he believed to be one of the murderers, had confided in him. After two hours Muldoon persuaded his caller to go with him to the police station and subsequently Gillies and his accomplice Ronald Jorgensen were convicted of the murders.

Muldoon held electorate clinics in his home in Kohimarama and also through-out the 1960s and early 1970s in the Glen Innes Plunket Rooms or the Glen Innes Library. Many of the constituents in Glen Innes did not own cars and it was easier for Muldoon to go to them than for voters from Glen Innes to make their way to Kohimarama.

He adopted from the first a policy of answering correspondence immediately, either with a considered reply or if he needed further information an acknow-ledgement followed up by a later letter. Over the first few years he wrote all his correspondence himself in longhand but from 1964 started to dictate to secretaries. He also was able to boast in his 1963 election pamphlets that he had 'asked more questions than any other member in the House' during parliamentary question time.

Muldoon consciously observed three rules of political conduct. First, he never lied, not just because it was immoral but also because it was impractical to do so. He always knew what he had said and was not constantly worried about being found out or having to change his story. Second, while trying not to start fights, he always gave more back to those who attacked him, on the assumption that they would think twice before attacking him again. Third, he always did his homework and then, once being sure of his facts and having made up his mind, he 'didn't hold his tongue but spoke out come what may'. In an address in 1961 he added that he carefully and precisely chose his words so that he could not be misquoted or misinterpreted and he always relied on facts not opinion.[9]

For over thirty years he was well served in Tamaki by very capable electorate chairpersons and secretaries, who built up the electorate membership, finances and organisation to be the strongest in the Auckland Division and arguably in the country. By 1963 Muldoon's pamphlets boasted that Tamaki had the largest membership in New Zealand. Vin Meade, Tom Rendell, Max Davies, Peter Wilkinson, Gavin Downie, John Tremewan, Richard Yates, Ian Shearer and Merle Bell successively chaired the electorate, while Murray Wilson, Bill Day, Len Abercrombie, Pam Forde and Brian Matthews gave long service as electorate secretaries.[10]

The most successful of Muldoon's grass-roots organisers was undoubtedly John Tremewan, who had joined the Junior National Party in 1953 and became chairman of the Auckland Divisional Junior National organisation in 1957. Tremewan was a teacher and subsequently a Training College lecturer. At the time Muldoon was very much the father-figure of the Auckland Juniors and, after working in other electorates, Tremewan moved to Tamaki in 1971 and became chairman first of the Kohimarama Branch and then in 1972 of the electorate committee. Under Tremewan the National Party's membership rose from 1400 in 1972 to over 4000 in 1975, a level maintained annually until 1979 when Tremewan, who was also deputy chairman of the Auckland Division from 1975 to 1979, became the National Party's Auckland divisional director. Until 1991, when Muldoon retired, Tremewan remained his most trusted local aide and confidant, for much of that time daily monitoring Muldoon's electorate answerphone and briefing him each week about electorate and divisional matters.

Even after shifting to Wellington, Muldoon attended most of the numerous social functions his electorate organised, and particularly if someone was having a birthday dinner party Rob and Thea would be there. When Tremewan celebrated his fortieth birthday, for example, the Tamaki activists gave him a surprise party after he arrived home from a divisional meeting at 11 p.m. At 1 a.m. Muldoon arrived accompanied by his police escort after having been at official functions. In later years, Muldoon restricted his attendance at business meetings in the electorate to the monthly electorate committee and the branch annual meetings.

Tamaki electorate members were active not only locally but also at the divisional and national levels of the party. Stuart Masters, the powerful divisional chairman 1967–80, and Colin Brenton-Rule, the equally influential secretary-director of the Division 1967–79, both belonged to the Mission Bay branch. Tremewan was Tamaki electorate chairman 1972–78 and deputy chairman of the Auckland Division 1975–79 before becoming divisional director in 1979. Simich served as a divisional counsellor and deputy chairman, David Morris as divisional publicity committee chairman, and Mavis Finlayson chaired the divisional women's committee.

By the 1970s opponents of the large number of prominent Tamaki members active in the Auckland Division started calling them the 'Tamaki mafia'. The term stuck and was later adopted by the group itself, though never by Muldoon. While his organisation was loyal to him and regarded him rather as their friend than their leader or prime minister, Muldoon also valued those who maintained his electoral base. He constantly referred to them and praised them in speeches. Muldoon, who was quite happy to use the term 'Rob's Mob', which the Tamaki organisation coined for the 1975 party conference, resented it when journalists referred to his electorate organisation as the 'Tamaki mafia'.[11] Far from being a mafia enriching themselves at the expense of others and operating ruthlessly to maximise their own self-interests, the Tamaki party workers, according to Muldoon, were the most generous in the National Party in providing funds to other electorates and spending weekends canvassing in marginal seats throughout Auckland. The Tamaki strength was continually deployed elsewhere, and its substantial financial reserves were from time to time given away to marginal seats.

Among the other new National MPs Muldoon found when he reached Wellington after the 1960 election were Duncan MacIntyre, a Hawke's Bay farmer and territorial brigadier who had been with Muldoon's Division in Italy and who had become MP for Hastings, and John Bowie (Peter) Gordon, a tertiary-educated farmer and World War II pilot, who had become MP for Clutha. All three men had considerable self-confidence, were prepared from the first to speak their minds, and were not overawed by authority. They believed that they 'could make a positive impact if we were prepared to ignore the political convention that controversial matters are to be avoided as far as possible'.[12]

In the House, Muldoon shared a backbench with a fourth new MP, Bill Brown, who had served long terms on the Wanganui Education Board, the Palmerston North Hospital Board, and the Manawatu Automobile Association. Because the chief whip, Jack Scott, insisted that at least one of the two seats on each of the Government's backbenches had to be occupied constantly, it was expected that each National MP would spend about half their time sitting in the House. Muldoon found this frustrating if he was not personally involved in the debate. He quickly arranged that Brown, who enjoyed listening to the debates, would be in the House most of the time. This freed Muldoon up for committee and other work outside the debating chamber, although he was always willing to return and speak at short notice if required.

Muldoon shared an office off the ground floor corridor with Bert Walker, the new MP for St Albans. MacIntyre and Gordon were in the office next door. These were the colleagues with whom Muldoon almost immediately developed the closest relations. At the first caucus, Holyoake told his new MPs that, besides 'breathing through their noses' for a while, they should each choose 'three roles in which they could carry a Marshal's baton and after succeeding in those look for the Field-Marshal's baton. He added that we should pick which of our cobbers we could trust to hold one's own views and express them on matters other than our own choices.'[13] Muldoon, MacIntyre, Gordon and Brown decided to act as a team and defer to each other's expertise. Muldoon 'was obvious for finance'; Gordon took health, transport and agriculture; MacIntyre was responsible for Maori Affairs, forestry and fishing; and Brown became the authority on education. The fact that their wives got on well helped knit the group even closer together.

Of the four only Muldoon was from the start a confident and fluent debater. MacIntyre was rather taciturn, rarely spoke at first in the House, and then never belligerently or controversially. Gordon also found the House difficult and preferred to be active in other arenas. Brown, a good constituency MP, was not a strong speaker. From the first, therefore, Muldoon was the most articulate and visible of the group.

Muldoon was still mischievous and particularly liked teasing Gordon, who could always be relied on to rise to any bait. Indeed Gordon believed that his often violent reaction led to his being given the nickname 'Hiss and Roar' by his close colleagues.[14] On one occasion Gordon was so provoked that he hit the end of the desk with his knuckles as he waved his arms furiously to emphasise his point. The 'next thing there was a line of blood spatter 14 feet up! Muldoon nearly split himself but next morning made arrangements to have the blood varnished into place . . . It was there until the room was decorated.'[15]

When Muldoon became under-secretary after the 1963 election, he moved into an office on his own some distance from the other National backbenchers, but shortly after his friends Gordon and MacIntyre also moved into a room nearby. As MacIntyre recalled,

> It was in this atmosphere that we worked and played together and cemented a bond of friendship which is strong enough to withstand the sometimes strong opposing views we held . . . It is probably at this time, since we were hard by the Press Gallery that we were bracketed and began to be thought of as a troika and as the 'Young Turks'.[16]

The term 'Young Turks' was coined by the long-time parliamentary journalist Ian Templeton because the troika were prepared to challenge senior National ministers as well as the Labour Opposition.

The office Muldoon and Walker occupied had once been inhabited by the controversial former Labour MP John A. Lee, who still left his coat and bag there when he visited Parliament. Muldoon, who claimed that he had admired Lee since the 1930s because of his 'courage', 'political oratory' and 'tremendous feeling for the underdog', said that he also shared Lee's and Seddon's view 'that a strong economy with its wealth fairly shared is the best action that a Government can take on behalf of the underprivileged'.[17] Over the following years until Lee's death he and Muldoon exchanged correspondence and shared a mutual admiration for each other. Muldoon described Lee as possibly 'the greatest political figure in our history who did not hold Cabinet office',[18] and Lee predicted publicly as early as 1963 that Muldoon was 'a coming force in politics' who 'excites approval and hostility but always arrives with a prepared brief. He lives not only on his wits but on his industry, and perspiration was as important as inspiration. He has plenty of guts and realises that there is no point in giving the soft answer to people prepared to heave a dead cat at him.'[19] Significantly, although all the Auckland MPs, both Labour and National, were invited in 1963 to attend the launching of Lee's autobiography, *Simple on a Soapbox*, only Muldoon was present.[20]

The older National and Labour MPs mixed freely together in Bellamy's members' bar, where racing not politics was the major topic of conversation. Muldoon and the younger National MPs wanted to discuss politics and started to have their evening drinks in their own rooms rather than Bellamy's. From time to time they also organised parties attended by some of the Press Gallery journalists, typists and librarians. Muldoon, Gordon and MacIntyre formed the core of a wider group of National backbenchers. The group, which regarded each other as friends as well as colleagues, included Brown, Logan Sloane, Harry Lapwood, Esmé Tombleson and Allan McCready, all of whom were first elected in 1960, and Bert Pickering, who came in to Parliament in a 1961 by-election. Muldoon also formed a reasonably close working relationship with two MPs elected in 1957, Doug Carter and Alf Allen, and with Lance Adams-Schneider, who had been elected at a by-election in 1959, and in time also with Colin McLachlan and Rob Talbot, who were first elected in 1966, and with Frank Gill, who entered the House in 1969.

The older National MPs, according to Muldoon, were very parochial, constantly talking about their own rural district or country town and the effect of government policies on it or on the sectional interests the MP represented in Parliament. In the 1960s many MPs still saw themselves as representing their constituency first and national matters were of secondary importance. Many indeed were unwilling to look at national implications at all. One such was George Walsh, MP for Tauranga. On one occasion Hanan and Muldoon gave short speeches on the situation in the Cook Islands. Walsh was asked to follow them. He gave a speech entirely on the orange industry in Tauranga and completely deflated the case concerning the Cook Islands made by his colleagues. On another occasion the National MPs Ernie Aderman and Bill Sheat had a violent debate with each other in the House over rates drawn from southern Taranaki for New Plymouth's harbour.

At mealtimes Muldoon did not always sit with other National MPs but joined whoever was there. Some older Labour MPs often sat with Muldoon, notably the aged Rex Mason, who was very set in his ways and was disgusted with many of his younger Labour colleagues, and Mick Moohan, who disliked many in his own party more than he did National. Moohan had formed a very close relationship with the Speaker, Sir Ronald Algie, to whom Holyoake had refused to give a cabinet post in 1960. For six years thereafter Algie and Moohan nursed their resentments over drinks in the Speaker's suite. Moohan detested his fellow Labour MP Norman Douglas, who had been John A. Lee's political deputy and business partner, and on one occasion gave Muldoon and Adams-Schneider a copy of a vicious pamphlet attacking Douglas in the hope that they would use it in the House. Moohan also passed on to National a public relations presentation prepared by Gordon Dryden for the Labour Party which enabled Muldoon to attack and embarrass Arnold Nordmeyer, whom Moohan also hated.[21]

Muldoon was honoured at being selected by Holyoake to move the Address in Reply at the opening of the 1961 session of Parliament. He declined an offer from the party's research director and speech-writer, Martin Nestor, to help him with the speech because he wanted to set out his own personal views rather than simply mouth what the party wanted.

When he rose to give what was also to be his maiden speech, Muldoon was irritated to hear the Speaker say that the speech should be non-controversial and that while a member should not read a speech he was sure that on this occasion other MPs would be indulgent if Muldoon read his. Muldoon saw this as a denigration of his ability as a speaker and later wrote: 'I never really forgave him for his belittling remarks, and my occasional subsequent clash with him as Speaker was certainly influenced by this episode.'[22] Algie reciprocated the dislike, and Muldoon noted that the Speaker rarely let him succeed with a point of order but cut him off half-way through and sat him down.

In his speech Muldoon paid a gracious tribute to his defeated opponent, Tizard, referring to Tizard's hard work on behalf of the electorate and saying: 'I hope that his voice will again be heard in this House – as the representative of some other electorate.'[23] Muldoon described himself politically as a Liberal and concluded that 'as a Liberal I find my only possible political home in the National Party'. He went on to criticise Labour for having built 5000 state houses in his electorate with virtually no amenities other than schools. He made a passionate plea for the teaching of Christianity in schools and criticised 'a sterile education system' which 'shuts out the greatest power for good that the world will ever know'.[24] He deplored the rise of pressure groups and sectional interests and warned that 'No inefficient industry could expect to lie snug under the blanket of protection.' He then went on to challenge New Zealanders to retrieve the pioneering spirit in attitudes to work and to improve management to produce and market well-made goods in an increasingly competitive world. This would also require more stable labour conditions and more flexible primary and secondary industries. Diversification and 'hard selling' internationally were essential. He also signalled that he personally did not see membership of the International Monetary Fund as a 'clear-cut issue'.[25]

Following Muldoon's and Walker's speeches, Holyoake, as was his custom, wandered over to speak to them. He commented that, 'while not the best, they were also not the worst that he had heard'.[26]

Muldoon's speaking style was simple, direct and somewhat repetitive. He spoke with authority, conviction and sincerity. He concentrated on a few major central points and his turns of phrase were telling though not memorable. He often used humour, sometimes wryly ironic but occasionally cruelly sardonic. Physically, he radiated energy and his compelling eyes, fascinating facial expressions and unique chuckle captivated audiences whether in a hall or watching on television. Throughout his career Muldoon wrote most of his own speeches even when using materials initially provided by others. He dictated a first draft which was then typed up so that the speech retained the cadences of the spoken rather than the written word.

Algie, who as Speaker watched Muldoon carefully in the House over the following years, was more magnanimous towards Muldoon than Muldoon was to him. He later wrote:

As a backbencher, he was always a hard worker. That was quite obvious in his speeches. He mastered his facts and presented them with force and confidence.

Anyone who took him on in an argument had to be equally or better prepared. He had, and has, a very sharp tongue and a very quick wit. He enjoys the great gift of being able to think quickly on his feet.[27]

At least one very experienced journalist, George Burns, shared Algie's opinions of Muldoon:

I think he is able, ambitious, courageous and, if in his opinion the need arose, ruthless . . . It was very noticeable that if the Opposition got on to something [in the adjournment debates] that could embarrass the Government, Muldoon was quickly into the act. He was the best diversionist I have seen in more than forty years of political observing. Within two minutes he had switched the discussion to something entirely different and rarely did the Opposition stick to their original point. He had been so provocative that they responded to his bait and spent the rest of the time arguing the topic he had introduced. This might not be statesmanship, but it is good Parliamentary tactics.[28]

It was as a frequent fill-in speaker during debates over his first three years in Parliament that Muldoon first developed his reputation as a 'counterpuncher' who saw attack as the best means of defence, and diversion and disruption as the easiest way to counter a Labour offensive in the House. Invariably, his tactics worked and subsequent Labour speakers abandoned their prepared strategy to reply or retaliate.

Muldoon not only developed a certain contempt for some of the older National backbenchers but during the 1960s clashed with a number of Holyoake's ministers. They in turn developed a dislike of their younger, more abrasive colleague. John Marshall, Tom Shand, David Seath, John McAlpine, Leon Götz and Percy Allen were never Muldoon admirers. In time Marshall, Shand and McAlpine emerged as the three senior ministers Muldoon particularly disliked and who in turn came equally to distrust and dislike him. On one occasion, for example, a journalist remembered Muldoon, as a backbench MP and after drinking too much, sitting in the Press Gallery at 1 a.m. 'bitching about Shand'.[29]

Holyoake allowed controversial matters to be debated in caucus until there was a consensus and until most MPs were prepared to accept the decision even if they had reservations. He would not allow ministers to force matters through against strong backbench opposition and on several occasions rebuked his deputy Marshall and other senior ministers for suggesting that major decisions would be taken by cabinet not caucus.

Holyoake advised that, before asking a question of a minister in the House or at the Public Expenditure Committee and perhaps embarrassing them, the more militant backbenchers like Muldoon should ask permission of the minister concerned. Marshall, according to Muldoon, 'always said no', as did Seath and McAlpine, but others such as Shelton and Hanan always said yes but warned the MPs concerned that they would have to take the consequences if the minister savaged them in reply.[30]

At first Holyoake clearly regarded Muldoon with some disquiet. Not only did Muldoon ignore Holyoake's often repeated advice to young MPs to serve an apprenticeship before asserting themselves but on at least one occasion he looked likely to cross the floor and vote with the Labour Party. Following the 1960 election the Minister of Finance, Harry Lake, presented a White Paper outlining the advantages for New Zealand of joining the International Monetary Fund and the World Bank. Muldoon was one of a small group of National MPs opposed to membership and had spoken out against it during the 1960 campaign, saying that he saw no advantage at that time in New Zealand becoming a member.

In caucus Muldoon, who argued that IMF membership had not been part of National's 1960 election policy, outlined what he saw as the disadvantages and with several other dissidents such as Percy Allen and Bert Walker continued to argue the matter with the Minister of Finance and Treasury officials. In the end only Muldoon remained opposed and he announced to caucus that he intended to cross the floor and vote with the Labour Opposition against the Bill's introduction. That night officials held a further lengthy meeting with him and the following morning Muldoon told Lake that he had been converted by the possibility that the IMF might be useful for loans in the future and would support the Government and the Bill after all. Holyoake and Lake were undoubtedly annoyed by his intransigence during the caucus considerations but were somewhat mollified by his last-minute conformity.[31]

In 1961 Hanan introduced into Parliament a Bill amending the 1908 Crimes Act. A majority of the National caucus led by Marshall forced Hanan, against his own views, to include in the Bill the retention of the death penalty. Not content with exercising his free conscience vote against the provision, Hanan, who knew that the Labour caucus would bloc vote against capital punishment, sought to persuade enough National MPs to vote with Labour to create a majority against the death penalty. He concentrated his lobbying on the new National MPs, sending them all the summaries of discussions he had had with the Chief Justices of Britain and the USA.[32]

Muldoon took a strong stand, saying that he had 'always had a great deal of doubt about the value of capital punishment', the only reason for which was 'the natural . . . desire for revenge'. Otherwise 'hanging cannot be shown to be a deterrent' and it 'solves nothing'. Although recognising that abolition would be against public opinion, he added that 'I cannot conscientiously vote for . . . the death penalty' and concluded that 'once abolished it must never return'.[33] The *Auckland Star* commented that 'By far the finest speech came from Tamaki's member, Mr R. D. Muldoon'.[34] In retrospect, Muldoon recalled his view as being that 'only God should take life because only God can give it', and he was later to base his opposition to abortion on the same principle.[35] When the vote was taken, the death penalty was defeated by 41 votes to 30. Six of the nine new National MPs elected in 1960 voted to remove it. Among the older National MPs only Hanan, Rev. Ernest Aderman, Gordon Grieve and Talboys voted against capital punishment.

Shortly before the 1960 election the National Party caucus had debated twice and at length whether it should include voluntary unionism as a plank in its policy platform.[36] Such a proposal had been endorsed by the 1959 National Party conference. A majority favouring voluntary unionism included Shand, Hanan, Talboys, Marshall and Watts, who was retiring at the 1960 election, but Holyoake, supported by McAlpine, John Rae and Tom Hayman, was opposed.

Following the 1960 election Shand, who became Minister of Labour, had second thoughts after discussions with unions, employers and departmental officials and with Holyoake proposed a compromise to which caucus finally agreed. If requested, a ballot of all members of a particular union would determine whether membership in that union would be compulsory or voluntary. Not one union chose to end the compulsion and in effect the wishes of the majority of the National Party and its caucus were thwarted.

Muldoon, Gordon, MacIntyre, Walker, Pickering and McCready were among the strongest advocates within the caucus for staying with a simple form of voluntary unionism but were unable to win against Holyoake and Shand backed by other senior MPs.[37] Two of the backbenchers were so incensed with Shand, who treated them with almost total contempt, that they physically attacked him – one, Geoff Sim, 'belting Shand with a stick' while the other, Allan McCready, 'tried to get him into a headlock'.[38]

Although Muldoon during his years in Parliament was not averse to attacking some unions and unionists publicly and suggesting that voluntary unionism could be looked at again, he never thereafter put a high priority on it and only reluctantly in 1983 accepted voluntary unionism when it was forced through caucus by Jim Bolger.

A year after his election to Parliament Muldoon gave a speech to the New Zealand Society of Accountants on his impressions of life as a new MP. He said his greatest satisfaction was helping constituents but his duties left him little time for a family life, for recreation or for reading simply for pleasure. He also noted that a successful politician obviously had to project a public image and he had learnt to act differently to the way he used to when he was a self-effacing accountant.[39]

Sometimes, particularly in the debating chamber, MPs can become personal or childish in their attacks on each other. From time to time political nicknames are used, only some of which become permanent or are remembered by posterity. Few now remember that Peter Fraser was called 'Piddling Pete', Norman Kirk was named 'Blossom' after a basking sea elephant on Wellington's beaches, Hanan was nicknamed 'Moses' and 'Foxy', Gordon became 'Hiss and Roar' or that Lance Adams-Schneider was for a time 'Apple Schneider'. More memorable were 'Kiwi Keith' Holyoake and 'Gentleman Jack' Marshall. For a time Muldoon was called 'Buddha' or 'Bonnie Robbie' by his Labour opponents and 'Mulders' by Gordon. A Labour MP, Paddy Blanchfield, accused the new MP for Tamaki of 'grunting and growling like a whale with a bellyache'. Those nicknames and descriptions were replaced permanently early in 1967 by 'Piggy', which was first used in attacks on Muldoon in the Victoria University students' newspaper

Salient. The origin of 'Piggy' Muldoon is a little unclear though the National Party's long-time research officer and speech-writer, Martin Nestor, believed that it was a variation of 'Biggy Muldoon', the subject of a sociological study *The Living and the Dead*, by W. Lloyd Warner, a professor at the University of Chicago. Biggy Muldoon was described by Warner as an Irish American politician 'born . . . on the wrong side of the tracks . . . a street-fighter, a brawler, and an all-round tough guy' who, despite his 'abusive language, fighting and other rough behaviour distasteful to the pious and respectable' was a very successful politician and long-time mayor of a New England community which always regarded itself as quiet, dignified and conservative. When Labour commenced referring to 'Piggy Muldoon', Holyoake told the National caucus to retaliate by attacking 'Piggy Kirk'.[40]

The 1957–60 Labour Government had pursued a vigorous programme of industrial development in depth. One proposal was to encourage Smith and Nephew, a British company, to build a new cotton mill at Nelson and to extend the main trunk railway to that city. Immediately following the 1960 election a group of backbench MPs including Muldoon commenced a campaign to stop the construction of the Nelson cotton mill and the Nelson railway extension.[41] Roy Jack was related to the owner of a men's shirt-making company in Christchurch, who was concerned at having to buy more expensive local cotton, and three local Canterbury MPs, McLachlan, Pickering and Walker, also opposed the mill. Muldoon was lobbied while cutting his lawns by an Auckland clothing manufacturer with whom he had gone to school and who lived near Muldoon in Tamaki.[42] The issue became publicly more controversial after a journalist, Bevan Burgess of the *Christchurch Star*, met the group of backbenchers and then wrote an article questioning the project.

The conflict over the cotton mill reflected a much more serious basic difference of opinion within cabinet and caucus over industrialisation policy. One side's views were summed up by Shand, who in a speech in Auckland argued: 'The time has come when sick industries must die and not be maintained by artificial means . . . it will be a happy day when industry is sufficiently competitive and there is no longer a welfare state for industries.'[43] The other view was expressed by Marshall, who as Minister of Industries and Commerce told Parliament: 'I would take the very opposite view and say that sick industries should be nursed back to health.'[44] Marshall also took the view in caucus that 'the agreement had been signed and that's the end of it'.[45] Muldoon became annoyed not just over the issue 'but that type of ministerial attitude to backbenchers'.[46]

In their campaign against the cotton mill, against other secret industrial agreements made by the previous Labour Government, and against the general industrialisation policy advocated by Dr W. B. Sutch, the Marxist-influenced Secretary of Industries and Commerce, the backbench National MPs were given support and encouragement by Federated Farmers, the Constitutional Society, various manufacturers and importers with vested interests, and the economist Professor B. P. Philpott of Lincoln College. They were all opposed to what they argued was another protected uneconomic industry which would result in higher prices and less variety of choice.

On 4 October 1961 during an adjournment debate Walker finally raised the matter in Parliament with a question which Muldoon had drafted.[47] Marshall replied and Muldoon then spoke. He said that, although Marshall's reply was 'not entirely satisfactory' and small manufacturers were worried, 'it would not be proper' for the Government to repudiate the contract.[48] By that time, however, the party organisation was bitterly divided over the issue, with Eric Holland claiming that it was a 'trial of strength between the party and the Minister' and another Dominion Executive member warning Holyoake in a letter that 'the cotton mill is threatening to tear the party asunder' and suggesting that Marshall should perhaps resign.[49]

The battle raged with a number of bitter caucus meetings between October 1961 and January 1962, culminating in two days of debate on the 11 and 12 January. Every MP was then asked to state where they stood and by this time Muldoon was firmly in the camp opposed to the mill. Holyoake finally declared that he personally would close it down the next day but that cabinet would discuss the issue taking into account the caucus opinions and would make a decision.[50] When caucus adjourned shortly thereafter for lunch, the backbench group celebrated their anticipated victory over drinks. Cabinet met at 7 p.m. the same night and the agreement was cancelled, the British company was paid £500,000 in compensation, and neither the mill nor the railway extension were built.

MPs often make their reputation through committee work. Muldoon and Gordon served on a Fishing Industry Inquiry which during 1962 sat for 239 hours over 46 days, considered 110 submissions and interviewed 138 witnesses. Consisting of five Labour MPs and five National and headed by National's Jack Scott, the committee toured the country hearing submissions. Muldoon later commented that 'we had never heard so many lies' from witnesses with vested interests.[51] In Invercargill the committee met with a senior National Party activist who was prominent in the oyster industry. He survived a series of questions from the Labour MPs but his relief was short-lived. He was then subjected to penetrating and hostile questioning from Gordon and Muldoon, who concluded by requesting a look at his accounts. He refused and was threatened with having to appear before the bar of the House. Subsequently, Gordon and Muldoon had to apologise to Hanan and the Invercargill National Party for losing them a strong supporter and donor to the party.[52] The committee made thirty-one recommendations all but one of which, concerned with trout farming, were subsequently implemented.

Muldoon was fortunate in 1961 in being appointed to the Public Accounts Committee, which in 1962 became the Public Expenditure Committee with enhanced powers. The Public Expenditure Committee reported in depth on the efficiency of government departments and made its members very well informed on all aspects of government so that they were able to participate with confidence in a wide range of debates in the House. The committee was one of the watchdogs looking for waste, inefficiency, theft, neglect and carelessness in the use of public funds. It scrutinised the expenditure of money voted by Parliament, and no one was exempt from its activities. It operated as a bipartisan committee and ministers often found themselves criticised or cross-examined by the backbenchers from their own party and not just the Opposition.

Shortly after Muldoon was appointed to the committee, its chairman, David Seath, handed over to Bill Sheat. Sheat, a lawyer and one-time economics lecturer from Taranaki, had stood twice as a Labour candidate before becoming a National MP and a very successful Under-Secretary for Works. He had resigned, however, and been re-elected as an Independent, before retiring from Parliament in 1954 and then again being re-elected as a National MP in 1957. A principled but very independently minded man, who had a powerful intellect and was a fearsome debater, Sheat by 1960 had accepted that his ambition to be a senior frontbench minister would never be realised. Although not a heavy drinker, he enjoyed the Bellamy's club-like atmosphere and over drinks encouraged Muldoon and other keen, young MPs to become bold, investigative committee members and not to be overly deferential to more senior colleagues.[53] They responded enthusiastically, much to the chagrin of some older ministers and MPs.

A subcommittee of the Public Expenditure Committee was appointed to examine the Tourist Hotel Corporation. It was chaired by Freer and included the 'Young Turks', Gordon, MacIntyre and Muldoon.[54] In 1964 they visited every hotel, prying not only into its management and finances but into everything else, including the drains in the bathrooms, the guttering on the roof and the soup in the kitchens. The report concluded that there was a case for having some loss-making Tourist Hotel Corporation hotels so that New Zealanders and overseas tourists could see some remote parts of New Zealand where it would not be a commercially sensible decision to build, but that there was no need to have state-owned hotels in places where private enterprise was able and willing to build and maintain them.

On one of its fact-finding tours, the committee flew on a Widgeon amphibian plane piloted by Captain Fred Ladd from Waitangi to Waikaremoana and then to Tokaanu. On the last leg, Ladd gave the controls to Gordon, who was a pilot. Muldoon, who was not a good air traveller at the best of times, became increasingly agitated and as Gordon came into land 'bashed Fred on the head and demanded he take over. Fred gave me a wink and nudged the pedals . . . We landed O.K. but Muldoon would hardly speak to me for hours!'[55]

The committee soon developed a reputation for its thoroughness and the public service started to take pre-emptive action, for example checking fire-extinguishers or clearing silt out of drains before the committee paid a visit. Once Gordon found a drain full of silt at the Wellington Training College. He went back and checked a month later and it was still full of silt.

In late 1963 Muldoon succeeded Sheat as chairman of the Public Expenditure Committee and encouraged the members even more than before to 'get stuck into' the departmental representatives who appeared before the committee and force them to justify their requests and defend their expenditure. Muldoon decided that he would never rule out a question or prevent a member following up, even though some of his colleagues asked what he regarded as muddled and interminable questions.

On one occasion all the members of the Road Safety Committee decided to get drunk while considering new drink-driving legislation incorporating the introduction of breathalysing and blood-testing. Muldoon, Brown, who was a former President of the Automobile Association, Doug Carter, Gordon, Martyn Finlay and Henry May all got drunk on whisky and gin they paid for themselves, while being blood-tested every half-hour by a doctor who pronounced on their ability to drive. At the end Muldoon called for a driver and took Gordon home but was amazed by Brown and Finlay, who decided to go off for a drink together.[56]

Muldoon worked hard on various caucus committees. In 1963, for example, he served on those dealing with the New Zealand Society of Accountants fidelity fund, the Fisheries Amendment Bill, the Shipping and Seamen Amendment Bill, business depreciation, district licensing trusts, hire purchase, tenancy laws, the Real Estate Agents Bill and the Motor Spirits Distribution Amendment Bill.[57]

He also continued to register his opposition to government policies and actions which disadvantaged the poorest of those he represented. On 10 August 1962, for example, he wrote to Holyoake listing seven reasons why he was worried about proposed increases in state house rentals based on income, asking for the decision to be reversed and suggesting the matter be discussed at the next caucus. Among his concerns were that rent increases would be a tax on overtime income, that it did not take into account total household income, that many of those affected were older people nearing retirement and that 'the means test idea is repugnant in itself'.[58]

In October 1963 Holyoake asked caucus members to suggest ideas for policy at the forthcoming election. Muldoon suggested three things: the abolition of stamp duty on owner occupied flats; a royal commission on public transport in Auckland; and a better housing policy.[59] Later in the meeting he made a comment recorded as 'Local body rates biggest issue in cities. Solution required.'[60]

In early 1963 Muldoon made an overseas trip with five other MPs: Roy Jack, Bert Walker, Henry May, Norman Douglas and Arthur Faulkner. They visited Singapore, Malaysia, Thailand, South Vietnam and the Philippines. Muldoon summarised the tour in *The Rise and Fall of a Young Turk*, emphasising particularly Vietnam where the delegation met President Ngo Dhin Diem and visited the cities of Saigon, Hué, Qui Nhon and Dalat.[61] What Muldoon saw reinforced his dislike of communists and he subsequently became a strong defender of US involvement in Vietnam and a critic of western television reports which he alleged showed only atrocities committed by the Americans and the South Vietnamese anti-communists. His recollections of Thailand were largely restricted to 'the worst attack of dysentery possible from a steak . . . Thai flies . . . had trodden on' and the group's Thai liaison officer, who crossed into China and 'came back with enough contraband Chinese goods to pay all his personal expenses for the trip'.[62]

The Philippines was dismissed as 'one of the most corrupt countries on earth . . . the American system of government gone mad.'[63]

Surprisingly Muldoon made no reference to Malaysia and Singapore. This may well have been because he absented himself in Singapore from official engagements. Lee Kuan Yew and his party had only been in power in Singapore for a couple of years and the New Zealand Government was very anxious to strengthen relations between the two countries. After considerable negotiations the New Zealand High Commissioner, R. Hunter Wade, who was to become one of New Zealand's most distinguished diplomats, persuaded the Singaporeans to host a ministerial dinner for the visiting New Zealand delegation and it became a major feature of the official programme. Hunter Wade recalled that when he went to the hotel to collect the MPs and take them to the dinner, he was told by Roy Jack that Muldoon had flatly refused to attend and

> had rudely rejected his leader's pleas not to offend the Singapore government . . . He hadn't said where he was going – to some dive, the leader suspected. As far as I recall . . . Muldoon never turned up for anything that had been arranged for the delegation and I doubt if I ever set eyes on him at all during their stay of several days . . . I had to explain to the Singapore government as best I could.[64]

Muldoon was in fact being shown round Singapore by his old friend Alan Jenkin, who lived there from 1954 until 1965. Jenkin recalled that Muldoon 'spent a couple of nights with him and they went to the most unusual places' such as the backstage of a Chinese opera, a temple where a medium went into a trance to talk to a monkey god, and a shop which made coffins and models of the hereafter for adorning Chinese funerals.[65]

At home in New Zealand, however, Muldoon was always conscientious and easy to find. Although already regarded as somewhat too independent and aggressive by some colleagues and commentators, he was also by the end of his first three years in Parliament being referred to by the *Auckland Star* as a 'vigorous debater', a 'strong advocate of Auckland interests, particularly pensioner housing', 'the most able of the 1960 crop of Parliamentarians' with 'a force of character and a depth of interest rare in New Zealand politics' and an MP whose 'views on rents have sent the blood pressures of Cabinet Ministers soaring'.[66] Muldoon was a presence and a talent that could not be ignored.

CHAPTER 7

The Under-Secretary 1963–66

MULDOON'S HOLD ON THE TAMAKI ELECTORATE WAS strengthened at the 1963 election by boundary changes which had cut off a solid Labour-voting area in the south-west. He increased his majority to 3754 and thereafter Tamaki was never again regarded as a marginal seat.

Holyoake after the 1963 election promoted David Seath, the Under-Secretary to Harry Lake, the Minister of Finance, to the cabinet as Minister of Internal Affairs. The Prime Minister gave the Under-Secretaryship to Muldoon. Muldoon was a marked contrast to both the much more easygoing Lake and Seath. Lake's principal private secretary, who had earlier worked for Walter Nash, Hanan and Nordmeyer among others, recalled that Lake, 'who didn't hit it off all that well' with Muldoon, was worried about how he could keep his new energetic and ambitious Under-Secretary busy.[1] Muldoon had inherited from Seath the farm workers' superannuation scheme, but that was almost completed. Lake decided to give Muldoon responsibility for the introduction of decimal currency and chairmanship of the Public Expenditure Committee, and hoped these duties would be enough to occupy his attention and time.

Lake was not a proud or ambitious man. Although a 'pleasant fellow', he was regarded by some public servants who worked closely with him as 'a lazy fellow' and 'perhaps not competent'.[2] He was also not a well man, sometimes did not bother reading and comprehending briefing papers from Treasury, and in the view of his private secretary 'never got on top of the job'.[3] He was happy to seek and take advice and frequently discussed financial matters with Holyoake, who kept a close watch on the finance area. Lake was also willing to delegate and gave Muldoon a relatively free hand as Under-Secretary. Although Lake sometimes gave pugnacious speeches, these were quite out of character and were in fact written by his more aggressive and politically partisan secretary, Jack Bryant.[4]

There was some suggestion that Holyoake knew Lake was not well, but clearly he did not favour the prospect of having the independent Shand in the finance portfolio. Muldoon may well have been appointed to relieve Lake of some of the detailed work and pressure in the House. Muldoon believed he had a good working relationship with Lake, although he did not appear to respect him much and subsequently damned him with faint praise as 'a modest, nice bloke who never felt diminished by his Under-Secretary's high profile'.[5]

As Under-Secretary to the Minister of Finance, Muldoon sat as Lake's proxy every Wednesday morning on the Cabinet Works Committee chaired by Percy Allen, the Minister of Works and a close friend of Holyoake's. Muldoon was relentless in questioning officials and if not satisfied would persuade the Public Expenditure Committee to hold up the matter for a further report. The bureaucrats took him so seriously that many started to rehearse their arguments before going to see him or appear before a committee which included him. It was a pattern that continued after Muldoon became a minister.

Allen came to resent deeply Muldoon's aggressive criticism and questioning of Ministry of Works projects and his junior colleague's apparent capture by Treasury and its formidable permanent head, Henry Lang.[6] Treasury's approach to papers from other departments was based on three questions: 'Is it within policy? Is it correctly costed? Is there provision for it in the programme and estimates?'[7] During 1965 and 1966 Muldoon and Treasury believed that the economy was running too fast and fought many battles with Allen and other spending ministers in an attempt to hold back the commencement of various projects. During the 1964–66 period the Works Committee also visited every university and technical institute in the country. These visits gave Muldoon information and insights that he drew on in the education debates he later instigated as Minister of Finance in 1968–69.

On Tuesdays Muldoon regularly attended meetings of the Cabinet Committee on Economic and Financial Policy, which often considered reports from an officials' committee chaired by the Secretary of the Treasury and including the heads of Customs, Industries and Commerce, Statistics, External Affairs and the Reserve Bank. Muldoon relished the access to information and asked the Government Statistician for detailed breakdowns of such things as movements in the consumer price index, the internal and external public debts and the marketing of primary products. He recalled that 'it was during this period that I really started to get the feel of the New Zealand economy'.[8]

Muldoon found the position of Under-Secretary 'a somewhat lonely one' because he was neither a member of cabinet nor any longer a backbencher. Unlike other MPs the Under-Secretary has to remain in his office when Parliament is not in session and sees few people apart from staff. Fortunately, in Muldoon's opinion, his chairmanship of the Public Expenditure Committee still gave him the opportunity between 1964 and 1966 to get out of the office, work with other MPs and get about the country.[9]

Not only senior ministers such as Shand and Allen had reservations about the new Under-Secretary. One young Treasury official who was not impressed on first meeting Muldoon was Bernard ('Bernie') Galvin, later to become Secretary of the Treasury and Head of the Prime Minister's Department during Muldoon's prime-ministership. Galvin prepared a detailed submission on taxation changes for Muldoon as Under-Secretary in 1964 and backed it with a detailed algebraic analysis. Muldoon dismissed it contemptuously as 'academic twiddle' and twenty-five years later Galvin remembered that Lang almost 'had to hold me down. It was not an auspicious start to our relationship.'[10]

Muldoon, however, continued to impress other observers, particularly in the Press Gallery. The *Auckland Star*, for example, which praised him as 'the man on the government benches who made the sharpest advance' in 1964, predicted that 'he will have reason to feel unjustly treated if he is not given full Cabinet rank in the next Cabinet review . . . He was quite outstanding on several occasions, always did his homework, and could speak fluently and, if need be, bitingly on any subject.'[11] That assessment was echoed by the *Evening Post*.[12]

In caucus Muldoon continued to express his opinion mainly on economic matters. For example, although still relatively junior, Muldoon had no hesitation in advancing his views on how National should organise tactically during the 1964 Budget debate in Parliament. He suggested that the main theme should be 'We can't borrow without savings' and that MPs in marginal seats should 'have latitude' in the content of their speeches while MPs in safe seats could 'keep to the Budget'.[13]

From the start Muldoon also showed himself to be an opponent of policies which would hit too severely on lower-income earners. At a caucus meeting on 13 February 1964 the Housing Minister, John Rae, outlined new policies on housing, including reviews of rents and mortgage interest rates in relation to earnings. Muldoon immediately argued that 'rents should be left alone and a man who gets a 3 per cent loan has a big enough burden'.[14] A decision was deferred until March when caucus overrode Muldoon's objections and agreed to a five-yearly review of mortgages with interest rates increased from 3 to 5 per cent if the mortgagee no longer qualified for the lower rate.[15]

Surprisingly, although many MPs commented in caucus on another Government proposal to allow trading banks to establish savings facilities, Muldoon did not express an opinion.[16] That did not mean he opposed the policy. Muldoon as Under-Secretary felt a need to be loyal to his minister Lake, who was taking the lead in the matter, and publicly Muldoon did defend the policy even to the extent of having a major row with his old friend Colin Busfield, who was the Assistant General Manager of the Auckland Savings Bank.[17]

Throughout 1964 and early 1965 there were other lengthy debates in caucus on such matters as the threatened takeover of the *Dominion* newspaper by Lord Thompson, the reorganisation of electricity supply, the construction of the Intercontinental Hotel, the huge Tongariro Power Scheme, railways and telephone charges, licensing hours, amendments to the industrial conciliation and arbitration system, and the development of an iron and steel industry. Muldoon had nothing to say on any of them.

In October 1964 Holyoake, not Lake, introduced a major caucus debate on the economy, giving a lengthy review of economic developments since 1960 before suggesting a public statement on the current recession and inflationary trends and steps being taken to address the problems.[18] Eighteen MPs participated in the succeeding discussion but, surprisingly, once again Muldoon was not one of them. By then he was becoming increasingly preoccupied with the changeover to decimal currency.

The team set up to plan and implement the introduction of decimal currency into New Zealand consisted of Muldoon; Syd Moses, a Wellington businessman who became chairman of the Decimal Currency Board; Jack Searle, a Treasury official who was the Board's secretary; and a number of other temporary staff, some seconded from other government departments. Among the latter were John Wybrow, a Treasury official who later became General Secretary of the Labour Party, and John Reid, a prominent Labour Party activist, who came from the Tourist and Publicity Department to be the press officer.[19]

Muldoon saw that his performance in introducing decimal currency would have a significant effect on his public reputation and chances of future promotion and was determined that none of the potentially controversial issues associated with the changeover would reflect adversely on him. People were worried about various things: conversion problems; the design and naming of the new banknotes and coins; the effect on prices; the fear that translating a shilling worth twelve pence into a ten-cent coin would devalue savings and wages by about 17 per cent; and the belief that converting cash registers and other machinery would result in higher costs being passed on to the consumer in higher prices. He also had to cope with the difficulty of not sitting in the cabinet which took many of the major decisions. He complained that 'frequently cabinet discussions were taken in my absence . . . without a full understanding of the difficulty that might arise' and 'on one or two occasions I had to ask for papers to be sent back to cabinet after they had been altered to produce a decision that was unworkable'.[20] There were protracted negotiations with office machine companies, especially over the cost of importing or converting machinery, and Muldoon was prepared to threaten that the Government would not hesitate to use the dual sanctions of import licensing and price control if the companies concerned attempted to profiteer from the changeover.

While Searle and his staff dealt with detailed technical matters, Muldoon decided he would 'act as front man in the public eye' rather than leave that task to Moses.[21] As a result he not only featured on television and in newspaper reports but became a frequent figure in cartoons. Some of his parliamentary colleagues thought he talked too much in public.

Early public disputes about the radio and television advertisements and jingles, which annoyed rather than educated people, and over the naming of the new currency unit – dollar, crown, royal, zeal, tui, or doubloon, etc.– paled into insignificance, however, against the furore raised by the design of the coins. Early in 1966 Cabinet endorsed the views of an advisory panel in selecting four stars for the one-cent coin, a flax bush for the two cents, a geyser for the five cents, a Maori mask for the ten cents, a rugby player for the twenty cents and a sheep farmer for the fifty cents. When the designs were leaked and published in the press, there was an immediate and widespread negative reaction. For once, Muldoon admitted, 'I was . . . at a loss to know what to do'.[22] Interviewed in Australia, he remarked to a journalist that some people would say that 'it doesn't matter what's on the coins so long as you have enough of them'.[23] This was reported back in New Zealand and provoked a dissenting view from Holyoake, who phoned Muldoon on his return to New Zealand and 'solemnly told me that the press would ruin me if I could not get out of this. I think he was only mildly exaggerating.'[24] Muldoon decided to announce that all the designs would be published and a nationwide poll would be used to select designs for the coin. The only design to survive was the ten cents but the controversy was defused.

A second controversy replaced it. Television's major current affairs programme in 1966 was called *Compass* and was produced by Gordon Bick. *Compass* decided to make a documentary on decimal currency which would include an investigation into possible price rises as a result of the changeover. Muldoon declared that this was a political not an administrative issue and that as such he, not Moses or Searle, should appear on the programme to answer any allegations. Because the programme was to be screened within three months of an election, however, and the New Zealand Broadcasting Corporation had a rule that no politicians could appear on TV during that period except in a scheduled election programme, Muldoon could not be used. Bick telephoned Muldoon and, when Muldoon again refused to let either Searle or Moses appear on the programme, told him that the programme would be screened without a reply to the criticism. Muldoon and Bick later disagreed diametrically on who threatened whom, but when the Director-General of the NZBC ruled that the programme would not be shown without balance, Bick resigned and moved to Australia after alleging political interference. He claimed that Muldoon had ended their acrimonious telephone conversation with the threat that 'we'll see about that' when Bick had said that the programme would screen without a representative of the Decimal Currency Board. When Bick revealed that he had a tape of a telephone conversation with John Reid, the publicity officer of the Decimal Currency Board, suggesting that Holyoake was responsible for delaying the programme until after the election, Bick was accused of phone-tapping and lost some of his public support.[25]

Muldoon's suspicion of state-run television and radio may well have influenced his attitude to deregulation of the electronic media. Faced with a challenge to the state monopoly of radio and television, Muldoon told caucus that he was convinced there was 'a place for private radio. Television is different and should be delayed for some time yet', he said, though he believed it 'would not be . . . worse than a second TV channel under the NZBC'.[26] The following week he again expressed support for private radio, observing that 'young people favour the pirates'.[27] Marshall, Shand and others were less sympathetic to a breach of the state monopoly of broadcasting.

In 1965 Muldoon received a US State Department foreign leader grant to spend three months in the United States travelling and studying topics of his own choosing. His major subject was the working of the US economy, especially taxation. He also looked at balance of payments problems and visited cash register firms to inquire about changing to decimal currency. During his visit, from 20 February to 20 April, he met various officials from the US Treasury, Federal Reserve Bank, Bureau of the Budget and US Mint. He also met a number of elected politicians and appointed officials in both Washington DC and various states.[28] Muldoon's American hosts became concerned that Muldoon was too intense and needed to relax. The State Department contacted the New Zealand Embassy in Washington and the first secretary A. C. (Fred) Shailes, who later became New Zealand's Auditor-General, was asked to intervene.[29] Shailes and his wife invited Muldoon for dinner and found him to be quite relaxed and very good company, but the suspicion remained that Muldoon was not really enjoying himself despite the fact that he received hospitality and went sightseeing in Washington DC, New York, Atlanta, Dallas, Phoenix, Los Angeles, San Francisco, Denver, Chicago, Detroit and Hartford.

During his visit Muldoon developed or confirmed a number of generalised views on the United States which he later recorded in *The Rise and Fall of a Young Turk*. He chided his Treasury guide on the number of US presidents who had been assassinated, described US culture as 'mush' which made Americans 'emotionally immature and warped', argued that the US 'political system formulated two hundred years ago is totally unsuited to the modern world' and is 'hopelessly corrupt', and concluded that 'it is almost impossible to be a successful politician in the USA and remain an honourable man'. Although he conceded that 'the ordinary American . . . is a warm friendly person', he deplored the fact that 'so many things have an overlay of insincerity'. Muldoon believed that the United States exhibited all 'the classical symptoms of the decline of a civilisation'.[30] These were not generalisations about the United States which one expected to hear from a National Party politician at that time. Muldoon also recalled that 'travelling from city to city was lonely', and although he enjoyed visits to the Rockies and the Grand Canyon, he needed 24 hours to recover from a test ride in an Iroquois helicopter at Dallas Airport.

His official report written and submitted on his return to New Zealand did not contain his general impressions but was restricted to precise observations on the US economy and balance of payments problems, New Zealand borrowing from the United States, taxation and electronic data processing, meat exports, the purchase of aircraft and military equipment from the United States, decimal currency, the IMF, ignorance of New Zealand in the United States, television and politics, and the Johnson presidency. In a series of discussions on balance of payments problems and ways of solving them he had received conflicting advice from bankers, the US Treasury, the Bureau of Budget and the Federal Reserve. Stability of the currency appeared to be the major priority.

The highlight of his visit appears to have been a day spent at Stanford University with the New Zealand-born economist, J. B. Condliffe; this was the beginning of a long-standing relationship between the two men. Muldoon noted that Condliffe's 'views on the expansion of the NZ economy are brilliant and far-sighted but in 1965 he told me that he saw at that time exactly the same signs as he saw in 1928 prior to the great crash of 1929. On balance, however, he felt that we would avoid such a crash.'[31] Muldoon readily admitted that Condliffe's views were reflected in his speeches and approach to economic management over the following three years or so.

Muldoon's report to the National Party caucus on his three months in the United States appears to have been a somewhat boring and superficial account and contrasted with that of Sir Leslie Munro, who at the same meeting summarised his impressions gained during a private visit to America.[32] Unlike Muldoon, who did not refer to Vietnam, Munro dealt with that topic at some length, stressing the Americans' need for support and friends. Munro's sentiments were echoed by McCready, Donald and Harrison, who had recently returned from an Asian tour. When Vietnam was debated at length the next day, fifteen MPs took part but as in all previous debates on the topic Muldoon was not one of them.[33]

He did, however, defend New Zealand's involvement in the Vietnam War publicly, for example in a bruising television encounter with Labour's Hugh Watt in June 1965, and elsewhere he argued that 'a withdrawal from Vietnam would be a betrayal of our collective security obligations, a betrayal of the people of South Vietnam and ultimately a betrayal of the people of New Zealand'.[34] But he continued to show little interest in the subject when it was debated frequently and at length in caucus during 1965 and 1966. There is no question that throughout the period 1964-66 his attention was focused almost entirely on economic matters.

One exception when Muldoon did feel constrained to speak out on a non-economic matter in caucus was in 1966. Muldoon became annoyed with lawyers in the caucus, including Hanan, Marshall, Riddiford and Jack, who sided with the Law Society and a majority of judges in opposing a clause in a Bill which would allow the Crown the right to appeal against inadequate sentences. This clause was also opposed by the Labour Opposition. Muldoon, supported by Tombleson and Talboys, noted that the clause was designed particularly for cases of 'child rape and cruelty to children'. The caucus minutes went on to summarise Muldoon's argument: 'Very bad not to take notice of public opinion. Large number of people who think we should take action and not leave it to the lawyers. Bill should proceed and not be emasculated. Fight the Labour Party if they want it.'[35] Muldoon and his supporters won the subsequent vote.

Concern about growing inflation led Muldoon in 1965 to advocate once again in the caucus restraints on expenditure, particularly on government buildings. Holyoake countered by arguing that New Zealand's growth rate was the fastest in the world and that there were ample overseas reserves which could be used and IMF loans were available at low interest if necessary.[36] Holyoake's strategy of borrowing in the expectation of an upturn in the economy was adopted rather than Muldoon's more cautious but electorally more dangerous approach.

Early in 1965 the National Party caucus debated the image of the party and the long-term strategy leading up to the 1966 election.[37] Gordon pointed out that the party was divided on the scope of private enterprise, to which Pickering replied that without 'more emphasis on competitive enterprise', 'the gradual dismantling of import control', and a 'determination to restore competition', there would be an impression that National was a 'Party without a purpose. No difference between the Parties.' With the Government moving towards committing combat troops to Vietnam, a decision which was approved two months later,[38] Shand suggested that National should 'concentrate on external affairs and defence'. Muldoon was surprisingly lacking in policy and vision in his observation that, because National was a second-term government whose major policy had been carried out, 'we will be judged on administration. Should focus on our men compared with Opposition.'[39]

The Government was concerned prior to the 1966 election with advice it was getting from Treasury, the Reserve Bank and the Monetary and Economic Council on the current economic situation and outlook.[40] Various reports indicated that measures designed to dampen inflation had 'had only a minor impact and that further measures were imperative'; that the 'government must be prepared, even though this is an election year, to implement a firm policy of economic restraint', including 'firmer control over its own expenditure'; that the estimated increase in total government expenditure of $52 million (8.8 per cent) should be cut to no more than $24 million (4 per cent); and that taxation, especially indirect taxation, should be increased. The Secretary to the Treasury concluded prophetically in one letter that 'if firm action is not taken to reduce internal demand, a rapid deterioration in the balance of payments could lead to a critical external situation.'[41]

Faced with the election, however, and trying to counter the Labour Party's campaign based around the slogan 'the economy is in a mess', Holyoake and Lake decided to minimise the seriousness of the situation and cover both internal and external deficits by drawing on foreign exchange reserves. Lake argued that while 'we are confronted with a deficit in our balance of payments . . . international reserves exist to get the country over short-term problems such as these which have arisen while we are building up export potential'.[42]

Labour chose a 53-year-old secondary school teacher, Mrs Irene Offen, to stand against Muldoon in Tamaki in 1966, but when she withdrew six weeks before the election a well-known barrister, Kevin Ryan, replaced her. [43] Muldoon believed that Ryan was the most formidable candidate Labour ever ran against him, but further favourable boundary changes and expensive housing construction appeared to have consolidated National's hold on the electorate. Muldoon felt safe enough to spend most of the campaign outside Tamaki supporting colleagues in more marginal electorates. In the widespread Taupo electorate, for example, he held meeting after meeting in the small isolated timber villages and hydro stations playing no small part in the re-election of his admirer Mrs Rona Stevenson by 275 votes over the author of this biography, who was the Labour candidate.

Muldoon centred his own campaign on four issues: the economy, which Labour claimed, with some justification, was in a mess; Vietnam; the comparison between Holyoake and Kirk as leaders; and trade union influence in the Labour Party. He also continued to stress his work as a local constituency MP, and Ryan, who with his identical twin brother canvassed extensively, soon discovered that 'Muldoon was well respected in Tamaki and was generally regarded as a hard worker . . . I found . . . even in Labour areas . . . convinced Muldoonists as opposed to Nationalites'.[44] Nevertheless, Muldoon's vote dropped by 397 votes compared to 1963, Ryan increased Labour's vote by 530, and Muldoon's majority was cut from 3754 to 2827.

By 1966 Muldoon's reputation as an aggressive debater had become something of a two-edged sword. Some voters admired his aggression, others were repelled by it. Muldoon's attacks on Labour also sometimes rebounded. In 1965, for example, in a 'display of verbal judo and karate' which 'left a dozen Opposition members tied up helplessly in knots of mingled pain and laughter', Muldoon perhaps subconsciously and injudiciously irritated his own as well as Labour's front bench. Replying to Rowling, who had praised the Labour front bench, Muldoon argued: 'It's remarkable to hear one of the backbench bunch say something complimentary about the frontbench bunch . . . we all know there's only one good thing the backbench bunch wants the frontbench bunch to do – and that's retire'.[45] Muldoon might have been referring only to Labour but National frontbenchers such as Allen, Shand, Marshall and Shelton, who had been repeated targets for the Young Turks, and even Holyoake, who was always sensitive to suggestions that older incumbents should retire, were probably not amused by Muldoon's general observation.

Muldoon aggravated his senior colleagues' suspicion and dislike of him by his performance at the post-election caucus. Muldoon told his colleagues that National had not done well at the polls because the farmers did not think highly of Talboys as Minister of Agriculture and in consequence there was an increased vote for Social Credit and the danger of a possible country party in the future. He then criticised National's election publicity – the responsibility of a committee chaired by Marshall – and the party's organisation. By implication he even insulted Holyoake by suggesting National had to learn how to use television effectively.[46] Holyoake was not impressed and Muldoon obviously confirmed the negative views of Marshall, Shand, Allen and others that he was too tactless, abrasive and undisciplined to be promoted to cabinet, where he was likely to be as independent and divisive as he was in caucus. Instead of a phone call from Holyoake inviting him to join the cabinet, Muldoon received a telegram which said 'Caucus preference suggests Peter, Duncan and David. Keith Holyoake.'[47] Muldoon was, in his own words, 'shocked and staggered' at his omission.[48]

While there were valid reasons for selecting Gordon, MacIntyre and Thomson, and Adams-Schneider had recently been ill, the omission of Muldoon surprised many commentators. According to the *Sunday Times*, for example, Holyoake, who had sole control over cabinet selection though he consulted other senior ministers, had ignored precedent in not elevating his two parliamentary under-secretaries, Muldoon and Adams-Schneider, who were generally regarded as equally hard workers but much better debaters than the three new ministers he had chosen.[49] Holyoake, however, was later to state in an interview that 'he looks for the qualities of a "judge" rather than those of an "advocate" in considering candidates for cabinet rank'.[50]

Muldoon's omission was even more of a snub when it is remembered that he had been one of the two backbench MPs on the National Party's Dominion Council since 1961 and, with Holyoake and Marshall, one of the three MPs on the Policy Committee since 1965. During the three years that he had been an under-secretary he had also relieved Lake of much of the chore of speaking to meetings of Rotary, Chambers of Commerce, National Party groups, and other business and community organisations.

MacIntyre, Gordon and Thomson did not know who else had been selected for cabinet when they arrived at Parliament in response to Holyoake's summons. They assumed Muldoon had been chosen also and were discussing what portfolio he might have got when Muldoon walked into the office and congratulated them.[51] Although obviously devastated, Muldoon was unusually gracious and by accepting Holyoake's rebuke without demur showed that he accepted the Prime Minister's leadership and was prepared to be less confrontational. Three months later, Holyoake appointed Muldoon Minister of Tourism and Associate Minister of Finance. Adams-Schneider also was added belatedly to cabinet as Minister of Broadcasting and Associate Minister of Customs. It may not have been a coincidence that at the same time Muldoon's major enemy in Cabinet, Shand, relinquished the chair of an important cabinet economic committee after a row with Holyoake over economic management and at a time of considerable economic uncertainty coinciding with a collapse in wool prices.

At the meeting of caucus on 10 February 1967 at which Holyoake announced the appointment of Muldoon as Minister of Tourism and at which Muldoon was also reappointed to the party's Dominion Council and appointed to the Dominion Publicity Committee, Holyoake and Lake also expressed to their parliamentary colleagues their concern at the rapid development of a serious economic crisis. After a widespread discussion (to which Muldoon did not make a contribution) it was agreed that Holyoake and Lake would issue a statement on the situation.[52] The Government also moved to dampen consumer demand. In February consumer subsidies on butter and flour were removed; funds for new state advances housing loans were reduced; state house rentals were increased by $12^1/_2$ per cent; postal, telephone and telegraph charges were raised; limits were announced on government expenditure; and hire purchase regulations, exchange controls and credit restraints were tightened.

On 21 February 1967, Lake died suddenly of a heart attack, the last of a series he had had over the previous three years. Muldoon became acting minister while Holyoake considered his options. He first offered the post to his deputy, Marshall, who declined.[53] Shand wanted the portfolio but Holyoake disliked Shand's forceful independence in economic matters which, throughout his prime-ministership, Holyoake kept closely under his ultimate though indirect control. Muldoon was appointed Minister of Finance, but Holyoake again warned him not to become too arrogant or independent by leaving him at the bottom of the cabinet rank order and giving him only the eighth and lowest seat on the Government front bench. At 45 Muldoon was New Zealand's youngest Minister of Finance since Joseph Ward in 1893. The only minister who sought Muldoon out to congratulate him and offer his full support was Shand, who added, however, that he would help Muldoon only as long as Muldoon pursued conservative economic policies.[54] Shand clearly had doubts about the direction of the Government's economic policy at that time, though this may well have been more an implied criticism of Holyoake's leadership and response to the current economic crisis than concern about Muldoon's ability or ideological orientation. It was not long, however, before Muldoon found himself at odds again not only with Shand but with other senior ministers.

CHAPTER 8

Minister of Finance 1967–69

A S MINISTER OF FINANCE, LAKE HAD BEEN AMENABLE TO THE
Prime Minister's wishes and suited to his 'steady does it' approach to
economic management. By 1967, when Muldoon took over the portfolio,
the times were changing. During the 1966 election campaign Muldoon had denied
repeatedly that there was an economic crisis but in less than three weeks after the
election wool prices collapsed. By April 1967 he was warning his Tamaki electorate
AGM that New Zealand was 'facing the worst balance of payments position in 30
years.'[1] The 1967 wool price drop was not a temporary setback, which would be
followed after a short time by a recovery in world agricultural commodity prices
and New Zealand's terms of trade. Instead, except for a brief high in 1972 and
1973, the terms of trade have remained below their level of the 1950s and 1960s,
generating structural problems which were to bedevil Muldoon's and his successors' economic management. As a World Bank report in 1968 on New Zealand's
economy concluded:

> During the last two years New Zealand has been undergoing a difficult period charac-
> terised by a large deficit on current account . . . The present balance of payments
> difficulties reflects the basic weakness of New Zealand: she is a high-income country
> over-dependent on exports of a small number of primary products . . . now facing
> prospects of a long-term price downturn . . . Only if the industrial sector becomes
> internationally competitive can the dependence of the balance of payments on a few
> agricultural commodities be reduced.[2]

The long-term deterioration of New Zealand's terms of trade would be exacerbated
by the entry of Britain into the European Economic Community and the oil shocks
of the 1970s. Muldoon came into a crisis situation and despite some initial apparent success never got out of it.

Caucus met on 2 March and, after paying respects to Lake, commenced with a
wide-ranging discussion of the political scene. Muldoon was not among the fifteen
contributors. Immediately after, however, he introduced a debate on the economy

by telling caucus it was clear that as a result of the drastic drop in wool and meat prices the 'farming community will take the most severe knock in income'. He was concerned that the resulting necessary 'press down of the economy should not be aimed at production' but should be 'directed mostly at consumers'.[3] He advocated delays in the start of government-funded capital works, and proposed various measures that would place more of the burden on the 'commercial community and higher-salaried' taxpayers. His specific proposals for consideration included a rise in indirect sales taxes across the board; increased taxes on spirits, beer, tobacco, petrol, overseas fares and travel; an import surcharge; an exchange tax, to effect a one-sided devaluation; a reduction in personal tax exemptions; a payroll tax for large employers; and a compulsory savings scheme for younger people. He stressed that these were only suggestions and that no decision had yet been made to adopt any of them.

During the discussion that followed, Holyoake argued that the 'only way of taking money out of circulation without increasing the cost of living is increased direct taxation', and that view was endorsed by most of the other nineteen MPs who commented. Luxton was the only MP who supported Muldoon's suggestion of cuts to government expenditure, though Hanan, Gair and Gordon wanted an increase in the social security tax rate rather than general income tax.

When caucus convened the following day, twenty more MPs contributed to the general debate before Holyoake asked caucus to indicate collectively what it thought of Muldoon's proposals. Tax increases on tobacco and spirits, increases in social security tax and motor vehicle registration charges, and the abolition of income tax rebates received the most support. Muldoon, when faced with a demand for a means test on the family benefit, argued that it would be better to leave the benefit alone and alter the wife and child allowances for income tax rather than breach the principle of universality.[4]

The debate within the National Government over how precisely to handle the economic crisis continued throughout April. Holyoake made it clear that, while he wanted 'to stabilise the economy', National 'should not overdo it' because of the 'psychological effect' on the nation. He admitted, however, that overseas funds were low and that reserves needed to be created.[5] Muldoon reiterated the need to balance direct and indirect taxation and kept presenting various alternative fiscal packages to caucus, explaining their comparative effects on the cost of living. In April increases in electricity charges averaging $12\frac{1}{2}$ per cent were announced, and in May sales taxes, duties and government fees were raised. The banks were directed to reduce overdrafts by 10 per cent. There were also cuts in import licence allocations.

On becoming Minister of Finance, Muldoon had started talking about 'flexible economic policies' and 'fine-tuning', by which he meant that problems in the economy should be addressed as they emerged, not dealt with all together subsequently in an annual budget. He did this by introducing the practice of 'mini-budgets'.[6] Muldoon's use of mini-budgets also meant that he always seemed to be on TV introducing, explaining and defending government policy. The first mini-budget was delivered on Thursday 4 May 1967. Muldoon moved to dampen down economic activity by increasing a range of indirect taxes and government charges. Some incentives were given to exporters and the fishing and tourism industries. By these means, it was possible to produce a less dramatic budget in June. Muldoon's mini-budgets and economic fine-tuning by regulation were not welcomed by all National Party supporters, some of whom feared what a Labour Minister of Finance might do with such 'arbitrary powers' which could breach the prerogative of Parliament.[7]

Muldoon's first major budget was presented to Parliament on 22 June 1967. In the eyes of at least one leading economist, Frank Holmes, that Budget was 'blacker than Nordmeyer's Black Budget of 1958' and Muldoon's firm tackling of the balance of payments crisis was followed by a substantial devaluation which effected 'the most successful short-term use of the exchange rate of the post-war era'.[8] In this budget Muldoon claimed that he was cutting the increase in government expenditure for 1967–68 to about 2 per cent, compared to about 9 per cent the previous year. He also identified clearly the specific economic problems facing the Government: an economic slow-down; a growth in unemployment; a drop in exports, especially wool, and of export receipts; a significant increase in the cost of invisibles; a run-down in the building industry; a credit squeeze; and a hold-up in government spending.[9] He was quite prepared to share this depressing scenario not only in confidence with caucus but also openly in an effort to educate and influence public opinion.

In September and October 1967, Muldoon made his first overseas trip as Minister of Finance. In Britain he sought the approval of the Labour Chancellor of the Exchequer, James Callaghan, and the Governor of the Bank of England, Sir Leslie O'Brien, for the New Zealand Government to borrow to repay a large sterling loan falling due. Muldoon then travelled to Trinidad, to attend his first Commonwealth finance ministers' meeting, and Washington DC to arrange loans from the IMF. Finally, Muldoon went to the IMF and World Bank meetings in Rio de Janeiro.

While at Rio Muldoon received a phone call from Holyoake informing him that the Government's advisers were recommending an immediate devaluation and that, at a secret meeting in Holyoake's house, Holyoake, Marshall, Hanan and Shand had been inclined to agree. Muldoon, who was always reluctant to manage the exchange rate, told the Prime Minister that such a move was not only probably unnecessary but could trigger a devaluation of sterling. Muldoon had assured the British that New Zealand would not devalue unilaterally and said to Holyoake that if the decision was made to devalue at that time he would resign.[10] Holyoake agreed not to act until Muldoon returned to New Zealand.

After Muldoon had returned to New Zealand, a decision was taken not to consider devaluation again until early 1968, but Britain's decision to devalue in November led to New Zealand not only following suit but adding on a further 5.15 per cent, making a total devaluation of 19.45 per cent. As Muldoon argued, the addition of 5.15 per cent 'gives us a greater safety margin and covers us for years to come' as well as maintaining parity with Australia.[11] Senior Treasury officials in retrospect agreed that Muldoon had been right and that, rather than devalue prematurely and unilaterally and then have to make a subsequent devaluation, it had been better to wait and act concurrently with the British.[12]

When in November 1967 Muldoon did recommend devaluation of the New Zealand currency, he also proposed concurrent legislation to abolish export incentives. This annoyed the manufacturers. Holyoake declared that the 'manufacturers and exporters have a right to be heard' before the Government agreed to abolish the incentives, but 'if legislation is required next session, we will do it and make it retrospective'.[13]

While the devaluation led to a price realignment, which facilitated the great export diversification of the 1970s, it also exacerbated inflationary measures. In Muldoon's view devaluation in 1967 failed to shift price relativities and correct the balance of payments problem. It reinforced his suspicions about lowering the exchange rate and made him even more resistant to advice recommending devaluation in the future.

Some weeks earlier, in October 1967, Muldoon had written to the Managing Director of the IMF explaining that New Zealand had recorded overseas exchange transaction deficits on current account of over $50 million in the year ending June 1966. He added that, 'with conditions tightening in the international capital markets, we have encountered difficulties in raising long-term loans abroad'.[14] New Zealand, therefore, was now forced to appeal to the IMF to make use of its reserve facilities and requested the IMF to agree to a stand-by arrangement of US$87 million for one year. Muldoon claimed that the Government's measures during 1966 to restrict government expenditure and restrain domestic demand had been more than negated by the unexpected drop in demand and price for wool which, for the 1966/67 season, had forced the Wool Commission to buy in nearly 650,000 unsold bales, or about one-third of total production for that year, at a loss of some $60 million in overseas earnings to New Zealand. The IMF agreed to New Zealand's request.

In September 1968 Muldoon again went to the Commonwealth finance ministers' meeting, this time being held in London, and to the IMF–World Bank meeting in Washington. He also visited Japan, Germany, Switzerland, France and England. He was particularly concerned with discussing with the Japanese delays in setting up the Comalco aluminium industry.

At the World Bank meeting in 1969 Muldoon clashed with Robert McNamara, the Bank's president, who believed that, as a wealthy, developed country, New Zealand had a very low priority compared to more needy countries seeking Bank loans.[15] New Zealand wanted a loan for its Development Finance Corporation and, risking giving a weapon to his political opponents back in New Zealand, Muldoon argued that over the past twenty years New Zealand had dropped from third to thirteenth place in the world in gross national product and that the terms of trade had moved very adversely against agricultural exporters such as New Zealand. McNamara had scheduled a ten-minute courtesy meeting with Muldoon but the meeting went on for an hour with McNamara's later appointments piling up outside, much to the disgust of his staff, as the two men argued.[16] Subsequently New Zealand received its loan.

During his overseas trips Muldoon usually fitted in a little relaxation: a nightclub in Rio de Janeiro; the Folies Bergère in Paris; a baseball game, dinner, a show, a party with expatriate New Zealanders in New York, Washington or London; visiting relatives or friends in England; 'clean and above board' geisha parties in Japan or watching women pearl divers; and regular 36-hour stopovers in Hawaii on his way home to New Zealand.[17]

Whereas Muldoon's 1967 Budget had been the shortest since 1951, his 1969 Budget, which included recommendations from the National Development Conference and a review of monetary policy, was the longest in twenty years, taking an hour and forty minutes to read. In the 1969 Budget debate Labour's former leader Nordmeyer, who was retiring at the election later that year, contrasted the Budget with his infamous 'Black Budget' of 1958. Nordmeyer pointed out that while the 1967–68 recession was in terms of the drop in wool receipts the worst since the war, some $63 million on the previous year, in the 1957–58 year New Zealand exports fell in every commodity except timber by a combined total of almost $93 million. Imports had also risen sharply in 1958 compared to a fall in 1967 and public debt rose only $22 million in 1957–60 under Labour compared to $182 million in 1963–66 under National.[18] It was a very telling attack on National and in an untypically gracious gesture when Nordmeyer concluded Muldoon crossed the floor and shook Nordmeyer's hand.

Muldoon's lifestyle as a minister was incredibly busy. Because there were financial aspects to most matters that went to cabinet, he found himself reading numerous papers and Treasury reports. Besides cabinet meetings on Monday and the weekly caucus meeting on Tuesdays, he had a cabinet committee meeting most days. He spent more time in the House than many other ministers, saw numerous officials and delegations, often addressed three or four meetings a week outside Wellington, and spent the first Saturday morning of each month back in his Tamaki electorate dealing with the problems of his constituents.

Unlike many other Ministers of Finance, Muldoon tried not to deal with matters more times than was necessary. He moved paper expeditiously and kept a relatively clear desk. There was no 'too hard basket', and if he had doubts Muldoon immediately rang the Secretary of the Treasury or some other official so that the matter could be resolved there and then. Each night Muldoon stayed in his office working until he had dealt with all the minor matters that had piled up during the day so that he started afresh the next morning, but he did not expect his staff to work the same hours if there was nothing specific for them to do. In that he differed with previous finance ministers, some of whom – like Walter Nash – insisted that their staff should stay, even if doing nothing, until the minister went home.[19]

Muldoon did not enjoy a close or friendly relationship with N. R. Davis, the first Secretary of the Treasury with whom he was associated. Personality rather than policy differences marred the relationship, and the situation was not helped by the fact that Davis was an ill man for much of that time. Henry Lang, Davis's successor, was a different proposition. Muldoon and Lang, over a long working relationship, quite often argued policy and because each liked to have the last say and their own way never became friends. But they certainly grew to respect each other's intellect and strong personality.

Some observers thought initially that Muldoon might have been captured by the talented and powerful Lang, who was the dominant figure in Treasury even before he became its head in 1969. One journalist speculated that Lang, 'the most competent Secretary of the Treasury we have had for a number of years . . . could well be using Muldoon as his mouthpiece'. On reflection, however, Burns concluded that was not the case but rather that 'at present we have the case of two very strong personalities who seem to collaborate in a remarkable way. On balance, I do not think that Muldoon would let the Treasury actually domineer him.'[20] He did not.

Lang, who remained Secretary of the Treasury until 1977, subsequently recalled that he at first appreciated having such an intelligent, hard-working and pragmatic minister who also revealed 'considerable integrity',[21] although privately others were of the opinion that Lang personally detested Muldoon. Lang certainly believed that Muldoon's agenda became increasingly dominated by the paramount objective of National winning elections, which Muldoon saw not only as a matter of party and personal interest but also as necessary for the continued good government and welfare of New Zealand generally.

Although Muldoon's strong personality and lack of imagination made him sometimes difficult to convince, his ability to grasp and understand complex arguments was excellent. He rarely initiated major policy, but he could read and digest numerous background reports and papers suggesting alternative actions and was decisive in approving or rejecting them. For example, in the preparation of the Budget alone there could be as many as 200 Treasury reports on specific policy areas. While the detailed text of the Budget was drafted by Treasury's Budget officer and the statistics in the Budget and estimates were also provided by officials, the main issues were determined by consultation between the Minister of Finance, the Prime Minister, the Secretary of the Treasury, cabinet and caucus. Muldoon himself always dictated in one afternoon the opening three or four and the closing pages of his Budgets. He personally edited them and would not tolerate changes after that unless in exceptional circumstances.

Muldoon had some vigorous arguments with his Treasury advisers over the years but always respected the independence of the public service and was prepared on occasions to be persuaded by good-quality advice. On other occasions Muldoon was able to persuade Lang and other Treasury officials that their Minister was right. Irrespective of who won the argument, Lang recalled that he usually 'went home like a wrung-out dishrag', while 'Muldoon was elated by the confrontation.'[22]

It also became obvious to his advisers that Muldoon found it difficult to admit a mistake or apologise for his behaviour by saying so. But he could indicate his regret, and if he had been particularly rude or unreasonable in imposing his view, officials to whom he owed an apology would often send him their pet project for approval the following day, confident that he would indicate his remorse by approving it.

Muldoon was scrupulously, even parsimoniously, correct in dealing with expenses and the perquisites of office. It was usual, for example, for free sets of new coins to be presented to the Minister of Finance, but Muldoon always rejected the free sets and insisted on buying them personally.[23]

Muldoon's rise in National's ranks during the 1960s had been rapid: a backbench MP for three years, then an under-secretary for three, and finally Minister of Finance from 1967 to 1972. He was probably at his most effective during the almost six years when he was Minister of Finance but not able because of Holyoake's oversight to win all his arguments with colleagues. He developed a reputation for decisive, orthodox economic management which seemed to have carried New Zealand through a major economic crisis brought about mainly by the disastrous fall in wool prices that commenced in December 1966. The fiscal and monetary measures taken in early 1967, the firm restraint on government expenditure in 1967 and 1968, the devaluation of the New Zealand dollar in November 1967 and a partial recovery in wool prices all contributed to a marked improvement in New Zealand's external accounts by 1969. By the end of the June 1968 trade year, external transactions showed a current account credit of $37 million, and Muldoon was able to start cautiously to reflate the economy and counter the drift towards recession and higher unemployment.[24]

As early as February and March 1968 Muldoon was admitting privately that he was concerned that his measures throughout 1967 had resulted in the economy being 'dampened down more than anticipated'.[25] He was also worried about the effect of his policies on the poorer sections of society. He opposed a suggestion in the Ross Committee Report on taxation reform that the Government should move more from direct to indirect taxation by imposing an 8 per cent sales tax to compensate for reductions in the rate of personal income tax, arguing that such a policy would increase both producer and consumer costs and fall most heavily on lower-income earners.

Muldoon's early public comments as Minister of Finance did not reveal a particularly right-wing stance. He argued, for example, that a person 'who is unemployed is not just a statistic' and that some 'theoretical economists fail to realise that economics are people – not just a lot of words and ideas in books . . . We must think in terms of people.'[26] On social security he observed: 'The Welfare State, in my view, has been used as a term of opprobrium more often than it should have been. In its best form it is a good thing and it will be retained, with the idea of putting a floor under people – not a ceiling above which they can't rise – a floor under the population.'[27] He not only defended the welfare state which the National Government had inherited from its predecessors but in some areas extended it.

In 1968, for example, Muldoon established an emergency domestic purposes benefit (DPB) for deserted wives and single women with dependent children, a benefit which Labour extended to all solo parents in 1973. This went beyond Muldoon's original intention. While National was critical of the extension, it did not make it a major issue but in 1976 set up a review committee. By that time, however, the DPB was not only meeting a real need in many cases but had also become much more widespread. Muldoon subsequently felt justified in retaining the benefit despite its increasing cost, partly because he believed that 'If someone needs help they'll get it' and partly because he tried 'never to antagonise a lot of people'. It was 'not good politics to take away from people something they've already got and which they valued'.[28] By the 1980s he saw the DPB as being an alternative unemployment benefit for women, many of whom, he thought, would be only too happy to go off it if they could get a job.

The economic crisis of the late 1960s also forced the Government to try to look more carefully at the future of the New Zealand economy and to bring together the public and the private sectors and representatives of the major interest groups in a National Development Conference. Such conferences on specific aspects such as agriculture, labour, industry, housing and exports had been held previously but the NDC, which met in plenary sessions in August 1968 and May 1969, was a comprehensive attempt to involve all major sector groups in the indicative planning of the economy and to create a consensus on policy direction. Although Marshall became its chairman, and Muldoon was appointed its deputy chairman, the NDC proposal appears to have grown out of a discussion between Muldoon and Lang and partly in response to the Labour Opposition's interest in indicative planning.[29] Holyoake supported the establishment of the NDC probably for publicity and electoral reasons, but it certainly was consistent with his pluralist, consensual style of government. The exercise resulted in the setting of ten-year targets and the establishment of sector councils and working parties to facilitate their achievement. The National Development Conference became a centrepiece of National's 1969 and 1972 election campaigns.

All cabinet papers prepared by departments were accompanied by a Treasury report which could and often did cover matters other than the financial costs or implications of the proposal. When these papers were discussed by the Cabinet Economic Committee, it soon became obvious that Muldoon's mind was usually made up and he looked to others to reinforce his views rather than to provide independent answers. This inevitably brought him into conflict with other ministers.

Muldoon's general approach to politics and government was based on a number of firmly held assumptions. One was that there never would be Utopia. 'The essence of life', he argued, 'is imperfection, the constant struggle for total efficiency.'[30] It is quite revealing that his goal was 'efficiency', not 'happiness' or a 'better world'. Muldoon was not a romantic in either his outlook or his relationships, and his rhetoric – prosaic and concrete, rather than poetic and abstract – revealed that fact about his personality. Although he claimed that he put efficiency ahead of public image, the claim was somewhat disingenuous. He was always striving to portray a calculated public image: the image of super efficiency.

In some ways the image reflected the reality. One journalist, introducing a published interview with Muldoon in 1969, observed:

> Mr Muldoon is soon offering proof that his highly successful television appearances don't give an artificial image of the man. He provides the same lopsided grin, avoidance of rhetoric or resounding platitudes. Those remarkable eyes efficiently peer, absorb and analyse. And there is the familiar flat voice, unflappably precise answers, occasional brusqueness over a dud question, the impression of an unshakeable confidence in his infallibility.[31]

In other ways, however, Muldoon was still the somewhat shy and insecure small boy, defiantly projecting a tough and independent image and using blunt words to conceal and defend himself and doing his best to prove to himself and others that he was someone who had to be taken seriously. He, therefore, welcomed suggestions that he was tough and ruthless, not afraid to take a stand and willing to accept the consequences of becoming unpopular with those with whom he disagreed. Muldoon admitted that he could be negative and abusive, and on occasions he 'enjoyed being offensive'.[32] He justified himself, however, by stating that as Minister of Finance he was 'the "perpetual" Opposition in cabinet', fighting to control his spending colleagues, and on the broader political scene he admitted that he could not expect to be liked. 'When I brought in extra taxes before Christmas I realised I was going to be one of the most unpopular people in the country'.[33]

Muldoon and his rival Shand were similar in that they chose not to make decisions simply behind closed doors but took issues out into the public arena and were willing to debate them openly and persuade public opinion via the media. One perceptive contemporary observer, who identified and analysed this development, was the Wellington academic Jack Shallcrass, a senior lecturer in Education at Victoria University and formerly deputy principal of the Wellington Teachers' College, who noted in early 1969 that

> Shand and Muldoon seem to me to be raising issues in public and inviting reply in a way that is quite unusual. One need not agree with them (and I seldom agree with RDM) to recognise that they are probing sensitive spots and clarifying issues in a way that is unusual in NZ in the modern era. Of course they understate as well as select for political purposes but this often seems incidental to the main issue. We're just not used to politicians trying to define issues and stimulate public debate.[34]

In a more detailed paper, Shallcrass argued that, with the growth of bureaucracy, the choice facing society and particularly politicians was either 'to hand over power to the elites or to revitalise the democratic processes . . . by encouraging and leading the widest possible public debate on all the public issues'.[35] Shallcrass concluded that Muldoon did the latter and was 'resisting the temptation to take more decisions after cabinet rather than after parliamentary discussions and by taking issues to the people especially through the mass media'. Muldoon, Shallcrass noted, was also 'the exception' to the 'pussyfooting and such obvious caution' that usually characterised politicians who appeared on television.

Some experienced journalists concurred with Shallcrass's assessment and admired Muldoon's performance as Minister of Finance in the late Sixties. O. S. Hintz, for example, noted that 'Whereas the Treasury is normally secretive, Muldoon insisted on telling the people what he would do in given circumstances . . . He proved himself to be the most forthright and forthcoming Minister of Finance since Coates.'[36] George Burns recorded: 'I am constantly amazed at his transformation now that he is Minister of Finance. He seems to have curbed his quick temper and has made a tremendous effort to appear to the public as a reasonable, pleasant politician.'[37] Burns, however, was concerned that 'just under the surface lies the old Muldoon . . . I have a distinct fear that if he ever becomes Prime Minister he would tend to become dictatorial'.[38]

At least one of Muldoon's senior colleagues, Norman Shelton, who saw himself as an administrator and someone who possibly talked too little and was content to be judged by his actions, felt, however, that Muldoon talked too much, particularly about other ministers' portfolios, and did not realise that 'the more you talk the more you have to answer.'[39] That was an opinion shared by others in the National Party, some of whom always believed Muldoon was in the wrong party. So did some outside observers. An Australian observer, for example, in 1969 noted that 'Mr Muldoon hardly represents the traditional image of the Nationalist [sic] Party. He is not self-effacing, paternalistic or patrician. He is an unabashed wheeler-dealer.'[40] That journalist might well have been reflecting the views of a group of Wellington businessmen who met regularly with Holyoake during the 1960s and influenced his views, particularly on economic and financial matters. They were not impressed with Muldoon's appointment as Minister of Finance, regarding him as 'a jumped up Auckland accountant' who was closer to Auckland manufacturers that to 'the Wellington National Party establishment of people prominent in the importing, banking and finance community.'[41]

Muldoon's public image and arguably also his private personality changed after he entered Parliament. Publicly he was seen increasingly as an arrogant bully who scathingly put down opponents and fools, or those he saw as opponents and fools. His extended family, however, regarded him, particularly before he entered Parliament, as 'a quiet, home-loving, almost introverted chap but with a natural, jolly sense of humour which was of the "chuckles rather than laugh" variety.'[42] Other people outside the family also saw glimpses of this more congenial Muldoon. At Hatfields Beach, for example, the Muldoons fitted easily into the holiday community each Christmas and New Year. In 1968 Muldoon came second in the men's race at the annual Ratepayers' and Residents' Association Boxing Day sports. He also acted as anchor-man in a tug of war, although it was abandoned after 1968 when the rope broke and Muldoon was buried under a pile of bodies.[43]

When Parliament was in session, Muldoon, even after becoming a minister, continued to be gregarious between 1967 and 1972. He was often found in the evenings drinking whisky or wine and enjoying discussions and impromptu office parties with fellow National MPs and members of the Press Gallery. The Press Gallery was in the view of many MPs a more mature and 'gentlemanly' group of journalists in the 1960s than it later became. Possibly because there were at first no women journalists in the Gallery, the MPs and journalists enjoyed a club atmosphere with unwritten rules of behaviour. Muldoon never turned journalists down and often gave off-the-cuff comments which he assumed reporters such as Peter Scherer, the *New Zealand Herald*'s parliamentary reporter who later became that paper's editor, or Ian Templeton of the *Auckland Star* and *Christchurch Star*, or Keith Eunson of the *Otago Daily Times*, would use responsibly. He and other MPs were later to become more suspicious and guarded as newer and younger members of the Gallery became less interested in merely reporting Parliament and more confrontational in their investigation of politicians and politics. One marked difference between Holyoake and Muldoon in their relationship with the Press Gallery was that whereas Holyoake was quite willing to play poker with journalists until 4 or 5 a.m., Muldoon did not but would stay arguing with them over political issues until 2 a.m.[44]

Although Muldoon socialised with and used the Press Gallery he had few friends among its members. An exception was the good-natured and astute David Inglis. Inglis, who represented the New Zealand Broadcasting Corporation, was almost the stereotype of the investigative reporter; a heavy drinker with a broken marriage, whom Muldoon remembered as the last reporter on the job at night and the first in the morning, a man totally committed to pursuing the news and the story behind it. Inglis was the only journalist to visit Muldoon at home on the day after the 1975 election to ask him for a reflective comment, and Muldoon genuinely grieved when Inglis died at a relatively young age from cancer.

Questioned about his pugnacious reputation by a journalist shortly after he became Minister of Finance, Muldoon replied that, 'It worries me that I should get the reputation for being unnecessarily aggressive, which I am not. I don't set out to have a fight, I just end up in them by not giving way. But when all is said and done, government and politics is all very largely argument . . . The issues are too big to let trivial considerations interfere with them, so in a way, I suppose I'm ruthless.'[45] When asked if power appealed to him, Muldoon observed to the same interviewer that 'the only power one has really is the power to persuade'.

As Minister of Finance between 1967 and 1969, Muldoon at first tried to control himself and present a somewhat softer public image. One opponent observed that

> RDM has changed his political personality, or more accurately his image, in recent years from that of a sharp, sardonic and biting person to one who is essentially calm, reasonable and only occasionally biting . . . I may of course have misjudged him earlier but if so it is an error that is widely shared. I'm convinced that many people still react to that older Muldoon image and hence do not give due attention to the import of the remarks of the present Muldoon.[46]

The apparent change was not to last. Muldoon after a fairly short time reverted to his earlier more aggressive image and reputation. He was seen accurately as energetic, decisive and willing to listen to people with something worthwhile to say. Not only did he not suffer fools gladly, however, he did not suffer them at all and told them so. Nor did he like or easily tolerate people with social pretensions or educational, as distinct from intellectual, arrogance. He understandably disliked wasting time. He had no patience with sycophancy or small talk and was not at ease in social gatherings where he was expected to back-slap, hand-shake, cheerily greet and casually chat with strangers. An exception to this were the poor, powerless, aged or uneducated with whom from time to time he came in contact as an MP. With these people he was invariably courteous, patient and kind.

Politicians and senior civil servants he expected to perform well and so, although very demanding of them, he rarely if ever complimented or thanked them. He reserved his comments for those who fell below his expectation of competence and the less efficient became justifiably scared of Muldoon. He never regarded public servants as friends but simply as professional officials doing their job, and the fact that some of those closest to him, he assumed with some justification, were Labour supporters he regarded as completely irrelevant. They were totally professional and good at their jobs and to Muldoon that was all that mattered. Their private political beliefs and loyalties were their own business. Senior civil servants generally remembered Muldoon, who never addressed them by their Christian names, as formal and courteous in his working relationship with them even if they did not like him or disagreed with his policies, whereas many disliked Holyoake and Kirk personally and resented those prime ministers' negative attitudes towards them and contemptuous treatment of them.

Many journalists and others who observed Muldoon on a day-to-day personal or professional basis saw him as a belligerent man who consciously provoked arguments, enjoyed controversy, and could not confine himself simply to debating views with which he disagreed. He was impelled not only to demolish his opponents' arguments but also to crucify his adversaries publicly.[47] He gave no quarter to opponents or interviewers but equally he expected no deference or mercy from them. He could on occasion reveal a vindictive attitude towards specific editors or journalists. Even his critics had to admit, however, that Muldoon's incomparable skill in the area of self-publicity, his willingness always to be interviewed or to offer a comment, and his cultivated directness made him during the 1960s and 1970s the most successful politician in using the mass media in New Zealand's history.

Shortly after Muldoon became Minister of Finance, a British television drama series, *The Power Game*, became compulsive Sunday night viewing for many New Zealanders. The leading character was a ruthless but seductively impressive businessman Sir John Wilder, played by the actor Patrick Wymark. Not only the Roman Catholic paper the *New Zealand Tablet* but also many other viewers quickly drew a comparison between Muldoon and the fascinating character Wilder.[48]

From time to time Muldoon's self-control slipped somewhat. In December 1968, for example, he was incensed by a relatively minor incident in Parliament. Thea had acquired a stray cat called 'Tibby' and when a newspaper reporter from the *Auckland Star* interviewed her on her views on the family budget and inflation she commented that because of the extra cost of feeding the cat she had asked her husband for an increase in housekeeping.[49] A new Labour backbencher, Trevor Young, suggested in Parliament that Mrs Muldoon thought more of her cat than she did about social security beneficiaries and Muldoon in a rage crossed the floor of the House, flourished his fist under Young's nose and threatened to 'fill in' anyone who brought words attributed to his wife into debates in the House. Muldoon admitted in retrospect that he came very close to punching Young. The incident did nothing to soften his aggressive image. Nor did his frequent battles with other cabinet ministers.

Muldoon found himself at odds in cabinet and caucus particularly with Shand, Marshall, Allen and Kinsella. In his first week in the post of Finance Minister he 'spent one morning with the Minister of Works, Mr Allen, going over item by item the Ministry of Works programme to see what could be cut out. It was hardly surprising that Mr Allen was not his cheerful self for the rest of the week.'[50] One of the major battles that developed between Muldoon and Allen was over the very expensive Waihou Valley Scheme which Muldoon wanted stopped unless it was funded largely by local rates. Allen, supported by the local Hauraki Plains MPs whose constituents wanted the scheme in order to prevent flooding, appealed to Holyoake who finally made a decision that it should go ahead despite Muldoon's objections.[51]

In May 1967 Marshall reported on the breakdown of wage talks with the railway workers' union and recommended to caucus that the union should be forced back to the Railways Tribunal and that an awarded margin for skill should be absorbed into a ruling rates survey, not made additional to it. Muldoon opposed both of Marshall's proposals on the grounds that the Railway Tradesmen's Association was a 'responsible union', that the Tribunal would only confirm its earlier decision, and that 'if Marshall's proposal is carried out there will be a strike and a big one'.[52] Although supported by Gordon, Muldoon found himself in a minority against Marshall, Shand and Holyoake, and Marshall's proposals were adopted. This was a prelude to a much more serious dispute over wages the following year.

Early in 1968 the Federation of Labour applied to the Arbitration Court for a general wage order of 1.7 per cent to compensate for inflation since the previous order. On the deciding vote of the judge the Court decided to make what became known as 'a nil order' and the trade unions erupted. Shand, who as Minister of Labour put a high priority on industrial peace, and Muldoon, who as Minister of Finance wanted economic stability and feared a wage–price escalation, became the major contenders in cabinet and caucus over what should be done. The two men, who had similar personalities, had never been friends but this dispute (in Muldoon's words) turned a 'rift' into a 'chasm'.[53]

In the deteriorating industrial situation Shand advised the employers to stand firm against more militant elements in the Federation of Labour, who were pressing for a 7.6 per cent wage increase, but he conceded to his parliamentary colleagues that some employers, faced with strike action, would probably give way.[54] Shand also was concerned that the Government had to make some immediate concessions so that the FOL's president, Tom Skinner, could offer something to his members and regain the initiative from the militants.

Most other National MPs, led by Marshall and eventually Holyoake, opposed any major concession or compromise as proposed by Shand. Muldoon amidst all the rhetoric simply noted that such a wage increase would 'aggravate' his problems with the economy and complicate the Budget he was scheduled to deliver within the next fortnight. Finally, after four days of discussion and negotiation, with Holyoake playing as prominent a role as Shand, it was decided, despite considerable opposition from within the National Party and from farmers, to amend general wage order regulations and overrule the Arbitration Court's nil wage order. Muldoon stated that 'we have made the right decision' and expressed his hope that the employers would support the Government and that National MPs would support Holyoake.[55]

Caucus agreed that the Employers Federation and the FOL should be asked to return to the Court and seek a review of the nil wage order, the Government anticipating that perhaps about 2 per cent might be awarded. This was acceptable to Muldoon. The Court did reverse its decision, but the union and employers' representatives outvoted the judge and awarded 5 per cent. Muldoon was furious at the inevitable effect on prices and his economic stabilisation policies. He launched a public attack on what he termed an 'unholy alliance' between the employers and the unions and particularly the large Auckland firm UEB Ltd, which had unilaterally given a wage rise of 5 per cent before the order was made, thus breaking the employers' unity and providing a precedent for the unions.

Shand retaliated by stating that Muldoon spoke for himself and that in bringing the employers and unions together he had the 'full support of the government' and had achieved 'a great victory for sanity'.[56] Muldoon subsequently believed and claimed that the wage–price spiral started by the 'unholy alliance' made his task as Minister of Finance in controlling inflation over the following four years very difficult.

The two ministers continued to differ over other matters. In October 1968, for example, Shand wanted the National caucus to support a Tenancy Amendment Bill which would permit owners of property to seek possession or rent increases if they had owned the property for seven years. Muldoon opposed the Bill on political grounds rather than on principle, arguing that it 'will affect everyone in a fair rented tenancy', but found himself in the minority of 9 out of the 38 MPs who voted on the proposal.[57]

Sometimes, however, Muldoon found himself arguing with Shand against his closest colleagues, one heated dispute being with Gordon, the Minister of Transport and Civil Aviation, over the purchase of planes for the National Airways

Corporation. The debate over replacement planes for NAC caused a division between those who wanted to buy cheaper planes from the United States manufacturer Boeing and those who wanted to buy British planes. The latter were concerned with pending trade negotiations with the British and argued that Britain was more important to New Zealand as a market for agricultural exports and as a source of long-term borrowing than the United States. The British case was argued by, among others, Muldoon and Shand, while the American case was advocated by a group led by Marshall and Gordon. A vote in caucus resulted in 22 votes for the Boeing 737 and 16 for the BAC 111 after Holyoake finally supported Gordon. Eight MPs wanted the decision delayed for further consideration. Muldoon also fought Gordon over the proposed extension of Wellington Airport, because he was reluctant to fund it at that time, and over the acquisition of the Union Steam Ship Company by the state, an issue on which Gordon finally got his way with the help of Holyoake's casting vote.[58]

Another minister with whom Muldoon clashed was Kinsella, the Minister of Education. Muldoon was concerned that New Zealanders were becoming used to incrementalism, and that the strong, well-educated, well-organised and articulate education lobby was particularly effective in increasing social expenditure. As Minister of Finance he spoke out about education as well as other policy areas such as industrial relations, not simply because he wanted to interfere in the portfolios of his ministerial colleagues but because he had to deal with the costs of the decisions they made.

In the 1960s and 1970s there was an explosive growth of tertiary education in New Zealand. Universities were built or rebuilt throughout the country. From 1963 Muldoon, first as Under-Secretary for Finance and later as Minister of Finance, sat on the Cabinet Works Committee where Treasury recommendations were often against proposed expenditure. Nevertheless, the committee, which visited every university, agricultural college and technical institute in the country, generally agreed either to upgrade and build new blocks or even in the case of Canterbury and Waikato universities to construct whole new campuses. Within a month of becoming Minister of Finance, however, Muldoon sent a memorandum to the Minister of Education expressing concern about overexpenditure on the university works programme and its continued growth.

Muldoon became concerned at the need for better justification of, and accountability for, the large sums of money being spent at first on bricks and mortar but subsequently on salaries and other continuing operational costs. As was to become his habit, he took the debate outside cabinet, caucus and the bureaucracy and used public speeches and the media to inform and influence public opinion. He started to question the justification for the expansion of tertiary education and query elements of the curriculum and what if anything went to make room for new subjects. Inevitably, as Minister of Finance he became a major protagonist in the public debates on education, constantly asking not only what needed to be done, and where, and how it was going to be funded, but also why it should be.

Muldoon started to suggest that resources should be reallocated rather than simply increased, not only in tertiary but also in primary and secondary education expenditure, because total expenditure on state education had risen from 10.1 per cent to 12.7 per cent of total government expenditure between 1957 and 1967.[59]

He objected to the rebuilding of half-empty schools in declining population areas while the burgeoning population of pupils in South Auckland were housed in prefabricated and overcrowded classrooms. This brought him into conflict with South Island and rural MPs. He also argued that many schools had been overbuilt for a temporary peak, as in his own electorate, where Tamaki Boys and Girls and Glendowie Colleges had become half-empty.

Muldoon did not say what his major critics said he had about education but his opponents read between the lines and attacked him for what he seemed to imply rather than what he actually said. Inevitably he came into conflict with various educational interest groups. A long-time friend, who was for a time president of the New Zealand Post Primary Teachers' Association, recalled that Muldoon

> made no secret to me of his antipathy to 'pressure groups' such as the NZPPTA and was angered by the fact that some of his criticisms of educational expenditure . . . were incorrectly taken to mean that he favoured a reduction in the education vote. He was at pains to tell me how it was not the size of the vote but the wastefulness of the expenditure that he was aiming to change. I found it impossible to convince my colleagues that he was at all sympathetic towards education.[60]

Tertiary education was a major topic of public and political debate when Muldoon entered Parliament and became much more so during the 1960s. The debate included a number of issues, most of which were covered in various reports and papers. Those reports questioned the preparation and success–failure rates of university students and the nature and utility of the courses they studied. In 1967, Kinsella, the Minister of Education, also presented to Parliament a statement on 'School and University Enrolment Projections for the Years 1967–80', which revealed, inter alia, that the number of secondary school leavers would rise from 37,500 in 1961 to 50,000 in 1970 to possibly 66,000 in 1979. The ratio of those leavers with University Entrance would over the same period go from 1:6 to 1:4.[61] Muldoon, who read these reports, received further information from Treasury, including projections which showed that total annual expenditure on universities – which had already risen 509 per cent between 1957 and 1967 – would be rising again from $32.4 million in 1967–68 to $60.5 million in 1976–77.[62] Subsequently, Treasury notified Muldoon that total university expenditure for 1978–79 was projected to be $78 million.[63] Prior to preparing his 1967 Budget Muldoon visited every university to discuss the topic with each vice-chancellor.

In his 1967 Budget Muldoon indicated that, because the university student enrolments had doubled to 24,000 over the previous nine years, expenditure on universities was increasing much more rapidly than that on any other area of education. He suggested that there was a need to reappraise this development, not only because of the budgetary implications, but also because the Education Training and Research Committee of the National Development Conference, of which Muldoon was deputy chairman, should be addressing New Zealand's future educational needs in its indicative planning. Critics immediately suggested that Muldoon's agenda was the reduction of university expenditure and the restriction of non-vocational education and pure research.

Muldoon justified his interest in education on the grounds that it was the fastest-growing item of expenditure in the Budget during the 1960s, growing at twice the rate of GNP, and that the economic crisis of 1967 necessitated his review of spending priorities. He was determined to get value for money and accountability by using a cost–benefit analysis approach. His suggestion that perhaps there should be a slow-down in the growth of arts, humanities and physical sciences, which did not directly relate to New Zealand's agriculture and industry, particularly enraged many academics, who saw his comments as an attack on both non-vocational tertiary education and university autonomy, especially in curriculum matters. He argued, for example, that some university students would be better employed studying applied education of vocational value to themselves and economic value to the country at technical institutes, rather than wasting their time on a 'fun subject' such as political science which was of little use to New Zealand.[64] He also suggested that the universities were turning out surplus numbers of unemployable graduates in law, architecture, the arts, and physical sciences rather than in biological sciences of greater value to the national economy.[65] These views became known by the term 'Muldoonism', which was applied not only to education but also to Muldoon's general utilitarian and interventionist approach.

By early 1968 the various universities, the University Grants Committee, and Treasury were also commencing work on the 1971–75 quinquennial grants for university expenditure, which was to be determined by 1970. Muldoon embarked on a campaign to keep those grants as low as possible. Throughout 1968 Muldoon made a series of provocative but very well researched, persuasively argued, and statistically illustrated public speeches on education: for example, to the Massey University branch of the Association of University Teachers on 13 February; to the National Club at Victoria University on 23 April; to Canterbury University students on 18 June; and to the Wellington Headmasters' Association on 8 August. His views were brought together in an address to the annual university students' conference at Curious Cove on 29 January 1969.[66]

In these speeches Muldoon raised a number of specific issues and questions. Could the current policy of open entry to universities be continued? To what extent could the Government accede to future requests for university funding? Could some rising additional costs be reasonably restricted? Were entry standards sufficiently high and would unsuccessful students, some 33 per cent of first-year full-time enrolments, have done better at technical institutions? Should there be an expansion of technical institutes rather than academic universities? Should biological sciences of value to the New Zealand economy and more vocationally oriented subjects be emphasised rather than the humanities, social sciences and physical sciences at both secondary and tertiary levels? Were too many of New Zealand's best young students taking subjects that forced them eventually to migrate overseas in search of opportunities lacking in New Zealand, thus creating a 'brain drain'?

Muldoon's address to the students at Curious Cove was a very substantial paper of twenty-three closely typed pages with his arguments well developed and substantiated with statistics. It was described in a lengthy and not totally hostile editorial in the Auckland University student newspaper *Craccum* as 'a reply to many criticisms that his first challenges brought forth, as well as an elaboration and clarification of his own position'.[67]

After showing the tremendous growth in spending on universities, Muldoon addressed the nature of tertiary education suggesting that, while a minority of students pursued pure knowledge, the majority were seeking training for a career as a doctor, lawyer, or engineer. Universities benefited individuals and also the collective economy and society. If financial and intellectual resources were limited, then it was essential that priorities be established. He went on to summarise the points he had made in speeches on the subject throughout 1968 and countered some of the criticism they had generated.

He addressed the financial as well as the personal cost of failure, calculating that the cost of students failing papers in their first year at university was at least $10 million. He suggested that tightening entry standards might mean the loss of some graduates but would make the expenditure on the universities more cost-efficient generally. He cited in support of his view a former chairman of the Grants Committee, Dr F. J. Llewellyn, at the time vice-chancellor of Exeter University. Llewellyn noted that Britain got as many graduates as New Zealand from only half the number of students and that 'the British student is selected in expectation of success' while 'for a New Zealand student, failure is part of his expectation'.[68]

Muldoon then dealt with the controversy over his 'brain drain' suggestion and his comments on technical institutes and applied studies of value to the New Zealand economy before concluding with the suggestion that research funds should be channelled into subject areas of immediate relevance to New Zealand.

One of Muldoon's critics, Jack Shallcrass, also spoke at Curious Cove. He rejected the allegation that Muldoon was a 'hostile hatchet man' and suggested that he was instead a 'potential Prime Minister' who was doing his job as Minister of Finance by asking how New Zealand could most efficiently spend its money. Where he was wrong, Shallcrass argued, was in simply using an economic measurement for judging educational expenditure.[69] Other critics were less complimentary or reasonable.

Following publication of his comments at Curious Cove, Muldoon found himself in an ongoing and heated debate with numerous academic defenders of the universities. One was Professor N. C. Phillips, vice-chancellor of the University of Canterbury. Muldoon and Phillips each produced three public statements in the course of a week. Phillips commenced by accepting that it was 'perfectly proper' for the Minister of Finance to be concerned about the rising costs of university education but stated that economic considerations had to be balanced by 'social philosophy'. If New Zealanders wished to maintain open entry to universities then there should be no attempt to thwart that policy by the arbitrary raising of entry standards or inadequate funding. If open entry was to be abandoned because it was not sufficiently high on the Government's list of priorities for limited expenditure, then that decision should be made openly and only after informed debate.[70]

Muldoon responded by accusing Phillips of having made a personal attack on him and having ignored the fact that he was simply asking for an informed public debate about the nature and future of tertiary education. Phillips, he argued, was ignoring also the fact of failure in the university system and was misrepresenting Muldoon's position on open entry and what was taught in universities. Open entry was 'the one keystone of policy that has been agreed between the universities and successive governments', and Muldoon noted that 'I have repeated many times that it is my view that universities and not the government should determine university policy'.[71] Phillips replied accurately and succinctly that 'if the government will not finance adequately a policy adopted by [the universities], the universities' freedom of choice is illusory'.[72]

After nearly two years of public agitation by Muldoon on the subject of university expenditure he suffered, shortly before the 1969 election, a major defeat in cabinet and caucus over the universities' quinquennial block grants. The University Grants Committee predicted a growth in student enrolments from 29,000 to 41,000 over the following five years. The UGC recommended that the total grant to universities of $19 million in 1969 should increase to $20.8 million in 1970; $24 million in 1971; $27 million in 1972; $31 million in 1973; and $34 million in 1974.[73] Kinsella, supported by Talboys and Munro, was in favour of the recommendation but Muldoon, backed by Gordon, a champion of technical education at the tertiary level, was opposed. Treasury countered with an alternative recommendation that the quinquennium should be shortened to a triennium and the dollar amounts cut considerably but subject to later reconsideration. Again Muldoon argued not from principle but from pragmatic politics, claiming 'the majority [of voters] are not concerned with universities, they are concerned with taxes. If we put the money in here, we do not have it to put into productive development.'[74] At the end of the debate, Holyoake declared that he and the Government 'would go with the Grants Committee. Their recommendations are at today's costs and will be higher.' That had to be accepted because he was 'not enthusiastic about restrictive entry to universities', which would be the logical outcome of inadequate funding.[75]

Muldoon rarely won a battle in cabinet or caucus during his first three years as Minister of Finance if Holyoake was opposed to his position, as on a number of major issues Holyoake indeed was. Sometimes it was difficult to predict which side of an argument the Prime Minister was on, because he tended not to show his own preference until a matter had been debated by others. Indeed, some of his colleagues uncharitably believed that on many matters about which he was not deeply concerned he simply put himself at the head of the majority when he summed up the cabinet or caucus consensus.

As Prime Minister and as a chairman, Holyoake was a master of the technique of obtaining a consensus, usually the result he personally favoured. His method was the opposite of the 'divide and rule' strategy. If there was a serious division in cabinet or caucus, he would suggest (as Duncan MacIntyre later recalled) that the minister concerned should 'go away, set up a committee, thrash out the problem, and come back when he got it sorted out and had something supported by the committee. There was no question of things going to the press and being argued out in public.'[76] Muldoon and Shand must have tried Holyoake's patience, because both tended to debate issues in the public arena as well as cabinet and caucus.

Even as Minister of Finance, Muldoon during the 1966–69 period did not have a free hand except when Budget timetables had to be met and Holyoake and cabinet had to trust Muldoon's judgement. On all other major economic decisions Holyoake expected to be consulted, let other ministers vigorously challenge Muldoon's opinions and advice, and from time to time overruled his Finance Minister in major policy disputes with Marshall, Shand, Allen, Gordon and Kinsella.

During the first six months of 1967, particularly, Muldoon and Holyoake worked very closely together meeting almost daily to discuss measures to counter the serious balance of payments crisis. Thereafter, as Holyoake's confidence in Muldoon grew, Muldoon gradually asserted his independence and control over economic management.[77] Muldoon, however, never made the mistake of over-estimating his own strength or underestimating Holyoake's ultimate role as the 'boss'. Holyoake's goodwill was essential to Muldoon, who was not popular with most of his senior cabinet colleagues. Whereas Holyoake handled people in a subtle way in order to get his views accepted while not alienating opponents, Muldoon was insensitive to the feelings of others and was more abrupt in telling them what to do. In public Muldoon deferred, sometimes somewhat sycophantic-ally, to Holyoake. He told an interviewer in 1968, for example, that Holyoake might not 'come across' in public or on television but was 'a most considerate fellow, utterly patient. A tremendous man on detail, and such detail as matters concerning the ideas and feelings of other people.'[78] Again, at the 1969 National Party Conference, Muldoon told delegates that 'the image of the Prime Minister has never been better . . . Nobody in the National Party stands within head and shoulders of Mr Holyoake at the moment'.[79] This led the poet Allen Curnow, writing in the *Herald* as 'Whim Wham', to jibe,

> There's Nobody in the Party
> Who stands as high as He,
> Head and Shoulders above them All –
> Even Me!

From 1967 on Holyoake often met informally late on Monday nights with Muldoon and three other ministers. Muldoon, Gordon, MacIntyre and McKay developed a habit of discussing over a bottle of whisky matters which had come up at cabinet earlier in the day. One night, in the midst of a passionate debate, Holyoake entered the room and said 'for goodness sake, shut up! You can be heard all over the building.'[80] Finding out what was going on, the Prime Minister got into the habit of joining the group for a drink and a chat thereafter.

Holyoake undoubtedly enjoyed the public praise and pledges of loyalty from Muldoon compared to the barely restrained impatience of his deputy Marshall, who believed Holyoake should stand aside in Marshall's favour, but the Prime Minister also realised that Muldoon's support was not altruistic. Muldoon needed more time to establish himself if he was to have a chance of contesting Marshall's succession to the leadership. That meant that Holyoake, not Marshall, had to lead National into the 1969 election, a situation both Holyoake and Muldoon wanted for their own personal reasons.

National entered the 1969 election campaign worried that inflation, unemployment, the fact that they had been in power for nine years, questions about Holyoake's possible retirement, and a much more confident Labour leader in Kirk would make winning a fourth term very difficult. Their fears were heightened by Holyoake's poor performances on television.

By 1969 many farmers, especially dairy farmers, faced with escalating costs and no corresponding increase in prices for their products, were becoming very critical of the Government's failure to hold wages and remove import controls. Muldoon warned his colleagues of the political aspect and the need to take action to counter Labour and Social Credit appeals to the farmers but rejected calls from worried caucus colleagues to augment farmers' incomes through budgetary measures.[81] He was reluctant, for example, to increase fertiliser freight subsidies, and even when it was finally decided to raise them he fought unsuccessfully to cut the amount proposed by Talboys.[82] He also opposed a milk subsidy to dairy farmers on the grounds that 'basically we are a low tax party', and he attacked assistance to the wool industry because National 'must not be seen publicly to be a farmers party'. Subsidies to the Wool Board would open the door to all the other farm groups.

Early in the campaign public attention seemed to be centred on the leaders Holyoake and Kirk, to the former's clear disadvantage. Kirk, for example, assisted by a rowdy and hostile anti-National audience demolished Holyoake in a nationally televised question-and-answer session at Victoria University, Wellington. Holyoake also lost control during his opening address of the campaign in Christchurch, though he consoled himself that votes would be gained for National from the reaction to the spectacle of an unruly rabble trying to prevent the Prime Minister talking to the people. National, nevertheless, decided to downplay the contrast between Holyoake and Kirk and allowed Muldoon to play a more prominent public role.

Muldoon was determined that Labour would not win the election by default and astutely diverted attention away from the leadership issue. He arranged for Treasury to calculate how much Labour's election promises would cost and enticed Kirk into retaliating. However, Kirk rejected Muldoon's invitation to debate on television, partly because he wanted to be compared publicly with Holyoake, not Muldoon, and partly because Labour's own secret estimate of its election promises was even greater than Muldoon's. Before long, most Labour MPs were concentrating their fire not on the Prime Minister but on the Minister of Finance and on Muldoon's handling of the economy and belligerent personality. That enabled Muldoon to point out clearly that Kirk was prepared to attack him at every opportunity but would not debate with him face to face. Kirk continued to state that he was only prepared to meet National's leader, Holyoake.

Other Labour MPs were less reluctant than Kirk to face up to Muldoon on television or radio, but invariably the results were disastrous for Labour. On 21 November, a week before polling day, for example, there was a televised debate on the current affairs programme *Gallery*. Muldoon and Labour's Dr Martyn Finlay ended a confrontation, which had been dominated by Muldoon, shouting at each other. The cameras remained on Muldoon who kept talking while Finlay was screaming, sometimes inaudibly, off-camera and the chairman, Dr Brian Edwards, was trying vainly to gain control of the situation.[83] While it was not an edifying spectacle, it was gripping television and highlighted Muldoon's fearsome and arrogant strength in debate.

Muldoon also traversed the country with a punishing schedule of public meetings over the three weeks of the campaign proper, at Auckland, Christchurch, Wanganui, Feilding, Wellington, Invercargill, Rotorua, Tokoroa, Auckland's North Shore, Napier, Gisborne and Kaitaia. Significantly, many of those meetings were in electorates held by backbench MPs who were later to be his key supporters in the 1972 and 1974 contests for the leadership of the National Party.

On the eve of the election the *Australian Financial Review* was observing that

> The Prime Minister, Mr Keith Holyoake, has taken a back seat. His deputy, Mr J. R. Marshall, is hardly in evidence. Instead the whole of the running by the incumbent Nationalist [sic] Party is being made by Mr Rob Muldoon, the Finance Minister and No. 8 in the Holyoake Cabinet . . . Should the National Party win . . . Mr Muldoon will be seen as the political general. He will become the de facto heir to Mr Holyoake.[84]

Holyoake desperately wanted to win the 1969 election, not least because he would be the first Prime Minister of New Zealand since Seddon to win clearly four elections in a row.[85] But he had serious doubts that he would win and many others – National and Labour politicians, and journalists and academic commentators – also believed that Labour would become the Government.

During the last fortnight and possibly the last week, however, Labour's potential victory slipped away. National's superior grassroots organisation helped it to hang on narrowly to a number of key marginals, and Labour's image was not enhanced by a highly publicised and unpopular seamen's strike during the campaign. Many commentators credited Muldoon's effective appearances on television as being the deciding factor, and certainly the polls revealed that voters saw him as New Zealand's most effective politician ahead of Holyoake, Marshall and Kirk.

Holyoake was relieved and delighted by the result, which gave National 45 per cent of the vote to Labour's 44 per cent and Social Credit's 9. National took 45 seats to Labour's 39, a majority of 6 compared to National's 8-seat majority over the 35 Labour MPs and 1 Social Crediter elected three years before. Muldoon retained Tamaki, more than doubling his majority to 6088 and increasing his percentage of the vote from 55.4 per cent in 1966 to 65.1 per cent in 1969.

At his first cabinet meeting following the election Holyoake told his colleagues, 'We've won, fellows, and we can thank one fellow – Muldoon'.[86] From that time on Holyoake clearly regarded his Finance Minister as a potential successor to the party's leadership and an alternative to his long-time deputy, Marshall.

CHAPTER 9

The End of the Holyoake Era
1969–72

THE CABINET WHICH HOLYOAKE SELECTED AFTER THE 1969 election was without two of the dominant ministers of the 1960s. Hanan had died suddenly in July 1969 and Shand died in early December. Holyoake unreasonably loaded his deputy Marshall with much of their work. Marshall kept Overseas Trade, though relinquishing Industries and Commerce, and picked up Labour and Immigration from Shand and the Attorney-Generalship from Hanan. Muldoon continued as Minister of Finance and chairman of the Cabinet Economic Committee.

Holyoake was in a difficult position in finding a suitable replacement for Shand as Minister of Labour, but Marshall was understandably far from impressed when he was appointed to the portfolio.[1] Indeed, he argued that he was fully committed as Minister of Overseas Trade, Attorney-General, Deputy Prime Minister and chairman of half a dozen cabinet committees and would be frequently overseas involved in EEC negotiations. Holyoake rejected Marshall's suggestion that Gordon, MacIntyre or Thomson should be appointed instead, and very reluctantly Marshall added to his already onerous load of portfolios what he saw as 'the most demanding, frustrating and thankless job in cabinet.'[2] There seems to be little doubt that Holyoake deliberately overloaded Marshall not only to keep him too busy to lobby for the leadership but also in the hope that Marshall would damage his reputation in the difficult Labour portfolio. Certainly, over the following two years Marshall's handling of industrial disputes in a non-confrontational manner led to considerable criticism within anti-union National Party ranks and brought him into frequent conflict with Muldoon.

The Young Turks retained a strong personal empathy as ministers even though the interests of their particular portfolios sometimes clashed. They could still get a chuckle out of each other through seeing, or sometimes creating, a humorous situation or making a ridiculous statement and Gordon and MacIntyre were quite prepared to 'tell Muldoon he was a mutt on occasions if we thought he was wrong'.[3] It was inevitable, however, that because of their different ministerial responsibilities and heavy workloads the three men saw less of each other and found themselves more often than before on different sides in debates within cabinet and caucus over policy and funding.

After appointing a Speaker, National had a safe working majority of five in the House, but Muldoon was not alone in believing that from the first and throughout the entire period 1969–72 the Labour Opposition under Kirk 'had the ascendancy in the House'.[4] The end of 1970 with Holyoake and Dan Riddiford in hospital and Marshall overseas and with Labour refusing pairs was a particularly trying time for the Government.

Inflation, which had been an evident problem before the 1969 election, became even more of one after it, fuelled by the increasingly high prices of imports and by wage and salary agreements reflecting double-digit annual rises in the cost of living. Muldoon and his colleagues were forced to introduce wage and other restraints in 1970 and 1971. They also increased taxes on petrol and cigarettes, raised Post Office charges and in October 1970 levied a 10 per cent surtax on incomes. In November 1970 a price freeze was announced, which lasted until replaced the following February by a complex price-justification system. A Stabilisation of Remuneration Act in February 1971 established a Remuneration Authority to hold, if possible, annual wage increases to a 7 per cent maximum. These were difficult and destabilising years for the National Government and its electoral support.

This extent of intervention and control by a government pledged to limit state intervention in the economy and dismantle controls over it was undertaken very reluctantly, as were the increased direct and indirect taxes levied by a government committed to lowering taxation. The new payroll tax introduced in Muldoon's 1970 budget was particularly controversial and unpopular with National's core support among businessmen. Muldoon's attempts to explain and justify it failed to convince the critics.[5] The measure undoubtedly cost National support and finance from the business community in the run-up to the 1972 election. Muldoon publicly admitted in hindsight that 'my greatest mistake as Minister of Finance during that period was the introduction of the payroll tax'.[6]

Muldoon and his colleagues blamed the 14 per cent wage increases in 1970 more on militant unions and weak employers than on justifiable cost of living catch-ups. Indeed, they argued that the wage increases were themselves a major factor in causing inflation, fuelling a wage–price spiral as employers gave in to the militant unions. Relativity adjustments were required throughout the wage-force, and the extra costs were then passed on to the consumer, thus instigating further wage claims. Muldoon wanted to stop the wage–price spiral but was annoyed by Marshall's apparent inability to control the militant unions; by employers who, Muldoon believed, gave in too easily to wage demands and then passed on the cost to the consumer; and by the Federation of Labour, which would not exercise wage restraint without effective controls on prices, rents and interest rates. Increasingly, Muldoon started to argue that his task as Minister of Finance was being made impossible by lack of wage restraint and by the militancy of unions, which caused more strikes and the loss of more workdays in 1970 than in any year over the previous fifty years except 1951. His comments were eventually to bring him into conflict not only with trade union leaders but with Marshall, as Minister of Labour.

The Minister of Finance was also annoyed when, following his 1970 Budget, a Trustee Savings Bank Bill to raise the level of deposits on which interest could be paid was successfully amended by the Labour Opposition after two National MPs, Seath and Munro, slept through a division in the House.[7] This was the first time a Government had been defeated in the House in forty years. Shortly afterwards, however, Muldoon himself slept through two divisions during the committee stages of the Local Authority Petroleum Tax Bill, and the Government only won by the casting vote of the Chairman of Committees. Admittedly, this was at 6.15 a.m. after an exhausting all-night sitting, and Muldoon excused himself on the grounds that he was taking anti-histamine tablets for a persistent sinus condition,[8] but it still made him a target for embarrassing Opposition and media comment.

The measures taken against inflation during 1970 did not work and prices rose in 1971 by 9 per cent compared to the 10 per cent of a year before. Unemployment reappeared and consumer spending subsided. Muldoon subsequently admitted that 'by the end of 1971 it was clear that while the measures we had taken were slowing down the wage–price spiral it was not happening quickly enough.'[9]

Difficulties in the farming sector of New Zealand's economy also led to Muldoon's having to budget in the 1969–72 period for fertiliser subsidies, assistance to dairy farmers switching to beef, funds for drought relief, an expensive cost adjustment scheme for farmers, grants to the Wool Board, and a stock retention scheme (labelled by Kirk 'a family benefit for sheep'). Many of those measures were pressed on a somewhat reluctant Muldoon by farmer MPs in the National caucus.

As Minister of Finance, Muldoon also agreed to Inland Revenue pursuing the Europa Oil Company and other Todd family group companies for non-payment of taxes and the diversion of overseas currency reserves by use of a system of paper companies, notably through a Todd subsidiary called the Pan Eastern Company set up in the Bahamas. Muldoon was totally unmoved by the fact that the Todd family had been generous supporters of the National Party from the time of its formation.[10] Although the Supreme Court had found in favour of Inland Revenue, that decision was reversed by a unanimous decision of the Appeal Court. Early in 1970 Muldoon approved an appeal to the Privy Council which by a majority of 3 to 2 found that Europa was liable for tax plus penalty payments totalling in excess of $5,400,000 for the period 1960–70. Muldoon had also moved earlier in 1968 to strengthen New Zealand's tax laws to catch the income of overseas subsidiaries when it was considered there had been a diversion to an overseas subsidiary.[11]

In May 1971 Muldoon opened an Auckland factory bottling Gilbey's Gin and agreed that the firm could use a photo of him being presented with a bottle of gin and a tray and glasses. An advertisement subsequently appeared in the *Auckland Star* and resulted in a petition to Parliament originating among Labour supporters in the English and History Departments at the University of Auckland requesting Parliament to censure Muldoon both for allowing his image to be used in the 'promotion of a commercial product' and for his 'promotion of the liquor trade'. A Labour MP also suggested that Muldoon had possibly breached a section of the Police Offences Act prohibiting ministerial patronage of businesses, and Muldoon was criticised for lowering the 'prestige and dignity of the House'.[12] Muldoon defended himself before the Petitions Committee, showing that a number of former New Zealand prime ministers – notably Seddon, Massey and Coates – had been used in advertising whisky, beer or gin. The Labour minority on the committee supported the petition which, however, was rejected by the National majority.

On Tuesday 27 July 1971, on the current affairs programme *Gallery*, David Exel interviewed Rudd Hughes, the President of the Auckland Seamen's Union over a dispute concerning the ship *Kawerau*. During the course of the interview Hughes admitted that he was a 'militant' and a 'communist', whose ultimate aim was 'violent revolution' involving the use of guns against 'a small class of bludging leeches at the top of the social scale'.[13]

During a follow-up *Gallery* programme two nights later involving Muldoon and another communist trade unionist, Bill Andersen, Muldoon commented that the communists exercised influence not only in the trade unions but also to a limited extent in New Zealand's universities, schools and government departments.[14] This led to a public statement by I. G. Lythgoe, chairman of the State Services Commission, that none of the communists employed in the Public Service held 'as far as we are aware . . . positions where they have any influence on policy.'[15]

Although 131 of 147 letters Muldoon received after the programme agreed with his stand, many of Muldoon's critics believed that he was launching an anti-communist and anti-union campaign to distract people's attention from the economy.[16] Not for the first or last time, comparisons were made between Muldoon and Joseph McCarthy, who represented Wisconsin in the United States Senate from 1946 to 1954 and whose intolerance of liberalism and witch-hunt against alleged communists led eventually to his censure by the Senate for bringing it into dishonour and disrepute.

In the television debate, Andersen, in rejecting Muldoon's concerns, asserted that there were 'no more than six' communists active as full-time officials in the New Zealand trade union movement.[17] Following the programme Muldoon obtained from the Security Intelligence Service a considerably larger list of communist trade union officials.[18]

In August 1971 Muldoon almost found himself in a libel case when W. 'Pincher' Martin, the president of the Seamen's Union, threatened legal action because Muldoon had referred to him on television as a communist. Muldoon accepted that Martin had never been a communist and that he had confused Martin with Rudd Hughes.

Muldoon's tendency to upset senior colleagues was again demonstrated in 1971 when he clashed with Marshall over the appointment of a Chief Industrial Mediator. Brian Brooks, a lecturer in law at the University of Auckland who had taken leave to become industrial relations manager for Alex Harvey Industries, was proposed unanimously for the post by a committee set up by Marshall to make the

To the Householder

Postage Paid

R. D. MULDOON
NATIONAL CANDIDATE
for
MT. ALBERT

for the
RIGHT APPROACH

MULDOON'S THE MAN FOR WAITEMATA

TO THE HOUSEHOLDER

POSTAGE PAID

Above: Muldoon stood twice unsuccessfully in Mt Albert in 1954 and Waitemata in 1957 before winning Tamaki in 1960.

Left: Muldoon in 1960 won the Tamaki seat from Bob Tizard and from that time on, especially after Tizard returned to Parliament in 1963 and later became a Labour Minister of Finance, there was a sharp rivalry between two of Parliament's most intelligent members.
NZ HERALD.

Above: Muldoon and Bert Walker about to give their maiden speeches in the 1961 Address in Reply debate. AUCKLAND STAR/NEWS MEDIA.

Left: The three 'Young Turks' in the National caucus after 1960 were Muldoon, Duncan MacIntyre (top) and J.B. (Peter) Gordon (bottom). NATIONAL PARTY PAPERS.

Above: Ralph Hanan was one senior minister whom Muldoon, as a new MP, admired. REDFERN PHOTOGRAPHICS.

Left: Tom Shand, a minister with whom Muldoon was frequently to cross swords. *NZ HERALD.*

Below: Muldoon, informally dressed at a social function, possibly the Orewa Rotary, in the late 1960s. The man with glasses behind Muldoon, also dressed informally, is Ed Buxton, the private secretary to the Minister of Finance. MULDOON PAPERS.

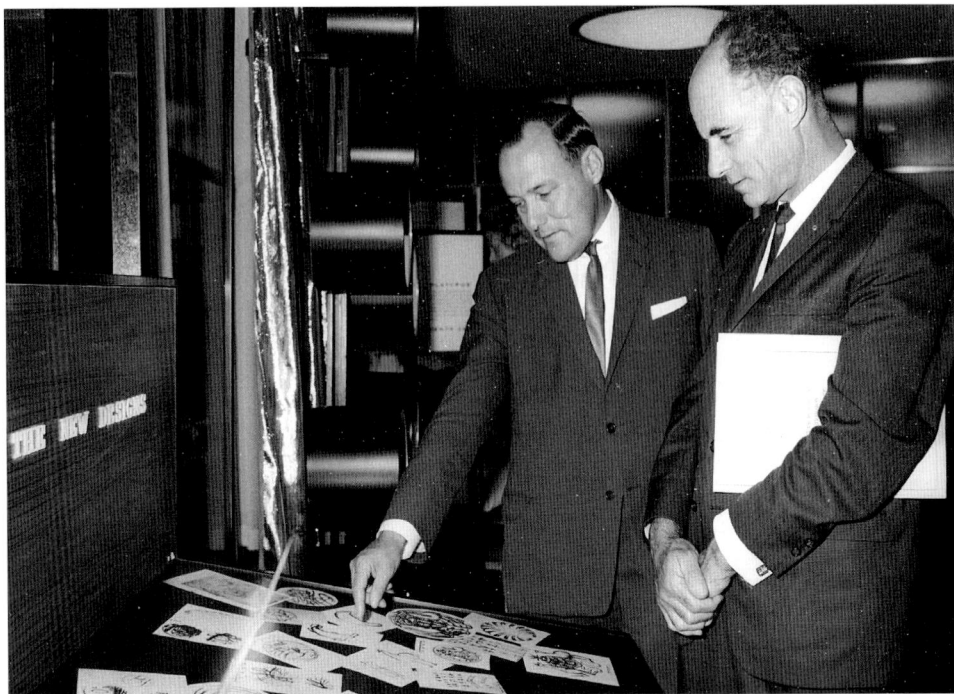

Above: Muldoon and Syd Moses, chairman of the Decimal Currency Board, examine designs of the new decimal coins. QANTAS PHOTOGRAPH/ MULDOON PAPERS.

Right: Presenting a set of decimal coins to the Queen. From left: Muldoon, David Thomson, Holyoake, Norman Shelton, Percy Allen, Gordon, MacIntyre, Marshall. MULDOON PAPERS.

Above: Muldoon (far left) debating tertiary education with students at the University Students' Congress, Curious Cove, Marlborough Sounds, January 1966. MULDOON PAPERS.

Left: Muldoon in a tug-of-war at the Hatfields Beach annual sports day. *AUCKLAND STAR*/NEWS MEDIA.

MR MULDOON WILL NOW BE MAKING MORE RADIO AND TELEVISION APPEARANCES ON BEHALF OF THE NATIONAL PARTY THAN HAD BEEN PLANNED ooo

THE BEST HEAD FOR IT ?

Left: Muldoon was the National Party's key to winning the 1969 election rather than the leader, Holyoake, or the deputy-leader, Marshall, as the cartoonist Ronken recognised. RONKEN/*WAIKATO TIMES.*

Right: Although Marshall replaced Holyoake as National's leader in February 1972, the calculating look on his new deputy's face boded ill for their future together. *NZ LISTENER*/NZ MAGAZINES.

Below: The cartoonist Lodge also suggested Muldoon might not be satisfied with being only deputy leader. NEVILLE LODGE/*EVENING POST.*

LODGE LAUGHS

"FEELS LIKE A GOOD FIT"

"FEELS A BIT ON THE SMALL SIDE"

PM

DEPUTY

RESIGNA

Left: Muldoon was ill with hepatitis during the latter part of the 1972 election campaign and here is seen with Thea reading telegrams and letters of condolence. *NZ HERALD.*

Below: Muldoon did not appear very happy at the opening of Matai Industries on the West Coast in 1973 with Kirk (left) and Kevin Meates (right). MARGARET HAYWARD.

Left: Labour MPs with whom Muldoon frequently found himself in dispute included, from left, Kirk, Joe Walding, Bob Tizard, Warren Freer and Dr Martyn Finlay. *EVENING POST.*

Below: Muldoon's replacement of Marshall as National's leader damaged his credibility when he subsequently warned the National Party Conference against encouraging challenges to sitting National MPs prior to the 1975 election. BROMHEAD/*AUCKLAND STAR.*

BY AND LARGE, THE TRADITION OF THIS PARTY IS NOT TO TACKLE SITTING MEMBERS...

BROMHEAD

Below: Coincidentally, Muldoon's first autobiography, *The Rise and Fall of a Young Turk*, was published shortly after he became leader and quickly sold an amazing 32,536 copies. His son-in-law, Kevin Williams, did the cover portrait and designed the cover. LIZ BROOK/SOPACNEWS.

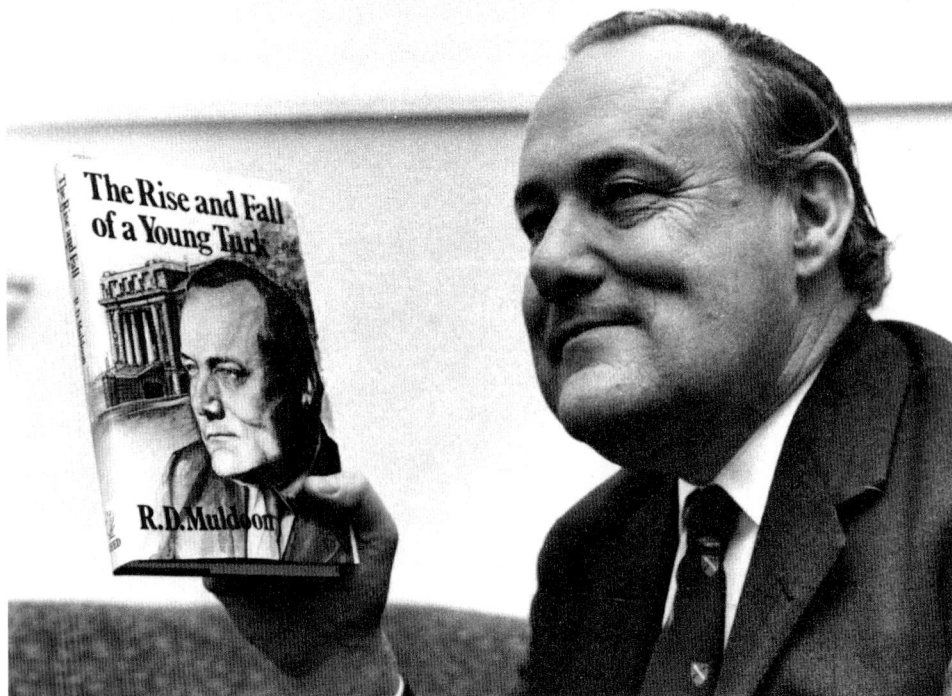

recommendation. Marshall and the Associate Minister of Labour, Thomson, also supported Brooks's appointment, but Muldoon led cabinet and caucus opposition to it. Caucus deferred the appointment while Marshall was overseas, but on his return he announced he intended to appoint Brooks despite the opposition within government ranks. Muldoon then expressed his attitude to the appointment publicly. Brooks withdrew his application and subsequently became secretary of the Auckland Clerical Workers Union.

On the TV programme *Gallery* and in comments to the *Sunday News* and *Auckland Star*, Muldoon attacked Brooks, a Labour Party activist and founder of a breakaway National Union of Teachers, as a 'way-out militant' and 'a way-out left-winger'.[19] Brooks sued Muldoon for defamation. A jury found that the comments made by Muldoon were defamatory, untrue, 'actuated by malice' and prejudicial to Brooks's selection.[20] Brooks was awarded $5000 damages, one-fifth of what he had claimed. Although the Government in keeping with precedent offered to pay the damages because Muldoon had been speaking as a Minister of the Crown, Muldoon in the face of Labour criticism announced that he would pay the damages and an equal amount in costs personally but would continue to speak out on matters of public interest and in future would no longer, as in the past, ignore defamatory statements made about himself. In the event Muldoon was not out of pocket because unsolicited donations from supporters more than covered the $10,000 involved. He declared shortly afterwards that, although he did not believe the libel laws should be amended, he did feel that controversial public figures such as himself should be tried by judges rather than by jurors who could be politically biased.

The Brooks incident did nothing to better the, at best, cool relations between Marshall and Muldoon. Their different approaches were clearly shown when both were interviewed about Brooks. Muldoon said that in the 'broadest sense' Brooks had a 'political background' and that he thought it was quite fair if Brooks got hurt playing in a tough game. Marshall, in contrast, said that he would not hurt anyone if he could avoid it and that he would never have made the comments Muldoon did about Brooks because 'I didn't think that the facts as I knew them justified the extreme condemnation of this young man.'[21] Marshall had tried to prevent the division between himself and Muldoon over Brooks becoming too public and at first refused to debate the matter on television. However, when Muldoon did appear on *Gallery* and discussed the matter, Marshall changed his mind and two nights later appeared on the same programme.[22] Marshall not only defended Brooks personally but expressed his opinion that Muldoon had gone beyond the right of any minister to express a viewpoint by interfering in 'the administration or detailed policy matters that are the immediate responsibility' of another minister, in this instance Marshall himself. He stated that the entry of the Minister of Finance into industrial relations matters generally was not helpful. As one journalist observed, 'The coldly furious Minister of Labour, Mr Marshall, left no one in any doubt that he resented the provocative excursions into industrial relations of the Minister of Finance, Mr Muldoon'.[23]

Of the 350 unions in New Zealand at that time the most militant and disruptive was probably the Seamen's Union, which caused Marshall a great deal of trouble. In November 1971 in the midst of a seamen's strike Marshall deregistered the Seamen's Union for defying a government directive to return to work, and a new union was subsequently formed. As a result of that action Marshall appeared to be strengthening his position within both the National Party and the electorate as a whole. A poll in the *Herald* a week after the seamen's dispute was settled found that 43 per cent of respondents thought Marshall would have the best chance of leading National to victory in 1972 compared to 20 per cent for Muldoon and 18 per cent for Holyoake. In another question, however, 33 per cent said Muldoon was 'the most effective person in political life' compared to Marshall, 28 per cent, Holyoake, 8 per cent, and Kirk, 7 per cent.[24]

Following the 1966 election there had been from time to time press speculation about a possible change in National's leadership. That speculation increased considerably after the 1969 election and even more so after Holyoake had a prostate operation in December 1970. Indeed, Marshall and his supporters, one of the most outspoken of whom was the irascible Sir Leslie Munro, undoubtedly thought Holyoake should have retired in Marshall's favour prior to the 1969 election. Holyoake resented the suggestion that he should retire and shared his concern with Muldoon, Gordon, MacIntyre and McKay at one of their late Monday night sessions.[25]

By the end of 1970 Holyoake's major allies and lieutenants – Lake, Hanan, Shand, Allen and Shelton – were dead, ill, or on the eve of retirement. A large section of the party organisation led by the Wellington divisional chairman, George Chapman, who in 1973 was to replace the pro-Holyoake Ned Holt as the party's president, was clearly pressing for a change of leadership from Holyoake to Marshall.[26] Marshall himself told Holyoake in a private and very blunt letter in 1971 that it was time Holyoake retired, a move which infuriated the Prime Minister. Holyoake showed the letter to the Auckland divisional chairman, Stuart Masters (among others), and told him that he might well go in 1972, the following year, but thought the party would be 'in real trouble if it elects Marshall as leader'.[27] Marshall, according to Holyoake, was 'a very good 2 i/c'. While Holyoake thought Muldoon was a possible leader, he wondered whether it might not be too soon to elevate him to the top job. On another occasion Holyoake confided in the president and five divisional chairmen of the National Party that he intended to retire before the 1972 election and thought Muldoon, not Marshall, his deputy of fifteen years, should succeed him.[28]

Holyoake became incensed by the pressure that built up to replace him during 1971, especially when Marshall after the successful completion of the EEC negotiations raised the question of Holyoake's retirement at the July caucus meeting shortly before the National Party's 1971 Conference. The debate was so heated that at one point Holyoake sent Percy Allen out of the caucus room to check whether the loud voices of Gordon and others could be heard by lurking journalists down the corridor.[29] Holyoake, with Muldoon's support, argued that a leadership change while Parliament was sitting would be a gift to the Labour Opposition and staved off the challenge by promising to make his position clear by December. At the conference in August Holyoake used his influence to re-elect his supporter Ned Holt as president of the party against a strong challenge from Chapman.

Holyoake was annoyed with Marshall for trying to push him out as leader, partly because he was well aware that he needed only one more victory at the polls to surpass Seddon's thirteen years as New Zealand's longest-serving prime minister. Equally, Marshall was frustrated by Holyoake's refusal to retire gracefully in his favour. There were, however, other reasons for the two men's alienation from each other.

Very few of National's leaders have been particularly friendly with their deputies, not only because of personality differences or rival ambitions but also because they usually were drawn from different ideological factions within the party. National was a coalition of three older parties: Reform, United and Democrat. There have always been divisions between rural and urban, interventionists and free enterprisers, moral conservatives and liberal humanists, supporters and opponents of the welfare state, collectivists and individualists, authoritarians and libertarians. Holyoake and Muldoon came from the more pragmatic, interventionist, collectivist and socially conservative wing of the party; Marshall from the more philosophical, legalistic, free enterprise, individualistic and liberal wing.

While Holyoake appears to have felt Marshall did not support him sufficiently in the House, cabinet and caucus, there was one issue which particularly annoyed him. He had for a long time resented Marshall's lack of support over New Zealand's involvement in the Vietnam War. During the agonised discussions in cabinet and caucus over this issue which led finally to the decision on 24 May 1965 to send New Zealand combat forces to Vietnam, most of the returned soldiers were prepared to approve limited support for the Americans. Although Holyoake had for several years resisted US appeals for such action he finally and reluctantly chose to accept the advice of the majority of his officials (though not of his Secretary of Defence, Jack Hunn) that New Zealand had to become involved.[30] Marshall, however, was very concerned about the destruction and suffering in Vietnam and sat silently through three cabinet meetings at which the question of involvement was debated and deferred.[31] Finally Holyoake agreed to send combat troops – 'the hardest decision Holyoake ever made', in the words of one of his colleagues, Gordon. Thereafter, however, it was clear that he did not trust or respect Marshall, who shortly after, and not coincidentally, became active in the Christian international relief organisation World Vision.

Marshall did share one characteristic with Holyoake; both were politicians of the 'chairman of the board' type, who tended to meld different groups together by a process of consultation and consensus, preferably by discussion in committees. Muldoon, on the other hand, was a direct and hard-hitting leader willing to debate in public. He did not avoid controversy, and indeed often seemed to provoke it, thereby dividing people sharply into opposing camps of those who agreed and those who disagreed with him. Consensus leaders tend to stress similarities and points of agreement; confrontational leaders highlight the differences and points of disagreement. As Muldoon told an interviewer, 'I believe that anyone in Government should lead. I believe in letting the people know what I think on whatever issues are current and then they can judge whether I am right or not. I dislike intensely Government behind closed doors.'[32]

All three men were clearly ambitious and enjoyed power. As a result they aspired to be or to remain prime minister. Only Muldoon, however, had to endure, far more than the other two, suggestions that he was power-hungry. In an interesting NZBC 'Lobby Report' interview in September 1971, Muldoon and Marshall, as Holyoake's most likely successors, were asked if power and its exercise was important to them personally. Muldoon replied modestly but somewhat disingenuously that no one had less power than a chartered accountant working for other people but that he was 'more interested in the job than the power that goes with it'.[33] When asked bluntly if he wanted to be Prime Minister, Muldoon answered simply, 'We've got a Prime Minister [Holyoake]'. Marshall on the other hand replied, 'I think that the ambition of most people is to get to the top. And at the appropriate time I would like to be Prime Minister of New Zealand.'

Some of the media comment on Muldoon was quite facetious. In another interview, Muldoon was told that a forthcoming issue of the women's magazine *Eve* would include a poll on New Zealand's sexiest politician and that Muldoon was 'way out in front' because he exuded power.[34] Muldoon's reply was that *Eve* was not a particularly reliable authority. In its horoscope the previous month it had noted that he turned 50 on 25 September and that his stars revealed him to be 'sweet and gentle of nature', a person who would make 'a successful interior decorator'. Muldoon agreed he was sensitive but ruled out any 'superfluous decoration'.

When it became obvious in late 1971 and early 1972 that Holyoake was at last seriously considering retiring from the leadership, Muldoon discussed the succession with many of his caucus colleagues. He became convinced that he would win the succession by a small margin. He realised that few of the older, retiring ministers and members would vote for him but did not fully appreciate at the time that some of the others who said flattering or supportive things to him were nevertheless going to vote for Marshall.[35] Although Muldoon's candidacy to succeed Holyoake was enthusiastically promoted by some of his friends and admirers, notably Colin McLachlan, Frank Gill and Logan Sloane, he was mistaken in believing he had the numbers in caucus in 1972 to beat Marshall. The former chief whip, Alf Allen, was convinced that National was going to lose the 1972 election and told Holyoake so.[36] He also told Holyoake that if he wished to remain leader then he would have enough votes in caucus to retain the post but that it would be better to retire after four election victories than after a defeat that year. If he did not stand, Allen told him, Marshall would beat Muldoon for the leadership. Allen advised Muldoon to nominate Marshall for the top post, take the deputy's post, and replace Marshall after the 1972 election defeat but Muldoon, convinced by his most ardent supporters that he had a majority in caucus, decided to force a ballot in the event of Holyoake vacating the leadership.

The National MPs met for a two-day caucus on 2 and 3 February 1972. The first business was a discussion of the economy introduced by Muldoon. He told his colleagues that his objectives during the forthcoming year would be to dampen down inflation, stimulate a sluggish economy, and win the election. He proposed 'a two months wages pause and price freeze for the same period' which 'would allow a little time to produce other solutions of a more lasting nature'.[37] Marshall then at some length outlined the current industrial situation, arguing that because the Government did not have the legal authority to impose a wage freeze, the co-operation of employers and unions in postponing wage settlements and slowing inflation would be essential.

After lunch, Holyoake, aware that there were people in both the National caucus and the party's Dominion Council who would raise the leadership question if he did not, introduced the matter by reading out a newspaper article suggesting a change. Holyoake, who later publicly said that the caucus had 'finally bowed' to his 'very strong wish to retire',[38] in fact at first left his retirement open. He told caucus that he was, if it wished, prepared to go, 'taking with him the aura of unpopularity due to difficult times' and giving a new leader a chance to win the election later that year.[39]

Talboys, supported by Munro, immediately suggested that members of caucus should vote 'yes' or 'no' on whether Holyoake should retire. Gordon then suggested an indicative ballot to see whom caucus wanted, with each MP writing one name on a piece of paper. Doug Carter, a Muldoon supporter, countered by proposing a three-way ballot between Holyoake, Marshall and Muldoon. Although Marshall later stated that no one rose in the caucus to suggest let alone urge that Holyoake should remain leader, in fact Alf Allen, George Gair, Lance Adams-Schneider, W. G. Tolhurst, Esmé Tombleson, Roy Jack, Leo Schultz and J. R. Harrison all said that they were not prepared to support any type of vote until Holyoake clearly indicated his wish to retire.[40]

Holyoake then intervened again in the discussion and announced that he could not accept just the blind loyalty of his colleagues and 'in the best interests of the party as a whole' he wished to retire. He declined to indicate whom he favoured as his successor. Five other MPs – Eric Holland, Norman Shelton, Jack Luxton, J. M. Rose and David Thomson – then said that they 'would not ask Sir Keith to step down'; but Holyoake confirmed that 'he had a strong wish to retire from the leadership' and the way was now open to elect a new leader.

Talboys again took the lead and suggested that MPs write either Marshall or Muldoon on a piece of paper. Marshall defeated Muldoon 28 votes to 16.[41] After Muldoon had congratulated Marshall and asked his supporters to help the new leader, Marshall nominated Muldoon as deputy leader, the nomination being endorsed unanimously by acclamation. Marshall spoke briefly to caucus and then Muldoon formally expressed appreciation to Holyoake for his leadership of the National Party and New Zealand.

The two other Young Turks did not vote for Muldoon. MacIntyre and Gordon had no hesitation, despite their friendship with Muldoon, in supporting Marshall. MacIntyre was a traditionalist, who accepted that Marshall as the deputy had earned the right to succeed Holyoake, and also he personally believed Marshall to be a better potential leader than Muldoon. Muldoon had proved himself as a finance minister, but MacIntyre had doubts about his ability as a commander able to handle people well.[42] For these reasons, MacIntyre supported Marshall in 1972 and understood why Marshall felt aggrieved by the Muldoon challenge. Gordon held similar opinions at that time.[43]

The day after Marshall became leader, caucus debated further methods of stabilising the economy.[44] Wages had gone up 40 per cent and prices 20 per cent over the previous two years and Holyoake strongly advocated a wages and price freeze. When the question of a freeze on rents and interest rates was also raised, Muldoon argued that it was 'almost impossible to control interest rates' and he did not want to reintroduce rent controls which National had so recently abolished. Marshall still favoured an agreed wage constraint rather than legislation or regulation and did not like Muldoon's observation that to be effective regulation would have to be retrospective to 1 December 1971. It was decided to impose a price and wage freeze for six weeks while the Government consulted and decided on longer-term economic policies.

On 27 March a package of proposals was announced which included control of wages and salaries by regulations administered by the Remuneration Authority. The Government undertook for twelve months not to increase charges or allow increases in the prices of electricity, postal and railway services, bread, milk, butter, sugar or other prices subject to the Price Tribunal. The pay-out to dairy farmers was reduced and the surplus put into reserve accounts. Company dividends and interest rates were also capped. In an attempt to stimulate the economy, company tax payments were deferred, social security payments were increased, sheep farmers were assisted, bank lending was freed up, and hire purchase regulations were relaxed. A cost of living order based on the Consumer Price Index for the nine months ending September 1972 was also signalled.[45] Muldoon set to work to draft a budget which would further induce economic growth while combating inflation.

Muldoon had difficulty putting together his 1972 Budget, presented on 22 June. He wanted it to be an expansionary one, but unfortunately such a Budget would involve a threefold increase in the deficit before borrowing, from $70 to $200 million. He did not want to increase expenditure to a point that would require tax increases the year after the election and he was having considerable difficulty meeting the demands and expectations of various lobbies, especially farmers. His caucus colleagues also were pressing for a wide array of increased items of expenditure. At one caucus meeting, for example, twenty-three MPs suggested extra expenditure on various items including farm stock and feed subsidies; increased tax incentives and deductions, including deductibility of payroll tax and private school donations; greater expenditure on old age pensions; lower charges for power and postal and telephone services; increased boarding allowances for country children; more expenditure on housing, regional development and country roads; and reduced income and sales taxes. One MP, Rona Stevenson of Taupo, suggested restraint by opposing any increase in the family benefit.[46] When Muldoon decided instead to increase the family benefit, Jack Luxton remarked at a later caucus meeting, 'This Budget shows we're a socialist National Party.'[47] Muldoon, who was trying to hold expenditure, also annoyed some of the farming MPs by commenting that if increased livestock 'production was such a good thing . . . why would they [farmers] need incentives?'[48]

The Budget reduced income tax by 7.5 per cent and increased investment allowances and export incentives. Social security benefits were raised in line with the recommendations of the Report of the Royal Commission on Social Security chaired by Sir Thaddeus McCarthy, which after two and a half years of investigation had endorsed the system set up in 1938. Family benefits were doubled, though income tax deductions for dependent children ceased. Welfare benefits were increased to take account of inflation and return them to the level relative to a working wage that they had been in 1960. There was considerably more expenditure on health, housing and education. Payroll tax was made tax-deductible and company tax would be reduced in December. As a result of the increased expenditure, the Government predicted a deficit to be covered by borrowing instead of a balanced budget. Although the Budget failed to stimulate economic recovery as far or as fast as Muldoon wished, it did lay the basis for a much more dramatic, albeit belated, economic upturn later in the year when dairy, wool and lamb prices improved sharply.

In May 1972 the property investment firm JBL crashed after expanding its activities to Australia and London. Some forty-seven companies within the JBL group were affected. There was criticism that Muldoon as Minister of Finance had been partly responsible for JBL's collapse by limiting participation in property syndicates which JBL depended on substantially for public investment funds. Indeed, some critics went further and accused Muldoon of hastening JBL's crash by a 'tax raid'.[49] Muldoon responded that 'regulations and controls' were sometimes necessary 'to encourage competitive private enterprise but in a manner compatible with the public interest.'[50] Because he had become concerned 'about certain aspects of syndication investment', the Government had legislated in 1971 to inhibit its growth by making new syndicates of more than ten members formed after 2 September 1972 to acquire real estate liable for tax on the same basis as companies.

In order to protect smaller investors in JBL and to try to salvage some of its more profitable companies, Muldoon appointed at the end of May a government receiver, D. L. Hazard, a move which enraged the ANZ Bank, which had appointed its own receiver shortly before and which believed that Muldoon's action might 'be disadvantageous to the Bank recovering its full loan'.[51] Muldoon believed that the collapse of JBL taught two lessons: 'that entrepreneurs who take in other people's money have a duty to those people over and above any strictly legal requirement' and that 'a high return necessarily means a higher than normal risk'.[52] He was also annoyed that high interest rates offered by such entrepreneurs and speculators forced up costs for more productive borrowers and for long-term economic development.

Experienced and perceptive journalists recognised and sometimes admitted that Muldoon understood them very well and was 'managing us all the time and we can't do a bloody thing about it' because 'he's a better journalist than most of us'.[53] Muldoon always enjoyed performing on television current affairs or talkback radio programmes. He was confident in his grasp of any subject on which he agreed to be interviewed and of his ability to think and answer clearly even in an interview in which he was under attack. Indeed he relished the cut and thrust of a tough debate or interview on television. When he went on television Muldoon was determined not just to leave his viewers with a general impression but a thought – 'one per appearance . . . maybe on rare occasions two'. His comments were easy for press, television and radio journalists to edit and report. They were simple, short, precise, sometimes humorous, sometimes cynical, and usually very effective statements. He also used rhetorical questions well and on television would look not at the interviewer but straight at the viewers inviting them to agree with him. He recalled that in the early days he used to watch playbacks of his television performances to perfect his straight-at-the-camera technique.[54]

Muldoon was not devious. On television he clearly distinguished between fact and opinion, always quoted others correctly and in context, justified his point of view, and openly expressed outrage when he believed he was being treated unfairly. He was ruthless in identifying and exposing errors of fact or quotation and made interviewers almost paranoid about being adequately prepared.[55] Muldoon had a great ability to turn the attack back on to journalists and become the interviewer-interrogator by responding, 'Where did you hear that?' or 'You haven't got your facts right' or 'You didn't understand what I said.' He expected interviewers not to be partisan or to comment publicly about how they got on with him.

One current affairs programme that Muldoon had mixed feelings about was television's prime-time *Gallery*, which he once described as having been a 'more effective opposition than the Labour Party' from the time of its inception in 1969.[56] Although one *Gallery* interviewer dismissed Muldoon's criticism on the grounds that the programme simply was 'revealing the true nature of New Zealand society' and that 'the capacity of programmes such as *Gallery* to undermine the Government's credibility lay in their power to inform rather than in the dialectical skill of their interviewers',[57] there is no doubt that many of the interviewers were critical personally of Muldoon and what he represented. Austin Mitchell later became a British Labour MP; Brian Edwards was a Labour Party candidate for Miramar in 1972 and, despite admiring Muldoon's courage, revealed his personal dislike of the man in his book *The Public Eye*;[58] David Exel went on to organise the 'Citizens for Rowling' campaign in 1975 before becoming the Labour Party's Public Relations Officer; Simon Walker helped organise Labour's 1984 campaign; and Geoff Walker, whom Muldoon publicly identified as being in his opinion 'the best current-affairs interviewer in my time',[59] subsequently helped organise some of the most disruptive Springbok Tour protests in Wellington in 1981. Only Dairne

Shanahan, whom Muldoon found 'charming and intelligent', was not considered by Muldoon to be politically and personally antagonistic towards him among the *Gallery* interviewers.

Muldoon did not stand on his dignity and participated even in programmes which could expose him to ridicule. One such episode was the pilot in late 1970 for a proposed *The Brian Edwards Show*. Muldoon was prepared to risk his reputation by appearing with Tim Shadbolt, the radical protester, Chris Wheeler, the editor of the satirical journal *Cock*, and Alister Taylor, the publisher of *The Little Red School Book*. The programme commenced with criticism of Muldoon's facial scar, alleged callous disregard for the poor, arrogant personality, lack of a sense of humour, and contempt for human values. Shadbolt called him 'A crapped-out ledger-keeper who can't even dance or sing!'[60] Muldoon, who was sitting with his wife in the audience, was then given the chance by Edwards to reply and in Edwards's words, 'For the next thirty minutes it's anything goes . . . And many of the blows are dangerously below the belt as Muldoon is accused of arrogance, ambition, publicity-seeking, deviousness and dishonesty, contempt for parliamentary democracy, the trivialisation of politics, lack of concern for the quality of life, a callous indifference to the needs of people and a dozen other crimes against humanity. He gives as good and better . . . At the end Muldoon is still smiling' and Edwards has to admit 'You may not like him . . . but you have to admit, the man's got guts.'[61] The NZBC programme committee, however, rejected both the pilot and the proposed new series of programmes hosted by Edwards, and although Muldoon publicly stated that he was 'astounded and disturbed' by the decision not to screen the pilot and waived any rights to sue for defamation, it was never shown.[62]

Not only communists, militant trade unionists, speculating businessmen, and some journalists were subject to Muldoon's criticism. He also questioned the consistency and fairness of some churchmen, particularly on the issue of South Africa. He clashed, for example, on *Gallery* with Bishop Pyatt, accusing the bishop and other clergy of letting their left-wing political views colour their public statements on behalf of the Christian church.[63] Muldoon was incensed by what he regarded as the 'selective conscience' of those who spoke out on moral and religious grounds on certain public issues. He was not the only National MP to speak out about churchmen becoming involved in political issues but he became the one most associated with the issue. In a *Gallery* programme in May 1972 the interviewer Exel pointed out to Muldoon that Marshall, Gair and Adams-Schneider had also said churchmen should keep out of politics.[64] Muldoon, however, denied that he personally had taken that position. On the contrary he stated, 'I believe that churchmen should speak out on issues' but added that he was concerned at their becoming involved in a 'band waggoning kind of way' in fashionable issues such as South African rugby tours. He suggested that 'there are far worse evils around the world that the churches should be devoting their attention to than a Springbok rugby team coming to New Zealand.' Muldoon subsequently enlarged on his views about religion and politics in the *Dominion*.[65] That article led to a critical editorial in the *New Zealand Law Journal* written by Jeremy Pope, the editor.[66] Muldoon took exception specifically to the accusation that he 'saw no religious or humanitarian ground for opposing apartheid', and Pope and the publishers of the *New Zealand Law Journal* were forced to apologise and admit publicly that, far from attacking freedom of dissent and the right of churchmen to become involved in political issues, Muldoon 'was in fact advocating that the Church should speak out on a wider range of public issues on religious and humanitarian grounds than it has done hitherto.'[67]

In 1970 the controversy over a proposal to raise the water level of Lake Manapouri erupted with a petition to Parliament signed by 265,000 people.[68] A commission of inquiry reported that the raising of the lake would damage its scenic beauty. In mid-1971 the Government decided not to raise the lake but to build a wide low dam capable of being raised in the future. The anger among conservationists particularly in Otago-Southland led to widespread protests and mass meetings and when National, unlike Labour, refused to give firm assurances that Manapouri would not be raised, Wanaka would not be flooded, and dams would not be built across the Clutha in the future, the public reaction was such that at the 1972 election four marginal National seats in Otago-Southland fell to Labour.

Even without Manapouri, Marshall faced a very difficult task at the 1972 election. Not only was Kirk a much more impressive and formidable opponent than he had been in 1966 and 1969 and the Labour Party better organised and funded than for many years, but National had been in Government for twenty of the previous twenty-three years, including the last twelve.[69] It was inevitable that Labour's election slogan, 'Time for a Change,' copied from National's successful 1949 campaign, would evoke a positive response from many voters who were not impressed with the National strategy which, as Marshall later admitted, 'relied on our record and promised more of the same'.[70] National's support had been steadily eroding since 1960 and as Brian Edwards, who unsuccessfully contested Miramar for Labour in 1972, concluded, 'In offering the country "more of the same" . . . National made its biggest mistake. The country did not want more of the same; it wanted action, excitement . . . and that was precisely what Labour promised . . . Labour said, "We will", and that was enough.'[71] The media also found Labour's lavish promises and the future orientation of its campaign much more newsworthy than National's backward looking defence of its record in government. Muldoon disliked the inexplicable change of National's advertising colours from blue and white to orange and black and wanted as National's campaign slogan 'National Puts People First'. Instead Marshall insisted on 'Man for Man the Strongest Team', which because of media focus on the leaders meant a contrast between the restrained and defensive Marshall and the ebullient and confident Kirk.

The contrast between Marshall's fatherly, reasoned, genteel style and Kirk's brutal, emotive and decisive performance, a foretaste of the Muldoon–Rowling contest three years later, was also a major negative factor for National in 1972. Marshall was the thoughtful, experienced administrator, not an enthusiastic and effective campaigner. Again, as Edwards observed, 'decisiveness induced credibility. Faced with the considered, weighed, balanced, "much can be said on both sides" sort of argument, audiences responded with voluble scepticism, interpreting what was sometimes sound and tempered reasoning as deceit . . . It was, it seemed, the style that mattered, rather than the substance. And the style had to be clear, direct and positive.'[72] Kirk, however, was careful not to offend voters by being too decisive, defusing the Springbok tour issue, for example, by promising that a Labour Government would not intervene to stop the tour.

Marshall and Muldoon argued, with some justification, that despite the difficulties faced during 1970 and 1971 the economy by 1972 was buoyant: overseas reserves exceeded overseas debt; export earnings and private savings were both rising; and inflation, though still causing some concern, had, with considerable difficulty, been halved in 1972 compared to 1970 and 1971 and brought at least temporarily under control. The Government had successfully defended New Zealand's position in the difficult negotiations over Britain's entry into the European Economic Community; the seamen's strike had finally been dealt with; and five new ministers – Gair, Gandar, Holland, Jack and Highet – had been brought into cabinet by Marshall to produce a younger and more dynamic executive team.

The opening meeting of National's election campaign, however, was a disaster. A broadcasting malfunction meant that television viewers in the South Island and the southern part of the North Island could not see Marshall's live address from Whangarei. Thereafter, Marshall had to endure a series of rowdy public meetings with the police being called in to eject dozens of demonstrators from the Christchurch and Auckland rallies. At Auckland, Marshall and his party were pelted with red paint bombs and firecrackers as they left the town hall.

Muldoon was a shadow of the dynamic 1969 campaigner. He had not been well since late October and continued to be ill throughout the election campaign. Although he attracted large audiences in provincial cities and towns such as Hamilton (1500 present), Invercargill (1000), Masterton (900), Tauranga and Blenheim (both 800) as he attacked the estimated $600 million cost of Labour's promises, he was struggling for much of the time. At the end of the third week he collapsed in Wellington and had to spend several days in bed and curtail his contribution to the final week's campaign. Hepatitis was diagnosed.

Even had Muldoon been well, however, he would not have been able to turn the campaign around as it was generally accepted he had three years before. Indeed, some commentators suggested that while at that time Muldoon rated highly in the polls as New Zealand's most effective politician, he was not as highly rated as preferred prime minister because voters also regarded him as 'the most obnoxious' politician in the country. Moreover, as Kirk was later to taunt, because he was so disliked Muldoon 'played perhaps the dominant role' in the defeat of the National Party in 1972.[73] Naturally, Muldoon rejected such an interpretation, as he did the suggestion that Marshall was solely to blame. In hindsight, he decided that nobody could have led National to victory in 1972.[74]

Governments are usually voted out by disappointed, frustrated and alienated voters shifting to the Opposition, and certainly in 1972 there were many such voters. Apart from those enraged by the Manapouri issue there were manufacturers worried about the removal of import licensing; employers angry at the payroll tax; farmers struggling with increasing costs and uncertain overseas prices, and annoyed with a government that seemed to be more interested in controlling the marketing of wool than the activities of militant unions; young families thwarted from owning a home by escalating property values and building costs and the scarcity and expense of mortgage finance; workers facing wage restraints at a time of unprecedented increases in the cost of living; young executives whose salaries were restricted by the Stabilisation Regulations and the Remuneration Authority and who were hit with a surtax on their incomes; and young people angry about a range of issues such as the Vietnam War, French nuclear testing, compulsory military training, abortion, homosexual law reform, equal pay and greater opportunities for women, and apartheid in South Africa, specifically Springbok–All Black rugby tours. Labour's position on many of these issues was more attractive in 1972 than National's.

A whole raft of National's seats in parliament were held in 1972 by majorities eroded in 1969 to dangerously low levels. A dozen of National's forty-six seats would fall to a relatively small but uniform movement of votes to Labour across the country, and others were also vulnerable.[75] Nevertheless, the outcome of the election appeared to have been an unexpected shock to National's leaders. Marshall and Muldoon both admitted subsequently that on election day they believed National had won.[76] Within an hour of the polls closing it became clear that there was a landslide to Labour. The National percentage of the total vote dropped 3.7 per cent to 41.50 while Labour increased 4.2 to 48.37. Fourteen National seats were lost and National was left with only 32 seats in Parliament to Labour's 55. Some commentators predicted that with that majority 'it is unlikely that they [Labour] will be defeated in 1975 or for that matter in 1978.'[77]

CHAPTER 10

In Opposition 1972–75

IN THE MONTHS FOLLOWING THE 1972 ELECTION DEFEAT THE National caucus over several meetings discussed its future strategy and tactics. A group led by Marshall, Gair and Talboys proposed what Gair called a 'rebirth', a fundamental reform of the party's policies, personnel, organisation and image. The strategy involved the party networking with the special interest groups in the economy and society.[1] Talboys also stressed the need to work on the 'nerve ends of nationalism'. Muldoon, supported by Gordon, was more conservative. He responded that there was nothing very wrong with the National Party as it was and that he was worried about 'too much rebirth' or changing National into a 'new party'. He commented that Kirk and the new Labour Government had the biggest majority since 1938 and that 'the average bloke will say that the new Government has got to be given a fair go', even though he believed the Labour Government would probably get itself into trouble.[2] National should be careful about attacking Labour for the first six months and should spend that time working out some positive new policies and building up its organisation. Muldoon observed that National MPs would 'have to work like blazes' and 'must learn from Labour's tactics' and predicted that, with a few new policies and better publicity, National could win the 1975 election.

Both approaches drew criticism from Holyoake. Recalling the success he and National had enjoyed in attacking Labour's 1958 'Black Budget' and destroying Nordmeyer's reputation, Holyoake advocated an immediate, sustained, no-holds-barred attack on Labour and especially its leader Kirk. The caucus records summarised Holyoake's advice. National 'must be brutal – for another twelve months totally destructive'. Whilst National MPs could start thinking about policy, they should not make it for twelve months, but 'be everyone's friends'. There was no question that 'Kirk [is] our problem' and that National had to 'cut him down . . . on every occasion.'[3] Holyoake reminded his colleagues that a one-man government was easier 'to shoot down' than a strong team and that Kirk's support of one-party African governments could be used to link him to the communists. At subsequent caucus meetings throughout 1973 and 1974 Holyoake continued to press for stronger attacks on Labour's credibility and morale, especially by targeting the government's weakest ministers.

One result of Holyoake's advice was that in early 1973 Gair convened a caucus committee that formulated and directed parliamentary questions designed to embarrass and discredit Labour ministers National perceived to be weak, specifically Fraser Colman, Michael Connelly, Henry May, Matiu Rata and Whetu Tirikatene-Sullivan. One Labour leader Muldoon insisted should not be asked any questions was Arthur Faulkner, whom Muldoon regarded as 'glib and unscrupulous' but very effective in the House.[4] Marshall also set up other caucus committees and Muldoon chaired the Economic Committee with Talboys as his deputy. The other members were Carter, Gair, Gandar and Walker.[5]

One of Labour's major policy planks at the 1972 election was regional development and among other promises Kirk stated that he would bring industry to Westport and Greymouth on the depressed West Coast of the South Island. Throughout the election campaign Kirk was assisted by a close and long-time friend, Kevin Meates, a Christchurch businessman and former All Black. Meates and his two brothers were keen to establish industry on the West Coast provided the Kirk Government was prepared to give them substantial freight subsidies, sufficient import licences, loans or government guarantees for loans and fast-tracked decisions by government departments.[6] After apparently receiving such assurances, though Kirk may never have been as committed and certainly not to specific subsidies as Meates believed or hoped, Matai Industries Ltd was established and among its directors were to be two appointed by the Government and one by the Opposition.[7]

Despite Meates's strong protestation, on the National Opposition's nomination Muldoon was appointed on 26 July 1973 as a director of Matai.[8] Meates was later to record that 'at all times . . . he acted in a non-political manner . . . to the best of his ability as a Chartered Accountant and he gave the Company invaluable guidance and advice.'[9] Kirk, in a blaze of publicity, opened Matai Industries' factories in November 1973, but was concerned that Meates wanted 'to double the Government guarantee, which was big money.'[10] Muldoon was also aware that the company, having not received a cent of regional or other subsidy, was facing a severe liquidity crisis and was barely solvent. He repeatedly from November 1973 approached Kirk, Finance Minister Wallace (Bill) Rowling and Trade and Industries Minister Warren Freer as the three ministers most involved with the project.[11] Muldoon's suggestion that it might be prudent to retrench somewhat was dismissed, but both Muldoon and Meates believed that assurances were given that further money would be injected into the company. Muldoon also proposed the appointment of a financial controller and one of his partners from Kendon Mills Muldoon and Browne was appointed in December to reorganise Matai's accounts and financial controls. However, Rowling was by that time receiving strongly worded expressions of concern from the Secretary of the Treasury about the management and future viability of the Matai development.[12]

Kirk appeared to support Meates and the project generally throughout and was insistent that there should be a big public opening in November 1973 of four factories producing woodware, metalware and plastics and employing 347 people in Reefton, Greymouth, Runanga and Westport. Meates, however, by August was telling Kirk that his own capital was fully committed and that if further funds were not forthcoming from Government then he and the other directors thought they should reduce staff and retrench to a more modest development with perhaps initially only one factory at Westport. Meates also felt that a recent 'meeting with Freer and Rowling . . . couldn't have gone worse . . . They do not understand'. He blamed 'Freer and Rowling for the buggering about' which was preventing the successful implementation of the scheme.[13] In a postscript Meates warned Kirk that Labour's constant attacks on Muldoon were counterproductive and provided him with repeated opportunities to counter-attack with devastating effect and gain publicity. As a result, 'Muldoon has had a feast – When will your cohorts learn to ignore him?'[14]

Muldoon might have been very sceptical about Kirk's promises in general and Matai in particular, but he was determined as a director, and with his own reputation involved, to do all he could to make the company successful. Shortly before Matai went into receivership the directors met Freer, Rowling, Fred Turnovsky the chairman of the Development Finance Corporation, and officials of Treasury and Trade and Industry.[15] Muldoon went straight to the heart of the matter and told Freer that Matai's directors had placed 'complete reliance on repeated assurances' of 'yourself [Freer], Mr Rowling and the Prime Minister that the Government would stand behind the company and we should not close down operations or sack staff.' Freer replied that he did not 'think that the situation was quite as clear' and Rowling added that 'Those assurances were not unqualified assurances.'[16] Muldoon responded that the company would not have gone to the West Coast without assurances of financial assistance, but the grants had not eventuated. When the Secretary for the Treasury, Lang, said that 'under no circumstances would the Government ever contemplate giving assistance of any kind without a feasibility study', Muldoon criticised Lang for breaching the 'spirit of co-operation' which might enable the company to survive. Muldoon added that he was on the board because the National Party Opposition had criticised the possible assistance the company had appeared likely to get from the Labour Government but he believed the project could be salvaged.

Although Kirk had discussed the matter the night before with the board's chairman, Ralph Thompson, one of two government nominees, he had not indicated that he was aware that Freer and Rowling intended to propose receivership. Meanwhile, however, Kirk had left for the Chatham Islands that morning and Thompson was unable to contact him. Freer assured the meeting that he had Kirk's 'full approval'. Kirk's agreement with Freer and Rowling made the Matai directors' position hopeless. Muldoon still pursued the matter arguing that, 'I think that the Ministers are making the wrong decision . . . the Government's policy on regional development will be set back immeasurably.'[17] Four days later, on 19 February 1974, Matai went into receivership.

Thompson placed on record Muldoon's integrity in not using anything as a politician which he had learnt as a director and also stated that 'I do not think we could have had a more loyal supporter of the scheme, at all times . . . available . . . to come to the Coast or Christchurch to advance the interests of the company . . . I couldn't wish for a better associate on the Board.'[18] When Freer, who had been conducting the negotiations, and Rowling, who had to make the final decision, decided to appoint a receiver, who would officially be appointed by the DFC, Muldoon demanded a public inquiry into the affairs of Matai unless Freer and Rowling went on record that he and the other outside directors had at all times acted in the interests of the company. He would not permit his political reputation to be prejudiced by any suggestion that he had not acted professionally as a director of Matai. He received that assurance, although in later years Labour politicians were to suggest in Parliament that Muldoon had not been an able company director.[19] Subsequently, Muldoon concerned himself with the need to protect Matai's unsecured creditors, such as small tradesmen and companies on the West Coast and he agreed to remain on the board to help the receiver throughout 1974. In September 1974 a decision was made to sell off the company's assets.

At the end of 1974, Muldoon launched a bitter public attack on Rowling and Freer and called for a public inquiry into Matai Industries, blaming the disaster primarily on the Labour Government's refusal to pay regional development grants to the company. In 1978 a $1 million claim was brought in the Supreme Court by the shareholders of Matai Industries against the Government, alleging breach of agreement for the setting up of industries in Westland, but because the plaintiffs could not produce written documents supporting their case and Kirk, who had died four years earlier, never concerned himself with the details of the project, the claim failed.[20] The Chief Justice made it clear in his judgment that he had to distinguish between political promises and binding contracts, and that the former had not become the latter. However, the Government finally paid out over $5 million from the Consolidated Fund and from Vote: Trade and Industry: Regional Development in respect of Matai Industries.[21]

While in opposition between 1972 and 1975 Muldoon was chairman of the board of Devon Investments, commercial mortgage finance brokers, among whose other directors were Sir Ron Scott and Peter Shirtcliffe, and also was chairman of Superannuation Investments Ltd, a company formed by a previous National Party leader, Sidney Holland. He was also a director of Simmental Beef Export Company Ltd and Lowndes Lambert (NZ) Ltd.

If Holyoake had been unenthusiastic about Marshall succeeding him as leader in 1972, by 1974 he was openly critical and prepared on a one-to-one basis to tell colleagues that Muldoon would be preferable, and in public heightened the sense of crisis in the National Party by observing that if National lost the 1975 election they would be torn asunder as a party and might have to 'pull ourselves up from the roots and start again' as in 1935.[22] That view was shared by others in caucus and elsewhere in the party who thought that the wrong decision had been made in 1972, as the election outcome had shown.

The Auckland Division, for example, continued throughout 1973 and early 1974 to criticise the morale and performance of the National caucus and its obvious inability to counter Kirk and the Labour Government. When George Chapman, the new party president, addressed the Auckland Divisional Executive in March 1974 delegates raised with him 'the Leadership of the Party' and 'the lack of communication with the man in the street.'[23] This was an implied criticism of Marshall in particular.

Unlike the four other regions of the National Party, the leadership of the Auckland Division was strongly supportive of Muldoon. The divisional chairman, Stuart Masters, the divisional director, Colin Brenton-Rule, and at least one of the deputy chairmen, Peter Dempsey, were all firmly convinced that Muldoon would be a better leader than Marshall. The other deputy chairman, Jim McLay, who was not averse to Muldoon, was soon to be replaced by the much more committed Muldoon lieutenant John Tremewan. Among the other Aucklanders on the Dominion Council, Doreen Bray, Mat Te Hau, Jack Ashby and Neil Austin were also supportive of Muldoon. Only Pat Baker, who was later to succeed Masters as divisional chairman, was lukewarm and was generally regarded as pro-Marshall.[24]

Not all of Muldoon's own electorate officials, however, were happy with Muldoon's priorities as Deputy Leader of the Opposition. Throughout 1973 he concentrated on attacking Labour in Parliament and on writing his first book, *The Rise and Fall of a Young Turk*. At successive electorate meetings in November two electorate deputy chairmen, Ed Smallwood and Doug Tillyshort, alleged that the electorate was not receiving sufficient attention from Muldoon as local MP and that people were complaining that they could not contact him and that he had not been seen recently in the electorate.[25] The discontent and criticism continued into 1974 and resulted in the Tamaki Electorate taking its concerns on the general state of the party to the Divisional Executive. There Tillyshort moved on behalf of Tamaki a motion deploring the apathy and lack of communication within the party and Remuera moved a similar motion. Both were carried.[26] The following weekend on Sunday 17 February a special meeting was held at Muldoon's home at which not only his local performance but also the 'apparent apathy and lack of general direction within the Party' was discussed. Tillyshort, Smallwood and a third deputy chairman, David Bagley, told Muldoon that National needed a 'dynamic and newsworthy' leader who could stop the party drifting and see that Kirk was 'knocked off the pedestal on which he had been placed mostly by the news media'.[27] Muldoon defended his own work in both the Tamaki electorate and Parliament but clearly did not satisfy all his critics.

Marshall told the caucus in mid-1973 that he saw 'no deep-rooted divisions' in it but that 'the quickest way to destroy the [National] party was to undermine the leadership'.[28] He suggested that someone from caucus should move a motion of confidence in his leadership during the forthcoming party conference. Immediately Frank Gill, Harry Lapwood and Doug Carter responded that leadership was not 'static', that leaders could be replaced, and that the wider party should not be given the impression that the leadership was unchangeable. Although Muldoon, who was present, did not take part in the discussion, Holyoake commented that the party was 'never entirely content with any leader' and suggested that Muldoon, not Marshall, should be prepared to deal with the question if it was raised at the forthcoming party conference in Christchurch.[29] Marshall admitted to the caucus that he realised that he was 'not a rabblerouser' and would, therefore, 'not try to speak for an hour' in his leader's address to the 1973 conference. He asked caucus members to encourage delegates to applaud. In the event, Marshall gave an excellent address, which drew from Holyoake the cryptic comment that 'We've just lost the next election.'[30] Those with him concluded that he meant Marshall had consolidated his leadership but could not win in 1975.

National's defeat in 1972 had not been the result of any one factor or any one person, but there was no doubt that the electorate as a whole had perceived Kirk to be a stronger leader than Marshall. Since the days of Seddon, political parties had been personified in their leaders, who often fought presidential-style elections which the most charismatic, confident or aggressive personality usually won. Successive governments were also known commonly by the leader's name: the Ward, Massey, Coates, Forbes, Savage, Fraser, Holland, Nash, Holyoake and Kirk governments.

Kirk was a very complex individual who, despite being a physically big man with an image of confidence and vision, was secretly insecure and also convinced that he would die at a young age and therefore could not afford to wait. He was contemptuous and suspicious of intellectuals, including caucus colleagues such as Martyn Finlay, Bob Tizard and Bill Rowling, but unnecessarily so because although lacking formal education, Kirk was an extremely intelligent man and was remarkably well-read. He also was a passionate man, capable of seizing the moral high ground in both domestic and foreign affairs through his ability to verbalise emotion and his highly uplifting and symbolic actions such as taking the hand of a small Maori boy and walking across the marae at Waitangi to symbolise New Zealand's bicultural history and future, or by sending a warship with a cabinet minister on board to protest dramatically against French nuclear testing in the South Pacific.

Marshall recognised that Kirk and Muldoon were different types of leader from himself and believed that they were more motivated than he was by 'power and the satisfaction of exercising power.'[31] He claimed that, unlike Kirk and Muldoon, 'I never sought to use power in a dictatorial way and indeed got no satisfaction – as some do – from forcing men to respond out of subservience or fear or weakness to dictates with which they do not agree but which they do not have the courage to oppose.'[32] To Marshall, leadership often was more influenced by events than events were influenced by leadership; leaders should, and ultimately could, only use their authority 'within the limits of the Party's policy and principles'; and, while a leader should exercise a guiding influence and carry ultimate responsibility as spokesman on major issues, 'policy making and the strategy and tactics of the party are more the product of collective thinking.'[33]

There were of course differences not only of personality or over tactics between Muldoon and Marshall. The two men also continued to differ on a number of key policy issues throughout 1973. On superannuation, for example, Muldoon favoured a universal scheme 'to be done on a Social Security basis'; Marshall, while leaving all 'options open', believed it should not be a 'universal compulsory scheme'.[34] Marshall thought that 'competition was the best regulator of prices', but Muldoon argued that it was impossible to 'go back to laissez faire' and 'free up the management economy'.[35]

Muldoon also disagreed with Gair and others who wanted the abolition of the Maori electorates and with Talboys and Gill over nationalism and defence issues. Supported by Holyoake, Muldoon told Gair that the Maori seats should remain until 'the Maoris asked for abolition',[36] and he warned his colleagues against 'too much flag waving' because the RSA was a 'spent force', there were 'not many votes in defence', and National should take care 'not to antagonise the young'.[37]

While overseas in October 1973 Muldoon attended the Commonwealth Parliamentary Association conference in London; visited Germany, Sweden, the Soviet Union and the United States; and had talks at the EEC, the IMF, and GATT. He particularly examined the topic of superannuation, which Labour had made a major item of policy, and extended his knowledge of international affairs.[38]

Kirk's dominance over Marshall continued beyond the 1972 election. While Marshall worked quietly and systematically behind the scenes, in co-operation with Chapman and the party's new general director, Barrie Leay, to renew National's organisation and rethink its policy, Kirk and Labour rode roughshod over the Opposition during the debates in Parliament. National MPs became worried about their performance in the House, particularly in the evenings. Gair observed: 'the feeling that came through quite a number from the caucus was a very strong, aggressive personality like Kirk needed somebody other than Marshall to oppose him. And Muldoon seemed to be made for the job.'[39] Marshall and his wife were ever-conscious of his earlier heart attack in 1964, and he was later to reveal in his memoirs that again during 1973 'my heart was causing a certain amount of alarm and consternation' and he was receiving medical treatment.[40] There was a widespread perception that National's leader had neither the will nor the capacity to cope with the tough and arrogant Labour leader and his colleagues. As Gordon later commented, Marshall had 'not enough fire in his belly'.[41] Only Muldoon among National MPs seemed able to counter the often personal and brutal debating style with which Kirk repeatedly lashed the Opposition. Had Kirk not existed, or had he died and been replaced by Rowling earlier than he was, National's caucus might not have felt compelled to reject Marshall and turn to Muldoon. But from about July 1973 Muldoon claimed that the possibility of a leadership change was 'raised with me regularly by caucus members'. He added that, while he listened, he refused to campaign actively to replace Marshall.[42]

Muldoon always responded to a challenge. Many Labour MPs genuinely hated Muldoon and most attacked him throughout his career with a cruel contempt and a selective viciousness which they rarely showed towards his colleagues. Perhaps that was because most also feared him. Muldoon infuriated them and deepened the animosity by his retaliation – he called it counterpunching. He kept with him in the House a large file of anti-Labour material, key statistics and significant quotes from Labour MPs and party officials which could be used if necessary in unexpected ways. He also frequently challenged the chair and pushed to the limit points of order and the Standing Orders of parliamentary debates.

Throughout 1973 and 1974 Muldoon found himself repeatedly at odds with the Speaker, Stan Whitehead. Prior to becoming Speaker, Whitehead had been one of Labour's most robust debaters and, unlike most Speakers, he continued to attend caucus meetings and take part publicly in partisan political polemic. Muldoon questioned Whitehead's impartiality on numerous occasions and believed that, while National was determined to disrupt and discredit the Government in the House, Labour MPs were equally responsible for the fractious, disorderly and personalised nature of many debates.

On Friday 27 July 1973 one debate got seriously out of control. Labour MPs including the Deputy Prime Minister, Hugh Watt, criticised National MPs particularly Thomson for taking their wives with them on overseas trips. Muldoon replied in a speech that Watt had taken his wife to Europe for a month's holiday. Watt interjected, 'Better than going with someone else's wife', to which Muldoon retorted, 'Well, the Minister would be a judge of that.' Watt, who had separated from his wife and then had a series of relationships, burst into tears and left the House but returned later, sitting dejectedly 'with his head in his hands'.[43] Kirk was furious and according to his secretary, who recalled that Kirk regarded Muldoon as 'evil', 'pointed a finger at Mr Marshall and said quietly, "Don't you ever let that creature (Mr Muldoon) do that sort of thing again."'[44]

The following Tuesday, when the House reconvened to discuss the Estimates of the Minister of Finance, Muldoon was sat down by the Chairman of Committees for refusing to apologise to the chair during a heated exchange over a point of order. Muldoon, supported by other National MPs including Marshall and Holyoake, challenged the ruling on the grounds that he had apologised and did not need to do it again, but following a fiery exchange he was ordered from the House.

Muldoon's clashes in Parliament with the Speaker, and the Chairman of Committees, led to concern and some criticism within the National caucus. Marshall raised the matter from the chair, stating that while Muldoon might well have been frustrated, he had to show 'discipline in face [of] provocation' and should 'avoid incidents' to which the public reacted badly. He was supported by the former Speaker, Roy Jack. Gill, Lapwood and Schultz, who were Muldoon supporters, agreed that Muldoon was 'tarnishing his image' and being hurt even within the National Party by such actions, but Gair appealed for the rest of the front bench to support Muldoon more in the House. Muldoon was unrepentant and contrasted his performance with that of the 'rabble' on Labour's backbench.

Not only MPs from both sides were criticising Muldoon publicly. At a meeting of the Public Expenditure Committee on 24 July 1973, Jack Lewin, the Government Statistician, referred to Muldoon's 'personal animus' and the 'unfortunate malleability of Treasury and the State Services Commission' when Muldoon had been Minister of Finance. The Secretary of the Treasury, Lang, responded: 'At no time did Mr. Muldoon direct me or attempt to direct me about what recommendations I should make on any issue concerning the Department of Statistics on which Treasury was asked to report.'[45] Muldoon defended himself in the House and Rowling, the Labour Minister responsible for the Government Statistician, declined to comment. A few days later Lewin became head of the Department of Trade and Industry.

Despite the misgivings of some of his beleaguered colleagues, however, Muldoon became in time their undisputed champion, standing between them and the savaging government majority. Marshall worked hard administratively and gained people's respect. Muldoon did the fighting politically and gained the headlines and eventually the sometimes grudging gratitude and loyalty of a majority of National's caucus.

Although Marshall recognised that Muldoon was a more aggressive and effective debater in the House than himself, he was confident he would remain leader and win the 1975 election. By early 1974, however, some of Muldoon's admirers, who had never accepted the 1972 selection of Marshall as irrevocable, were moving among the caucus advocating a change. Although Muldoon did not openly plot a coup, he did little to discourage it. Marshall lived with his family in Wellington. In Opposition, Muldoon flatted with Talboys, Gordon, Thomson, Talbot and Venn Young in a house in Hawkestone Street. Late at night, after Marshall had gone home, Muldoon would remain drinking and chatting with caucus colleagues, reviving their flagging spirits and discussing ways of attacking the government. Gair, Gill, Sloane, McLachlan, McCready, Walker and Lapwood were the core of the draft-Muldoon group, with Gill and Sloane responsible for most of the lobbying of their colleagues. Significantly, none of them except Gair was a senior National MP. They had growing support, however, from National's front bench. Many of those who had supported Marshall in 1972 had retired or been defeated. Marshall estimated that, of the 16 MPs who left Parliament in 1972, 11 were his supporters and only 5 Muldoon's.[46] Others, such as Adams-Schneider, Gordon, and Talboys, who still preferred Marshall personally, now felt that only Muldoon could counter Kirk and give National a chance of winning the 1975 election.[47] The impression grew that Holyoake also favoured a change to Muldoon, an impression Holyoake did nothing to deny. Slowly, a consensus built up among the MPs that a change of leader was both necessary and inevitable.

Gordon, for example, who had supported Marshall in 1972 and who played golf with him several times a month, recorded in 1974 why he felt Marshall was no longer suitable as leader.[48] Caucus meetings were 'slack' under Marshall's chairmanship. They 'inevitably started late' and Marshall 'suffered a legacy from his Teheran heart attack of never having a get-up-and-go attitude', which meant he only performed well in 'one debate while we were in Opposition'. Gordon noted that 'Members were upset that they could never find him except in exceptional circumstances before 9.30 and sometimes 10 a.m. when the members themselves started at 8 or 8.30. Quite often important matters such as adjournment notices were held up waiting for him to arrive.'[49] By contrast Muldoon, in his own words, 'for years always roamed around the members' offices keeping up with their day to day problems and ideas.'[50]

By early 1974 Muldoon's attack on the Labour Government's handling of the economy and on its controversial compulsory superannuation scheme was attracting considerable press comment, much though not all of it favourable. The *Sunday News*, for example, in March declared, 'It's all Rob Muldoon, working away like a one-man rock-grinding machine.'[51] 'Gallery George', in *Truth* a few months later, went even further, observing that 'I've been around for some time but never before have I seen such a concentration of venom directed against one hard-working, dedicated man . . . Are the 55 Government Members panicking because of just one man among them? Why else do they have to perform like a frightened school of minnows in the presence of one barracuda?'[52] He went on to point out the David and Goliath nature of the battle with Tizard as Minister of Finance, for example, being able to call on all the expertise of the Treasury, Reserve Bank, and government economists, specialists, statisticians and departments, while 'Rob Muldoon is on his own – a former Minister of Finance, two years out of office, armed only with memories and the fruits of his own labours'. Unlike the press, Muldoon did not see himself at that time as a 'one-man band' and indeed commented that '1973 in the House was Brian Talboys' year as far as the Opposition was concerned and there was no more effective debater on the Government side either.'[53]

During 1974 a new phenomenon appeared, talkback radio on the Auckland station Radio I. Both Labour and National tried to use this opportunity to criticise their opponents and to publicise their own personnel and policies. Muldoon was particularly aware of the potential and in June addressed a National Party seminar on the topic 'The content of what should be said by callers and the techniques involved.'[54] He was to retain an interest and expertise in talkback radio for the rest of his life.

Chapman and Gair both believed that the reorganisation of the party and the growing realisation that National might just have a chance of winning in 1975 made a leadership challenge even more attractive to some MPs.[55] By July 1974 a public opinion poll had Labour and National both on 44 per cent with Labour trending down and Muldoon polling 40 per cent compared to 13 per cent for Marshall as the most impressive non-Labour politician.[56] When National MPs believed that it would be at least 1978 before National could return to office there was no urgency to remove Marshall until after the 1975 election; but as the caucus became somewhat more aware of how brittle Labour's huge majority was, even before the death of Kirk and the economic downturn following the first oil shock in 1974, the need to have a dynamic leader became more evident. Leadership could be the deciding factor at the 1975 election.

The challenge to Marshall was initiated by Gair and Gill, who discussed the matter with Muldoon over lunch at Gill's home at Mairangi Bay during the Christmas–New Year holidays at the end of 1973. Muldoon said he could not campaign for the post but did nothing to dissuade the move.[57] Throughout the first half of 1974 his supporters worked towards creating a consensus for change. Marshall subsequently claimed he was unaware of what was going on, though nearly everyone else in caucus was. This ignorance was in itself an indictment of Marshall's leadership and a revelation of how few loyal supporters he now had. It seems incredible that no one alerted Marshall, isolated though he tended to have become, but certainly he was not warned by those with the prime responsibility for doing so. Muldoon as deputy had a vested interest in not doing so and the two whips, who were supposed to keep the leader in touch with caucus opinion, were not only strong Muldoon supporters but two of the most active conspirators. The senior whip was Harry Lapwood and the junior whip Colin McLachlan, two of Muldoon's drinking friends. Lapwood, in particular, bitterly resented Marshall. When Marshall had selected his cabinet in 1972 Lapwood, who had been in Parliament since 1960, was not included. When he asked Marshall why he had been overlooked, Marshall had told him bluntly that he was not cabinet material and that he drank too much.[58] That does not, however, explain why senior MPs who were Marshall's friends, such as Talboys or Gordon, did not impress on Marshall earlier than they eventually did the seriousness of the challenge to his leadership.

On 3 April 1974 Marshall left New Zealand for a six-week overseas tour. By the time he returned on 15 May there were widespread rumours within the party of a challenge to his leadership. Muldoon, who according to Gordon played throughout a 'minimal role himself in the challenge',[59] had certainly not encouraged a change during Marshall's absence, and Gair in retrospect believed that on the contrary 'Marshall's absence seemed to put a moratorium' on the campaign to replace him.[60] As one academic observer noted subsequently, 'to have attempted to move definitively at this time during the leader's absence would have been construed as an overly ambitious deputy stabbing Marshall in the back. Muldoon . . . wished to "inherit" . . . Moreover, he was probably insufficiently sure of his numerical support'.[61] Muldoon had been overconfident in 1972. What he did do, however, was seize the opportunity provided by Marshall's absence to perform very creditably as a leader and allow his admirers to contrast his aggressive and effective performance with that of Marshall's to the latter's detriment.

On his return from overseas Marshall appeared to realise that his position had weakened but not by how much. Muldoon, in private consultations with Marshall reporting on events during the leader's absence, did not alert him to the situation, but Chapman, Leay and Symmans went to Marshall and told him that his MPs were in revolt.[62] At first Marshall refused to believe them. When Chapman suggested Marshall ask the MPs, he replied that it was not his style, he had been invited to be leader, and he would remain so without lobbying until requested to step down. Marshall subsequently invited all the MPs to dinner in two groups but it was too little too late to shore up his position.

Marshall had widespread support within the party organisation and might well have been able to mobilise it behind him had he wished and had he acted earlier and more decisively. Despite his inaction, however, the rumours of discontent in the caucus and of the possibility of a leadership challenge were discussed at a meeting of the Dominion Executive on 12 June 1974. The party was preparing to spend a great deal of money on publicising its leader in the run-up to the 1975 election and wanted to be sure who that leader would be. Egan Ogier, chairman of the Wellington Division and a Marshall supporter, prior to lunch gave notice that in the afternoon session he would move a motion that the Executive ask caucus to support Marshall strongly as leader for the next election, thus hopefully ending any further speculation. Marshall and Muldoon were both absent but Adams-Schneider, the sole MP present, immediately contacted Talboys and together they advised the Executive that it was doubtful caucus would give such an assurance and that, indeed, such a resolution by the Executive in support of Marshall might produce the opposite result to its intention. Talboys told the Executive that although most MPs respected and wanted to be loyal to Marshall, most believed that only Muldoon was a match for Kirk. The Executive, nevertheless, voted without dissent to ask caucus to declare that the party was united behind Marshall and that there would be no change of leader before the next election.[63] Chapman, a long-time Marshall supporter who had been opposed by Muldoon when he was elected president in 1973, conveyed the resolution to both Marshall, who welcomed it as an endorsement, and Muldoon, who said he did not believe the Executive's motion reflected the current thinking of a majority of caucus. Marshall agreed that Muldoon could sound out other members of caucus and Muldoon subsequently spoke to nearly all on a one-to-one basis.

MPs can be and often are very self-centred when it comes to retaining their own seats or advancing their cabinet prospects. The National Party organisation in reforming itself had overhauled its candidate selection procedures and hoped to have all sitting MPs reselected by 30 September 1974, a year before the 1975 election. While the MPs were happy to have early confirmation of their candidacies, they were worried that the party was allowing, even encouraging, open challenges to sitting members. Caucus believed that Marshall should be making it very plain that no sitting MP should be challenged. Marshall tended to take the view that selection was a matter for the party organisation, not the caucus. Muldoon, on the other hand, clearly suggested that he understood his colleagues' concern and as leader would make it plain to the National Party Conference scheduled for 26–29 July that there should be no challenges to sitting MPs. While Muldoon denied that deals were made with about seven MPs who feared challenges in their electorates, he admitted that, 'I am not stupid. They know precisely that I would tackle the party.'[64]

Marshall was slow to appreciate the seriousness of his position and the extent of Muldoon's support. Once he did start consulting MPs during the latter part of June, however, he found his position dangerously eroded. On 27 June, shortly before going into caucus, Talboys and Gordon, who had both supported Marshall in 1972, advised him that not only would he be overwhelmingly defeated if he forced a ballot in caucus but that Talboys and Gordon had themselves decided to vote for Muldoon, as had three other senior MPs who had once been strong Marshall supporters: Gair, Adams-Schneider and Thomson.[65] Marshall then on 2 July circulated a long statement setting out his record and position and saying that while he did not intend canvassing for support, he wanted colleagues to say in a secret ballot whether or not the leadership issue should be top of the agenda for the next caucus meeting on Thursday 4 July. The letter and ballot were distributed and subsequently collected by the whips. Muldoon, as soon as he received Marshall's letter, also circulated a shorter letter to every member of the National caucus including Marshall, though Marshall in his *Memoirs* subsequently denied receiving it.[66]

Responding to Marshall's memorandum, Muldoon agreed that 'a unanimous vote of support in the Leader' had been passed at a meeting of the Dominion Executive three weeks previously. He then noted that Talboys and Adams-Schneider had pointed out to the Executive that 'the decision as to who should be our leader must rest with caucus', and expressed doubt whether caucus would support the Executive's unanimous decision. Following the Executive meeting Marshall, Muldoon and Chapman had discussed the resolution 'at some length' and Muldoon told the others 'that I do not believe that our present leader will beat Kirk during the four weeks of an election campaign, and that those views are shared by many, many people who have approached me throughout the country.' Muldoon told Marshall and Chapman that if a majority of MPs wanted to retain Marshall then he would continue to support him also, but he had wanted permission to approach MPs individually to confirm their views. He had spoken with 28 of the 30 other MPs. The two he assumed would be irrevocably hostile to him and would not be worth contacting were Percy Allen and David Thomson.[67] Thomson was hurt by being taken for granted and told Muldoon so. Muldoon apologised and Thomson subsequently became one of Muldoon's firmest supporters. Muldoon concluded his letter by asserting that only 'three or four are disinclined to see any open discussion of the matter . . . The remainder have indicated to me that the electorate, as far as they are concerned, and they themselves, wish to see a change of leader.' Muldoon claimed that Chapman, Talboys and Gordon had independently found from their discussions with MPs that Muldoon had majority support and suggested that MPs convey their wishes individually in writing to Marshall, so that preferably the leadership question could be resolved without a formal challenge and vote.

When the votes were counted on the night of Wednesday 3 July, there was a clear majority in favour of opening up the leadership. It was not as overwhelming, however, as Muldoon and his supporters hoped for or later claimed. According to Marshall, 19 MPs wanted a leadership vote and 13 opposed it.[68] It was also clear that a vote which Marshall would probably lose might split the party. The next morning Marshall invited Gair to his office and Gair, who was not as unbiased an adviser as Marshall might have thought, told the leader he would be lucky to get three or four votes and strongly urged Marshall not to stand for re-election when caucus met later that morning. Marshall was reluctant to divide the party or demonstrate by a formal vote the disunity in caucus.[69] As soon as caucus met at 10 a.m. on Thursday 4 July, Marshall announced his resignation as leader. At a caucus meeting the following Tuesday, 9 July, Muldoon was elected to the leadership unopposed with Talboys becoming deputy leader and Gordon being given the number three ranking on National's front bench. Although Muldoon was elected leader unanimously and with acclamation, a note of caution was sounded by Talboys, who in moving Muldoon's nomination noted that, 'There is concern in the minds of many members of caucus, as in the minds of people outside, that Rob must be prevailed upon to find an image that is not always as aggressive as he can be.'[70]

When Muldoon had challenged Marshall for the leadership in 1972, he had asked Holyoake for his support. Holyoake replied by asking, 'Have you got the numbers, my boy?' When Muldoon said 'Yes', Holyoake responded, 'I don't think so.' In 1974 when Muldoon canvassed Holyoake the former leader repeated the same question. When Muldoon again answered in the affirmative, Holyoake on that occasion stated, 'I think you have too.'[71]

The role of Holyoake in the 1974 leadership change was neither impartial nor passive. He started to advise individual MPs that he personally preferred Muldoon to Marshall and believed National would only win in 1975 if Muldoon became the leader. When Marshall became aware of a possible leadership challenge he approached Holyoake for support and was devastated when Holyoake admitted that not only did he know of the challenge but he was not prepared to help Marshall against it. Marshall believed that his almost fifteen years as Holyoake's deputy had earned him Holyoake's loyalty, but Holyoake, like Muldoon, saw loyalty as a relative virtue, not an absolute. Holyoake and Muldoon supported totally, and in Muldoon's case sometimes to a fault, those who were totally loyal to them. Neither felt any obligation to followers or colleagues who were not themselves totally loyal. Holyoake believed Marshall had not always sprung to his defence when as Prime Minister he was attacked during the 1960s, and he still resented the pressure Marshall had put him under to retire after 1969.

Holyoake was also the only MP who let slip to the press that there might be a change of leadership. Throughout the three weeks prior to Marshall's resignation, despite the Dominion Executive resolution, the discussions at two caucus meetings, the letters to all MPs from both Marshall and Muldoon, the private meetings held by Muldoon with all but two MPs, and the intensive lobbying by Muldoon's supporters, no one in the Press Gallery appeared to be aware of the situation. On the night before the 4 July caucus meeting a large group of MPs and journalists were drinking in McLachlan's room. Holyoake who was present hinted that the journalists might expect a change in leader. His remark was treated as a joke by all the reporters except one from Radio Windy, which on its 9 a.m. news bulletin the next morning correctly predicted that Marshall would resign that day.[72]

Following the change of leadership, Chapman stated publicly that the Dominion Executive had not unanimously endorsed Marshall a few weeks before but had simply 'asked the caucus to tell it who was going to be the leader of the party at the 1975 election'.[73] Forewarned by Marshall of his intention to stand down, Chapman had contacted all five divisional chairmen of the party and obtained their agreement to ratify the impending caucus selection of Muldoon. Although Chapman announced that 'it is the grass roots of the party, the ordinary members, who have expressed a desire for change',[74] the replacement of Marshall by Muldoon was certainly not universally welcomed throughout the party organisation. In the Auckland Division, where many of the key activists were Muldoon admirers, his selection was popular, though more so among the rank and file than among the more senior party officials.[75] The Divisional Executive immediately passed unanimously and with acclamation a motion noting 'with pleasure' Muldoon's election as leader.[76] In Canterbury and Otago-Southland opinion was divided. The Wellington and Waikato divisions were from the first suspicious of, if not hostile to, Muldoon. Most of the more prominent Wellington activists liked Marshall and distrusted Muldoon. In the Waikato, in an Executive debate on 7 May 1974 on whether Marshall or Muldoon was preferred as leader, eighteen speakers favoured Marshall, two Muldoon and one was undecided. The Division resolved, 'That we as a Division support our present leader Jack Marshall'.[77] A few weeks later when Muldoon replaced Marshall, the divisional chairman, Jack O'Halloran, expressed great sadness at the party's 'grievous loss' and reports from the electorates revealed only Carter's Raglan came out strongly in favour of Muldoon.[78] Not all prominent, older National Party members outside Auckland were upset by the change of leader. In addition to the Holyoakes, Hanan's widow, for example, wrote to Muldoon that she was 'delighted' and that 'I know Ralph's eyes would have sparkled to see you at the helm for he saw you as the brightest star on the horizon.'[79] She also praised Muldoon's 'interest in human problems and in social welfare'.

In contrast, Muldoon's accession to the leadership concerned some younger urban liberals in the party who had in 1973 organised themselves into a ginger group called Pol-Link. Pol-Link believed that National had got out of touch with younger people and that 'for us to stick to our present policies or to revert to old style conservatism would be to sound the death knell.'[80] To them Muldoon personified a reassertion and continuation of the old-style Holyoake tradition which they were seeking to reject. The 1974 National Party Conference in Auckland shortly after the change of leader was an unpleasant affair. A number of Dominion Councillors, led by Julian Watts and John Schnellenberg of Wellington, both Pol-Link members, bitterly lamented the removal of Marshall and made their views known at the councillors' meeting immediately preceding the conference. Particularly in the informal discussions among delegates off the floor of conference, there was considerable sympathy and support expressed for Marshall and widespread condemnation of Muldoon and criticism of the caucus for changing the leadership.

Some political observers suggested that Marshall had also damaged Muldoon with a speech 'delivered with consummate political skill' at the conference.[81]

Marshall's speech, which made it clear that he believed he had been deposed unjustly, turned the attitude of Marshall's supporters towards Muldoon from coolness into hostility, and from that time Muldoon's many critics outside the National Party had allies within it. Muldoon never managed to win over the most critical.

At the conference church service on 28 July Muldoon was embarrassed to be given to read a passage of Scripture chosen by Dean Rymer before the change of leadership but which in the circumstances should have been changed.[82] The passage was John Chapter 15 which commenced, 'I am the true vine' and went on to say that other unproductive branches not attached to the vine would be thrown into the fire and burned. This appeared by implication to be adding insult to the injury Marshall had sustained.

Muldoon was further embarrassed at the conference when he asserted from the platform that he believed no one in the hall would advocate the legalisation of marijuana. He was rendered uncharacteristically speechless when his son Gavin, sitting with the Young National delegation at the front of the hall, called out, 'I would.'[83]

The day he was ousted as leader, Marshall described his successor as 'critical, aggressive, abrasive and destructive'. Commenting on those attributes, Muldoon subsequently admitted, 'I'm sure they're accurate but I'm equally sure that they're not complete'. He observed, 'I think I've got other qualities' as well.[84] Muldoon accepted that he polarised people but denied he did so deliberately, arguing rather that he said what he thought on the issues of the day and some people agreed with him and others disagreed. All knew, however, where he stood on the issue. He also conceded that his counterpunches were often harder than the provocation and that he was prepared to use personal attack against opponents when he believed they had also descended to personalities. But he protested that 'Someone's got to attack me personally, before I respond.'[85]

Even after becoming leader, Muldoon continued to distrust and despise the Speaker and in an article in *Truth* on 6 May 1975 commented adversely on the Speaker's ability and impartiality. As a result he found himself brought before Parliament's powerful Privileges Committee on a charge of contempt.[86] He also continued to speak out controversially on other topics. In the weeks following his selection as leader, for example, he made some controversial comments about young Maori and Pacific Islanders who, often because of drunkenness, committed crimes. He suggested that the former should be prohibited from living in the cities and sent back to their whanau or extended family in the rural areas, while the latter should be deported back to the Pacific Island from which they came.[87] Although he continued to express such sentiments, he was quick to condemn an embarrassing article published by the Tamaki Young Nationals critical of racial equality and suggesting that dark-skinned people were inherently inferior.[88] Trade unions also came under attack, with Muldoon accusing some union officials of being industrial wreckers who intimidated those of their members who disagreed with militant tactics. Despite attempts to get specific examples from him, Muldoon continued only to generalise, once again leading to accusations that he was making political capital out of a fallacy.[89]

The British television personality David Frost decided to host a television panel debate on 'the state of the unions' in New Zealand. The programme was pre-recorded on the afternoon of Sunday 25 August 1974. Among those participating were Muldoon and the trade unionists Tom Skinner, Bill Andersen and Tony Neary.[90] Originally the programme had been designed as a debate between Kirk and Muldoon in front of an invited and participating audience drawn from the unions, the Labour Party and the National Party. Kirk, however, was too ill and Skinner took his place. When Muldoon started to overwhelm Skinner, Andersen and Neary, who personified the left and right wings of the trade union movement, both started to interject and were soon involved in angry exchanges with Muldoon. Pandemonium reigned and even one of Muldoon's greatest admirers who was present thought he went too far and 'didn't come over well'.[91]

Frost and the unionists challenged Muldoon to produce evidence which he claimed to have of intimidation and ballot-rigging in union affairs and suggested that even if he did have correspondence alleging such actions they were probably exceptions not the rule in union affairs. Muldoon expressed regret that Skinner and Neary were not honest enough to acknowledge awareness of the 'gangsterism' that existed in the union movement, and the debate which raged for almost an hour and a half became very heated.[92] He was particularly offended by Neary's implication that he was following the example of Hitler in seeking to destroy trade unions preparatory to establishing a dictatorship.

Skinner, Neary and others always claimed that Muldoon's 'wild public statements about alleged gangsterism in unions and rigging of ballots' were made without any evidence and that he did not have the correspondence he claimed to have.[93] In fact Muldoon had in his possession at that time letters and affidavits alleging recent illegalities or intimidation in five different unions – the Freezing Workers, Drivers, Engineers, Boilermakers, and Pulp and Paper Workers – but was reluctant to use names and details publicly because he feared retaliation against his informants.[94]

Even after the filming of the programme ended, members of the audience continued to debate among themselves and with Muldoon. Thea took strong exception to comments the Labour MP for Eden, Mike Moore, had made about her husband and told him so, and other female members of the National Party roundly abused Skinner and Andersen, the latter being struck with a handbag. When the programme was finally shown, many National Party supporters more used to Marshall's dignified courtesy and calm reason were appalled by the combative image Muldoon projected and the programme reinforced a negative judgement of him already formed by a further incident in which he had been embroiled later the same day.

When the filming of the programme on the unions ended, Muldoon left the studio and went to a meeting of the Landlords' Association, which was being held in the Peter Pan Cabaret in Auckland's Queen Street.[95] Muldoon had been invited to address the meeting by the Wellington businessman Bob Jones.[96] A crowd of about forty demonstrators abused those entering the meeting, including Muldoon, who was booed and jeered at and greeted with cries of 'Heil Hitler'. Firecrackers were exploded and flour bombs thrown. The nineteen police present, however, prevented the protest getting totally out of hand. At the end of the meeting, which was disrupted temporarily by a bomb threat, Muldoon and some 150 invited guests mixed socially while enjoying food and drink. Muldoon's inhibitions may well have been loosened not only by the adrenalin released from the Frost debate and the meeting but also by alcohol consumed at the end of the day. Indeed, Jones believed that by the time he came to leave the Peter Pan Muldoon 'was roaring drunk'.[97] A uniformed police sergeant assured Muldoon that the situation outside was under control and Muldoon decided to leave by the front door. A plainclothed police sergeant at that point suggested he should leave by a side door which also opened into Queen Street, but Muldoon chose to continue out by the front door. Despite the demonstration organisers' assurances to the police that there would be no violence, 'without any real warning the demonstrators violently attacked the police, quite obviously with a view to attacking Mr Muldoon'.[98] Muldoon vanished under a scrum of demonstrators and was pushed up against his car. Aided by a policeman he broke clear. According to a witness, described by the police as 'a reputable and independent bystander', Muldoon, who 'was white with rage', was immediately 'accosted by two or three demonstrators . . . Muldoon charged into the demonstrators. I could see his arms going like pistons but did not see any blows land. The demonstrators retreated about 12 ft. down the road. One fell. I do not know whether or not he was struck by Mr. Muldoon or stumbled accidentally.' The Commissioner of Police noted that 'Mr Muldoon did receive injury as the result of his being assaulted, but I am sure he would have been more violently assaulted had it not been for the actions of police present, several of whom were even more seriously injured.'[99] Muldoon blamed the Progressive Youth Movement in particular for the violent street clash. He had been hit in the face by a flour bomb, kicked in the leg by a young socialist son of parents active in Muldoon's own Tamaki National Party organisation,[100] shoved up against his car and, as he told a reporter, generally 'knocked about a bit'.[101] When he saw a 'couple of them coming at me', he 'clobbered one of them and he went down'.[102] Recalling the incident several years later, Muldoon wrote, 'it was obvious to me that the demonstrators were out to do physical damage, so I thumped the demonstrator as hard as I could and he went over backwards'.[103] Muldoon had then chased a group of demonstrators down the street allegedly calling out to them 'one at a time and you're welcome'.[104] Labour's deputy leader, Watt, immediately criticised Muldoon saying that street brawling was not in keeping with the dignity of the position of Leader of the Opposition.[105]

While many of National's traditional members and supporters were appalled by the street brawling of their new leader, others both within and without the party saw Muldoon's reaction as a natural, understandable and even admirable reaction to provocation. As Bob Jones observed in retrospect, 'that night provided the foundations for the evolvement of "Rob's Mob": for the transfer in allegiance of mainly male, normally Labour-voting ordinary Joe, not from Labour to National, but Labour to Muldoon. This was the sort of street-fighting leader they usually only dreamt about.'[106]

The daily newspapers almost universally condemned Muldoon's belligerence and reported that a worried National Party wanted to curb its new leader's abrasiveness in public.[107] The Peter Pan Cabaret scuffle, which was 'too much to stomach for the average National Party member',[108] and Muldoon's appearance on the Frost programme on trade unions[109] were cited as particularly negative incidents. Following the release of the police report on the Peter Pan incident, however, a *Dominion* editorial concluded that others in the media, particularly television, who had presented the incident as a 'brawl' with Muldoon in the wrong, were overlooking the fact that he had done nothing at the time to provoke the demonstrators, who were 'determined to assault him whatever the circumstances' and that Muldoon had every right to defend himself.[110]

Not all the protests against Muldoon provoked his retaliation or received media attention. For example, on 21 March 1975 two North Shore teenagers, aged 18 and 16, threw a pie in Muldoon's face at Auckland airport and he complained to the police. Later a lawyer arranged for the boys to visit him at his home and apologise. Muldoon accepted the apology, withdrew his complaint and asked the police not to prosecute.[111]

Muldoon rejected criticism, including some from within the National Party, of his aggressive performance on the Frost programme, arguing that people at least knew what he was thinking and where he stood on issues.[112] The *Auckland Star*, however, suggested that while National supporters wanted more action than they had seen when Marshall was the leader they did not want 'three-ringed circuses every day', which was what they were getting from Muldoon.[113]

The National Party was also very sensitive to the media's practice of portraying the party as a 'one man band' and motions were passed asking for more publicity to be given to the Deputy Leader and other key MPs.[114] As Highet reminded the critics, however, Muldoon 'can't please everybody' and party officials should be doing their best 'to convince our own membership that Mr. Muldoon is the right man in the right job at the right time and not run him down . . . he was a magnificent leader' though 'there had been difficulties over Mr. Muldoon's image'.[115] One of the organisers of Muldoon's coup against Marshall warned party officials that 'Bob Muldoon was [National's] only hope in November' and that 'the Labour Party must try to destroy him because they feared him.' All members of the National Party had to try to counter 'the vilification campaign against Mr. Muldoon by Labour and the leftist media.'[116]

In his leader's address to the August 1974 Dominion Council, Muldoon conceded that he was open to criticism for some of his recent actions such as the 'Peter Pan' incident but intended in future to appeal to the uncommitted voters with positive, concise and clear policies. After Kirk's death on 31 August, he stated that National had been working on a strategy to defeat Kirk rather than the

Labour Party, but new tactics might have to be adopted in the light of Rowling's style.[117] Chapman in response noted that it had to be recognised that 'we had elected as our Leader the most controversial MP since Bob Semple.'[118]

On other occasions Muldoon tried to defend himself by suggesting that he was being judged not by the totality of his behaviour but by a few negative incidents, particularly repeated television showing of lapses where he overreacted or slipped up and was seen in a bad light.[119] But usually he neither explained nor apologised, adopting a seemingly arrogant attitude of take me or leave me, love me or hate me, agree with me or disagree with me.

Muldoon had an astute political instinct for issues of concern to large sections of the public and the ability and audacity to exploit them. There is no doubt that he was a populist politician who imposed his own personality on the issues of the day and was not afraid to divide society by playing upon emotion and prejudice, although he also used facts and reason very effectively. Muldoon was adept at identifying a threat to the economy, society or nation and then putting himself forward as the person honest, strong or intelligent enough to deal with it. He was in many ways a master of the politics of division and diversion and was not reluctant to scapegoat unpopular minorities. His appeal to the 'decent bloke' and the 'ordinary New Zealander' meant that he often defined those people by attacking others who were not: the trade union gangster with a Liverpool accent; the financial speculators and swindlers; the rent-a-mob demonstrators; the ivory tower academics and trendy leftist students; the Maori radicals with European ancestry; Pacific Island overstayers; and thieves and bashers whose criminal activities threatened the security of law-abiding citizens.

By mid-1975 Muldoon was attracting enormous crowds wherever he spoke and had in the view of many journalists 'emerged as New Zealand's most divisive political figure in living memory, polarising emotions for and against himself in a manner that brings out the worst in opponents and supporters'.[120] Labour was pursuing 'a deliberate policy of attacking him with all the invective they can muster . . . retaliating in extravagant, emotive condemnation', but even while attacking his aggressive, abrasive and divisive influence his critics still had to admit that, 'If for some he is a devil, for others he already represents a new political messiahship.'[121]

There was some resentment among traditional National Party members about the influx into the party during the 1970s of former Labour Party supporters, and even former communists, attracted by Muldoon. One long-term party official remarked that before Muldoon became leader, 'I could have gone into a room and known it was a National Party gathering just by glancing around but [after] I'd go to the National Party gatherings and think I was at the local football club . . . He brought a whole new group in.'[122] Challenged even by members of his own Tamaki electorate committee on this, Muldoon replied, 'It's rather like gathering in lost sheep. We should rejoice when they come.' His audience erupted in laughter. Behind Muldoon's head on the wall of the Sunday School hall in which the meeting was being held was the text, 'Rejoice with me for I have found my sheep which was lost. Luke 15 v. 6'.[123] On another occasion when questioned about his appeal to some non-traditional National voters, Muldoon responded, 'I think there are some people who believe National should be the party of the "correct" people. But there aren't enough people of that kind to win any election in this country. The election is won by the ordinary bloke.'[124]

CHAPTER 11

The 1975 Election

ULDOON WAS ELECTED LEADER ON 9 JULY 1974. THE
following day his first autobiography *The Rise and Fall of a Young Turk*
was published. Within four months it had been reprinted three times
and had sold over 28,000 copies. The timing of this publication was fortuitous and
certainly was a very positive start to both his leadership of the National Party and
his extended campaign over the following seventeen months to win the 1975
election. On 1 December 1972 David Elworthy, the chief editor of the publishers
A. H. and A. W. Reed, had written to Muldoon saying that although his firm had
some time before seen the first draft of a biography of Muldoon by Denis Wederell,
they had felt at the time that 'we would much prefer to see a book written by the
man himself.'[1] After further negotiations it was agreed that Muldoon would write
such a book and would receive 12.5 per cent royalties up to 5000 copies and 15 per
cent thereafter.[2] A contract was signed on 5 February 1973 and Muldoon delivered
the completed manuscript on 1 February 1974. It was to be the first of four such
books Muldoon wrote over the next ten years.

Muldoon's publishers were delighted with *The Rise and Fall of a Young Turk*.
The vice-chairman of Reed told Muldoon after reading the typescript that 'it was
so honest, comprehensive, non-aggressive and non-defensive . . . I enjoyed your
writing tremendously', and Reed's chief editor predicted that the book would be
'the New Zealand bestseller of 1974'.[3] Elworthy subsequently recorded that the
'unprecedented demand . . . has caught us all by surprise – booksellers, printers
and publishers . . . *no* political book published by any New Zealand publisher has
sold well in the past . . . Comparatively few books published in New Zealand sell
more than 5,000 copies.'[4]

The Rise and Fall of a Young Turk was written in longhand and then typed up.
The three subsequent autobiographical books, *Muldoon* (1977), *My Way* (1981),
and *Number 38* (1986), and his *The New Zealand Economy: A Personal View* (1985),
were typed up from dictation onto a recorder. Muldoon tried to write a chapter
each week, planning its theme and structure and collecting material in between
other commitments. He then dictated about 5000 words for each chapter over the

weekend. All the books were written in a remarkably short time and fitted in around a busy life. Muldoon, for example, agreed to write the second book, *Muldoon*, on 19 November 1976 and delivered the typescript to the publisher on 30 April 1977. *My Way* was commissioned on 8 August 1980 and the manuscript was delivered on 31 January 1981. Muldoon's books were, he commented, his own recollections and views and were certainly not intended to be balanced and objective.[5] Although all his books were written clearly, *The Rise and Fall of a Young Turk* was much better written than the three later autobiographical works, which were more episodic reminiscences. They lacked systematic chronological development and meandered from interesting analysis and fascinating insight to boring and superficial narrative and self-serving opinions, which also sometimes repeated material from the earlier books. He had a good eye and memory, however, for humorous incidents.

Besides discussing his life, Muldoon used the books to record his personal values and views. He clearly respected courage, intelligent pragmatism and humanitarianism but despised abstruse and non-practical political or economic theory. He also disliked ideas and influences imported from overseas rather than ones which had evolved indigenously within New Zealand's own history and culture. Patriotism and a genuine belief in helping the poor and the powerless through the social security system are two repeated themes. His books were not the memoirs of a retired politician – balanced, reflective, enjoying the advantage of hindsight – but were very much the work of an active politician anticipating a long future and seeking to present his qualities and opinions in the best possible light. He saw the making of New Zealand into a creditor nation with greater overseas reserves than overseas debt in 1972 as his greatest achievement and the National Superannuation policy of 1975 as the social contribution which gave him most satisfaction.

Certainly, *The Rise and Fall of a Young Turk*, which finally sold some 32,500 copies and earned him over $25,000 in royalties, was much more successful commercially than any of the other books. It had a curiosity value in that it was unusual for a New Zealand politician to write such an autobiography at all, let alone at a midway point in his career.[6] Even though Muldoon took orders in caucus for copies of his second book, *Muldoon*, and everyone except Roy Jack bought at least one, that book did not sell as well to the general public and the publishers asked Muldoon not to publicise the number sold because 'it would cause difficulties within the trade'.[7] *My Way*, which had a print run of 15,000 copies, sold 9240, with the rest remaindered. Muldoon received royalties on that book of some $15,000.[8] Only 4000 copies of *Number 38* were printed in 1986 and they were largely presold to bookshops prior to publication.[9]

The Rise and Fall of a Young Turk was a major factor in preventing the publication of a well-researched and more objective biography of Muldoon. Denis Wederell, the editor of the Manawatu *Evening Standard*, carefully carried out research during the late 1960s and collected a great deal of material before drafting the outline of a biography which he hoped to write and publish before the 1972 election. The publishers A. H. and A. W. Reed, however, decided in 1969 that such a book would not be viable because a book published by them on the 1969 election had not sold well and a book on Muldoon would have to compete with proposed biographies of Ralph Hanan and Walter Nash.[10] Reed also felt that Muldoon needed 'a few more laurels and a few more scars' before he was a substantial enough figure for a publishable biography. Reed's editor, G. C. A. Wall, thought his company's decision not to publish a biography by Wederell was 'all wrong'. He told Wederell, 'Muldoon's star is in the ascendant; come Labour or come National in November [1969], he'll stay in the public eye; he's the best subject for political biography this century bar maybe Savage and Fraser; the day must come.'[11] By 1972, when Wederell was prepared to take the project up again, Muldoon had decided that he would write his own autobiography, which Reed preferred to publish rather than a biography.[12] Wederell placed all his research material and the draft of his book in the Alexander Turnbull Library.

In 1978, shortly before the election of that year, a Wellington journalist, Spiro Zavos, drawing heavily on Wederell's research and using and reinterpreting Muldoon's first two autobiographies, published a biography *The Real Muldoon*. Zavos, who had over a period of years observed and discussed Muldoon with a friend and colleague, Warwick Roger, was motivated into writing his biography by dismay at the 'naivety of Citizens for Rowling . . . I was infuriated by their fanaticism and by their . . . ramming uninformed opinions down the throats of well-informed educated people. Their total misreading of Muldoon was one of my prime motivations.'[13]

As a result Zavos wrote a not totally unsympathetic analysis of Muldoon and criticised both Labour's obsession with him and Labour's consistent abuse of him. While Zavos's conclusion that Muldoon was a much more effective politician than Rowling was not surprising, his observation that Muldoon was much more accessible than Kirk 'to ordinary people' such as the Irish peace activist Mairead Corrigan or the Maori gangs was a revelation. So also were his comments: 'I think of Walter Nash's love of people in the mass, but not being able to stand them as individuals. Muldoon . . . attacks trade unionists in the mass, but when Toby Hill, a militant, was in hospital, Muldoon was one of the few politicians to visit him.'[14]

Most controversial at the time, however, was Zavos's astute overall assessment that Muldoon, despite his intelligence, hard work and tenacity, was an essentially cautious politician who did not take risks, and whose political philosophy was 'reactionary and sterile . . . short-term and reek[ing] of expediency'.[15] Muldoon, said Zavos, was a superb manager of detail but lacked any great vision. Prophetically, Zavos observed: 'There is something of the Ted Heath about Muldoon. Both men became leaders of a Conservative party despite low social backgrounds. Both were solitary . . . determined to be leaders. When Heath failed, the Party turned on him with a fury reserved only for those who pushed it into positions . . . it has no interest or stomach for.'[16]

Muldoon attacked what he saw as numerous inaccuracies in Zavos's book and with his cousin Laurie Browne and friend Harry Julian went to Avalon to debate the book with Zavos on television.[17] Muldoon also wrote a letter to the *Listener*, a publication he once described as 'that precious journal of the effete left',[18] detailing what he claimed were '30 factual inaccuracies' in a three-page extract of Zavos's book which the *Listener* had printed. Muldoon was particularly incensed with the suggestion, originating from the Labour MP for Mount Albert, Warren Freer, that Muldoon's mother had been an active member of the Mount Albert Labour Party. That suggestion was to be vehemently denied by Muldoon until his death.[19] Freer may have confused Muldoon's mother with Muldoon's grandmother and aunt, both of whom were Labour partisans. Some years later Muldoon again attacked Zavos's biography in the third of his autobiographies, spending about half the three pages he devoted to Zavos condemning Zavos and Freer for inaccuracies concerning Muldoon's mother's Christian name and political allegiance.[20]

The Labour leader Kirk and Muldoon did not like each other but they did respect each other's political abilities and strength. Neither was afraid to attack the other. Following his 1972 election victory, for example, Kirk with heavy sarcasm publicly baited Muldoon by saying that there were two people mainly responsible for Labour's 1972 election landslide and that modesty compelled him to admit that Muldoon was more responsible for it than he was.[21] According to one Labour MP, Kirk was strangely excited by the change of National's leadership from Marshall to Muldoon. He told the Labour caucus it would improve National's performance in the House and appeared to be looking forward to debating with Muldoon.[22] But then Kirk died suddenly.

Muldoon sometimes did regret his off-the-cuff quips and particularly in hindsight one made at Kirk's expense. At a meeting when Kirk was in a public hospital for a varicose vein operation, Muldoon told him to get better quickly because a pensioner needed his bed. Six months later, when Kirk returned to hospital and died, on 31 August 1974, journalists and political opponents accused Muldoon of having callously attacked a dying man.

Subsequently, however, Muldoon was very supportive of Kirk's widow and son. Learning that Ruth Kirk was entitled as Norman Kirk's widow to a pension of only $2921 per annum, Muldoon wrote privately to Rowling that, 'I would be most happy to support any consideration that could be given to increasing the pension for Mrs Kirk.'[23] The annuity was raised to $5422.

On another occasion Muldoon was incensed not only with the media's treatment of three of his colleagues but also its dismissive attitude to John Kirk, who had succeeded his father as Labour MP for Sydenham. In October 1975, Muldoon wrote to R. G. Collins, the chairman of the board of TV1, taking strong exception to a *Seven Days* current affairs programme in which his friends Gill, Schultz and Walker were named as the three worst National MPs in Parliament and John Kirk, who had replaced his father a year before, was similarly dismissed on the Labour side. Muldoon wrote of 'John Kirk, who coming into the House under tragic circumstances, has done his best to support his mother and father in the face of vicious criticism inside his own party and has had at the same time a positive contribution to make.'[24]

Following Kirk's unexpected death, National strategists were at first very worried that the new Prime Minister Rowling and the Labour Party would call an early election in late 1974 or early 1975. The National Party's President believed that such an election could well be won by Labour. National had not healed the division resulting from its leadership change; Muldoon was being attacked as 'a naughty boy who was doing us harm overseas by his remarks'; National's candidates were by March 1975 only half chosen; policy was undecided; membership and finances were down on previous election years; Rowling had enjoyed tremendous media coverage and success on his recent overseas tour; and the Labour Party's public relations campaign was 'tremendous'.[25] In the event, although a majority in the Labour cabinet favoured going to the polls, many backbench Labour MPs were worried that some might lose their seats. Finally, Rowling decided against an early election, and this gave Muldoon a chance first to consolidate and then to extend his reputation and appeal as alternative prime minister.

Although in public Muldoon was seen as a brutal debater attacking Labour personalities rather than policies, in caucus he often spoke well of Labour opponents and at first was prepared to treat Rowling with respect. Whenever he did, Holyoake rebuked him. For example, in January 1975, after several colleagues had dismissed Rowling merely as a 'nice little bloke', Muldoon, while agreeing that he was 'not within a roar of Kirk', suggested that Rowling was a man who 'speaks his mind' and could be 'a dangerous opponent'. He should not be 'overestimated' but he should be 'watched carefully'.[26] This was a view Muldoon had had ever since Rowling had entered Parliament in 1962 at a by-election in Buller. Speaking after Rowling's maiden speech in Parliament, Muldoon publicly praised the new Labour MP for his 'clarity of thought and his delivery' and predicted that 'he will be an asset to the Opposition'.[27] Holyoake, however, dismissed Rowling in caucus as 'not impressive' and as a 'schoolboy in a man's job' and at a subsequent meeting Holyoake again urged his caucus colleagues to 'laugh at Rowling. We've got to brand him as an inoffensive and ineffectual Prime Minister.'[28] Holyoake was also much more hostile than Muldoon towards Labour's other MPs. In May 1975, for example, Muldoon in caucus referred to the Labour MP for the marginal seat of Whangarei, Murray Smith, as 'a good guy' who should not be attacked personally. Holyoake immediately retorted, 'We should remember there is no such thing as a nice young Labour Member.' He added that Muldoon and others should also remember 'the story is that "Wallace Rowling is a disaster".'[29]

Much of the onslaught against Labour ministers in Parliament was instigated and co-ordinated not by Muldoon but by Gair who, following the change of leadership, organised rotating teams of four or five National MPs to maintain a sustained attack on a designated minister. In question time in the House ministers should win. They have access to information, can answer any way they wish, and have helpful supplementary questions from their own backbenchers. But in 1974 and 1975 Muldoon targeted Labour's weakest ministers and, in the opinion of at least one astute Labour observer, 'tore them to pieces'.[30]

Rowling came under pressure to present a stronger image from many within the Labour caucus and party organisation who were more used to Kirk's casual brutality. Although one or two Labour officials advised Rowling that he should not try to emulate Muldoon or Kirk, he was persuaded by others to launch personal attacks on Muldoon, Talboys and other National MPs, for example, deriding 'miser Muldoon' and 'deputy parrot Talboys' at the 1975 Labour Party Conference. Muldoon retaliated in kind at the National Party conference, saying of Rowling that he had seen 'shivers moving round his body, looking for a spine to run up'. Lesser Labour MPs were also lashed by Muldoon, Mat Rata being told that the five happiest years of his life were the ones he spent in Standard II and Michael Bassett being described as the only man in the House who could eat a banana sideways.[31] Muldoon believed that Rowling's timidity had prevented him calling an early election, which he might well have won following Kirk's death, and throughout subsequent years was to damn Rowling publicly with faint praise as 'a nice bloke' but one who, unlike Muldoon, found it difficult to say 'yes' or 'no'. Rowling was a capable and compassionate man, but he lacked Kirk's or Muldoon's presence, flair and instincts. Whereas Muldoon seemed forever on the offensive and kept his comments, especially on television, simple and direct, Rowling presented himself increasingly as a defensive person, uncertainly rehearsing involved arguments in public, appearing to say 'on the one hand . . . on the other hand' without decisiveness or conviction.

Rowling was in fact much more than a 'nice bloke'. In many ways he matched Muldoon for intelligence and determination. As Minister of Finance, perhaps because he was an economist, he showed himself more willing to accept Treasury advice and take hard decisions than did Muldoon, whose rhetoric and reputation were always stronger than the reality.[32] Although Rowling is remembered as a Labour leader who lost three elections in a row to Muldoon, in only one of those, 1975, was he decisively beaten. Indeed, in 1978 and 1981 Rowling's Labour Party polled more votes than the Muldoon-led National Party, but on both occasions the first-past-the-post electoral system did not accurately reflect the voters' wishes in the number of seats each party won.

In November 1974, anticipating the possibility of the Rowling Labour Government calling an early election, Muldoon undertook a series of public meetings that looked almost like an election campaign: Hamilton (18 November), Paraparaumu (19 November), Masterton (20 November), New Plymouth (21 November), Tamaki social functions (22 and 24 November), Mosgiel (28 November), Whangarei (2 December), Christchurch (4 December), Levin (5 December), and Taupo (9 December). This laid a solid basis for further campaigning throughout the following year.

From 8 February until 17 March 1975 Muldoon as Leader of the Opposition was overseas visiting Indonesia, Singapore, Malaysia, Japan, Iran, Germany, the European Community in Brussels, and the United Kingdom.[33] While in London, where he met a wide range of Labour Government ministers, British businessmen and bankers, and Margaret Thatcher, who had recently been elected leader of the Conservative Party Opposition and whom Muldoon described on his return as a 'remarkable woman full of vitality',[34] he also had talks with the Canadian Prime Minister, Pierre Trudeau. His visit to Britain coincided with that country's renegotiation of British membership of the European Community.

The revival in National Party enthusiasm and activity generally in 1975 was reflected in the increase in the membership of Muldoon's Tamaki electorate from 2289 at the end of 1974 to 4410 in 1975, the largest membership of the twenty-four electorates in the Auckland Division[35] and organised into eight local branches, a women's executive drawn from five local women's sections, and a Young Nationals' branch.[36] This was in marked contrast to the situation in mid-1973 when, with the membership at a mere 744, the electorate had been unable to confirm the selection of the party's then deputy leader as its official candidate because its strength was below the required minimum of 2000 members.[37]

Muldoon's television personality and the direct and controversial nature of his views and the way he put them resulted in larger and larger crowds turning up to his meetings. He continued throughout 1975 the regular public meetings which he had commenced holding in various New Zealand centres during the latter part of 1974. Many of those meetings attracted several thousand people with the one in the Rotorua Sportsdrome on 21 May being attended by a phenomenal 4000.[38] The series culminated with a public meeting on Saturday 11 October at the Wiri Wool Store in South Auckland and Muldoon was astounded and somewhat nervous when, arriving on a very wet night, he found himself speaking to a crowd variously estimated at between 5000 and 7500.[39] Muldoon found several features of his massive meeting at the Wiri Wool Store in 1975 amusing. Security was very tight and Muldoon at 5 foot 5 inches tall found himself flanked by two 6 foot 6 inches tall policemen, which he believed must have been a sight. His son Gavin, who looked like a young protester, was also stopped and searched by the police before being permitted to enter the meeting.

Two themes dominated his meetings and were hammered home repeatedly in unambiguous, everyday language: Labour's alleged economic mismanagement, notably its 'borrow and hope' policy, which was shattering New Zealand's economy; and 'creeping socialism' whereby, according to Muldoon, the centralised state controlled by Labour was fast eroding the freedom of ordinary New Zealanders and moving the country in the direction of those controlled by a politicised bureaucratic elite. He appealed particularly to the disaffected, the fearful and the angry in the New Zealand electorate with a mixture of nostalgia, belligerence, confidence in his own ability and his clear grasp of the problems, even if he did not have all the solutions.

Muldoon also targeted certain specific groups. For example, on Saturday and Sunday 27 and 28 September he opened the St. Barnabas Anglican Church centennial fair in Christchurch; went to services at the Christchurch Revival Fellowship and New Life Centre before lunching at the New Life Bible College; and preached the sermon at the evening service at St. Barnabas. He also spent a weekend on 18 and 19 October on a marae at Gisborne formulating the National Party's Maori election policy.

National's advertising agency by the middle of 1975 was delighted that 'Rob Muldoon is coming through so clearly' and believed the momentum he was creating could be consolidated simply by highlighting the problems the Labour Government was experiencing and matching them with solutions proposed by National.[40] Muldoon, however, at about the same time was becoming worried that 'our campaign is coming to a peak too early', and he was also angry that he was becoming personally involved in too many points of order in the House. He told his caucus colleagues, 'If nobody gets up, I do', and suggested that most other MPs were 'experienced enough to help' rather than leave it to him.[41]

In July 1975, following an enthusiastic ovation at the National Party conference, Muldoon gave a lengthy and memorable interview to Ian Fraser on the *Seven Days* programme on Television One.[42] Muldoon made a comment which was to haunt him for the rest of his life and beyond the grave. Asked if he had 'a vision of society or a philosophy that you want to implement', Muldoon replied that he 'had a tremendous feel for the New Zealand way of life, which is a cliché, but is none the less real. A way of life where there is no inherited position, where you judge a man for what he is rather than where he comes from' and where people could take 'advantage of the country, the fresh air, the clean water, the beaches, the mountains, the forest', which New Zealanders often took for granted.[43] When the interviewer then suggested that Muldoon was 'a preserver rather than a reformer', Muldoon admitted, 'Yes I am. I am a preserver. I lived in a very good time in New Zealand.' Fraser ended the interview by querying, 'If as you confidently expect you're the Prime Minister after November, what's the one most important thing you'd like the people of this country to ascribe to the Muldoon leadership?' Muldoon revealingly replied, 'That when I go, I left this country at least as good as when I took it over.'

Ever after, this modest comment was quoted repeatedly as a sorry admission that Muldoon had no vision. That was unfair. Admittedly, he was no radical who saw constant movement towards some distant Utopia as the ideal, but he was a man who had a deep appreciation, based on his own experience, of the many blessings he and other New Zealanders enjoyed and which had been built up by previous generations. He also had a wary scepticism about the reality of any perfect society promised by dogmatic ideologues who believed that the welfare of future generations could be achieved by the suffering of individuals in the present. Nor did his comment rule out the possibility of leaving New Zealand better than he found it; indeed, he suggested that through pragmatic reform he would. All Muldoon was saying was that New Zealanders in the 1950s, 1960s and early 1970s had many advantages and a very good quality of life and that, in the face of many impending threats, especially to its economic security and prosperity, he did not want New Zealand to regress during his tenure of office as Prime Minister. Indeed, in an interview given a few months later, immediately following the 1975 election, Muldoon did promise to 'preserve and enhance . . . the unique life-style of this country'.[44]

While some critics saw Muldoon's populism as either lack of vision or even akin to socialism, in fact it was a very mainstream conservatism: he believed in preserving and slowly improving the status quo. He valued democratic government; private enterprise operating within limits set by the state; individual initiative complemented by collective concern; freedom and self-reliance yet also the need to give people equality of opportunity and a 'fair go' especially when 'down on their luck' – and he disliked experts, elitists and pressure groups.

Although the management of the economy and superannuation were to be the two major issues throughout 1974 and 1975, Muldoon was very conscious of the importance of non-economic issues, some of which had been highlighted by the advent of the Values Party at the 1972 election. In regard to the environment, Muldoon and others in the National Party were determined that the 1972 election fiasco, when National had mishandled widespread opposition to the raising of the water level in Lake Manapouri, would not be repeated in 1975.⁴⁵ That had cost National four marginal seats in Otago-Southland. With the help of Venn Young and Hugh Templeton, and after considerable correspondence with Dr. A. F. Mark, the chairman of the Manapouri Guardians, Muldoon promised in a speech at Blenheim to match any public commitment given on Lakes Manapouri and Te Anau by Rowling, and also to establish a Lakes Manapouri and Te Anau Authority with a majority of local members and with much wider responsibilities and powers than the existing guardians.⁴⁶ He guaranteed that any future changes to the lake levels would be made only on the recommendation of the guardians.⁴⁷

Clearly related to the environment was the nuclear issue. Between 1964 and 1976 no nuclear-powered US warships visited New Zealand because of doubts of legal liability in the event of a nuclear accident while in port. The possible reinstatement of the visits of such ships was raised as an issue at the 1972 election. Subsequently, the Americans told the Kirk Government that they would indemnify New Zealand for any mishap. Labour's Minister of Defence, Arthur Faulkner, told the Americans to raise the matter again after the 1975 elections. In the lead-up to the 1975 election National became concerned about anti-nuclear sentiment in New Zealand and particularly about attempts to establish a South Pacific Nuclear Weapons Free Zone and bans on nuclear ship visits to New Zealand. Holyoake felt that the matter was such an 'emotional issue' that National 'can't oppose' it going to the United Nations, but Muldoon, backed by Talboys, opposed supporting both the Nuclear Weapons Free Zone and the ban on nuclear ship visits and argued that National should 'make clear publicly [that] this runs counter to membership of ANZUS'.⁴⁸ New Zealand voters had to realise that they could not have both ANZUS and a ban on US naval ships. Although the Americans observed a 'neither confirm nor deny' policy, Muldoon said it was perfectly obvious what the situation was. He accepted that the ships were almost certainly nuclear-armed, stating in retrospect, 'No nuclear-capable vessel was going to be so far from its home port without nuclear weapons aboard. It would be totally illogical for it to be two weeks away from its home port and be incapable of doing its job.'⁴⁹

Another controversial issue was immigration. This issue touched not only the argument propounded by Values since 1972 for a no-growth, sustainable economy and environment. It also reflected rising public concern about the pressure of immigration on housing, health, education and employment in urban areas such as Auckland and about the apparent rise in violent crime, some of it associated with illegal immigrants, or 'overstayers', from the Pacific Islands. A major division occurred in the caucus over National's immigration policy for the 1975 election, particularly the section relating specifically to limits on Pacific Island immigration into New Zealand. Venn Young argued that National did not want 'to be painted as a racist party', and with Holyoake and Jim Bolger (who had been elected in 1972 as MP for the King Country electorate) tried to have the section deleted from the proposed manifesto. Gair, who 'argued strongly for facing the facts and not sidestepping the Polynesian issue', and Gill, who felt the policy was 'watered far enough already', defended the proposal, which was eventually endorsed after Muldoon predicted that it would have a positive effect on the results in the Auckland marginal seats of Eden, Birkenhead and Auckland Central.[50]

There is no doubt that Muldoon also deliberately played the All Black–Springbok card for political reasons at the 1975 election, irrespective of the sincerity of his own views on the issue. One confidant, Frank Gill, bluntly told the Auckland Divisional Executive shortly before the election: 'Sporting contacts with South Africa had been mentioned by Mr. Muldoon as an election issue simply because wherever he went in the marginal areas which we had lost and must regain he was asked this question and great interest was expressed in it.'[51]

Two other issues which cut across party lines in 1973 and for some years after were the legalisation of abortion and homosexuality. Prime Minister Kirk was strongly opposed to both, and Muldoon also came out on the side of the anti-abortionists. That clearly reflected the mail he was receiving. For example, in September 1974 he received 1057 letters against abortion and only 179 in favour.[52] On the homosexual issue, however, Muldoon went in the opposite direction to the unsolicited advice and even threats he received from many National supporters. Of the 125 letters he received in July–August 1974 nearly all opposed the private member's bill introduced by the National MP for Egmont, Venn Young, which would have legalised homosexual acts in private between consenting adults.[53] Many writers praised Kirk's strong homophobic stance and contrasted that with Muldoon's support for the Bill.

When homosexual law reform was discussed in the National Party caucus in August 1973, Holyoake, who noted that he had 'always been against reform', tried to have the matter referred to a committee of inquiry, thus delaying both the reform and the requirement that MPs might have to vote on the matter.[54] Muldoon opposed such a strategy and moved that MPs should have a free vote on any such proposed legislation, and a show of hands revealed he had the support of a majority of caucus. During an earlier caucus debate, Muldoon had expressed concern that National was 'behind the times' on homosexual law reform.[55] Muldoon, admittedly only after much thought, had decided to support Young's Bill because 'Parliament would be distinguishing between something that is distasteful to most people, "sinful" or even obnoxious and something which is a crime punishable by law. It would certainly not be condoning homosexual activity but categorising it as something less than a crime.'[56] By favouring decriminalisation, Muldoon angered homophobes, but by refusing to accept homosexuality as normal behaviour he also continued to antagonise the gay community.

The 'great majority' of Muldoon's Tamaki electorate and branch committee members were strongly opposed to the Hospitals Amendment Bill, moved by the Labour MP Dr Gerald Wall, which sought in 1974 to prevent therapeutic abortions at the Remuera Abortion Clinic and other private hospitals. They told Muldoon that the issue was one of 'the individual's freedom of choice' and advised him to oppose the Bill.[57] Local opinion in Tamaki reflected the general view within the National Party's Auckland Division, whose Executive had already recorded a motion, carried without dissent, that if abortion was legal then it was the right of an individual to choose whether it should be performed in a public hospital or a private clinic.[58] When Wall introduced the Bill into Parliament on 30 August 1974, however, Muldoon spoke in support of it. Muldoon's clear stand on the issue was a contrast to that of the new Prime Minister, Rowling, who admitted in retrospect, 'I did sit on the fence . . . deliberately' because 'my opinion wouldn't have been seen as just that of Bill Rowling, MP for Tasman but as that of the Government'.[59] In an article written for *Truth* Muldoon considered both sides of the abortion debate before saying how he would vote. He concluded that in his mind, 'There is no doubt that the human foetus is in the form of a child at a very early stage of pregnancy. It cannot be that the proper way to deal with an unwanted child is to kill it before it is born. I was one of those whose vote helped to abolish capital punishment in this country in 1961 . . . My vote will oppose the killing of an unborn child.'[60]

The National caucus endured another lengthy debate on abortion at its meeting on 26 March 1975. Holyoake was concerned that MPs would be forced to choose either to legalise or restrict abortion and suggested that if pressed MPs should 'run for cover'.[61] Muldoon advised MPs only to 'answer for yourself' and to stress that the abortion issue was one for individuals not parties. Gair, who believed that women had a right to make a choice, responded that Muldoon as leader would set the pattern for the National Party and asked him to 'say as little as possible'. A few weeks later Muldoon again requested 'a free-for-all' debate in caucus on the abortion issue, stressing again that 'we are in a free vote and free speaking situation', and he pleaded with MPs to 'maintain the serious tone of debate throughout and avoid heat or acrimony'. He added that he was 'more concerned with the welfare of the party than the fate of this Bill' and, that 'everyone who votes against the Wall Bill will be branded pro-abortion and for the Bill will be branded as SPUC'.[62] Highet, Gair and Holyoake challenged Muldoon's analysis and Holyoake, who announced he would not be in the House for the debate, then suggested 'that Muldoon should speak first and then get right out of it' when the Bill was debated in Parliament.[63] The abortion debate of the mid-1970s would bitterly divide not only the country but also the National Party, and was to become particularly divisive in the East Coast Bays electorate of the staunchly anti-abortion MP, Frank Gill. It also drove a wedge between Muldoon and his former ally Gair, who became the most prominent pro-choice advocate in the National caucus.

The debate on abortion reflected a growing involvement of women in politics, particularly through the Women's Electoral Lobby (WEL). Muldoon believed that two thirds of the women involved in WEL were Labour supporters and that in many people's minds WEL was related to 'women's lib'.[64] He recognised, however, that with some women WEL had 'quite an influence' and took consolation from the fact that some WEL activists such as his own electorate deputy chairpersons, Anne Miller and Lois Morris, belonged to the National Party. Holyoake lamented the fact that 'few men [were] willing to contradict women' publicly.[65] Of particular concern to Muldoon was a questionnaire which WEL asked all candidates to complete prior to the 1975 election. Although Muldoon was worried about the marking and grading system generally, he believed he would receive fair treatment because one of the WEL women interviewing him, Helen Eisenhofer, was a good friend.[66] Gill suggested that National MPs could just 'pretend sympathy', but Muldoon responded that all National MPs and candidates should treat both WEL and its questionnaire seriously and answer honestly, and he pointed out that some Labour MPs would also score badly.

Muldoon was not threatened by the campaign for more women in Parliament or more policies specifically designed for women, and indeed, according to Marilyn Waring and others, he was supportive of both.[67] Throughout his leadership he found it a source of concern that he could not get more women candidates selected for winnable seats, but he also believed that 'ordinary women' with family responsibilities, especially the upbringing of children, were understandably reluctant to submit themselves and their families to the onerous and even traumatic life of a member of Parliament. As a result Muldoon suggested that women who went into Parliament were not typical of their gender and were drawn largely from those who were not particularly interested in family life or traditional female roles.

The selection of the 22-year-old Marilyn Waring as a candidate in 1975, however, delighted Muldoon. He invited her to attend the caucus meeting on 26 March 1975 and assured her, 'we wanted a woman and will help all we can'.[68] As a member of the Opposition research unit, Waring had worked for Gair researching and writing National's housing policy and had also prepared speech notes on that topic for Muldoon. Although she thought Muldoon did not know her name or recognise her, Waring in hindsight had no doubt that Muldoon did what he could to help her win the nomination for Raglan because he wanted a woman MP. At the selection meeting for National's candidate for Raglan each aspirant was asked to answer an unseen question posed by the party leader. Muldoon surprised not only Waring but most others present by asking what should be in National's housing policy at the forthcoming election.[69] Muldoon's patriarchal attitudes did not prevent him from recognising the talents of women colleagues in caucus and the party organisation such as Waring, Rona Stevenson, Esmé Tombleson, Colleen Dewe, Jenny Shipley, Katherine O'Regan, Ruth Richardson and Sue Wood – though

Richardson was always an economic opponent and personal critic of Muldoon, Waring and Wood eventually found themselves alienated from their socially much more conservative leader, and Muldoon never made any secret of the fact that he found Stevenson, Tombleson and Dewe much more congenial colleagues personally and politically than he did Waring, Richardson or Shipley.

Because 1975 was International Women's Year and considerable publicity was being given to women's issues, interests and opinions, it was decided that National should bring together its policies of particular interest to women and specifically identify ways in which a future National Government would remove disabilities affecting them.[70] The policy document covered such matters as maternity leave, family law, a family law court, family planning, and easier and non-adversarial divorce. Muldoon was concerned specifically to remove as far as possible the 'conflict situation' in divorce proceedings which led to 'terrible problems' for those involved.[71] Breakdown in marriages should be accepted without blame having to be proved and apportioned. There were no women in the National caucus between 1972 and 1975 and as a result the women's policy for the 1975 election was written largely by women outside Parliament, notably Julie Cameron, Natasha Templeton, Margaret Young and Waring, with the assistance of David Thomson.[72]

One of the other major debates within the National caucus prior to the 1975 election was over Muldoon's proposal to make local body rates on non-commercial, owner-occupied properties tax deductible. Muldoon argued that this would be particularly good for beneficiaries.[73] He encountered strong opposition from rural MPs who, like Holyoake, were 'concerned about the cost of our policies' or, like Harrison, saw tax deductibility and rate relief at the expense of tax payers as 'anathema'. Muldoon responded that 'this is not a farmers' party', that it would be a 'fatal blunder to accept farmer thinking', and that 'we can't buy farmers over and over again'. The majority of caucus finally agreed to accept the policy. Muldoon also pointed out to Holyoake that National would be making only one big, expensive promise at the forthcoming election, National Superannuation.

Labour suffered not only from the oil shock and a downturn in New Zealand's terms of trade after 1974 but from trying to implement its own extravagant and paternalistic 1972 election manifesto. The Labour Government had set out vigorously to develop New Zealand's industrial base with direct assistance through a government-owned Development Finance Corporation and to try to insulate the New Zealand economy from adverse overseas influences, especially imported inflation. Labour also tried to control inflation with a range of price controls and subsidies, while at the same time it increased expenditure markedly on health and education and extended social welfare benefits including the domestic purposes benefit. Wage demands at home and 'stagflation' (stagnating growth plus high inflation) in the world economy soon undermined the Government's economic strategy and social agenda. The collapse in economic growth around the world coupled with escalating prices for imported oil and declining prices for agricultural exports shattered New Zealand's economy, and by the end of 1974 the Government was clearly in political as well as economic trouble.

Privately Muldoon did not entirely blame the outgoing Labour Government for the economically difficult situation he inherited in 1975. The first oil shock had clearly not been Labour's fault but its misfortune, and Muldoon in retrospect felt that the 'only fault one could pin on Labour was that Kirk freed up the economy too much and had to clamp down before the oil shock resulted in such a shocking downturn in the terms of trade'.[74] There was no doubt, however, that Muldoon saw himself as a much better manager of the economy, especially when it was in difficulty, than Kirk, Rowling or Tizard and he certainly campaigned on that. His major real difference of opinion with Labour in 1975 was not over the economy generally but over the specific issue of superannuation.

During 1973 Muldoon chaired a caucus committee which examined Labour's proposed compulsory superannuation scheme and possible alternatives to it. While he recommended initially that all options be kept open, by September 1973 he was identifying what he regarded as the weaknesses of the Labour proposal. It was, he argued, a small, costly pension which might well be reduced in times of high inflation. It would be half a century before the first full superannuation payments would be made. It was bad for the self-employed and women not in paid employment. There was a low lump sum option. The size of the fund could well upset the investment market, raised the prospect of government majority shareholding in public companies, and would require a large, expensive administration. There was also some concern about the viability of a funded scheme at a time of long-term, double-figure inflation.[75]

With the help of Gill and Gair among others, Muldoon developed an alternative National Superannuation Scheme funded out of taxation and not through a separate compulsory fund. This would be the sole major, long-term policy initiated by National in its first three years of office if it won the 1975 election. National Superannuation was presented simply and very effectively to the voters. Three criticisms of the Labour scheme were highlighted: it would concentrate the capital in government hands; it would discriminate against women and non-workers; it would not start paying out its full benefit for many years. Against that, three advantages of the National policy were stressed: a housewife would receive as much as a working man; the National Superannuation would be universal and paid in addition to any private retirement income; and every existing pensioner would receive around a 70 per cent increase. National claimed that the additional cost would only be slightly more than the Labour scheme and that as a taxation-based scheme the income would not be eroded by inflation.[76]

In many ways National Superannuation was the universal pension scheme based on citizenship advocated but not introduced by the Labour Party prior to 1935. The National scheme extended in modified form the existing pension to 80 per cent of the average ordinary-time weekly wage, less tax. This would be paid to everyone who had lived in New Zealand for at least ten years and had reached the age of 60. The indignity of a means test would be removed; those who received the pension would be able to continue working if they wished; non-earners such as housewives would qualify as well as wage and salary earners; wives would be paid separately from their husbands; and six-monthly adjustments would be made in accordance with future alterations in the average wage. The existing Labour superannuation scheme would be abolished and contributions already made, together with the employers' contributions, would be returned to account holders free of tax.

Challenged that the scheme penalised savers and reduced everyone to the same level, Muldoon claimed that to the contrary it provided a secure minimum for everyone but did not discourage people from saving more.[77] Without a means test the superannuation would be paid to everyone, including women outside the workforce, and retired people would be taxed on their total income from all sources. Some would still enjoy more than others as a result of their hard work, good fortune or thrift, but no one would thenceforth fear deprivation in their old age. In order to insure that the scheme was affordable and sustainable Muldoon had Dick Jessup, an actuary of the National Provident Fund, check out the figures for National's superannuation policy, which was released on 24 June 1975.[78]

Four National MPs retired at the 1975 election – Marshall, Percy Allen, Carter and Sloane. In caucus Muldoon paid warm personal tributes especially to Carter and Sloane, describing the latter as one of his 'closest personal friends', a tribute reciprocated when Sloane spoke later. Muldoon also went out of his way to praise his defeated rival for the leadership, noting that Marshall was held in 'tremendous respect and affection' in the party, the country and 'all round the world' and that his '25 years of great distinction' as a politician would ensure 'his place in history' as 'one of [the] great figures of New Zealand politics and government'.[79] Marshall in a brief response made a perfunctory reference to his 'mixed feelings' about Holyoake and Muldoon.

Throughout 1975 National strategists had become convinced the Labour Government was heading towards defeat but anticipated that Labour as a last resort would mount 'a concerted attack . . . at Rob Muldoon . . . Expect dirt.'[80] Certainly, throughout 1975 Labour had tried to fuel the divisions within the National Party by the distribution of 'Bring Jack Back' car bumper stickers and later in the year launched a major attack on Muldoon personally through the 'Citizens for Rowling' campaign.

The Citizens for Rowling campaign, or what most observers soon correctly realised was much more a Citizens against Muldoon campaign, was spearheaded and launched on October 23 by twelve prominent, mainly academic citizens. Each wrote a short statement on why they preferred Rowling to Muldoon and these were published in a 16-page pamphlet. The contributors were Sir Edmund Hillary, Bishop Paul Reeves, Professor Geoffrey Palmer, Dr Muriel Blackburn, Walter Scott, Sir Jack Harris, Professor John Roberts, Richard Campion, Rev. Dr. John Hinchcliff, Jack Shallcrass, Jeremy Pope, and David Exel, the former television current affairs interviewer and at that time a public relations consultant who had conceived and started to organise the campaign as early as April 1975. Although ostensibly a spontaneous and independent initiative organised by Rowling admirers outside the Labour Party, in fact the campaign was from the first organised by Exel and Bob Harvey, Labour's major public relations consultant.[81] Essentially the campaign compared Muldoon's high-profile, divisive leadership style with Rowling's low-key, consensual approach. It was alleged that if New Zealanders voted for Muldoon they would be choosing authoritarianism, confrontation, intolerance and demagoguery; if they voted for Rowling they would be choosing reason, conciliation, toleration and moderation. The election of Muldoon would change New Zealand from a tolerant and caring community into a bitterly divided and callous society, or so the Citizens for Rowling predicted.[82]

Many of the 2500 people who agreed to their names being used in newspaper advertisements, and whom Muldoon subsequently dismissed as 'these precious people who presumed in their arrogance' to advise 'the ordinary bloke',[83] were Labour supporters or sympathisers. Others were less politically committed people who genuinely liked and respected Rowling irrespective of his party and were annoyed at the constant and unfair denigration of Rowling, not only by Muldoon and the National Party but also by the Wellington businessman, Bob Jones. As Neary observed and Jones himself freely admitted, Jones had been 'tormenting' Rowling 'with posters, signs, advertisements and stunts . . . showing a mouse in the image of Rowling caught in a trap' and a week before the election Jones had a friend dressed in a mouse suit burst into a live TV interview of Rowling by Brian Edwards, ridiculing and devastating the Prime Minister.[84] Neary was typical of those who admired Rowling's 'fairness, his kind of strength, available when needed but not for display, the organisational skills . . . a consensus man . . . who listened . . . weighed up mood and argument and brought extremes together'.[85] There is no doubt, however, that most if not all of those who became Citizens for Rowling, or Clergy for Rowling, or Lawyers for Rowling, were also anti-Muldoon and were perceived as such by most New Zealanders.

Muldoon was alerted to the Citizens for Rowling campaign by a number of people including Walter Murphy of the Political Science Department at Victoria University, Wellington. Murphy sent Muldoon a copy of a letter from Exel circulated to staff at the university asking them to support Rowling and Labour because Muldoon and National did not represent a 'style of government consistent with the values University people traditionally endorse'.[86] The staff members were being asked to pay $5 or $10 and allow their names to be used in advertisements as 'Citizens for Rowling'. Muldoon was hurt by what he felt was 'a massive exercise in character assassination', and he was angered further by what he regarded as the hypocritical double standard of people who were claiming to be opposed to personal attacks and divisiveness in politics. He issued a press statement attacking the personal motivation of several of the initial twelve 'Citizens for Rowling' and made a populist appeal by arguing that 'none of the people involved has to worry about their own comfort, whether they will have a job next year, or a home, or be able to cope with the cost of living generally'.[87] Subsequently, he was to suggest that Citizens for Rowling supporters should offer their resignations from public positions since they disliked so much the thought of a Muldoon-led Government and after the election most did, including John Jeffries as chairman of Air New

Zealand and Bishop Paul Reeves as chairman of the Environmental Council. Sir
Jack Harris was dismissed as chairman of the Tobacco Industry Board.

The Citizens for Rowling campaign, however, at first appeared to be working,
with a poll taken a fortnight before the election showing that voters preferred
Rowling to Muldoon by a margin of 65 per cent to 35 per cent and, ominously for
Muldoon in the light of that preference, the issue of leadership had replaced the
economy as the main campaign issue.[88] But the campaign started too early and
after its initial impact Muldoon's supporters had time to counter-attack. In
hindsight, it is clear that the Citizens for Rowling campaign was misguided in
conception, ill-timed and ultimately counter-productive. Many people were
annoyed by the personal denigration of Muldoon and the implication that they
could not make their own minds up but had to be advised by arrogant elitists, and
they wrote to tell him so. Typical of such letters was one from a Glen Innes
constituent and head of the technical department and evening classes at Tamaki
College, A. C. A. McDonald, who told Muldoon that over the years he had
discussed Muldoon with many people.[89] 'Almost without exception' those people
had said Muldoon had given them 'the maximum consideration' and even when he
disagreed with them or could not help had courteously explained in detail why.
Muldoon had 'never differentiated between Labour Party supporters or National
Party supporters' and 'there was never any suggestion of intolerance of other points
of view'. Nothing seemed to be too much trouble for Muldoon and irrespective of
the outcome he had 'then called personally at their door to tell them what you have
done'. McDonald told Muldoon that he was politically neutral but was so annoyed
at the distortion and misrepresentation of Muldoon's nature and attitudes that he
felt he should write and was prepared to be quoted.

Among other letters were a number from Labour members and voters such as
Rev. John Drew, a former freezing worker who had become a social worker and the
minister of Porirua Baptist Church, who suggested the formation of a 'Clergy for
Muldoon' list to counter 'Clergy for Rowling'.[90] Perhaps the most surprising was
from Douglas Smith, until July 1975 the chairman of the Tamaki Labour Representation Committee, who wrote: 'I deplore unscrupulous personal attacks and
character assassinations' and 'I reaffirm my belief in your personal integrity and
proven ability.'[91] In the NZ Herald and Otago Daily Times letters to the editor ran
ten to one against the Citizens for Rowling campaign and the ratio in the Dominion
and Christchurch Press was negative by a ratio of five to one.[92]

Holyoake was enraged by the Citizens for Rowling campaign and said so
unequivocally at a public meeting at the Berkeley Theatre, Mission Bay, on
Monday 17 November. Wearing a 'Rob's Mob' lapel badge produced by the
Tamaki National Party, Holyoake launched a spirited defence of Muldoon and a
scathing attack on Citizens for Rowling. He told the audience in Muldoon's
Tamaki electorate that, 'In his long political career he had never witnessed such
poisonous and vitriolic attacks as those being waged against Mr Muldoon . . .
scurrilous and insidious character assassinations.'[93] Holyoake called on 'ordinary
New Zealanders to flood Mr Muldoon's office in Parliament Buildings with

telegrams of support.'[94] In the following days over 5000 such telegrams supporting Muldoon were received from all over the country. Many were from individuals but others were signed by fifteen or twenty people. While the majority simply said 'We fully support you' or a variation of that sentiment, others referred more specifically to the Citizens for Rowling campaign, for example: 'Average New Zealanders do not appreciate innuendos or attempts to discredit you' (Dunedin); 'Anything Rowling can only go in one direction' (Ohaupo); 'Deplore Labour Party smear tactics' (Glenfield); 'You've got them shaken, rattled and Rowling' (Hokitika).[95]

Although Muldoon refused to approve a Citizens for Muldoon counter-campaign, Bob Jones had no such reservations and organised and published two days before the election a list of 100 Muldoon endorsers. The list contained fourteen former or current All Blacks, including Colin Meads, Fergie McCormick and somewhat more ambivalently Ron Jarden.[96] Muldoon's Tamaki electorate committee also produced and distributed car bumper stickers which read 'Citizens for what's his name'.[97]

The momentum of National's election campaign was increased by an effective publicity and advertising onslaught devised by a three-person team from the public relations firm Colenso. Muldoon refused to be groomed and ignored instructions not to look straight at the television camera, a technique he had used effectively for nine years. He welcomed, however, the campaign slogan which Colenso developed from a phrase out of Muldoon's speech to the 1975 National Party conference. Muldoon had stated that, 'National will preserve and enhance the things that make New Zealand the way we like it.' That was abbreviated and altered to 'New Zealand – The way you want it.'[98] Many people sensed during the 1970s that something was wrong with New Zealand's economy, and there was a widespread general mood for change despite uncertainty as to what precisely should be done. Muldoon's and National's 1975 slogan, 'New Zealand – The Way You Want It', implied that ordinary people would be consulted and would have a say in a future which they would find acceptable.

National prepared and showed seven different animated advertisements, twice each on TV1 and twice each on TV2. The advertisements covered the issues of industrial relations, freedom, superannuation, women's rights, the economy, housing, and cities. The cost of the preparation of National's television campaign, including $5000 for Muldoon's closing address, was $47,500 out of a total advertising budget of $202,100.[99] The seven animated commercials varied from 64 to 84 seconds and were produced at a cost of $2000 per minute or $16,700 in total by the American cartoon film maker Hanna Barbera.[100] Subsequently Muldoon vehemently denied suggestions that the US Central Intelligence Agency had been involved in or had subsidised the creation of the Hanna Barbera cartoons.[101]

National also produced a huge volume and variety of pamphlets in 1975, including four on superannuation with a print run of 1.5 million copies. The manifesto and fifteen pamphlets on other topics meant that in total National distributed over 7.5 million copies at a cost of $152,000.[102]

National's stereotyping and appeal to popular prejudices evident in its 1975 election advertising was reminiscent of the scare tactics used by conservative parties earlier in the century. Labour's moderate social democracy was portrayed as akin to Stalinist communism, with threats that the re-election of the Rowling Labour Government could spell the end of freedom and democracy in New Zealand.[103] The campaign was even more focused than previous ones on personalities, emotions and sweeping allegations, and the general condemnation of Labour was accompanied by repeated assertions that National, and in particular its leader Muldoon, was stronger, much more competent and experienced, more sensitive to the wishes of the 'ordinary' New Zealander, and more committed to individual freedom and choice than Labour and Rowling.

While Labour criticised loudly and somewhat sanctimoniously National's use of cartoons depicting dancing Cossacks and brown-skinned overstayers, the Labour Party was not above using on television in 1975 an advertisement of a child holding a pig while a background song alluded to a dictator. No one believed Labour claims that this was in no way directed against 'Piggy' Muldoon. National undoubtedly oversimplified and created stereotypical myths in an attempt to destroy Labour and discredit Rowling in 1975, but Labour countered by creating its own oversimplified propaganda, not least of which was the crude portrayal of Muldoon as a dictator and a bully.

Although he had been effectively campaigning already for over a year, Muldoon commenced his official 1975 election campaign on Tuesday 4 November. After a four-day break at his Hatfields Beach bach, he arrived in Hamilton where he lunched with the Women's Electoral Lobby and in the afternoon visited Huntly. That night he spoke at an opening rally in the Founder's Theatre at 8 p.m. The campaign opening was more a television presentation than a traditional address and was designed to show Muldoon as a man equally at ease in the corridors of power or with the family at the beach. It presented him as a person of 'wit rather than any malice' and in a confident and bantering mood. It even showed the somewhat disrespectful slogan 'Vote Piggy'.[104]

The speech itself began with praise of the 'New Zealand way of life' and the need 'to preserve and enhance' what most other countries were still seeking. Muldoon specifically mentioned New Zealand's climate, geography, small popula-tion, high material affluence and multi-racial and multi-cultural society, which together made up what he regarded as the best quality of life in the world. A sound economy was the number one priority, not as an end in itself but as a means to an end, the base for the welfare state, which assisted those in the community who were disadvantaged. Then Muldoon summarised the many problems facing New Zealand: inflation, borrowing, overspending, housing, law and order, sporting contacts with South Africa. He identified some of the solutions in the areas of immigration, farming, manufacturing, tourism, fishing, superannuation and voluntary unionism. He then touched on health, education, social security, broadcasting and regional development. He promised a Human Rights Commis-sion. Finally, he referred to National's experience and expertise and stressed the importance of policies covering particularly women, young people and the family unit. The theme repeated throughout was 'New Zealand the way *you* want it.'

Muldoon also unveiled the large board containing a comparison between 1972 and 1975 that he was to use frequently during the campaign. It was entitled 'Before and After a Labour Government'.

	1972	1975
Costing of Living Increase	5.5%	15+%
Cost of Food Increase	2.3%	11.03%
Average House Price	$13,696	$25,205
Average Building Section Price	$3,875	$8,717
Average Farm Price	$65,464	$123,889
Unemployment	9,075	9,760

Among the many telegrams of congratulations and good wishes Muldoon received following his Hamilton address were messages from Sir John Grace[105] and Sir Jack Butland[106] and 341 students at Hamilton Girls High School.[107]

Over the following twenty-four days Muldoon addressed twenty evening meetings and twenty-four other public meetings during the day. The evening meetings were packed, from the 1250 at the opening in Hamilton, with similar numbers in Hastings and Oamaru, to 1600 in Palmerston North, 2000 in Wellington and Masterton, 2500 in Invercargill, and 3000 in Dunedin. Even the smallest meetings drew audiences of 800 or 900.[108] Certainly the meetings were well organised by the National Party organisation, but people were keen to attend and the huge attendances were themselves news as well as what Muldoon said at the meetings.

The 1975 election campaign was remembered as a happy time with lots of fun by those who travelled with Muldoon. Muldoon was accompanied by Thea, Rob Hole, his private secretary, Peter Acland, his press secretary, Margaret Neich, his secretary, and usually about half a dozen journalists.[109]

On election night, 29 November, Muldoon with Tremewan, Richard Yates and their wives had a quiet meal at the Grammar Club and listened to the early results on the radio. The trend was clear from the start of counting the votes and as Muldoon and the others drove to the Mission Bay Women's Bowling Club in Kohimarama, where the Tamaki party members had gathered, they heard on the car radio that National had taken New Plymouth. By the time they arrived at the Bowling Club, the crowd waiting for New Zealand's new Prime Minister was wild with excitement, in marked contrast to the dismal scene in the same hall three years before.

Muldoon had predicted at National's pre-election campaign caucus in mid-October that Labour would retain only about 25 seats at the forthcoming election.[110] In the event they held 32 to National's 55, an exact reverse of the situation following the 1972 election. Partly because Muldoon was happy to commit his Tamaki activists and financial resources to the marginal seats of

Birkenhead and Auckland Central, and there was virtually no canvassing or election-day activity in his own electorate, the swing to National in Tamaki itself at the 1975 election was at 4.6 percent, the smallest percentage gain in the Auckland Division. Labour actually won the special votes in Tamaki by eight, a remarkable indication of the relatively little effort put in by National. Even so, Tamaki now became the second safest National seat in New Zealand, with Muldoon taking 62.38 per cent of the valid vote to Labour's 26.88.[111]

CHAPTER 12

Power, Personality and Political Process

IN CONSTRUCTING HIS FIRST CABINET AFTER THE 1975 election, Muldoon first invited his caucus members to submit their opinions to him. Twenty-seven MPs did make recommendations, with twenty-nine people being mentioned.[1] Most nominated full possible cabinet lists, and the more senior MPs indicated their own preferred portfolios. Only a couple of new MPs responded, notably Jim McLay, the MP for Birkenhead, who put forward a full cabinet list. Reflecting their previous responsibilities in Opposition, there was a clear consensus that Talboys should have Overseas Trade (17 nominations); Adams-Schneider, Industries and Commerce (19); MacIntyre, Agriculture (16); Gair, Housing (22); Gordon, Labour (18); Venn Young, Environment (15), Maori Affairs (13) and Land (12); and Holland, Energy (14). There was a division of opinion over Education between Gandar (10) and Templeton (10) and Foreign Affairs between Holyoake (11) and Talboys (9). Gandar received nine nominations for Minister of Agriculture. Although not proposed by a majority, Gill was named as a possible Health Minister (13) or Minister of Social Welfare (11); Highet as Minister of Internal Affairs (11); Wilkinson as Attorney-General (10); McLachlan, for Transport (8); Bill Young, for Works (6); and Lapwood, for Tourism (5). One interesting nomination for cabinet was the one-term MP, Bill Birch, who got thirteen mentions divided amongst almost as many portfolios, while the other one-term MP, Bolger, was named eight times for a variety of cabinet posts. Bolger and Birch also received the most mentions for under-secretary, eight and six respectively.

Significantly, only nine of the twenty-seven respondents specifically proposed that Muldoon should hold the finance portfolio as well as the prime-ministership: Bolger, Highet, MacIntyre, McLay, Walker, Wilkinson, Venn Young and two anonymous submissions. No alternative emerged, however, from the consultation process, and the general preconception that Muldoon would again become Minister of Finance was indicated by the fact that not one MP nominated another person for that position. Wilkinson received fifteen nominations for Associate Finance

Minister and Gair three, including a strong memo from himself to Muldoon advocating such an appointment.

Muldoon should never have been both Prime Minister and Minister of Finance. Prime Ministers have enough to do running a cabinet team of opinionated, ambitious and often vain ministers without also handling a detailed portfolio such as Finance, which preoccupies their time and which periodically brings them into conflict with colleagues wanting more money to spend. The Prime Minister is like the captain of a ship with overall authority and cannot simultaneously run the bridge, the engine rooms, the kitchens, the radio room and the radar system. It was an arrogant presumption on Muldoon's part that any person could do both jobs and equally presumptuous to judge that no one else in the caucus was capable of doing one of them. Muldoon's major problem as Prime Minister was his unwillingness to surrender the finance ministry. He also had the misfortune to become Prime Minister and Minister of Finance at a time when the days of budget surpluses, full employment and a favourable balance of trade were over. Ministers of Finance are seldom praised and are often abused both by the public and by cabinet colleagues whose spending suggestions they must frequently oppose. Muldoon fought so many battles as Minister of Finance that he was not able to rise above the day-to-day detail of the finance portfolio and look at the broader and longer strategic picture or subsequently to bring the party or electorate behind him when he assumed his prime-ministerial role. MacIntyre was only one of Muldoon's senior allies who believed that his major weakness was not his leadership ability but his dual roles as Prime Minister and Finance Minister.[2] Muldoon accumulated too much power in that there was no independent chairman of cabinet and caucus to whom other ministers could appeal in their inevitable disagreements with the Minister of Finance.

MacIntyre, who had been returned to Parliament as MP for the Bay of Plenty, after having been defeated in Hastings three years before, took the unusual step of arguing in writing against the appointment of five senior colleagues, all but one of whom were regarded as among Muldoon's closest friends and supporters: Highet, McCready, McLachlan, Lapwood and Walker. Muldoon appointed all five although in offering them their portfolios he made it plain that McCready, Lapwood and Highet were being appointed only for three years after which he would replace them with younger ministers. McCready and Lapwood accepted the condition but Highet insisted on being reconsidered in three years' time.[3] Gandar also advised Muldoon not to include McCready or Walker in the cabinet, as did one of the anonymous respondents who also opposed Lapwood and Allen.

Muldoon did not agree with those of his colleagues who dismissed Walker and McLachlan. Both had the advantage of being South Island MPs, and Muldoon respected Walker because of his skills as an accountant and his concern for people. He believed that Walker was the local constituency MP par excellence, always door-knocking, offering and available to help people in need. Although many of Muldoon's critics jeered at his close friendship with McLachlan, whose intelligence and competence as a minister they despised, one close observer, Patrick Millen, the long-time Secretary to the Cabinet, saw McLachlan as 'an interesting and likeable man who occasionally had devastating bouts of shrewdness and got the point when everyone else missed it'.[4] Millen, however, also conceded that McLachlan, who was 'the Apostle John in the Muldoon Cabinet', for 'most of the time didn't know what was going on'. Muldoon and McLachlan, incidentally, owned in partnership a number of racehorses such as the aptly named Noodlum and Macdoon.

Muldoon followed Holyoake in not always selecting ministers solely for their intelligence, expertise or interest in a particular area. Other factors such as loyalty and the ability to be part of a team were taken into consideration, as was the need for a geographic balance in the cabinet. In 1975, for example, Muldoon felt that John Luxton, a North Island MP, was very unfortunate in finally being omitted in favour of 'three or four South Island MPs who were no better if at all compared to Luxton' on merit, but were preferred because of their location.[5] Muldoon also believed that in cabinet selections there will always be some disagreement when subjective judgements are made by different people concerning another's ability or contribution. Unlike Holyoake, Muldoon did not require those whom he appointed to cabinet to give him on their appointment an undated but signed letter of resignation.

The final cabinet selection closely resembled the views of Muldoon's caucus colleagues and, to a lesser extent, the aspirations of individuals themselves. Sixteen ministers received the positions a majority of their caucus colleagues indicated that they should have, while the remaining four received one of the portfolios for which they were deemed most suitable by their peers. Seven received the post they had asked for; three others got one of the positions for which they had nominated themselves; and eight were chosen by Muldoon for positions which they had not requested but for which they had received the most nominations. Nevertheless, there were some significant disappointments and surprises, even among those chosen for cabinet.

One of Muldoon's close allies, Gill, a former Air Commodore, was very disappointed when Muldoon refused to appoint him Minister of Defence and insisted that he take the Health portfolio. Muldoon wanted Gill to prepare an alternative to the outgoing Labour Government's white paper on health and to resolve the controversial computerisation of the Health Department, but he admitted in hindsight that Gill had not been the ideal person to be Minister of Health at a time of debate over abortion, since he was easily the most conservative of National's MPs on that issue. Although friendly, Muldoon and Gill were never really friends and could and did disagree strongly with each other on occasions. In 1976, for example, Gill, offended by something Muldoon had said or done, astonished a senior National Party official by threatening to go to Muldoon's office and 'fill him in'.[6]

Among others who did not get what they asked for were Gandar, who desperately wanted Agriculture and put up a strong argument against the Education portfolio Muldoon insisted on giving him; Walker, who requested Postmaster-General and Broadcasting but got Social Welfare; and Templeton who wanted Education but got Postmaster-General and Broadcasting. Muldoon may well have given MacIntyre and Gandar their desired minor portfolios of Maori Affairs and Science respectively to sweeten his unwelcome decisions regarding their major ministerial responsibilities. Allen, Bolger and Comber became under-secretaries, which meant that the major omission from the ministry was Birch, who had received thirteen nominations for cabinet and six for under-secretary. Muldoon wanted Birch as his chief whip.

Muldoon could be, and increasingly became, irritated by the personalities of some of those he appointed to his cabinet. Holland had a hearing problem, which annoyed Muldoon in cabinet meetings. The Prime Minister disliked what he saw as Gair's bonhomie, Gill's sometimes uncontrollable arrogance and Templeton's academic mannerisms.[7] In time he grew to detest Gair personally, although he always recognised Gair's intellectual calibre and acknowledged that he was a 'hardworking, capable and conscientious' minister 'who could be left to get on with it' without any 'support or supervision'. Muldoon's one openly admitted criticism of Gair, apart from his support for abortion, was that, in Muldoon's opinion, 'if there were eight possible decisions on an issue Gair would find a ninth'. Gair's willingness to consider a wide range of alternatives, which Muldoon saw as a fault, was much more appreciated by senior civil servants, one of whom, a Director-General of Education, recalled that Gair was, unlike Muldoon, 'Wonderfully polite, courteous and gentlemanly . . . prepared to spend time listening to and respecting other views before pulling the discussion together and making a decision'.[8] Another, the chairman of the State Services Commission, believed that Gair was 'far more able than any of his colleagues' except Muldoon. He was a 'superb chairman of officials' meetings, got full contributions from everyone', with 'everyone working willingly and well together'. He 'listened to arguments even if he didn't agree with them' and was 'always impeccably polite and appreciative'.[9] Gair's barely concealed ambition to be Minister of Finance and perhaps one day leader of the National Party, however, threatened Muldoon.

Although MacIntyre had been a Marshall supporter, he was pleased for Muldoon when he became leader and subsequently Prime Minister. Muldoon, for his part, did not hold MacIntyre's lack of support in the leadership contest against him when he returned to Parliament in 1975.[10] Indeed, Muldoon ranked MacIntyre fourth in the cabinet after himself, Talboys and Gordon, the same order as in the Marshall ministry of 1972. He did not, however, give MacIntyre the portfolios he requested, his former responsibilities for Lands and Forests, where MacIntyre felt he had unfinished business. Instead, MacIntyre became Minister of Agriculture, a post he did not want, though at his insistence he also retained Maori Affairs from 1975 until 1978 when Muldoon felt the position should be held by one of National's Maori MPs, Ben Couch. As Minister of Maori Affairs, MacIntyre owed a considerable debt to 'Hori' Hanan, Holyoake's Minister of Maori Affairs 1960–69, and to Norman Perry, who had run the YMCA in the Maori Battalion overseas during World War II. In turn MacIntyre was able to influence not only Muldoon on Maori attitudes and concerns but also Bolger, who as MacIntyre's Under-Secretary 1975–7 chaired the Maori Affairs Committee and developed a genuine and long-term commitment to attempting to resolve Maori grievances.

The most serious dispute over Muldoon's 1975 cabinet selection was between Muldoon and the most senior of his colleagues after Talboys. Gordon confidently expected to get the cabinet posts he wanted, especially Transport. Muldoon and Talboys called Gordon into Muldoon's office and after teasing him about Transport told him that he had been given Labour and State Services. Gordon was furious and shouted at Muldoon, 'Oh bugger that!'[11] He picked up a pile of *Time* and *Newsweek* magazines on the corner of Muldoon's desk and threw them in the Prime Minister's face. One had an open staple which scratched Muldoon's forehead resulting in copious bleeding. Gordon was horrified, but Muldoon was amused and insisted that Gordon take him for lunch where there was considerable speculation as to the cause of the leader's marked face.[12] Muldoon's refusal to take Gordon's preference into account led to a deterioration in their previously close personal relationship.

Gordon, as Minister of Transport, and Muldoon had clashed a number of times between 1966 and 1972 over major transport policy and Gordon believed that this was at least a factor in Muldoon's decision in 1975 not to reappoint him to transport. Gordon felt that it was adding insult to injury when Muldoon appointed his close friend McLachlan to the job Gordon coveted. As a result, Gordon had no compunction in exposing McLachlan's ignorance and incompetence at every opportunity, and the besieged Minister of Transport repeatedly turned for support to the Prime Minister. An angry Muldoon saw Gordon as 'stabbing his great friend McLachlan in the back'[13] and supported McLachlan on a number of disputed issues: extensions to Wellington airport; nepotistic appointments to the National Airways Corporation board; and, most important, the amalgamation of NAC and Air New Zealand. Despite being intensively lobbied by Morrie Davis of Air New Zealand and Fred Dobbs, the National Party's publicist and a close friend of Muldoon, Gordon remained opposed to the merger. At short notice Muldoon insisted that Gordon fly to Paris to chair an OECD committee, and while Gordon was absent forced the amalgamation through cabinet. In his final speech in the House before retiring at the end of 1978, Gordon, recollecting his most satisfying achievements, referred to Wellington Airport and commented that it would have to be extended further. Muldoon interjected, 'Hey, careful', and when Gordon persisted added 'That's just cost you a job.'[14] Gordon believed that his conflict with McLachlan led to Muldoon vetoing his appointment to the board of Air New Zealand following his retirement from Parliament. As an alternative, Muldoon did offer Gordon the High Commissioner post in London, an appointment Gordon did not want and which he declined.

Despite their disappointments at their portfolios, at first MacIntyre and Gordon tried to keep up the strong empathy with Muldoon which they had built up and enjoyed as 'Young Turks' in the early 1960s and as younger ministers in the Holyoake and Marshall cabinets. The three after 1975, for example, revived their old habit of meeting late at night to relax and to discuss problems over drinks. With informal camaraderie they teased each other, enjoyed getting a chuckle out of various situations and were quite prepared to call a spade a spade. As MacIntyre recalled, 'friendship didn't stop Muldoon telling you you were a bloody fool if you put something up to him he thought was foolish' and for their part Gordon and MacIntyre had no compunction in telling Muldoon to his face that 'he was a mutt on occasions when we thought he was wrong'.[15] The fourth senior member of cabinet, Talboys, was more aloof and separate from the troika and indeed not only did not attend the late-night gatherings but did not even know about them.

Muldoon was determined from the start that public servants would advise ministers and carry out policy but that politicians would make the decisions. Immediately after the 1975 election he called together all the permanent heads of government departments. Without preamble he stated, 'This is the National Party's election manifesto. If it's in it, you do it! If it's not in it, forget it!' He pointed out that he would not consider any other new policies costing money during the government's first term.[16]

In 1975 the Rowling Labour Government, on the advice of Millen, the Secretary to Cabinet, and Robin Williams, chairman of the State Services Commission, was in the process of setting up a separate Prime Minister's Department. In the past the small cabinet office was under the control of the Secretary of Foreign Affairs and the Prime Minister had very little administrative and policy support. On the change of government in 1975 Muldoon was asked by Millen what he wanted and found his personal views matched those of Millen and Williams. At its first meeting cabinet agreed to Muldoon's proposal that 'the Prime Minister's Department should be administered as a Department of State separate from the Ministry of Foreign Affairs'.[17] It was decided to have three autonomous units in the Prime Minister's Department: the Prime Minister's Office, an Advisory Unit, and the Cabinet Office. The Prime Minister's Office and the Advisory Unit were under the control of the head of the Prime Minister's Office, during Muldoon's tenure successively Bernard Galvin and Gerald Hensley. There was also a Chief Private Secretary, successively Hilton Wells, Ed Buckton, Harold Hewitt and Ken Richardson. Although the Cabinet Office was officially under Galvin and Hensley, Millen was fiercely independent and largely kept the office neutral.

Not all Muldoon's staff liked or respected him. Wells and Gray Nelson were two secretaries inherited from Kirk's and Rowling's office and found their new boss much harder to work for. Indeed Nelson, who worked for five prime ministers, disliked Muldoon's policies and his personality and character and 'grew to hate him'.[18]

Muldoon was particularly impressed with Buckton and Galvin, both of whom he suspected had never voted anything but Labour, and indeed Galvin had already been designated to head up the new department if Rowling won the 1975 election. That did not worry Muldoon. As far as he was concerned they did their jobs efficiently and with complete integrity and on only one occasion did he ever refer to what he discerned to be their contrary party allegiance. On the Monday following the 1978 election in which National's large majority had been slashed, as Muldoon walked through the office he commented to Buckton and Galvin, 'You must have been pleased with Saturday's result.'[19] Muldoon judged Galvin, whom he saw two or three times a day, to be 'the best public servant I have ever worked with'. Muldoon recalled that he 'could get Galvin into my office and say "We have a problem" and explain it to him. Unlike others Galvin didn't reply, "I'll give a report next week." He would think the thing through there and then, make immediate progress and get the issue underway.'[20] Galvin for his part quickly learnt how best to argue with Muldoon. It was counter-productive to take a diametrically opposed view and tell Muldoon he was wrong or tell him there was only one possible course of action. One had to present and compare alternatives and think through the problem with him. In the end Muldoon made the decision and sometimes did reject advice, but on other occasions he allowed himself to be persuaded by the logic of the argument.[21]

Muldoon after 1975 was less impressed with his other major adviser, Lang, the Secretary to the Treasury, with whom he had crossed swords on a number of occasions over the previous ten years. Muldoon, who met with Lang every Monday morning at 9.45 a.m. before cabinet started at 10.30 a.m., admired Lang's intellect and determination but felt that as a civil servant he was too inclined to try to determine policy rather than simply advise the Minister of Finance and then implement the decisions made by the politician. Lang favoured Labour's Superannuation Scheme, which he had helped devise, more than National's alternative, and his arguments with Muldoon over this and over Muldoon's proposal to tax overseas travel funds also harmed the relationship. When Lang in 1976, at a time of considerable economic difficulty, decided to retire early at the age of 56, apparently to establish a retirement career, Muldoon was annoyed. He felt Lang had put his own interests ahead of his public service duty in not staying on as Secretary of the Treasury until he reached 60 and as a result, although Lang had been head of the Treasury for eight difficult years, Muldoon opposed a knighthood for him and the Cabinet Honours Committee concurred with a lesser honour.[22]

Galvin had replaced Frank Corner as head of the Prime Minister's Department. Corner, who had held that position concurrently with that of Secretary of Foreign Affairs from 1973 to 1975, continued in the latter role until 1980. Although Talboys was the Minister of Foreign Affairs and Overseas Trade, Corner was also a major adviser on foreign affairs to Muldoon, especially on the Prime Minister's major overseas trips. The relationship between Muldoon and Corner was never a particularly friendly one, though both men observed the formalities. Corner had become between 1972 and 1974 an almost unqualified admirer of Norman Kirk personally and of what Corner regarded as Kirk's moral foreign policy in regard to Africa, especially opposition to apartheid. He also supported recognition of and closer relations with China and nuclear disarmament, specifically the negotiation of a nuclear weapons free zone in the South Pacific. Corner was very disappointed with Muldoon's more pragmatic and less idealistic position: his equation of New Zealand's foreign policy with its overseas trade interests; his ambivalent attitude to Africa, specifically the reversal of Kirk's rugby boycott decision; and his complete lack of enthusiasm for nuclear weapons free zones.[23] Muldoon was more comfortable with Corner's successor, Merwyn Norrish, who was Secretary of External Relations and Trade from 1980 to 1987.

Among Muldoon's very loyal personal staff, Margaret Mouat (née Neish) was very significant. As a young and junior typist in the Minister of Finance's office from October 1965 she chose to go with Muldoon into Opposition in 1972 and devoted herself to working for him, particularly after the death of her husband in an air crash. Mouat remained with Muldoon, except for a number of short breaks, throughout his period as leader of the National Party, resigning finally in August 1986. She not only acted as his personal secretary and typed up the manuscripts of his books but also over the years collected and filed many of his papers. She organised annually a birthday party for Muldoon attended mainly by female secretaries, librarians, researchers and other staff around Parliament with whom he had worked over the years. Muldoon dedicated his second book, *Muldoon*, to her. Mouat recalled that, although in later years he used to introduce her as 'my fierce little secretary', she was in fact terrified of him at first and 'one look from those little blue eyes would freeze me to the spot'.[24] In time she grew more comfortable working for him and while he might never show appreciation or say 'Thanks', even when she was working from 6.30 a.m. until 10.30 p.m., in other ways he was 'a secretary's dream' and 'a joy to work for'. He was organised, 'never needing to be chased up', a person who 'moved paper superbly', and who rarely altered anything after it was typed up.[25] In a reference written for Mouat, Muldoon repaid the compliment: 'Her ability, application and personal loyalty have been quite outstanding . . . I have not met anyone like her in my career for attention to detail and dedication to the task in hand.'[26]

Muldoon said that as Prime Minister and Minister of Finance he was able to spend almost 100 per cent of his time, interest and energy on the job without constant unrelated chores and distractions. Unlike ordinary citizens there was always someone else to take care of meals, appointments, travel arrangements, the technical side of correspondence, and the numerous other things one usually did for oneself. It was, therefore, much easier for him to organise and use his time than when he did not hold office.[27]

The Advisory Group within the reorganised Prime Minister's Department was sometimes referred to as the Liaison Unit or more commonly the 'Think Tank'. It never included more than about eight hand-picked members whose task was to provide Muldoon with expert advice, particularly on the economy, independent of the state bureaucracy. Its members also liaised with individuals and interest groups throughout the country.[28] The group carried out detailed analysis of special topics and issues, and individually and collectively its members helped Muldoon think through various problems and alternative solutions. Despite the calibre of Muldoon's Advisory Group it was never really a long-term strategic research think-tank but much more a unit dealing on an ad hoc basis with current events and specific problems and providing a liaison between the Prime Minister, the bureaucracy and major interest groups. Muldoon's Advisory Group enabled him to react quickly and knowledgeably to events by giving him independent expert information and advice, keeping him abreast of ongoing developments, reaching out to interest groups while policy was in formative stages, and to some extent controlling and co-ordinating the flow of information between the Prime Minister and the public and private sectors.

Each member of the 'Think Tank' was chosen for his or her expertise, ability and personality, and as far as Muldoon was concerned their personal political persuasions were totally irrelevant. In retrospect Muldoon claimed that in the eight and a half years he was Prime Minister he 'never got a dud' in the unit which, he believed, had been extremely valuable.[29] The team was led at first by Galvin, head of the Prime Minister's Department and formerly Assistant Secretary to the Treasury. Galvin had degrees in mathematics and economics from Victoria University College, Wellington, and a Master's degree in public administration from Harvard. Galvin was given a free hand to make the other appointments. Muldoon never once refused a suggestion by Galvin or his successor, Hensley, that someone should be appointed to his advisory group. In 1981 when Hensley congratulated Muldoon on his election victory, Muldoon simply laughed, said it was close, and then added, 'I doubt whether I got a majority of votes from my Advisory Group.'[30] The other inaugural members of the Advisory Group were Len Bayliss, an economics graduate who had worked for the Bank of New Zealand, the Reserve Bank, the Treasury, the Monetary and Economic Council, and, on secondment, the Bank of England, and the only person appointed to the unit at Muldoon's personal request; John Beckett, a Rhodes Scholar and graduate in engineering from Auckland University and in management studies from Oxford, who had returned to New Zealand as deputy director of economic planning for the Railways Department after working as a management consultant in London; John Wood, a graduate in English from Canterbury University and Oxford, who had served in both the Ministry of Foreign Affairs and Treasury; and N. W. Stirling, who with an MCom and BSc had been an investigating officer with Treasury. Others were subsequently added, notably Dr Graham Scott, a consulting economist from Auckland, who had earlier worked in the United States for a number of years and whose speciality was energy research and development, and Helene Knox (née Wong), a young sociologist and later theatre director who became Muldoon's adviser on social affairs and his chief liaison with Maori gangs – although he also used other contacts such as Denis O'Reilly, a detached social worker with Black Power, especially in Wellington and Hawke's Bay, and Harry Tam, who developed work schemes with the Dunedin Mongrel Mob. Muldoon's press secretary, Gerry Symmans, attended all meetings of the Advisory Group and was also briefed on everything that was going on by Galvin.

The 'Think Tank' met with the Prime Minister at 4 p.m. every Friday afternoon for about two hours and among other matters checked through the cabinet agenda for the following Monday. Muldoon, who grasped their memos, documents and arguments very quickly, listened to his advisers intently and questioned and debated with them as they thought through various issues. The discussion was blunt and intimate, but always conducted formally and courteously on Muldoon's part. Subsequently, short reports of a page or two were written up and fed into the cabinet system. Members of the unit would also discuss the matters informally with individual ministers, civil servants and key individuals in the community. Because members of the Advisory Group automatically attended meetings of any officials committee set up, even if the civil servants did not want them there, Muldoon was kept up to date on what was going on and the main arguments rehearsed. The Friday briefings accompanied by summary memos made him better informed than some ministers were by their own officials.

The members of the Advisory Group also got into the habit of inviting their spouses and partners to join them about 5.30 p.m. on Fridays after their meetings and shared drinks and fish and chips in Galvin's office. Muldoon was not invited and never once chose to gate-crash. Nor did he choose to socialise with Galvin or other officials in his department, although when Galvin remarried quietly during a lunch-hour without telling him, the Prime Minister, on reading of the event in the *Evening Post*, banged on Galvin's door and told him he was 'cross because you didn't tell me' and then demanded that they break out the champagne.[31] Muldoon stayed on celebrating for a long time.

Because most of his cabinet had been ministers under Holyoake and Marshall in 1972, Muldoon's 1975 cabinet was a very experienced one and did not take long to come to grips with executive responsibilities. Muldoon presided over a very strong cabinet committee system. If a minister could not persuade a cabinet committee, then there was little if any hope of winning agreement in cabinet, which tended largely to confirm cabinet committee recommendations. The key Cabinet Economic Committee was chaired by Talboys and included Muldoon, Gordon, MacIntyre, Adams-Schneider, Gair, Holyoake and Wilkinson. It met every Tuesday at 10.30. Gill chaired the Cabinet Social Affairs Committee; Gordon the State Services Committee; and Bill Young the Works Committee. There were various other cabinet committees on such matters as Defence, Expenditure, Legislation, Transport, Honours, and, subsequently, National Development. Following the 1975 election Muldoon also set up thirty-two caucus committees to cover specific parts of National's election manifesto and keep his large number of backbenchers busy.

Muldoon promised a new style of government whereby the public would have greater access to information through the publication of government documents and by the readier availability of ministers to the press.[32] As chairman of cabinet and caucus he also was much more forthcoming than Holyoake and Marshall had been in sharing information with colleagues and in permitting wide-ranging and frank exchanges. The almost unanimous retrospective judgement of his colleagues was that between 1975 and 1978 Muldoon chaired both cabinet and caucus very well. While he could show impatience and anger, he rarely lost his temper and was willing to permit vigorous debate, including disagreement with his own views. He was also willing to accept a consensus that went against his own position, but 'his grasp of the issues, logic of argument and force of personality usually meant he was able to sway the majority'.[33]

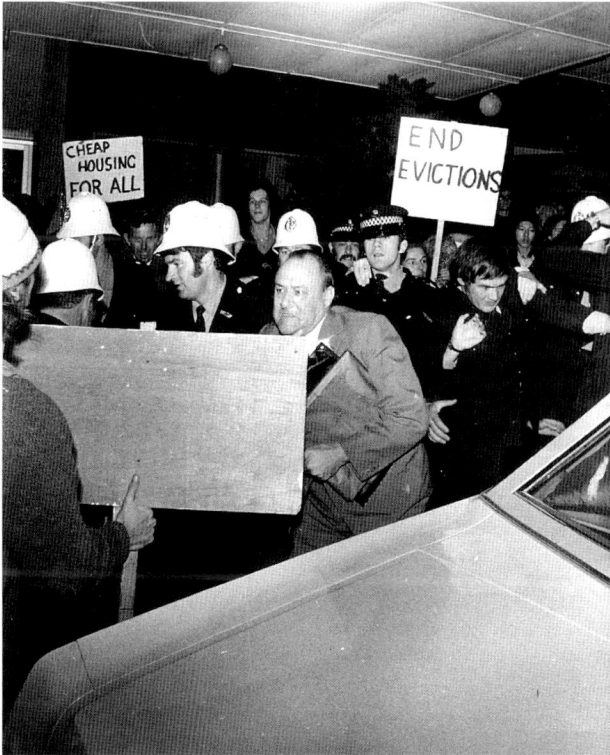

Above: While in Opposition, between 1972 and 1975, Muldoon flatted with five other National MPs in a Hawkestone Street house. At breakfast, from left, Muldoon, Talboys, Talbot, Gordon, Harrison, and Venn Young.
IAN MACKLEY/*EVENING POST.*

Left: Fighting with demonstrators in 1974 showed that Muldoon could counter-punch physically as well as verbally. *NZ HERALD.*

Top right: Many in the National Party always regarded Muldoon as a mixed blessing to their party, as Bromhead suggested. BROMHEAD/ AUCKLAND STAR.

Centre right: Rob and Thea for a number of years spent the New Year holidays cruising on the *Sirdar* with their friends Helen and Fritz Eisenhofer. MULDOON PAPERS.

Below: Election meeting at the Wellington Town Hall, 1975. EVENING POST.

Above: Muldoon's meeting at the Rotorua Sportsdrome on 21 May 1975 was attended by over 4000 people.
PETER FENWICK.

Left: Muldoon used charts to good effect throughout the 1975 election campaign.
NZ HERALD.

Muldoon in Britain in 1976. *FINANCIAL TIMES*.

Above: National Superannuation was a vote-winner in 1975 but its sustainability was to be an ongoing issue for the rest of the century. MULDOON PAPERS.

Right: 'New Zealand – The Way You Want It' was a very effective 1975 election slogan. MULDOON PAPERS.

Below: The National Party Caucus elected in 1975. Note Sir John Marshall standing at the top of the steps. EVENING POST.

Top: Four Secretaries of the Treasury, from left Dr. Graham Scott (1986–93), Bernie Galvin (1980–86), Noel Lough (1977–80), and Henry Lang (1968–77).
MARGO BREMFORD/*DOMINION*.

Above: Colin McLachlan was Muldoon's closest caucus friend and confidant after 1975.
CANTERBURY-WESTLAND DIVISION OF THE NATIONAL PARTY.

Above: At the South Pacific Arts Festival, Rotorua, 1976. MULDOON PAPERS.

Top left: Brian Talboys, Muldoon's deputy 1974–80 and nearly his replacement as leader in 1980. NATIONAL PUBLICITY STUDIOS.

Bottom left: George Gair worked closely with Muldoon in 1975 but after differing strongly with Muldoon on abortion was increasingly perceived as a rival. *NZ HERALD.*

At Waitangi Day, 1976. MULDOON PAPERS.

The policy process during Muldoon's term as Prime Minister was very clear and rarely varied. New or altered policy was the responsibility of the minister in charge of the particular portfolio. The minister was assisted by his ministry or department drawing not only on its own professional expertise but also on officials committees involving other departments, on caucus committees, and on specialists from outside government. Once the minister was satisfied, a cabinet paper was prepared and sent on to the cabinet office, which in turn forwarded it to the Prime Minister for a report by the Prime Minister's Department; to the Minister of Finance for a Treasury report on the financial and economic implications of the proposal; and to other ministers whose portfolios might be affected. All the reports were then referred to an appropriate cabinet committee. As one senior civil servant noted:

> in Sir Robert's time officials committees were used to good effect . . . [and] senior officials from the originating ministry/department, plus officials from Treasury, the SSC, Prime Minister's Department, and other 'reporting' departments, attended the cabinet committee meetings . . . This provided an opportunity for ministers to obtain further information, or to cross-examine officials on the opinions their departments had expressed . . . Any attempt on the part of a minister or department to push something through without proper consultation was quickly pulled up.[34]

In cabinet Muldoon liked to be carefully prepared and did not appreciate having to deal with unscheduled matters or unforeseen problems. Nor did he tolerate any waste of time. He expected his ministers to prepare and present short papers for their colleagues to read prior to the cabinet meeting. They were expected to show the relevance of proposals to the party's election manifesto, indicate the extent of caucus support, and be willing to argue the case against opposition. Ministers were required to concentrate primarily on their own portfolios and not continually tell colleagues how to run theirs. Muldoon insisted that ministers read the thirty or so papers on each Monday's cabinet agenda. He had a rule that if a minister had a question on a cabinet paper while reading it over the weekend that minister should ring the colleague responsible for the paper and seek an answer. Muldoon would not allow such questions of clarification to be asked in cabinet meetings. Thus cabinet meetings tended to be shorter under Muldoon than they had been under Holyoake.

Most ministers were afraid to attend cabinet ill-briefed and expose themselves to Muldoon's penetrating questioning. During the meeting he would move quickly and informally through the non-controversial items. This would usually leave about half a dozen more difficult matters on which to concentrate. Muldoon objected to matters being raised that were not on the agenda, which was sent out on Thursday afternoon with supplementary agendas on Friday afternoon and, for very late items, during the weekend. He also had a rule that nothing would go through cabinet without the necessary Treasury, State Services or Works reports. Usually cabinet decisions were made by consensus. When a straw poll was taken it had to be a clear majority for a decision to be approved. A one- or two-vote majority was usually, though not always, seen as too close, and Muldoon would defer the decision until a clearer margin of support appeared. Once a decision was taken, however, he would not allow a minister to return to an earlier item on the agenda or seek to reopen a matter. The Secretary to Cabinet, Millen, kept longhand notes of cabinet meetings and because his writing was so difficult to decipher would take the notes to Muldoon's office after the meetings and read them out to the Prime Minister. The notes were used in the preparation of letters and memoranda and for recalling points made during cabinet deliberations and were then attached to the duplicate set of cabinet agendas and papers which Muldoon retained personally as Prime Minister.

Muldoon was able quickly and clearly to absorb and understand a vast amount of information over a wide range, then get straight to the point in discussing or explaining it. His intelligence, grasp and recall of detail, capacity to identify key issues and points, forceful personality, ability to persuade, and access to information and analysis (from Treasury, the Reserve Bank, and the Advisory Group within the Prime Minister's Department) all together enabled him to dominate cabinet discussions. This was quite apart from the fact that as both Prime Minister and Minister of Finance he occupied the two most important positions and as Prime Minister was responsible for the composition of cabinet, the agenda, chairing the discussion, and summarising the consensus. In cabinet, however, Muldoon was not just a chairman but, in Finance and also in other areas such as Labour and Foreign Affairs, played an active and often decisive role in discussions. He frequently led or intervened in ways that countered or minimised the contributions of other ministers with whose views he disagreed and was not averse either in cabinet or caucus to eyeballing a dissident member and cutting that member down. Muldoon often in cabinet or cabinet committees, in questioning policy advice particularly from Treasury, would make comments such as, 'How's this going to affect people out there?' or 'You're not even thinking about the effect on people of these proposals'.[35] Once he had a majority in cabinet he was able to use executive collective responsibility, his own mana and powers of persuasion, and clever use of the whips, especially Birch, to sway a majority of caucus.

Many of those around Muldoon in cabinet and caucus were to varying degrees sycophantic. His closest political allies and friends such as McLachlan rarely questioned his authority or decisions, and in return Muldoon protected them with absolute loyalty. He could be extremely tolerant and compassionate when dealing with individuals who had been blindly loyal to him. Others who were more independent, and often more capable than some of the loyalists, were intimidated and reluctant to disagree with him or challenge him openly. Not all the ministers who supported Muldoon loyally in cabinet and caucus, however, were (as his critics alleged) incompetent sycophants or frightened of him. Certainly, in the early years of the third National Government, Talboys, Gordon and Gill were not and MacIntyre, Thomson, Adams-Schneider and Birch were also universally recognised as not only loyal but very capable. In cabinet Gill and MacIntyre in particular, according to Millen, said what they liked and showed no fear of or deference to

Muldoon.[36] MacIntyre and Thomson were also two of the most liberal of National's MPs, MacIntyre with a genuine interest in Maori affairs and Thomson regarded by Waring as one of the men most sympathetic towards women's affairs in general and her position as a young liberal woman MP in particular.[37]

Undoubtedly most of Muldoon's ministers and backbench MPs had a ambivalent 'love–hate' attitude towards him. They admired his ability but were repelled, even if fascinated, by his personality. It is doubtful, however, that Muldoon dominated and frightened his cabinet and caucus more than Richard Seddon, W. F. Massey or Peter Fraser had theirs.

Nevertheless, it is undeniable that Muldoon's autocratic tendencies became much more apparent after 1975. He had never been happy when he was opposed by political rivals, colleagues or advisers, and although he was prepared to allow a fair discussion he often made up his own mind early and then sought to reinforce his position or persuade others to his own view. Muldoon's impressive intellect and very efficient work habits enabled him to cope with the onerous day-to-day demands of being both Minister of Finance and Prime Minister, but the joint positions after 1975 gave him too much personal power. His personality, according to those who worked closely with him, changed after he became Prime Minister.[38] He became more isolated from most of his colleagues and eventually stopped socialising with them in the evenings. Eventually Muldoon's evening sessions with Gordon and MacIntyre gave way to drinks with McLachlan. Fewer MPs dropped into his office for a chat as they had done throughout the 1960s and early 1970s. Muldoon was genuinely fond of a few friends such as McLachlan, Harry Julian and Fred Dobbs with whom he could relax, drink, joke and tell stories. They were not only completely loyal and would not gossip about and embarrass their friend, but they did not make demands of him or take the opportunity to push an issue or seek an advantage. Muldoon became more difficult to work with and less fun to travel with. He became much more conscious of his status as Prime Minister and as a result behaved much more formally. Probably because of his background, he was not socially relaxed, especially in new situations or with strangers, and was always somewhat worried about doing or saying the wrong thing. He also became brusque, even on occasion rude and arrogant, in his attitude to colleagues, advisers and some civil servants and less tolerant of other views or criticism. On the phone as well as in person Muldoon was invariably abrupt. He simply barked 'Muldoon' and then launched himself straight into the business about which he had called. Some of his colleagues used to tease him by commenting on the weather or something equally mundane.

Muldoon realised that many people were frightened of him and offended by his manner, but he argued that he did not set out intentionally to be rude or aggressive. It was just that he was a very busy person with little time to waste in everyday relations. What he believed was a formal and businesslike manner, others perceived as abruptness or even hostility.[39] Muldoon as Prime Minister did not like anyone going into his personal office without an appointment. The best way to get things done was to put a request in writing and Muldoon would respond usually in a short time by returning the memorandum with either approval, disapproval or a short comment scrawled across the bottom. He was quite single-minded when dealing with any matter, giving his total attention to the matter in hand and not being diverted by other tasks, even if they were more important or more interesting. A creature of habit, he disliked changes in arrangements, even minor ones, inside or outside the office.

Muldoon was not only ill at ease with strangers but indeed was comfortable only in familiar surroundings. His new ninth floor office in the Beehive was colour-coordinated with light walls, creamy furniture and tobacco-brown carpets but Muldoon turned it into an interior decorator's nightmare by insisting on moving from the old Parliament Buildings his favourite electric blue, velvet wing chairs and his huge, dark mahogany desk, which had belonged to Seddon and which had to be sawn in half to get it into the ninth floor office.

Unlike most ministers Muldoon kept a very clean desk. Correspondence was usually read only once and a reply dictated or scrawled across the bottom for a secretary to draft more fully. If Muldoon had doubts on any subject, he immediately rang the Secretary of the Treasury or another responsible official either for supplementary information or to resolve a problem. He needed to know everything so that he could put the pieces together and come to his own conclusions. Reports also were dealt with methodically, with the main points swiftly identified and critically analysed. Muldoon had no 'too hard' basket into which recommendations and decisions vanished indefinitely. People might not always like or agree with his decisions, but he could not be accused of dithering. He disliked leaving things undone and one of his favourite sayings after a cabinet or committee discussion or towards the end of a day in the office was 'That's got things tidy.'[40]

Most ministers rely on notes, guidance and even full texts of speeches prepared by departmental officials or personal press officers and speech writers. Muldoon was exceptionally good at preparing his own speeches. He used departmental briefs only on formal occasions and in the finance field usually prepared his own speeches. He had a phenomenal ability to return after a weekend with half-a-dozen tapes of the following week's speeches to be typed up during the Monday. They rarely needed revision in their typed form. Muldoon tended to build a series of speeches around one theme and delivered them from engagement to engagement irrespective of the audience. In fact he was talking not so much to any particular group but to the press and through them to the wider public. Of course as Minister of Finance and later Prime Minister, Muldoon did have on his staff people who could carry out research and draft speeches and press releases. One was the former Press Gallery journalist Ken Hancock, who left Muldoon after a row. Hancock got into a vicious argument with one of Muldoon's office staff over the use of a copy machine and when Muldoon refused to back him he resigned, aggressively telling the Prime Minister that he did not need to provide him with a reference. Muldoon did not, an action he subsequently admitted was a mistake which he regretted.[41]

According to two chairmen of the State Services Commission, Muldoon was 'absolutely impeccable' about the independence of the State Services Commission and 'accepted with perfectly good grace one or two appointments' which he personally would not have made to senior posts in the public service.[42] The personal political views of his officials never worried him provided they were competent in their official duties, and nearly every civil servant interviewed by the author also commented on the courteous formality with which Muldoon usually treated them.

Rarely if ever did Muldoon praise anyone. The closest he came to it was usually to tell someone 'That's reasonably tidy' after reading a report or memo. Nor did he apologise overtly if he was rude or unreasonable. When he calmed down, however, he would try to restore the relationship by inviting the offended official or colleague in for a drink or five minutes of pleasantries. After one major row with Hensley, the head of the Prime Minister's Department arrived back in his office to find a brief note from Muldoon's secretary saying, 'PM wondered if you and your wife would like to have lunch with the Prince and Princess of Wales in nine months time?' Hensley realised Muldoon was apologising for the row. [43] He did not treat civil servants as friends and insisted on addressing them as Mr Buckton or Mr Galvin. On only one occasion over nine years did he ever address Galvin, the head of his Prime Minister's Department and later Secretary to the Treasury, by his first name. After an exhausting and frustrating day in China and after sitting through an interminable lecture on China's revolutionary view of education, Muldoon on returning to the hotel exploded, 'For Christ's sake, Bernie, get me a drink and one for yourself.'[44] That was also one of the few times Galvin ever heard Muldoon swear.

Although few of them liked him, most senior Treasury officials respected Muldoon's intelligence and work habits.[45] There was never any question that he comprehended the advice and background material provided to him, although there was some complaint that he did not always accept the advice. Muldoon could be and understandably was often abrupt and rude if senior civil servants or cabinet colleagues tried to bluff him, either by presenting shoddy papers or by not taking the trouble, as Muldoon always did, to read and comprehend documents before a discussion. Perhaps because he was an accountant he detested inexactitude and sloppy thinking. He also disliked procrastination. Unlike most ministers, Muldoon did not make his officials wait for decisions. On most non-controversial matters which did not require lengthier consideration, papers sent to him by Treasury in the morning were usually returned with his signature or comments by the afternoon. As the head of the Prime Minister's Department from 1980 to 1987 commented, Muldoon 'lived for the dispatch of business'.[46]

It was sometimes difficult to know what Muldoon really thought. In public, and even among colleagues and confidants, he was always positive and intent on creating the impression that he had the answers and the ability to deal with any problem. Throughout his career he projected an image of extraordinary self-confidence and determination, and of a man who saw things in black and white. He also, in public, strongly defended decisions and policies made in cabinet, caucus or the party organisation even if he personally had opposed them in private or had reservations about them. But despite his strong and decisive image Muldoon tended to be too timid and pessimistic about what voters were prepared to tolerate in economic restructuring, deregulation, and the reform of the welfare state, apart from a relatively brief period during 1976 and 1977.

The public Muldoon was different from the private man, who was very dependent on the understanding, care and support of his wife Thea. Her calmness and common sense and her undoubted influence on her husband may well have reinforced his finer characteristics, such as his sensitivity for those in need, and curbed his less positive ones, such as his aggression and vindictiveness. As one of his ministers later observed, Muldoon was 'totally unforgiving of people who postured themselves into a position and then didn't perform'.[47] He also never gave an inch in an argument or publicly admitted to making mistakes. He believed in 'an eye for an eye' and always responded in kind if attacked. Pugnacious and intimidating in public and in Parliament, and portrayed by opponents as a loud-mouthed bully, Muldoon was, however, on most occasions reserved and proper when meeting strangers. Complex and basically shy, he was not naturally gregarious, was awkward in the presence of people he did not know, and had no small talk. As the party's president, Chapman, recalled, 'Muldoon was not an easy mixer at social functions or even on a one-to-one basis. He was not a meeter and greeter like Holyoake was.'[48] When Muldoon did converse, he was often gruff in manner and sparse in words. Another person who observed him frequently at social functions recalled that, 'he would slip away behind a bookcase, rubber plant or corner' rather than move confidently among guests whom he did not know personally.[49] He could 'talk, grizzle, growl and joke with close friends', according to one admirer, but particularly when he was Prime Minister did not have time even to spend with friends and when he made time had to be more careful about what he said.[50] He also in the 1980s became much more defensive, isolated and suspicious. In the earlier years he had received brickbats and bouquets but in the later years there were many more of the former and few of the latter.

In the course of a day many people had appointments to see the Prime Minister and Minister of Finance. Interviews with Muldoon could often be measured in seconds rather than minutes, and people were shown in and out of his office sometimes at breathtaking speed. Meetings with major interest-groups were invariably formal, businesslike and courteous. Muldoon would invite a delegation into his office; ask them to explain what they wanted; would listen intently, grunting occasionally; ask whether anyone else had anything to say; and would then respond, showing respect to those who had presented well-prepared arguments, even though he did not agree with them, but demolishing those who had not. Muldoon respected those who had integrity and stood up for their convictions but could and did bully sycophantic colleagues, advisers or suppliants and less able or less principled opponents. He was equally brisk, and brusque, in dealing with written material. The long-time Cabinet Secretary, Millen, recalled that Muldoon could read a submission faster than anyone else he had ever met and could then dictate a concise and precise response which rarely needed alteration. When dictating, Muldoon could also often accurately recall a key fact or sentence from a document without recourse to it even if it had been a long time since he had read it.[51]

In his approach to political management, Muldoon was undoubtedly an interventionist. He accepted without question that the government should be involved actively in the planning and management of the economy and in building and maintaining a society in which all people had access to education, health care, housing, recreation, and support in times of misfortune or old age. He believed that politicians, not bureaucrats, businessmen, academics, farmers, bankers or trade unionists, were the legitimate guardians of the public interest in a democracy and that only politicians responsive to the will of the people could bring a degree of harmony out of the competing vested interests within society. He was also an interventionist in that he personally involved himself in the day-to-day affairs not only of his own finance portfolio but of other ministers' responsibilities – in labour, education, industries and commerce, and foreign policy and trade.

Very much a man of his times, embodying contemporary values and perspectives, Muldoon was not just an interventionist for the sake of intervening. New Zealand was a very regulated economy as the result of its historical development. Most of its economic infrastructure had been built either by, or with, considerable state input, and successive governments of every political persuasion had for a century managed the system and tried to balance the interests of differing sectors of society such as farmers, manufacturers, importers, workers and professional people. Muldoon was prepared to deregulate, but in a managed way which did not divide New Zealanders too starkly into winners and losers. His ideal society was a peaceful, fair, egalitarian, prosperous and racially integrated society, but it seemed to him many contemporary pressures, and much of the policy advice he received from Treasury, especially after 1978, attacked the very foundations of that type of society. Those pressures had to be resisted and that policy advice had to be rejected, or New Zealand's society would collapse and be catastrophically transformed. Nor was Muldoon's interventionism synonymous with socialism. There were elements of both socialism and capitalism, collectivism and individualism, radicalism and conservatism, protectionism and free trade, regulation and deregulation in Muldoon's eclectic policies and actions.

Muldoon had definite views on what was ideologically and politically right or wrong, good or bad, and could not stand what he called 'political neuters', those people who pretended to be totally apolitical. Rather he respected and preferred to deal with people who had thought about things and who had firm views, even if their views differed from his own. But because New Zealand is a small and intimate society, it is almost impossible to have a detached debate about ideas and policies. The debate very quickly descends to personalities, so that what is being said often becomes less important than who is saying it, and people who disagree over issues also begin to question the motivation and integrity of their opponents. Muldoon was always prone to attack the messenger as well as the message, and in turn he too became demonised in the minds of many of those whom he had attacked and who in return criticised his attitudes, principles and policies.

Much of his venom was directed at those who wore their conscience on their sleeve or adopted a holier-than-thou attitude. Muldoon absolutely loathed hypocrites and believed Parliament was full of them. That was reflected in his abruptness. If someone commenced a statement with 'I assume . . .' or 'With respect . . .' he would snap, 'Don't assume' or 'Don't "with respect" me', and as one of his closest officials observed, 'bricks would rain down on the head' of the person who had used the despised term.[52] Conversely, many of his critics or those attacked by him were so antagonistic to him personally that they never gave him any credit or benefit of the doubt when considering his actions, views and motivation. Muldoon was able to debate intellectually with intellectuals but not when, at meetings or on television, he was explaining or appealing to the ordinary voter. On such occasions he adopted a populist and simplistic approach which often infuriated intellectuals.

Muldoon's rise to political prominence and power coincided not only with a long-term structural decline in New Zealand's economy and a transformation in its society but also with the advent of television and the end of the mass-based traditional two-party system. People became less partisan in their identification with political parties and reacted more personally to the perceptions they formed of leading politicians competing on television. The media and politicians have always had a love–hate relationship. They need each other but their mutual dependence is balanced by mutual distrust and even mutual contempt. Muldoon fascinated and fed the press, though many journalists and interviewers disliked him. Despite his contempt for many in the media, he nevertheless relied particularly on television to appeal directly to the voters. He was quite prepared to accept that television would only provide him with short soundbites, so he simplified his comments and asserted rather than explained the positions he took. He realised that the nature of television news and current affairs was to trivialise, sensationalise, personalise, and present politics and politicians in as combative a way as possible. Entertainment, or what later became known as 'infotainment', became more important than balanced education in the presentation of news and current affairs. Politicians like Muldoon realised they would be judged by the viewing public, the voters, primarily by the impact they made through their television performances. As one journalist in retrospect noted, through television Muldoon 'was, incessantly, in everybody's living rooms, stirring hate and devotion'.[53]

Journalists, he contended, were there largely to report the news, in his case what he as Prime Minister or Finance Minister said or did. Too many journalists, however, were not in his opinion disseminating information but editorialising, interpreting and even challenging it. As a result he frequently questioned their accuracy and objectivity and regarded many as political opponents. His weekly press conferences became battle-grounds and were later described as such by the radio journalist Sharon Crosbie:

Oh the nervous excitement on press conference day. The equivalent of the Normandy landings week after week. Sir Robert manning the gun emplacements . . . Wave after wave of journos would hit the beaches. Hours of preparation had gone into question lines that generals back behind the lines (the editors) guaranteed . . . would drop Sir Robert in his tracks and leave him sobbing piteously as the position known as Fort Muldoon was overrun and the fourth estate flag was run up the pole. Time passed. The dream faded . . . Sir Robert never lost a fight. It was trench warfare at its finest and fiercest and it went on for years. The flower of polytech journalism courses fell back and died in the mud and heard above them, borne on the wind, the sound they dreaded most . . . Hah, hah, hah.[54]

During the late 1970s television interviewers also deliberately engaged in what Ian Fraser has described as 'adversary interviewing'. They not only asked questions eliciting information and opinion but were direct, aggressive and argumentative in pursuing a line of questioning.[55] In an interview following the 1978 Budget, Fraser tried to show that Muldoon had written a political rather than an economic document and had abandoned his 1977 Budget belief that tax reform was very important and long overdue. Muldoon threatened to walk out of the interview four times, telling Fraser that 'this line of interviewing will stop or the interview will stop'. Fraser persisted and a very angry Muldoon at the end of the programme flung the microphone on to the chair and drove away from the studio without removing his make-up. Almost every newspaper and radio station in the country commented and quoted Fraser as saying 'interviewers could not be intimidated'. Muldoon, however, never again consented to be interviewed by Fraser and his refusal to co-operate eventually led to Fraser being replaced by David Beatson as the frontman for Television's 1981 election-night coverage.[56]

One observer, who interviewed Muldoon frequently throughout his political career, has graphically described his television style:

> He liked to think of himself as a boxer, a counter-puncher, but I do not think that fitted him. Boxers fight by Queensberry rules; Rob Muldoon fought by Rob Muldoon's rules. He was a television prodigy, who could harangue like Castro, patronise like de Gaulle, and abuse like Paisley. . . . He saw the studio, press conference or platform as battlefields, and walked on to them with two aims – dominate the occasion, intimidate the participants. Sometimes he ignored the interviewer and barked directly into the camera, full-frontal. He ignored normal conventions about media access, and simply took out any observer he thought was getting in his way. . . We have not had a politician to match him for gall, balls and gunfire.[57]

CHAPTER 13

Turbulent Times:
SIS, Abortion, the Moyle Affair,
and the Governor-General

ULDOON INHERITED FROM KIRK AND ROWLING THE 'SUTCH Case' and an inquiry into the Security Intelligence Service. Dr William Ball Sutch had been Secretary of Industries and Commerce from 1958 to 1965 and had served New Zealand in a variety of other capacities prior to that from the time he joined the staff of Finance Minister Gordon Coates in 1932.[1]

Ironically there were some significant similarities between Muldoon's approach to economics and those of the more Marxist influenced Sutch. To both, the social ends were more important than the economic instruments used to obtain them. Both saw the insulation of a dependent economy and the maintenance of full employment as the priorities. They were quite prepared to use import controls, import substitution, government planning and intervention, exchange controls, and subsidised farming and manufacturing to achieve those goals. Both were cultural as well as economic nationalists and both, incidentally, were very arrogant in assessing their own intelligence and abilities in comparison to those who disagreed with them.

Although never a member of the Communist Party, Sutch made no secret of his interest in and admiration for the Soviet Union, which he visited on three occasions in 1932, 1937 and 1946. The British, from 1937, and the Americans, from 1947, were suspicious of Sutch as a security risk and in 1958 the Nash Government, which appointed him Secretary of Industries and Commerce, gave the United States Government a written assurance that no classified material of US Government origin would be made available to Sutch or to his department.[2] Sutch retired in 1965. Between April and July 1974 routine SIS surveillance of D. A. Razgovorov, the First Secretary of the Soviet Embassy and a career KGB intelligence officer, identified regular night-time meetings between Razgovorov and Sutch.

After consulting the Solicitor-General, the SIS advised Prime Minister Kirk on 2 August 1974 not to prosecute Sutch but to seek an explanation from him for his contacts with Razgovorov and to declare Razgovorov and two other Soviet diplomats involved persona non grata. Instead Kirk instructed the SIS to continue the surveillance and to establish what information or government contacts Sutch still had access to. Kirk also authorised phone taps and bugging of Sutch's office by the SIS.[3] Kirk died on 31 August and on 13 September his successor Rowling, with whom Kirk had previously discussed the matter, was fully briefed. With Rowling's approval it was decided that the police would intervene at the next meeting between Sutch and Razgovorov with a view to identifying what material, if any, Sutch was passing to the Soviets. On the night of 26 September the police interrupted a meeting at Holloway Road but Razgovorov claimed diplomatic immunity; another Soviet Embassy member, V. F. Pertsev, drove off in his car with the material handed over by Sutch and delivered it to Alexei Makarov, the second in charge of the Soviet Embassy; and Sutch, although he denied that he had been regularly meeting Razgovorov, was formally charged under the Official Secrets Act.

The Attorney-General, Dr Martyn Finlay, reluctantly agreed to Sutch being prosecuted and a trial by jury was conducted in the Wellington Supreme Court 17–21 February 1975. Sutch was found not guilty and following his acquittal there was considerable public criticism of the SIS, which led to Rowling deciding to review the Official Secrets Act and also on 8 August 1975 to set up an inquiry into the SIS conducted by the Chief Ombudsman Sir Guy Powles. Powles submitted his report to Muldoon on 6 May 1976. It contained ten findings and 28 recommendations and led to the drafting later in the year of a Security Intelligence Amendment Bill and in 1978 the establishment of a committee chaired by Sir Alan Danks to consider freedom of information.[4] The SIS Bill was largely written by Galvin, who chaired the Security Officials Committee, and Millen, who was its secretary.[5] Many people on the left of politics were very sceptical about the prosecution of Sutch and suspicious about the role of the SIS in spying on left-wing academics, unionists and peace activists.

That antagonism had been aggravated by the apparent role of at least some SIS personnel in a campaign to discredit key figures in the Labour Government prior to the 1975 election. The SIS, for example, was implicated in the leaking of police job sheets regarding interviews with a Labour MP who was the Labour Party's senior vice-president, Gerald O'Brien. The material was clearly intended to embarrass the Labour Government, but although a Security Intelligence officer was forced to resign, he always denied that he had given the information to a businessman who was a former acquaintance in the Territorial Army.[6] The businessman passed the material to Rowling instead of using it – as probably had been originally intended – to embarrass the Labour Government. Subsequent suggestions that the leaked documents were part of a National Party plot to discredit Labour were denied totally and angrily by Muldoon.[7]

Suspicions still remained in Labour Party, academic and trade union circles that not only the SIS but also the police might be exceeding their authority by investigating citizens who legally disagreed with Government policies. Shortly after the 1975 election, K. B. Burnside, the Commissioner of Police, recommended officially that Muldoon as the new Prime Minister should listen to a tape in which an undercover policeman code-named 'R' and a paid civilian informant known as 'Sparrow' reported on the operations and proposed future activities of the Halt All Racist Tours (HART) organisation. Burnside admitted that 'in the past infiltration of such like organisations by police agents has been considered unethical' but then asserted that 'this organisation is not all it seems to be on the surface . . . They are in fact a radical agency who are prepared to force their will on our society by terrorist activities of the worst possible kind.'[8]

The tape, which in transcript covered nearly nineteen typed pages, dealt largely with the HART national conference in Wellington on 28–29 February 1976. Among claims made in the tape were that some HART activists proposed to disrupt sporting fixtures by means including the breaking down of fences, the destruction of softball diamonds, the burning of rugby clubrooms, the assaulting of South African sports people, an invasion of the softball field during a game, explosions in the street, the use of aeroplanes and helicopters which would drop various objects, and the use of heavy vehicles to block streets and disrupt traffic. Burnside was particularly worried about injury to members of the public from any possible use of explosives. The Auckland delegation was accused of being very radical and only with difficulty restrained by moderates such as Trevor Richards. The briefing confirmed Muldoon's existing suspicions of and hostility towards HART.

At the same time the Security Intelligence Service was raising Muldoon's concern about and rekindling his antagonism towards the Socialist Unity Party and other New Zealand communists. The whole question of communism, the Soviet Union, possible espionage and subversion had been raised by the Sutch case and the resulting Powles Report on the SIS. Following that report Muldoon requested details of communist influence in the New Zealand trade union movement and received them in August 1976.[9] The SIS briefed Muldoon on the activities of the SUP and the Communist Party of New Zealand in the union movement and reassured him that although about a third of SUP members held office in various trade unions, those parties had at that time virtually no representation at or influence on the Federation of Labour. At the 1975 FOL Conference, for example, out of 300 delegates only ten were known to be members of the SUP and only one a member of the CPNZ. SUP members did, however, have some influence on a few individual unions and SUP members did undergo general ideological training at the Soviet Union's expense at the Institute of Social Sciences in Moscow. The SIS identified forty-five members and nine recent former members of the SUP and CPNZ who held office in the trade union movement.

Some of Muldoon's own National caucus thought that the SIS and the police were going too far in investigating New Zealand citizens who were simply exercising their democratic and legal rights as peace or anti-apartheid activists, trade unionists, academics, or political party members. The new MP for Hamilton West, Mike Minogue, was a lawyer and a former mayor of Hamilton who before his entry to Parliament had clashed with Muldoon over education and local body finance. Almost from the first Minogue acted as if he was an independent rather than a National MP. He called the Government's roading policy 'bloody crazy',[10] criticised the growth of cabinet executive power at the expense of parliamentary democracy,[11] and condemned bureaucratic secrecy which blocked access to information.[12] By 1977 his campaign had became more strident as he alleged that New Zealand was well on the way to becoming a police state.[13] This was an observation seized on with glee by Muldoon's many political opponents. In caucus Minogue expressed serious concerns about the SIS Bill and Muldoon's attitude towards dissent. Minogue was particularly concerned about the SIS undertaking surveillance against protesters and also argued that public servants would be subject to much greater surveillance by the SIS and commented that this was 'outrageous'.[14]

Muldoon's growing impatience exploded after Minogue was interviewed in a *Dateline* television current affairs programme on 12 September 1977. Minogue's long, pre-recorded interview was edited and much of its balance removed. In the programme Minogue attacked the SIS Bill and argued that it inadequately protected the basic rights of individuals in a democratic society. He also appeared not to have confidence in Muldoon as Minister in charge of the SIS. The night it was broadcast Muldoon was entertaining the heads of the New Zealand SIS and its British equivalent. They watched and were appalled by the programme. Muldoon publicly criticised Minogue's comments as 'extravagant, unwarranted and disloyal' and as 'patently absurd' and threatened to oppose his reselection as a National candidate at the 1978 election.[15]

Minogue responded publicly and in caucus by explaining that his comments had been distorted by the omission of other references in the interview favourable to the Bill and also to Muldoon personally but remained unrepentant regarding his central criticism.[16] He noted that his comments had been pre-recorded several days before he had seen a copy of the Bill and that, although they had been made about the Powles Report and he had stressed that he had not seen the Bill, his comments had been edited so that it appeared that he was in fact criticising the Bill. Muldoon told Minogue that he did not need to cross the floor as he had threatened to do because the Prime Minister would look at the Official Secrets Act with a view to removing any danger to civil servants which Minogue feared as a result of the SIS Bill. Muldoon also stated publicly that he had made his earlier critical comments about Minogue because he had thought Minogue was being interviewed live, whereas it had been a heavily edited pre-recorded interview which did not fully or accurately reflect Minogue's position.[17]

Muldoon complained to the Broadcasting Corporation of New Zealand's Complaints Committee that the TV programme had greatly distorted Minogue's remarks and quoted him out of context and that the political scientist Keith Ovenden, 'presented as an independent commentator', was Sutch's son-in-law. The Labour MPs Rowling and Hunt had also been on the programme dealing with the SIS Bill and the Powles Report but although Muldoon, as minister in charge of the SIS, had agreed to an interview neither he nor any other official government spokesman had been included in the programme. Muldoon said that he would not in future agree to be interviewed by Simon Walker, and that interviews with Brian Edwards, Gordon Dryden and Ian Fraser should be shown unedited. The Complaints Committee found in favour of Muldoon's complaint and detailed numerous ways in which the unedited interview with Minogue had been edited to give a totally wrong impression of his views, but a great deal of harm had been done in Muldoon's opinion.[18]

Minogue had certainly expressed the disquiet of many voters, including some within the National Party, concerning the powers, activity, competence and integrity of the SIS and had undoubtedly damaged both the Government's and Muldoon's public images. As a result when he continued to speak out independently and critically it came as no surprise to Minogue when Muldoon invited him to the Prime Minister's office one night. After handing him a full glass of whisky and inviting him to sit down, Muldoon without further preamble stated, 'You have no future in this party. You will resign and spend the rest of your term as a National Independent or an Independent, as you will.'[19] Minogue replied, 'I think you are a bloody poor judge of character. Goodnight.' He put down his glass undrunk and left the office. This exchange set the scene for the relationship with Muldoon over the following seven years, though the two men never again discussed the question of Minogue's resignation. Following his defeat at the 1984 election, Minogue did cease to be not only an MP but also a member of the National Party.

In August 1976 *Truth* ran a story alleging that Waring, another MP from the Waikato, was in a lesbian relationship with a woman who had left her husband and three children to live with the MP.[20] Muldoon learnt of the matter during a cabinet meeting. After sending cabinet staff from the room, he told his cabinet colleagues and asked all of them to support Waring and refrain from any comment on the matter. Only Gill refused. Muldoon then got Chapman to contact all five divisional chairpersons with the same request and despatched Birch to tell Waring's parents about the article and how he intended responding to it. Waring was unaware of Muldoon's reaction until the following morning when the Prime Minister invited her to his office and advised her not to say anything to anyone about the matter and if possible to go into hiding for a while.[21] He also placed National MPs at each end of the corridor to Waring's office to stop her being bothered by reporters and gave her a question to ask in the House so that she would still be seen to be doing her job as an MP. Although Rowling was waiting at her desk in the House to assure her that Labour would not exploit the situation, and Waring also received messages of support from Finlay and other Labour MPs, some National and Labour MPs did subsequently criticise her lesbianism. Muldoon retaliated in private by saying, 'She's just a kid; why are they picking on her?'[22] Muldoon's position was quite clear. Provided it was not illegal a person's sexual orientation or activity was that person's business and should have no relevance at all to their public office or the loyalty they should be able to expect from their party leader and colleagues. Waring's Raglan Electorate Committee passed a unanimous vote of confidence in their MP and she was also supported publicly by a wide range of other people who agreed with her electorate chairman's comment that 'Marilyn Waring's private life is no one else's bloody business'.²³ For a time there was speculation, however, fuelled by Waring thinking aloud publicly, that she might quit politics or stand as an independent at the 1978 election.²⁴

While Muldoon was more conservative socially than Waring, the two generally agreed on economic matters and sometimes, indeed, found themselves on the same side on other issues as well. Many more conservative MPs such as Brill and Dail Jones, for example, believed that recognition of property rights in what Muldoon termed the 'many valid de facto relationships' in New Zealand 'undermines [the] rights of the family' and condoned 'living in sin'.²⁵ When asked if the matter could be made a conscience issue and a free vote, Muldoon declared that it was a policy not a conscience issue, and by a vote of 20 to 17 caucus agreed to recognise de facto marriages in determining property rights. Muldoon and Waring, however, disagreed on a tough approach to drug traffickers. Waring was concerned about the police using listening devices to obtain evidence and also pointed out that many older people smoked marijuana but Muldoon, while admitting that 'public indignation doesn't always make good law', was determined to respond to public outrage against drugs and believed that, because selling drugs was 'an offence of greed', convicted drug dealers should have their properties confiscated.²⁶

Waring found herself totally opposed to Muldoon on the abortion issue which re-emerged when Gill decided in 1977 to introduce into Parliament a conservative Contraception, Sterilisation and Abortion Bill. The Prime Minister had been undoubtedly forewarned of Gill's intention at a dinner he had with Gill and the Roman Catholic Cardinal at the home of the Wellington lawyer and anti-abortion leader, Des Dalgety, on 13 April 1977.²⁷ Muldoon stressed to his caucus that the Bill would be 'hotly contested in principle and detail' and appealed to MPs to 'please restrain your feelings' because although it was a 'serious issue' it was, in his opinion, 'not sufficiently important for any of my MPs to lose [his or her] seat on this.' It was a matter of the 'least said – soonest mended'.²⁸ He told caucus he wanted the Bill dealt with as quickly as possible, preferably within two months, to minimise the damage it would cause.

The abortion debate in caucus, however, was nasty, and the pro-abortionists felt that Muldoon was chairing it badly and favouring Gill over Gair, who was leading the liberal pro-choice faction and intended to move an amendment to Gill's Bill. At one point Muldoon observed that, in his opinion, the Gair amendment was 'dead'.²⁹ Muldoon also at first refused Gair the right to speak in caucus because he had spoken in cabinet, but the issue was a conscience matter not one of collective ministerial responsibility. When the liberals tried to prevent Gill introducing his Bill by arguing that the Royal Commission on the subject was still sitting and nothing should be done until it reported, Muldoon said he had to allow the Bill to be moved in Parliament because he had sent out letters promising to do so during the election.

Not only the caucus but the party organisation was divided over the issue. When the Gill Bill was passed by Parliament late in 1977, the Auckland Divisional Executive at its first meeting in 1978 found itself faced with a motion moved by Gair's North Shore and McLay's Birkenhead electorates. They asked the Division to pass a resolution stating that the recent legislation on abortion was 'unacceptable to the majority of the New Zealand public' and that the Division 'records its disapproval' and 'calls upon Parliament to repeal this part of the legislation immediately'.[30] After an hour's heated debate in which twenty-three people spoke, the motion was carried by 30 votes to 28. Muldoon was not impressed with what he saw as an attempt by Gair and his supporters to bring abortion back on to the agenda in an election year after he had pleaded with his caucus to get the matter tidied up and out of the way before the end of 1977 so that it would not continue to divide and damage National in 1978. He was even more incensed when it was reported to him by the Auckland Divisional and Tamaki Electorate chairmen that there were rumours that pro-abortionists were working to remove Malcolm, Wellington, Birch and Dail Jones as National candidates for their respective seats and that, because a majority of activists in Muldoon's Tamaki electorate were pro-abortion, he should avoid the issue at his own electorate's AGM because, as his chairman warned, 'I don't think you can win and I don't want you buying into the wrong side of the fight'.[31]

Just before the 1978 election, Muldoon invited Waring to his office and told her again that he did not want abortion to be a major election issue. Waring responded that it would be, irrespective of what she did, and that she intended only to visit electorates with pro-choice National candidates. She could not campaign for anti-abortionists. Muldoon found this attitude difficult to understand or accept and told her so. As far as he was concerned abortion was a conscience issue and he would campaign for National candidates regardless of their personal stance on the issue. While there was never much affection between Muldoon and Waring, neither of them over eight and half years wasted energy on attacking the other personally. Each knew where the other stood, listened attentively and courteously to each other's arguments, and agreed to differ without rancour. Only on the night in 1984 when Muldoon called an early election did he ever abuse Waring personally and then, according to her and the recollections of others present, 'he made up for himself'.[32]

Muldoon's reaction to Gair's role in the abortion debate was much more negative. There is no doubt that Muldoon's growing personal antipathy towards Gair, who was often mentioned as a more civilised and democratic alternative leader to Muldoon and who made no secret of the fact that he thought that at the very least he should take the finance portfolio from Muldoon, was worsened by the abortion debate. During the second reading of the Contraception, Sterilisation and Abortion Bill the strained personal relationship between Muldoon and Gair was irrevocably broken when Muldoon said that he would be very disappointed if the Member for North Shore used the abortion issue to advance his personal ambition.[33] For years after, the two men hardly spoke to each other socially, even when sitting in adjacent seats on the flights to and from Wellington and even though both continued to respect each other's talents and strengths. They kept their relationship very businesslike, communicating through cabinet papers and discussions at formal meetings. Gill and Gair's relationship was also damaged irreparably by the abortion issue but others who took opposite sides in the debate remained close personal friends and collaborators in the future, for example Gair and Birch or Waring and Malcolm.

Muldoon might have been willing to defend Waring against both National and Labour MPs who attacked her lesbianism, and he also might have been prepared to support the decriminalisation of homosexuality, but he was not above seeking to put down an opponent on one occasion by suggesting that he might be a homosexual. Muldoon's tendency to counterpunch with ruthless and devastating effect, and sometimes to hit well below the belt, was exemplified possibly more than at any other time late in the evening of 4 November 1976. Labour decided to try to prevent Muldoon from following usual procedure in dealing with supplementary estimates and a very bad-tempered debate raged for three hours.[34] In the opinion of the Social Credit MP, Beetham, Labour MPs were enjoying 'baiting the bull' but 'Moyle got gored' by the 'aggravated, liquored-up and clearly dangerous' Muldoon.[35] During that time numerous points of order were raised and MPs on both sides became enraged. Abused as a fascist, Muldoon retaliated by attacking Russell Marshall, who had compared the Prime Minister's Advisory Group with Nazi Germany's propaganda department, as 'the red reverend, the representative in this country of the communist party'. In the midst of a barrage of Labour interjections, the Labour MP Frank Rogers laughed. Muldoon who thought the laughter came from Colin Moyle, remarked, 'I shall forgive the effeminate giggles of the member for Mangere, because I know his background.' An understandably angry Moyle, in turn, descended to personalities responding, 'Would it be in order . . . to accuse the Prime Minister of being a member of an accountancy firm that did things that were dishonest?' To that Muldoon, who had been drinking earlier in the evening and was perhaps even more belligerent than usual, replied, 'It would be in order if it is in order for me to accuse the member for Mangere of being picked up by the police for homosexual activity.' Not only Moyle and his Labour colleagues were devastated by Muldoon's implication; so were some National MPs.[36] The Speaker forced both Moyle and Muldoon to withdraw their remarks and apologise.

Had the matter stopped there, no one would have emerged with very much credit but the damage could have been contained. Although Muldoon's partners in the Auckland accountancy firm of Kendon, Mills, Muldoon and Browne were very hurt, indignant and somewhat apprehensive of the effect on their business of the unjust accusation Moyle had made against them, they issued only a brief press statement and decided to make no further comment. There was no loss of clients and most people simply saw both Moyle's comments and Muldoon's as being politicians grossly overstepping the boundaries of propriety.[37] On reflection, Moyle realised that his comment in the House about the accountancy firm of which Muldoon was a partner was indefensible, even though parliamentary privilege protected him from legal action. He also realised that Muldoon was using it to justify his response. On 16 November, almost a fortnight after the incident, Moyle

wrote to Kendon, Mills, Muldoon and Browne, confirming that his various
television and radio statements were a 'withdrawal and apology' and that 'I express
my regrets if the incident has caused your firm any embarrassment.'[38] Muldoon's
comments about Moyle, however, continued to provoke ongoing controversy.

Almost a year and a half before, Moyle at 11 p.m. on 17 June 1975 had invited
an undercover policeman in a Wellington street near a nightclub run by the
flamboyant homosexual Carmen to join him in the then Minister of Agriculture's
car. After ascertaining Moyle's identity the policeman had warned him of the perils
of inviting strangers into his car late at night in a somewhat dangerous area. Later
that night the constable mentioned the incident at a debriefing attended by ten
policemen and was asked by a senior sergeant, his superior, to type up a report
which was then given to an inspector. The following day Moyle had contacted a
chief superintendent and in a meeting with him claimed to have been carrying out
private research into homosexuality in preparation for a debate in Parliament on
the decriminalisation of homosexuality. The police decided that the Minister of
Police, Hon. Michael Connelly, should be sent the file with the suggestion that 'for
a Cabinet Minister to engage in such conduct was, under any circumstances, most
unwise.'[39] Connelly in turn suggested that Moyle discuss the matter with the
Deputy Commissioner of Police, R. G. Walton, who advised Moyle that his actions
were open to misinterpretation and that, while no offence could be established on
the evidence available, similar conduct might result in proceedings. The file was
subsequently put in the Commissioner's safe in case there was any further question
as to actions of the police in the matter.

How did Muldoon learn of the incident involving Moyle and the police?
Within three days twenty-five police employees were aware of the incident
according to a confidential police memo dated 20 November 1975.[40] In addition
Moyle's cabinet colleague Connelly, the Minister of Police, had been sent the file
with a covering letter, though he later could not recall reading it, and had
mentioned the matter twice in passing to the then Prime Minister Rowling.
Muldoon claimed that he had been told about the incident by a member of the
parliamentary Press Gallery, David Inglis, who had heard about it through the
police-journalist grapevine.[41] One of Muldoon's colleagues, Templeton, however,
has suggested Muldoon had been also alerted to the matter by a policeman who
had telephoned Muldoon while Templeton was in Muldoon's office.[42] Muldoon
always denied this and said he did not speak to the police about the matter before 5
November 1976.

However Muldoon learnt about the police file on Moyle, it is significant that
the information was not leaked or used during the 1975 election campaign, one of
the dirtiest in New Zealand's history in terms of character assassination of leading
politicians on both sides. Only in the heat of the moment, when alcohol had
loosened Muldoon's inhibitions and three hours of sustained vituperation from
Labour's front bench had enraged him, did he lash out with the accusation and
then only after Moyle had attacked the honesty of his accountancy partners. What
Muldoon did was wrong, but Moyle had provoked him and the subsequent though

temporary destruction of Moyle's parliamentary career resulted more from his and Rowling's subsequent handling of the issue than from any continued vindictiveness on Muldoon's part, though not only most Labour supporters but some in the National Party also put the blame for the disgraceful episode almost entirely on Muldoon.

One National MP, Minogue, believed, or perhaps hoped, that Muldoon's comment about Moyle would destroy Muldoon and told one of his colleagues so the same night.[43] Minogue expected that Labour would defend Moyle and attack Muldoon, asking where his information had come from, the SIS or the police, and demanding his resignation for a gross abuse of power.

Other National MPs challenged Muldoon over the Moyle affair. McLay at the end of the following caucus meeting asked for a discussion and said the media would expect caucus to consider the issue.[44] Muldoon responded that McLay had given a good reason for not discussing it but would put it on the agenda for the next meeting. The following week McLay told Muldoon that he had certainly been provoked but had not needed to respond in the manner he had. Muldoon 'in a firm and sharp but not angry response' replied that if people attacked him he would attack back. After no one supported McLay but several other MPs had defended Muldoon's action, caucus moved to the next business.

That did not mean all other National MPs except Minogue and McLay supported what Muldoon had done, even allowing for the provocation. Talboys, Gordon and MacIntyre who, according to Gordon, all lacked 'the killer instinct' had been growing increasingly concerned at the viciousness that was entering politics and were appalled by Muldoon's attack on Moyle.[45] But they felt that they had no option but to defend him publicly by arguing that Moyle was equally, if not more, to blame.

Labour's leader Rowling was already angry with another Labour MP, the party's vice-president Gerald O'Brien, regarding allegations of homosexual conduct earlier in the year. The so-called O'Brien affair originated in a leaked police interview and the apparent involvement of police, an SIS agent and territorial army officers. Although Moyle was one of Rowling's closest friends and colleagues, and Rowling was determined that he should be exonerated, he was adamant that the Labour Party's attitude should be the same towards both Moyle and O'Brien and that they should vindicate themselves or go – a view not shared by the party's president Arthur Faulkner, who believed they should both be supported without reservation.

On Friday 5 November, the day after Muldoon had made the allegation in Parliament, Moyle rose to make a personal statement in Parliament. He told a tense House that he had never been 'arrested, apprehended or "picked up"' by the police but that while driving home the previous year he had seen a man he suspected could be a burglar and had stopped. The man had approached him and identified himself as a policeman. The following day Moyle had discussed the matter with Assistant Commissioner Walton who said Moyle had been mistaken for the burglar's contact man and that the 'the whole matter was completely innocent'.[46]

Following that statement, Muldoon and his Minister of Police, McCready, met with the Commissioner and Assistant Commissioner of Police, who refused to reveal the contents of the file on Moyle. In the light of Moyle's statement to Parliament earlier in the day and after receiving advice from the Solicitor-General, they were prepared to say that Moyle's statement in Parliament 'varied in some respects to the Police record of events' and that homosexuality had been suspected though no offence had been disclosed. As a result Muldoon two hours later rose in the House and challenged Moyle's statement and asked Moyle if the police file could be tabled. Rowling defended Moyle and asked how Muldoon knew what was in the file when the police had earlier that day refused Moyle permission to see it himself until they had taken legal advice. Apparently unaware that Connelly had seen the file and was aware of the discrepancies between its contents and Moyle's statement, Rowling called for the true facts of the matter to be made public.

That afternoon Moyle wrote to the Commissioner asking for confirmation that he had not been 'arrested, apprehended or picked up'. The Commissioner and Assistant Commissioner met Moyle on 10 November and told him that while he had not been 'arrested or apprehended' he had been 'picked up'. Moyle then told the two senior policemen that in 1975 he had been investigating a conspiracy involving territorial army officers and people with links to the police and SIS who were seeking to discredit the Labour Government and that one of those suspected was possibly the Assistant Commissioner. For that reason he had to make up a cover story about researching homosexuality because he had been unable to tell Walton what he was really doing the night he picked up the policeman. He thought the policeman was another person he was meeting secretly and who would give him information about the group of conspirators including Walton. Unfortunately, the person who arranged the aborted meeting, the only one who could collaborate the story, had died three weeks before. The Commissioner assured Moyle that only he, Walton and Connelly had seen the file and that Muldoon had not seen it or been given details of its contents. But the police could not publicly corroborate Moyle's statement to Parliament without giving a false impression. Burnside told Moyle, 'If you want a written answer it will be given but you may not like it and therefore it is considered in your best interests to leave the matter as it is.'[47]

By then, however, Muldoon, who was under pressure from not only the Labour Party and the Press but also some in his own party who were outraged by his attack on Moyle, was counter-attacking hard after initially trying to defuse the issue. He was helped by Rowling's call for an inquiry and by sympathy, even among some of his critics, for the provocation to which he had been exposed. Rowling also made another error in insisting on Sir Alfred North, a former President of the Court of Appeal, as commissioner undertaking the inquiry.[48] Muldoon intended appointing a retired senior magistrate, Leonard Sinclair, but acceded to Rowling's insistence. While Rowling got his inquiry and his choice of commissioner, Muldoon managed to have included in the terms of reference the differences between Moyle's public statements and the police records, and whether

Muldoon and others had seen police files to which they were not entitled. Rowling failed to have the commission investigate what evidence the Prime Minister might have had at the time he made his devastating insinuation about Moyle, even though it had been put forward as a hypothetical question rather than a statement. North, however, did cover this in his report, stating that Muldoon was acting on hearsay from the Press Gallery and not from prior acquaintance with the police report. Muldoon also gave North a very short time to report – four weeks. Because of the short time-span North chose to deny Moyle the right of legal representation, even though Moyle was in effect on trial. In retrospect one can see this as a terrible breach of Moyle's rights.

Largely overlooked at the time were the constitutional implications of what was happening. Muldoon and Rowling agreed on a commissioner to conduct the inquiry but setting up such an inquiry appeared to be contrary to centuries of tradition that the legislature was separate from the judiciary and that Parliament had exclusive sovereignty in its own affairs and in investigating and disciplining its own members. No resolution of the House had authorised North to examine statements made in the House by a member of Parliament or to report in a way which could destroy the member's reputation and career.

North presented his report on 21 December 1976. He found that the police had not made the file on Moyle available to Muldoon or McCready. The only politician with access to it was the former Labour Minister of Police but North found, nevertheless, that so many police and journalists knew of the incident that it 'in June 1975 very rapidly became known in the "corridors" of Parliament'.[49] He then compared Moyle's three stories: to the police about investigating homosexuality; to Parliament about burglars; and then to the Commissioner of Police and the Commission of Inquiry about a political 'dirty tricks' conspiracy possibly involving the Deputy Commissioner of Police, and concluded that 'the belated attempt by Mr Moyle to present a totally new explanation for his conduct that night was unwise'.[50] North concluded: 'I see no reason why I should attempt to adjudicate whether in the climate of today it is more wounding to refer to a senior Member of Parliament as having homosexual interests or to accuse a Prime Minister of being a member of an accountancy firm engaged in dishonest practices. Both were indeed very serious allegations to make.'[51]

Moyle decided to resign from Parliament and fight a by-election to clear his name. On 12 February 1977, however, partly under pressure from Rowling, he announced his withdrawal from the Mangere by-election following the release of North's findings which, according to Moyle, resulted from 'terms of reference deliberately designed to avoid the main issue of the Prime Minister's actions to whitewash both him and the police and to crucify me.'[52] Moyle had been prepared to vindicate himself in a by-election, which he undoubtedly would have won, but despite the strong support of both the party's national president and Auckland regional chairman, the unexpected entry into the candidate selection process of David Lange proved to be the last straw to a man shattered, at least temporarily, by the events of the preceding three months. Lange was eventually to replace Moyle as

Labour candidate and MP for Mangere, and within two years he also replaced
Rowling as Labour's leader.

Ironically, the same week that the Moyle affair erupted in Parliament, some
senior figures in the Labour Party had been plotting to replace Rowling with
Moyle as Labour's leader, a move of which Muldoon always claimed he was
unaware.[53] Muldoon, however, realised that the North Report had ended any
chance of Moyle becoming Labour's leader and told his caucus so.[54] Interestingly,
although Muldoon felt that the North Report had vindicated him and was furious
when Moyle later attacked North for 'intracranial disability', the Prime Minister at
first resisted press pressure to publish the full North Report on the grounds, as he
privately told the National caucus, that 'This would destroy Moyle . . . I don't
want it published.'[55] It was inevitable, however, that the continued speculation and
selective leaks would eventually result in the release of the North Report. Some
fifteen months later, in April 1978, in response to continued pressure from the
media, the Labour Opposition and Moyle himself, Muldoon agreed to the
publication of the full report.

Muldoon had defended himself throughout the controversy by stating that
Moyle and other 'people should know me by now that they can't get away with
attacking under protection of Parliament associates of mine who are unable to
defend themselves in the house . . . They must know I will retaliate.'[56] After the
Moyle affair, other MPs were even more reluctant to provoke Muldoon than
previously for fear that he would answer their criticism with a personal attack
which revealed publicly something they wished concealed. That widespread fear of
retaliation created a frightening climate. Labour MPs would have been even more
paranoid had they realised that Muldoon had a file of material on some of them
containing letters from various people alleging sexual misconduct and criminal
activities and suggesting Muldoon use the material in the House. None of that
material was ever even hinted at by Muldoon.

One other controversy that persisted throughout Muldoon's term of office as
Prime Minister was the ownership and use of land at Bastion Point. Bastion Point,
a prime piece of land on Auckland's waterfront within Muldoon's Tamaki
electorate, had been part of a 690-acre block originally the home of local Maori,
Ngati Whatua Tamaki Makaurau. From 1868 the land had been acquired by the
Crown through a series of compulsory and negotiated purchases. While part of it
had been subsequently subdivided and built on privately, other land had been
used for state houses which were used partly to accommodate Maori evicted from
the pa at Okahu Bay in 1951. Another large area was vested in the reserves known
as Savage Memorial Park and Orakei Domain. In 1976 Cabinet decided to dispose
of some 60 acres remaining between the existing housing and the reserves. A mix
of private and state housing was the main proposal, though some of the land was
added to the recreational reserves and a further nineteen acres was designated for a
marae and Maori housing.

There was considerable opposition to the proposal not only from the local
Maori but also from the Auckland City Council and environmentalists. On 5

January 1977 local Maori and sympathisers led by Joe Hawke occupied the site and claimed it to be Ngati Whatua land. Muldoon himself received over 1000 letters and petitions, most of the latter containing more than twenty names. The overwhelming majority opposed the sale of Bastion Point for private housing and many sought the restoration of the remaining unused land to Ngati Whatua.[57]

Venn Young, the Minister of Lands, was unable to convince the protesters to change their minds and support the Government's proposals[58] and eventually a cabinet committee of Young, Muldoon, MacIntyre and Holland was authorised by cabinet to discuss the proposals and the issue generally with Ngati Whatua elders.[59] On 27 February 1978 cabinet agreed to a revised settlement of the Bastion Point Maori land dispute following a meeting between Ngati Whatua elders and cabinet ministers two days before.[60] An Orakei Block (Vesting and Use) Act 1978 created a Ngati Whatua Trust Board which for a payment of $257,000 loaned by the Maori Trustee received 11.6 hectares of land for Maori residential use. Almost 12.5 hectares were set aside for a recreational reserve and 1.7 hectares were vested in the Housing Corporation. The land handed over to Ngati Whatua included thirty-three existing state houses and units in Kitemoana Street.

The settlement, which Muldoon saw as generous and which was estimated to be worth about $2 million, was condemned by Hawke and the Ngati Whatua protesters who had occupied the site and whom the Government was trying to remove by a Supreme Court injunction. Finally, on 25 May 1978, 506 days after Bastion Point was first occupied, 600 police backed by the army forcibly cleared the site, arresting some 230 protesters.

Debate continued over whether more of the land should be returned to the Maori, whether it should be used for housing or reserves, and if for housing whether it should be 'low cost medium density' or more expensive housing. Even after some of the land was transferred from Crown Lands to the Housing Corporation in February 1978, the type of housing to be built remained controversial throughout 1978 and 1979. While Young, the Housing Minister Holland, and, after 1978, Holland's replacement Quigley were agreeable to building 'medium density' and 'medium cost', rather than 'low income', public rental housing, Muldoon favoured 'medium cost private housing' and warned Quigley that any other development would 'have my total opposition, both as Member for the district and as Minister of Finance'.[61] By the time the Government in 1981 finally resolved the matter and moved to build thirty-nine Housing Corporation units on the site, the dispute was not so much over what type of housing should be built but over whether the land should simply be handed back to Ngati Whatua. When in early May 1981 building contractors moved in to prepare the site for residential housing, Maori protesters, supported by the Auckland Trades Council and others, reoccupied Bastion Point. Muldoon announced immediately that 'The Government will certainly not permit any occupation of Bastion Point or any intimidation of the people working there'.[62] Following a discussion in National's caucus on 18 May it was decided to use the police to demolish all buildings and remove all people from Bastion Point in one day.[63] It was not until 1987 that a new Labour

Government, following a Waitangi Tribunal report, reversed the decision, ceded the land to Ngati Whatua, and paid $3 million to the local Maori.

Not all National MPs were totally supportive of their Government's handling of the Bastion Point controversy in particular or of Maori land claims in general. In May 1978, for example, MacIntyre, Bolger and Couch moved in caucus that Mount Egmont should be renamed Mount Taranaki and given back to the local Maori iwi which had indicated that it would dedicate the mountain as a national park. The MPs believed that such an action, in contrast to the situation at Bastion Point, would show that the National Party was sensitive to the grievances of Maori over past land confiscations and was prepared without excessive pressure from protest groups to try to redress them. Muldoon, Venn Young, Friedlander, Thomson and others, who formed a majority, opposed such a move, especially in an election year, and clearly believed that it would raise Maori expectations about the return of other disputed land.

Muldoon developed a strange personal relationship with Maori gangs, notably Black Power and, to a lesser extent, the Mongrel Mob. He used members of his Advisory Unit, social workers such as Denis O'Reilly, and gang leaders such as Rei Harris as contacts, and from time to time met gang members at secret, informal meetings.

The relationship between Muldoon and O'Reilly was an interesting one. O'Reilly, who had started but never finished training for the Catholic priesthood, had later, while a student at Victoria University, become active in the Tenants Protection Society. He then became a detached social worker with Black Power gang members, organising work trusts funded by the Government but administered through Presbyterian Social Services. While recognising that some gang members were evil, O'Reilly took the view, which was shared by Muldoon, that many others could have their attitudes and behaviour changed and be integrated into society if they were provided with work, an income, an education, a family home and pride in their traditional culture. The marae, sports clubs and work trusts could be used to provide bridges between the gang members and the authorities and community. Although they agreed on the gangs, O'Reilly and Muldoon frequently and bluntly in correspondence and conversation differed with each other over other matters, notably Muldoon's handling of the Bastion Point and Springbok tour issues.

On one occasion, accompanied by Galvin, Muldoon spent an afternoon visiting gang members who were working for the Te Kaha Trust, organised by O'Reilly at sites around Wellington. Later that evening he met a group of twenty or thirty Black Power members at the Royal Tiger Tavern.[64] The Prime Minister, whose small stature meant that he was largely obscured among the Maori gang members, put some money on the bar and for several hours chatted with them over rounds of beer. Eventually, the management became nervous, closed the bar and called the police. When Galvin met the police and told them that there was no problem and that Muldoon was present the police refused to believe him until the Prime Minister himself pushed through the throng and asked them what they wanted.

The police asked the Prime Minister and the gang members to leave and as Muldoon recalled, 'to save trouble . . . we all went up to a house where some of them were living and we had our drinks and our discussions there.'[65]

At the house in Elizabeth Street, the party became very lively. One cheeky young gang member kept flicking beer from the top of his glass at the Prime Minister. Everyone was watching but Muldoon ignored his tormentor until he had almost finished a glass of whisky, when he suddenly threw the dregs into the young man's face and burst out laughing. According to O'Reilly, 'everyone was impressed at the way Muldoon dealt with the incident'. Another gang member swapped his patched leather jacket for Muldoon's suit coat and proceeded to stand on the table and parody one of Muldoon's recent calls for young Maori in trouble to be returned to the marae. Galvin again had to explain to sceptical police that the Prime Minister was present and that everything was in order when irate neighbours called out the police.

Muldoon's continued interest in finding accommodation for gang members, turning gangs into social clubs, and encouraging gangs to contract through work trusts was balanced by his tough rhetoric and support for the police against the gangs' violence and criminal activities. It was very much a 'carrot and stick' approach. Counselled by friends and supporters such as Whina Cooper and Graham Latimer, Muldoon also favoured young Maori, including gang members, returning to their marae and learning their Maori culture to give them alternatives to their gang subculture and identity. As he wrote to O'Reilly, 'I have never doubted that the one thing that will bring your boys back to the point where they can live with even an uneasy acceptance with society is that they get back in touch with their Maoritanga and that, equally importantly, the Maori people get back in touch with them . . . this goes back to my "back to the marae" statement in *Young Turk* which caused all the left-wing intellectuals and bleeding-hearts to come down on my head and claim that I was a racist.'[66]

O'Reilly, who visited Britain to study its race relations in 1977, persuaded Muldoon in 1978 to go to Islington while the Prime Minister was in England. There Muldoon met the radical West Indian, or Afro-Caribbean, theatre group Keskidde. Muldoon helped O'Reilly and others to bring the Rastafarians to New Zealand where they became a model for Maori theatre with a political cause.

Muldoon was less sympathetic towards environmentalists. In 1977, for example, when Venn Young, the Minister for the Environment, supported by Shearer and Waring, proposed bringing together planning and environmental protection in an Environmental Protection Bill, Muldoon observed that such legislation was 'the thing we didn't need'.[67] Supported by Gair and Cooper he went on to argue that New Zealand was 'over-legislated' and that while 'we are all environmentalists, audits and reports are a nuisance' which 'slow down' and 'add to costs'.

In March 1977 Muldoon reshuffled his cabinet. Bolger was promoted from Under-Secretary to Minister of Fisheries. Gair exchanged Housing and Associate Minister of Finance for Energy Resources, Mines, Electricity and National

Development, taking the first three from Holland, who received Housing, and the fourth from Talboys, who retained Foreign Affairs and Overseas Trade. Wilkinson exchanged Statistics for Postmaster-General with Templeton, who also became a new Associate Minister of Finance. The catalyst for the reshuffle was the departure of Holyoake from Parliament after nearly forty years as an MP.

On 7 March 1977 the Queen, who was in New Zealand, announced that New Zealand's next Governor-General would be Holyoake, who would immediately resign from cabinet and from Parliament. Although Muldoon stated that the appointment will 'I am certain, be warmly welcomed throughout New Zealand',[68] it was not. The Labour Party was incensed not only by the choice of Holyoake but also by the fact that Muldoon delayed notifying Rowling until half an hour before the controversial appointment was made public.[69] The Secretary to the Cabinet and Executive Council, Millen, believed that, although by convention at that time the Leader of the Opposition was not consulted but simply informed, on this occasion Rowling should have been given sufficient time to object if he wished. As it was, Rowling's objections could not be made privately but were expressed publicly, causing concern not only to Holyoake and Muldoon but also the Queen.[70]

Muldoon tried to defuse the controversy by issuing a lengthy press statement pointing out that people should be appointed to positions because of their quality and ability, not their political persuasion. He compared Holyoake to John Jeffries, a prominent Labour Party activist and 'Citizen for Rowling' whom Muldoon's Government a year before had appointed to the Supreme Court.[71] Muldoon strongly criticised the news media for the way it had accepted Jeffries without comment on his political allegiance and activities but had criticised the Holyoake appointment. Not only Labour and the press were lacking in enthusiasm for Holyoake's shift from partisan political leader to symbol of constitutional unity. A number of National MPs, including Talboys, who believed 'priests and politicians should not be Governors General',[72] disagreed with the precedent of appointing a politician as Governor-General and, although the appointment of a New Zealander was welcomed, caucus members reported widespread reservations and opposition within the broader National Party membership to the idea of having a former politician as Governor-General.[73]

Worried about the appointment, the way it was made, and the public reaction, Millen, without Muldoon's knowledge, prepared a paper on the issue and sent it to Buckingham Palace where it was considered by the Queen herself.[74] Subsequently, Muldoon on a visit to Britain was given by the Queen's Secretary new procedures for the future appointment of a Governor-General. When the Prime Minister returned to New Zealand and passed on the new procedures to Millen, Millen was very careful not to let Muldoon know that they were almost verbatim the suggestions he had made, including early consultation with the Leader of the Opposition.

Holyoake was delighted with the appointment and indeed was so emotional that he burst into tears when the Queen signed the warrant in the Executive Council.[75] That may have influenced his comments about Muldoon when

Holyoake gave his farewell address to caucus. Holyoake referred to all the leaders he had served under with one notable exception, his deputy of fifteen years, Marshall, whom he ignored entirely. Forbes had been 'much under-rated'; Coates had exuded 'charm' and 'charisma'; Holland had been 'ebullient, strong, vital'; and Muldoon was 'the most brilliant man with whom I have been associated in Parliament in 40 years'.[76] Not everyone in New Zealand shared Holyoake's admiration for Muldoon.

Many people's perceptions and judgements of Muldoon were reinforced by the way he was portrayed by David McPhail in the South Pacific Television satirical programme *A Week of It*. While Rowling was usually portrayed as weak and confused, Muldoon came over as hard, cynical, arrogant but also as a rather likeable anti-hero. Muldoon himself was not worried by McPhail's clever portrayal of him, and when in 1978 television management decided that the political caricaturing should stop, Muldoon issued a press statement that *A Week of It* was one of his favourite programmes and that he would be 'very happy to see the political caricatures continued'.[77] He also enjoyed the numerous newspaper cartoons based on his comments and actions, purchasing from the artists many of the originals with which he decorated the walls of his home office.

Although some Labour MPs realised privately that while 'Muldoon's image was that he was anti-Maori, anti-Pacific Island, decisive, a tough economic decision-maker, and an uncaring person, in fact he was the opposite',[78] there is no doubt that to most Labour supporters Muldoon personally symbolised many things they detested. The Opposition's hatred of Muldoon led one of his supporters to observe that 'the Labour Party . . . are using hatred of Rob Muldoon as the one thing which can bring them together. It's sad; it's ugly; but it's true, I fear.'[79] But not only Labour supporters disliked and feared the Prime Minister. So also did members of protest groups and some journalists. Sarah Campion, a founding member of CARE and supporter of HART, 'compared him with Hitler' because 'both leaders were appealing to the lowest in us all – to our greed, racism and ignorance',[80] and the journalist Tom Scott, after praising Kirk and less enthusiastically Marshall, lamented that 'much of the sourness, depression and division that currently besets the country can be laid at the feet of one man, Robert David Muldoon.'[81] The climate was such that as a result of anonymous threats on his life Muldoon, in July 1978, was given two armed personal bodyguards by the police, and security was increased considerably at his public appearances and meetings.[82]

Although Muldoon was hurt by the enmity and criticism, he refused to accept that any of it was justified. Rather than restrain his aggression he became even more insulting towards his opponents and told his caucus never to compliment the Opposition: even 'if you can't kick 'em, never kiss 'em'.[83] Muldoon found it hard to forget or to forgive personal criticism of himself, especially his motives or integrity, but his appeal to anti-intellectual, anti-liberal, anti-feminist prejudices within the electorate offended even many in National's own caucus and party organisation. There was also a growing fear within the National Party as well as among Labour supporters that Muldoon was too susceptible to flattery, tended to see himself as omniscient and omnipotent, resented being questioned or contradicted, and was prepared to surrender first principles and consistent policies in order to win elections and retain power for its own sake.

There were rumours throughout Muldoon's career that he was, like many other MPs, sexually promiscuous. Among women with whom Muldoon had an affair or to whom he made advances, according to various informants, were two prominent women in Wellington, one of them a close and long-time friend of both Muldoon and his wife; the sister of a prominent businessman; the wife of a cabinet colleague; the daughter of another National minister; the wife of a Labour frontbencher; a Press Gallery journalist; a prominent radio personality; a television interviewer; several National Party admirers; and three parliamentary secretaries. Most of these people, when questioned by the author about the supposed relationship, admitted that Muldoon in social contexts and sometimes after drinking had flirted with them but all denied that they ever had an improper sexual relationship with him. Such rumours, however, were very distressing to Thea and especially from 1978 when Muldoon found himself the butt of a scandalous public campaign against his alleged sexual promiscuity.

Shortly before the 1978 election a series of mock newspaper posters entitled *The Double Standard* started appearing around Wellington streets. They were the work of several anonymous Wellington women and almost half of the 47 headlines, which continued until 1985, were personally anti-Muldoon.[84] Other were directed, either generally or specifically, at what was seen as the sexual hypocrisy of other MPs. The anti-Muldoon headlines were quite explicit, for example: 'Adulterer Muldoon Stabs Moyle'; 'Mystery Solved: P.M.'s Loose Screws Turn Up in Posh Suburb'; 'Rooting Pig Shot in Ngaio: P.M. Safe'; 'P.M. panics: Ayotollah Bartlett Collects Stones'; 'Noodlum Loves True Lady. What a Mix-Up'; 'P.M.'s Pen is Busier than Basil's'; 'P.M. Admits: I Can't Say No To A Good Ruck'; 'P.M. Brags: I Stuffed Glen Eagles: I'll Do Laura Norda Next;' 'Beware Of The Pig That Pokes'.

Muldoon most years managed to relax for a few weeks over Christmas and New Year at his bach at Hatfields before cruising with Thea and a couple of friends on the *Sirdar*, a launch owned by Ken Butland, whom Muldoon had known since the 1940s, and Peter Cornes. While holidaying with Thea and Fritz and Helen Eisenhofer on Cornes's boat, in early 1978 Muldoon suffered a back injury which left him in pain and having physiotherapy for a number of years afterwards.[85] The party had been joined for an evening dinner by the Yugoslav ambassador who was a friend of the Eisenhofers. He arrived with a case of Yugoslav wines and plum brandy and insisted that the brandy should be tossed down like vodka, not sipped slowly. One bottle was 'polished off before dinner', which was consumed with 'a variety of beautiful Yugoslav wines'. After dinner Muldoon set off down a flight of steep steps. There was a loud crash and the Prime Minister was found stunned at the bottom. He was in agony for the rest of the voyage and barely able to move. Indeed, when the boat got to Little Barrier Island where they had permission to land he was determined to go ashore but had to crawl on hands and knees over the boulders on the beach because his sore back prevented him standing upright. Muldoon's chronic back problem was, however, one of the least of his problems in 1978 and subsequent years.

National's 1976 conference at Rotorua marked the height of Muldoon's popularity within the party. Over 2000 wildly enthusiastic delegates and supporters packed the Rotorua Sportsdrome for his Saturday night leader's address and the tremendous reaction was well captured by a Bromhead cartoon which showed the National Party in the palm of Muldoon's hand.[86] Even at that early stage, however, there was press speculation that some National MPs and party officials were plotting to replace Muldoon with a more 'civilised and democratic' leader. As one loyal caucus supporter, Rob Talbot, recalled, Muldoon was 'never accepted by upper-crust blue-bloods of the party including many in my own electorate of Ashburton'.[87] There were other more specific complaints about Muldoon. Within a year of the 1975 election Bob Jones was complaining that the National Government 'have succeeded in alienating themselves from just about every sector possible' and was calling for the removal of 'a maze of controls currently inhibiting people's liberty and productivity'.[88] And in the Auckland Division of the National Party its chairman was having to respond to criticism that Muldoon was appointing non-National people to statutory bodies. Stuart Masters asserted that 'over the years Mr Muldoon has appointed people on the basis of expertise, not necessarily in all cases on their political allegiance'.[89] Because MacIntyre, once seen as a potential leader, appeared to have become the 'forgotten man in National', the dissidents were reported to be looking to Talboys or Gair for a suitable alternative.[90] In 1976 and even 1977 there was no real danger of a challenge despite such speculation, but it did indicate correctly that there were those in the National Party who never wholeheartedly accepted Muldoon as leader.

By late 1977 and throughout 1978 reservations about Muldoon were being expressed more widely and openly within National's ranks. Although in terms of membership and finance the National Party's organisation ended 1977 in a relatively strong position, the economic recession, the abortion controversy, and Minogue's public stand on the SIS Bill undoubtedly had damaged the party's unity and morale. In Muldoon's absence from the October Dominion Executive meeting, several senior party officers were very outspoken. Chapman commented that 'an election in the near future would result in a loss for the National Party'; Egan Ogier said 'the Parliamentary team had damaged the Party's ability to win in 1978'; and Dorothy McNab claimed that 'Parliamentarians were losing touch with the people, and leading the Party back into a 1972 situation'.[91] Muldoon retaliated by reporting back to the National caucus after a subsequent meeting that the leadership of the party organisation in the Dominion Executive were a 'very keen' but 'inbred group' of men and women who were 'not close to events'.[92]

Muldoon was not, however, unduly optimistic about winning the 1978 election despite his huge majority, and as early as April 1977 exhorted his caucus colleagues to 'get stuck in' and 'attack Labour who are more aggressive and more effective' in the House. 'If we fall behind, 1978 is hard. If people feel Labour can win, it's hard for us. If they become credible, we can lose. That's what happened in 1972 compared with 1969.'[93]

As the election came closer, the National Party's Treasurer rejoiced in the early and full payment of divisional levies, a successful national raffle, a record central business house collection a third up on 1975, and a donation from Fletcher Holdings almost two and a half times more than at the previous election.[94] The party's president and general director, however, were less sanguine about the build-up to the election. In a lengthy letter they told Muldoon that the party's polling revealed 'a dramatic shift of opinion both against yourself and our Party, in recent months'.[95] While Chapman and Leay believed that 'the prime reason must be the economic measures which have had to be taken, and the consequent impact upon individual living standards and employment prospects', three other factors had contributed to the fall in Muldoon's and National's support: the public conflict among National MPs over the abortion issue; a feeling that the Government 'is not tough enough on Unions, especially the freezing workers union'; and Muldoon's leadership. They told Muldoon:

> The renewed debate of your style of leadership has also done harm to public support for our Party, and perhaps has done even more harm within our Party organisation. Regrettably, the upsurge on this debate arose from a press conference you gave just before the Christmas holidays involving the abortion issue. The press reports of this conference seemed to unleash all the pent up frustration on the abortion issue, particularly from women, both within and outside the Party . . . Other incidents which fuelled the flame included the television coverage of your public meetings in Marton during the Rangitikei By-Election; your personal intervention in the Freezing Works dispute and (apparent) support for the Freezing Workers' Union; the series of attacks on your leadership by the *Christchurch Star*; and finally the method in which the Moyle Report was released. The release of that report proved for many to be the last straw in a cumulative sense, and has harmed your support within the National Party. It is our view that public opinion polls do not yet fully reflect the full impact of your public image.[96]

This was an extraordinary letter for a party's president and general director to send to a party leader a few months before an election.

Perhaps even more extraordinary was that Chapman and Leay then went on to tell Muldoon what he should do to address the 'marked drop in support for our Party amongst farmers, and amongst women because of the abortion issue'. They thought Muldoon should 'commit himself publicly' to the Wallace Committee's proposed amendments on abortion, which 'would enhance your support amongst women voters'; use the forthcoming pre-election budget to restructure personal taxation rates, assist farming, and enunciate clear 'overall economic policy direction and objectives'; act strongly against militant unionists; and improve his public image. On the last of these suggestions they wrote:

Within the Party, the biggest concern has been your apparent inability in recent months to convey clearly your overall assessment of problems and issues through the media to Party membership in particular and the public in general. Looking back ourselves, the only time we can recall your receiving favourable television coverage in recent months was your address to the Orewa Rotary Club and your interview with Bob Lowe. We believe that instead of the press conference being your best medium as they [sic] once were for spreading your message, it has become your major stumbling block. In our view the press conference has become a confrontation situation between yourself and certain members of the Press Gallery, and the game of trapping the Prime Minister takes place at every opportunity and little else is reported. We think that less frequent press conferences, combined with selected individual interviews on television, radio and with favourable newspaper outlets, would convey a clearer message to the electorate, and lead to a quick improvement in your Prime Ministerial image.[97]

Whereas in 1975 Muldoon's leadership had been regarded as a very real electoral advantage by the National Party, by 1978 there were many in the party who regarded their leader as a liability. That changed perception was not simply because of Muldoon's personality but also because of his performance in foreign policy and his management of the economy.

CHAPTER 14

Foreign Policy and Overseas Trade
1975–78

BEFORE BECOMING PRIME MINISTER IN 1975 MULDOON HAD
shown little interest or expertise in foreign affairs and admitted that
because of his preoccupation with 'the financial and economic side of
government . . . I've had very little to say on foreign policy.'[1] That changed
dramatically after 1975 and as one observer noted, 'Mr Muldoon has taken full
advantage of the wide latitude his position as Prime Minister provides for
involvement in foreign affairs'.[2] This was not all that unusual. Only the prime
minister has access to other heads of government such as the presidents of the
United States and France or the prime ministers of Britain and Australia, and only
heads of government attend CHOGM or the South Pacific Forum. Thus, of
necessity, there are times in practice when a New Zealand Prime Minister will be
his or her own Foreign Minister even when a colleague officially holds the portfolio
and is responsible for most of the day-to-day work.

As Prime Minister, Kirk had pursued a much more positive and moral foreign
policy overseas than had former National Party leaders such as Sidney Holland or
Holyoake. Muldoon also was, like his mentor Holyoake, more concerned with
pragmatic economic rather than idealistic moral considerations and saw New
Zealand's foreign policy primarily, indeed almost exclusively, in terms of its foreign
trade. Muldoon always equated New Zealand's foreign policy with trade because 'at
the heart of our dealings with the outside world is . . . trade. We must do that if we
are to maintain living standards for our people.'[3]

As Prime Minister and Minister of Finance between 1975 and 1984, therefore, Muldoon played an active and at times dominant role in determining policy
in both foreign affairs and trade, even though the day-to-day oversight of both
was in the hands of first Talboys (1975–81) and then Warren Cooper (1981–84).
Muldoon kept foreign affairs and trade together because he believed that the
Minister of Foreign Affairs carried more weight internationally and had a direct
line to the US Secretary of State and the British Foreign Secretary, whereas
Ministers of Foreign Trade tended to be regarded as relatively minor and had

access only to less senior counterparts overseas. In practice the portfolio was split with the Ministers of Industries and Commerce, Adams-Schneider (1975–81) and Templeton (1981–84), handling much of the detailed trade negotiations, particularly with Australia.

As with his approach to most policy areas, Muldoon eschewed high principle in favour of pragmatism, or, as he liked to express it, he preferred realism over naive idealism. He was contemptuous of what he termed 'sanctimonious humbug about a moral foreign policy'[4] and said that was one reason why he had no very high regard for the United Nations. He saw it as a pontificating body which pressed New Zealand for contributions to aid agencies such as UNESCO, FAO, and WHO but did little else that was useful. Largely irrelevant to New Zealand's economic or security interests, in his opinion, it often seemed to pass hypocritical motions which most member states ignored but which a few countries such as New Zealand were criticised for not observing. Realistically, he argued, New Zealand was a tiny country of little geographic, economic or strategic significance. It could have an influence beyond its size, but only very slightly, and then only if it impinged on the relationship between the major powers. In trade and security New Zealand was an almost totally dependent economy and state.

That did not mean New Zealanders could not have independent views which sometimes were expressed bluntly. Muldoon proved to be as outspoken, pugnacious and controversial in the foreign policy arena as he was in domestic politics. Often his comments reflected his own instincts and prejudices rather than the informed opinion of officials or diplomatic niceties. His statements were also directed frequently at popular opinion in New Zealand and were not designed to flatter or impress foreign dignitaries. Although well briefed, Muldoon could be, and often was, mistrustful and at times contemptuous of the Ministry of Foreign Affairs, whom he regarded, with some exceptions, as 'a bunch of prima donnas and socialists'.[5] Muldoon recognised, quite correctly, that many Foreign Affairs officials, in particular its head, Corner, had been enthusiastic admirers both of Kirk personally and his idealistic approach to nuclear arms control, apartheid, and warmer relations with India and black Africa. They had far less sympathy with Muldoon and his external policy perspectives and priorities. Indeed, Corner subsequently made no secret of the fact that his personal dislike for Muldoon and disagreement with the Prime Minister's attitudes to and comments on foreign policy matters were exacerbated by his (Corner's) despair and frustration at the premature death of both Kirk and the policies he had initiated, pursued and come to symbolise in international affairs.

Muldoon preferred the advice of the Advisory Group within the Prime Minister's Department and the Intelligence Council, both chaired by Galvin, and in dealings with international financial institutions such as the IMF and the World Bank relied more on Treasury than on the Ministry of Foreign Affairs. In using the Prime Minister's Department, especially the Advisory Group, Muldoon, probably not consciously, tended to bypass the Ministry of Foreign Affairs in much the same way as President Nixon in his first term had used Henry Kissinger and senior advisers in the White House to freeze out the US State Department from real influence on vital subjects. Muldoon received copies of all Ministry of Foreign Affairs cable traffic and, in the words of the then Secretary of Foreign Affairs, that 'cables traffic was sifted out to enable Muldoon to exercise censorship and control without consultation with his Minister [of Foreign Affairs] or the Minister's staff. It also enabled Muldoon to detect when Talboys might be about to score a success, and then intervene either to undermine it or take it over for his own political benefit.'[6] Muldoon wrote many of his own major speeches in foreign policy as he did in finance, though he used briefing papers and speech drafts provided by Foreign Affairs and Treasury. He asserted, however, that he was not prepared to let others put words in his mouth because he knew usually what he wanted to say and 'my all-round experience was greater than those whom they'd get to write a speech – a relatively junior officer'.[7]

Muldoon usually performed well at overseas conferences and particularly relished meetings of the IMF and World Bank. He was not overcome by either the occasion or the reputation of other leaders, usually from much larger and more important states, but nor did he play at being an international statesman and try to push his views on others. The notable exceptions were his refusal to allow New Zealand to be pilloried for its stance on sporting contacts with South Africa and his preoccupation with Third World debt. Muldoon, despite what some critics alleged, was genuinely colour-blind when dealing with South Pacific, African, Caribbean and Asian leaders and got on well with many of them. But he did believe that some had a double standard when it came to South Africa; that boycotts would hurt black and coloured South Africans as well as white; and that Governments had no right to direct sports bodies and individual sports people.

Muldoon became a strong advocate for the expansion of unrestricted world trade, particularly in agricultural commodities, and he pushed hard for the reform of the international finance system and the restructuring of world debt, especially for developing countries heavily burdened with similar balance of payments problems to New Zealand's. As he told a meeting of the Governors of the IMF in 1977:

> We cannot say to a poor country 'We will pay you much less in relative terms for your goods than we used to pay, but you need not worry as we will lend you the balance at market rates of interest providing you take steps to lower the standard of living of your people.' New Zealand is uniquely placed to understand these difficulties because . . . we have suffered more than most from declining terms of trade and the impact of international protectionism.[8]

While such speeches had little effect on the industrial countries' leaders, they did gain Muldoon and New Zealand some sympathy and support from leaders of developing countries in Africa, Asia and Latin America. On Third World debt his officials believed that, while he had a point, the topic became a fixation and that Muldoon kept saying it even when it was apparent that he was offending British and US bankers and others in the IMF and World Bank. Muldoon's crusade on

Third World debt was to become even more important to him in the 1980s as the topic also received more widespread international attention.

Although he ate the wrong foods, drank too much and never exercised, Muldoon displayed great stamina when travelling and was rarely ill on overseas trips. On one occasion in India, for example, a country which incidentally Muldoon never liked, Galvin, Hewitt, Symmans, Geoff Datson and others were taken ill. Meeting Galvin's wife in the corridor Muldoon growled, 'I feel like Napoleon retreating from Moscow.'[9] He was a good travelling companion, whose mischievous sense of humour was ever-present and allowed him to see the funny side of things, but he was also fastidious about punctuality and found it difficult to turn down invitations even when the programmes prepared by the New Zealand embassy or the host countries were excessive. Muldoon's style was demanding if not dictatorial. He could and did 'chew the head of one ambassador every trip' when something went wrong,[10] and among senior diplomats a number developed a deep and abiding dislike of the Prime Minister.

As in domestic politics so also in international forums Muldoon could be stubborn, persistent and outspoken. Once his mind was made up he rarely changed it or retracted or apologised for positions he had taken or statements he had made. His sometimes simplistic and instinctive approach to foreign policy, with things being right or wrong, win or lose, and his blunt, confrontational manner dismayed many of the more sophisticated and diplomatic senior officials in the Ministry of Foreign Affairs.

Muldoon's difficulty in maintaining a light conversation with strangers was noticeable at functions at both home and abroad. He did not enjoy chatting generally with others around a formal dinner table or becoming friendly with other leaders at CHOGM, OECD or IMF meetings. Those leaders such as Margaret Thatcher, Ronald Reagan, Lee Kuan Yew or Helmut Schmidt whom he saw as realistic, tough, highly intelligent and prepared to speak out unequivocally – a reflection of his own self-image – he admired and frequently praised.[11] Muldoon was to enjoy particularly a long and warm relationship with Thatcher, even though their economic views were very different. Each admired the other's strength and directness, although Muldoon always thought Thatcher was more open-minded than she really was. As one of his advisers recalled, 'Muldoon only deferred to God, the Queen and Thatcher, though sometimes I think he equated himself with the first of them.'[12]

Muldoon was much less complimentary about some other world leaders and frequently made comments which shocked senior officials in the Department of Foreign Affairs and Trade because they contradicted carefully thought out policies being pursued at the United Nations or elsewhere overseas or offended foreign leaders personally. As a result Talboys, Corner, and various New Zealand ambassadors frequently found themselves engaged in damage control. One of the most serious incidents involved the President of the United States.

Muldoon's view of President Jimmy Carter as a dangerously naive politician too concerned with morality rather than realism in foreign policy, was reinforced by

Muldoon's friend Armistead Selden, the US Ambassador to New Zealand. Although a Southern Democrat like Carter, Selden had been appointed by Carter's predecessor the Republican President Gerald Ford and made little attempt to conceal his dislike of Carter. In two speeches in Sydney and Auckland in March and April 1977, Muldoon referred to Carter as the 'President of the most powerful country in the world' but also 'a peanut farmer from Georgia', and then gratuitously put down the President's family by adding that 'brother Billy is a beer-drinking, petrol station attendant, and sister is a peripatetic evangelist'.[13] Even though Muldoon went on to mention Carter's 'Christian morality', 'no hint of political scandal', 'willingness to speak out on moral issues', successful business record, and 'apparently a brilliant' naval career, the damage was done. Not only Americans and the Ministry of Foreign Affairs but also many New Zealanders of every political persuasion were aghast at Muldoon's arrogant, if factual, description of the President and his siblings. The central argument in Muldoon's address was that Carter did not understand 'the realities of America's role in the world' and that while Carter could talk 'about human rights, a moral foreign policy' he had not thought through its implications in practice, namely 'Is America going to declare war on every government that is infringing human rights, and, if not, just how are they going to carry out such a policy?'[14] This public questioning of the competence of America's President would have been shocking enough without the personal slights, and few accepted the view of Muldoon and one or two of his advisers and defenders that the 'peanut farmer' comment only looked offensive when taken out of context and sensationalised by reporters hostile to Muldoon and did not really damage relations between New Zealand and the United States.[15]

In May Muldoon visited Europe for a meeting of the OECD in Paris. At the end of one session, shortly before leaving for a meeting with the French Prime Minister, Muldoon was advised that the US Secretary of State, Cyrus Vance, would like to see him. Vance, who was accompanied by the US Ambassador to the OECD, Herbert Salzman, coldly informed Muldoon that his denigration of the President of the United States was unacceptable and that Muldoon's official visit to the United States later that year would be cancelled.

Muldoon was shattered. The meeting with Vance had delayed him so much that, accompanied by a police motor-bike escort, Muldoon, Corner, and the New Zealand Ambassador to France, John McArthur, had to speed through rush-hour traffic across Paris to make his scheduled appointment with the French Prime Minister. Muldoon was still so shocked by his confrontation with the Americans that even though the Prime Minister Raymond Barre tried gently but persistently to find out what Muldoon wished to discuss, Muldoon found it difficult to respond and the meeting ended after a few vacuous civilities.

Back at the hotel, Muldoon summoned Corner and asked if he could use his friendship with Salzman to get the Americans to reconsider and relax their position. Corner and Salzman, with the help of another friend in the US State Department, Philip Habib, subsequently arranged for Muldoon's visit to be postponed rather than cancelled and in November 1977 Muldoon was received in

Washington.[16] The State Department arranged for him as part of the official itinerary, however, to visit a peanut farm and nut-packing factory in Carter's home state of Georgia so that Muldoon would be left in no doubt that the President was associated with a highly developed and lucrative big business and had not been a small, backwoods dirt-farmer. When Muldoon gave Carter a copy of his second autobiography, *Muldoon*, at a 2½-hour meeting at the White House, Carter passed over a copy of his book, *Why Not the Best?* and a pair of peanut cufflinks. Muldoon also had talks with Vance, National Security Adviser Zbigniew Brzezinski, and various other US cabinet secretaries and senior officials before embarking on a three-week promotional tour of the US. Despite their meeting, however, and despite Talboys enthusiastically endorsing Carter's foreign policy, the relationship between Muldoon and Carter never improved and there was considerable relief in official New Zealand circles when Carter lost the 1980 presidential election and was replaced by the much more 'realistic', aggressive and anti-communist Reagan to whom Muldoon could relate more enthusiastically.

Another international figure whom Muldoon found it difficult to respect was Shridath (Sonny) Ramphal, the Commonwealth Secretary-General. Muldoon always regarded Ramphal as an administrative secretary who should not try to influence the policies of individual Commonwealth countries or indeed of the Commonwealth as a whole. His major criticism of Ramphal, however, who had been Attorney-General of Guyana (a one-party state led by Forbes Burnham, President for Life), was that Ramphal was prepared to criticise New Zealand's sporting contacts with South Africa while 'he would never utter a word of criticism against the Third World countries of the Commonwealth whose practices in Government were, in some cases, deplorable'.[17]

The foreign leader whom Muldoon probably most disliked – and who recipro-cated the dislike – was Australia's Prime Minister Malcolm Fraser. There has always been considerable trans-Tasman rivalry if not antipathy at all levels and Muldoon and Fraser were not the only two prime ministers who seemed unable to tolerate each other or be present without the creation of an unpleasant incident between them. Muldoon's predecessor Kirk and his successor Lange also disliked and in return were detested by their Australian Labor counterparts, Gough Whitlam and Bob Hawke. Nevertheless, the antagonism between Muldoon and Fraser was particularly deep and long-lasting. Muldoon had no sympathy with Foreign Affairs advice that New Zealand's relations with Australia should be managed with the greatest delicacy and tact. The physical attributes and social backgrounds of Fraser and Muldoon were in direct contrast – Fraser, a tall, polished, wealthy grazier; Muldoon, a short battler from the wrong side of the tracks. Although they both led conservative parties and shared similar views on some matters, Muldoon found it difficult to restrain himself when Fraser lectured him on racism, particularly in the light of Australia's historic and contemporary treatment of Aboriginals. The two men were totally unable to mix socially together and at Commonwealth Heads of Government meetings Muldoon did everything he could to have Fraser excluded from playing a prominent role, especially in regard to African matters such as the Rhodesian settlement or the Gleneagles Agreement on sporting contacts with South Africa.

Talboys, rather than Muldoon, was the best-informed, most perceptive and most forward-looking of National's ministers in his grasp of New Zealand's changing place in the world. He understood that, as he told the 1976 National Party Conference, 'Over the next 25 years, we will have to reorganise our economy to break free of the suffocating squeeze, the gradual tightening circle of boom and bust and access to markets. We will have to become more open, more internationally competitive and more export-orientated – not just in agriculture but in manufacturing, services, and across the board.'[18] New Zealand's relationship with Australia and reorientation into Asia were particular concerns of his.

While Muldoon's perspective and sometimes priorities differed from those of Talboys and the Ministry of Foreign Affairs, causing them some confusion, embarrassment and even anger, in hindsight he admitted his admiration for Talboys, who with John Marshall had served New Zealand well. Talboys and Marshall were both 'highly intelligent and nice blokes' whose work in retaining New Zealand access to the European Community and in freeing up trade with Australia had been crucial. Muldoon was especially appreciative of all the 'awful travel' Talboys had undertaken, especially in Europe, where New Zealand had 'nothing to bargain with except a very limited amount of goodwill' from the British and the Germans.[19]

On Europe, as on other matters, Muldoon was often reluctant to take expert advice. At one meeting of the Cabinet Economic Committee chaired by Talboys to consider an important matter regarding a New Zealand approach to the EEC, it was known that Muldoon had a strong view which Foreign Affairs believed was completely mistaken on the facts. A senior Foreign Affairs official, Ian Stewart, a long-time specialist on EEC affairs, was delegated to call every minister on the committee and acquaint them with the facts. When the meeting started not one of the ministers who had earlier appeared convinced by Foreign Affairs spoke or disagreed with Muldoon. Finally, the officials were asked if they wanted to add anything. According to the Secretary of Foreign Affairs, Stewart 'spoke his piece, courteously and with objectivity. Muldoon glared at him and spoke again, menacingly. Stewart restated the clear facts. Muldoon then snapped: "You speak too strongly, Mr Stewart. Stop it!" Muldoon had played his trump card. After that a civil servant has only two choices: be silent or resign.'[20]

Britain's accession to the EEC in 1973 had been a serious blow to New Zealand, necessitating a radical diversification of the New Zealand economy, export products and overseas markets. While Protocol 18 to Britain's Treaty of Accession gave New Zealand special access for dairy products until 1977, New Zealand was keen to negotiate further access beyond that date, especially for butter, 80 per cent of which went to Britain and for which there was no alternative market. Britain also took 75 per cent of New Zealand's lamb exports. Talboys and Muldoon both stressed New Zealand's close relations with Europe in general and Britain in particular but, while trying to maintain as much access in the future as possible, concurrently started to cultivate and develop alternative markets.

One non-traditional target for the expansion of New Zealand's overseas trade was the Middle East, which after 1974 became much more important as a source of oil and as a potential market for meat, dairy products and other foodstuffs. The Labour Government had sent a goodwill mission to nine countries in the region in February 1974 and later that year had signed a trade agreement with Iran. In the period 1973–81 New Zealand exports to the Middle East grew from just under $9 million to just over $440 million, which helped balance the $526 million of imports, almost entirely petroleum, which New Zealand imported from the Middle East in the 1980–81 trade year.[21]

While most of the trade was with Iran, Iraq and Saudi Arabia, Muldoon took a personal interest in a proposal to build a cold storage facility in Bahrain. In 1976 the Prime Minister of Bahrain visited New Zealand, angry that Australia's Prime Minister, Fraser, had dismissed out of hand a proposal that Australia should develop a close economic relationship with Bahrain. Muldoon, who had visited Iran in 1975, took the suggestion more seriously on the basis that there were advantages in New Zealand having a trade partner among the more conservative, smaller Arab States. He discussed the matter with his Advisory Group, especially Galvin and Jack McFaull, and it was decided that once a causeway was built between Bahrain and Saudi Arabia the former could perhaps become 'the Singapore of the Gulf States'.[22] The New Zealand Government would take a 49 per cent ownership of a joint venture Bahrain–New Zealand Cold Storage and Warehousing Company and the cold store was built in eighteen months following the signing of an agreement between New Zealand and Bahrain in 1978. Although officials of Foreign Affairs and Trade had put a lot of work initially into the project, Muldoon decided that it should come under the control of his prime-ministerial office. McFaull was put in charge of the operation reporting directly to Galvin, Muldoon and Talboys. Unfortunately, the causeway was not built and the cold store, at a disadvantage compared to others built on the mainland, was not used by New Zealand exporters and by 1980 was regarded as a failure.[23] Of particular interest, however, was the fact that the project was not one officially developed by the Ministry of Foreign Affairs, the Department of Trade, the producer boards or the private export sector, but was 'an unusual, indeed unique, example of the Advisory Group playing a determining role in the formulation, implementation and execution of an important policy initiative'.[24]

Another region with which the Labour Government had tried to strengthen links was the much closer South Pacific. Muldoon decided that he would deal personally with the other small South Pacific states by regularly attending meetings of the South Pacific Forum and by cultivating close informal relations with other South Pacific leaders.[25] He became very much his own minister of South Pacific affairs. Muldoon realised that he would have to overcome the legacies of National's crude racist portrayal of Pacific Island overstayers during the 1975 election and the dawn raids by police and immigration officials which Gill unleashed after the election. As Tupuola Efi, the Prime Minister of Western Samoa, observed, that had 'generated a measure of ill-feeling in some of the Island countries'.[26]

Muldoon attended his first South Pacific Forum meeting as Prime Minister in March 1976 when the leaders met at Rotorua. He subsequently attended further meetings in 1976 at Nauru in July and Suva in October and thereafter, although often inundated with other responsibilities and at considerable inconvenience, always made time to be present at Forum meetings. In nine years as Prime Minister he did not miss one meeting and noted that on two occasions he returned to New Zealand from Forum meetings on the day he delivered budgets in the evening.[27] In cabinet and caucus he was a strong advocate of New Zealand aid to South Pacific states as being of more value than aid spent elsewhere in the world.[28] The importance of reliable shipping in the region to encourage trade instead of aid was of particular concern to Muldoon.

The South Pacific Forum at its meeting in Nauru in July 1976 had on its agenda a recommendation to establish a regional shipping line. Although Australia had serious reservations, Muldoon was quick to endorse the previous New Zealand Labour Government's support for the proposal.[29] Muldoon's continued support in the years thereafter, especially after 1980 when he persuaded his friend Harry Julian to become a director, brought him from time to time into conflict with the Australian Prime Ministers Fraser and later Bob Hawke and the Fijian Prime Minister Ratu Sir Kamisese Mara, none of whom were keen on their countries funding the Forum Line.[30] Muldoon did not help, in 1983 at a Forum meeting in Canberra, by labelling Australian bureaucrats, and by implication Australian politicians, 'Pacific ignorant'.[31]

There is no doubt that Muldoon consciously set out to take the initiative and to become more influential in the South Pacific Forum than Fraser, who unlike Muldoon did not attend all its meetings, and to make New Zealand more liked and respected than Australia in the region. He also wanted to keep the region as – in the words of one senior adviser – 'a nice, quiet, peaceful backwater'.[32] This involved the region being politically cohesive by excluding any Soviet influence, and Muldoon used his position to qualify the South Pacific Forum's support for a nuclear weapons free zone in the South Pacific and opposition to the storage and testing of nuclear weapons by getting the Forum to agree that existing defence pacts such as ANZUS and the free passage of ships on the high seas would not be affected.

Among those Forum leaders with whom Muldoon did develop a friendly relationship were Tupuola Efi of Samoa, after initially disliking each other; Michael Somare and Julius Chan of Papua New Guinea; Robert Rex of Niue; Hammer DeRoburt of Nauru; and Tom Davis of the Cook Islands. Muldoon always remained somewhat contemptuous of Albert Henry and critical of his corrupt and inefficient management of the Cook Islands and did not enjoy a close relationship with the Tongans, who for a time seemed to be flirting with the Soviet Union, or the Fijians. He found Fiji's Ratu Sir Kamisese Mara particularly difficult and antagonistic. Mara was offended by New Zealand's negative attitude towards Air Pacific, had reservations about the Pacific Forum Line, and resented New Zealand restrictions on imports of orange juice from Fiji, but Muldoon admitted that

Mara's negative attitude might not have been 'some deep-seated antipathy towards New Zealand' but 'just Rob Muldoon'.[33] The other Pacific leader with whom Muldoon had a mutually antagonistic relationship was Walter Lini of Vanuatu, whom Muldoon saw as a Cuban-aligned Marxist.[34] He regretted that Bougainville, with its mineral wealth, had not become part of the Solomons instead of being attached to Papua New Guinea.[35]

Muldoon's personalised confrontational approach to foreign and trade policy did not stop with insulting an American President, rebuking the Commonwealth's Secretary-General, feuding with an Australian Prime Minister, or disliking some South Pacific leaders. He also embarked shortly after his election as Prime Minister on a dispute with Japan, which New Zealand accurately viewed as potentially a major trading partner. In February 1974, in order to protect its own domestic producers, Japan had banned imports of beef from New Zealand. Partly as a result, the balance of trade between the two countries for the June 1975 trade year swung heavily against New Zealand.[36]

Muldoon had been talking publicly about the importance of Japanese trade and the desirability of complementary, reciprocal, long-term trade agreements since a visit to Japan when he was Minister of Finance in 1968. When he revisited Japan as Prime Minister in April 1976, he warned the Japanese that their treatment of New Zealand beef imports could lead to Japan losing access to fish in New Zealand's about-to-be-established 200-mile economic zone. The Japanese agreed to joint New Zealand–Japan economic consultations but the dispute was not resolved over the following year and Muldoon finally announced in May 1977 that 'no agreements will be signed with any Japanese fishing organisations until we can get an assurance of regular access for our farm products on to the Japanese market.'[37] In July 1977 an *aide mémoire* was prepared and delivered to the Japanese Government detailing what New Zealand was seeking in the way of access for dairy products, beef and timber to the Japanese market in return for granting the Japanese fishing rights in New Zealand's 200-mile zone.

Despite further discussions between Muldoon and Japan's Prime Minister Takeo Fukuda, a visit for intensive talks by Talboys to Japan, and negotiations between New Zealand's and Japan's top foreign affairs and trade officials, the Japanese predictably refused to create a precedent that would be dangerous in dealing with much more significant trading partners. New Zealand had been polite and patient but had got nowhere. The Japanese appeared to be saying yes but doing nothing. Muldoon was frustrated and angry and in early 1977 and early 1978 made a number of undiplomatic comments: for example, that Japan was motivated by 'commercial imperialism' and 'steadfast adherence to blind self-interest'; that 'Japan has achieved, by peaceful means, what it failed to do during the war'; that Japan must become 'a good international citizen in trade terms'; and that 'Japan has to be dragged kicking and screaming into the international community.'[38] Needless to say, Corner and other Foreign Affairs professionals were devastated by another example of Muldoon's interference and undiplomatic language. There was some justification to Muldoon's argument that the Japanese needed to be embarrassed into movement, but his language was too extreme and as a result the Japanese felt deeply insulted. Both the Labour Opposition and some officials in the Ministry of Foreign Affairs felt that Muldoon's policy stance and rhetoric were counter-productive in improving trade with Japan, and even Muldoon started to question the wisdom of being too intransigent.

While the Japanese did not respond publicly to Muldoon, they did send a 'special envoy' to New Zealand, Zenko Suzuki, a former Agriculture Minister, to negotiate the dispute in February 1978, but agreement could not be reached and on 1 April 1978 Japan stopped fishing within New Zealand's economic zone. At an informal meeting in Melbourne in May, Muldoon and Suzuki agreed that a further attempt should be made to resolve the dispute. Muldoon invited the Japanese Minister of Agriculture, Ichiro Nakagawa, to visit New Zealand in June. Although the Muldoon–Nakagawa communiqué issued at the end of their discussions was rather bland, Muldoon believed that he and Nakagawa had also reached an unwritten 'gentlemen's agreement' whereby Japan would informally increase New Zealand access to its market while New Zealand would relax its prohibition on Japanese fishing. A subsequent treaty drafted by officials, however, was signed only after Muldoon initially rejected it because the consideration of 'New Zealand interests' referred to in the document did not specify access to the Japanese market for New Zealand's agricultural products. Muldoon relented and agreed to the treaty only after exchanges between the New Zealand and Japanese governments clarified what each side intended, even though Muldoon accepted that there was some continuing disagreement over the interpretation. As far as Muldoon was concerned, the Japanese had at least recognised that there was a need for New Zealand to expand its meat and dairy exports to Japan on a stable and secure basis, though there was no specific provision for such expansion.

The treaty was signed and came into effect on 1 September 1978 and three days later Bolger, the Minister of Fisheries, announced quotas for Japanese fishing vessels. Six weeks later the Japanese announced a 10 per cent increase in its global import of beef, which allowed Muldoon and Talboys somewhat tendentiously to claim a connection and a victory for his tactics.[39] While imports from Japan rose from $335 million in 1975 to $1,708 million in 1984, New Zealand's exports to Japan over the same period rose from $185 million to $1,311 million. The growth, however, may well have occurred despite rather than because of Muldoon's blunt negotiating style and language. Muldoon did not appreciate the complexities of Japanese policy consensus building and also was deluded in believing that New Zealand had the ability to force the Japanese to make an exception to their general protectionist policy by accepting the concept of reciprocity in trade with New Zealand.

The South Pacific, the United States, Australia and Japan were not the only countries to engage Muldoon's attention after he became Prime Minister. China was to become a nation which fascinated him. On 9 April 1976, accompanied by his wife, officials including Corner and Galvin, and a press contingent, Muldoon embarked on his first extended overseas trip as Prime Minister. The trip had originally been planned in the expectation that Rowling would still be Prime Minister and was to be the first time that a New Zealand prime minister visited the European Economic Community without first having consultations on the way with the British. It was hoped that this would impress upon the Europeans that New Zealand was indeed an independent nation. The move had the support of the British Government. Muldoon shortly after the election took over the arrangement but after briefings told Corner that the Governor-General, Sir Denis Blundell, thought the Queen would be insulted if Muldoon visited the European Commission without first paying his respects to her. Corner responded that he did not think that the Queen would take the slightest offence and that 'the idea that a New Zealand Prime Minister should visit the Queen before going to another country was an old-fashioned one'. Muldoon replied icily: 'I *am* old-fashioned' and insisted that arrangements be made for him to see the Queen and British ministers before visiting any foreign countries. [40] Muldoon was probably the last New Zealand prime minister to attach more importance to the relationship with Britain than his officials believed it was really worth in practice.

After a visit to Disneyland in Los Angeles, where he amazed those with him, including twenty US Secret Service agents, with the child-like glee with which he toured the attractions, he flew to London. There he had meetings with the Queen, Prime Minister James Callaghan, Commonwealth Secretary-General Sonny Ramphal, Opposition leader Margaret Thatcher, and various other politicians, businessman, bankers and journalists.

Muldoon had been impressed by the Irish peace activist Mairead Corrigan who, on a visit to New Zealand in 1976, suggested that some of the Irish involved in the troubles in Northern Ireland should be able to seek sanctuary and start a new life in New Zealand. The Prime Minister instructed the New Zealand High Commission in London to investigate the proposal, and Denis McLean paid two visits to talk with peace movement leaders in Belfast.[41] As a result of his reports the Government agreed to accept about ten people initially but when McLean submitted the names the Minister of Immigration, Frank Gill, who was a Roman Catholic, rejected five Protestants who had been involved in anti-IRA activities. McLean, and Corrigan, whom McLean told, were very annoyed but not as furious as Muldoon when McLean informed him at a dinner during the Prime Minister's visit to London.

Over drinks with McLean, Galvin, Buckton, and Symmans following the dinner, Muldoon 'tore strips' off McLean for telling Corrigan. McLean responded that he was committed to the scheme and was annoyed at Gill's obstruction. By about 1.30 a.m. after a 'lengthy and ugly scene' Muldoon's rage abated but not before he had rung Gill in New Zealand and demanded, 'What have you done with my bloody Irish?'[42] The Prime Minister then decided he would go to Northern Ireland to see the situation first-hand and talk personally with the peace activists the following weekend, which had been kept free of official functions and meetings. Although Galvin did not think such a visit could be arranged at such short notice and the British were also reluctant to allow foreigners, even from the

Commonwealth, to visit Northern Ireland for the purpose of involving themselves in the troubles, McLean with the help of a friend who later became Permanent Head of the Foreign Office arranged the visit with the RAF and the British Army. During a fascinating weekend and with heavy security, Muldoon toured housing estates and shopping centres, received military briefings on the situation, and met representatives of the peace movement. Despite his personal interest in and endorsement of the scheme to rehabilitate Irish in New Zealand, the scheme failed. Only a few were eventually resettled in New Zealand and most of those did not stay but returned to Ireland.

The next stop was Paris for talks with President Valéry Giscard d'Estaing and Prime Minister Jacques Chirac. The state banquet for Muldoon started disastrously and became worse as the evening progressed. Five minutes before Muldoon left the hotel for the dinner at the President's palace he summoned his secretary to his hotel room. When Gray Nelson knocked on the door, Muldoon threw it open and stood there dressed in his dinner suit minus the trousers. Thea had given them to a maid to iron but the maid, not realising it was urgent, had thrown them in a laundry basket and gone off duty. After Muldoon had abused the secretary as 'a hopeless, good-for-nothing bastard' for not insuring the dinner suit was ready, Muldoon was outfitted in the trousers of the member of the New Zealand delegation most similar to him in height and weight.[43]

At the banquet a number of French women, during the early part of the dinner, discussed Muldoon in their own language but in his hearing. The French had obviously been briefed about some of the less favourable aspects of his personality and reputation. During the formal speeches later in the evening Muldoon, much to the consternation of his hosts, spoke in French. French officials took Galvin aside afterwards and complained that they had not been informed that Muldoon spoke French and apologised for the disparaging remarks which the women had made about him and which he may have heard and understood. Galvin might have been less concerned had he heard a discussion between one of the French women and Corner. Muldoon, who had learnt some colonial French in the Pacific during World War II but had not had cause to speak it since, had read a simple speech prepared for him by the New Zealand Ambassador to France. Unfortunately his accent and general command of the language led one bewildered French woman to ask Corner in what language his Prime Minister was speaking.[44]

From France Muldoon and his entourage travelled to South Korea for discussions with President Park Chung-Hee and Prime Minister Kyu Hah Choi and then on to Japan for meetings with Prime Minister Takeo Miki and most of the other senior Japanese politicians and an audience and lunch with the Emperor and Empress of Japan. The subsequent seven-day visit to the People's Republic of China, however, was the highlight of the trip as far as Muldoon was concerned.

Muldoon's visit to China from 28 April until 5 May 1976 was primarily to confirm New Zealand's interest in developing links with that country following the establishment of normal diplomatic relations by the Kirk Government in December 1972. While Muldoon was fascinated by visits to the Great Wall of

China, the Imperial City, and the tombs of the Ming Emperors, and was honoured by a state banquet in the Great Hall of the People, the most important parts of the visit were two days of talks with Chinese leaders led by Premier Hua Guofeng and an audience with Chairman Mao Zedong.

Mao was physically very frail and could not move unaided. The fifteen-minute meeting with Muldoon at 8 p.m. on Friday 30 April 1976 clearly tired and distressed China's leader. The conversation consisted of only ten short grunted comments from Mao, which his interpreters had difficulty deciphering, and an equal number of brief responses from Muldoon. A shared concern about the Soviet Union was expressed; New Zealand's friendly relations with Japan were mentioned; and Mao observed that 'Japan and New Zealand don't like our [nuclear] tests. You should curse us.' Muldoon replied, 'We are opposed to nuclear war and nuclear tests and must protest. But we understand your situation.'[45] Mao concluded that underground tests in the future would be better than atmospheric ones.

The more detailed talks between Muldoon and Hua on Thursday and Friday 29 and 30 April revealed the extent to which both leaders, and their foreign policy advisers who prepared the background briefing papers, were concerned with the perceived threat from the Soviet Union. Muldoon's advisers, for example, suggested that he needed to 'express general concern, without giving the totally bleak assessment the Chinese are prone to' concerning the United States losing ground to the Soviets because of détente, which was 'oversold in the United States', and because of the 'lack of direction . . . and loss of morale generally' and 'indecision and a lack of purpose' as a result of Vietnam and Watergate.[46] New Zealand did not, however, 'believe that the power balance has shifted decisively towards the Soviet Union'. Muldoon was also told by the Ministry of Foreign Affairs to 'mention that you had been concerned about aspects of the Labour Government's attitude to the United States, which seemed equivocal and unclear. Your Government has moved quickly to restore confidence and certainty to the relationship e.g. approval of visits by nuclear-powered vessels . . . ANZUS is the cornerstone of our security links.'[47]

Muldoon accepted and elaborated on these themes and in a major prepared statement for the first meeting with Hua spelt out the position on foreign policy that he and his Government were to pursue throughout the following eight years. He accepted that the United States was 'going through a period of political instability . . . uncertain as to their future and not disposed to be engaged in foreign commitments of any kind' but believed that, following the 1976 presidential elections, the US would return to 'a more stable, a stronger, and perhaps even a more active position in world affairs . . . and particularly in respect of the Soviet Union.'[48] Unlike Hua and the Chinese government who believed that 'nuclear conflict between the superpowers was inevitable', he saw little likelihood of nuclear war but was concerned that the Soviet Union would take advantage of any opportunity it had to expand its influence in any part of the world. New Zealand was a geographically isolated country but its isolation was threatened by the expansion of Soviet naval power into the Pacific and the fact that Soviet land-based, long-range, ballistic missiles could reach New Zealand. ANZUS was the key to New Zealand's defence against any future Soviet aggression in the South Pacific region. Muldoon recognised, however, that 'In New Zealand there is a strong body of opinion which is totally opposed to the use of nuclear power for any purpose, peaceful or otherwise. A good deal of that opinion is associated with the Labour Party.' He argued that while the National Government would oppose the testing and proliferation of nuclear weapons and was prepared to explore proposals for nuclear weapons free zones, including one in the South Pacific, it did not believe that nuclear-powered vessels, especially from the United States, should be banned from visiting New Zealand ports.

In the course of his discussions with Hua, Muldoon predicted that while the EEC had 'built up the economic strength of Western Europe' he had 'never felt that in terms of history the EEC is a concept that will continue, if we are talking in terms of 50–100 years'; expressed his belief that 'there must be in East Timor a proper opportunity for self-determination'; and observed that the independent states of the South Pacific, excluding Australia and New Zealand, 'want no kind of alliance or association with any great power at all, whether the United States, the Soviet Union or any other great power'.

Hua responded with a detailed analysis of world affairs which centred on China's contention that 'the Soviet Union has become the main hotbed of a world war.' He argued that 'the United States is . . . on the defensive while Soviet social imperialism is on the road of expansion and in the offensive position' and that this 'will in the final analysis lead to a major world war'.[49] Hua warned the West against 'appeasement' and 'a kind of Munich mentality' or seeking to pacify or divert the Soviet Union by directing its attention eastward.

Elaborating for a further hour and a half on this theme the following day, however, Hua added that, in his opinion, 'the Soviet Union is but a paper tiger – outwardly strong looking, and inwardly weak.'[50] He detailed the Soviet Union's internal difficulties: 'lopsided development of its war industries, while the non-military industries remain very backward. Its failure in agriculture . . . growing dissatisfaction of the Soviet people and the national contradictions within the Soviet Union . . . In carrying out aggression and expansion the Soviet Union sows the seed of its own defeat.' He then went on to detail China's attitudes to and relations with Japan and South Korea.

Muldoon was impressed with Hua personally and convinced by his arguments. He told Hua: 'On your remarks regarding the Soviet Union we find little to disagree with' and 'We agree very largely with your analysis of the situation in Asia/Pacific, Southeast Asia and the Indian Ocean'.[51] On his return to New Zealand Muldoon declared: 'I don't see any threat from China'.[52] Indeed, much of Muldoon's subsequent anti-Soviet rhetoric in New Zealand appeared to reflect China's perception of the Soviet Union and the USSR's supposedly imperialistic threat to establish its hegemony in the Pacific.

The trade discussions with China were somewhat less consensual, for, although New Zealand's trade had expanded rapidly from $2 million in 1972 to $43 million in 1978,[53] Muldoon had to explain to the Chinese that the New Zealand Government was not in a position to control the direction of New Zealand's trade and guarantee balanced bilateral trade.[54] He did, however, stress that New Zealand genuinely wished to see growth and diversification in its bilateral trade with China and would seek to remove any discrimination that existed against trade with that country. To that end a Most Favoured Nation Trade Agreement was signed between China and New Zealand.

Muldoon was visibly annoyed when the Chinese insisted that the agreement was not important enough to be signed by him or his Chinese counterparts. Instead they would be witnesses to the signing by New Zealand's Ambassador and a Chinese official. Despite Muldoon angrily arguing that he should sign for New Zealand, especially when he saw all the cameras present, the Chinese could not be moved.

Following the official meetings in Beijing, Muldoon attended the May Day festivities on the Saturday and a farewell banquet, soccer match and fireworks display. On Sunday over two million cheering and clapping Chinese lined the route of Muldoon's motorcade at Shanghai. After visits to Suzhou (Soochow) and Guangzhou (Canton), Muldoon returned to Hong Kong and then flew back to New Zealand.

Muldoon was fascinated with China as a country and was keen to revisit it in the future. During his second visit in 1980 for lengthy talks with Hua, who had become Chairman of the Communist Party, and Vice-Chairman Deng Xiaoping and new Premier Zhao Ziyang, Muldoon praised the courage of China's leadership for the economic restructuring of their country which they were undertaking. His visit coincided with the Chinese National People's Congress meeting to approve revolutionary economic changes combining planning and market.[55] When asked just before the 1981 election what he would miss most if National was defeated the following Saturday and he ceased to be prime minister, he replied, 'Not going to China for a third time.'[56] That did not mean he did not find some aspects of his visits to China irritating. The food and the obligatory and lengthy ideological harangues were not to his taste and he was not impressed by the standard of some of China's manufactured products. On his visit to China in 1980, for example, a toilet collapsed under Muldoon. Thea had to get Galvin and Harold Hewitt to extract the Prime Minister from the wreckage. Galvin never forgot dragging a wedged and chuckling Muldoon from the floor while they joked about 'the seat of government'.[57]

While Muldoon moved quickly and enthusiastically to endorse the Kirk–Rowling Labour Government's initiatives in the South Pacific, the Middle East and China, he was less enthusiastic about the growing attention it had paid to black Africa and its apparent undermining of ANZUS. He reversed the ban on visits to New Zealand ports by US and British warships if nuclear-powered or possibly nuclear-armed, and he overturned the Labour Government's refusal to allow sporting, especially rugby, contacts with South Africa. Both were issues that were to divide New Zealanders and lead to increasing opposition to Muldoon over the following eight years, and the nuclear issue was to be the catalyst for the 1984 snap election which effectively ended the Muldoon era in New Zealand politics.

Kirk had advocated from about 1963 a nuclear weapons free zone in the South Pacific, and his government initiated a resolution to that effect in the United Nations which was passed on 29 November 1975, the day the Labour Government was defeated at the 1975 election. The decision was ratified in the UN General Assembly, 110 votes to none, with 20 abstentions, on 11 December even though Muldoon, as incoming Prime Minister, made it plain that he saw the ban as nonsensical and a danger to the continuation of the ANZUS Alliance.

Muldoon's Government announced on 28 June 1976 that nuclear-powered and possibly nuclear-armed warships from the United States and Britain would be permitted to visit New Zealand ports again. Such visits had commenced in 1960 when the then Labour Government had welcomed the nuclear submarine USS *Halibut*. No nuclear-powered ships had visited since 1964 and in 1971 the National Government had imposed conditions on the visits of ships which might carry nuclear weapons. In 1972 the Kirk Labour Government had banned all warships which would not confirm that they were not nuclear-armed. The Muldoon Government's decision was apparently a rejection of the South Pacific nuclear weapons free zone which the Labour Government and other smaller South Pacific states had advocated at the United Nations. While Muldoon was happy not to see a proliferation of nuclear weapons or of countries possessing them, he believed the ship-visit ban and a total nuclear weapons free zone were both incompatible with strategic realities and New Zealand's membership of ANZUS. He also argued that even the defeated Labour Government had told the Americans that, as the result of the US Congress in 1975 deciding to accept responsibility and pay compensation in the very unlikely event of an accident during a visit, it would reconsider ship visits once the 1975 election was out of the way.[58] The eventual visits of the USS *Truxton* in August 1976 and the USS *Long Beach* in September of the same year resulted in widespread protests both on and off the water. Muldoon characteristically dismissed the protesters as including not only 'New Zealanders who are genuinely apprehensive' but also those 'who owe less allegiance to their country and their people than they do to an aggressive foreign power'.[59]

Subsequently, in November 1977, returning to New Zealand from the United States, Muldoon stopped in Hawaii for talks with Admiral Weisner, the US Commander in Chief Pacific. According to the then Secretary of Foreign Affairs, 'At some stage, completely out of the blue, for the subject had not been touched upon even remotely, the Prime Minister said to the Admiral: "I want you to send nuclear ships to New Zealand." The Admiral was taken aback and replied: "But I have no plans at present for sending any ships to New Zealand." "Send them," said Muldoon. "I want them."'[60]

Muldoon was less concerned with the morality of nuclear weapons than with protecting New Zealand's security and trade. He argued that New Zealand was 'totally vulnerable if we do not retain the freedom of the sea lanes' and that trade, foreign and defence policies went together.[61] The United States and ANZUS were the major guarantors of New Zealand's security, especially against the Soviet Union. That position undoubtedly reflected the views of National Party voters on the nuclear ship visit issue, as a Foundation of Peace Studies public opinion survey revealed in 1978.[62] Only 12 per cent of National supporters were opposed to visits by US nuclear-armed ships compared to 45 per cent of Labour supporters, 36 per cent of Social Credit supporters, and 81 per cent of Values supporters.

The new government's stance on sporting contacts with South Africa also had widespread support. Among National voters only 3 per cent wanted the government to prohibit travel to South Africa by New Zealand sports people, compared to 13 per cent of Labour voters, 6 per cent of Social Credit voters and a nil return for Values voters. Indeed only 6.6 per cent of all voters according to the poll were prepared to approve a government ban on travel even though 49 per cent of all voters including 39 per cent of National supporters wanted the New Zealand Government to 'support efforts to end apartheid and bring about black majority rule in South Africa'.[63] As three prominent political scientists concluded, 'it is clear . . . that any policies involving direct restrictions (as opposed to the exercise of influence through official discouragement of travel by sportsmen, as provided under Gleneagles) on travel by New Zealanders to South Africa will have scant support' from the New Zealand public.[64]

It can be argued that Muldoon should have taken a more principled and courageous stand and tried to lead rather than follow public opinion, and particularly the opinion of National voters, but that would be to assume that he was simply following public opinion against his own instincts and judgement. Muldoon was not a hypocrite. On both these matters he acted in the way he did because his correct assessment of public opinion at that point coincided with his own genuine views and reinforced them. Despite criticism, he was able to convince himself that as a democratic leader he was following not just his own inclinations but also the will of the majority of voters, and that his actions were thus both principled and realistic. What he failed to take into account sufficiently was that public opinion can change over time. That was certainly to be the case on both nuclear ship visits and sporting contacts with South Africa in the 1980s.

The growing unease over the exclusion of New Zealanders of Maori descent from All Black teams playing the racially selected South African Springbok rugby teams during the 1940s and 1950s had erupted in the 'No Maoris, No Tour' protests of 1960. Although that tour went ahead, by 1967 public opinion had hardened and when the South Africans again insisted on an all-white team Prime Minister Holyoake asked the NZRFU to reject the invitation and the tour was cancelled. In 1970 a tour did go ahead after the South Africans agreed to the inclusion of Maori players who were classified 'honorary white', but by then the issue was not simply discrimination against Maori but revulsion against South Africa's apartheid system. In 1973, although they had promised at the 1972 election not to interfere, Kirk and the Labour Government changed their minds and banned a Springbok tour of New Zealand.[65]

Kirk had stated unequivocally in 1972 at the Labour Party conference that, while Labour was opposed to apartheid which was abhorrent to most New Zealanders, 'a Labour Government would not stop the tour', because Labour had

> always endorsed the view that such decisions are made by the sporting body concerned, not the Government . . . The Labour Party is not in the business of directing private organisations who are acting within the law. We do not believe that limiting the freedom of New Zealanders will extend the freedom of others. Surely that is the difference between a democratic and a totalitarian society . . . In a democratic society there is an inalienable right to freedom of speech, freedom of art, writing, cultural and sporting pursuits.[66]

That position, abandoned by Labour in 1973, was subsequently taken up and defended by Muldoon.

National's 1975 election policy was quite unequivocal; 'there will be no political interference in sport, in any form'.[67] Muldoon himself went further than the policy by indicating just prior to the election that a Springbok rugby team would be welcome to visit New Zealand.[68] Almost immediately after the election, Abraham Ordia, the President of the Supreme Council for Sport in Africa, announced that African countries would boycott sporting competitions, including the Olympics and Commonwealth Games, if New Zealand allowed sporting contact with South Africa.[69] Public opinion polls, however, until the Soweto massacre of June 1976 continued to reveal that a clear majority of New Zealanders supported an All Black rugby tour of South Africa.[70] This strengthened Muldoon's resolve to ignore domestic protests and warnings from the Africans and from the United Nations and Commonwealth secretary-generals.

Muldoon typically and aggressively continued to attack his opponents personally as well as debate the issue. He accused anti-apartheid groups such as HART (Halt All Racist Tours) and CARE (Citizens' Association for Racial Equality) of 'spreading lies about New Zealand' in a treasonable fashion, although in response to pressure from both home and abroad he also became publicly more critical of apartheid and expressed concern about the broader negative consequences to New Zealand of All Black–Springbok tours.[71] It became clear, however, that the Rugby Union was determined that the 1976 All Black tour of South Africa would go ahead.

In June 1976, the same month as the Soweto massacre in South Africa, Ordia visited New Zealand to discuss the matter but Muldoon brusquely, indeed insultingly, refused to meet him. The Government also appeared to give its blessing to the tour when the Under-Secretary for Sport, Ken Comber, attended the official farewell function for the All Blacks and stated that 'The All Blacks left for their South African tour with the blessing and goodwill of New Zealanders and the New Zealand Government.'[72]. Black African nations were enraged and as a result there was a last-minute partial African boycott of the Montreal Olympic Games in July.[73]

Muldoon defended his government's refusal to stop the All Blacks from touring South Africa by taking away their passports by arguing that to be consistent he would have to stop sporting contacts with other countries such as the Soviet Union, Brazil, Uganda, China and India, where repressed ethnic groups were also inhumanly mistreated. Pressed by one television interviewer in a lengthy discussion on sports and politics, however, Muldoon frankly admitted that the 1976 All Blacks went to South Africa with his 'good wishes' both as a private citizen and as Prime Minister, despite his Government's formal disapproval of racially selected teams.[74] He further enraged his opponents by conceding that he would not have interfered in a sporting tour of Germany even if it had been 1933 and the Nazis were slaughtering the Jewish community.[75]

Holyoake, as Minister of State, led the New Zealand delegation to the United Nations General Assembly in October, where he spoke in the general debate and had numerous discussions with African and other foreign ministers. He explained and tried to justify New Zealand's continued sporting contacts with South Africa, but admitted that 'the Olympic boycott had shocked New Zealanders and had brought home to them the depth of African feeling against the oppressive racial policies of the South African Government'.[76] Holyoake also stated that the New Zealand Government would in future discourage sporting bodies from playing with South Africa. Muldoon, however, refused to accept in full a resolution of the UN General Assembly which not only condemned apartheid but called on all member states to 'refuse visas to South African sportsmen and deny facilities for their own sportsmen to visit South Africa'.[77]

By mid-1977 the National caucus was not so united on the issue as Muldoon wanted or the public generally assumed. A significant group led by Talboys and Holyoake, and including with varying motivations and degrees of conviction Waring, Shearer, Gandar, Birch, Malcolm, Cooper and Bolger, believed that the Government should not encourage, recognise or welcome sports contacts with South Africa and should make that policy very clear to the sports bodies, especially the New Zealand Rugby Union. With the exception of Waring, the anti-tour faction did not want the Government to ban tours but argued that it should actively seek to 'discourage sporting contacts with South Africa' rather than more passively 'not encourage them'. Muldoon, however, tended more towards vocal backbenchers such as Robert Fenton, Ben Couch and Norman Jones who, in the words of Jones, bluntly argued that 'to discourage is to interfere' and that this would be seen as repeating Kirk's and Labour's about-face on an election promise of non-interference in the decisions of sporting bodies about whom they chose to play against.[78] There is no doubt that on this issue Muldoon put domestic political perspectives and priorities ahead of foreign policy considerations and as one senior official observed, put 'domestic pragmatism before international pragmatism'.[79]

Pressure against New Zealand continued to build internationally, and a much more serious boycott of the 1978 Commonwealth Games in Edmonton, possibly by as many as fourteen African countries, started to look likely. When the host country, Canada, indicated that it might oppose New Zealand's participation,

Muldoon and the National Government realised that, at the very least, they would have to express publicly, strongly and repeatedly New Zealand's abhorrence of apartheid and of racially selected sports teams such as the Springboks. It was also clear that the issue would be raised at the Commonwealth Heads of Government meeting in London in June 1977 and that only Britain would be likely to support Muldoon's position on non-interference. Australia and Canada would side with the Africans.

Just before the 1977 CHOGM opened in London, Fraser gave an informal dinner at the Savoy for Muldoon and other senior members of the New Zealand delegation. He clearly intended it as a gesture of goodwill, but Muldoon was in no mood to be placated particularly after it had been reported to him that Fraser's Press Secretary had said that the Australian Prime Minister was going to 'tidy up Muldoon on this sporting issue'.[80] Early in the dinner Fraser made a comment about the need for aid to underdeveloped countries. Other listeners thought it was a reasonable remark but Muldoon, who appeared to mishear or misunderstand it, saw it as implied criticism of New Zealand's position on rugby contacts with South Africa and 'took strong umbrage putting not only Fraser's peace-offering dinner but also Australian-New Zealand co-operation during the conference into ruins.'[81]

Muldoon took the view that his 1975 election promise not to prevent rugby tours by and of South Africa took precedence over the danger of the Common-wealth collapsing over the issue. New Zealand was clearly isolated on the issue and Muldoon's stubbornness was not only upsetting other Commonwealth leaders but also the Queen, who saw her own twenty-fifth Jubilee celebrations being disrupted as well. When it became obvious at the conference that a unanimous resolution by the Commonwealth leaders was unlikely without some compromise, a group consisting of Muldoon and four other leaders from Canada, Jamaica, Nigeria and Tanzania agreed on what became known as the Gleneagles Agreement. The Gleneagles Agreement was a clever strategy by Ramphal to allow New Zealand to accept a consensus on the matter without Muldoon appearing to break his election promise.

Muldoon took no staff with him to Gleneagles and did not discuss the issue of apartheid and sport or any of his speeches or press releases on the subject with Corner, who had accompanied the Prime Minister to CHOGM. After discussion and agreement on the main points to be included in the agreement, Ramphal, with the help of officials in the Commonwealth Secretariat, prepared a draft which was then amended to meet the views of Pierre Trudeau of Canada, Michael Manley of Jamaica, and Muldoon. Muldoon had the word 'ban' replaced by 'persuade', and also wanted explicit reference to New Zealand's laws which did not give his Government the power to deny passports or visas to sportspeople. When the leaders returned from Gleneagles to London, the amended draft was shown to Callaghan, Fraser and Kaunda before being adopted formally.

The Gleneagles Agreement imposed on all Commonwealth governments an obligation to dissuade sporting bodies from having contact with countries practising apartheid. The document commenced by stating that, 'The member countries of the Commonwealth . . . have long recognised racial prejudice and discrimination as a dangerous sickness and an unmitigated evil' and that 'apartheid in sports, as in other fields, is an abomination'.[82] The signatories accepted that it was 'the urgent duty of each of their Governments vigorously to combat the evil of apartheid by withholding any form of support for, and by taking every practical step to discourage contact or competition by their nationals with sporting organisations, teams or sportsmen from South Africa or from any other country where sports are organised on the basis of race, colour or ethnic origin'. They fully acknowledged that 'it was for each Government to determine in accordance with its laws the methods by which it might best discharge these commitments'.

When he returned to New Zealand with the Gleneagles Agreement, Muldoon complained that he was 'amazed and appalled at the volume of material . . . most of it a pack of lies' that HART and CARE had distributed overseas, particularly allegations that he and his Government were racists, and he was also angry at the Australians, especially Fraser, who was 'no friend of New Zealand'.[83] When Fraser had 'wanted to sit in' on the drafting of the Gleneagles Agreement, Muldoon had successfully opposed it because he did not want 'it said Fraser settled the matter'.[84]

Muldoon also issued a press statement drawing New Zealanders' attention to the Gleneagles Agreement and stating that it would be sent together with the Government's views to all sporting bodies contemplating contact with a country such as South Africa. He weakened the appeal, however, by prefacing his statement with the assurance that 'decisions on sporting matters will be left to the sportsmen themselves in accordance with National's 1975 election campaign promise' and that 'under a National Government there will be no political interference in sport in any form'.[85]

In December 1977, Muldoon told his caucus, 'We are in trouble . . . It's . . . beyond Gleneagles. Things we can't accept – visas, awards, co-operate with HART and CARE . . . We said we would stick to Gleneagles' and 'decided to abstain' on the UN resolution on sport and apartheid.[86] Talboys pointed out that 'All the Commonwealth will disagree with us with the exception of the United Kingdom' and that 'may have an effect on the Commonwealth Games'. Muldoon responded that he did not 'want to be branded if the Commonwealth Games fail' but was thankful 'we are not the only country' involved.[87]

In June 1978 Ramphal, who was acting in a very partisan way because that was what the overwhelming majority of Commonwealth leaders wanted, wrote to Muldoon assessing the impact of the Gleneagles Agreement over the previous twelve months since it was signed. He noted that it was the general expectation of Commonwealth Heads of Government that as a result of Gleneagles 'there were unlikely to be future sporting contacts of any significance between Commonwealth countries or their nationals and South Africa.' Ramphal believed that 'all Commonwealth Governments have adhered to their obligations' and that as a result the Edmonton Commonwealth Games would be an 'unqualified success'.[88] At the last moment, however, Nigeria withdrew its team, in part because it believed New Zealand was still maintaining sporting contracts with South Africa.[89]

The Gleneagles Agreement and whether or not Muldoon's Government took it seriously was to become a contentious issue over the next few years. Although the Gleneagles Agreement, despite the withdrawal of Nigeria, saved the 1978 Commonwealth Games and appeared to have brought about consensus among the Commonwealth's leaders, it did not really satisfy anyone and it raised expectations in both the Commonwealth and New Zealand that a scheduled visit to New Zealand by the Springboks in 1980 or 1981 would not go ahead. That expectation underestimated the self-centred intransigence of the New Zealand Rugby Football Union.

Between 1975 and 1978 Muldoon made a number of other overseas trips in addition to those already discussed. In early August 1977, for example, he spent a week in Singapore, Kuala Lumpur and Bangkok. He attended an ASEAN meeting; had talks with a Japanese delegation which included Prime Minister Takeo Fukuda, Minister of Finance Iichiro Hatoyama, and Minister of International Trade Tatsuo Tanaka; was briefed on the drug traffic situation in Thailand; dined with the King of Thailand and his family; and held discussions with, among others, President Soeharto of Indonesia, President Ferdinand Marcos of the Philippines, and Prime Minister Lee Kuan Yew of Singapore.

A less pleasantly memorable trip was to a Commonwealth Heads of Government Regional Meeting in Sydney in 1978. Shortly after arriving in Sydney on Sunday 12 February, Muldoon met his Australian counterpart Fraser for bilateral talks at the Hilton Hotel. Unfortunately, the meeting took place after a dinner aboard a boat cruising around Sydney Harbour. Fraser and Muldoon each had one official with them and Corner, who accompanied Muldoon, was devastated when Muldoon, who Corner believed was drunk, started to abuse and taunt Fraser, challenging him to open Australia's markets to New Zealand's much better and more efficiently produced dairy products. As Corner recalled, 'the language in which he did so was of the kind that would be the prelude to a fight in a bar'.[90] Despite considerable provocation from Muldoon, who 'said some terrible things about Australia and Australians, Fraser remained cool and courteous but later told his office manager M. J. Cook that there was to be no written record kept of the discussions'. The notes taken by officials were destroyed.[91] The talks finished at 11.10 p.m. and the leaders then met with the press until midnight. At 12.37 a.m. there was a violent explosion in George Street outside the hotel. The bomb blast, aimed at the Indian Prime Minister, killed two rubbish collectors, critically injured a policeman and seriously wounded a young New Zealand worker in the hotel. Security was doubled, the hotel cordoned off, and the meetings continued throughout Monday. In the evening Muldoon left the hotel and visited the injured New Zealander in hospital. The explosion and the wounding of a New Zealander were in hindsight symbolic of what was to happen to New Zealand diplomatically at CHOGMs over the next few years as the New Zealand Rugby Union moved closer to hosting a Springbok tour.

CHAPTER 15

National Superannuation and 'Restoring New Zealand's Shattered Economy'

MULDOON MADE ONLY TWO MAJOR ELECTION PROMISES AT THE 1975 election: to replace Labour's compulsory, funded superannuation scheme with National Superannuation; and 'restoring New Zealand's shattered economy'.[1]

In April 1975 the Labour Government's earnings-related, employer-subsidised, compulsory contribution superannuation scheme had come into force. The more one paid into the fund, the higher would be the retirement income, but the scheme did not cover those not in paid employment such as housewives. Labour saw the scheme not only as paying retirement incomes but also as a means of increasing savings in a fund which could be invested in developing the economy. By reducing discretionary consumer spending it also dampened inflation.

On the first working day after the election Muldoon summoned the recently appointed Auditor-General Fred Shailes and told him that the new Government intended scrapping the Government Superannuation Scheme and wanted to stop collecting subscriptions immediately.[2] Shailes, who as Assistant Secretary of the Treasury had with Lang, the Treasury Secretary, and Hutton Peacock, the Government Actuary, been prominent in devising the existing scheme and who thought it was better than National's proposed alternative, realised there was no point in arguing with Muldoon about this matter. Shailes told Muldoon that National had such a majority that he would as Auditor-General not make any difficulties if Muldoon stopped collection, even though it would strictly be illegal until legislation had been passed. Muldoon gave Shailes a written assurance that legislation would be passed before the end of the session. At a cabinet meeting on 15 December, after considering advice from the Solicitor-General, it was decided that the compulsory requirement for people to pay into the existing superannuation scheme would cease immediately and refunds of previous contributions would be made following tax returns after 31 March 1976.[3]

Muldoon and the Government were accused of acting illegally, although Muldoon claimed they were merely following precedent, as when the previous Labour Government had ended compulsory military training before they had amended the law.[4] Nevertheless, a legal action was brought against Muldoon, and Chief Justice Wild found against the Government.[5] Although the judgment had little practical effect, opponents of Muldoon were able to claim that he had acted illegally in pre-empting the decision of Parliament. They could not, however, prevent National replacing the Labour scheme with National Superannuation.

National Superannuation was, as Walker, the Minister of Social Welfare, proudly declared, 'the most generous social welfare benefit ever paid in New Zealand'.[6] Muldoon and his supporters never accepted the argument that New Zealand could not afford such a generous and costly superannuation scheme,[7] and they also defended it on the grounds that the elderly had earned such security and without the indignity of means tests. As Walker noted, older New Zealanders 'had gone through two world wars and the great depression of the 1930s. They had been taxed hard to compensate for costs and for reconstruction after the second world war, and . . . their savings had been eroded by inflation' over recent years.[8]

The National Party claimed that its scheme would cost a net $275 million a year after allowing for existing old age pension and superannuation payments, while Labour's would have required $250 million a year. As one economist observed, that was a misleading comparison because National's scheme would involve payments, without additional income, out of general tax revenue from 1978 while the Labour scheme would only commence paying out fully some fifty years later and after the building-up of a large, invested contributory fund.[9] The whole political and economic scene during 1975–78 was overshadowed by the implementation and financing of National Superannuation, and many other policies were delayed. The second oil shock of 1979 meant the total rethinking of National's other policies and strategies.

Muldoon realised that the introduction of National Superannuation would make it difficult, particularly during a time of economic recession, to remove the fiscal deficit (the gap between government income and expenditure before borrowing) and thus to balance the budget. In particular, holding or lowering the rates of taxation would require careful control of expenditure on the welfare state: health, education, housing and social security payments – notably the unemployment and the domestic purposes benefits. Muldoon, therefore, asserted the principle of compensatory savings. If a minister wanted funding for a new policy, it had to be bought by identifying some other expenditure that could be given up.

Under the Kirk-Rowling Labour Government the budget deficit had by 1975–76 risen to 9.1 per cent of GNP, reflecting a dramatic increase in government expenditure from 29 per cent of GNP in the year ending March 1973 to over 40 per cent in the year ending March 1976.[10] Within one year Muldoon, with firm restraints on public service staffing, cuts in spending, and increased income tax revenue reflecting inflation, was able to reduce the budget deficit to 3.9 per cent and expenditure as a percentage of GNP to 35.1 per cent.[11] By 1978, however,

Muldoon's success in reducing government expenditure and the budget deficit was being threatened by the cost of National Superannuation. While he was able to hold health and education expenditure and reduce state housing expenditure, the cost of National Superannuation markedly increased expenditure on social security transfers both as a percentage of total public expenditure and as a percentage of GNP.[12] The cost of National Superannuation cancelled out the savings Muldoon was able to make from firm spending restraints on other social expenditure and as a result prevented him from cutting total public expenditure and reducing taxation dramatically and permanently.

Within New Zealand, as elsewhere overseas, the debate over the costs of maintaining a universal and generous social welfare system and also over the economic and social effects of high rates of income tax grew, with Muldoon increasingly seen as an impediment to, rather than a leader of, restraint and reform. Public frustration, particularly found among long-time National Party supporters, and based on the belief that too few taxpayers in the private sector were sustaining too many non-producing beneficiaries and a massive bureaucracy, led to growing opposition to Muldoon and public questioning of whether New Zealand could afford any longer to maintain the welfare state in its existing form.[13] Muldoon's philosophical commitment to a comprehensive and universal welfare state from the cradle to the grave and his determined attempts to maintain it were eventually to isolate him from a younger generation of National Party MPs and voters, advisers in Treasury and the Reserve Bank, and Labour Party politicians led by Roger Douglas, all of whom subscribed to free market and anti-state values and policies commonly referred to as the 'New Right'.

Labour's 1975 White Paper on Health and its attempt to computerise the health service had proved electorally unpopular. Muldoon and his Health Minister, Gill, saw no reason for a monolithic, centralised health system and favoured the existing decentralised system. The new National Government did believe that, because health expenditure was very high, every effort had to be taken to get the maximum benefit from the money spent. Clearly funds spent on preventive health, health education and early diagnosis could reduce the amount spent on later more expensive treatment. Muldoon also was quite prepared to increase taxes on alcohol and tobacco and directed the extra money so raised into community health care.[14]

While Muldoon sought a 10 per cent overall cut in government expenditure in his 1976 Budget, the cut in Education was only 1 per cent, and that almost entirely in capital works and in administration.[15] Muldoon warned teachers, however, that his ability to fund education depended on the state of the economy as a whole, and that while the education system would not go backwards, 'it certainly does mean, in present circumstances, no giant leaps forward'.[16] As a result there were few new initiatives in education between 1975 and 1978, though the Government did continue Labour's programme of integrating some, mainly Catholic, private schools into the state system, restored A and B bursaries,[17] and increased funding for rural pupils, children with special needs, and early childhood education.

Muldoon also revived a 'back to basics' debate, which was to become more intense in future years. He asserted that 'children today are not as well grounded in the basics as they were many years ago' and stated that, 'I . . . cannot ignore growing public criticism arising from the failure of many students – primary and secondary to reach satisfactory levels of attainment in basic subjects.'[18] His emphasis on basics and on applied, vocational learning also made Muldoon somewhat suspicious of the more radical proposals in the report of a committee set up by the previous Labour Government to examine social education. The committee reported in 1977 and emphasised the importance of spiritual values and human relationships. Although officially entitled *Growing, Sharing, Learning*, the report became much more commonly known as the Johnson Report, after its chairman Garfield Johnson, and much of the controversy and debate about the report revolved around its recommendations on sex education.[19]

The Minister of Education, Les Gandar, who was much more liberal about education than the Prime Minister, believed that fears about the standard of basic skills in education were exaggerated, as were concerns about the Johnson Committee's Report, which Gandar by and large accepted and opened for a year of public discussion. Muldoon's perspectives and comments on both, however, were reinforced by a former teacher and National backbencher Merv Wellington. After Gandar was defeated at the 1978 election, Muldoon replaced him with Wellington, who more accurately reflected Muldoon's own views on education.

Another matter of concern was that the average price of a house had doubled as the result of inflation, speculation and massive immigration between 1972 and 1975. By the time National took office, however, immigration had fallen dramatically and the reduction in immigration, and indeed a net emigration after 1976, reduced pressure on the state to provide housing. Housing was one area in which the Muldoon Government moved decisively to reduce the role of the state. Fewer state houses were built for rent, and Housing Corporation mortgages for private homes became less freely available. Tenants were also encouraged to purchase the state houses they rented. The Government's liberalisation of the private financial sector in 1976, however, led to a greater availability of long-term first mortgages and the easing and standardisation of interest rates. The previous policy of holding interest rates artificially low had channelled funds into the speculative purchase of property instead of into more productive areas, thus forcing up urban property prices, which had almost doubled in three years under Labour. National introduced tax-exempt savings schemes and inflation-proof bonds for people saving for homes, removed stamp duty on first homes, and enabled people to take out Housing Corporation loans for existing as well as new houses.

Although Muldoon was concerned to hold government expenditure and reduce the budget deficit, he was not prepared to hurt low-income and young families or the elderly. As a result he not only pushed ahead with National Superannuation but also reformed the tax system to help low-income families with young children.[20] His 1976 Budget introduced a tax rebate equivalent to $6 per week for the principal income earner earning less than $140 per week in a family with at least one child under five years of age.[21] His 1977 Budget increased the rebate to $9 and the income limit to $150.[22] This amounted to an increase in take-home pay of up to 15 per cent over the two years. The 1977 Budget also contained a new rebate for single-income parents, including solo parents, with a child under the age of 10 and was worth up to $4 for those on low incomes. In his 1978 Budget Muldoon simplified the tax structure, reducing it from nineteen to five steps, and altered the tax scales in such a way as to further increase the after-tax income of single-income families relative to those with second incomes.

In retrospect, Muldoon admitted that it 'may be seen as excessively conservative that women should stay home and look after the kids', but he believed that two-income families were often 'of necessity rather than choice' because of the high cost of housing, especially in Auckland.[23] Muldoon did not accept that direct family support was the ideal answer because it created a poverty trap in which, as wages increased, the state assistance was abated. However, despite all his good intentions he found the dilemma impossible to resolve and was unable to devise a system that was equitable and effective.

These efforts to assist single-income and young families were not only motivated by compassion for the plight of the poor, especially children, but were also an attempt to strengthen the traditional family unit. National's 1975 election manifesto had stressed that 'the family is the basic unit of our society' and that 'all social welfare policies should encourage or be compatible with good strong family life'.[24] After the election National set up a Cabinet Committee on Family Affairs, which concluded that since the 1960s there had been a disturbing rise in solo-parent families, either as the result of separation and divorce or through young unmarried women choosing to keep babies and raise them on their own rather than marry the fathers or give their children up for adoption. As the Minister of Social Welfare told Parliament, in 1965 one in twelve marriages broke down but by 1976 it was one in three.[25] National was concerned that the domestic purposes benefit, which Muldoon had introduced in 1968 as an emergency benefit and which the Labour Government had extended after 1972 to all solo parents, was a major contributory factor. Between 1972 and 1977 the number of people receiving the DPB rose from 6000 to 28,400, and the cost from $6.5 million to just over $100 million.[26] National moved both to ensure that those receiving the DPB were in fact solo parents and not living in de facto relationships and also to cut the benefit for the first six months a person received it to make it less attractive. Neither measure stopped the growing number of marriage break-ups or unmarried teenagers keeping their babies but they did earn the Government considerable criticism from women's groups.

In the lead-up to the 1975 election Muldoon had talked much about the need to restore what he termed New Zealand's 'shattered economy', although he had not proposed any radical or dramatic new initiatives. Rather, he predicted, the following three years would 'almost totally be devoted to tidying up our economic problems without any attempt at creating long-term changes in the New Zealand economy . . . there will be no fundamental restructuring of the economy'.[27] There is no doubt that in 1975 the New Zealand economy was, as Muldoon argued, in great difficulties and he received at the election an extraordinary mandate to restore it. He did not address the structural problems, however, but followed traditional fiscal and monetary policies of weathering what was seen as a temporary recession with the minimum possible damage to the productive sector and the minimum amount of unemployment. Regulation provided only temporary relief by moving the problem around while trying to minimise increases in inflation, costs, interest rates, unemployment, budget deficits, balance of trade deficits, public debt, and pressure on the value of the New Zealand dollar.

At the 1975 election, Muldoon had attacked Labour's 'borrow and hope' approach and had raised expectations that after the election he would implement firm macroeconomic restraints and would also deregulate the economy to prevent its erosion. But he feared a political backlash from manufacturers, farmers and unions if he went too far too fast, and the results of the 1978 election eventually reinforced his belief that one of the reasons National had lost in 1972 was because such groups feared deregulation.

While Muldoon was quite clear in his mind that New Zealand was facing its most serious economic crisis since the Depression of the 1930s, he freely admitted in hindsight that in 1975 neither he nor any other contemporary New Zealand politician nor any of the official advisers expected the downturn in New Zealand's terms of trade to last not three to five years but twenty.[28] As a result he followed, as his predecessors both National and Labour had, the short-term strategy of holding government expenditure and borrowing to bridge what was seen as a temporary shortfall, on the assumption that the terms of trade would eventually recover. New Zealand's terms of trade, which had dropped a staggering 40 per cent between 1973 and 1975,[29] did not recover. While the quadrupling of the price of oil had created both inflationary and recessionary pressures – stagflation – around the world, New Zealand was hit particularly hard. The rise in the cost of imported fuels, imported industrial goods and transport was accompanied by a decline in returns for agricultural commodities such as New Zealand had traditionally exported. Reliance on a very restricted range of pastoral exports – wool, meat and dairy products – and an unhealthy dependency on the British market meant that New Zealand had either to export three bales of wool or three lambs for every two it had previously or else broaden its variety of exports and develop new markets.

Initially Muldoon, who believed that he had resolved an earlier crisis in the terms of trade after 1966, set out to encourage greater export volume in order to earn more overseas funds and thus to maintain the domestic economy, full employment, and existing levels of social welfare expenditure. His ability to transfer resources to the export sector was, however, hindered by his wish to maintain as far as possible the full employment, education and health systems, and social welfare benefits which New Zealanders had come to expect over the previous thirty years. This restriction on his policy options was strengthened by his unwillingness to ignore the very many vested interest groups such as farmers, manufacturers and unions who felt threatened by suggestions of more radical economic restructuring, deregulation, and the removal of subsidies and protection.

Encouraged by Treasury, Muldoon did move swiftly and firmly in 1976 and 1977 to cut domestic spending in order to reduce both internal inflation and the large deficit in the balance of payments. Those deflationary measures combined with a decline in farmers' incomes, however, led to a sharp contraction in economic activity and by 1978, despite a large net emigration, the highest level of unemployment since the 1930s.[30] Muldoon was annoyed by the outcomes resulting from following his officials' advice and realised that, faced with an election in 1978, he would need to reflate the economy at least partially and start to look at longer-term and more radical ways of fundamentally restructuring the economy, reducing imports, and increasing exports.

Although Muldoon accepted the necessity of some deregulation and attempted also to hold government expenditure, he chose not to follow the radical free-market reforms that were to become associated with Thatcher in Britain, Reagan in the United States, and, after 1984, Douglas in New Zealand. He did remove some controls, including some liberalisation of the finance sector. He was also tough on public expenditure during the 1975–77 period, but this resulted in some contraction of the economy in subsequent years and Muldoon became worried about causing a serious recession and damaging industries essential to New Zealand's future. Fear of creating unemployment made him back away from his earlier tough policies to combat the serious fall-off in New Zealand's terms of trade in the mid-1970s. Instead, he sought to restructure the New Zealand economy through pragmatic and increasingly complex ad hoc intervention in the day-to-day running of the economy; by the use of farming subsidies to increase the volume of production and export subsidies to both farmers and manufacturers to encourage the earning of foreign currency; and eventually through what became known as the 'Think Big' industrial development projects to maximise the use of New Zealand's energy resources for import substitution, especially of liquid fuels, and to create downstream industries such as aluminium and steel both to conserve and in the longer term earn overseas funds. Apart from the heavy and unwelcome state regulation of, and intervention in, the economy, the subsidies caused considerable inflation in farm land prices, beyond what was rational in terms of the farms' real productive capacity and economic return, and led to heavy overseas borrowing not just to buy time until the terms of trade improved but also to provide the massive capital investment needed for the energy and other major industrial diversification projects.

The new National Cabinet met three times immediately after the election, on 12, 15 and 18 December 1975, to discuss briefing papers prepared by the Officials Economic Committee under the chairmanship of Lang on the current economic situation and overseas exchange transactions and borrowing.[31] Those papers made depressing reading. According to Treasury, 'Falling export prices, a growing deficit in external payments and a squeeze on liquidity at a time when costs and prices were rising, led to a contraction of economic activity early in 1975. Consumer spending slowed, stocks rose and production dropped . . . The consequential effects on employment were largely countered by an expansion of Government spending and the provision of special employment.'[32] Government expenditure, rising at 38 per cent per annum, was increasing at over double the rate of income from taxation at 16 per cent. The widening deficit had to be funded from borrowing. As a result, New Zealand's official overseas debt had risen from $465 million at 31 March 1974 to $1,859 million at 30 November 1975, with large amounts of that debt due for repayment in 1979 and 1980. The Treasury briefing papers argued that 'In the short to medium term economic policy changes are needed to reduce the Balance of Payments deficit, the rate of inflation, the Government deficit, liquidity, consumption. These policies have to be so devised as to at the same time insure adequate investment, particularly for export, maintain high levels of employment, and preserve our capacity for economic growth.'[33] There was some hope in that 'the rate of contraction has slackened', 'import prices are not rising as steeply', and 'much improved prices for this season's wool and meat and some dairy products augmented by devaluation' would increase farm incomes and should help stimulate economic activity.

The new ministers were particularly shocked by the summary of overseas exchange transactions for the previous three years.[34]

	1972–73 $m	1973–74 $m	1974–75 $m
Export receipts	1,773	1,748	1,658
Import payments	−1,249	−1,849	−2,375
Net cost invisibles	−199	−233	−350
Current account balance	325	−334	−1,067
Overseas reserves	1,094	594	564

Treasury predicted some improvement in 1975–76 but still estimated that the current account deficit would be −$650 million and that forecasting was 'even more hazardous than usual' and 'the deficit could be greater than anticipated'. However, they expected at the worst 'a moderate recovery' and at the best, reflecting the views of the United States and Japan, 'a more rapid and sustained recovery together with a resultant more significant improvement in New Zealand's terms of trade'.

New Zealand's worsening balance of payments made an increase in exports and the restructuring of the economy unavoidable but there was considerable debate about how best that could be done. Devaluing the New Zealand dollar would give exporters higher returns and greater incentives but would raise even further the already escalating price of imports and fuel inflation. Overall it would switch income from domestic consumers to exporters. The removal of import controls and protection from domestic manufacturing would help combat inflation but would, at least in the short term, increase already unacceptable levels of unemployment. Muldoon wanted export-led growth but he was equally determined to stop inflation and minimise unemployment. He therefore chose initially to use export incentives to compensate exporters for the overvalued exchange rate and the higher costs resulting from import controls and the protection of domestic industry.

The outgoing Labour Government at its last cabinet meeting on 9 December, faced with a 10 per cent OPEC price increase, higher tanker freight charges, and the devaluation of the New Zealand dollar in August, had decided that the price of motor spirits should be increased by 5 cents a litre, diesel by 4.7 and fuel oil by 3.4. This was conveyed to Muldoon by Tizard, the outgoing Labour Minister of Finance, and confirmed at National's second cabinet meeting on 15 December.[35] Three days later the cabinet decided to increase railway charges across the board by 30 per cent minimum, with some passenger fares rising 64 per cent. Those charges had been frozen since November 1971 and Railways had lost $48 million the previous year.[36] Post Office charges for all services were also raised, letters by 100 per cent from 4 to 8 cents and postcards and private boxes by more than 100 per cent (3 to 7 cents and $7 to $20 respectively). Individual telephone charges were increased 41 per cent.[37]

Muldoon at first appeared to be moving decisively to combat Treasury's predictions of a 15 per cent inflation rate, a $1.2 billion budget deficit, and a $650 million balance of payments deficit in 1975–76.[38] In the months immediately after the election he removed subsidies on milk, bread, eggs and butter; raised electricity prices 45 per cent, rail fares 64 per cent, and postal and telegram charges 100 per cent; and increased the tax on beer and spirits. He removed most interest rate controls in an effort to reduce distortions in the finance market and to encourage savings; closed some branch railway lines; froze state service staffing levels; restrained public works; and in May 1976 imposed a year-long wage and salary freeze. It soon became obvious that a likely result of the deflationary policy and attempt to cut the budget deficit would be the higher unemployment Muldoon desperately wanted to avoid.

Until October 1977 the Muldoon Government's economic policy was clearly deflationary, designed to moderate inflation and adjust to the large drop in the terms of trade in 1974. Treasury estimated that by March 1977 real personal disposable income per head had fallen over the previous three years by 7.5 per cent and real private consumption per head had fallen 5 per cent.[39] Nevertheless, export volumes rose strongly during the period from mid-1975 until mid-1977, by 17.8 per cent for the year ending June 1976 and by 10.7 per cent for the year ending June 1977. Manufactured exports rose by 23 per cent and 25 per cent during the same two years. The drop in real personal disposable incomes, however, which was 6.3 per cent during 1977–78 made a total fall of 13.8 percent over four years. This led to a major recession in the domestic economy and a sharp rise in unemployment.

Muldoon's Budget on 29 July 1976 had declared that domestic inflation and fiscal restraint would continue to be his major economic concerns during the coming year. The growth in Government expenditure, which had increased from 30 per cent of GNP in 1972–73 to 42 per cent in 1975–76, could not be allowed to continue, he stated.[40] His Budget would reduce the percentage to 36 for the following year.

Prior to the 1975 election Muldoon, while still favouring a detailed, regulated monetary system, had asked Frank Holmes and Len Bayliss to comment on the possibility of freeing up interest rates, and especially on the possible effect of this on savings banks. Even before the 1976 Budget, Muldoon had moved on 2 March to implement Treasury recommendations that the new Government should relax financial regulations. He was concerned, however, that deregulation of the financial markets should free up housing finance, foster productive investment in farming and export industries, and through competition lower interest rates to borrowers, not lead to a rise in interest rates. He always believed that 'Interest is a dead cost; it achieves nothing', and that 'high interest rates are a major impediment to farmers and manufacturers borrowing for development, expansion, growth in production, and generation of employment'.[41]

The liberalisation of New Zealand's financial sector and the removal of most interest rate controls in March 1976 was a very significant economic reform and allowed banks and other financial institutions to compete for funds on a relatively open market, although the finance sector was not fully deregulated until after the fall of Muldoon's Government eight years later. Muldoon, who had been responsible for regulations on interest in 1972, had been won over by two of his closest advisers in 1976, Galvin and Bayliss, to the more deregulated position advocated by the Reserve Bank and, somewhat more belatedly, by Treasury. One international financial journal, *Euromoney*, described Muldoon's financial reforms as 'possibly the boldest single decision made by any New Zealand politician since the 1945 war'.[42] Muldoon had been motivated in making this change not by free market principles but by a pragmatic realisation that controlling banks simply permitted fringe financial institutions, often speculative and unstable, to manipulate the system.

The collapse of Securitibank Ltd on 9 December 1976[43] damaged a large number of corporate and personal depositors and bill-holders. Muldoon was concerned at the effects on Securitibank's investors and borrowers and also the likelihood of similar possible failures and asked for a report from R. W. R. White, the Governor of the Reserve Bank.[44] White reported to Muldoon that there were seven large corporates with unsecured deposits in Securitibank, while 51 other corporates and 4350 smaller investors who held bills were likely to be adversely affected. He advised Muldoon that 'all the large borrowers are involved in property development . . . [and] will be in danger of insolvency' and that there will be a 'grave effect on a large number of individuals'.[45]

Not only investors in property or merchant banks were facing insolvency; so also were many farmers. Farmers were the most important sector in earning New Zealand's export income and they were the backbone of the National Party's electoral support as well as of the economy. By 1975, however, there was considerable concern that farmers since the 1960s had suffered a severe decline in their incomes, especially relative to the rest of the community.[46] While much of this was caused by external factors negatively affecting New Zealand's markets and

Above: Muldoon enjoyed his visits to China. MULDOON PAPERS.

Centre left: Muldoon discussed the Soviet Union's intentions and China's nuclear tests with Mao Zedong, shortly before Mao's death. MULDOON PAPERS.

Bottom left: Although their economic policies differed markedly, Muldoon and Margaret Thatcher, seen here with Denis Thatcher, admired each other personally. MULDOON PAPERS.

Above: Muldoon is clearly apprehensive about the reception he is about to receive from President Jimmy Carter and US Vice-President Walter Mondale at the White House following Muldoon's reference to the 'peanut farmer from Georgia'. MULDOON PAPERS.

Left: Muldoon enjoyed a more cordial relationship with Carter's successor as US President, Ronald Reagan. Behind Muldoon and Reagan is Lance Adams-Schneider, at that time New Zealand Ambassador to Washington. MULDOON PAPERS.

Right: Thea and Rob with Mickey Mouse on a visit to Disneyland 1976. MULDOON PAPERS.

Above: Muldoon and Labour leader Bill Rowling with Yugoslav Ambassador Karapandya in 1978. *Evening Post.*

Left: The foreign leader Muldoon probably disliked most was the Australian Prime Minister Malcolm Fraser. *Press.*

Below: Muldoon appeared to be constantly at war with the media, especially television interviewers. Bob Brockie/*National Business Review.*

Right: Muldoon was very menacing when dealing with interjectors. *OTAGO DAILY TIMES.*

Below: Muldoon's relationship with National Party president George Chapman was never personally close, though they worked well together between 1974 and 1978. *DOMINION.*

CREDIBILITY GAP ?

Left: Muldoon's claim that the basic issue at the 1978 election was his credibility compared to Labour's drew this response from the cartoonist Bill Wrathall. BILL WRATHALL/*NZ TRUTH.*

Below: Although he won the 1978 election, Muldoon and the National Government saw their massive majority seriously reduced. SIR GORDON MINHINNICK/*NZ HERALD.*

"Wait for it! Wait for it!"

Below: Not everyone welcomed the appointment as Governor-General of Holyoake, seen here with Muldoon, Talboys and German President Scheel. MULDOON PAPERS.

Right: Among the journalists Muldoon criticised most was the *Listener* columnist and cartoonist Tom Scott. TOM SCOTT/ NZ LISTENER.

Below: The driving force behind Think Big was Bill Birch, here seen with conservationists protesting mining on the Coromandel. WAIKATO TIMES.

Left: The Closer Economic Relations with Australia Agreement was seen by Muldoon as one of his Government's major achievements but it owed much more to Hugh Templeton (seated left at the signing) and Brian Talboys than to Muldoon. EVENING POST.

Right: The Motonui methanol plant was one of the more successful Think Big projects. TARANAKI NEWSPAPERS LTD.

Muldoon enjoyed visiting schools such as this one at Raglan in 1980, when the children were fascinated by his unique grin. MULDOON PAPERS.

terms of trade, internal costs also cut farmers' net incomes. Not only did farmers have to pay higher prices for both imported and locally manufactured goods as the result of protection and import controls, but during the 1960s and 1970s they were also faced with dramatic increases in land values, wages, killing charges, transport costs, machinery prices and interest rates. Farmers were understandably angry that the overvalued exchange rate meant that they did not receive full compensation in New Zealand dollars for their exported produce.

The protected nature of the New Zealand economy and large increases in costs further transferred income from the farming to the secondary and service sectors of the economy. Muldoon recognised this fact when he noted in his 1976 Budget that 'the share of the farming community in total private income has dropped in percentage terms to an alarming degree'.[47] Others in the senior levels of the National Party were also concerned.

Shortly before Muldoon's 1976 Budget, the National Party's president, George Chapman, wrote to Muldoon saying that he and all five divisional conferences of the party wanted 'substantial support for farming in the July Budget'.[48] Specifically the party wanted the maintenance of existing levels of subsidies on fertiliser, weed control and pest control; 'production incentives for increased livestock numbers . . . by paying grants for additional stock held'; 'taxation incentives on sale of increased livestock'; 'significant reductions in Estate Duty'; and additional finance available through the Rural Bank. Chapman concluded by arguing that 'To date all Government measures have been aimed at restraint of expenditure and demand, cutting Government costs, restraining imports, etc. The measures suggested would emphasise that part of our solution to the present economic crisis is increasing the volume of exports.'[49]

Many farmers saw subsidies as a very poor alternative to a freeing-up of the economy, which would allow them to escape excessive costs, and to the devaluation of the New Zealand dollar. Muldoon, however, was also under considerable pressure from the protectionist leaders of the FOL and of the Manufacturers' Federation, such as Sir Laurence Stevens and Sir Earle Richardson, who wanted tariffs left as they were.[50] They convinced him and Adams-Schneider that the removal of interest controls and protection would lead to an unacceptable rise in unemployment and that devaluation would fuel inflation. He decided instead to compensate farmers and increase both their production for export and their incomes by a number of incentives and subsidies, although everyone, including Muldoon, realised they could not be sustained indefinitely.

In 1976 he introduced the Livestock Incentive Scheme to encourage an increase in livestock numbers. In 1978 the Supplementary Minimum Prices (SMPs) scheme placed a floor under the prices paid to farmers for meat, wool and dairy products, and the Land Development Encouragement loan scheme offered, through interest and principal rebates, cash grants to farmers to increase production. In 1979 a tax rebate on the domestic added value of exports was initiated through the Export Performance Tax incentive. Other measures included low-interest loans for farm purchase; tax rebates for fencing, drainage, roading and depreciation; fertiliser subsidies; and the removal of various government charges. The most controversial of these measures were SMPs, which Muldoon saw as 'a targeted devaluation' because although 'the value of the New Zealand dollar was too high... we let it remain high. . . to avoid any pressure on prices. . . as we were struggling to bring down the rate of inflation. . . . What we gave the farmer as an SMP was the equivalent of the increase that he would have had from devaluation.'[51] The Government undertook to pay farmers the difference between minimum prices set at the start of each season for all major pastoral products and the actual market price reached during the season. This was not dissimilar to the support system at the centre of the European Economic Community's Common Agricultural Policy. It was hoped that this would not only give farmers a more reasonable return on their investment and labour but would give them confidence to increase production.

The export incentive schemes devised in 1976 and 1977 were seen by Muldoon as short-term incentives to increase both agricultural and manufacturing exports quickly, but over succeeding years they proved harder and harder to remove, especially when defended by pressure from the exporting sector.[52] Concurrently Muldoon started to reduce tariffs and protection of less efficient industries. Although stock numbers and exports did increase as a result especially of SMPs, the subsidies and tax incentives encouraged quantity rather than quality, discouraged diversification from traditional products, and raised the price of farmland to artificially high levels. Even people who admired Muldoon as a person and who were committed National Party stalwarts became concerned at the longer-term effects of subsidies. Sir Roderick Weir, for example, observed in retrospect that 'too many people were buying land in expectation of capital gains and were simply capitalising subsidies. Without export subsidies their equities vanished.'[53] Subsidies also made it more difficult to balance the Budget.

Muldoon was always reluctant to devalue, partly because his 1967 devaluation had had only a limited effect. Any gains exporters received had been largely eroded by the effect of imported inflation as a result of the lower exchange rate, and its consequential wage and cost increases. Instead he declared that 'my Government intends to continue to implement . . . policies of incentives, regardless of the sector . . . whether it be farming, forestry, the export and production of manufactured goods, tourism, or the fishing industry . . . by means of the carrot rather than the stick'.[54]

Many farmers recognised how unsatisfactory subsidies and export incentives were and became more, rather than less, frustrated and annoyed by being made in effect welfare beneficiaries because the Government was not prepared to risk the cost of dismantling protection and devaluing the currency. The result, as some perceptive contemporary commentators noted, was deep disenchantment with Muldoon and the National Party, who were seen as being more concerned with the interests of urban manufacturers and even trade unionists than National's traditional farming constituency.[55] That disillusion came to a head with Muldoon's decision to end a freezing industry dispute in early 1978 by subsidising freezing workers' wages.

Manufacturers as well as farmers were encouraged to produce for export by the use of export incentives. The strategy was not just to increase exports but also to move resources away from industries that produced solely for the domestic market and consumed costly imports to industries which would earn foreign exchange. Muldoon adopted a 'winners and losers' approach to manufacturing and used Treasury, the Ministry of Industries and Commerce, the Development Finance Corporation and his own Advisory Group to identify those industries which should be encouraged by assistance. He announced in his 1976 Budget that over the following year research and discussions would identify specific ways in which export-orientated businesses could receive incentives.[56] The review could not be completed in time for the 1977 Budget although that Budget did offer some special treatment and concessions to 'those productive activities which are of high priority because they are making an outstanding contribution to economic growth and the balance of payments.'[57] Not until 1979 did a new system of export incentives come together, based on the principles that incentives should apply only to net foreign exchange earnings after deducting the foreign exchange costs of imported content and that the incentive should apply to a firm's total exports not simply to an increase in its exports.

Muldoon's incentive schemes for farmers and manufacturing exporters increased government intervention in and control over the economy. They demonstrated clearly both his reluctance to trust the free market, particularly when there was rampant inflation, and his belief that governments were able, as he expressed succinctly in retrospect, 'to pick the potential winners and support them'.[58] The very recipients of such subsidies, however, resented having to accept them as a very inferior alternative to deregulation of the economy and the reduction of their costs and they also became increasingly frustrated by, and annoyed at, the extent of government control and bureaucratic interference in their activities. They were concerned at increasing levels of government expenditure and the high rates of taxation and borrowing necessary not only for the economic subsidies, rebates and incentives but also for the social services of health, education and social welfare.

Understandably, some observers became concerned at the extent to which the Government was intervening to protect and subsidise farmers, manufacturers, exporters, wage and salary earners, families, retired people and those unable to work through illness or unemployment. Many voters resented the way large, relatively wealthy, entrenched interest groups seemed to be able to defend and advance their own privileged vested interests while criticising government expenditure on other groups. From the late 1970s free market critics of the Government, and of Muldoon in particular, were suggesting that the Government should stop trying to pick winners and should stop trying to restructure through subsidies and incentives. Instead, through deregulation and the operation of an automatically operating free market, the economy should be allowed to become more rational, efficient and productive, even if in the short term the reconstruction of the economy would be painful for many people in terms of business failure or unemployment. That inevitable human cost was unacceptable to Muldoon.

Muldoon's economic philosophy was not intellectually sophisticated. As he wrote, 'Put my own way, economics is not money, or wealth, or resources, but people; their hopes, their fears, their reactions to stimuli or to adversity.'[59] In making economic decisions Muldoon was always conscious of what his policies and actions would do to individual people, to families, to communities. Having experienced hard times himself in his youth, he was determined to hurt people as little as possible, and this consideration led to self-imposed limits on the economic and social policies he was prepared to countenance. It was a humane approach to government which he shared with many others of his generation, both National and Labour. The public interest was the concern of government and that prevented him pursuing free market or anti-state policies which would create a laissez-faire economy, in which only the fittest or more fortunate would prosper, or which would cut back the welfare state from social security in time of need to a mean-spirited minimal charity.

Muldoon and others believed that he had received a mandate to implement real change in 1975 but there is little doubt he lost the opportunity and the will and became preoccupied with managing as best he could an increasingly malfunctioning economy and a welfare state also in urgent need of reform. His conservative, reactionary style did not resolve major structural problems but merely delayed more radical systemic reform. Temperamentally and philosophically Muldoon was opposed to laissez-faire New Right economic and social theories. Muldoon was too concerned at the human pain radical reforms such as those introduced in Britain and the United States by Thatcher and Reagan would cause, and he also believed such policies would lead to his government being voted out of office by understandably angry voters. He concluded, after discussing such solutions with Tom Skinner, that if he went down that policy road the trade unions would confront the Government with a general strike that would surpass the 1951 waterfront dispute. Although Skinner conceded that the Government would eventually win, Muldoon was not prepared to risk the economic dislocation and social division that such policies and such industrial action would produce.[60]

Because, Muldoon argued, wage negotiations and settlements and industrial unrest had an impact on the economy as a whole, it was inevitable that the Minister of Finance would be concerned about industrial relations. Muldoon had not enjoyed a close working relationship with Shand or Marshall when they had been Ministers of Labour and was determined from 1975 to have someone in that portfolio with whom he felt comfortable. Neither Gordon, from 1975 to 1978, nor Bolger, from 1978 to 1984, were content, however, to defer completely to him, and from time to time there were quite serious disagreements with each of them. One cause of tension was the very close relationship Muldoon developed with Skinner, the president of the Federation of Labour. Almost every Sunday morning when Muldoon was in Auckland he met Skinner at 11 a.m. There the two men, 'who got on very well', over 'a couple of gins . . . vetted proceedings' on industrial matters and sometimes agreed to decisions which Gordon found anathema, such as 'Muldoon's notorious decision to pay freezing workers' which was 'a Tom Skinner thought'.[61] Gordon also saw Skinner privately and informally about half a dozen times a month, and Skinner would often forewarn the Minister of Labour about Muldoon's thinking on various matters. Both Muldoon and Gordon admitted that they did what they could to help Skinner 'maintain mana' in the trade union movement in order to strengthen him against left-wing challenges,[62] but Skinner undoubtedly used his access and friendship with both Muldoon and Gordon to persuade them to accept policies which many of their colleagues in the National Party disliked.

Three major problems faced Muldoon and his Government in their relations with the trade union movement: the desire of a significant section of the National Party to legislate for voluntary trade union membership; the question of rising unemployment; and the impact of excessive wage settlements on inflation and costs to producers. Like Holyoake's Government before him, Muldoon in dealing with industrial relations had to balance the expectations of National's farming and employer constituencies against the need to support Skinner and, most import-antly, to prevent the grave damage to the New Zealand economy that would be caused by a major strike or a long hold-up in production, especially during the killing season. Despite his strong anti-union rhetoric and frequent public clashes with more militant union leaders, Muldoon was determined to avoid a serious industrial confrontation. Although he had supported Talboys and Gill, who wanted a firm commitment to voluntary unionism at the 1975 election, he was relieved when Holyoake and Gordon, who both argued strongly in caucus against it, were able to achieve a compromise which left the question of compulsion up to compulsory ballots of individual unions rather than the more radical legislative repeal of compulsory unionism.[63] He also tried hard to hold unemployment, which in January 1976, shortly after he took office, registered 10,617.[64] Twelve months later the figure had only risen slightly to 11,276 but by October of 1977 it had jumped sharply to 17,155, and during early 1978 it exploded to 46,894 by July.[65] Nothing like that had been seen since the 1930s.

Throughout the 1960s, 1970s and early 1980s successive National govern-ments worked on an incomes policy which would have the support of government, employers and unions. All three groups, however, were divided between moderates and militants and as a result the rhetoric from the leaders was often more confrontationally aggressive than the negotiations behind the scenes. Not only Skinner and the employers' leaders but also Holyoake, Muldoon, Shand and Gordon had to satisfy their constituencies' prejudices while seeking to achieve agreement on wages and avoid major strikes or industrial hold-ups, especially in the season when export produce was being shipped. The disastrous effect of the 1951 waterfront dispute on New Zealand's economy and society was a constant reminder of the need to avoid the breakdown of consensus or compromise. Muldoon particularly was prepared to agree to wage–tax trade offs as Minister of Finance in order to get the unions and employers closer in wage bargaining.

Muldoon believed that 'we will only achieve price stability if the whole range of government economic measures, particularly fiscal and monetary measures, are supplemented by an effective incomes policy'.[66] That required, however, 'the consent and support of the majority of the general public' and could not be simply imposed on them except for a relatively short period of time. The trade unions would need to accept wage increases lower than rises in the consumers' price index if inflation was to be controlled and unemployment minimised. Because the Labour Government imposed a statutory incomes policy during 1975 the unions were given and accepted a general wage order in January 1976 which was considerably less than the rate of inflation over the previous year. They were adamant, however, that in 1976 there should be a return to free wage bargaining and an end to constraints on wage increases.

In response Muldoon on 15 May 1976 announced a twelve-month freeze on wages, salaries, professional charges, directors' fees and rents, accompanied by a cost-of-living increase of 7 per cent or $7, whichever was the less. Muldoon accepted that this freeze was an 'extreme form of government intervention' but he saw no real alternative in the circumstances.[67] The freeze enraged the unions, and following a special conference of the Federation of Labour there was widespread strike action. Indeed, 1976 became the worst year for industrial disputes since 1951. More than twice the number of working days were lost as in the previous year. Finally, the Government agreed to a partial lifting of the freeze through an 'exceptional circumstances' clause, which was designed to deal with serious pay anomalies.[68] The Government also established in December 1976 an independent Wage Hearing Tribunal to consider general wage orders, and that Tribunal awarded a pay rise of 6 per cent from 14 March 1977, much to Muldoon's disappointment.[69]

Skinner, in a presidential address to the May 1977 FOL conference, blamed the Government's intervention in wage negotiations between employers and workers for the unpleasant industrial climate and the increase in strikes.[70] Muldoon responded by agreeing to 'a freeing-up of wage bargaining procedures' even though 'this involves a risk of wage escalation'.[71] He appealed to the FOL and the Employers' Federation to be responsible by 'keeping wage settlements to a level that will not prejudice the nation's economic recovery'.[72] Although Muldoon overruled Gordon, his Minister of Labour, and in May 1977 extended the wage freeze for another three months until the 14 August, thereafter there was a return to freer wage bargaining for the first time since 1971.[73]

Problems with freezing workers and boilermakers during 1977 appeared to signal a rise in industrial militancy and a shift away from moderate union leadership personified in Skinner to militants such as Ken Douglas and Bill Andersen who were the leaders of both the Drivers' Union and the Socialist Unity Party. Muldoon and Gordon decided that the Government 'had to give a victory to moderates before Anderson [sic] takes over' because 'a stable wage system' was the 'only way to beat inflation'.[74] Quigley was concerned that the agreement between Government, employers and moderate union leaders might be a 'social contract', but Muldoon denied this, saying that it was simply the 'best of a bad job', and he was 'frankly not sure if it will work'.

In November 1977, with Muldoon overseas, industrial problems in the freezing works and at the Tokoroa pulp and paper mill worsened. Gordon was totally opposed to a suggested 23 per cent increase on current rates, which he believed the employers were on the point of offering the freezing workers, and decided that regulation would be necessary to reduce that figure to an acceptable 7 per cent.[75] Although he thought Skinner 'will react reasonably', he did not believe the freezing workers or the FOL generally would. Gordon was also worried about the effect a closedown of the freezing works and the loss of overseas earnings would have on the economy. He categorically ruled out, in response to a query from Quigley, the use of non-union labour to break the strike.

Many of the National Government's supporters believed, correctly, that Muldoon, despite talking tough, was too inclined to give in to union pressure. That perception was confirmed in March 1978 when Muldoon personally intervened in the dispute, which threatened to shut down the freezing industry at the height of the killing and export season and when most farming areas were also suffering a serious drought. In consultation with his Ministers of Agriculture and Labour, the Prime Minister chaired several meetings designed to achieve a settlement of the long-running dispute. He made it clear that while the companies could not pay everything the unions were asking, they would have to increase their offer and absorb, not pass on to farmers, much of the additional cost. He also suggested that settlements should favour lower-paid workers rather than those on higher rates.[76]

The unions rejected Muldoon's proposals and gave notice of industrial action from 20 March. Muldoon then decided that the difference between the union's claim (on an annual basis $32 million) and the companies' offer ($18 million) should be shared equally by the unions dropping their claim by one third of the difference, the companies absorbing one third of the difference, and the Government providing a subsidy for one third of the difference ($4.696 million each). The unions called off their proposed strike and the Government moved to amend the Economic Stabilisation (Slaughtering and Processing Charges) Regulations 1977, which limited increases in remuneration that could be claimed as passed on costs in calculating killing charges to farmers.[77] The agreement increased the freezing worker wage bill overall by 10.8 percent with a variation from a minimum rise of 7.6 per cent to a maximum rise of 17.3 per cent. Such rises needed to be seen in the context of a 14.3 percent rise in consumer prices in the year to March 1978.

The solution was opposed by Gordon and by the Minister of Agriculture, MacIntyre.[78] Farmers, in particular, were outraged by the unprecedented arrangement, which was seen as the Government not only giving in to militant union demands but also using taxpayers' money to increase freezing workers' wages beyond what the freezing works were able to pay even after raising killing charges to farmers. Muldoon replied to his critics by arguing that the situation was extraordinary; that farmers' liquidity would be damaged severely if the one million head of stock slaughtered each week were not put through the freezing works. The drought made retention on the farms very difficult without severely depleting foodstuff stored for the coming winter. Above all, New Zealand could not sustain disruption to its exports. He concluded that 'the cost to New Zealand taxpayers . . . is relatively small compared with the losses to the farmers and the nation which would have been caused by a strike and the disruption in our exports.'[79] The fact that having such a strike and the resulting damage to exports and the economy was not a good way for the Government to start an election year also was undoubtedly in Muldoon's mind, though he did not mention it in his public utterances at the time.

Muldoon was personally responsible for the 1976–77 wage freeze, its extension in late 1976, and the freezing industry settlement in 1978. The actions were extremely interventionist and involved rejecting the views of other key ministers, notably the Minister of Labour, and of officials, and they provoked strong opposition from groups such as employers and farmers who traditionally supported the National Party. But Muldoon's intervention was erratic, veering from confrontation to compromise with the unions, from wage freeze to free bargaining, from telling employers to be firm in resisting wage demands to subsidising them in paying wages which they claimed were untenable. Critics argued that he failed to stop either wage inflation or the achievement of unreasonable settlements by the abuse of militant union power. He also failed to get consensus on incomes policy and admitted in retrospect that it went on far too long and that 'the Government, employers and unions never got it right'.[80] Following the freezing industry settlement in March, which even Muldoon admitted was a 'compromise' which contrasted with the 'tough line preached' by the Government during the lengthy negotiations, he was challenged by Bolger, who asked bluntly and rhetorically, 'What have we achieved?', and Quigley who said it was a 'No win situation' which was 'strangling the farming industry' and 'losing credibility' for the Government.[81] Quigley questioned Muldoon, 'When will you deliver on policy? You must answer.' Muldoon responded that he was prepared to deregister militant unions if he had to. Muldoon, however, saw both employers and unionists as being at fault in the long-running freezing works dispute, and he had a high regard for some freezing worker union leaders, notably 'Blue' Kennedy. He warned his colleagues that in settling the dispute the Government 'must be careful not to be undemocratic' and that there was 'no way of legislating men back to work'.[82]

National's caucus was again divided by the dropping of prosecutions against freezing workers at the start of the next killing season. Prosecutions against some freezing workers arising out of the 1977–78 dispute were pending at the start of the 1978–79 season. Muldoon invited Knox and Ken Douglas to meet him, Bolger and Gavin Jackson, the Secretary of Labour. The Prime Minister told the FOL leaders that if the prosecution of the Ocean Beach freezing workers got to court they would be found guilty and either fined or gaoled, which would lead to a 'stoush' between unions, employers and the Government. He asked Knox and Douglas what they could do to prevent such a situation. Douglas replied that there would be no problem if the prosecutions did not proceed and Knox asked what would happen if no evidence was given. When Jackson answered that the judge would probably throw the cases out, Muldoon exclaimed, 'That's it, Jackson, you offer no evidence.'[83] According to Douglas, this was typical of Muldoon's 'what is necessary to fix it' approach rather than a more ideologically committed position. Muldoon was supported in caucus by Talboys, Bolger and Gordon in arguing that there would be no start to the killing season without the dropping of prosecutions. Quigley and Brill disagreed and declared that there should be no interference with the process of law.[84] Quigley later commented that 'nobody will believe us' if the Government said that there had been no political interference in the judicial process, and expressed his view that National should have acted as a 'law and order party' in seeing the law was enforced.[85] When it was suggested that the Secretary of Labour had not acted properly, Gordon indicated that he would resign as Minister of Labour if caucus passed any resolution critical of the Secretary.

The debate over the prosecutions spilled over into the caucus meetings on 29 September and 3 October 1978 when the report of an inquiry into the freezing industry was also discussed. By then the Invercargill MP Norman Jones was threatening to cross the floor, even after Muldoon pointed out that 'If the season hasn't started on election day, it'll cost us the farmers' vote . . . I wouldn't want to lose our mixed farming seats.' Muldoon also suggested that 'This is the only issue that could cost us the election . . . A shambles could beat us.'[86] In the end only five hardline MPs voted against dropping the prosecutions, though others undoubtedly sympathised with them.

Muldoon also used his influence to prevent the Government taking a hard, confrontational line in disputes involving other militant unions. During a long debate on industrial action on the BNZ site and the possibility of deregistering the Boilermakers Union, for example, a move Gordon opposed, Shearer, who supported deregistration, asserted that 'People want blood'.[87] Muldoon responded, 'This isn't worth a total stoppage . . . This is not one for blood.' Supported by Talboys and McLay, Muldoon and Gordon persuaded the majority of caucus not to deregister the boilermakers. At the same meeting of caucus Muldoon persuaded caucus not to intervene directly in the Kawerau timber mill dispute.

By late 1977 it had become clear that the world economy was unlikely to help New Zealand overcome its economic difficulties in the immediate future. With the terms of trade remaining low, inflation and unemployment rising, strikes threatening, and widespread farmer discontent, Muldoon decided that he needed to stimulate the economy. There was a risk that such a strategy might fuel inflation and cause a blow-out in the budget deficit through increased expenditure. The 1977 Budget had already projected increased expenditure of 24.3 per cent, compared to only 2.7 per cent in 1976, largely as the result of the introduction in February 1977 of National Superannuation.[88] Nevertheless, for political and social reasons, Muldoon decided to stimulate the economy because 'We don't want any more unemployment'.[89]

He introduced a mini-budget on 28 October 1977 having told his caucus that '1978 will be difficult for New Zealand . . . If we don't stimulate now unemployment will go up. We don't want that. So we run [the] balance of payments deficit up . . . We take a risk but a necessary one. Things could deteriorate in New Zealand very rapidly.'⁹⁰ The mini-budget, which clearly reversed the deflationary strategy of the previous two years, eased lending for housing and consumer goods; introduced a $25 per child supplementary family benefit; increased expenditure on public works; expanded job training and employment schemes; cut income taxes across the board by 5 per cent from 1 February 1978; and increased assistance to farmers and exporters.⁹¹ Muldoon's actions on farming ran into opposition in caucus from Bolger and Quigley. When Quigley asked for permission to speak and vote against a farm mortgage vendor bond scheme, Muldoon refused, telling him that he was 'exaggerating' and 'seldom consistent'.⁹² Bolger, supported largely by urban MPs such as McLay and Malcolm, was successful in opposing a proposed increase in export levies for meat. Following that vote Muldoon suggested that in future caucus should 'reserve unpopular decisions for essentials'; that is to say, to minimise them so that the Government had a chance of retaining its popular support 'We want to win the 1978 election', he said, and the economy, in his view, was starting to favour Labour.⁹³ That assessment was based not only on Muldoon's own instincts but also on public opinion polls, which by May 1977 had found Labour and National tying for support.⁹⁴

Monetary policy was subsequently eased in February 1978 and the Budget that year further reflated the economy, particularly by expenditure on SMPs to farmers. As a result the increase in unemployment slowed but inflation, the budget deficit and the balance of payments deficit, all of which Muldoon seemed to be getting firmly under control in 1976 and 1977, started to rise again. Muldoon was also concerned that the rate of private sector credit should not grow at more than 15 per cent per annum, which was the actual annual growth rate during the early part of 1978. In August 1978 he took steps to slow the expansion of liquidity in the economy by regulation, by a government cash loan, by higher rates of return on Treasury bills, and by allowing the Reserve Bank to operate more freely in the open money market.⁹⁵

When Muldoon had returned from his overseas trip in November 1977, he had addressed caucus on the state of the New Zealand economy and especially on the increase in production concurrent with the contraction of overseas orders for New Zealand's traditional exports. In the absence of the freeing-up of agricultural trade globally and in the face of rising unemployment in New Zealand, he suggested that there should in future be six criteria for investment beyond simply the profit goal of creating 'money for the sake of money'.⁹⁶ Those criteria were: 'Is it good for New Zealand?'; 'access to markets'; technology coming from research and development; the use of New Zealand resources; 'minimising the rate of unemployment'; and New Zealand ownership of resources. These were to become important guidelines to Muldoon in developing his economic strategy and policies over the remaining six years of his administration.

On Christmas Day 1977, in the midst of the freezing works dispute, the Speaker of Parliament, Sir Roy Jack, died, precipitating a by-election in the National Party's rural stronghold of Rangitikei. The collapse of farm incomes, the reaction to the freezing works situation and the Government's handling of it, and general discontent with the National Government destroyed National's majority. The Labour vote in the electorate collapsed, with many Labour supporters voting tactically for the Social Credit leader Bruce Beetham, who was that party's local candidate. Beetham won the by-election on 17 February 1978, and it became even more obvious than before that National would have to move to shore up its vote before the election later that year.[97]

After the by-election, Muldoon warned his caucus that the press would be on Beetham's side and that he should be treated as a backbench Opposition MP not a party leader and should certainly not be listened to in the House with 'rapt attention'.[98] Nor should National MPs 'be drawn into an analysis of Social Credit', which would raise its profile further. A few months later, however, Muldoon relented somewhat and offered Beetham the third speaking place after himself and Rowling in the Address in Reply debate, telling his caucus that it was 'Be kind to Beetham week'.[99]

The loss of Rangitikei to Social Credit in the February by-election, and public attacks by farming leaders on the Government in general and Muldoon and MacIntyre, the Minister of Agriculture, in particular, led Muldoon to announce that his June 1978 Budget would be a 'farmers' budget'.[100] Labour's deputy leader, Tizard, correctly observed that it was more accurately 'a rural seat retention scheme' for the 1978 election.[101] In March Federated Farmers had demanded that the Budget should include $100 million of assistance to farmers.[102] Muldoon responded with increased subsidies for fertiliser; drought relief payments; suspensory loans for horticulture; land and irrigation development; and other Budget items which together – and excluding the cost of SMPs, which were also introduced – came to $109 million in a full year.[103] The Budget included further income tax reductions and public service salary increases. The deficit before borrowing was projected to be nearly 7 per cent in 1977, but in fact rose to 9 per cent during 1978–79.[104]

As a percentage of GDP, however, the budget deficit had been reduced and some other economic indicators also suggested that by 1978 the Government's economic policies were having the right effect. Inflation was down, despite the removal of consumer subsidies and higher government charges, from 16.9 per cent in 1975–76 to 12 per cent in 1977–78.[105] The budget deficit had been reduced from 9 per cent to 4.7 per cent of GDP in the same period.[106] The balance of payments deficit was down from $960 million for the year ending June 1976 to $463 million for the year ending June 1978.[107] The one economic indicator, however, that was not moving the way Muldoon wanted was unemployment. In April 1977 registered unemployment, excluding those on subsidised work schemes, was 4100 or 0.61 per cent of the labour force. By April 1978 it had risen to 19,800, or 1.84 per cent, a situation causing considerable public concern and adverse comment.[108] By the 1978 election 21 per cent of respondents in the *NZ Herald*-NRB public opinion polls were identifying unemployment as their main concern.[109]

As a result of his measures in late 1977 and 1978 Muldoon encouraged a consumption-led recovery in the domestic economy with a strong increase in retail trade, manufacturing activity and business confidence. But investment expenditure continued to fall, there was a relatively high flow of funds from the private to the state sector, and the money supply continued to grow quickly, partly fuelled by an almost 20 per cent increase in trading bank credit during 1978.[110] Predicted strong rises in salaries and wages during 1978–79 would also fuel inflation. Unemployment, including those in subsidised employment, was projected to be between 45,000 and 55,000 in 1979 and to include a significant minority of skilled workers as well as a majority of unskilled. It was also anticipated by the end of 1978 that inflation would accelerate and the balance of payments would deteriorate in the following two years. Treasury warned the Government: 'Unless future investment is primarily in internationally competitive industries our ability to increase activity and employment beyond 1979–80 will be limited by the balance of payments constraint to an even greater extent than it is now.'[111]

In September 1978, shortly before the election, the Economic Monitoring Group of the New Zealand Planning Council, chaired by Dr Donald Brash, published the first of what became an annual series of reports on *Economic Trends and Policies*. The report stated bluntly that 'we face a structural problem, rather than a "normal" cyclical situation . . . Self correcting forces are still at work both here and overseas, but have been overlaid with unusual, non-recurring influences such as oil prices, an explosion of wage costs in many countries, currency upheavals, and a reluctance of Governments in some major trading countries, for various reasons, to adopt the usual counter-cyclical policy measures.'[112] Among the report's recommendations were the extension of SMPs for agriculture; tax incentives for exports; removal of price controls and controls on foreign investment; reduction of the Government deficit; control of credit expansion; and tax reform. The use of incentives by the Government should be balanced by a greater use of market forces.

Although Muldoon realised that he had been unable to satisfy the economic expectations he had aroused at the previous election, he still believed that he would beat Labour at the 1978 elections, at least partly because in his opinion the Labour Party was 'deeply divided' and was 'no longer a workers' party', having fallen into the 'hands of middle-class intellectuals'.[113] He also realised, however that there was widespread concern about the apparently worsening economy and about his own personality, which was under constant attack not only from his Labour opponents but also from some of his own party and sections of the media. The Heylen Research Centre found that whereas 38 per cent of respondents to their polling were dissatisfied with Muldoon in February 1976, by September 1977 it had reached 51 per cent. Muldoon's only consolation was that Rowling's disapproval rating had risen from 29 to 62 per cent over the same period.[114]

Nevertheless, some journalists continued to be more sympathetic to Rowling than to Muldoon, who was faced with sustained criticism during the 1978 election year. The *Christchurch Star*, for example, published a series of editorials suggesting that voters should 'sack Muldoon . . . New Zealand no longer needs – if it ever did – his style of leadership. He's bad for this country; he's bad for the National Party.'[115] The editor of the *Christchurch Star* undermined his anti-Muldoon campaign, however, by nominating Minogue as the alternative. Most voters realised that the real choice in 1978 was still, as it had been in 1975, between Muldoon and Rowling.

Defending criticism of his own leadership Rowling told a television interviewer that Muldoon engaged in 'grubby politics . . . windbagging . . . in order to offset some of his weaknesses' and that 'one Muldoon is too much for this country . . . a rotten Prime Minister.'[116] There was no doubt, however, that during the 1975–78 period Muldoon continued to dominate Rowling in Parliament. As a senior Gallery journalist, Richard Long, observed, 'Muldoon in the House has this dominant voice, he speaks in newspaper headlines, repeats a catchy phrase to make sure that it ends up in the newspapers. Mr Rowling on the other hand in spite of his voice lessons cannot dominate in the House, and even when he makes a simple point he often qualifies it out of existence.'[117] It came as some surprise, therefore, when, during the 1978 election campaign, Rowling appeared to perform far more effectively and impressively than did Muldoon.

As he had done three years before, Muldoon started his 1978 election campaign in Hamilton and on Monday 30 October and in the following four weeks addressed a total of nineteen evening meetings and numerous whistle-stop gatherings during the day. Under the party's election slogan, 'We're keeping our word', he stressed his attempts to repair the economy over the previous three years; talked about encouraging production and exports; reminded voters of the National Superannuation Scheme, the tax cuts and the increased support to single- and low-income families; and asked people to judge whether he or Rowling was the more credible leader. He was able to point out that when he came to office, export receipts were $1658 million and three years later in 1977–78 they were more than double at $3418 million.[118] Imports over the same period had increased by only 26 per cent. Many voters remained unconvinced.

Muldoon and the National Party were devastated by the results of the 1978 election. On election night, 25 November, they appeared to have lost nine seats, although Hunua and Kapiti were subsequently held through a Supreme Court petition and a magisterial recount.[119] National also failed to win back Rangitikei from Social Credit. Although National still had a comfortable majority in the House, it dropped 7.8 percentage points in its vote, at 39.8 per cent actually polling marginally fewer votes than the Labour Opposition on 40.4 per cent. Only the 1977 electoral boundaries redistribution, which had favoured National, and a diversion of protest votes into Social Credit had prevented the Government's defeat.

Contemporary observers were surprised at Muldoon's inability in 1978 to repeat his dominance over Rowling during the election campaign. The media was much more favourable towards Rowling and the Social Credit leader, Beetham, than it had been in 1975, and Rowling himself projected a more positive and confident style and image. Muldoon, on the other hand, was surprisingly tentative and his aggression appeared counter-productive. In the month before the election his support as preferred Prime Minister fell from 60 to 48 per cent while Rowling's rose from 30 to 38.[120] National and Muldoon were also on the defensive in 1978, having to justify their policies and actions over the past three years, and were busy trying to explain why they had not, as promised in 1975, repaired New Zealand's shattered economy.

The caucus meeting following the 1978 election was a restrained and even sad affair.[121] Although National had been returned to office with a comfortable majority, its vote nationally and its majority in the House had both been slashed. Moreover a number of the surviving MPs had very small majorities in their electorates. Muldoon had lost through defeat or retirement some of his strongest personal supporters in cabinet and caucus such as Walker, Lapwood, McCready, Dewe, Edward Latter and John Lithgow, the last of those observing that 'I'm a Rob Muldoon man' and saying that he thought some of the harder decisions should have been taken by some of the other ministers.[122] Two of Muldoon's more capable ministers, who did not always agree with him, Gordon and Gandar were also going.

Ten new National MPs elected in 1978 were more in favour of deregulation and saw their election as owing less to Muldoon than those elected in 1975.[123] Most disliked his personality and his policies and formed an alternative caucus to push for delicensing the meat industry and road transport, deregulating the labour market, and freeing up the finance sector.[124] They also supported Bolger's attempts to extend shop trading hours and introduce voluntary unionism. Muldoon was unenthusiastic about, and in some cases totally opposed to, all these changes. The group also struck up a rapport with McLay, Quigley and Gair.

Muldoon observed at the post-election caucus meeting that the smaller majority would require more discipline from National MPs over the following three years, and told them: 'In caucus you are entitled to say what you want to, but if you miss a decision you can't come back later and say you didn't agree. We try to get a consensus. We try to avoid votes if we can. Voting against your colleagues in the House is a serious matter and should not be taken lightly. Politics is a team game all the way. You're either in the team or not.'[125]

Waring then asked for 'a softer image on some issues', while Shearer noted the 'criticism in his electorate which he was obliged to record'. Muldoon took these comments as criticism of his leadership and replied that the 'Party would have to accept him as he is. He was not proposing to change.' Quigley, who wanted better communication through the media and more private enterprise, and Adams-Schneider, who said he was also 'aware of criticism of the leadership', then spoke before Ken Comber, John Elliott, Ben Couch, Rob Talbot and Aussie Malcolm praised Muldoon. Gandar estimated that he would have been beaten by a greater majority had Muldoon not been leading National, and Talboys ended the discussion by reminding caucus that, 'the quickest way to destroy a party or a Government is to attack its leader . . . Labour will try hard to destroy Muldoon', who would again lead National into the 1981 election. National's task over the next three years was to 'look after its leader'.[126]

Criticism of Muldoon personally and the Government's policies generally were more forthcoming from the National Party organisation. Muldoon freely admitted to his party's Dominion Executive at its post-election meeting that, along with the negative issues such as industrial relations, unemployment, overseas borrowing, law and order, taxation and abortion, all of which had cost National votes, 'Muldoon as portrayed by the media' had also been a factor in the Government's relatively poor result.[127] He stated, however, that 'he did not propose any change' in his style of leadership. In response, Murray Reeves and Valerie Forbes of Waikato, Roy Johnston and Julian Watts of Wellington, Dorothy McNab of Otago, and Murray Hunter of Canterbury all blamed Muldoon's style of leadership for the result, but Muldoon had left the meeting at lunchtime and so missed the comments most critical of him, particularly those from the Wellington and Canterbury-Westland divisions.

Following the election, Muldoon also addressed some 600 party members in Auckland and at length analysed the campaign and the results. He largely ignored the fact that although National had won a reduced majority of 10 seats Labour under Rowling had actually polled slightly more votes. National's share of the vote had slumped from 48 per cent to just under 40 per cent in three years and was the lowest share of the vote National had polled since its establishment in 1936. Muldoon concluded that the important thing was that National had won and that there would be little change in the style of Government over the next three years.[128] Many of those at the meeting saw the results as disappointing, indeed even a disaster,[129] and the Auckland Division subsequently and unanimously passed a motion endorsing a call by the party president George Chapman for the Government in future to adhere to the principles of private enterprise in its planning and decision making.[130] Muldoon, however, seemed to believe that what the electorate had rejected was his relatively hard economic line after 1975 and thereafter became very cautious in his approach to restructuring and deregulating the New Zealand economy.

CHAPTER 16

Economic Restructuring and 'Think Big' after 1978

FOLLOWING THE 1978 ELECTION, MULDOON WAS FACED WITH replacing six ministers. Gordon's throat problems and his unhappiness with the Labour portfolio (instead of his first love, transport) had led him to announce as early as October 1977 that he would retire from politics at the 1978 election.[1] Two other ministers, Lapwood and McCready, also retired; Walker and Gandar had been defeated; and Wilkinson's high blood pressure forced him to move to the backbenches. Muldoon's range of choice in constructing his new cabinet was constrained by the defeat of Colleen Dewe in Lyttelton, because Muldoon certainly intended to promote her, and by uncertainty over the result in Kapiti, where Barry Brill also appeared unlikely to hold his seat.

As he had done in 1975, so after the 1978 election Muldoon invited all members of the National caucus to indicate who should be in cabinet and what positions they should hold.[2] He received 31 replies, not counting his own and Talboys'. The only nominees for Finance were Muldoon, who received twelve nominations; Adams-Schneider, who received two; and Templeton, one. Talboys received fourteen mentions for Foreign Affairs and Overseas Trade; MacIntyre eleven for Agriculture, twelve for Labour and eight for Maori Affairs; Adams-Schneider nine for Trade and Industry; Thomson eight for Labour; Gair eight for Energy and five for Education; Highet thirteen for Internal Affairs; McLachlan nine for Transport; Venn Young eleven for Lands; Templeton ten for Education; McLay eleven for Justice; Cooper nine for Tourism; and Holland nine for Housing. Bolger, the new minister whom Muldoon had brought into cabinet in 1977, and Bill Birch, the chief whip, received ten nominations for Agriculture and twelve nominations for Works respectively. Gill, who received ten votes for Health, told Muldoon that he did not want either Health or Education but wished to retire from Parliament and be appointed either High Commissioner in London or Ambassador to the United States. Muldoon gave him Defence and Police and promoted him along with Templeton to the front bench to replace Gordon and Gandar. Apart from proposing Brill as Minister of Justice and Attorney-General, Gill made no other written recommendations to Muldoon. Five backbench respondents strongly opposed the reappointment of Holland and McLachlan as ministers.

When he announced his new ministry, Muldoon gave some existing ministers new portfolios which neither they nor their caucus colleagues, judging by the written recommendations, thought were the ideal ones. Gair received Health and Social Welfare; Templeton Customs; and Bolger Labour. The President of the Federation of Labour, Skinner, had predicted that Muldoon would appoint Bolger to replace Gordon as Minister of Labour.[3] Skinner noted that Muldoon had a deep interest in the Labour portfolio and from time to time even took it over in practice so would need a minister with whom he could liaise closely and who would share the Prime Minister's perspective on industrial relations.

Because Muldoon's combative temperament and heavy responsibilities as Prime Minister and Minister of Finance made it difficult for him to lead business in Parliament in a careful and calm way, he appointed Thomson, whom he trusted and who was suave and diplomatic, Minister of State, Minister of State Services, and to a new position as Leader of the House responsible for the day-to-day running of parliamentary business. Muldoon was not the only one who hoped that now he himself would be less involved in the endless points of order and day-to-day clashes over procedure, which hurt his public standing.

Muldoon made several surprise choices of new cabinet ministers. He had been impressed with Merv Wellington's backbench performance, especially on educational issues, over the previous three years and had no doubt about choosing him.[4] Muldoon ignored the caucus consensus which was clearly for Templeton, and indeed Wellington had received only three nominations for cabinet (one each for Police, Social Welfare and an unspecified position). Gandar, Muldoon's Minister of Education 1975–78, was much more liberal and a more conciliatory personality than either Muldoon or Wellington, who held the portfolio from 1978 to 1984. In particular, Gandar had been reluctant to abandon the Johnson Report on education, which he had inherited from the previous Labour Government, even though many of the report's recommendations were strongly opposed in cabinet, caucus and the National Party organisation. There was also a suspicion that Gandar had been more interested in tertiary education and in his Science portfolio than in primary and secondary education. Muldoon believed that a Minister of Education was faced by more pressure groups than any other minister and that those groups were very well organised, very articulate, and often very extreme in their views. Most wanted more money, even though education already had a huge budget, and unless a minister was very strong and prepared to be unpopular it was difficult to say no to them. Muldoon chose Wellington to replace Gandar because he had a conservative, 'back to basics' approach to education and in Muldoon's opinion the strength of personality to say no to the pressure groups.

Although Brill was his first choice for Attorney-General, and McLay only got that portfolio when Leay incorrectly informed Muldoon that Brill would be defeated narrowly in his electorate, that did not mean that McLay would not have been in the cabinet. On the contrary, Muldoon intended including him anyway at the expense of one of the last four he finally chose, but had not intended giving him Justice, even though McLay received eleven nominations for that portfolio to Brill's four.

Muldoon claimed that three MPs were not considered for inclusion solely on health grounds: Wilkinson, who had very high blood pressure; Holland, who had suffered a stroke in 1972 but who had recovered and had served as a minister from 1975 to 1978; and Norm Jones. The latter two, who did not appreciate Muldoon's reasoning, were very disappointed and in Holland's case the Canterbury-Westland Division of the National Party unsuspectingly played a role. The leaders of the Division, led by the chairman Murray Hunter, felt that Muldoon's friend McLachlan was becoming a liability to the party and told Muldoon that the Division would not be too upset if he dropped one of the Division's ministers. Because they were embarrassed they did not stipulate and Muldoon did not request a name. When Muldoon dropped Holland, the Division's officers remonstrated with him and said they had meant McLachlan. Muldoon, who had undoubtedly realised that at the time, simply chuckled and said he thought they had meant Holland.[5]

One of the most unfortunate MPs was Holyoake's son-in-law Ken Comber, who had been an under-secretary to Highet from 1975 and who received twenty nominations for cabinet covering a wide variety of possible portfolios. One of those nominations came from Highet, who was summoned to Muldoon's office. After 'a curt nod and no preliminary talk, Muldoon said, "I see you think Comber should replace you. . . . I'm inclined to agree with you."'[6] Highet then asked if Muldoon had been satisfied with his performance and when Muldoon replied that he had been Highet inquired, "'Then what is this all about?" Muldoon said, "We'll leave it as it is: you as Minister and Comber as Under-Secretary."'[7] Comber remained an under-secretary as did Keith Allen, who received less than a third of Comber's support.

The new ministers besides Wellington and McLay were Birch, who became Minister of Energy and National Development; Derek Quigley, who was given the portfolios of Housing, Tourism and Works; Ben Couch, who got Maori Affairs and Postmaster-General; and Warren Cooper, who became Minister of Tourism. Rob Talbot and 'Aussie' Malcolm became new under-secretaries.

Waring recalled that she 'just about fell off my chair' when Muldoon, without any prior consultation, announced at caucus that she would be chairperson of the very influential Public Expenditure Committee.[8] This was a major position for an MP of only three years' experience and even more so in the light of Waring's youth and controversial first term. Muldoon, however, knew that Waring had similar views and values on the economy to his own and that she had the intellectual capacity and drive to cope with complex investigation and analysis. He was also well aware that she would not be intimidated by ministers or senior officials. In one way the appointment was a consolation prize, because Muldoon had rejected a suggestion from Gair that Waring should become Gair's under-secretary in Health and Social Welfare, though she was given the chair of the caucus committees on both.

Muldoon also lost one of his long-time trusted office staff in 1979 when Margaret Mouat resigned to travel overseas. Muldoon through Harold Hewitt asked Jenny Edwards to take her place. Edwards had worked in the General Assembly Library from 1964 to 1969 and had got to know Muldoon at the frequent informal parties Doug Carter held in his office on Friday evenings. Muldoon had helped her get first a job in the World Bank Library in Washington DC in 1969 and then a position as social secretary and personal assistant to the New Zealand Ambassador to the United States. In that post she organised the details of all Muldoon's visits to Washington throughout the 1970s, including an 'annual pilgrimage to look at Dali's "Last Supper" at the National Gallery.'[9] Edwards accepted and worked for Muldoon in his Wellington office for the following four and a half years. During that time she accompanied him on 75 trips within New Zealand and 8 overseas and incidentally in 1981 in the course of her duties met and married Prince Charles's police bodyguard, becoming known thereafter as Jenny Officer. Muldoon insisted that she have her wedding reception at Vogel House.

Following the 1978 election Muldoon also decided to stop his practice of holding a regular post-cabinet press conference.[10] Although he argued that he wanted individual ministers to make their own public statements on matters raised in cabinet concerning their portfolios, thus changing the image of the Government as a 'one-man band', there was no doubt that Muldoon's deteriorating relationship with the press was a strong factor in his decision to discontinue the press sessions. Muldoon had become suspicious and annoyed especially at the way television used sound bites from his press conferences. On one occasion, for example, he was quizzed by reporters after a caucus meeting for about twenty minutes on the abortion issue. Finally a journalist asked a question on another topic but before Muldoon could reply someone interjected, 'Prime Minister, one more question on abortion.' Muldoon responded, 'We've had enough on that question.' Later that evening television news used that response in such a way as to suggest Muldoon was refusing to discuss the abortion topic.[11] By February of the following year, however, one newspaper at least was lamenting that Muldoon was needed back on television to explain government policy and actions because the public were tired of watching 'ill at ease and fumbling' ministers such as McLachlan making 'a muck of things'.[12]

Muldoon's predecessor as National's leader, Marshall, had deplored the 'politics by personal denigration' exemplified in the Moyle affair,[13] and Marshall became much more openly critical of his successor in the latter part of 1978. Following the election he wrote to Muldoon suggesting changes in Muldoon's image and policies. Muldoon replied that if he needed advice he would turn to Holyoake 'who led us to four successive victories' rather than to Marshall 'who led us to by far the party's greatest ever defeat'. He also added that Marshall had throughout his parliamentary career 'failed to understand what makes the ordinary New Zealander tick'.[14] The negative comments about Muldoon which Marshall made as an election-night commentator on television and elsewhere not only upset Muldoon but many other National Party members and supporters. One, who admitted that

Muldoon 'certainly has irritated many people' but 'has worked untiringly, and, I think, successfully, for the good of the country', wrote to Marshall telling him so.[15] Marshall replied that he had suppressed his concerns for three years but the massive drop in National's support at the 1978 election 'calls for corrective action . . . Rob Muldoon's style of leadership was one, and only one reason, for the loss of support for the Party, but, it is a fact, that a significant number of people refrained from voting, or voted against us for that reason.'[16]

Marshall criticised Muldoon not only in private correspondence but publicly and repeatedly and suggested that Muldoon should give up the Finance portfolio because as Prime Minister and Minister of Finance he was too dominant in cabinet and caucus and because National needed to change its economic policies and 'return to its private enterprise base' by cutting government expenditure and lowering income taxes.[17] Throughout December 1978 and all of 1979, Marshall continued to criticise the Muldoon Government, calling on it not only to revitalise private enterprise but to curb the power of the state, to 'observe the rule of law', to protect individual freedom, to reduce taxation, to foster greater teamwork in cabinet, and to restrict spending on social welfare.[18]

The now open conflict between Muldoon and Marshall throughout 1979 made many people within the National Party decidedly uncomfortable, particularly if there was any suggestion that they were siding with Marshall. Gordon, for example, when he joined Marshall as a member of the Board of the National Bank, felt constrained to write to Muldoon assuring the Prime Minister that, 'I want you to know that this acceptance is in no way a disloyal act to you or the team . . . to assure you of my continued support and to clearly indicate that this is not anything of a personal clique or a "ganging up" with Sir John.'[19]

In July 1979 Marshall wrote to Muldoon saying that proposed legislation to allow cabinet to reduce income tax by executive instead of legislative action would remove one of the 'safeguards against the abuse of power' and alienate National Party supporters.[20] Marshall noted that 'so far I have refused to add to the mounting volume of criticism' though 'the press have asked me to comment'. Muldoon replied that Marshall was 'taking an exaggerated view of a relatively trivial matter' but that 'your previous public comments have done so much damage to the Party that you once led that one further comment is not likely to alter the situation greatly'.[21]

When Marshall wrote again to Muldoon in late 1979 making some policy suggestions, Muldoon retaliated by accusing Marshall of embarrassing cabinet ministers by approaching them on behalf of his clients, notably Comalco, seeking preferential treatment. Marshall, understandably, was appalled and replied in a relatively restrained letter that he had never approached a minister 'on the basis of asking for special treatment'. He also observed pointedly that he was enjoying his retirement and could recommend it to Muldoon.[22] Muldoon responded with unconcealed hostility, accusing Marshall of 'an enormous capacity for self-deception'. He claimed that unlike Marshall he had not publicly engaged in a personal debate 'except in the mildest of terms' but was now going to express his feelings in private. After telling Marshall that he should not be acting for the Comalco consortium because of his previous role as a minister negotiating with Comalco, he questioned whether Marshall was behaving honourably by laying himself open to the charge of 'influence peddling'.[23]

Marshall, however, was not alone in his criticism of Muldoon and particularly the National Government's economic policies after 1978. Within the upper levels of the National Party organisation Muldoon had many opponents. Even the president, Chapman, who in early 1978 had claimed that the period 1975–78 would be remembered in New Zealand's history as the 'Muldoon economic miracle' which had seen a very good recovery in the context of the energy crises and the very negative world economy,[24] became more critical of the Government's performance. Chapman's call echoed Marshall's in early 1979 for a return to the basics of private enterprise and individualism and the virtues of self-reliance and thrift, and Muldoon took it personally.[25] He refused to allow Chapman to attend caucus meetings to convey to MPs the views of the party organisation. This was regarded by many senior members of the party as an insult not just to the president but to the party itself.

Within caucus Muldoon's most persistent and irritating critic continued to be Minogue who, for example, attacked Muldoon's 1979 Budget on the grounds that it did not address forcefully enough the need to develop rapidly New Zealand's indigenous energy resources.[26] Minogue returned to his public attacks on Muldoon in October 1979, accusing the Prime Minister of being 'damaging to the office he holds, to his party . . . to New Zealand' and speculating that Muldoon might not remain National's leader much longer.[27] A few days later his Waikato colleague Waring supported Minogue's right to make those comments, although she stopped short of endorsing them.[28] It was not surprising, therefore, that by September 1979 the press was speculating that Muldoon was becoming increasingly isolated within the National Party, with younger and more right-wing MPs and party officials and members unable to relate to or respect the Prime Minister's personality, tactics or policy decisions.[29]

The debate over Muldoon's personality was in many ways related to a much more important and complex debate over New Zealand's economy, a debate which was to become more divisive and bitter within the National Party for the rest of the term of the Muldoon Government and beyond. Muldoon was very influenced by the Japanese, who had largely insulated their own domestic economy while trading, on their terms, with the rest of the world, and who, with the Singaporeans, had developed an economic model mixing free market capitalism with a considerable amount of state involvement, incentive and assistance.

By late 1978 Muldoon, however, was being advised to address structural problems in the New Zealand economy. The Economic Monitoring Group to the New Zealand Planning Council in its first report, for example, stated in September 1978 that in order to maintain past growth rates and employment 'without incurring higher balance of payments deficits, the economy has to be restructured to offset the effects of the shift in the terms of trade arising from the energy price change'.[30] New Zealand could no longer wait for an upturn in the world economy in general and primary product prices in particular to improve its terms of trade and stimulate domestic growth and employment. In January 1979 the Planning Council published *Economic Strategy: 1979*, which advised the Government to liberalise import controls. According to the report, 'insulation has been a major factor in sustaining inflation and weakening the export drive'.[31] This proposal to liberalise import licensing reflected advice concurrently being given to Muldoon and his Government by the OECD, the Reserve Bank and Treasury. Muldoon's apparent reluctance to accept the advice led to widespread criticism of him both publicly and, within the National Party itself, privately. As one journalist noted, 'Suddenly it was respectable to criticise Muldoon.'[32] Within caucus the more market-orientated minority, which included McLay and Quigley, had been greatly strengthened following the 1978 election by the addition of pro-marketeers such as Ian McLean, Michael Cox, Doug Kidd and Geoff Thompson. Even the new chairman of Muldoon's Tamaki electorate, Richard Yates, told his MP and other local party members that, 'Perhaps, like me, you have received a lot of adverse comments. . . fiercely critical of the Government' and requesting 'a return to free enterprise. . . symptomatic of a feeling throughout much of the Western World.'[33]

Internationally, neoclassical free market economic views were becoming dominant, replacing the more paternalistic, interventionist and protectionist Keynesianism of the post-1930s Depression era. In March 1979 an IMF mission spent ten days in New Zealand looking particularly at New Zealand's exchange rate. Although Treasury officials took the view that the exchange rate should remain unchanged unless it would clearly promote a significant increase in the volume of New Zealand's exports the mission was unconvinced. Instead the IMF report suggested that New Zealand should devalue by 'a substantial initial adjustment in the rate' and then make future, frequent, smaller adjustments as required.[34] The IMF also wanted appropriate and tighter monetary, fiscal and wage policies to support the devaluation.

The 'firm policies applied in 1976 and 1977' had, the IMF recognised, resulted in a number of significant achievements: the substantial reduction of the current account deficit; the reduction in the rate of inflation; an improved restructuring of foreign debt; the improved functioning of the financial system and the strengthening of the instruments of monetary control; a recovery in economic activity since late 1977; and unemployment 'at least temporarily' arrested. But unfortunately there were still a number of serious problems facing the economy, notably the sharp increase in the size of the budget deficit before borrowing in 1978–79; the accelerating expansion in domestic credit; the recent 'worrisome escalation of wage increases'; and the recent rise in the price of liquid fuels. Because in the short term, at least, exports were expected to remain unchanged in volume terms while the cost of imports surged upwards, New Zealand might well, the IMF predicted, see a doubling of the balance of payments deficit on the current account during 1979–80 to about 6 per cent of GDP. Because private capital inflows were expected to remain weak, there would need to be large government borrowing from overseas. Inflation, much of it imported, would in all likelihood rise to about 15 per cent per annum. In conclusion, the IMF warned that the Government would have to make 'significant policy changes' and 'the longer these changes are delayed, the greater the risk that draconian measures would become inevitable in the future.'[35]

While recommending that the Government should follow a firm monetary policy, reduce the budget deficit by several hundreds of millions of dollars, and dampen down excess liquidity, the IMF mission did not think it appropriate 'to rely exclusively on a policy of demand restraint. . . Such a policy would probably involve a very high cost in terms of unemployment and emigration . . . and would not be sustainable for very long.' Rather 'demand restraint should be accompanied by structural policies designed to allow. . . a marked improvement in the underlying balance of payments position and a satisfactory rate of growth and employment creation.'[36] Because the 'already high tax burden' and the budget deficit prevented reliance on further incentive schemes to boost production and exports, a substantial devaluation appeared to be the best way of increasing exports, rewarding farmers and taking up spare manufacturing capacity in exports. But it would fuel inflation and would, therefore, concurrently require direct government intervention to restrain wage increases. While a gradual dismantling of import licensing would increase efficiency, the restructuring of the economy did not require as 'an essential precondition' the 'immediate substantial reduction in protection afforded domestic industry'.[37]

After 1978, however, Muldoon found the range of economic and fiscal policy options open to him limited by the political situation he was in, and this worried and depressed him. Labour had got more votes than National at the election, and the recession was going on and on and had been worsened by the second oil shock. He became uncertain about what to do and looked for alternatives to radical economic restructuring, deregulation and the slashing of the budget deficit.

His 1979 Budget was concerned with the balance of payments situation which he saw as 'the main factor limiting New Zealand's growth rate'.[38] In the Budget Muldoon attempted reforms of the exchange rate, export incentives and import licensing. In all three areas, however, the Minister of Finance moved far more cautiously than his critics wanted. In particular, he was not prepared to risk the manufacturing business failures, unemployment and industrial strife which would, he believed, inevitably follow a radical reduction of import licensing and tariff barriers. As he told the Auckland Young Nationals, 'My Government does not propose to destroy the efficient manufacturing industries which employ thousands of New Zealand workers in the interests of some theory put forward by desk bound advisers who have no fear of being put in jeopardy from any cause whatsoever . . . if we accepted that advice, we would do untold harm, not just to individuals, but to companies, to employers, to organisations, which have been built up by the patient toil of New Zealanders over many years.'[39]

Throughout 1979 and 1980, Muldoon, while claiming that the country was in the worst economic crisis since the Depression of the 1930s, tried to convince his party that the Government was determined to get the maximum rate of income tax down to 50 per cent by a shift to indirect taxation[40] and intended to remove protection from inefficient industries.[41] He also strongly defended the construction of major energy projects and emphasised the necessity of ending the wage–price inflation cycle.

In retrospect Muldoon admitted that 'one major miscalculation during my second term as Minister of Finance between 1975 and 1984' was to believe that the fall in the terms of trade was only cyclical and temporary.[42] Believing that what he saw was a recession, he moved to cushion its effect on low- and single-income families through rebates, increased family benefits, tax cuts and first home assistance, and by seeking as far as possible to minimise unemployment. He was by nature cautious and found radical restructuring alien, although at first he was prepared to move in that direction provided the social cost and the political damage were not too great. By 1979, however, he had lost confidence in his ability to plan for the long term and argued that 'in today's conditions, it is not possible to set out even in a short, let alone a medium term, plans in detail for the very simple reason that basic assumptions are being changed virtually from week to week, by events which are occurring in the international economy'.[43]

While Muldoon and his colleagues were still determined to make structural changes in the economy to make it more efficient and productive and to diversify both products and overseas markets, there was increasing debate over how best those changes could be made. A growing group of younger advisers in Treasury and the Reserve Bank, together with a few in Muldoon's cabinet and caucus, favoured greater use of market forces and deregulation of the finance and labour markets. Others were more willing to support the Government intervening as it had done throughout the previous century for various reasons: to control inflation; to protect New Zealand's foreign exchange position; to manage wages through an income policy involving tripartite agreement among the Government, employers and unions; to maintain employment; to ease the dislocation of structural change, especially in the farming sector; and to develop new industries financed largely by borrowed capital. The dramatic drop in the National Party's share of the vote at the 1978 election and the impact of the second oil shock in 1979, however, made Muldoon less committed to deregulation and moved him much more firmly into short-term intervention in the economy while his longer-term growth strategy, later known as 'Think Big', as distinct from what he said was Labour's 'think small' approach, was implemented.[44]

Muldoon was not opposed to cautious restructuring of the economy to make it more efficient and shift resources into exporting, but in March 1979 had warned his advisers publicly that 'I do not agree with some of the methods that have been proposed . . . Those who have advised us to use the stick rather than the carrot are notified that their advice is unacceptable.'[45] Incentives and subsidies rather than the freeing-up of controls and protection were to be the preferred means. Muldoon's approach, therefore, ran counter to that which proposed the greater use of market forces and less government intervention in and distortion of the competitive free market.

In an effort to reduce government spending Muldoon in 1978 had established a Committee of Officials on Public Expenditure (COPE). The committee, chaired by the Secretary to the Treasury, included the Chairman of the State Services Commission and the Commissioner of Works and Development with power to co-opt other permanent heads as appropriate. It reported through the Cabinet Committee on Expenditure to cabinet and was charged with reviewing all government departments and programmes with a view to eliminating any expenditure which no longer reflected the Government's current economic and social objectives. COPE assessed economic activities and expenditure according to three criteria: export potential; potential to reduce unemployment; and potential to reduce imports. There were also to be constraints on the funding of hospital and educational boards and research organisations. COPE presented its first report to cabinet on 18 December 1978, accompanied by another paper on 'State Services Staffing Policy and Ceilings'.[46] It was decided that, in addition to an overall 'sinking lid' for reducing staffing by 1.5 per cent per annum across the public service, any new programmes or extra staff would require cabinet approval following recommendations from both the Cabinet Committee on State Services and the Cabinet Committee on Expenditure.

Throughout 1979 Muldoon sought to fund the budget deficit to a greater extent than in the past by the sale of government securities to the private sector rather than by forcing financial institutions to invest even more in government stock through the compulsory reserve ratio requirements. This had the effect of controlling high levels of domestic credit albeit at the cost of higher interest rates generally. The Government also started to remove price controls and remove or reduce subsidies on basic foodstuffs such as bread, milk and butter, resulting in a 'one off' inflationary effect. Government charges for electricity and railway services were raised to rates nearer their true costs. Although Muldoon was not an enthusiast for shifting taxation from direct income tax to indirect consumer taxes, because he believed such taxes penalised poorer people and would also lead to compensatory wage claims that would hinder his fight against inflation, he did announce in May a 10–20 per cent sales tax on a wide range of goods including petrol, lawnmowers, caravans and boats. The move was partial, discriminatory and unpopular, and was seen simply as a means of raising more revenue for the Government and not part of a consistent restructuring of the tax system. There were no income tax cuts to reflect the shift to indirect taxation.

Muldoon was surprisingly uninterested in a fundamental reform of New Zealand's taxation system. The problem was not so much that New Zealanders were excessively taxed compared to other developed countries, and indeed in 1980 New Zealand was thirteenth on a table of the eighteen leading industrial nations.[47] Rather, even ignoring the potential inflationary effect, the problem was that over three-quarters of New Zealand's tax revenue came from personal income tax, which fell very heavily on wage and salary earners who found themselves on high marginal rates of tax at relatively modest levels of income. The alternative was to widen the tax base by a shift from direct to indirect tax but critics argued that indirect consumption taxes were unfair to poorer people who spent their entire income on necessities. Private sector companies, farmers and self-employed professionals were also avoiding income tax because of the many rebates, concessions, exemptions, incentives, and loopholes available. There were numerous other problems and anomalies in the tax system such as the need to have very high nominal wage increases to leave a worker with a reasonable after-tax raise, the disincentive to work overtime, and the incentive to avoid or evade tax. Muldoon responded to critics of the tax system and his failure to reform it by claiming that he was more concerned with reducing the total tax take than in shifting it from direct to indirect. He was prepared to accept income tax cuts as alternatives to wage increases, but the only taxes he seemed willing to introduce were those which targeted luxuries, fringe benefits and unearned, speculative capital gains. Nevertheless, partly as a result of pressure from many within the National Party itself, Muldoon in July 1981 set up a tax reform task force headed by a Wellington accountant, P. C. McCaw, to prepare a report which would be submitted after the election.

One major though limited move towards freer trade was the decision by the Muldoon Government to expand an existing trade agreement between New Zealand and Australia. Through a New Zealand–Australia Free Trade Agreement concluded in 1965, the two countries had reduced or removed duties on certain products which they traded with each other. In March 1978, largely through the work of Talboys, it was decided by Australia and New Zealand to reaffirm the objective of trade liberalisation and closer relation between the two countries. Muldoon was surprised by the Nareen Declaration following discussions between Australia's Prime Minister Malcolm Fraser and Talboys at Fraser's farm in 1978.[48] Adams-Schneider, who was close to New Zealand's protected manufacturing lobby and not a free-trade enthusiast, was in charge of trans-Tasman trade at that time and Muldoon was not prepared for such a development when Talboys agreed to a draft produced by Fraser.

The negotiations advanced further in 1979 when Doug Anthony, the Australian Deputy Prime Minister, came to New Zealand for NAFTA talks with Talboys and Adams-Schneider. Anthony believed that NAFTA had come to the end of its usefulness and was too concerned with trivia and suggested that Australia and New Zealand should 'start again and look at total free trade across the Tasman'.[49] Talboys took Anthony to see Muldoon and it was agreed that a suitable new agreement should be negotiated. It took three years.

After lengthy negotiations, in which Talboys and Templeton were prominent, and during which Templeton in particular became annoyed at the extent to which Muldoon sometimes became involved and at the end claimed the credit, NAFTA was replaced by a much more ambitious free trade agreement, Closer Economic Relations (CER), which was signed in December 1982 and came into force on 1 January 1983. The final CER agreement came together following dinner at Vogel House. The wives retired for coffee in the lounge and Muldoon told the waiters to stop serving drinks to the men so that they kept clear heads. Then Muldoon and the key New Zealand negotiators convened in the library and the Australians led by Anthony had a final consultation at 10 p.m. on a warm summer's night under floodlights on the lawn before the New Zealanders and Australians met together to resolve the last details. At one point Muldoon and Anthony met separately to resolve an Australian request for a larger quota of tomatoes. Galvin tried to influence Muldoon from a distance by gesticulating upward. The Prime Minister walked over and said 'What do you want Mr. Galvin? Up the Aussies or offer them more?'[50]

Muldoon was not a major proponent, architect or builder of CER and throughout the first few years of discussions was unenthusiastic and pessimistic about a new, enhanced form of NAFTA.[51] By mid-1981, however, influenced by Talboys, Templeton and Galvin, Muldoon had become converted to the CER concept and thereafter tended to take more interest in it and also to take more credit for it. Although he was years later to regard CER in hindsight as one of his Government's major achievements, it was one concluded despite him rather than because of him. The agreement resulted from the vision and the work of Talboys, Templeton and keen officials rather than the Prime Minister.

Not all New Zealand's economic problems in the late 1970s could be blamed on oil price increases. The second oil shock compounded the other inflationary pressures of increased government spending, rapid rises in wage rates, new indirect taxes and escalating non-oil import prices. There were serious external pressures but they were exacerbated by Muldoon's unwillingness or inability to attack some of the domestic economic problems. While his 1979 Budget had been generally welcomed as a further move towards restructuring of the economy through cautious deregulation, the 1980 Budget was widely criticised as an uninspiring and defensive document. It certainly disappointed the more free-market exponents in the National caucus and party.

In July 1979 Muldoon freed up foreign investment in New Zealand, removing some controls on foreign ownership of New Zealand companies and raising the amount of private overseas investment allowed before government approval was required. He wanted to make it 'clear beyond question that such investment was welcome' and argued that such foreign investment should be seen not as a sell-off of New Zealand's assets but as a means of assisting its economy to grow.[52] He was not, however, prepared to remove controls entirely or to allow a totally deregulated market because, as he noted in his 1980 Budget, 'I do not . . . take the view that a "more market" approach is universally valid. In some areas the market works imperfectly . . . The Government has a role in ensuring that in some cases the interests of the private investor – whether foreign or New Zealand – coincide with the interests of the nation.'[53]

Muldoon was still faced at the start of 1981 with an inflation rate for consumer prices which at 16.4 per cent was higher than most of New Zealand's major trading partners: Australia (10.3), the United States (12.6), and Britain (15.9).[54] This, of course, kept interest rates high and threatened the viability of the Government's growth strategy and the battle to reduce unemployment. Unemployment had risen almost 30 per cent during the previous year.

The 1981 Budget was not one calculated to guarantee a resounding election victory later in the year. Commentators and critics argued that it did nothing to restructure the economy, reform taxation, alleviate unemployment, combat inflation, curb government spending, or promote investment, production and exports.[55]

The economic historian John Gould has labelled the freeing-up of the financial sector from government controls between 1975 and 1978 as the one major structural reform Muldoon's Government made in monetary policy.[56] The general decontrolling of interest rates, greater flexibility in trading and savings bank activity, the reduction of government security requirements, the relaxation of regulations governing private money market dealers and private sector credit, and a more active secondary market in government securities, all together constituted a significant liberalisation.

Towards the end of 1981, however, Muldoon became very concerned at what he regarded as excessive growth in the money supply and private sector credit. Financial institutions other than banks were competing for deposits with the banks and the Government, thus forcing up interest rates on deposits and subsequently creating higher rates on the funds they attracted and lent out again. In October, only weeks before the election, he announced that the Government had drafted regulations which would be used to hold down interest rates if necessary. Muldoon was immediately attacked by the finance houses and free market critics.

One other significant act of deregulation was the removal of restrictions on the days and hours shops could be open. In November 1980, largely at Bolger's initiative and insistence, Muldoon's Government passed legislation providing for shops to be open for trade on Saturdays and also widened the range of goods that could be sold on Sundays. This reform had a marked social as well as economic impact. It also annoyed the trade unions, who saw the extension of shop hours as the start of an erosion of the five-day, forty-hour working week and the end of the traditional weekend of leisure and recreation. The unions, however, saw this dispute with the Muldoon Government as minor compared to the ongoing battle over wages.

As Jonathan Boston has observed, by the 1970s it was widely believed in Western economies that 'decentralised wage fixing, a high level of unionisation, a low level of employee deference, strongly held notions of co-operative justice . . . and vigorous conflict over income shares' resulted in 'self-interested, maximising behaviour by individual bargaining groups' which 'instead of securing collective benefits brought collective ruin i.e. low economic growth, inflation, and high unemployment'.[57] While Muldoon had attempted to allow free wage bargaining from August 1977 until 1979, high wage settlements and accompanying industrial disruption proved unacceptable in the context of the Government's efforts to counter inflation, foster growth, and reduce unemployment.

Muldoon rejected as socially and politically unacceptable a tight monetary and fiscal policy which would lower inflation at the cost of a marked increase in unemployment and adverse effects on lower income workers, which was broadly the strategy that would be taken by his Fourth Labour Government successors.

Although he often criticised the unions, he also found it difficult to restructure and free up the labour market by weakening their organisational strength or by removing the minimum wage. Instead, he leaned heavily on a corporatist incomes policy and process involving consultation, compromise and agreement between the Government, union leaders and employer representatives to combat wage inflation. For almost a hundred years the state had itself sought to be involved in fixing wages by, on the one hand, persuasion and threats and, on the other hand, legislation and regulation. Muldoon, like his predecessors, tried not to act arbitrarily or unilaterally but by achieving a consensus with the trade unions and the employers. His insistence on being personally involved in industrial matters, especially wage settlements, was understandable because of their importance to economic management generally, but his intervention and comments as Minister of Finance, and after 1975 also as Prime Minister, often complicated the situation and also annoyed successive Ministers of Labour – Shand, Marshall, Gordon and Bolger.

On 6 July 1979 the Federation of Labour applied to the Arbitration Court for a minimum living wage to be granted under the General Wage Orders Act of 1977. Muldoon was not opposed to such a minimum wage and in his 1979 Budget had already moved to double the family benefit and increase rebates to families on lower and/or single incomes. But while he stated that 'the Government has no objection to the spirit or intention of this application', he was concerned that the actual amount claimed by the FOL was only a little less than the average wage. As a result the Government repealed the legislation but sought to soften union reaction by simultaneously issuing a 4.5 per cent general wage order and passing a Remuneration Act giving the Government authority to fix wages and conditions by regulation.

Several of the major wage disputes during mid-1979 involved the threat or use of strike action by unions and resulted in large settlements between unions and employers. The Drivers Federation agreement with the Road Transport Association in September, for example, in effect gave drivers an increase of about 19.5 per cent, which threatened to be reflected in other industrial awards that had historical relativity to the drivers. Muldoon immediately warned that the settlement was a clear inflationary threat to the economy and had been achieved by intimidation rather than by conciliation and arbitration.[58] He warned the unions and employers that if they did not reduce the settlement then the Government would. His threat to intervene was supported by the Employers' Federation and Federated Farmers. When the drivers and their employers persisted, cabinet prepared regulations limiting the increase to 9.5 per cent. The FOL Executive called a 24-hour general strike.

Muldoon left for a month overseas and in his absence cabinet decided not to issue the regulations limiting the drivers' award but, led by the Minister of Labour, Bolger, sought to find a compromise solution. The drivers' award went to the Arbitration Court for a ruling and the Acting Prime Minister, Talboys, announced that the Government would abide by the Court's decision.[59] The Court altered the detail of the agreement but overall the drivers gained a similar increase to what had been originally decided. The Government was somewhat more successful in intervening with the storemen and packers and the boiler-makers awards but ran into trouble with tradesmen at the New Zealand Forest Products mill at Kinleith.

The tradesmen at Kinleith had during 1978 lost their traditional parity with tradesmen at the Tasman pulp and paper mill at Kawerau. When Forest Products refused to restore the relativity, the Kinleith mill was closed by a strike between 8 January and 29 March 1980. Forest Products offered a maximum of an 18 per cent increase, which the pulp and paper workers accepted, but the tradesmen held out for 22 per cent. Bolger again refused to become involved in the dispute initially, but when the company at the end of February finally agreed to a 20.5 per cent increase to restore parity with Kawerau, Muldoon announced that the maximum should be 18 per cent.[60] The Prime Minister also again started to blame commun-ists for the industrial problems and released a new list of 32 alleged SUP members active in the trade unions.[61] The strike continued throughout March until Bolger worked out a compromise which largely met the strikers' demands.

Thereafter the Government moved from selective intervention against specific large wage settlements by individual unions towards tripartite talks which involved the Government, Federation of Labour, and Employers' Federation and which would include wage–tax trade-offs. Such a trade-off can help to retain the purchasing power of incomes while restricting increased wage costs and the inflation that would follow when those costs were passed on to the consumer. Without cuts in government spending elsewhere, however, the tax foregone means that the wages are in effect being subsidised by increased budget deficits before borrowing. The wage–tax trade-off also raised again the possibility of the Govern-ment seeking to collect more revenue from indirect taxation on spending on goods and services rather than from direct taxes on incomes.

Muldoon tried throughout the latter part of 1980 and early 1981 to persuade the unions to accept income tax cuts as equivalent to wage increases.[62] When the FOL annual conference in May 1981 voted against a wage–tax trade-off, Muldoon warned that the alternative would again be wage regulation, especially if the unions put forward 'excessive wage demands'.[63] He added that without agreement on tax cuts in lieu of wage increases he would not include any tax cuts in his 1981 Budget, even though the unions and many observers believed that in an election year he was likely to give tax cuts anyway. In the event there was no agreement and there were no tax cuts.

New Zealand's manufacturing sector had for a generation relied heavily on government import controls, which protected it from competition, and many manufacturers had become dependent also on imported raw materials, capital equipment and components – these imports being an inefficient use of New Zealand's overseas earnings and foreign exchange loans. Muldoon wanted to move New Zealand's industrial base away from such products to those using New Zealand raw materials or energy resources and which would either save New Zealand foreign exchange through reducing costly imports, for example of liquid fuels, or would earn foreign exchange through new energy-based exports, for example of steel and aluminium.

As part of its strategy to restructure the economy, the Government had the Industries Development Commission examine the manufacturing sector and particularly its protection from imports and the extent to which it would be adversely affected by exposure to greater external competition. Manufacturers were seriously concerned when the Government indicated that it might reduce or remove protection in areas such as plastics, television, footwear, glassware, motor vehicles, and textiles. Laurence Stevens, the president of the Manufacturers' Association, declared that restructuring should not be directed solely at manufacturers but should be part of a much broader restructuring and rationalisation of the economy.[64] Muldoon reassured the manufacturers that he understood their concern and personally guaranteed that there would be no undue haste and no destruction of efficient industries.[65]

The most important economic policy plank in the National Government's 1981 election campaign was its 'Growth Strategy', which became more commonly known as 'Think Big'.[66] 'Think Big' started as a disparate number of ad hoc policies and projects, not the apparently clear, comprehensive, long-term and interrelated strategy which the later adoption of the term 'Think Big' implied. The two major objectives of the strategy were to make New Zealand strategically much less dependent on scarce and costly overseas liquid fuels and to use New Zealand's energy resources to create new industries which would diversify the New Zealand economy and move it away from almost total dependence on the production and export of a narrow range of agricultural commodities.

The 'Think Big' projects fell into three categories: those using Maui gas, such as the methanol and ammonia-urea plants at Waitara; those involved with alternatives to imported liquid fuels, such as the Motonui synthetic fuel proposal, the Marsden Point oil refinery expansion, and compressed natural gas (CNG) and liquid petroleum gas (LPG); and those involving high energy use (of electricity, gas and coal) to develop secondary industries, such as the third aluminium potline at Tiwai Point, a second aluminium smelter at Aramoana, and the New Zealand Steel expansion. In addition, further oil and gas exploration, a massive increase in the quantity of traditional farm exports, the rapid development of forestry, fishing, tourism and horticulture, and the electrification of the North Island Main Trunk railway between Palmerston North and Hamilton were also regarded as part of the 'Growth Strategy'. It was a high-risk strategy from the first but a drop in world oil prices in the mid 1980s made it much more so than when the schemes were originated.

The large, expensive, energy-based projects were the most dramatic parts of an overall economic development programme based on diversification, import substitution, and the export of new products. The projects, which involved co-operation between the Government and multinational companies, were very capital-intensive. Much of that capital would be borrowed overseas but it was hoped that in the longer term the strategy would produce a much more balanced and diversified economy, save and earn overseas funds, provide employment, and insulate New Zealand from future energy shocks and balance of payments crises. Until the projects were completed, however, there were clearly short-term costs and risks in draining investment and labour resources away from farming and small businesses, in increasing New Zealand's overseas debt, and in provoking the wrath of both environmentalists and those who believed the Government should not be so directly and heavily involved in 'picking winners' and planning, funding, developing and owning major industries.

The 'Growth Strategy' was in some ways a response to a number of factors outside the control of Muldoon and his Government. In May 1979 Maui natural gas came on stream with the Government committed by a previous Labour administration decision in 1973 to buy it for thirty years whether or not the gas was used.[67] In addition to the 'take or pay' gas, as the gas came out it was accompanied by a light oil condensate and there were obvious advantages in utilising that condensate obtained with the gas. By 1979 it was clear that the gas would not be needed for electricity generation and there was no obvious alternative market. In the same year there was a sizeable electricity surplus. If the surplus power could not be sold at a reasonable price, then the costs of constructing the power stations and generating electricity could not be recovered or the loans serviced from income. Clearly there needed to be downstream industries to use both the surplus gas and electricity, pay for the cost of their generation, and cover the capital costs of creating the new secondary industries. The second oil shock in 1979, which was accompanied by and which partly caused a worldwide recession, convinced the Government that it needed to develop quickly energy-based industries and also an alternative supply of indigenous liquid fuels.

Most governments, analysts and commentators had believed that the first oil shock in 1973–74, which led to a fourfold increase in the price of oil imports to New Zealand, was a temporary problem which could be survived by borrowing and such strategies as carless days until the terms of trade returned to normal. That indeed seemed to be happening in 1978, when most industrialised nations found themselves paying somewhat less for imported oil than they had done in 1974 immediately after the first oil shock. New oil supplies had come on stream in Mexico, Alaska and the North Sea, and demand slackened in the West.

In December 1978, however, there was a revolution against the Shah of Iran, from whose country New Zealand in that year imported 40 per cent of its total oil imports. In the months that followed, Iran stopped exporting, international oil stocks ran down, OPEC raised oil prices, and throughout the Western world there was pessimism concerning the long-term future availability and cost of oil. When Iran and Iraq went to war in September 1980, there was further dismay. By March 1979, oil cost NZ$12.88 a barrel; by December 1979, $24.22; by March 1980, $28.74; by December 1980, $34.00; by March 1981, $37.00; and by December 1981, $41.50.[68] With the advantage of hindsight, although some observers such as the *Economist* were saying it as early as 1979,[69] it can be seen that between 1979 and 1981 it was the fear of shortage rather than a real shortage that pushed oil prices to record heights. An OPEC agreement on 29 October 1981 held out some hope that oil prices would stabilise around a price of US$34 and might even decline somewhat in the future, but by that time New Zealand was committed to the development of new energy industries.

The energy planners in the late 1970s worked on projections that future oil supplies imported from overseas could cost as much as US$60–70 per barrel and certainly no lower than US$20, but by 1986 the price had collapsed down to US$8.50, before rising to about US$15, where it remained until the Gulf War of 1990. On the evidence available it was believed that oil was a finite resource and shortages would lead to high prices, but in fact there was more oil available then generally thought and high prices led to increased supply and eventually excess of supply over demand, forcing the price down. As a result the projects in hindsight could be and were seen as uneconomic, but they were under way and had to be completed. The Labour Government in 1986 abolished both the Energy Research and Development Committee and the Liquid Fuels Trust Board and moved to deregulate and then privatise the energy sector.

In New Zealand during the late 1970s, however, the Muldoon Government following the second oil shock was forced to address the resulting drastic increase in the economy's balance of payments deficit; to recognise for the second time in five years the country's critical vulnerability to interruptions in the supply and dramatic rises in the cost of imported oil; and to shift the focus on energy planning firmly on to the future supply of liquid fuels. The diversion to Japan of a tanker of oil heading to New Zealand revealed New Zealand's vulnerability, and there was a sense of real crisis and urgency over the need to develop liquid fuels and other energy projects. It was not just a question of cost in overseas funds or the prospect of running out of fuel but of the importance of self-sufficiency in the interests of the sovereignty and security of the state. Many in the Government and among its advisers saw the situation as akin to a wartime crisis, with the prospect of transport grinding to a halt, factories closing and crops rotting in the field.[70]

Prior to the 1978 election, the National Party's General Director, Barrie Leay, had suggested publicly that New Zealand should move away from traditional but in some cases 'irrelevant' industries and invest in new industries utilising the country's natural resources and raw materials.[71] That view became much more widely held in the National Party during 1979 and 1980. While the 1978 election campaign had focused on restructuring of the economy largely by deregulation, the focus in 1981 was on bold, positive, visionary growth with a strong element of nationalism mixed with the economics. The involvement of the Government in planning and providing capital was very much in the tradition of New Zealand's history, for ever since 1840 much of the country's economic infrastructure had been built and financed by central government. By 1979, however, such activity ran counter to a new initiative in Western societies to roll back the state and to privatise state-owned enterprises.

Times change. People often act in good faith or according to the information available to them at the time. Only later, with the advantage of more information and hindsight, do they see that they acted wrongly and/or in ignorance. Certainly, most of the expert advice available to the Government both inside and outside New Zealand prior to 1981 argued that because New Zealand was energy rich but exposed in relation to oil the prospect of converting gas to liquid fuels was an attractive one. The New Zealand Planning Council, for example, was very supportive of the energy projects and argued that because 'there were limits to the extent to which the additional investment requirements of the energy programme should be financed through reductions in potential consumption growth . . . recourse to the use of foreign capital would be an appropriate means of filling the gap between domestic financing capabilities and the whole cost of the energy programme'.[72] Although the Planning Council recognised that 'the increased imports of capital goods which could be financed by foreign capital, and the costs of servicing, would at least temporarily enlarge the balance of payments deficit on current account and deter the achievement of keeping it at about 2–3 percent of GDP', the Planning Council 'saw no objection to this if it were directly related to major projects designed to reduce import dependence or increase exports'. In the Council's opinion, 'All the major projects have the potential to earn or save enough foreign exchange to recover the foreign currency costs, and thereafter to make a major contribution to the balance of payments'.[73] Even with hindsight and taking into account that the Government and its advisers got future oil price scenarios wrong, it can be argued that most of the energy projects were still producing and earning or saving considerable sums of overseas funds twenty years after they were initiated, and the longer they run the greater their contribution to the New Zealand economy and particularly its balance of payments will be. The results were nowhere as good as National hoped or predicted in 1981, but neither were they as bad as critics such as the Labour Government after 1984 claimed. Indeed, they would have been even better had Labour not changed some of the rules retrospectively once the schemes had been started, for example by changing the baseline cost of synthetic fuel from that of other petrol from the refinery to the cost of imported fuel. By 1986, compared to the price of imported fuel, the Government, as a result of assurances to the refinery and the oil companies, was losing 58 cents on every litre of synthetic gasoline it sold to the refinery and motorists were paying 38 cents a litre more than they should have been for petrol.[74]

In 1974 Norman Kirk had set up a New Zealand Energy Research and Development Committee chaired by Dr Colin Maiden, the vice-chancellor of the University of Auckland and a former research and development manager for General Motors in the United States. That committee soon identified the fact that transport fuels were New Zealand's major energy problem, damaging New Zealand's balance of payments, contributing significantly to inflation, and necessitating carless days. Considering that most experts at that time predicted that oil prices would continue to rise, Maiden and other members of the committee recommended that the cheap, unused gas and the condensate from the Maui field should be used for liquid fuels to make New Zealand 50 per cent self-sufficient and so to insulate New Zealand from future oil shocks.[75] In 1978 a Liquid Fuels Trust

Board was set up with Maiden again in the chair. Maiden also became chairman of a new Synthetic Fuels Corporation set up in September 1980.

One of Muldoon's most significant new ministerial appointments after the 1978 election was that of Birch as Minister of Energy, National Development, Science and Technology. As chief whip between 1975 and 1978, Birch had also chaired a caucus committee which had helped the then minister, Gair, put together the 1978 election policy to use natural gas as a primary energy source and for fuel. Muldoon told Birch on his appointment to 'get those sums together and we'll decide on how to use the natural gas'.[76] Birch was a doer who once he had made up his mind on a course of action pursued it with missionary zeal, never faltering, and relentlessly getting things done as quickly as possible. He decided to move faster than his predecessor Gair and asked the new Liquid Fuels board for reports by September 1979, halving the time the board had originally been given. Despite some Treasury concern, Birch also speeded up decisions about CNG, pipeline gas, the methanol plant and synthetic fuel, pushing them through meetings of officials and the Cabinet Economic Committee. Birch also chaired the ad hoc cabinet committee on national economic development, which dealt with the growth strategy. Although Muldoon was a member he rarely attended. Those regularly present besides Birch were Bolger, Falloon, Templeton and Venn Young. With Muldoon's approval, Birch also invited Frank Holmes, the chairman of the Planning Council, and officials from Treasury and the Reserve Bank to be present and to take part in discussions.

Initially there were three arms to the liquid fuels policy. First was a synthetic fuel plant to produce petrol from natural gas at a cost of about US$25 a barrel. Secondly, the Whangarei refinery, which had been in production since 1964, would need to be expanded to balance the fuel supply by producing more diesel and aviation fuel. The refinery's configuration was dependent on the decision to proceed with the synthetic fuel plant, which would need construction of a hydrocracker at the refinery to make it capable of producing diesel and jet fuel. A delay in the decision on synthetic fuel would necessitate a delay in determining the nature of, and making the final decision to expand, the refinery. Thirdly, some of the gas would be used to produce chemical-grade methanol both as an export revenue earner and also as a possible fuel extender to be blended with gasoline. The last of these developments could be built reasonably quickly to give a stream of export earnings.

The Iraq–Iran war which led to the second oil shock appeared to confirm the energy strategy, and the Government simultaneously decided to use New Zealand's energy resources generally to diversify and develop the economy and increase employment and exports and to support several major industrial projects, notably the Bluff and the proposed Aramoana aluminium smelters and the New Zealand Steel expansion. Integrated energy planning was required to bring together oil, electricity, coal and gas, and so the Government created a Ministry of Energy, at first under Gair (1977–78) and then under Birch (1978–84). In 1980 an Energy Advisory Committee under the chairmanship of Professor Ray Meyer, dean of engineering at the University of Auckland, was set up to advise on energy planning and facilitate public input to the process.

Muldoon was not the originator or the major player in the 'Think Big' energy and industrial growth strategy, although he was supportive and as Prime Minister and Minister of Finance became a major contributor to and defender of the strategy and therefore very closely identified with it. The key political figure in the strategy was Birch, who was very enthusiastic, grasped advice quickly, and then very effectively implemented policy. Birch was a hard-working administrator and a clever political operator in cabinet, caucus and the bureaucracy. He also enjoyed a special and mutual relationship of trust and respect with Muldoon. That relationship became very important.

Muldoon's support was critical in the cabinet's decision to adopt a recommendation from Birch and the Liquid Fuels Trust Board that fuel should be produced by a new and unproven Mobil method rather than by a proven South African Sasol process favoured by many officials and private sector interests. At first Muldoon was uncommitted, but after thoroughly examining the two proposals he came down decisively in favour of Mobil.[77]

On a second decision, over who would construct and own the chemical-grade methanol plant, Muldoon and Birch differed. Birch, supported by Talboys, McLay, Quigley and Bolger, favoured a 90 per cent privately owned consortium involving BP, Fletchers, Challenge, Shell, ICI, Japanese interests, the Government and public shareholders. The alternative was a partnership between the wholly government financed and controlled Petrocorp and Alberta Gas, with Petrocorp holding a controlling 51 per cent of the shares. Gair, Adams-Schneider and most officials supported the Petrocorp–Alberta Gas option. The BP Consortium wanted to build a plant capable of producing 2000 tonnes a day, while the Petrocorp scheme was for a more modest 1200 tonnes. Birch was confident that he had the numbers to get a cabinet decision in favour of BP but Muldoon, who asked Birch for a full briefing the day before, then argued very persuasively in cabinet for Petrocorp. When it was clear that there was no consensus Muldoon took a vote, which to Birch's surprise and disappointment Petrocorp won by, according to Birch's memory, one vote.[78]

Cabinet meetings which had to discuss and decide on the 'Think Big' projects were faced with an almost unbelievable amount of complex documentation to be read, comprehended, analysed and resolved. It was only natural that many in cabinet were content to defer to Muldoon and other key ministers such as Birch who appeared to be, and undoubtedly were, better informed. For example, at cabinet on 28 September 1981 there was consideration of a secret report on the expansion of New Zealand Steel including possible co-operation with BHP, which 'could be the forerunner of a trans-Tasman steel community'; and detailed consideration of the synthetic gasoline project which, a fortnight before, cabinet had agreed should proceed subject to three conditions.[79] The conditions were review of contractual arrangements, final confirmation of planning consent, and adequate lending arrangements. Because it looked possible that Labour would win the 1981 election, Mobil wanted a fourth condition, allowing it to withdraw and to be compensated. Cabinet declined that request, however, and instead postponed the final decision until after the election, even though it was estimated that the delay would increase by some $30 million the capital cost of the project, and its later completion could cost a further $75 million in lost foreign exchange. In the event, when the Mobil synthetic petrol plant was built it was completed without major problems, on time and below budget.[80]

In contrast the expansion of the Marsden Point oil refinery, first commissioned in 1964, was originally estimated in 1979 to cost about $500 million. Even in 1981 when approved by cabinet the cost had been revised up to $1035 million. As a result of inflation, currency devaluation, changes in design, bad management and horrendous industrial strife, which doubled the construction time, the project, according to one estimate, eventually cost $2450 million.[81] When the price of imported petrol dropped as low as $10 per barrel in 1986 the refinery became uneconomic, though by that time New Zealand had become 60 per cent self-sufficient in petroleum fuels.

In addition to the North Island energy surplus from the Maui gas, there was also an electricity surplus in the South Island from the overbuilding of hydro stations. Over the Christmas–New Year holidays of 1980–81, Birch spent some time with Muldoon at the Prime Minister's Hatfields Beach bach discussing the possibility of using the surplus for increased aluminium production and incorporating all the energy and growth projects into a development plan. Birch believed that the creation of the energy projects led logically to the creation of manufacturing schemes to use all the new power generated, but Muldoon needed to be convinced that the latter in particular were good projects and good politics. Indeed, members of the caucus energy committee at first saw Muldoon as a major stumbling block, not only to the downstream industries but also to the initial energy development plans which Birch, supported by Kidd and Brill and advisers outside Parliament, was keen to see adopted. As one caucus energy committee member later recalled, Muldoon, far from being the initiator and driving force, was one of the last converts in caucus to the comprehensive 'Think Big' strategy and overall slogan, but because he was Prime Minister and Finance Minister he subsequently had to promote and defend the policy and eventually shoulder the blame when it became discredited.[82] It also appears clear, however, that Muldoon was more supportive of Birch in 'Think Big' matters and less inclined to listen to Treasury doubts about some of the projects and processes associated with them after Birch played such a critical role in defending Muldoon during the aborted 'Colonels' Coup' in 1980.

Although Birch was the minister most responsible for the 'Think Big' strategy, he admitted in retrospect that it would not have been possible without Muldoon's personal interest and support.[83] Both men appreciated that there were risks involved but decided, on the advice available at the time, that the risks were worth taking. They wanted to achieve balanced economic development and growth, protect New Zealand from external economic shocks and threats, especially in the liquid fuels area, and expand secondary industries to combat unemployment. Birch, for example, hoped optimistically and some would say unrealistically that the 'Think Big' growth strategy would create about 410,000 new jobs by 1990: 150,000 in agriculture including horticulture; 100,000 in manufacturing; 5000 employed directly on the major projects; and a further 155,000 created by the foreign exchange earnings from those projects, this estimate being based on an assumption that every $1 million of overseas earnings had historically created 161 jobs in the domestic economy after allowing for a multiplier effect.[84] In the event, by 1989 the five major projects were directly employing 3601 people and indirectly employing another 9002.[85]

The major metal-smelting projects in the growth strategy were designed not only to use up surplus energy, substitute for imports, earn foreign exchange through exports, and create employment but were also aimed at regional development, especially in the South Island. By 1979 there was a surplus of electricity and in March, Birch, the Minister of Energy, and Cooper, the Minister of Regional Development, announced concessions in the price of electricity to large users in the South Island with further incentives for export-orientated industries.[86]

The use of aluminium was growing rapidly worldwide at the time, and it was a very energy-intensive product. Cheap power was a critical factor in international companies' deciding where to locate a smelter and another consideration was that Australia had the world's largest commercial reserves of the raw material, bauxite. Two new proposals were submitted to the Government. Comalco, which was US- and Japanese-owned, had been producing aluminium at its Tiwai Point smelter at Bluff since 1971. During the following ten years it had produced 1.2 million tonnes of aluminium, of which almost 80 per cent had been exported.[87] Although the price the company had paid for its electricity was secret and had been renegotiated upwards under threats from the Government, it was still much lower than the price other consumers paid. At the end of 1979 Comalco began to discuss with the Government a third potline at Tiwai Point. By July 1980 agreement had been reached on the third potline and Comalco was in discussions with the Government over a second smelter at Tiwai Point. The second proposal was for a new smelter to be built by a consortium of Fletcher Holdings, Alusuisse and the Australian company CSR, which eventually was named the South Pacific Aluminium Consortium. Their preferred site was at Aramoana near Dunedin. Environmentalists, who had been attacking the location of a smelter at Aramoana for some years, became much more vociferous in 1980 and 1981.[88] Some of the critics, such as Paul van Moeseke, Professor of Economics at Otago University, questioned not only the environmental impact but also the economic rationality of the second smelter. Although Government ministers such as Birch and Adams-Schneider dismissed van Moeseke's arguments, he received widespread public support especially from the Coalition for Open Government, the Federation of Labour, the Association of Economists, the environmental pressure-group Energy-watch, the Environmental Defence Society, the Royal Forest and Bird Protection Society, and various local power boards. While Birch was the most prominent public defender of the scheme on the Government's side, he had throughout the support of Muldoon, who, however, was adamant that the price paid for the electricity should not be ridiculously low.

Although on 28 September 1981 the Government approved the construction of the Aramoana smelter, three days later Alusuisse, which was going to provide the technology, withdrew from the South Pacific Aluminium Consortium at least partly because Muldoon adamantly refused to lower the price of electricity to the level they wanted.[89] The consortium partners claimed that overseas power prices were lower than New Zealand's, and it was also apparent that the price of aluminium was falling worldwide as consumption growth slowed and production increased. Fear of oversupply was concurrently causing the postponement or abandonment of other proposed smelters overseas. It was, therefore, not surprising that the Fletcher-led consortium found it very difficult to replace Alusuisse with a new partner, and the second smelter was never built.

New Zealand Steel was a government-sponsored company set up in 1965 to utilise indigenous resources of ironsands and coal. Its successive chairmen, Woolf Fisher and Alan Hellaby, had been discussing with governments throughout the 1970s the possible expansion of the New Zealand Steel mill which had been built at Glenbrook in 1969. When they met cabinet ministers to push their case in 1972, they found that Muldoon, unlike his more enthusiastic colleagues, was 'cautious and somewhat critical' of the proposed expansion.[90] Nevertheless, New Zealand Steel carried out further feasibility studies, including the development of a pilot plant and a new process for producing flat steel. In 1978 members of the board and senior management again met the Cabinet Economic Committee and reopened negotiations with the Government. Discussions continued for three years.

With the 1981 general election campaign about to commence, three of the National Government's 'Think Big' projects were in trouble or delayed – the Aramoana smelter, the Mobil synthetic oil plant, and the Marsden Point oil refinery, which was still waiting for the Synfuel decision. That made much more imperative a decision on the other major metal smelting project, the New Zealand Steel expansion which would utilise coal, electricity and gas, expand ironsand mining sixfold, and increase steel production from 150,000 to 775,000 tonnes per annum.[91] Serious doubts about the viability of the project, however, had been raised by Treasury and the Prime Minister's Department, with almost all officials opposed to the expansion, and by September 1981 there was a strong likelihood that the Government would pull out of the steel project, particularly when the strain on energy and financial resources created by other more desirable projects was taken into account. Such concerns were, however, dismissed by New Zealand Steel. Because National wanted to enter the election campaign with at least some 'Think Big' projects finalised, cabinet on 27 October approved the New Zealand Steel plan, finalising also two other agreements: the ammonia-urea and methanol plants.[92] In the opinion of at least one of Muldoon's senior and closest advisers, the final decision to approve was done quickly for political rather than economic reasons.[93]

Muldoon, however, according to the managing director of New Zealand Steel, was 'very searching in his inquiries' and 'showed considerable courage in deciding to proceed'.[94] The Prime Minister told New Zealand Steel that he could not commit a future government but would give the company a letter of intent, and tenders were called for the construction of the steel mill. The project was plagued by union demarcation problems which led to extra costs and delays; interest costs also rose; successive National and Labour ministers insisted that local manufacturing be used instead of cheaper imports; and after the change of government in 1984 New Zealand Steel was forced to take over the separate, 60 per cent government-owned construction company and its debts, although the Government in return wrote off $1.138 billion in loans as part of the deal.[95] Under the original conditions of sheltered shareholders, preferential energy costs, market protection, guaranteed loans, and the company not being required to take over the new plant until it was in full production two years after commissioning, the company believed that it would make a profit and export the bulk of its product. As such New Zealand Steel was a classic example of a protected, government-supported industry, but that protection and support were to be abruptly removed after 1984. Without government involvement, limited protection or subsidy, the project became uneconomic. Even at the time the Government agreed to proceed, the New Zealand Steel project had been somewhat marginal and required protection.

Supporters of the New Zealand Steel expansion such as Birch, Ingram and Hellaby, however, always believed that despite substantial cost overruns, to a large extent due to industrial disruption on the Glenbrook construction site, the original agreement was a reasonable one. After 1984 the new Labour Government's 'resolve to cancel the commitments to market protection, financial support by way of guarantees, coal and electricity price levels and other elements in the development package had the accumulated impact of making the project unworkable', even though (as the board of New Zealand Steel argued) 'current projections show that if the original agreement had been maintained the project would have proved commercially acceptable and there would have been no need for the debt conversion as now proposed.'[96] In 1987 the Government, which had taken over the debts of NZ Steel, some $2,508 million, sold the company to Equiticorp Holdings for $327 million. New Zealand Steel subsequently became a wholly owned subsidiary of the Australian steelmaker BHP Ltd.

'Think Big' went well beyond intervention in the economy. It involved state-led and state-funded development of New Zealand's industrial infrastructure on a huge scale reminiscent of that undertaken by Julius Vogel and Richard John Seddon in the latter part of the nineteenth century. It was a determined and very ambitious strategy in which the Government would provide the vision, leadership and much of the venture capital to move the country away from its vulnerable overreliance on a commodity-based economy. While increased production and exports from traditional agricultural products would still be vital to New Zealand's economic health, that would be balanced by energy-based projects and a greater emphasis on technology. Muldoon's determined attempt to build energy projects, plant more forests, expand farming and foster more manufacturing was not just an economic policy but also a conscious attempt to create a secure and self-sufficient nation.

The Labour Government which came to power in mid-1984 was in no doubt that 'Think Big' was an almost total disaster. Roger Douglas, as Minister of Finance, was to estimate that the Synfuels, methanol, ammonia-urea, refinery expansion and New Zealand Steel projects cost about $8 billion.[97] Of that amount, the Government had had to take over or write off some $7.8 billion in debt, and initially even after that some of the projects were not seen as commercially viable. Another evaluation has put the government's assumption of loans and other write-offs at over $8 billion with the additional cost of identifiable inefficiencies and cost overruns in the electricity sector adding another $3 billion. The addition of opportunity costs would further increase the total to well beyond $11 billion.[98]

'Think Big', even in hindsight, is difficult to attack or defend as a whole. There is no doubt that it did diversify New Zealand's economy and reduce its dependence on imported fuels. Some projects were sound and ultimately successful. Others were reasonable in the circumstances at the time and on the expert advice available. The steel mill expansion was at first the most controversial but even that project, it can be argued, was only rendered indefensible by a complete change in government policy towards protection and subsidies and the effect of devaluation and high interest rates on loans after 1984. The refinery expansion and the ammonia-urea plant were also not economic propositions, especially when the refinery, like the steel mill, also experienced huge construction cost overruns. That does not mean, however, that there was not considerable dispute at the time about such things as the desirability of the strategy generally; the way it was so speedily implemented; the details of the specific projects; or the wisdom, or the lack of it, in the Government taking all the risks in enterprises such as the oil refinery when it would have been better to have greater private sector involvement.

Concerns about the 'Think Big' growth strategy included the desirability of heavy industry; the extent of government involvement and ownership; the massive capital investment involved and the possible diversion of funds from agriculture and small business; the shortage of skilled labour and the resulting effect on wage demands; the increase in overseas debt and debt servicing; construction delays, industrial strife and cost overruns on some projects; the efficacy of new technologies involved; the involvement of overseas firms and the resulting transfer of expected profits abroad; the possible waste of natural resources; the diversion of government attention and involvement from overall restructuring of the economy and deregulation to specific large projects; the questionable existence of future export markets for steel and aluminium; the secrecy, speed and environmental impact of the development; and doubts whether the capital intensive projects would provide sufficient jobs as promised to make a significant impact on unemployment.[99] Most of these concerns, openly expressed at the time by Rowling and the Labour Opposition, proved to be well founded. Even within the National Party many people had doubts about the strategy. Although FOL leaders in public criticised

National's 'Think Big' strategy, there was, however, privately within the union movement considerable admiration for the concept and approach, especially related to the energy projects.[100] The gamble was clearly whether New Zealand's growth rate and exports could be increased sufficiently and maintained long enough to pay for the development.

When Highet in November 1980 announced to the National Party in Auckland that the Government's 'massive industrial growth on the energy front' would be presented under the slogan 'Think Big', to distinguish the Government's approach from Labour's 'think small' perspective, neither the strategy nor its name were welcomed with any great enthusiasm.[101] Subsequently, cabinet ministers such as Quigley, Cooper and MacIntyre addressed meetings of Auckland party officials to try to convince them of the virtues of 'Think Big'. Quigley, for example, pointed out that it had taken 20 per cent of the earnings from meat exports to pay New Zealand's bill for oil imports in 1972 but by 1979 it had taken 100 per cent.[102] The development of agriculture, fishing, forestry and energy-intensive products such as aluminium, he added, would have a dramatic effect not only on the New Zealand economy generally but on specific districts where the development would take place. The three main objectives of the growth strategy, Cooper stressed, were to save or earn overseas funds; to become about 50 per cent self-sufficient in liquid fuels; and to provide employment.[103]

Other National MPs remained unconvinced. In December 1980 Minogue returned to his attack on Muldoon, condemning the 'Think Big' policy, especially the proposed second aluminium smelter, and suggesting as an alternative the encouragement of small and medium businesses in the private sector.[104] Minogue was not alone in caucus in also expressing misgivings about the constitutional, moral and legal implications of fast-tracking the major developments.

In an effort to speed up the process and remove obstacles to the 'Think Big' projects, the Government passed in December 1979 the National Development Act. Opposition to the Act was led by a Coalition for Open Government formed in September and headed by the former Ombudsman, Sir Guy Powles. The Coalition opposed the speed, secrecy and lack of public consultation which would result from the legislation and also expressed concern about the lack of environmental safeguards in the speedy utilisation of natural resources. Although only five of 341 public submissions gave unqualified support for the Bill, arguments against were largely dismissed by the Minister of National Development, Birch. Muldoon, however, agreed to some amendments following debate within National's caucus. The most important was a provision allowing for the Court of Appeal to consider a Government decision under the Act. Not all the critics were satisfied and three National MPs – Minogue, Shearer and Waring – voted with the Opposition in favour of parliamentary ratification being required for government departures from Planning Tribunal recommendations. Shearer later recalled going to Muldoon to explain why 'because of his environmental principles . . . he would have to vote against the Bill . . . Muldoon simply listened and said at the end, "Well you have to vote against it then." That was all that was said or done and there was no attempt to force me to change my mind or any criticism of me.'[105] Underlying the action of the three dissident MPs from the Waikato was concern that arbitrary executive power was being further strengthened by the National Development Act.[106] Supporters of the Act countered that it provided the Government with the power to cut through bureaucratic red tape, act decisively and get some projects under way before the 1981 election. The controversy over 'Think Big', the Government's dramatic intervention in the economy, and the apparently dogmatic arrogance of executive power all fuelled growing criticism of Muldoon both within and without the National Party.

CHAPTER 17

The Colonels' Coup 1980

IMPORTANT THOUGH IT UNDOUBTEDLY WAS, THE ECONOMY WAS not the only issue or matter that concerned Muldoon during his second term as prime minister. Within days after the return of the National Government at the 1978 election, the nuclear ships visit issue revived when the American ambassador requested diplomatic clearance for a nuclear-powered submarine, USS *Haddo*, to visit Auckland in late January 1979.[1] Talboys told Muldoon that, although 'the timing is not particularly convenient coming as it does during the holiday period . . . when the yachting season is at its height', the relatively limited protest against the USS *Pintado* earlier in 1978 suggested that the visit should be accommodated.[2]

Another issue of significant concern to both Muldoon and the general public was the Thomas affair. Arthur Allan Thomas had been convicted of the murder of Jeanette and Harvey Crewe at Pukekawa in June 1970. A second trial in 1973 also resulted in convictions although many people believed either that Thomas was clearly innocent or that, at the very least, the Crown had not proved him guilty beyond reasonable doubt.

Muldoon started to take an interest as early as May 1972 in the conviction of Thomas and was soon publicly expressing his unease about the verdict.[3] After becoming prime minister, he had a substantial correspondence with the Thomas supporters Pat Booth and Dr Jim Sprott and on 26 November 1976 met the two men to discuss what could be done.[4] The Secretary of Justice and the Solicitor-General and most other ministers, however, were opposed to any political interference in the judicial process. Among Muldoon's close colleagues only MacIntyre, who took an ongoing interest in the matter and who in 1977 wrote a lengthy, reasoned letter to Muldoon raising doubts about Thomas's conviction, wanted action to overturn the verdict.[5]

Following the publication in 1978 of a book by a British journalist[6] who argued that Thomas's conviction was a serious miscarriage of justice, Muldoon and McLay, the Minister of Justice and Attorney-General, authorised an investigation by the barrister R. A. Adams-Smith who reported to the Prime Minister in 1979.

Although Muldoon believed Thomas should not have been convicted, he also accepted that the final decision on freeing Thomas was McLay's. It was a personal decision as minister not a collective cabinet one. The Prime Minister expressed his relief and support when McLay told him that he was going to recommend a pardon.[7] Subsequently, a royal commission found that Thomas had been wrongfully convicted on very unsatisfactory evidence and recommended that Thomas receive substantial compensation to which Muldoon agreed. The Thomas Retrial Committee even after Muldoon's death was still recording its deep gratitude for Muldoon's 'vital contribution' to the freeing of Thomas.[8]

On 28 November 1979 an Air New Zealand plane crashed on Mount Erebus in Antarctica with the loss of 257 lives. On 11 June 1980 Justice Mahon was appointed by the Government as a sole royal commissioner to inquire into the tragedy. He reported on 16 April 1981. Muldoon was pleased that Mahon's report 'demolished the argument that the sole cause of the crash was pilot error' because he had met both pilots who lived in his Tamaki electorate. But he was not pleased with the suggestion that there had been 'an orchestrated litany of lies' by unidentified Air New Zealand witnesses and commented that 'it would have been better if Mr Justice Mahon had phrased his views less elegantly and more precisely.'[9]

Worried about the possible destruction of Air New Zealand's credibility, Muldoon read the report carefully. From the first he felt uneasy about it and commented to Hensley, 'There's something funny about this . . . If the plane was programmed to fly into a mountain from take-off, why have a pilot?'[10] With the aid of his staff and McLay he sent a detailed list of questions to the Air New Zealand board concerning the matters Mahon raised. He queried particularly the lack of written reports, the destruction of documents, and the fact that Mahon was given copies not originals of other documents.[11] Muldoon, however, finally appeared to accept the board's view that the accident occurred as a result of a combination of factors and was not impressed when Mahon suggested that Muldoon's confidence in his advisers might be sadly misplaced.

The Labour Opposition's politicisation of the issue a few months before the 1981 election also concerned Muldoon; Rowling was criticising him for looking after 'a clutch of personal political friends', particularly Des Dalgety, the Wellington lawyer and anti-abortion campaigner who was the board's deputy chairman.[12] Muldoon retaliated by saying that he was distressed that his involvement in the matter was regarded in such a way, because as Minister of Finance he held the shares of Air New Zealand and the Government was responsible for appointing board members. If Mahon believed Air New Zealand board members or management had conspired to present false evidence, then he should have named the people concerned and given them a chance to refute the allegations. Muldoon also pointed out that this was not the first time a royal commission's findings had been questioned and criticised.[13]

Air New Zealand challenged Mahon in the Court of Appeal and following the Court's unanimous decision that Mahon's finding that there had been a 'predetermined plan of deception' by Air New Zealand had been made 'in disregard of

basic principles of natural justice', Muldoon publicly challenged Mahon to answer
three questions:

a) Who were the conspirators?
b) Who told the lies?
c) What evidence have you to support your answers to questions (a) and (b)?[14]

Mahon was shattered by the decision of the Court of Appeal and decided to retire
immediately because he took the Court's finding to mean his credibility as a judge
had been destroyed and that he was 'incapable of distinguishing truth from
falsehood'.[15] A few weeks later he wrote a longer, more formal letter, again noting
that 'my judicial position has been compromised by the way in which the Court of
Appeal handled this case'.[16] He requested that the Government exercise its
discretion and pay him a pension which he would supplement by part-time
university teaching because convention prevented him returning to the bar. He also
asked if the Government would appeal the decision to the Privy Council on the
grounds that the Court of Appeal as a whole had 'misconceived the true nature of a
Royal Commission', and that Justices Woodhouse and McMullin should not,
because of their family and other connections, have taken part in the appeal.
Woodhouse and McMullin had presented a minority report totally exonerating Air
New Zealand of giving false evidence. Mahon had known in advance of the Court
of Appeal hearing that Woodhouse and McMullin had children who were
employed by Air New Zealand but when given the opportunity to object to their
sitting had not done so.[17]

Muldoon and McLay diverged strongly over the Mahon report on the Erebus
disaster and there were heated exchanges between the two when Muldoon sided
with Air New Zealand and McLay defended Mahon. At one point, indeed, McLay,
who wanted to reject Mahon's offer to resign, nearly resigned himself when
Muldoon favoured immediate acceptance. Mahon did resign and subsequently in
1983 the Privy Council also found that there was no evidence to substantiate
Mahon's charge that Air New Zealand's management had been guilty of a 'litany of
lies' and a 'conspiracy to deceive'. Nevertheless, there were many in the public who
felt that Air New Zealand had been too quick to blame pilot error and to minimise
other contributing factors to the tragedy and that Muldoon had been too partisan
in defending the board and senior management of the airline.

In December 1979 the Soviet Union invaded Afghanistan. New Zealand was
informed on Boxing Day. Muldoon was at his bach at Hatfields Beach and rang
Galvin at his holiday home at Otaki to tell him to go to the Soviet Embassy in
Wellington and receive a note from the Soviet ambassador.[18] When Galvin arrived
at the embassy dressed in shirt and shorts the police refused to allow him in so
Galvin had to ring Muldoon back at Hatfields. Unfortunately the telephone
operator thought Galvin was a drunk or crank caller and for some time refused to
put him through. When Galvin finally did get the note and managed to speak to
Muldoon, Muldoon informed him that the situation was complicated by the fact

that the Security Intelligence Service had evidence that just before Christmas Ambassador Sofinsky had secretly passed over money to the Socialist Unity Party.

The SUP had clear instructions from the Soviet Embassy never to approach it directly for funds, but the Soviets had for years purchased many copies of the SUP's newspaper, *The New Zealand Tribune*, as a means of indirectly helping the party. On this occasion, however, the KGB courier had not delivered the expected money and the printer of the newspaper was refusing to print it until the money was forthcoming. A phone call to the embassy asking for the funds urgently and a response to the effect that the ambassador, who was going to Auckland, would deliver it was intercepted by the SIS. The SUP always claimed that 'Sofinsky gave Jackson champagne and caviar not money' as a Christmas present at their meeting, although admitting that on other occasions the Soviet Embassy did help the SUP with trips for its members to visit the USSR, tickets on Russian cruise liners to raffle, books and magazines, and subscriptions to the SUP's newspaper. Large sums of cash were, the SUP insisted, never involved.[19]

Any action against the ambassador over the funding of the SUP would be seen as retaliation by New Zealand over Afghanistan, and as a consequence New Zealand's substantial and growing meat and dairy trade with the Soviet Union might be also damaged. At the very least the Soviets would retaliate by expelling the New Zealand ambassador to Moscow if New Zealand expelled Sofinsky. The Intelligence Council, chaired by Galvin as head of the Prime Minister's Department and consisting of the heads of Foreign Affairs, Defence, Police and the SIS, met and divided on what action should be taken in regard to Sofinsky. Galvin and Corner, the Secretary of Foreign Affairs, wanted Sofinsky expelled but the others, especially Air Marshal Richard Bolt, who pointed out that the SIS tape of the transfer of money at the motel was so difficult to decipher that it was not clear Sofinsky was one of those talking, were reluctant, and Muldoon was informed of the split. Muldoon decided to consult New Zealand's major allies, and officials were sent to brief the Americans, British, Canadians and Australians. All except the Americans, who were cautious, advised New Zealand to expel the ambassador and that was done on 24 January 1980.

Subsequently, New Zealand took further action over Afghanistan when, following Government persuasion, nearly all its athletes withdrew from the 1980 Moscow Olympics. Muldoon, however, would not intervene officially to prevent athletes going to Moscow because, as the US Embassy in Wellington advised the US State Department after Ambassador Anne Martindell had met Muldoon, he 'apparently intends to do the bare minimum required by the Gleneagles Agreement as the 1981 Springbok tour grows closer to hand' and 'clearly does not intend to take any action [in regard to the Moscow Olympics] now which might expose the Government to criticism in 1981 that he is being inconsistent.'[20]

In 1979 Muldoon was frequently overseas. He attended an OECD meeting in Paris from 7 to 17 June, travelling via Washington DC for talks en route with Robert McNamara, the head of the World Bank. At the OECD meeting, Muldoon made a speech attacking agricultural protectionism, which one New Zealand economic historian has described as 'one of the most important speeches made to that organisation by a politician'.[21] The following month he attended the South Pacific Forum, held that year in the Solomon Islands, and also visited Kiribati for its independence celebrations. The 1979 CHOGM meeting was held in Zambia and Muldoon, after attending that, had a comprehensive visit to Western Australia on his way home, being out of New Zealand from 28 July until 15 August.

The Commonwealth Heads of Government Meeting in Lusaka in August 1979 was largely dominated by the future of Rhodesia-Zimbabwe, even though that topic was placed late on the agenda. Britain saw the independence of Rhodesia-Zimbabwe and the movement to majority black rule there as a matter between it and its former colony and not, as many other Commonwealth countries believed, a matter for the Commonwealth as a whole. Nearly all the Commonwealth leaders also wanted an unqualified condemnation of the white racist breakaway regime led by Ian Smith. It was clear that Britain was largely isolated on the issue, but Muldoon had met the newly elected British Prime Minister Mrs Margaret Thatcher during a visit to London in June and told her that New Zealand would follow Britain's lead on that issue.[22] He confirmed that assurance during a private meeting between himself and Thatcher on Tuesday 1 August at the start of the Lusaka CHOGM.[23] He suggested that perhaps the Gleneagles Declaration might be a model for resolving the divisions at CHOGM over Rhodesia-Zimbabwe. If the key figures could be got together privately, a solution might be hammered out. While he did not want New Zealand on such a committee, Muldoon thought Kaunda and Nyerere could help, as could Ramphal who 'had the ability and was essentially well-disposed'. Nigeria would be a problem and in Muldoon's opinion 'Fraser's policy was one of excessive appeasement'. Thatcher, however, told Muldoon that she did not want a Commonwealth committee or declaration on the issue and that it was something Britain had to resolve, though eventually the British did accept a Commonwealth cease-fire monitoring force and Commonwealth observers for Zimbabwe's first democratic elections. She also disagreed with Muldoon's suggestion that Ian Smith had to go in the interests of a settlement which would stop the fighting and lead to a democracy based on black majority rule. While Thatcher saw the issue as largely a 'battle between black and white', Muldoon suggested to her that 'superimposed on this was the problem of tribalism'.

On Friday 4 August Nyerere and Thatcher read very carefully constructed speeches which dealt exclusively with Rhodesia.[24] Nyerere argued that, although Rhodesia now had a black president, prime minister and parliamentary majority, Britain still needed to establish a democratic constitution, hold democratic elections and end the fighting. Thatcher accepted this analysis in her speech but again stressed that the responsibility was Britain's alone, which as anticipated drew some negative comments from Nigeria and Uganda. When Muldoon spoke, he drew attention to the extent to which Thatcher's and Nyerere's speeches overlapped and he also emphasised a Kenyan suggestion that there must be no retribution after the war. A six-person group (with representatives from Britain, Australia, Jamaica, Nigeria, Tanzania and Zambia) was then established to try to produce over the weekend a consensus on the issue as the basis for a CHOGM statement which eventually became known as the Lusaka Declaration on Racism and Racial Prejudice. This committed the Commonwealth to working actively to rid the world of racism.[25]. Although the text of the declaration was not to be tabled until the Monday morning, it was decided to distribute it in confidence to the heads of government at an Australian Government barbecue on Sunday evening. By that time, however, Fraser had unilaterally passed it to the media to meet the Australian press's deadline, an action that had Thatcher 'hopping mad', particularly as Fraser in briefing the press gave the impression that he rather than Nyerere, Kaunda or Ramphal was the architect behind the successful outcome and that Thatcher had been forced to make significant concessions.[26]

The major overseas trip of the year was over four weeks spent between 17 September and 15 October in Washington DC, London, Bremen, Malta, Belgrade, Bucharest and the Gulf states. During this tour, Muldoon chaired meetings of the boards of governors of the IMF and World Bank in Belgrade. He would again chair meetings of the IMF in Manila in December the following year and during 1979 and 1980 he was reported to be interested in retiring as prime minister if he could win appointment as president of the World Bank.[27] He consistently denied such rumours. He also opened the New Zealand Embassy's new building in Washington DC; launched a New Zealand Shipping Company vessel in Bremen; attended a Commonwealth finance ministers' meeting in Malta; paid an official visit to Romania; and opened the cool store in Bahrain and a milk-recombining plant in Dubai. Most of Muldoon's expenses were met by the IMF and the governments of Malta and Romania, although neither country impressed Muldoon. In Malta, for example, Prime Minister Mintoff requested a meeting with Muldoon, who left the official reception for finance ministers early to be at Mintoff's office by 7.45 for the scheduled appointment. Mintoff then kept Muldoon waiting for half an hour and at 8.15 Muldoon 'informed the Prime Minister's aide that he could not wait any longer and returned to the hotel'. Muldoon's scheduled Pan Am flight from Belgrade to Bucharest was cancelled at the last minute and he had to drive across the border to Timişoara and catch an internal Romanian flight to Bucharest, where he visited a number of industrial plants and agricultural enterprises and lunched with the Prime Minister Ilie Verdet. Muldoon did not meet the president of Romania, Nicolai Ceauşescu, because he was absent from the country during his visit.

In 1980 Muldoon again made several lengthy overseas trips. On 25 May he left New Zealand and flew first via Sydney and Bali to Jakarta, where he had talks with President Soeharto before carrying on to Singapore for dinner with Lee Kuan Yew. Talboys, on his way back to New Zealand, was also at the dinner and the next morning, Saturday 31 May, Muldoon and Talboys met for discussions at 9 a.m. before the Prime Minister flew on to Bahrain and London. On arrival in London, he went to the Lyric Theatre to see a performance of *Middle-Age Spread* by the New Zealand playwright Roger Hall. Unfortunately Muldoon became ill shortly after the performance started and was taken back to his hotel by his private secretary. He recovered sufficiently to travel the next day to Paris for meetings of the OECD. On Wednesday 4 June, after lunching and meeting with President Giscard d'Estaing, Muldoon flew to Zurich where he spoke at a dinner on the subject 'Prospects for New Zealand in the 1980s'.

After leaving Switzerland on Saturday 7 June, he flew to San Francisco where he spent a quiet Sunday lunching at Sausalito, relaxing in the Golden Gate Park and attending a performance of the stage show *Beach Blanket Babylon Goes to the Stars* at the Club Fugazi. After making a speech at a reception for American banks on Monday and being presented with the keys of San Francisco City by the Mayor, Dianne Feinstein, he flew to Honolulu on Tuesday 10 June and then on to New Zealand.

One of Muldoon's strongest lieutenants in cabinet, Frank Gill, who had not been well for some time, had indicated to Muldoon following the 1978 election that he did not want to return to cabinet but wished to be appointed as either ambassador to the United States or high commissioner to the United Kingdom.[28] Gill's persistence led finally to Muldoon's agreeing, against Talboys' strong objections, to appoint Gill to Washington.

Gill assured Muldoon that his seat of East Coast Bays would be held easily in a by-election. Others in the party were not so sure. Both the electorate organisation and the party's vote in that electorate had been seriously divided by Gill's authoritarian manner, which made him insensitive and intolerant to the divergent views found in a voluntary grassroots organisation, and particularly by his dogmatic stand on the abortion issue. In 1978 a number of pro-abortion National Party supporters had put up a National Alternative candidate who had fragmented Gill's vote. Gill's assurances, however, were accepted by Muldoon without any attempt by the Prime Minister to check with the party organisation. Muldoon admitted later that he did not even realise that Social Credit had polled a large vote in the East Coast Bays in 1978.[29] Muldoon's old friends, Alan and Geraldine Jenkin, who were at that time respectively electorate chairman and chairwoman of the Woman's Section, did not share Gill's confidence but were not asked for their opinions.[30] The party president, Chapman, later recalled that it was 'perhaps the only occasion I was not consulted by Muldoon on an organisational matter' and that the first he knew was 'a telephone call from Muldoon that Gill was going to Washington and a by-election would be held'.[31]

While Muldoon's major blunder was causing the by-election in the first place, he proceeded to compound the error rather than recover from it. He showed a distinct lack of enthusiasm for National's new candidate, the economist and merchant banker Dr Don Brash, whom the selection committee chose in preference to Sue Wood or Bill Rayner. Wood was the party's Woman Vice-President and Muldoon's favourite, and Rayner a long-time local party activist. Muldoon recognised Brash's ability but believed he was too much associated with Friedmanite New Right economic policies. Brash had hosted Milton Friedman during his visit to New Zealand and had also been putting papers into National's policy committee advocating a flat income tax at a rate of 30 cents in the dollar. Muldoon had refused to meet Friedman and his wife Rose during their visit and had also rubbished Brash's flat tax proposals at the policy committee meetings.[32] Tremewan, Muldoon's trusted right-hand man in the Auckland party organisation, told the Prime Minister and senior party officers the day before the by-election campaign opened that National's organisation in the electorate had been divided into four camps as a result of the selection of Brash as candidate: they comprised (1) 'Brash supporters, cock-a-hoop and working hard' who were 'foolish optimists who expect a 5,000 plus majority'; (2) disaffected 'Rayner supporters who resent Brash as Johnny-come-lately'; (3) 'Sue Wood supporters' who feel the party is unsympathetic to women candidates; and (4) 'a fourth group of people with their feet on the ground'.[33] He reported, somewhat enviously, on the Social Credit campaign but believed the National organisation could match it. The danger, he predicted correctly, was the probable collapse of the 'soft' Labour vote to Social Credit.

Some of Muldoon's other actions also had the effect of undermining National's campaign. Shortly before the by-election he raised the tolls on the Auckland Harbour Bridge. He became involved in an undignified public dispute with the journalist Tom Scott and savaged various television interviewers. He appointed his crony, the much-criticised McLachlan, to fill Gill's position on National's front bench. That was seen as a gratuitous insult to much more competent younger ministers, such as Bolger, and a sign that Muldoon was contemptuous of the views of his critics in caucus and the party's organisational leadership, who had opposed strongly even McLachlan's reappointment to cabinet in 1978. Nearly everyone also agreed that the opening meeting of the by-election campaign on 19 August was a disaster, and Muldoon himself was enraged when he found himself speaking to a half-filled hall. After opening the campaign Muldoon then left on a seven-week overseas trip.

He attended the Commonwealth Heads of Government meeting in India; a Commonwealth finance ministers' meeting in Bermuda; the annual meeting of governors of the IMF and World Bank in Washington DC; addressed the General Assembly of the United Nations in New York; and paid state visits to China and Mexico.

Back in New Zealand, the East Coast Bays by-election continued to go badly for National. Pat Baker, the Auckland divisional chairman, warned the Divisional Executive a week before polling day that National was in danger of losing the seat to Social Credit.[34] At the meeting the Executive also passed a motion deploring the timing of Muldoon's announcement of his decision to allow an increase in tolls on the Auckland Harbour Bridge. One MP, Winston Peters, strongly defended Muldoon's political honesty in making the announcement before rather than after the election, but he was in a small minority. At the end of the meeting Brash reported that 'he had met a surprising degree of disillusionment, which could lead to a protest vote' and that 'there was a widespread contention that the Prime Minister was responsible for personality politics'.[35]

In contrast to National's inept performance, the Social Credit candidate Gary Knapp and his team ran a superb campaign and managed also to convince a large number of traditional Labour voters that the only way to defeat National in the East Coast Bays was to support Knapp. As a result Social Credit on polling day 6 September won the seat with Labour a distant third. Social Credit's leaders believed they owed a great deal to Muldoon. It was his policies that had created dissatisfaction in Rangitikei in 1978 so that Social Credit was able to get Beetham into Parliament, and it was his miscalculation in East Coast Bays in 1980 that allowed it to double its representation.[36]

When the press contacted Muldoon in New Delhi, he commented at length on the result. The abbreviated version published in New Zealand selectively highlighted his adverse comments about National's inadequate organisation and an implied criticism of Brash. Muldoon's temper and reaction were not helped by a hoax call from a Labour Party activist claiming to be Brash and abusing Muldoon for costing him the seat. Muldoon's reported statements in turn provoked widespread and ongoing criticism of him in the media as various National Party officials and MPs defended Brash and the party organisation and blamed Muldoon for the defeat.[37] Muldoon realised that his comments immediately following the defeat had been injudicious and tried to excuse himself by arguing that there had been a misunderstanding and that he did not say he 'put the whole blame on the party organisation'.[38]

The meeting of the Auckland Divisional Executive after the East Coast Bays by-election was a very angry one. The divisional chairman commenced with an attack on the absent Muldoon. Baker 'refuted utterly the comments made by the Prime Minister about the state of the organisation being the cause of the loss'. Rather, National voters 'were disillusioned by the style of the Leader and there was some confusion about the direction of current National Party policy . . . only Caucus could effect a change in either.'[39] The president, Chapman, made a number of observations about the way National's growth and economic policies were not understood and the way the Government appeared to penalise its own supporters most. Ross Armstrong from Gair's North Shore electorate then moved a motion that the positions of leader and deputy leader should be made 'reviewable and reconfirmable at least once in the period between each General Election'. This was seen as a direct attack on Muldoon and was lost 26 votes to 29. Muldoon was then invited to address the December meeting.

The disastrous loss of the East Coast Bays seat, however, had clearly provided the catalyst for the growing opposition to Muldoon within the party. It reinforced the doubts and questions raised by the massive shift in votes against National at the 1978 election. Chapman recalled that almost the whole of the party 'rose up in arms criticising Muldoon and his attempt to blame the organisation for what was clearly an error of judgement on his part' in causing the by-election.[40] Concern was expressed over Muldoon's combative style and interventionist economic policies. Various hurt feelings within caucus and a real fear that National would lose the 1981 election with Muldoon as leader also combined to create a mood for change among many in the caucus. The result was the so-called 'Colonels' Coup', an attempt during October–November 1980 to replace him with his deputy, Talboys.

Talboys, at the time 59 years of age and in Muldoon's absence overseas performing impressively as Acting Prime Minister, was the only credible alternative. The media started to praise Talboys' performance and suggested that his leadership style was reminiscent of Holyoake's consensual leadership in stark contrast to Muldoon's 'one man style'.[41] There was general agreement among the dissidents that other possible contenders – Gair, Quigley, McLay or Bolger – would not be acceptable to enough of their caucus colleagues to obtain a majority. Apart from Talboys, only MacIntyre might have commanded such support before a recent marginal lands board scandal, in which he was found to have acted unwisely though not improperly in regard to a loan application from his daughter and son-in-law, and he was loyal to Muldoon anyway. As one senior civil servant recalled, 'MacIntyre had the sharpness of Muldoon, was more decisive than Talboys or Templeton, and was more flexible than Gill. He usually had a twinkle in his eye and officials always felt, even if he disagreed with them, that MacIntyre respected their right to have their say.'[42]

Holyoake, years before, had identified Talboys as a potential National Party leader. Certainly Talboys, a likeable and, in the eyes of some of his fellow MPs, an 'intensely good person' who might well have become 'the best Prime Minister we'd had', enjoyed nearly all the attributes of success. He was physically a most impressive man with a charming personality. A developed all-rounder, he had a BA degree, had been a journalist and a farmer and had a wide range of ministerial experience – Deputy Prime Minister and at various times Minister of Agriculture, Education, Industries and Commerce, Overseas Trade, Foreign Affairs, and National Development. Moreover, he commanded the attention of the House as one of its best debaters. When provoked he could retaliate mercilessly though he never descended to the lowest levels of abuse. He was seen as having the ability to synthesise the caucus team, respect others' opinions and feelings and get people working together rather than constantly being at war with each other. He possessed a mind that analysed problems and ranged over alternatives and implications. He also had a somewhat visionary view of New Zealand's place in the Asia–Pacific region and in a future world with a diversified economy and new, complex trading patterns. One former colleague, who admired Talboys and believed that he 'would have been a good, perhaps a great, prime Minister', also believed, however, that he 'wouldn't have lived long' because he 'worried too much about difficult things' and 'sweated over decisions'.[43] Undoubtedly Talboys was less decisive, less pragmatic, and less ruthless than Muldoon.

The organisers of the revolt were Quigley, McLay and Bolger – arguably the three most able of Muldoon's younger ministers. Paul East labelled the conspirators 'the Colonels' and McKinnon told the press. The label stuck. The 'Colonels' were aided by five 'sergeants'. Michael Cox, who was later to become McLay's 'numbers' man in the 1984 and 1985 leadership contests, and Bruce Townshend, who performed the same function for Bolger on both occasions, were active in lobbying and counting the votes for Talboys. They were helped by Ian McLean, Doug Kidd and Tony Friedlander, the chief government whip. Dail Jones, the junior whip, was also sympathetic to the planned change. Kidd found out about the coup from Brill at Auckland airport when he returned after four weeks overseas. As soon as he reached Wellington he discovered McLay, Bolger, Quigley, Cox, McLean and Townshend plotting in a Beehive office. Kidd produced a duty-free bottle of Scotch and the conspiracy was sealed.

From the first Chapman was 'fully informed' about and was sympathetic to the challenge, having been visited at party headquarters and briefed by Cox, East, Kidd and Townshend. There was considerable support within the organisation, especially at the Dominion and Divisional Executive levels, for such a change. Gair, although taking little part in the lobbying, gave his support and acted as the group's link with a somewhat reluctant Talboys, who had to be persuaded that a majority of his caucus colleagues were determined to remove Muldoon and that, therefore, he would be filling a vacancy and not really challenging an incumbent leader to whom hitherto Talboys had shown impeccable loyalty. Although throughout the party's history none of National's leaders and their deputies had ever really liked each other, they had managed to work generally well together and Talboys certainly recognised and respected Muldoon's many personal strengths and contributions to the party. But he also valued the team system and was prepared to accept the consensus of caucus if it decided he should replace Muldoon. He refused, however, to lobby intensively on his own behalf or give his total commitment to achieving the change. The best Gair could get out of Talboys was that, while he would not challenge Muldoon, he would accept a draft. As one of Talboys' supporters recalled, 'All Talboys had to do was state, "Yes, I'm a candidate for leader" and he had it won. But he couldn't make up his mind.'[44]

Talboys' reluctance to lead the revolt and leadership challenge openly led to an attempt by Muldoon's opponents to get a majority of the caucus to sign a letter stating that 'If the majority of caucus members wish to change the leadership I will join them'. The signed statements were put in an envelope with the MP's name on the outside and handed to Holland, who acted as the 'postbox'. Holland kept the envelopes in a wire basket which he carried with him even into the House. When a majority handed over their envelopes then it was hoped that Talboys would commit himself and Muldoon would recognise that he no longer enjoyed the confidence of a majority of his colleagues. Two days before Muldoon returned to New Zealand, Holland was holding 28 signed letters, and several other MPs who refused to sign anything had also indicated that they would support Talboys.

Although the calibre of the anti-Muldoon activists was extremely high, once it became obvious that a revolt was afoot a number of equally competent and determined loyalists counter-attacked on Muldoon's behalf. Friedlander, although an active conspirator, felt it was his duty as chief whip to let the Prime Minister know what was happening. Friedlander discussed the situation with MacIntyre, who said he would advise Muldoon. Friedlander also approached Aussie Malcolm and told him that a challenge was planned; that Talboys was the candidate; the names of those who had organised and were supporting the coup; and Friedlander's belief that they had the numbers. Friedlander may well have hoped that Malcolm would join the opposition to Muldoon. Both MacIntyre and Malcolm, however, were incensed as much by the way the challenge was being mounted as by the revolt itself. MacIntyre, who believed that 'you don't have to love a leader to admire his qualities', saw the plotters as acting in 'an underhand, Mafia-style way' and said they should have 'fronted up to Muldoon'. Malcolm was angry at the conspirators' 'audacious disloyalty' and argued that if you 'want to have a go at the old bastard have it while he's here, not overseas'. Both felt that Muldoon had his faults but despite them was still a better leader than Talboys, who was 'shaking with indecision'.

Over whisky the two men, with MacIntyre 'as cool as a cucumber', discussed their strategy for defending Muldoon. Malcolm first leaked news of the plot to Frank Early, the *Auckland Star*'s reporter in the Press Gallery, in order to get the conspiracy out in the open. He then decided to compile an information base for Muldoon which was subsequently given to the Prime Minister by MacIntyre on Muldoon's return from overseas. Malcolm recruited as his lieutenants Barry Brill, John Elliott and Leo Schultz. None of the three knew who the other two were. Their task was to circulate among the other MPs and prepare a list indicating whether their colleagues were pro or anti Muldoon or still uncommitted. Over a fortnight Malcolm drew up three lists, all of which revealed that Muldoon's supporters were in a minority. There was little doubt that had Talboys agreed to a vote at that time he would have won. In all, the Muldoon camp, with Bill Birch and David Thomson playing increasingly pivotal roles, eventually compiled seven lists over a period of about three weeks. They revealed the following divisions within the caucus: pro-Muldoon 21, 21, 19, 18, 24, 28, 33: anti-Muldoon 28, 28, 28, 27, 26, 22, 17. On the initial count, 4 of the 21 Muldoon supporters were doubtful and 10 of the 28 opponents. By the fifth count there were no doubtful supporters in the 24 Muldoon votes but there were question marks over 8 of the 26 opponents. The final check revealed 33 Muldoon supporters, all of whom were confirmed, 12 intransigent antis and 5 doubtful antis.[45] Only on the final two counts, when the challenge was collapsing for want of a candidate and in the face of fierce pressure from Muldoon himself and strenuous lobbying on his behalf by MacIntyre, Thomson, Malcolm and Birch, did Muldoon have the numbers in caucus to defeat a challenge from Talboys had it eventuated.

By the time he returned to New Zealand, Muldoon was well apprised of the situation. Not only MacIntyre and Thomson had phoned him. Talboys, as Muldoon's deputy, decided to tell Galvin what was happening so that he could pass it on to the Prime Minister. The Auckland divisional director John Tremewan cabled a warning to Muldoon in California. Muldoon's Tamaki electorate chairman, Richard Yates, informed Muldoon that, although 'our loyalty in Tamaki has not wavered', particularly since the East Coast Bays by-election membership renewals and recruitment had virtually ceased and in Tamaki as in the rest of the country morale was low. The key officials in the electorate had decided that they needed to meet Muldoon privately and urgently on his return to New Zealand to discuss the problems with him.[46] Chapman and Leay also wrote to Muldoon informing him of the significant unrest in the caucus and the party and used the president of Federated Farmers to courier the letter to Muldoon in Mexico.

In their letter to Muldoon, Chapman and Leay reported that since he had been overseas the political climate had changed dramatically and 'there have been major problems in attaining membership and money'.[47] They criticised Muldoon for failing to provide 'direction and leadership', for 'indulging in trivia such as the Tom Scott affair', and for failing to explain properly the major energy and development proposals. Chapman and Leay then bluntly went on to say:

> The East Coast Bays by-election result has caused a shock wave of major proportions. Your reported comments from New Delhi, that the organisation was to blame and the wrong candidate was selected, have caused a New Zealand wide wave of hostility within the party of a severity not experienced since the Moyle affair . . . we believe this crisis will have far more serious consequences than the Moyle affair . . . organizationally and politically, we consider National is now in a 1971 situation. An alarming mood has been unleashed by the East Coast Bays by-election, which has been laying dormant since the 1978 campaign . . . The Springbok invitation, the Fitzgerald affair, the *Truxton* visit and the AFFCO closure have worsened the depressed atmosphere following the by-election . . . All this has led to a crescendo of voices from within the Party calling for your replacement . . . We also feel that it is our responsibility to inform you that there are clear indications that heads are being counted within Caucus at the present time and that there are a significant number of Members who could be persuaded to support a change in the leadership of the Party right now.[48]

If Muldoon were to retain the leadership, Chapman and Leay suggested he would have to 'embody National's Growth Strategy and Economic Policy into a total package'; 'introduce a Mini Budget outlining the package and giving personal tax incentives aimed at increasing production'; appoint a Minister of Finance independent of the Prime Minister so that the Prime Minister's role was seen publicly as a leader-chairman role, and not as a 'judge and jury of every economic issue'; and 'reshuffle Cabinet by promoting junior Ministers who are doing well, and allowing all Ministers more status by being seen to be in control of their own portfolios.' They appealed to Muldoon to regain his 'impish . . . sense of humour' and refrain from arriving back in New Zealand 'ill-tempered and blaming others for recent events' which would do 'immeasurable damage to yourself'. They also wanted much more liaison between the leader and the party headquarters, noting that, 'At no time were we consulted by you about the state of the party organisation or whether, in fact, a by-election should be precipitated in East Coast Bays'. Chapman and Leay concluded, 'Finally, in our view there is now a serious threat of a total rejection of your present style of leadership by the electorate at next year's General Election. A continuation of personal attacks, trivia and bad humour, will see a major defeat for the National Party in 1981.'[49]

On Sunday 12 October, Muldoon flew from Mexico to Hawaii, arriving in Honolulu at midnight. According to his official trip diary, on Monday he 'stayed in suite all day and made numerous phone calls to New Zealand' before departing at 11.45 p.m. for New Zealand. One call was to Chapman who found Muldoon 'very fully briefed on the situation'. On the same day McLay, Quigley, Kidd, Cox and Bolger met at Bolger's home to discuss the situation. During the meeting Bolger was called to take three long phone calls, one of which was from Birch and another from the chief lobbyist for the Catholic Church.

MacIntyre and Tremewan met Muldoon at Auckland airport at 6.40 a.m. on Wednesday 15 October and further briefed the Prime Minister. Malcolm's third canvassing list of caucus members handed to Muldoon on his arrival revealed a 28–19 split in favour of Talboys with three caucus members not identified. Muldoon then gave a press conference before catching a flight to Wellington. The Prime Minister realised that Talboys, who had left for overseas the day Muldoon returned, was not enthusiastic about the challenge and that the caucus majority supporting his deputy was unstable. Therefore he immediately took his campaign via the media to the public in a successful effort to get 'Rob's Mob' to put pressure on the dissident MPs. He told the press conference at Auckland airport that he was a 'bit long in the tooth' to change his style of leadership, but that it had been 'a mistake to take the public for granted' in the East Coast Bays by-election.[50]

A meeting of the National Executive of the National Party had been moved forward a week to the day Muldoon arrived back. Within hours of arriving home, Muldoon was facing in person a barrage of criticism from the leaders of the party organisation. Chapman opened the Dominion Executive meeting by lamenting that 'the East Coast Bays by-election has shattered the image of National being an unbeatable party'.[51] Two Auckland members of the Executive then moved a motion expressing confidence in Brash as the candidate again for East Coast Bays at the 1981 election and that was carried unanimously. Chapman then invited members of the Executive 'to share with the leader the critical state of the party' and 'criticisms of the Leader's style of leadership, particularly his vendetta with the news media'. The attack on Muldoon was led by the five divisional chairmen, all of whom were remarkably forthright and specific in fronting up to Muldoon with a wide range of criticisms.

Muldoon replied at length, dealing sequentially with the points made by his critics. He accepted that there were a number of economic areas such as taxation, interest rates, unemployment and death duties where the Government had to do more. Reshuffling cabinet was 'not a simple matter'. National certainly needed to explain its growth strategy better, though in his opinion it should be clear to all that 'National thinks big, Labour thinks small, and Social Credit does not think at all'. He wanted to see the Marginal Lands Board controversy finished but believed the ministers involved had 'absolute integrity'. Finally, 'The Prime Minister stated that everything that could have gone wrong in the East Coast Bays by-election had gone wrong. He said that his statement in New Delhi had been thirteen pages long . . . He said that he had no criticisms of the candidate.'

There followed a two-way discussion between Muldoon and several Executive members during which Auckland's Dr John Priestley dryly commented that 'Mr

Muldoon was the best communicator National had but in many areas the wrong message was being communicated.' Priestley subsequently, after Muldoon had left the meeting, moved and it was carried unanimously, that 'That Dominion Executive requests the National Party Caucus, as a matter of urgency, to review the style of government, its policies and the communication of policy to the electorate, to ensure that the National Party avoids what will otherwise be certain defeat in 1981.'[52] Significantly, in light of the discussion, the review of the party's leadership was not specified in the motion, but Gair, who was present, promised to 'reflect the concerns of the party as accurately and as frankly as possible at the next caucus meeting'.

Muldoon started to lobby individual MPs personally. On his arrival in Wellington, for example, he found Friedlander and Quigley talking in the parliamentary car park and brusquely ordered Friedlander to come to his office at 9 a.m. the next morning. As soon as Friedlander entered the room Muldoon asked him whom he intended to vote for. Friedlander replied that Muldoon was still fighting the 1975 election and that National would only win in 1981 with Talboys. Muldoon quietly replied that Friedlander was wrong; National could only win in 1981 with Muldoon. Other MPs who were thought likely to support the coup either did not do so or withdrew their support following Muldoon's return. The conspirators, for example, took for granted that the three Waikato dissident MPs, Waring, Minogue and Shearer, would support the coup against Muldoon. Shearer was overseas and Waring was delegated to brief him on his return. To her and the Colonels' horror, Shearer immediately went to see Muldoon to tell him about the plot and give him a list of the MPs who had agreed to support Talboys.[53]

Within forty-eight hours of Muldoon's return to Wellington half the MPs who had signed letters supporting a leadership change had changed their minds, including one of the Colonels, Bolger, who believed that without a declaration from Talboys and with core anti-Muldoon support dropping to about 15 MPs the coup was doomed to failure. His co-conspirators were shocked to hear on the radio early Thursday morning that, as one recalled, Bolger was 'no longer in the trenches with them'. McLay, Quigley, Gair and the 'sergeants' determined to press on to the bitter end, even after it was obvious Muldoon would win, because, as Kidd noted, they wanted to hurt him and teach him a lesson.[54]

Muldoon's opponents were desperate to obtain a decision from Talboys that he would contest the leadership. On the Wednesday evening Chapman was approached by a leader of the coup who assured him they still had sufficient signatures to change the leadership. The president was asked to contact Talboys in Germany to confirm his availability. Chapman did so but Talboys declined to accept formal nomination at the caucus on Thursday 16 October and said he would wait until his return to New Zealand the following week before making his decision. Earlier the same night Muldoon, MacIntyre and Thomson had jointly phoned Talboys in Bonn. It was a very unpleasant discussion with Talboys left feeling badly abused. More important, MacIntyre, previously a friend of Talboys, told the Deputy Prime Minister that because Talboys had not been prepared to front up to Muldoon and challenge him openly, even if he won a majority over Muldoon in caucus, MacIntyre would refuse to serve in a cabinet led by Talboys, and thereby ended their friendship.

The next morning, just before caucus met, Thomson phoned Talboys again and told him that Birch's count of caucus now had Muldoon leading Talboys by 33 votes to 12.[55] That was not strictly correct and the more accurate margin in Muldoon's favour was probably 33 to 17. The twelve listed as still openly opposed to Muldoon were Cox, Friedlander, Holland, Gair, Dail Jones, Kidd, McLean, McLay, Minogue, Quigley, Townshend and Waring. Five other MPs were listed at the end as undecided but probably anti-Muldoon: Bell, Gray, Luxton, Peters and Templeton. The last five to switch to Muldoon raising his support from 28 to 33, according to Birch, were Bolger, Austin, Elworthy, Highet and Wilkinson.[56] The conversation was recorded by Thomson, who asked Talboys, 'Please tell me where you stand on the leadership of the Party'.[57] The Deputy Prime Minister finally replied:

I think we would be better to stick where we are. I am concerned that if we make a change we would do ourselves more harm than good. If Caucus is determined to make a change I will not refuse. My attitude is I am his right hand and I support him and I will continue to support him. I am not there. But if Caucus is determined to make a change then I cannot refuse to serve. My advice to Caucus is that we should continue with what we have. It's basically about style and attitude. Let Rob find out for himself. If he's prepared to adjust let's stick with him.[58]

A Muldoon supporter, Don McKinnon, had placed the East Coast Bays by-election on the caucus agenda. McKinnon was furious with the result in the supposedly safe electorate adjoining his own marginal seat. He believed National had done nearly everything wrong during the by-election campaign and wanted the débâcle discussed fully. Such a discussion would obviously involve the leadership question and would take place with Muldoon present and Talboys absent. Muldoon admitted publicly that his leadership was under threat and when asked by journalists if he had the confidence of caucus conceded that he 'wouldn't go as far as to say that'. He believed, however, that Talboys would only consider the leadership if the caucus was determined to make a change.[59] Following the caucus meeting, at which, in the absence of an alternative, no challenge eventuated, Thomson, with Muldoon and MacIntyre present, again rang Talboys in Bonn and suggested that Talboys issue a press statement saying, 'I am Muldoon's right hand. I support him and I will continue to support him.' Muldoon added in his distinctive scrawl that Talboys should also state publicly that, 'I am not a candidate for the leadership. I have never been a candidate.'[60]

Sure of victory and seeing no need personally to lobby further, Muldoon left Wellington and over the weekend of 18–19 October relaxed in Auckland. On Saturday, after seeing individual constituents with problems and having morning tea with the Tamaki Young Nationals, he dined with a group of old friends at the home of Lance and Sharon Julian. Sunday was spent sailing with Julian on the Waitemata Harbour before in the evening launching a soccer coaching scheme and then returning to Wellington.[61]

On the Monday morning following Cabinet, however, Muldoon showed little intention of changing his style in response to the criticism or coup pressure. He commenced his post-cabinet press conference by refusing to recognise a question from Tom Scott and ordering a member of the Prime Minister's staff to 'Take him away will you'.[62] Muldoon then went on to tell the journalists that he had 'overwhelming support' from party members for his leadership, that the caucus 'flow is all one way', and that 'Talboys says we shouldn't make a change'.[63]

Talboys returned to New Zealand on Tuesday 21 October and was met at the airport by Thomson who the same day had notified Muldoon that, after reconsideration, 'it is Jim McLay's view BET [Talboys] should NOT contend against RDM [Muldoon]'.[64] Although Talboys talked with several members of caucus he found little will for change. Talboys told caucus at its meeting on 23 October that he would not contest the leadership. No one else spoke. It was obvious to Talboys that even if he had the support of a majority in caucus, and Gair and Quigley still thought he should test it, and even if he surprisingly did defeat Muldoon, the victory would not be worth winning. The cabinet and caucus would be badly split and Talboys believed that Muldoon in revenge might well destroy the party. Although he enjoyed his job, Talboys found his relationship with Muldoon and the working environment unpleasant and subsequently accepted without resistance Muldoon's terse suggestion in a private meeting that he should announce his retirement from Parliament at the next election.[65] The attempt to change the leadership was now well and truly over. Following the caucus meeting Muldoon and the other MPs went to a state luncheon to farewell Holyoake as Governor-General.

After the coup collapsed, Thomson, Birch, McKinnon, East and Rex Austin went to see Muldoon and suggested that in an effort to reunify caucus Muldoon should forgive and forget. Muldoon replied that he might be able to forgive but he would never forget. He then saw individually most of the conspirators. Friedlander, for example, was phoned and invited to have a drink with the Prime Minister. Muldoon asked Friedlander how old he was. When Friedlander replied, 'Thirty-five', Muldoon said, 'You've got time yet. You'll never become a Minister in my Government until you come to me and apologise and also say you have confidence in me as leader.' Friedlander never did, though subsequently Muldoon took him into cabinet.

At MacIntyre's suggestion, Cox, McLean, Kidd and Townshend went as a group to see Muldoon in his office. Muldoon accused them of being 'wet behind the ears', of having damaged the party and Government and of possibly costing National the next election. He suggested that they should publicly state that and apologise. The four told Muldoon that he had damaged the party more than they ever would and that it was the Prime Minister who would cost them the election. Robin Gray was then summoned to Muldoon's office. When he suggested that certain things needed to be changed if Muldoon's leadership was to be supported, the Prime Minister told him, 'I'm not going to negotiate with you'. Gray responded along the lines, 'Well, if that's so it's no good talking to you. Good day, Prime Minister' and walked out of the office. McLay and Bolger partly rehabilitated themselves in Muldoon's eyes by finally accepting their defeat, but Muldoon's deep-seated personal dislike of Gair and Quigley was aggravated by their refusal to concede anything.

One casualty outside caucus was Muldoon's Press Secretary, Gerry Symmans, who had always admired Talboys more than he did Muldoon. Symmans had resented Muldoon's insistence that he accompany the Prime Minister on his long overseas tour and on their return to New Zealand was not dismayed to discover the extent of Talboys' support. He told Hensley that, after discussing the coup with various MPs, he was convinced Muldoon was gone.[66] Despite the leadership crisis and the fact that the press was pushing Muldoon hard, Symmans took a week's holiday and left Wellington. Following the failure of the Colonels' Coup Muldoon sacked Symmans, who should during those difficult days have been a main barrier between the Prime Minister and the Press Gallery.

Talboys announced his intention to retire from politics on 7 November, a fortnight after his return to New Zealand.[67] Muldoon immediately let it be known that he wanted MacIntyre, whom almost everyone in the National Party caucus and organisational leadership regarded as a 'great guy', able, calm, with a dry sense of humour, as the new deputy, despite the Marginal Lands Board situation, and stated that publicly. He also declared that Quigley was unacceptable to him.[68] Gair and McLay ruled themselves out of the race for the deputy-leadership on the grounds that, like Muldoon, they were both Auckland MPs and threw their support to Quigley.[69] Bolger and Birch, who were close personal friends, both wanted to contest the position against MacIntyre and Quigley. Muldoon made it plain that if MacIntyre pulled out then Birch was the Prime Minister's preferred alternative.[70] It was decided not to take the vote on the deputy-leadership until the first caucus meeting in February 1981.

Over Christmas and the New Year holidays there was intense lobbying during which Quigley's position appeared to be strengthening. In the past National's deputy leaders had been contrasts to the leader and Quigley, as a relatively young farmer-lawyer representing a South Island rural electorate and holding right-wing ideological views, would certainly have complemented Muldoon's older, business, Auckland, urban, interventionist characteristics. But the differences were too great for either man to be comfortable with such a relationship, and the dogmatic personalities of both men made compromise even more difficult. Muldoon also did not want to see one of the most unrepentant leaders of the rebellion against him rewarded by being made his deputy and heir apparent. Muldoon lobbied very hard for MacIntyre as deputy leader. When a member of the National Executive at a meeting prior to the caucus vote exclaimed, 'If MacIntyre is elected deputy leader, I'll resign', Muldoon retorted, 'If he's not elected, I'll resign'.[71]

In mid-January Quigley announced that MacIntyre was no longer a serious contender and that the choice of deputy leader was between himself and Bolger.[72]

He also pointed out that the party was choosing a deputy leader, not a leader, and that a contest for the top position when Muldoon finally went would have to involve Gair and McLay. The following week Birch let it be known that he was supporting MacIntyre and would only contest the vacancy if MacIntyre withdrew his nomination.[73] Muldoon then stated publicly that caucus had to give him a deputy he could work with and that if MacIntyre chose to withdraw then Birch would become the front runner for the position.[74] He continued to lobby forcefully for MacIntyre arguing that Quigley was 'an extremist' and stressing that the selection of MacIntyre, who had no desire to become leader, would leave open the question of who would eventually succeed Muldoon in a way the election of Quigley or Bolger would not.[75] MacIntyre actually referred to himself as taking on a 'caretaker job'.[76]

At the caucus meeting on 4 February MacIntyre was elected deputy on the second ballot, defeating Quigley, albeit very narrowly, after Bolger was eliminated on the first ballot. Although the actual voting figures were not announced in caucus it was generally believed that on the first ballot Quigley led MacIntyre by 23 votes to 20 with Bolger trailing with 7 votes. On the second ballot MacIntyre, according to Quigley and his supporters, polled 26 votes to Quigley's 24, apparently picking up all but one of Bolger's 7 votes. McKinnon, however, who counted the votes and later took them home to burn, subsequently revealed that the margin was somewhat greater than most believed.[77] Muldoon clearly had asserted his authority and denied his critics even the consolation prize of deputy leader.

In a cabinet reshuffle following MacIntyre's election as deputy leader, Muldoon rewarded a number of other leading loyalists during the abortive Colonels' Coup. Birch and Cooper, previously ranked thirteenth and eighteenth in cabinet, were promoted to the fourth and eighth places on the Government front bench. Malcolm joined the cabinet as Minister of Immigration and Shearer as Minister for the Environment and Science and Technology. Quigley, in the light of his strong showing in the vote for deputy leader, was promoted from sixteenth to ninth in cabinet ranking, but lost the sensitive post of Associate Minister of Finance, adding Tourism to his Housing portfolio. Bolger, whose defection had been seen by his fellow conspirators as having sealed Muldoon's victory over the pro-Talboys faction, was promoted from ninth to fifth, thus becoming a front-bench minister. The promotion of Birch and Bolger ahead of Gair, Quigley and McLay was seen as giving them an edge in the future when Muldoon did retire or was replaced.[78]

CHAPTER 18

The Springbok Tour
and the 1981 Election

T HE DIVISION WITHIN THE NATIONAL PARTY OVER ITS leadership was soon submerged, however, by a much more widespread division within New Zealand society over a South African rugby tour of New Zealand. To many New Zealanders opposed to the Springbok tour the issue was simple. As Paul Reeves, Anglican Archbishop of New Zealand and later Governor-General, said, the choice was 'to give our support either to the victims of apartheid or to those who maintain that system'.[1] Reeves spoke for all the major churches in the country, which were united in their opposition to the tour.

Talboys genuinely and deeply detested apartheid and the South African Government and was determined as far as possible to seek the NZRFU's compliance in boycotting sporting contact with that country. When in early 1980 it became known that the NZRFU Council was considering inviting a Springbok rugby team to tour New Zealand in 1981, Talboys wrote a carefully and forcefully argued letter to the NZRFU chairman Ces Blazey.[2] Talboys noted that he was 'deeply concerned that a South African tour is even . . . considered' and that such 'sporting contact gives the appearance . . . of condoning the apartheid policies of the South African Government'. He warned that the Council's decision would determine how 'New Zealand is judged in the international arena'. Even though the decision would be made by the sporting body and not the Government, Talboys pleaded with the NZRFU to 'take fully into account the grave responsibilities it had under the Gleneagles Agreement'.

The NZRFU ignored the Government's request, the Gleneagles Agreement, and the widespread concern expressed by many others within and without New Zealand. On 15 September it announced that it had 'decided to issue an invitation for a merit-selected South African team to tour New Zealand in 1981'.[3] The NZRFU Council rejected any suggestion that this condoned apartheid and went on at some length to argue that in its opinion all South Africans, irrespective of race, now had equal opportunity to be selected for the Springbok team.

The announcement provoked widespread opposition within and without New Zealand. There were a series of critical statements by Commonwealth and African leaders. One of the first condemnations came from Ramphal, the Commonwealth Secretary-General, who expressed his 'revulsion' at New Zealand's 'contempt' for its obligations under the Gleneagles Agreement and for its alignment with and support of apartheid.[4]

Talboys immediately responded with a public statement that he personally had 'tried through the years to persuade New Zealanders how intense is the abhorrence of the indignity of apartheid in other Commonwealth countries' but believed the 'Government has done everything its power, short of coercion, to bring home to sporting organisations . . . their responsibility in terms of the agreement'. He believed the 'selfish decision' of the Rugby Union, not typical of that made by other sporting bodies, would have adverse consequences not just for rugby but for the whole of New Zealand.[5] The statement was sent to Ramphal with a long covering letter in which Talboys reiterated: 'In case there is any misunderstanding, I should like to underline to you that the New Zealand Government is opposed to the Rugby Union's decision, and that it made its opposition very clear to the Rugby Union before the decision was taken.'[6]

Talboys also sent another letter to Blazey in which he wrote: 'I am quite astonished that in more than four pages of statement [announcing the invitation to the Springboks] not a single mention has been made of the Gleneagles Agreement, to which I drew particular attention in my letter to you dated 9 April . . . That Agreement was a direct consequence of the All Blacks' tour of South Africa in 1976, the first casualty of which was the 1976 Olympic Games following the boycott by Africa and other countries.'[7] He argued that the decision went 'well beyond the administration of your amateur sport' and concluded that 'It remains my hope that your Council will reconsider its decision'.

When the Rugby Union remained adamant, the Supreme Council for Sport in Africa, among others, proposed that the New Zealand Government should refuse visas to the Springboks, as the Australian and Canadian Governments had done to Springbok sportsmen. Failure to do so might well adversely affect the 1982 Brisbane Commonwealth Games.[8] Talboys reacted more in sorrow than in anger at the African threat, noting that the New Zealand Government in general and he in particular had done their best to persuade the Rugby Union but that it was not New Zealand's tradition 'to abridge the freedoms of its citizens'. In a three-page statement, however, he did not specifically address the issue of denying visas to the Springboks.[9]

Talboys continued to pressure the Rugby Union's Council in the hope that as late as December, after the Council had reaffirmed its original decision, it would rescind the invitation. He pointed out that 'The Union may . . . deplore the intrusion of politics into sport and into the sport of Rugby in particular. But it cannot deny that the intrusion has taken place, in South Africa'. He stated, 'What the Rugby Union cannot do, in all conscience, is to behave as though it is free to act in the interests of Rugby alone when it knows that the action which it contemplates will have consequences for the whole nation . . . The inescapable reality is that . . . New Zealand and not just the Rugby Union will be judged . . .

the judgement will be harsh, should the tour proceed . . . For the sake of other New Zealand sportsmen, to avoid dividing and damaging our society, and for the sake of the international reputation of our country, I urge your Union to think again.'[10]

Others in the National Party shared Talboys' concern. Sir John Marshall publicly advocated that the government should stop the tour taking place and a motion that the Auckland Division of the National Party 'regrets the decision of the Rugby Union to invite the Springboks to tour New Zealand' was lost by 24 votes to 30 only after speakers against stressed the rights of individuals to make such decisions rather than governments.[11]

In May Muldoon sent Hensley to explain to the Rugby Union the consequences of their going ahead with the Springbok tour. When Hensley returned to the Prime Minister's ninth floor office in the Beehive and told Muldoon that the tour was going ahead, Muldoon sat for a long time with his head in his hands. Finally, in a sombre mood, which Hensley never again saw him in, the Prime Minister said through his hands without lifting his head, 'I can see nothing but trouble coming from this'.[12] Until that moment, Hensley believed, the Prime Minister genuinely hoped, and indeed expected, that the Rugby Union would make the right decision and call off the tour. There was no way, however, that Muldoon was going to break an election promise and like Kirk order the Rugby Union to do so.

A number of other Commonwealth governments contacted Muldoon during mid-1981 urging him to stop the tour and some such as Nigeria threatened New Zealand with boycotts and sanctions if he refused to act. Muldoon, who bitterly resented what he saw as the selective morality of some of those who criticised New Zealand while involved in or silently condoning tribal genocide in black African countries, responded fiercely pointing out that New Zealand respected the individual rights of its citizens and the rule of law. He told the Nigerians that their threat, for example, to have the Commonwealth finance ministers' conference removed from New Zealand was 'a gross insult to my government and my country' and if that happened New Zealand might well not only withdraw from the Gleneagles Agreement but would place on the Commonwealth meeting agenda an examination of member countries' domestic records in respecting human rights and racial harmony.[13]

Muldoon was somewhat more conciliatory, though no less direct, in his replies to Antigua, Lesotho, Jamaica, Tanzania, Zambia and Zimbabwe.[14] He told President Kaunda of Zambia, for example, that 'My Government has made it very clear to the New Zealand Rugby Union that we do not wish the tour to take place. Over many months we have told the Rugby Union, both publicly and privately, that the proposed tour will do immense damage to New Zealand and . . . the whole Commonwealth.' But he admitted to President Julius Nyerere of Tanzania that persuasion had not completely stopped New Zealand participation in the Moscow Olympics in 1980 and was clearly not sufficient to stop the rugby tour in 1981. While New Zealand 'would comply albeit reluctantly' with a Commonwealth trade embargo against South Africa, it was not prepared to 'interfere with the freedom of our sportsmen', he wrote to Prime Minister Mugabe of Zimbabwe.

Following discussion in cabinet and the Government caucus on 2 and 6 July, Muldoon made a last public appeal to the Rugby Union. On radio and television on the evening of 6 July Muldoon delivered what the *Auckland Star* called a rather 'baffling message'.[15] Most other observers agreed. After recalling that South Africans and New Zealanders had fought and died together in the Second World War, observing that many South Africans opposed apartheid, summarising police advice, and alluding to the Moscow Olympics, Muldoon explained why his government would not order the cancellation of the tour. He would compare the record of critics of New Zealand's race relations and human rights with New Zealand's record at the next CHOGM. He concluded by telling the Rugby Union to 'think well before you make your decision'. There was no direct request for cancellation.

Talboys was not the only one who believed that 'if Muldoon had taken a stronger view of Gleneagles he could have got the Rugby Union to call the tour off, but the way Muldoon interpreted and presented Gleneagles emphasised that the decision was theirs and gave the Rugby Union a get-out.'[16] Talboys admitted, however, that while 'Muldoon would never have made a statement asking the Rugby Union to call the tour off', had Muldoon wanted to do so 'caucus wouldn't have supported it and even I am not sure I could have said "Thou shalt not."' Muldoon's broadcast, however, was hardly an appeal calculated to persuade the Rugby Union to abandon the tour and on 10 July the union announced that it would go ahead. The Springboks arrived on 17 July and the first match was held on the 22 July at Gisborne.

The tour predictably divided New Zealand society and even many families. The conflict was about more than apartheid, sport or South Africa. It was also symbolically, on the one hand, a generational and attitudinal clash between the traditional, semi-colonial values and perspectives held by an older generation and especially those living in rural and small-town New Zealand and, on the other hand, the more liberal, internationalist, post-colonial values and perspectives towards which a younger generation and especially those living in urban Auckland and Wellington were moving. Much of the passion and commitment generated by the 1981 tour controversy was over what kind of New Zealand, not simply what kind of South African, society New Zealanders wanted. Not all those involved as participants or observers, at the time or subsequently, realised that, but Muldoon was one of those who did. As one HART leader has recalled, 'He clarified the issues and highlighted growing tensions and divisions in New Zealand society in such a way that helped ensure the issue was always centre-stage'.[17]

Games took place in siege conditions behind fences, barricades and police cordons.[18] Demonstrations and marches against the tour became larger and more difficult for the police to control and the second Springbok–Waikato game at Hamilton was abandoned on police advice after protesters occupied the playing field. While Muldoon made it plain that the tour would not be cancelled by his Government for political reasons, he also agreed that it could not go ahead if the police could not control the situation. Police Commissioner Walton, who had looked at civil disturbances elsewhere in the world, including Britain, believed that the police could either confront the protesters in a violent way or could retreat to a minimalist position and attempt to defuse the situation. Initially, Walton chose to protect rather than contain the demonstrators and to keep protesters and rugby supporters apart. The neutrality of the police was shown at the Springbok–Waikato game at Hamilton where the police did not stop demonstrators breaching an unguarded perimeter fence and where once about 150 protesters occupied the playing field, the police did not remove them but protected them from the enraged crowd of some 28,000 rugby supporters.

Muldoon, who was overseas visiting the United States and Italy and attending the wedding of the Prince of Wales, was disturbed when Hensley rang to tell him about the cancellation of the Waikato–Springbok game at Hamilton. When Hensley commented that he thought that Walton had made a wise and courageous decision to call off the match, Muldoon responded angrily, 'You do, do you? Well, I don't!'[19] Advised that cabinet in his absence was wavering about the continuation of the tour Muldoon let it be known that in his opinion the issue now at stake was the rule of law and order and that the tour must go ahead or the demonstrators' illegal tactics would have succeeded.

On Tuesday 4 August Muldoon convened and chaired a meeting in Parliament Buildings. The meeting, proposed by Dr R. Moodie and the NZ Police Association, lasted for two hours and was attended by Muldoon, MacIntyre and Couch representing the Government and representatives of the NZ Police Association, HART (Halt All Racist Tours), CARE (Citizens' Association for Racial Equality), SPIR (Stop Politics in Rugby), and the NZRFU; the Race Relations Conciliator, Hiwi Tauroa; Commissioner Walton and Deputy Commissioner K. O. Thompson of the Police; and officials from the Prime Minister's and Cabinet Offices.[20]

Muldoon commenced by stating the objective of the meeting, which was 'to diminish the tension and conflict aroused by the Springbok tour'. He noted that it would be difficult to keep the meeting's proceedings confidential because those present would have to consult their organisations. He asked people to 'speak out' and to avoid euphemisms such as 'postponing' when people really meant 'cancellation'. He then asked the NZRFU chairman to comment on any circumstances in which the tour could be cancelled. Blazey replied that the NZRFU only the previous week had decided the tour should proceed and that any shortening of the tour would also be rejected. Muldoon commented that 'that was not very helpful'. A spokesman for HART then said that he could not commit his organisation to any compromise, while representatives of the pro-tour lobby group SPIR argued that other countries including Canada and Australia still had sporting contacts with South Africa and that it was hypocritical to boycott sport but not trade. This led to a series of testy exchanges between Muldoon and the SPIR representatives. When HART said it was 'committed to campaign against the tour but it did not want confrontation with the Police', Muldoon said that 'HART could do as it wished' – provided the law was obeyed and respected: 'that was the only constraint'. In his opinion, 'New Zealand was caught in a dilemma where there were relatively large numbers at either extreme'. The meeting then discussed a paper prepared by Tauroa, which proposed the cancellation of the last test in Auckland as a symbolic gesture of New Zealand's opposition to apartheid and that on that day anti-apartheid rather than anti-tour marches be organised throughout New Zealand. At all other games still left in the tour, time should be set aside for an anti-apartheid and anti-tour speaker to address the crowd. The NZRFU should also state publicly that it would no longer support rugby exchanges with South Africa until significant changes had been made to South Africa's apartheid laws. Blazey and HART's spokesman, Michael Law, responded that their organisations would consider Tauroa's proposals but doubted whether they would be acceptable. Muldoon replied that 'part of the art of leadership was to persuade one's supporters that they were sometimes wrong . . . otherwise a leader would only be pushed along by those behind'. He still hoped there could be found 'a basis for reconciliation'.

The following day, 5 August, a demonstration in Auckland saw an escalation of violence. The ad hoc Cabinet Committee on Springbok Tour: Law and Order (Muldoon, MacIntyre, Thomson, Couch and McLay) met with Commissioner Walton.[21] It was reported that some protesters had been armed with pick handles and iron bars and that there had also been, a fortnight before, an unlawful attempt to take an aircraft to use in protest against a tour match in Gisborne. It was obvious that the protest movement, especially in the larger cities such as Wellington and Auckland, was stretching police resources to prevent the concentration of the available police at the major protest venues. Although the Christchurch and Wellington City Councils wanted the first and second rugby test matches in those cities called off, the Commissioner of Police advised the committee that law and order could be maintained without breaching the Government's instruction that games should be cancelled if 'it is considered the police are using too much force to maintain order, even though such force is within the law'.[22] It was decided in the light of a clearly deteriorating situation that up to 100 former members of the police be sworn in for support duties; that up to 1000 special constables be recruited from Civil Defence, police and Territorial Army units; and that police cadets be sworn in as temporary constables.

Muldoon later claimed that he believed in 1980 and 1981 that it was 'in the interests of New Zealand as a whole that the tour should not proceed and I made this view clear to the Rugby Union. It is not true to suggest, as some commentators and political opponents have done, that I was insincere in my public opposition to the tour. It was necessary, however, for me to be consistent with the platform on which we campaigned in 1975 and I made it clear to the Rugby Union and to the public that the National Government would not direct the Rugby Union to cancel the 1981 tour as Norman Kirk had done in 1973.'[23]

Not all Muldoon's National caucus colleagues, however, believed he had done all he could to stop the tour, or had ever really intended to do so. Waring, for example, who claimed that she was one of only three National MPs – the others were Talboys and Malcolm – who were totally opposed to the Springbok tour from the very start, believed that the Prime Minister, was a 'man of his times' whose 'own sentiments were anti-boycott' and who was following a 'calculating and unscrupulous . . . marginal [seats] retention strategy'.[24] Within the upper levels of the National Party organisation there were also a number of opponents of the Springbok tour who wished Muldoon had taken a stronger stand against it. They included Wood, Leay, Murray McCully and Julian Watts.[25]

Others who were usually critical of Muldoon such as Beetham and Minogue believed that he had no option but to allow the tour to continue.[26] Even with the advantage of hindsight, Social Credit's leader could not see how Muldoon could have acted differently and been true to both himself and what he believed the majority of New Zealanders expected him to do, and Beetham gave Muldoon his total support on the issue. Minogue also agreed with Muldoon that divergent points of view had to be tolerated in a democracy and people had to have the liberty to do what they liked provided they remained within the law. It was very dangerous for any group to be able to impose its intellectual, moral or spiritual views on others. In Minogue's opinion Muldoon had to uphold the democratic tradition and not try to advance democracy in South Africa by curtailing or compromising it in New Zealand. Minogue, however, believed Muldoon 'failed abysmally' to convey the essence of the argument and simply appeared as an 'insensitive, dictatorial character pandering to rugby rednecks'. As a result the Springbok tour did incredible damage to both New Zealand and to the National Party.

In a press interview given in March 1981 Muldoon estimated that 'public opinion was fairly firmly against' the tour but that much of that opposition was because people feared demonstrations and violence, not because they were strongly opposed to sporting contacts with South Africa.[27] Indeed, some people thought that sporting contacts would help break down apartheid more effectively than a boycott. The Gleneagles Agreement, however, took a contrary view and the combination of New Zealanders who opposed the tour on principle and those who feared division and disruption did constitute, in Muldoon's opinion, a majority who did not want the Springboks to come to New Zealand. In response to a question by a journalist as to his personal views, Muldoon responded, 'I thought I had made that clear. You have asked me that question week after week at my press conferences, and I have said I don't want them to come. How many more times do I have to say it?' Pressed as to whether he thought support for the tour would translate into votes for National at the 1981 election Muldoon said he did not and that 'whatever happens in the context of the Springbok tour is more likely than not to damage the chances of the Government'.[28]

Privately, Muldoon also told his party's Dominion Executive that 'the Government could not win on the Springbok issue'.[29] That assessment was confirmed by party officials and professional advisers. Tremewan, the Auckland divisional director, for example, told Muldoon, 'The most confusing and alarming factor is the spin-off from the Tour, CHOGM, etc. It seems that we are in trouble with our own natural constituency . . . in East Coast Bays, Tamaki, Remuera and Epsom'. He added, 'the relatively affluent middle class . . . hated the sight of the

Police confronting demonstrators and they worry deeply when we are portrayed in the press as being at loggerheads with the Black Commonwealth'.[30] Fred Dobbs, like Tremewan another of Muldoon's personal friends, and National's publicity consultant, warned Muldoon that 'The Springbok issue remains an unhappy intrusion which undoubtedly is costing points. Whilst I would like to believe your philosophical statements, I think the majority of people would want it played in Antarctica. The posture of protecting our individual rights is like God Defend New Zealand – we know the words, what do they mean?'[31]

Despite the widespread and understandable public perception that he personally favoured the Springbok tour, Muldoon frequently stated that he included himself among the 54 per cent of New Zealanders who according to polls opposed the tour;[32] that 'I wish that the tour had not taken place';[33] that 'I said that the Springbok tour would be a disaster. I believe I was right';[34] and that the Government 'repeatedly advised the Rugby Union of . . . the damage it would cause New Zealand'.[35]

As the tour progressed and some of the protests became more disorderly, Muldoon and other senior National politicians tried with some success to shift the debate onto the law and order issue. Muldoon, for example 'made it clear that he considered the issue was no longer one of apartheid but one of law and order',[36] while MacIntyre stated after the cancellation of the game at Hamilton that the protesters' 'undemocratic, violent and unlawful methods' meant that 'it is no longer a question of "pro-tour" or "anti-tour". The issue is now one of law and order.'[37] Because of the involvement of the Workers' Communist League in Wellington and the Progressive Youth Movement and Maori radicals in Auckland, Muldoon was able to attack 'members of subversive organisations' who were using the Springbok tour to polarise New Zealand politically and in August issued a statement to that effect 'prepared by the Security Intelligence Service'.[38]

The Security Intelligence Service also analysed the 'extent of subversive participation in the protest movement' noting that members of the Socialist Unity Party 'have maintained a low profile' but other 'hard-liners, often with little in common with each other, have sought by violent confrontation with the Police to demonstrate "the oppressive forces at work in the fascist, capitalist State". In doing so they have clearly outdistanced themselves from the underlying ethic behind the movement itself.'[39]

Following the tour Muldoon convened a meeting of interested parties at Parliament Buildings on 23 September. HART declined to attend.[40] During a lengthy discussion, Muldoon stated that 'whereas sport and politics might have been separate at one time the 1977 Gleneagles agreement had changed that'. He also recognised that 'Africans had very deep feelings about apartheid in South Africa . . . partly because they saw the Blacks in South Africa as being similar to themselves and partly because of their own colonial past and their belief that a majority was being oppressed by a minority'. He was concerned about New Zealand's international image but 'the problem now was how to take a stand against apartheid which would not infringe individual rights' in New Zealand.

Even though it was election year and there were major domestic issues causing serious and ongoing concern, Muldoon still made four overseas trips during 1981. From 14 to 26 April he was in Japan and Korea. In Japan, where he was accompanied by his Deputy Prime Minister MacIntyre, he had talks with Emperor Hirohito and Prime Minister Suzuki and various meetings with Japanese businessmen, bankers and officials. He also visited many centres outside Tokyo. In Korea, Muldoon had meetings with President Chun Doo and Prime Minister Duck-Woo Nam and visited Panmunjom, where the armistice had been signed, and the Hyundai motor company and shipyards.

In late July he spent a week in Washington DC and London, lunching and meeting with President Ronald Reagan and Secretary of the Treasury Donald Regan and hosting a dinner at the New Zealand Embassy attended by Vice-President George Bush, before attending the wedding of Prince Charles and Lady Diana Spencer at St Paul's Cathedral. While in London Muldoon also met Commonwealth Secretary-General Ramphal and Foreign Secretary David Owen and listened to a speech by Thatcher in the House of Commons on the British economy.

In August Muldoon was at the South Pacific Forum in Vanuatu and in late September and early October, shortly before the 1981 election, attended the CHOGM in Melbourne. Muldoon hosted Lee Kuan Yew of Singapore in New Zealand for ten days before flying with him to the CHOGM meeting in Melbourne in September 1981. From the first, Muldoon was, according to one senior adviser, 'in battle order'.[41] He started by 'tearing a strip' off Laurie Francis, New Zealand's High Commissioner to Australia and a former chairman of the National Party's Waikato Division. Tense and scratchy, Muldoon was not in a mood to be pleasant or build bridges with anyone. It was inevitable that New Zealand was going to be criticised over the Springbok tour and Muldoon wanted to head off the criticism by questioning aggressively his critics' record on race relations and human rights. Muldoon was under constant pressure from other Commonwealth leaders and from the press and had brought with him Fred Dobbs, who was his personal media adviser, his friend, and the National Party's long-time public relations consultant. Muldoon met journalists at frequent press conferences throughout the CHOGM and also addressed 200 people at a National Press Club gathering. He gave individual interviews to the Canadian Broadcasting Commission, ABC television and radio, the Melbourne *Age*, the Australian *Truth*, and a representative of South African newspapers. He lunched privately with Thatcher and also held another meeting with Thatcher, Fraser and Trudeau.

Taking a very aggressive stance, Muldoon refused to concede that the New Zealand government could have done more to implement the Gleneagles Agreement and savagely abused New Zealand's critics such as Mugabe, who labelled Muldoon 'a racist'.[42] He attacked 'empty agreements' and 'hypocrisy' but also apologised somewhat half-heartedly to Mugabe for saying that the African leader would have difficulty understanding New Zealand's position on the tour because he had 'been in the jungle shooting people.'[43] He claimed that throughout the dispute New Zealand had not breached Gleneagles and had tried to persuade the Rugby Union to abandon the tour. New Zealand, however, as he had earlier pointed out, observed the liberty of the individual 'regardless of race, colour, creed or political belief. I ask each of you if you can honestly say the same about your country. If you cannot, then you are not qualified to sit in judgement on my country.'[44] Much of Muldoon's rhetoric was interpreted as domestic electioneering rather than as a serious attempt at dialogue with New Zealand's many critics within the Commonwealth.

Before leaving early on the last day of CHOGM, Muldoon sent a letter to the chairman, Fraser, setting out New Zealand's position on Gleneagles and on the tour in an uncompromising way; suggesting that the records should show that New Zealand would withdraw from the Gleneagles Agreement if sporting boycotts continued against New Zealand as a result of its sporting contacts with South Africa; and asking for the letter to be read into the minutes. When Hensley handed the letter to Fraser, the Australian Prime Minister threw the letter down and told Hensley that there was no way he was going to read it into the minutes. Fraser and Trudeau led the opposition to Muldoon's proposal and the CHOGM meeting later formally rejected the letter and its inclusion in the communiqué.[45]

Because the Queen was attending the Melbourne CHOGM it had been decided that she would make a short visit to New Zealand from 12 to 20 October, before returning to Britain. The timing was not really suitable coming just before a New Zealand election and being open to interpretation as an election ploy by Muldoon. The timing, however, could have been worse. Muldoon had persuaded the Australian Prime Minister Fraser, who hosted CHOGM, to move the dates for CHOGM forward so that the Queen did not in fact arrive in New Zealand at the start of the election campaign proper, which would have been even more embarrassing to her than it undoubtedly was anyway.[46] Even so both the British Government and Buckingham Palace were worried that the visit would be taking place between the disastrous Springbok tour and what would clearly be an acrimonious election campaign and the Secretary to Cabinet had to reassure the Palace that there would be no trouble and that Muldoon was not simply using the Royal visitors for party political purposes.[47] Cynics still, however, accused Muldoon of using two tours – the Springbok tour of August–September and the Royal tour of October – to try to win the November election.

At the start of the 1981 election campaign Waring collapsed and was admitted to hospital where for five days she was allowed no calls or visitors. Muldoon came to Hamilton to open his campaign on 2 November and unexpectedly and on his own turned up at Waring's bedside. He confided in her his doubts about winning but assured her that her seat was safe and that she should not worry but take as long as she liked to recuperate. Waring recalled that he was 'very human', showed 'quite genuine concern', and that there was absolutely no suggestion that he was glad his controversial young anti-tour colleague was 'out of the way'.[48]

National should not have won the 1981 election and indeed the title of a study published just before – *Election '81: An End to Muldoonism?* – suggested that it would not.[49] Inflation and unemployment were both high; there was a serious balance of payments deficit; the Springbok tour had divided the nation bitterly and while it might have helped the Government retain some rural and small town seats it certainly cost National urban and suburban marginal seats; and the 'Think Big' growth strategy, which National identified as the central issue of its campaign, was very much a two-edged sword. But Muldoon was still a very effective campaigner on both public platform and more importantly television and in the four weeks of the campaign addressed twenty-eight public meetings. Again and again he told those audiences, and through press reports of those meetings the wider electorate, that New Zealand had in 1975 been heading towards bankruptcy. It had been 'spending three dollars abroad for every two that we are earning' and inflation had been 15.7 per cent. After 1978 the situation had been worsened by the second oil shock. Muldoon claimed that increases in exports and reduction in imports had by 1981 largely stabilised the situation but that only National's longer term economic growth strategy could give New Zealand economic security.[50] Wherever Muldoon went there appeared to be protesters, and he never sought to appease them or even ignore them but went out of his way to taunt them.

Two days before the 1981 election Muldoon confided in Hensley that National might well lose the election but that he was fatalistic about the prospect.[51] Leay, the National Party's Director-General, alone among National's head office personnel was reasonably optimistic about the likely result, telling Muldoon a few days before the poll that National would get 42 per cent of the vote or better to Labour's 35–37 per cent and Social Credit's 20 per cent.[52] He believed that, because during this campaign there was 'No Big Norm, No Abortion Issue, No Moyle Affair, No Freezing Works Settlement', National would double its majority, winning back Rangitikei and East Coast Bays from Social Credit and Hastings, Taupo, and Western Hutt from Labour. He was correct only in his prediction about Taupo, which National's Roger McClay finally wrested from Labour with a majority of 14 votes. Overall, National's share of the vote dropped a further percentage point from 40 in 1978 to 39 in 1981. National lost four seats – Miramar, Wellington Central, Kapiti and Hunua. For the second election in a row, Rowling and the Labour Party gained more votes than Muldoon and National but had to accept the bitter reality that New Zealand's first-past-the-post electoral system and the distribution of votes throughout the country had given them fewer seats in Parliament. Social Credit with a fifth of the total vote was even more discriminated against, winning only 2 out of 92 seats. Devastated in the major cities, National only held office by retaining the marginal provincial towns – New Plymouth, Gisborne, Whangarei, Invercargill and Taupo – largely because of the growth strategy and the Springbok tour. If fewer than 500 voters had changed their minds in any two of six seats, Labour might have become the Government.

One of the new MPs was John Banks who had won the Whangarei seat. Although Banks was a free marketeer who was immediately identified as a kindred spirit by another new MP, Ruth Richardson, Banks admired Muldoon and was indebted to him. Ideologically Banks might have been more with Richardson than with Muldoon, but emotionally he had a deep loyalty to the Prime Minister. Banks's father was a well-known criminal and rumours concerning Banks had led to Chapman and Leay excluding him from consideration for Onehunga in 1978. When told of this by two Auckland officials, Clem Simich and Chris Horton, Banks accepted their advice to contact Muldoon after failing to convince Chapman and Leay, who had continued their opposition even after Banks's accountant had detailed his assets and income and Banks had forwarded information from the Wanganui police computer obtained from the Privacy Commissioner and references from senior police officers. Muldoon asked Leay, 'What evidence is there that this apple has fallen close to the tree?' When Leay replied, 'None', Muldoon ordered that Banks should not be judged by his parents but by his own character and achievements. Banks subsequently was shortlisted and became candidate for Roskill at the 1978 election before winning Whangarei in 1981.[53]

At a Dominion Executive meeting ten days after the election, Chapman commented that 'while National could not claim a victory at this stage, it had not lost' largely because of 'a tremendous result' in the Waikato Division.[54] Muldoon blamed the media for the poor result and suggested that by 1984 'the growth strategy would be a lot more visible'. After recounts, National, with 47 seats in the new Parliament to Labour's 43 and Social Credit's 2, clung to office with a majority of one after appointing the Speaker.

At first, however, it had appeared as if the two Social Credit MPs, Beetham and Knapp, might hold the balance of power, or as they called it 'the balance of responsibility', in the new Parliament. Immediately after the elections, Millen, as Clerk of the Executive Council and a link between Cabinet and the Governor-General, decided that he should examine what would happen in the event of a hung Parliament in which Beetham and Knapp held the balance of power.[55] Millen approached the Governor-General, Sir David Beattie, and others and then suggested to Beetham that he postpone a planned holiday in Fiji for a fortnight. Beetham unfortunately went straight to the press and said that Millen had said he had a good chance of holding the balance of power. Muldoon subsequently summoned Millen and accused him of exceeding his authority, and the exchange was so heated that Millen stormed out of Muldoon's office.

Beetham had said before the election that if Social Credit MPs held the balance after it they would not be part of a coalition government but would support a minority government (whichever major party took office) on finance or confidence motions, and then vote independently on each other piece of legislation. Muldoon did not contact Beetham after the election but Rowling did. He had already met secretly with Beetham several times before the election to discuss the possibility of an electoral alliance, despite public opposition from his deputy Bob Tizard. Now he phoned Beetham, who suggested that talks about Social Credit supporting a Labour minority government should wait until the final results were announced.[56] In the event the Muldoon National Government survived for a third term.

After the election Muldoon enjoyed a number of informal dinner parties with close colleagues and friends. He hosted one for Holyoake, Comber, Brill and Bill

Young and their wives at Vogel House on Tuesday 15 December; was a guest of Des Dalgety, together with the Birches and Bolgers, on Wednesday 16 December; and dined with the Eisenhofers on Friday 18 December. The 15 December dinner was a 'thank you' to Comber, Brill and Young who had all lost their seats as Muldoon had predicted to them that they were likely to do, partly at least because of the Government's stand on the Springbok tour.[57]

CHAPTER 19

Third World Debt,
the Clyde Dam,
the Quigley Affair, and
Bob Jones's New Zealand Party

I N CHOOSING NEW MINISTERS AFTER THE 1981 ELECTION,
Muldoon rewarded two MPs who had remained loyal to him during the
Colonels' Coup – Falloon and Talbot – but also selected Elworthy, who had
initially supported Talboys. The Prime Minister ignored the abilities of the most
recalcitrant of his younger backbench critics, McLean, Cox, Gray, Kidd and
Townshend, all of whom, admittedly, had only been in Parliament for three years.
Waring was a more controversial omission, having a much stronger claim for
promotion in terms of ability, her six years in Parliament, her experience chairing
the Public Expenditure Committee, and her gender. Muldoon, however, had
doubts about her independent and controversial stance on key issues and her probable unwillingness to conform to the doctrine of collective cabinet responsibility.

The retirement of Talboys left a vacuum in Foreign Affairs and Trade. Muldoon
considered three people for the post: Templeton, who desperately wanted it but
whom Muldoon chose to keep in charge of Industries and Commerce; Gair, who
like Templeton, in Muldoon's opinion, would have done the foreign affairs task
well but might have been less effective in trade; and Cooper.[1] The choice of Cooper,
a man with a warm, easygoing personality and a dry wit but with no background
or even apparent interest in foreign affairs and overseas trade, came as a surprise to
everyone. Cooper discovered that he was the new Minister of Foreign Affairs and
Overseas Trade when he arrived in Wellington and found a message to call into
Muldoon's office. Muldoon, who had already seen all his other ministers, told
Cooper, 'I've only got two portfolios left, Foreign Affairs and Overseas Trade. I
want you to have them.' Cooper was astounded. Muldoon, however, made it plain
to Cooper that he was getting the job because Muldoon wanted someone with 'a
street-smart approach', who 'wouldn't get carried away with gilt and chandeliers',

and would not 'see New Zealand or himself as a Don Quixote making Nicaragua or South Africa of greater priority than facilitating the expansion of New Zealand's overseas trade.'[2] Cooper's strong stance on keeping politics and sport separate also commended him to Muldoon. In practice Cooper concentrated largely on the trade side of his portfolio while Muldoon in effect added the foreign affairs side to his already immense workload as Prime Minister, Finance Minister and, from time to time, de facto a second Minister of Labour.

The ranking of ministers was significant. Muldoon's promotion of McLay from seventeenth before the election to ninth after it indicated that McLay was being rehabilitated after the Colonels' Coup and could well be a rival in future to more established ministers such as Birch, Bolger, Gair and Quigley as a potential successor to Muldoon.

As was usual the new cabinet at its first meeting after the election considered a number of briefing papers prepared for the incoming Government.[3] The meeting commenced with a discussion of Closer Economic Relations (CER) with Australia, which would supersede the New Zealand Australia Free Trade Agreement (NAFTA). The central objective of CER was the 'gradual and progressive liberalisation of trade across the Tasman on all goods produced in either country on a basis that would bring benefits to both countries.'[4] It was envisaged that the current import base would increase by 10 per cent in real terms every year and would evolve beyond visible trade to other aspects of the economic relationship.

Cabinet then turned its attention to the current economic situation and noted that during 1981 there had been 'a significant recovery in economic activity with rising production and increased real expenditure but little change in the employment situation'.[5] Unfortunately, also, so cabinet was told, 'export prospects have deteriorated and this, together with a rise in import volumes is leading to a deterioration in the balance of payments. A large Government budget deficit and rapid growth in Private Sector Credit are contributing to an expansion in money supply with potentially serious effects in price and wage inflation.'[6] The forecast was for unemployment and the balance of payments situations to deteriorate further during 1982; for there to be little real economic growth; for prices and costs to continue to rise between 15 and 20 per cent; and for further entrenchment of the wage–price spiral. The Government's budget deficit over the next two years would probably be in the vicinity of $2500 million annually. There was little discussion of the report though Muldoon observed that demand for the New Zealand dollar was being weakened by the fear of devaluation. The current account deficit in New Zealand's overseas exchange transactions had gone from $1067 million in 1975 to $488 million in 1978 but by 1981 was again up to $724 million and officials predicted it would be well over $1000 million in 1982 and 1983.[7]

Muldoon's determination to increase New Zealand exports even went as far as having cabinet approve at its first post-election meeting an export programme grant of $366,691 to Red Seal Laboratories, a firm owned by the family of the Labour MP Roger Douglas, to cover 64 per cent of the expenditure on a campaign to promote its health products in Australia.[8] Cabinet at its first meeting also approved the electrification of the North Island Main Trunk railway line between Hamilton and Palmerston North at an estimated cost of $141.8 million over the following six years[9] and received an interim report from the Task Force on Tax Reform.[10] That report suggested 'a significant restructuring of personal income tax rates' for middle-income earners. The shortfall would be 'made up by increasing the role of indirect taxes'. Muldoon expressed his disappointment in the report and felt it was 'not helpful', which provoked disagreement from Quigley.[11]

Muldoon was frequently overseas during 1982 and 1983. In May 1982, for example, he spent three weeks in France, Britain and Ireland. He chaired an OECD meeting in Paris; visited Dublin for discussions with Ireland's Prime Minister Charles Haughey; and had three days of discussions in London with British businessmen, bankers and politicians, the Queen, and Thatcher. A few weeks before he arrived in London, war had broken out between Britain and Argentina over the latter's invasion of the Falkland Islands. Foreign Affairs thought that the British were being silly over the Falklands and that New Zealand should not become involved. When they told Muldoon this at a briefing the Foreign Affairs officials were 'savaged' by the Prime Minister, who told them that they did not appreciate the importance of 'keeping the British on side' if New Zealand was to continue having access to the European Community for New Zealand's butter.[12] New Zealand had to be seen to be supporting the British although Muldoon agreed that New Zealand should not become involved in the fighting.

Muldoon summoned the Argentinian ambassador to New Zealand to break off diplomatic relations but the protest was initially something of a farce. The Prime Minister commenced his statement by assuring the ambassador that he should not take his remarks personally, at which time it was discovered that the ambassador did not speak English. There was an embarrassed ten minutes of silence in the Prime Minister's office while Muldoon's staff rang Foreign Affairs and asked them to send a Spanish-speaking official to translate. When the translator arrived Muldoon proceeded to humiliate the ambassador by haranguing him aggressively about his country's actions.

Following the sinking of HMS *Sheffield*, Muldoon, after considering and rejecting the possible deployment of the SAS or Orion aircraft, asked cabinet to approve the deployment of a New Zealand frigate to assist the British by freeing up one of their warships in the Indian Ocean. Muldoon admitted that 'it was not a great gesture' but its announcement during his visit to London certainly earned him favourable publicity and Thatcher's heartfelt thanks. There can be no doubt that Muldoon genuinely wanted to align New Zealand with Britain over the Falklands issue, but he was also aware that by supporting Thatcher and Britain at a low point in the conflict he would cement his relationship with Thatcher and give New Zealand credit with the British Government and public that could be useful in future negotiations with the European Community over continued access for New Zealand primary exports.

In the second half of 1983 Muldoon made another five overseas trips which removed him from Wellington for about eight of the last twenty-four weeks. In

June he was in Yugoslavia and Greece attending a UN Conference on Trade and Development and holding talks with the prime ministers of both countries. In August he chaired the South Pacific Forum in Sydney. In late September and early October he attended the Commonwealth finance ministers' conference in Trinidad; addressed an IMF and World Bank joint annual meeting in Washington DC; and delivered speeches to the UN General Assembly and the Foreign Relations Council in New York and to the School of Government at Harvard University. In November he visited Perth, Adelaide and Melbourne, giving addresses to businessmen in each city. Later in November he travelled to a Commonwealth Heads of Government meeting in New Delhi.

While overseas Muldoon worked hard but he also found time to enjoy himself. During his visits to Europe, for example, he travelled down the Rhine participating in the centennial celebrations of Mueller-Thurgau wine; watched an Arsenal-Southampton soccer match; attended a performance of *Hobson's Choice* at the Theatre Royal; went to the Chelsea Flower Show; and visited a cousin in Suffolk. While in New York he spent a Friday night at a Broadway show, *La Cage aux Folles*; spent Saturday cruising the Hudson River, visiting Central Park and, at the Metropolitan Opera, listening to Joan Sutherland in Donizetti's *Daughter of the Regiment*; and spent Sunday morning in the Botanical Gardens and the afternoon at a gridiron football game. Muldoon while travelling overseas could and did laugh at himself and was even prepared to make himself a spectacle to get a laugh from his travelling companions. On one occasion when visiting Kiribati on the *Monowai* Muldoon and those with him went for a swim. To everyone's surprise an 'extraordinary vision appeared in huge blue shorts and an enormous Mexican hat.' It was the Prime Minister in mischievous mood.[13] Most of the time, however, Muldoon was neither sightseeing nor joking. Increasingly, while overseas he took every opportunity to draw attention to what he argued was a global economic crisis – the danger to the international monetary system and the world economy of Third World debt.[14]

In 1944 representatives of 44 countries had met at Bretton Woods, in New Hampshire, to design a new monetary system for the post-war era. There was agreement that fixed exchange rates were desirable and that competitive devaluation of currencies was senseless. The International Monetary Fund (IMF) was established to maintain order in the international monetary system and a World Bank was created to promote general economic development. All countries that joined the IMF fixed their exchange rates to the US dollar, which in turn was convertible to gold at a price of US$35 per ounce. Currencies could not be devalued by more than 10 per cent without IMF approval. The World Bank, or as it was officially known the International Bank for Reconstruction and Development (IBRD), concentrated its lending to less developed nations for major public-sector projects.

In the late 1960s, President Johnson increased US government spending to finance both the Vietnam War and at home his 'war against poverty' welfare programmes. The expenditure was balanced not by tax increases but by a substantial and inflationary increase in the money supply, which led to a deterioration in the US trade balance and speculative pressure against the US dollar. In August 1971 President Nixon announced that the US dollar was no longer convertible into gold. Subsequently the US dollar was devalued by about 8 per cent against foreign currencies and the fixed exchange-rate system was replaced by floating exchange rates that were formalised at an IMF meeting in Jamaica in January 1976. Exchange rates became much more volatile and less predictable and depreciation in a currency appeared to lead to imported inflation rather than to a boost in exports, especially where the country concerned was exporting goods for which there was a limited demand.

Muldoon had first become interested in the international economic order during the debate in 1961 over whether or not New Zealand should join the IMF and the World Bank.[15] He was very concerned at that time about the possible loss of sovereignty in economic matters and decided initially to cross the floor and vote with the Labour Opposition against the legislation. Lake, the Minister of Finance, had caucus briefed by Treasury officials and Muldoon found himself alone in continuing to oppose membership. He then spent considerable time in the library studying the topic. Finally, although still worried about the sovereignty aspect, he was convinced that New Zealand might need access to the Bank's funds in a few years time and so reluctantly, the night before the Bill was introduced, changed his mind and decided to support it. Because of the background work he had done Muldoon was able to take an informed and reasonably prominent role in the subsequent debates.

His interest grew when from 1967 as Minister of Finance he started to attend international economic conferences, including meetings of the Governors of the IMF. In 1976, at a meeting of IMF Governors in Manila, Muldoon spoke for the first time on the subject of Third World debt which thereafter was to become almost an obsession to him. The quintupling of oil prices in 1973 led to a large transfer of income from oil-importing to oil-exporting countries. The former countries were forced to cut imports, increase exports and often borrow, while the oil-rich countries not only spent on imports but also invested overseas in shares and property. When the second oil shock doubled prices between 1979 and 1980, the US Federal Reserve drastically tightened monetary policy. This sent interest rates soaring throughout the world. In order to service the rising debt repayments, developing countries in particular were forced to expand exports even further to generate foreign exchange and as a result the primary commodities markets became chronically oversupplied. Prices slumped and the problem was exacerbated by a continued rise in the price of manufactured imports. New Zealand found itself in a similar situation to most of the developing countries and primary product exporters.

Muldoon believed that the IMF's hard-line monetarist policies were likely to be counter-productive. He thought that that if the IMF was too tough in enforcing austerity on Third World countries encumbered by debt, then their economies would collapse, civil society would disintegrate, and the resulting populist or military dictatorship would abandon the IMF's policies and bring to a halt the creation of free market economies and the democratisation of their political systems. Constantly in various speeches at numerous forums he drew attention to what he believed was an inextricable relationship between economic stability and social, political and strategic stability, although (as he admitted in hindsight) 'without any great success'[16] until about 1982, when the problem of Third World debt became more widely recognised as a major issue.

Because the Bretton Woods agreement had been largely destroyed in the early 1970s, Muldoon firmly believed that a new mechanism was needed to stabilise the world monetary system. He also wanted the rules of the IMF changed so that developing countries could borrow money at lower than normal rates of interest from the IMF, and possibly from a consortium of private sector banks, in order to restructure those countries' increasingly unsustainable debt. Many countries only turned to the IMF when they had got into serious trouble because the IMF's conditions for loans earlier were too strict and caused too many social and political problems. Muldoon realised that converting the Americans to reform of the IMF and the world monetary system would be a difficult task but believed that it was essential.[17] He saw New Zealand as having similar economic problems to other developing and agricultural-commodity exporting countries and believed such states were unfairly treated by the wealthier, industrialised OECD nations.

Lange and Labour regarded Muldoon's views and speeches on Third World debt and the international monetary system as 'a political red-herring – a distraction from pressing domestic issues' and concluded that 'the international significance is accurately reflected by the level of their international media coverage – virtually nil'.[18]

Throughout 1982 Muldoon, however, took every opportunity in speeches within New Zealand to express and develop his views on reform of the global economy, especially the financial system. It was his major topic in addresses to the Wellington and Auckland branches of the NZ Society of Accountants (14 and 23 July); the Canterbury Club (13 August); the Wellington Chamber of Commerce (19 August); the Hutt Valley Chamber of Commerce (27 September); and the NZ Manufacturers' Federation annual conference (20 October).[19] He also raised the matter at a Commonwealth finance ministers' meeting and at the joint annual meetings of the IMF and World Bank in Toronto in September 1982 and in a speech to the Asia–Pacific regional meeting of Commonwealth Heads of Government in Suva on 14 October.

Thatcher responded at length to a copy of the Suva speech which Muldoon sent her. She commenced by noting that 'I found myself in agreement with nearly all your analysis' and added that Muldoon was 'right to say that growing protectionism and the international debt situation should be looked at together as threats to the international trade and payments system of the free world'.[20] She also concurred with his complaint that agricultural protectionism was particularly damaging to Third World countries and that this had not been recognised in the General Agreement on Tariffs and Trade. While noting that Muldoon was also correct in his appreciation of the pain involved in cutting back subsidies and budget deficits, Thatcher stressed the importance of the free market in facilitating economic changes provided that 'inflation and monopoly . . . the main forces damaging its performance and its ability to provide sustained growth and jobs' could be controlled. She offered qualified support for the reform of GATT, the IMF and the international currency system.

Because some of Muldoon's initial speeches on international monetary reform embarrassed many of his officials and academic economists, Galvin, Dr Rod Deane, the chief economist and later deputy governor of the Reserve Bank, and Tim Groser and Simon Murdoch of the Prime Minister's Department took the Prime Minister's ideas and rewrote them in a way which made them from a economist's viewpoint academically more respectable and tenable and more in keeping with conventional thinking. Muldoon was not offended and indeed thanked the officials for their help in developing and expressing his ideas in ways that would make them more acceptable in international forums,[21] especially to President Ronald Reagan and his Treasury Secretary Donald Regan and to the managing director of the IMF, Jacques de Larosière, all of whom were far more conservative about IMF policies and far less sympathetic to the social problems that harsh austerity conditions demanded by the IMF imposed on debtor countries.[22]

In late January 1983 Muldoon flew to Davos in Switzerland to attend a European Management Forum Foundation symposium. There, on Thursday 27 January, he gave the opening address before participating in a session on 'new dimensions of world leadership'. Muldoon, in his most carefully developed and polished exposition of his views, proposed that the world community should, as it had in 1944 at Bretton Woods, 'develop a co-ordinated set of policies to govern international trade and payments for the rest of this decade and beyond'.[23] Failure to do so would result in serious 'economic, political and indeed strategic consequences for the West' as well as for the more indebted and vulnerable developing economies. Muldoon was particularly critical of lending 'by the private banks with very little thought or with excessive optimism as to the capacity of the countries to pay it back'. He noted that some forty countries by 1982 had debt servicing liabilities which exceeded their entire earnings from the export of goods and services. This was a structural, not a cyclical problem, of concern to lenders as well as borrowers. He condemned IMF austerity programmes imposed as a condition of assistance to heavily indebted countries. While some reform conditions were necessary, if those conditions were too severe they might well be counter-productive economically and even endanger democracy in the countries concerned. He argued further that 'financial dislocation and protectionism feed on each other' and that global free trade would continue to be hindered by the unresolved problems of the international financial system.

After Davos, Muldoon stepped up his international campaign. He sent copies of his Davos address to numerous people, including the presidents, prime ministers and finance ministers of almost every country in Europe and North America and many others in Asia, Africa, Latin America, the Middle East and the South Pacific.

He also wrote to the heads of US, British, Swiss, Japanese, German and Dutch banks; the Director-General of GATT; the Secretary-General of the United Nations; the Secretary-General of the Commonwealth; and major world newspapers. Most responded and while some replies, such as those from President Reagan and Australia's Prime Minister Bob Hawke, were formal and non-committal, many others expressed agreement with Muldoon's proposals and encouraged him to pursue them further. Britain's former prime minister Edward Heath, for example, referred to Muldoon's Davos speech as 'one of the most far-sighted and eloquent statements to have been made on the problems of international payments and trade by any political leader for some time', while Julius Nyerere of Tanzania suggested that the IMF probably required radical reform rather than just strengthening and refurbishment.[24]

In his role as would-be reformer of the world economy, Muldoon continued speaking out on the topic overseas during the latter part of 1983 and in early 1984: at the Reform Club in London (17 May); the UN Conference on Trade and Development in Belgrade (7 June); the Los Angeles World Affairs Council (17 September); the Commonwealth finance ministers' meeting (22 September); the Washington Press Club (28 September); Harvard University (5 October); Colombia University (28 February); Berkeley University (5 March); and the East–West Center, Hawaii (10 March).[25] A revised version of his Davos speech calling for 'a second Bretton Woods type conference' which could 'set underway a systematic process looking to significant changes and adjustments in the structure of trade, payments, developments and exchange rates' was also published in the prestigious *Foreign Affairs* journal in June 1983.[26] Throughout these speeches and publications he criticised the political 'paralysis by analysis' and the 'gaggle of summits' and 'communiques that no-one reads' which prevented effective action to overcome both Third World debt and increasing trade deficits.[27]

The Commonwealth finance ministers had agreed at their annual meeting in September 1982 to establish a group of nine economic experts to examine Muldoon's proposal for a new Bretton Woods style conference on the international financial situation. The report was presented to and discussed by the finance ministers at the September 1983 meeting and was welcomed by Muldoon for endorsing the major thrust of his ongoing campaign.[28] He became chairman of a Commonwealth finance ministers' working party to explore ways in which an international consensus and action plan on the issue could be achieved during 1984. In the event, his election defeat in mid-1984 was to remove him from the international scene and the rescheduling of Third World debt, and a strategy to revive growth in debtor countries which emerged in 1985 became the Baker Plan, named after the then US Treasury Secretary James Baker. The Baker Plan was far less radical and generous than Muldoon had envisaged and by 1989 was largely acknowledged as a failure. It was replaced by another, more successful, debt-reform plan called the Brady Plan after a new US Secretary of the Treasury, Nicholas Brady.

Sensitivity to Third World opinion at this time even affected Muldoon's attitude to matters other than the debt question. In 1983, for example,

Wellington, as Minister of Education, was looking for items in the Education vote which he could cut in order to reallocate funds to new priorities. He disliked what he regarded as the wasteful expenditure and left-wing political agenda of UNESCO and deleted New Zealand's annual membership subscription. His officials were devastated but could not openly disagree with their minister. Renwick, the Director-General of Education, however, contacted Muldoon indirectly through Hensley, suggesting that it would be better to work for change within UNESCO than to leave it. When Wellington's proposal came to cabinet the following day, Muldoon, who was cultivating Third World support for his crusade against Third World debt, intervened and had the membership funding reinstated.[29]

Muldoon realised immediately after the 1981 election that if Waring, Minogue or any other National MP voted against the Government on any issue he would become dependent for a majority on the two Social Credit MPs, Beetham and Knapp. According to voting records kept by the National Party Research Unit, the Social Credit MPs voted 80 per cent of the time with the Labour Opposition.[30] Despite that, the Social Credit leader, Beetham, respected and supported Muldoon's campaign for international monetary reform and he also appreciated Muldoon's 'instinctive empathy for the ordinary bloke's concerns and a belief that the Government should attend to those concerns'.[31] Beetham trusted Muldoon more than he did Labour's leaders and believed that Muldoon's social conscience was much deeper and more genuine than that of most other MPs irrespective of their political allegiance. Moreover, the Social Credit leader believed that the Prime Minister 'could rarely be faulted on his facts . . . One could question his interpretation but not his facts and he won nine out of ten arguments because he had the facts.'[32] Muldoon was usually pleasant and courteous in his dealings with Beetham and when the two men visited Antarctica together in 1982 they got on, according to Beetham, remarkably well. All this made it easier for Muldoon when he found that he had to persuade Beetham and Knapp to support him in 1982 over legislation to build the Clyde high dam.

At a press conference on 27 May 1982, Muldoon announced that the National caucus had decided earlier that day to proceed with the Clutha River high dam at Clyde primarily because the high dam would be about $150 million cheaper than two low dams and would be completed earlier, which was an important factor in the overall growth strategy.[33] He admitted that three National MPs had reservations about legislating to fast-track the high dam proposal and overturn a judicial decision delaying the project because the Government had not obtained a water right. Muldoon also expressed uncertainty as to whether there was a majority in Parliament to pass such validating legislation.

Birch was convinced that the building of the Clyde high dam was vital to National's energy and economic growth policies. According to one National caucus member opposed to the overriding of the courts, Birch had an 'inordinate influence on Muldoon' over the decision to push ahead with the dam's construction.[34] Certainly, it was Birch who briefed and persuaded the National Party's Dominion Executive. Birch argued that the options open to the Government were to stop the work and go back to the Planning Tribunal and then probably on appeal to the High Court; to invoke the National Development Act, which would probably involve a lengthy delay; or to legislate to overrule the judicial system. There was no debate within the Executive after the Chairman of the Otago-Southland Division had responded, 'the people of the South Island were of one voice . . . they wanted it.'[35]

On 28 June, following a cabinet meeting, Muldoon announced that work could not continue on the Clyde dam because without legislation legal moves would probably delay the project for several years. As a result the workforce would have to be laid off.[36] Ten days later, the Government caucus approved a Bill authorising the Clyde dam to go ahead. With Minogue committed publicly to voting against the legislation, Muldoon realised that he needed either the support of the Labour Opposition, which was under pressure from the NZ Workers' Union to support any move to complete the dam; or from MacDonell, the Labour MP from Dunedin Central, who favoured such legislation; or from the two Social Credit MPs. Beetham and Knapp had stated unequivocally on 2 July that they had not wavered in their opposition to the Clyde high dam, that 'it is impossible' that they might change their minds, and that they intended voting against the Bill.[37] At first Muldoon took them at their word.

On 3 June Quigley briefed Labour MPs on the Clyde high dam and on 9 July Birch, Friedlander and McLay met Rowling and other Labour leaders to discuss a Labour compromise proposal on the dam problem.[38] The Government ministers rejected Labour's suggestion because it involved work on a low dam which had not been designed and which would produce only one-third the energy of a high dam.

Although Social Credit had campaigned at the 1981 election against the Clyde dam, Beetham, Knapp and two other prominent Social Crediters, Patricia Woczik, the environmental spokeswoman, and Terry Heffernan, decided to visit Otago and discuss the matter with local farmers and construction workers. They then reassessed their position in an attempt to show that they were taking seriously the fact that on this issue at least Social Credit held what they called the 'balance of responsibility'. Beetham and Knapp were convinced that Muldoon and the Government would, if necessary, override the judiciary in the Clyde dam impasse by an Order in Council if they could not get a majority for empowering legislation in Parliament. The two Social Credit MPs believed that the matter was best resolved in Parliament and not simply by the Executive. They were also persuaded by the fact that $30 million had already been spent on preparatory work at Cromwell; that some 600 workers and their families would be unemployed if the work did not continue; that the low-dam option would result in more serious silting; that a high dam would make it possible to set up an inexpensive and extensive system of irrigation; that without the high dam power pricing would be set at a level that would make the controversial proposed aluminium smelter at Aramoana impossible; and that the power from the high dam would remove any possibility of the construction in the foreseeable future of a nuclear power plant in New Zealand.[39] Beetham and Knapp decided that in return for various concessions and safeguards they were prepared to change their minds and support the Government on the high dam. They announced their decision on 13 July.⁴⁰

Muldoon immediately told a press conference that, after examining Social Credit's conditions for supporting empowering legislation, 'there is not one single thing that I can think of that the government was not prepared to do before the Social Credit people asked us'.⁴¹ Five hours of detailed negotiations involving Beetham, Knapp, Birch, Friedlander and McLay took place over the next two days. It was agreed to withdraw the Government's empowering bill and to allow opponents of the high dam to exhaust their legal avenues. In the meantime, however, work on the high dam could continue because Social Credit agreed to support future empowering legislation if that became the only way to complete the project.⁴² In what Beetham described subsequently as 'the toughest bargaining session I've ever been in in my life', Social Credit received assurances on irrigation and power pricing but were uncertain whether the concessions were sufficient to satisfy their supporters, many of whom were annoyed by the reversal in the Social Credit MPs' position.⁴³ Muldoon, who joined the discussions towards the end, made it plain, however, that he would not make any more significant concessions although he was prepared to accept 'some cosmetic or symbolic improvements'. He pointed out that if Social Credit backed out and changed its mind again after having gone so far it would look ridiculous and he was prepared to point that out to the press if in fact Social Credit did withdraw to its former position. Beetham and Knapp capitulated, believing that they had enough to justify their support for the high dam. Muldoon, however, then walked out of the room and gave a press conference which much to Beetham's chagrin portrayed National as having won a major victory.⁴⁴ The Labour Party immediately attacked Social Credit for its about-face. Publicly and politically the Clyde dam became very damaging to Social Credit, and an angry Labour Opposition took every opportunity to condemn Beetham and Knapp for apparently caving in or selling out to Muldoon.⁴⁵

Muldoon subsequently contacted the Auditor-General and asked Shailes whether the Government could move to carry on construction of the Clyde dam with a guarantee that empowering legislation would be passed as soon as possible. Shailes replied that the situation was different to the superannuation precedent in 1975 in that Muldoon now had a small and unpredictable majority and could no longer guarantee the outcome of a vote in Parliament. Muldoon responded that the two Social Credit MPs had promised to support the legislation, and after Shailes had rung and checked with Beetham the Auditor-General gave his agreement.⁴⁶

The Solicitor-General on 23 August advised the Government that there were no grounds for appeal against the decision of the Planning Tribunal stopping the Clyde high dam, and Muldoon then decided that he had no option but to legislate.⁴⁷ A new empowering Bill was prepared and discussed with Beetham before being pushed through Parliament not only with the votes of the two Social Credit MPs but also with the very reluctant support of two younger National MPs, Richardson and Upton, who had publicly questioned the need for and the morality of the legislation.⁴⁸

Muldoon's problems in trying to govern with a majority of one were increased when Social Credit, following negative reaction from its supporters over the Clyde dam issue, decided to adopt an unqualified position of opposition to the Government in future. Beetham announced in November 1982 that 'Anything is preferable to the Muldoon administration', suggested that Labour withdraw pairs in the House, and promised that Social Credit would change from abstention on no-confidence votes to voting with Labour in favour.[49] This made it much more important that all National MPs vote for government measures but Muldoon, with reason, doubted the reliability of a number of his caucus colleagues. While he had always regarded Waring and Minogue as likely to cross the floor, the major threat to his strategy and policies he now saw as coming from a more ideologically committed right-wing faction which had considerable support in the upper echelon of the party organisation.

Following the 1981 election, the Party's Dominion Council had held a meeting which considered a number of papers prepared to examine the party's identity, philosophy and future direction.[50] They concluded that the years of affluence in New Zealand had ended during the 1970s and that, although New Zealand had coped quite well in responding to change, it would have to do much more in the future if it wanted to create export markets, attack unemployment, improve education and maintain social services and a free, fair and relatively equal society. Leay suggested that National must pursue 'smaller government, lower taxes, less government in our lives, less regulation and restrictive laws' and 'provide more equal opportunity, more freedom of choice, more reward for effort and achievement, recognition of excellence and praise for the risk takers'.[51] There was a general consensus on the Council that not only should the National Government be less interventionist both economically and socially but that it would need to pay much more attention to urban and younger voters, National having since 1975 become very much an older, more rural and more provincial party in terms of its membership and its parliamentary representation.

Muldoon himself, however, was less willing to reject intervention and regulation or to woo younger urban voters at the expense of National's older, more conservative electoral support. Nor was the Prime Minister inclined to placate the major interest groups. There was no doubt that Muldoon's Government did many things which offended powerful sectional interests both within and outside the National Party. While there had been increased economic growth and a shift towards a more open and internationally competitive economy, a reduction in inflation, and some deregulation, the pace of change was too slow and there were too many ad hoc adjustments, many of which ran counter to the overall direction.

Much of the intervention was also arrogant in manner, although Muldoon was more sensitive in dealing with the poor and the powerless than he was with many of National's more traditional supporters. Many of Muldoon's caucus colleagues saw as one of his flaws his 'terribly soft spot for people' and 'sense for the underdog' which made him always 'weigh up the lives of those he was affecting' when considering economic policies and actions.[52] They saw this as 'genuine concern' not 'political cynicism' or worry about losing votes. Indeed, Muldoon often seemed to realise that his concern for the unemployed, the welfare beneficiary, the low-paid family, the aged, and the Maori, most of whom did not and would not vote National, cost him support from wealthier sections of the community who traditionally did.

The 1982 Budget was a difficult one to prepare. It involved major cuts in Government expenditure and Muldoon was not impressed when his Associate Minister of Finance, Falloon, told the press that the Cabinet Expenditure Committee was looking at cuts of between 6 and 9 per cent if the budget deficit was to be kept under control. Muldoon was at the time thinking more in terms of 3 per cent.[53] Preparation of the Budget also involved consideration of some 120 documents from Treasury and other government departments and also the report of the Task Force on Taxation Reform (the McCaw Committee), which had been set up in July 1981 and which had reported in April 1982. Among its recommendations was a shift from direct to indirect taxation by means of a goods and services tax.[54]

Caucus had a passionate debate on the indirect tax proposal, with Cox in particular arguing for the introduction of a Value Added Tax (VAT) similar to that in Britain. Muldoon and a majority of National MPs were worried, however, that such a tax would increase the cost of basic necessities and hurt disproportionately the less well-off; thus they rejected the proposal.[55] During the debate, Falloon reported that some reform was necessary because senior officers in Inland Revenue believed that the existing income tax system 'had lost its integrity completely' and that 'people were choosing whether or not to pay tax'.[56] The Prime Minister requested further information on this allegation.

Muldoon, who had no empathy or sympathy at all for those who sought tax evasion loopholes, was enraged by the subsequent Treasury and Inland Revenue reports, which drew his attention to lawyers, doctors, accountants and urban businessmen who were avoiding tax by taking advantage of tax shelters such as farms. Not only did they write off their primary income for tax purposes but their investment often led also to tax-free capital gains. For example, in one case put before Muldoon several professional men in a partnership wrote off 82 per cent of their $2,731,524 income over three years, 1979–81, through claiming losses and farm incentives and deductions on a large sheep and cattle station in the Wanganui district.[57] In addition such investment in rural land was often short-term and motivated not only by tax avoidance considerations but also by a speculative rise in property values which greatly increased land costs for farmers. Muldoon and his Associate Finance Minister discussed the issue late in the 1982 Budget round, and although they realised it would be very unpopular with many National supporters, decided to do something about it. The result was the Income Tax Amendment (No. 2) Bill.[58]

The tax idea incorporated in the Bill was put forward initially by Bruce Townshend, the MP for Kaimai, who earlier in the year had expressed concern about tax rip-offs in the kiwifruit industry. The matter was 'discussed about six times in caucus and Muldoon was very negative and antagonistic during the first four meetings' and even during the last two meetings 'when the mood in caucus as a whole moved . . . Muldoon had to be dragged into this.'[59] However, 'once caucus made the decision Muldoon was resolute in advancing it'.[60] McLay, Bolger, Falloon and Friedlander continued to oppose the measure in both cabinet and caucus on the grounds that for six years the Government had been encouraging people to invest and spend in horticulture, especially kiwifruit, but was now deciding to change the rules and tax them retrospectively.[61]

Muldoon originally intended the measure only to stop syndicates from writing off personal income tax in this manner, but when it was discussed in caucus some MPs argued that the measure discriminated against small investors, who had to become syndicate members, while leaving large individuals taxpayers untouched.[62] Finally, it was decided that no one would be permitted to offset more than $10,000 in any one year and that if the property was sold within ten years of its being purchased then the tax had to be paid out of the capital gain.

Although Muldoon could justify his actions on moral grounds and by arguing that he was closing tax loopholes and keeping farm costs down, many people saw the measure as retrospectively taxing people who had made business decisions which were perfectly legal at the time they were made. Although it would have been very difficult for Muldoon to have made the legislation apply only to people who bought land after its passage, inside cabinet and caucus there remained a minority, which included Bolger and McLay, who doubted the wisdom of the legislation.[63]

The Income Tax Amendment (No. 2) Bill was very controversial and proved particularly unpopular among National voters. It was seen as a capital gains tax, imposed retrospectively and on people part way through an investment and development programme. While it was meant to dissuade investment for capital gain or tax evasion purposes only, it also restricted investment in agriculture, especially horticulture.[64] Stormy meetings of party members were held, especially in the Auckland and Canterbury divisions, and resolutions were passed condemning the legislation.[65] As the Auckland Divisional Executive noted in a motion passed 'almost without dissent', it 'deplores the philosophy, economics and politics of the Income Tax Amendment (No. 2) Bill'.[66] Nor did the passage of the legislation end the opposition and National MPs started to distance themselves from the measure. Questioned at an Auckland divisional meeting in 1983, for example, all four MPs on a panel 'spoke not only against the Bill, but advised they too were surprised with its introduction and knew nothing of the reasons behind the Bill, and were in fact against the whole section of the Bill' even though they had discussed the issue numerous times in caucus and had voted for the Bill in Parliament.[67]

Little wonder that by 1982 there was a widely held view that not only had the National Party lost control over its parliamentary wing but that cabinet had become largely unaccountable to the caucus and that both cabinet and caucus were failing to check the Prime Minister and Finance Minister. Certainly Muldoon began to feel besieged by pressure groups, the Labour Opposition, and critics within his own party. His unwillingness to give way was, as his deputy observed, perceived as, and to an extent became also in reality, 'sheer, bloody-minded pigheadedness'.[68]

In 1981 the anti-Muldoon faction in caucus had been strengthened by the election of three new MPs with reputations as 'back-to-basics' private enterprisers. Ruth Richardson, John Banks and Simon Upton, it was believed, would crusade for more right-wing economic policies and for a curbing of Muldoon's interventionist style of government.[69] At the first caucus meeting she attended Richardson bravely challenged Muldoon but failed to receive the support she expected from Banks, who quailed under Muldoon's frightening glare.[70] While Banks came to like and admire Muldoon, Richardson remained an intransigent critic, leading Muldoon to confide to the Auckland divisional chairman that 'whenever I put out the hand of friendship or reconciliation to Ruth Richardson I get my arm chewed up to the elbow'.[71]

In June 1982 Quigley made a speech to the Young Nationals' Conference. He questioned the 'Think Big' growth strategy, which he believed New Zealanders neither understood nor supported.[72] Most attention had been paid to the very large, expensive projects utilising gas, ironsands, electricity, forestry and horticulture, which had squeezed out investment necessary for the expansion of traditional and smaller industries. Quigley questioned the quality, as distinct from the quantity, of the growth planned; suggested that the Government should be playing a more passive economic role and encouraging private enterprise more; and attacked the negative influence of excessive government regulation, licensing and intervention in the economy.[73] He doubted that New Zealand's economic base was strong enough for such a comprehensive and costly expansion as 'Think Big'.

Questioned by journalists at a post-cabinet press conference about his reaction to Quigley's comments, Muldoon restrained himself to responding that he disagreed with Quigley's views but refused to condemn his colleague for expressing them publicly.[74] Birch, however, was enraged and told Muldoon that the Prime Minister should retaliate more forcefully against what Birch argued was an intrusion by Quigley into Birch's area of ministerial responsibility and a clear breach of collective cabinet responsibility. When Birch said that he intended 'to tackle Quigley' publicly over his comments, Muldoon told Birch that he was not prepared to tolerate a public fight between two of his ministers and would deal with the matter himself.[75]

Muldoon tried repeatedly but unsuccessfully to talk to Quigley prior to cabinet and rang four times before the meeting to ask Quigley's private secretary where he was.[76] When Quigley arrived at cabinet Muldoon took him aside. Muldoon told him that his comments 'had offended, embarrassed and angered his cabinet colleagues and done considerable damage in the eyes of the public to the National Party and the Government'. He offered Quigley the options of either apologising publicly to his colleagues and refraining from making such remarks in public in the future or standing by his statements and resigning from cabinet.[77] Muldoon made it plain that Quigley was quite entitled to criticise 'Think Big' and, if he wished, the Government as a backbench MP but not as a minister. As the Prime Minister later told one interviewer, a minister 'can thump the table if you like, but once a Cabinet decision is made you either go along with it or you resign, there are no half measures'.[78]

Quigley chose to resign from cabinet. He indicated that he might also resign from Parliament.[79] That would have precipitated a by-election in a seat (Rangiora) that National was not guaranteed to hold. Loss of the seat would have destroyed the Government majority and forced an early election. The Dominion Executive, appalled at the thought, requested Quigley to stay in the caucus. It also invited him to replace Cooper as a keynote speaker at the party's forthcoming annual conference, a move seen by many to be an endorsement of Quigley and his views and a rebuke to the party's leader. Throughout New Zealand there was considerable anger within National party ranks at Quigley's sacking from cabinet for stating openly what many party members also believed, but a number of newspaper editors felt that 'Mr Quigley asked for it'[80] and that 'he was surely ingenuous if he imagined that he could remain in cabinet' after breaching collective responsibility and publicly criticising agreed and major cabinet decisions.[81]

There were many MPs and party members who agreed with Jim Gerard, the chairman of the Canterbury Division, when he claimed that '1982 was the worst year' in the party's history because of 'issues such as the Aramoana smelter, the Clyde Dam, the "Quigley Affair", the wage and price freeze and the Income Tax Amendment (No. 2) Bill; issues that were created by the National Government'.[82] This was also clearly a criticism of the party's leader.

Muldoon recognised the existence of Quigley's support and the growing New Right faction within the National Party, observing publicly that 'We've got a number in Caucus. Indeed we have got some in Cabinet. So long as they work with the team there is no problem . . . there's a place for them . . . But they are not the National Party' – which was and had to be much more broadly based.[83] Muldoon believed, however, that if the right wing could muster all its supporters and shape the party to its image it might be able to win a mere ten seats, including his own of Tamaki, but would lose all the marginal and even semi-safe National seats such as Rangiora (held by a prominent right-wing leader).

Early in 1983, despite Muldoon's dismissal of them and sensing the reaction to the Income Tax Amendment (No. 2) Bill, the right-wing faction in caucus and the party organisation renewed their attack on him. Quigley and Cox in March made their views public, and soon other MPs were also speaking out openly at party meetings or to the press.[84] For example, in successive meetings of the Auckland Divisional Executive, Dail Jones predicted National would lose the next election; Bruce Townshend, while defending Muldoon for having 'maintained the highest possible standard of living for the highest number of people over the past five years', conceded National was 'hurting the very sectors who vote National'; and Geoff Thompson observed that 'the National Party was shooting itself in the foot' and 'the electorate was . . . looking for leadership'.[85] Gair also expressed doubts about the likely outcome of the next election.[86] Such criticism and pessimism were echoed loudly at the Auckland, Wellington and Canterbury-Westland divisional annual conferences during May.[87] That provoked a defence of Muldoon and the Government's policies over subsequent months by Muldoon loyalists such as Birch, Malcolm, Wellington and Templeton.[88] It was now clear to everyone how deeply the National caucus and party organisation were divided.

In September 1983 Fred Dobbs, the chief executive of Dobbs-Wiggins-McCann-Erickson, who had handled a number of National's previous election campaigns and who was a personal friend of Muldoon, sent the Prime Minister a confidential report on National's election prospects the next year.[89] Dobbs noted that incumbent governments throughout the western world, irrespective of their political orientations, were unable to cope with the problems of economic recession, unemployment, inflation, high interest rates, union troubles, erosion of living standards and poor economic growth rates. In New Zealand voters were saying, 'The Government has had 8–9 years to fix the position and has not done so. We might as well give the Labour Party a chance – we have little to lose.'[90] He concluded that 'it can be assumed that as of now the Government has lost the next election' but went on to suggest ways in which National might fight back. While improvement in the economic and social indicators would help, it was important that the pressure should be taken off the Prime Minister. Other ministers should answer Opposition criticisms and 'the Prime Minister must be seen by the voters as an understanding father, aware of their problems and doing his best to help. He should never be bitter, sarcastic or carping. He must be respected, admired and perhaps loved.'[91] Even had Muldoon been able to accept this advice, it was too late for him to soften his image.

In October Dail Jones publicly questioned whether Muldoon should stay in office. He argued: 'In a proper Westminster system the person responsible for handling his portfolio in that messy shambolic fashion would have resigned.'[92] Jones added that clearly he was 'not a member of the Muldoon Party'. [93] According to Jones, Muldoon was deviating even further from National's philosophy and was running a socialist-type economic management policy. Thus, he claimed that there were now four parties in Parliament: National, Labour, Social Credit and the Muldoon Government.[94] A few weeks afterwards, joined by Quigley and Richardson, Jones defied the caucus majority and crossed the floor of the House to vote against interest rate controls.[95] During the debate in the House, Muldoon criticised his dissident backbenchers for supporting 'usurious interest rates' and for being so ideologically driven by their free market beliefs that they thought that 'if everything was let go things would be all right. "They are wrong," the Prime Minister said. "Everything would not be all right. Everything would be all wrong."'[96]

Despite the three defections Muldoon won a narrow majority in Parliament with the support of the two Social Credit MPs and two alienated Labour members, Kirk and MacDonell, after he had made it clear that if defeated on the Bill he would call an early election. The Prime Minister then asked Wood, who had by now succeeded Chapman as party president, to meet Quigley, Jones and Richardson, and also Waring and Minogue, who had crossed the floor and voted against the Government during the debate on the Industrial Law Reform Bill, which abolished compulsory union membership. Muldoon wanted the president to obtain assurances from the five that they would not cross the floor during 1984 and further embarrass the Government during an election year. Failure to obtain those assurances would precipitate an early election. Wood received the assurances and Muldoon believed he would be able to continue governing through to the scheduled November 1984 election.[97]

The Prime Minister warned the caucus and the party's Dominion Executive early in December 1983, however, that if the Government's one-seat majority was again threatened during 1984 he would call an early election, perhaps as early as April.[98] In Muldoon's opinion, National would do worse at the polls at an early election than it would in November, when he believed the Government's policies in increasing production and exports and destroying inflationary expectations would be more obviously successful. Muldoon concluded that while National MPs had always had the right to vote according to their individual consciences, and he personally had 'no difficulty' with any National MP crossing the floor when the Government's majority was secure, 'he could not have a situation where every backbencher had a right of veto' over Government policy and actions.[99] In response the Executive resolved on a motion moved by Wood and seconded by Reeves, the chairman of the Waikato Division, 'to uphold the right of National Members of Parliament to a free vote except on confidence issues, and expects members to use this freedom responsibly'.[100]

Wood was far from happy, however, when one National MP, Doug Kidd, decided to introduce another anti-abortion Bill towards the end of 1983. She told Muldoon that understanding Kidd's action 'is beyond me' and 'will carve up the Caucus and the organisation and we will not recover before the election . . . the timing is political suicide'.[101] The president also wrote to each National MP pleading with them to oppose the introduction of the legislation as it was 'divisive', 'contentious' and 'foolhardy' and would do 'serious damage' to the party.[102]

More damage was, however, about to be done to the National Party's re-election prospect by a new party formed by Muldoon's former admirer and ally, Bob Jones. Jones was a very intelligent man who could be both charming and arrogant, sometimes at the same time. He thought quickly and spoke and wrote clearly, fluently and persuasively. He frequently exhibited, like Muldoon, a mischievous sense of humour. Again like the Prime Minister he called a spade a spade, held many of the establishment in contempt, and was not afraid of revealing his personal prejudices or of shocking those who were politically correct or morally sanctimonious.

Jones had met Muldoon for the first time ten days after the 1972 election when Muldoon opened a commercial building Jones had built in Masterton. Over the following ten years the two men became friendly, although as both always admitted never close friends.[103] Jones had launched Muldoon's book *My Way* in

1981; Muldoon had invited Jones to functions in Vogel House; and Muldoon had been a guest at dinners and parties on 'three or four occasions' between 1972 and 1982 at Jones's home, including a memorable 1974 Christmas party. As Jones records it, Muldoon chased Jones's 'Labour activist sister, who had been taunting him all night . . . outside and around the house, then suddenly there was silence.'[104] Other guests on investigation 'found her drowning him, now without most of his clothes, in the shallow end of the swimming pool' and 'pulled my sister off Rob, who spluttered to the surface', whereupon some thirty of the other prominent guests also dived into the pool.[105]

The relationship between the two men had deteriorated during the latter part of 1982, despite the fact that on 25 September Muldoon had opened the refurbished Southern Cross Hotel in Dunedin for Jones and in return Jones had used the occasion to give the Prime Minister a surprise sixty-first birthday party and had flown Muldoon's two daughters from Auckland to join in the celebrations. Jones, never one to mince his words, was becoming increasingly and publicly critical of some of the Government's actions, such as the wage and price freeze, the compulsory wearing of seat belts and the random stopping of motorists by traffic officers.[106] Gair had pushed through cabinet and caucus the proposal to legalise the random stopping of drivers as a means of reducing accidents caused by drivers who had been drinking alcohol. Muldoon had actually opposed the measure both in caucus and at a Dominion Executive meeting but had found himself in a minority on both occasions.[107] Nevertheless, as far as Jones was concerned, it was Muldoon's Government that had made the decision. The tension between the two men was revealed a few months later at a National Party fundraising debate in Invercargill where Muldoon remarked, I'm not sure whose side Bob Jones is on any more' and an irritated Jones had responded, 'I know whose side I'm on . . . But by God, I think I speak for everyone here when I ask you, Rob, whose side you're on?'[108] On 20 January 1983 Jones announced that in protest at the Government's interventionist and increasingly socialist style practices he would stand as a independent candidate against Templeton in National's sole Wellington seat of Ohariu at the next election, and subsequently a bitter personal war broke out in public between Jones and an aggrieved Templeton.[109] Jones portrayed his campaign as a counter to National's shift into 'socialism' and an attempt to 'turn Muldoon around and . . . wake him up.'[110]

Jones's candidacy provoked a groundswell of support from disaffected National Party voters, particularly but not solely from younger entrepreneurial urban liberals.[111] Many of those who disliked and had suffered financially from the Income Tax Amendment (No. 2) Bill or from the freeze on prices and interest rates rallied to Jones and in August 1983 at a function at a Wellington hotel Jones launched the New Zealand Party. Ironically, as far as the Income Tax Amendment (No. 2) Bill was concerned, Jones was later to record, 'Actually I endorsed the thrust of the Bill insofar as effectively it amounted to a removal of subsidy although naturally I was contemptuous of its retrospective element.'[112] In announcing the party's formation Jones stated that he and other former National supporters 'could not stand what was happening any more – retrospective legislation, the abandonment of philosophy, a totally controlled economy, bullying tactics'.[113] This was a direct and devastating attack from an unexpected source on Muldoon and what was termed 'Muldoonism'.

During the following nine months the New Zealand Party, or as Muldoon always insisted on calling it 'the Jones Party', easily displaced Social Credit as New Zealand's third party. The success of the New Zealand Party during that period was almost entirely due to Jones's personal energy and charisma and to the incredible amount of time and money he was prepared to commit to maintaining and extending the party. His extraordinary ability and experience as a high-profile communicator enabled him to capture and exploit the media to keep himself and his message continually visible to a fascinated electorate. His meetings around the country attracted huge crowds; thousands joined the New Zealand Party; campaign organisations were set up in almost every electorate; a strong professional staff was recruited nationally; funds flowed in; imaginative and detailed policy was developed; and some excellent candidates were chosen.[114] From being initially a splinter party protesting at Muldoon's and the National Government's deviation from the principles of liberalism and conservatism, the New Zealand Party started to present itself and to be regarded by some observers as a possible replacement for National on the centre-right of the political spectrum. At the very least, by splitting National's vote and contributing to its defeat, the New Zealand Party's intervention would achieve its primary objective of removing Muldoon as leader and forcing the National Party to return to more individualistic and private enterprise principles and policies.

Jones still admired Muldoon as an extraordinary man but believed that philosophically he had moved too far from the free market and the rights of the individual and personally had become, especially after 1981, 'contemptuous of everyone around him, arrogant, intolerant, marked by venom and hatred'.[115] Much of that attitude, however, Jones believed was 'bluff' and certainly, although Muldoon always referred to the New Zealand Party as 'the Jones Party' or 'the Greedies', his public attacks on Jones and his party were relatively mild during the year between the New Zealand Party's formation and the 1984 election.

Although the National Party's membership had held up remarkably well throughout a very difficult 1983 and at the end of that year numbered some 140,000, party officials were expressing concern about holding crucial marginal seats in the face of Labour Party challenges. Muldoon himself frankly admitted to the National Party's Executive that National's re-election chances were also threatened if Jones persisted until the election.[116] At first, however, Muldoon thought Jones was simply stirring and playing a prank. Even after the New Zealand Party emerged, the Prime Minister did not believe Jones would be prepared to make the tremendous commitment in time, emotion and money to lead the new party through to the next election. Muldoon was sure that Jones would soon become impatient with and irritated by many of the people who rallied to the New Zealand Party. Muldoon might well have been correct and had the

1984 election taken place in November, not July, of that year Jones might have given his crusade away. As Jones himself observed in retrospect, 'By June 1984 I had a tiger by the tail but I was fed up with it and burnt out. I wouldn't have seen it out to November.'[117]

The New Zealand Party provided an acceptable alternative to National not only for some urban voters but also for many farmers who had become alienated from the Muldoon Government. Like the New Zealand Party, Federated Farmers was also totally opposed to the 1982 Income Tax Amendment (No. 2) Bill, which almost stopped the sale of horticultural properties and forced people through tax penalties to hold on to properties much longer than they had intended. That opposition did nothing to improve relations between Muldoon and Federated Farmers.

Muldoon had a genuine sympathy for farmers but he did not really understand them, and many of his policies, intended to offer short-term relief and compensation for his unwillingness to deregulate or devalue, had become built in, so that they were distorting market signals and standing in the way of the rational restructuring of New Zealand's agricultural production and exports. Once Talboys retired, Muldoon really had only MacIntyre left to advise him on agricultural policies because younger farmer MPs, who could have helped him, such as Bolger and Falloon, were never close enough to him to be able to influence him sufficiently.

Federated Farmers leaders such as Rob Storey, the farmers' New Zealand president between 1981 and 1984, and his predecessor Alan Wright, viewed Muldoon as an ultra-conservative holding up more progressive National Party MPs who wanted to lower the exchange rate, deregulate transport and freezing works, and remove import controls.[118] Increasingly, Federated Farmers leaders told Muldoon, often in MacIntyre's office late at night over whiskies, that his paternalistic protection and subsidising of farmers was not what they wanted.

Muldoon became incensed by the criticism Storey and others, such as Earl Richardson, the president of the Manufacturers' Association, were levelling at him over his refusal to devalue and deregulate. In 1983, as Storey recalled, Muldoon wrote to both men saying that 'he had natural enemies in the economy and that if Richardson and I continued saying what we were about deregulation we would be in that number'.[119] That was an amazing letter for two key sector leaders, who represented people who usually were politically aligned with the National Party, to receive from a National Prime Minister and illustrated the extent to which Muldoon had alienated himself from much of National's traditional support base. As one of Muldoon's caucus colleagues observed, however, it also showed that 'he wasn't open to capture by vested interests'.[120]

Muldoon dancing during his installation as Leʻasapai by the villagers of Siumu, November 1981.
JOHN NICHOLSON/*EVENING POST*.

Above: The Springbok rugby tour in 1981 led to massive protest marches in New Zealand's major cities and violent confrontations outside many matches. *DOMINION*.

Right: Protestors storm the fences at Rugby Park, Hamilton. The game was abandoned and thereafter the Government took its stand on the law and order issue. *WAIKATO TIMES.*

Left: The Springbok tour and the Royal tour of 1981 were both thought to have helped in the re-election of National at the 1981 elections, which followed shortly after. Here the Queen entertains the Muldoons, the Rowlings, and the Beatties at dinner on the royal yacht *Britannia* on 12 October 1981. MULDOON PAPERS.

Above: Third World debt and the reform of the international monetary system became almost an obsession of Muldoon's during the 1980s. Here he addresses students at Harvard University on the subject in 1983. MARTHA STEWART/MULDOON PAPERS.

Muldoon's critics included many within the National caucus, notably (clockwise from top left): Marilyn Waring; Michael Minogue; Derek Quigley; Ruth Richardson. ALL NATIONAL PARTY PAPERS.

Left: Muldoon at a judo club in Dunedin, July 1983. *OTAGO DAILY TIMES.*

Below: Muldoon could not persuade Ken Douglas (left) and Jim Knox (centre) to accept a wage–tax trade-off as a means of combating inflation while maintaining workers' incomes. *DOMINION.*

Right: Muldoon and the Governor-General Sir David Beattie at Government House after Muldoon asked for the snap election in 1984. *NZ HERALD.*

Below: Wellington businessman Bob Jones and Muldoon had a roller-coaster relationship between 1972 and 1992. They went from friendship, which included Muldoon launching Jones's book *Jones on Property* in 1977, to bitter enmity when Jones founded the New Zealand Party and split National's vote at the 1984 election, to reconciliation when Jones organised a dinner in Muldoon's honour in 1992. *DOMINION.*

Muldoon suffered from a chronically sore back but he could well be feeling for a knife as he watches the new leader Jim McLay, accompanied by his deputy Jim Bolger and party president Sue Wood, talk to the press after caucus ousted Muldoon. *NZ HERALD.*

McLay and Bolger might have ousted Muldoon as leader but they were far from certain that he would not attempt a comeback, as the cartoonist Scott noted. TOM SCOTT/*EVENING POST*.

CHAPTER 20

The Freeze: Unions, Consumers
and Finance Houses

FARMERS, URBAN BUSINESS AND PROFESSIONAL PEOPLE WERE
not the only sections of the community enraged with Muldoon and his
Government between 1981 and 1984. National had never enjoyed a friendly
relationship with the trade union movement but the situation had worsened for
various reasons; for example, changes in the leadership of the Federation of Labour;
the introduction of voluntary union membership in 1983, at the insistence of
Bolger and against Muldoon's reservations; industrial disruption to key 'Think Big'
projects; and the imposition of a wage and price freeze. Industrial relations
problems not only took up too much of the Minister of Labour's and indeed the
Prime Minister's time but also often dominated cabinet and caucus meetings and
the television and radio news and current affairs programmes. Despite all the
effort, including many late-night negotiations, industrial relations proved to be a
no-win situation for the Muldoon Government.

The Employers Federation, led by its director Jim Rowe and with Max
Bradford as first its planning and policy co-ordinator and then its director of
advocacy, decided in 1978 to reject the Swedish corporate model of strong
employers and union organisations working in partnership with the government.
Instead they started to advocate a deregulated, decentralised and internationally
more competitive labour market with a greater emphasis on bargaining over a
whole industry or site. Muldoon did not agree and indeed was moving in the
opposite direction towards more regulation, more intervention and more tripartite
consensus, especially on wage settlements and levels.[1] In the words of one of its
leaders, the Employers' Federation became increasingly 'worried about Muldoon's
affinity to blue-collar workers and unions' (but did not express those worries in
public) and judged Muldoon to be certainly 'far more sympathetic to the workers'
than those who replaced him after 1984.[2]

Muldoon, however, was concerned at the growing number of industrial disputes
at Marsden Point, the Clyde Dam, the Huntly Power Project, the steel mill
expansion at Waiuku, the Forest Products Kinleith plant, and in the freezing

works, and he encouraged the employers to settle as quickly as possible, even if it was costly, rather than risk interruption to export growth. The employers for their part feared a wage–cost blow-out unless the labour market was deregulated and inflation controlled. While Bolger, as Minister of Labour, was committed to voluntary unionism as his highest priority, Muldoon sided with the Employers' Federation in arguing that reform of the wage-bargaining system was of greater importance.[3]

Muldoon had for many years had a reasonably close rapport with Skinner, the FOL president. In public and to their respective constituencies both men attacked each other but in private they pragmatically made arrangements to their mutual advantage. When the economy and industrial relations deteriorated and criticism of Skinner became more widespread in the union movement, he decided to retire. His successor was the FOL Secretary, Jim Knox. Unlike Skinner, who was as much a politician as a unionist, Knox was almost the stereotypical working-class warrior. To Knox the solidarity and glorious defeat of the 1951 waterfront dispute, in which he had participated, were sacrosanct. Trust in a Tory politician like Muldoon and compromise with a Tory government and the capitalist 'bosses' were unthinkable. Warm, loyal, with a reputation for honesty, strength and militancy, Knox lacked the ability and the personality to work creatively and productively to find new long-term solutions to the industrial crises and the rising unemployment that were symptomatic of a deteriorating economy and an obsolete system of industrial relations and wage bargaining. Although Muldoon always respected Knox's position and was invariably polite to him, the Prime Minister found it difficult to communicate with Knox intellectually or personally and could not persuade the new president of the FOL to work with him to their mutual advantage.[4] That proved disastrous as Muldoon sought to hammer out a wage–tax trade-off and a new system of wage bargaining by enterprise, rather than by individual unions, during the freeze.

Muldoon's relationship with Ken Douglas, the new FOL secretary, was more complicated. Douglas was also national chairman of the Socialist Unity Party and with a fellow drivers' union leader, G. H. 'Bill' Andersen, was at that time one of the two most prominent New Zealand communists. Despite Muldoon's public antagonism towards the SUP, Douglas in retrospect could not recall one stormy private meeting with Muldoon.[5] Even when he had been drinking, the Prime Minister was never personally antagonistic or offensively abusive to Douglas, although he did debate Douglas's arguments fiercely. In Douglas's words, 'Muldoon never ran off at the mouth and pontificated until he had heard, knew and understood the facts.'[6] The mutual respect between Muldoon and Douglas was noted by employers' representatives, who recalled that Douglas, and the FOL economist Alf Kirk, were always well-prepared, which impressed Muldoon, had a sophisticated approach, 'took no nonsense from the Prime Minister', and could deliver on agreements which the 'fractured and indecisive' employers seemed unable to do.[7] Personalities were not the main problem, however; there were substantive differences over the issues.

Muldoon did not take an ideological or inflexible position in industrial relations. On one occasion, for example, cabinet resolved that a stoppage at Marsden Point should be resolved by midnight the following Tuesday. After debating all day the Federation of Labour Executive met Muldoon, Bolger, the Minister of Labour, and Birch, the Minister of Energy, in Bolger's office at 11 p.m. and put forward a compromise proposal.[8] Bolger said it was not acceptable and that the Government insisted on complete compliance with cabinet's decision. Muldoon intervened and asked Douglas to go over the compromise again and then asked whether such a compromise meant that the FOL would order a return to work the following day. Douglas responded in the affirmative. Bolger tried again to intervene but was told by Muldoon to wait a minute. After a short period of silence while Muldoon thought about the matter he said the compromise was acceptable. Bolger started to disagree but was cut off by Muldoon who said, 'Mr Bolger, you weren't listening. That is acceptable to my Government.'[9] Muldoon realised that the FOL was trying to extract itself with some dignity from a very messy situation and he was prepared pragmatically to allow it to do so provided work resumed. Bolger, the FOL believed, was 'prepared to go over the edge' and force a showdown.

Prior to 1981 a working party consisting of representatives of the FOL, the employers and Treasury, and chaired by Galvin, was attempting to reform the wage-setting system. The unions became irritated by Muldoon using speeches and press releases to try to influence both the current wage rounds and the working party. Douglas, in exasperation, told Muldoon that 'if he wanted to influence the negotiations he should get a chair and become involved directly in the negotiation'.[10] Muldoon responded that that was 'fair enough' and that in future there should be a tripartite system of government, employers and unions to provide a forum at which wage-setting could be discussed. He added that it was important that all these parties had access to accurate information and that there was no reason why the Treasury briefings to cabinet should not be made available to the employers and unions. The Secretary of the Treasury, Galvin, immediately objected on the grounds that such advice was confidential and sensitive but was overruled by Muldoon, who said that he had confidence in the integrity and discretion of the people involved and that access to information was essential if there was to be a realistic consensus on wage settlements which could work in the interests of the nation. If his trust was misplaced then naturally the flow of sensitive information would have to be cut off.

Such consultation with, and consensus among, the leaders of the major sectional interest groups was rare and fragile, however. The build-up in inflation, the continued low level in New Zealand's terms of trade, the slow recovery after the second oil shock, and world recession during the early 1980s, all made it increasingly difficult for Muldoon to retain by such means the economic security and social stability that the post-World War II generation cherished. On one occasion Muldoon lamented to Hensley that it 'Must have been great in Holyoake's day when John Ormond, Jack Acland, Tom Skinner and others could have a meeting in the PM's office and work things out.'[11]

While the FOL wanted substantial wage increases in order to improve the living standards of lower-paid workers and produce a wage-fuelled Keynesian demand impact on the domestic economy, Muldoon and Treasury rejected such a 'wage-led growth' approach as leading to further inflation and unemployment. They countered with a policy of 'export-led and investment-led growth' by 'further dampening inflationary expectations which would allow real interest rates to decline from their historically high level, and by holding and reducing unit labour costs.'[12]

Muldoon accepted that a more deregulated, decentralised and flexible labour market would make it much more difficult for the Government in future to control wage fixing and settlements, and for that reason he was determined to reduce both inflation and inflationary expectations. He was concerned, however, that the unemployed and the lowest-paid workers should be protected through a 'social wage' involving the 'explicit use of tax and social welfare policies'.[13]

In early 1982, after three years of negotiations, Muldoon believed that it might be possible to repeal the 1979 Remuneration Act and return to free wage bargaining without increasing inflationary pressures.[14] He offered a 5 per cent wage increase, though consumer inflation was over 15 per cent per annum at the time, but he also promised tax cuts in a wage–tax trade-off which he subsequently delivered in his 1982 budget. When the FOL negotiators took the proposal back to their Executive, it was quickly rejected. Muldoon was furious at the unions' rejection of his offer and the Cabinet Economic Committee decided to impose a settlement. In the face of both union and also employer intransigence there appeared to be no alternative to deregulation of the labour market, which Muldoon believed would fuel inflation, damage production and exports and hurt the lowest-paid and most vulnerable wage-earners, except for a wage and price freeze.

Muldoon had been warned by Treasury that the unions were refusing to accept wage restraints and that employers, who could not be relied on to take a firm stand, were discussing unacceptably high wage increases. Reluctantly, the frustrated Prime Minister decided that he would impose a twelve-month wage and price freeze while talks continued on wage-fixing procedures and the wage–tax trade-off. He also hoped that the freeze would bring home the seriousness of the situation and that it would lower inflationary expectations, which he considered to be a most important factor in keeping inflation alive and flourishing.[15] Muldoon's faith in regulation as a last resort in the extreme form of the wage and price freeze was accepted by a majority of his docile colleagues and by most of the public at the time.

Some of Muldoon's closest economic advisers, however, were opposed to the freeze. When he told Hensley and Galvin what he proposed, they rushed out, with the help of Graham Scott, Treasury's Assistant Secretary in charge of economic policy, a paper criticising the strategy.[16] They argued that the wage and price freeze did not tackle the basic economic problem but simply postponed dealing with it while making a future solution even harder. They warned against the build-up of pressure within the economy and predicted that the freeze could not and would not last more than three months. Although they argued with Muldoon for several weeks, particularly about how such a freeze could be eventually ended without tremendous problems, Muldoon was adamant and finally rang Galvin at home one weekend and told a depressed Treasury Secretary, 'You've lost. I want regulations next week.'[17] Muldoon then rang all of his ministers individually and, after nearly all agreed, he put the freeze on the agenda of the next cabinet meeting and it was imposed. Some time later Muldoon asked Hensley what day it was and when Hensley gave him the date Muldoon gleefully replied, 'No. It's now 110 days since we introduced the freeze.'[18] His advisers might have been wrong about the three months but they were to be proved right about the difficulties of coming out of the freeze.

In an address on economic policy delivered on 22 June 1982 Muldoon announced that 'inflation is our number one enemy' and that 'the Government has passed regulations to institute a wage and price freeze to apply from midnight tonight for a period of twelve months'.[19] Directors' and professional fees, rents and interest rates were also covered. There would be substantial income tax reductions from 1 October 1982 and 'the incomes of Social Welfare beneficiaries and national superannuitants will be protected'.

The day after the freeze was announced the Federation of Labour rang Muldoon and asked to see him. Muldoon, who according to one senior union leader was 'always accessible – more so than any other politician', agreed.[20] On entering the Prime Minister's office, the unionists were asked 'What do you want?' and responded 'How to end the wage-freeze'. When Muldoon replied that it had only been on for a day, the FOL observed that imposing the freeze had been easy but ending it would be harder and they were not sure what Muldoon hoped to achieve by it because the unions would simply make bigger claims at the end of the freeze. In retrospect the FOL leader Ken Douglas believed that the unions' unwillingness to accept a wage–tax trade-off was a mistake. Instead the FOL decided to concentrate on arguing for a 'living wage' and were unwilling to concede that workers might be better off as Muldoon suggested with a combination of wage increases and tax reductions than with a gross wage rise which was then taxed.[21] The FOL's intransigent stance was not only against the long-term interests of its members but also made it extremely difficult for Muldoon to end the freeze.

Muldoon did find it, as his advisers had predicted, very difficult to end the freeze and at the end of twelve months it was extended when the FOL again rejected three options for ending it. At a critical meeting on 23 February 1983 attended by representatives of the Employers Federation, the FOL and the Combined State Unions, Knox remained adamant that there should be a $20 per week general wage order before the FOL would agree to the ending of the freeze and he also continued to reject tax cuts in lieu of wage increases.[22] The Employers' Federation was also reluctant to end the freeze without agreement on a long-term and radical reform of the Industrial Relations Act, a suggestion immediately opposed by Knox. In early March, the presidents and chief executives of the employers', manufacturers' and retailers' organisations, the Chambers of Commerce and Federated Farmers, who met monthly in what they called 'The Top Tier' to co-ordinate their approach to Government and the Federation of Labour, agreed, at a meeting with Falloon, the Associate Minister of Finance, to support the extension of the freeze for another year until February 1984 while they tried to reorganise New Zealand's wage-fixing structure and procedures.[23]

Negotiations continued throughout 1983. Finally, in mid-December the FOL and the Combined State Unions wrote to Muldoon recognising that inflation had fallen and that there had been downward adjustments to the tax scales. The workers' organisations were now prepared to agree to a 'constrained bargaining round' following an end of the freeze provided that determinations for state employees were renegotiated alongside private sector awards.[24] The same day the Employers' Federation also agreed conditionally to a wage round in 1984 but added that 'In the absence of agreement on wage reform . . . we could not accept the wage round option' because of the danger of a 'resurgence of inflationary expectations'.[25]

As a result of these letters, Muldoon and Treasury were optimistic that the negotiations could at last be resolved 'provided the parties can negotiate a reformed wage fixing system' and, following consultation, the wage agreements could be tied to welfare and tax policies to be implemented in Muldoon's 1984 Budget.[26] Unfortunately, although the Long Term Reform Committee met twenty-eight times, by the end of February 1984, despite areas of significant agreement, two questions remained unresolved.[27] The unions continued to resist the employers' insistence on enterprise bargaining in which all unions on large sites negotiated wages jointly rather than union by union; and they also rejected Muldoon's and the Government's insistence that the state, as the representative of the broader public interest, should have power in law to intervene in wage settlements if it believed those settlements were clearly against that public interest.

Although Muldoon allowed the price freeze to end, he made it clear that price surveillance would continue and that, because the FOL Conference had twice before, in 1982 and 1983, rejected agreements with FOL leaders, he would not authorise general wage orders or the commencement of the 1984 wage round until the FOL Conference endorsed whatever long-term wage-fixing proposals were finally agreed to by the FOL, the employers and the Government.[28] Subsequently, Muldoon extended the wage freeze regulations indefinitely until he could get agreement on the new wage-fixing regulations and accompanied his decision with a general wage increase of $8 per week from April. (This represented an increase of 2.9 per cent for those on the average ordinary wage, a higher percentage for those paid below the average, and a smaller percentage for those paid above.) His move was accepted by the Employers' and Manufacturers' Federations and by Federated Farmers but was bitterly rejected by an upset FOL president Knox, who threatened to challenge the Government and attempt to break the freeze by direct negotiations with individual employers.[29]

Muldoon's wage and price freeze, which he extended to rents and interest rates, brought him into conflict not only with trade unionists but also with bankers and the finance houses.[30] He was already disliked by the latter group, who resented the

Prime Minister's tardiness in deregulating financial markets. As a result of the freeze, inflation had dropped during late 1982 and early 1983 from about 17 per cent to about 6 per cent, but interest rates remained largely unchanged in the 14–18 per cent range. In March 1983, anticipating the need to borrow heavily to fund his budget deficit, Muldoon offered a new short-term government security, Kiwi Stock or KISS at 13 per cent on call after a month or 15 per cent on call after a year. This was the most attractive place to put short-term money and soaked up $1.4 billion in three months at the expense of banks, building societies and finance houses. As a result, interest rates rose even further on the uncontrolled commercial bills market. Kiwi Stock was taken off the market in June and interest rates then tended to decline.[31] Largely as a result of KISS Muldoon was able to fund 'entirely by net borrowing in New Zealand' the deficit to be met by borrowing of $1.137 million for the first quarter of the financial year.[32]

Muldoon's 1983 Budget was an extremely difficult one to put together. His options were severely limited. Government expenditure had risen 13.1 per cent the previous year with the deficit jumping by 79 per cent.[33] Muldoon could not balance the budget by raising income taxes, because he had cut them as part of his imposed wage–tax trade-off the previous October. Increased indirect taxation would fuel price increases during a price and wage freeze. National Superannuation could not be cut because of Muldoon's promises to the electorate. His desire to increase production, economic growth and exports made him reluctant to trim his budget deficit by reducing or removing subsidies and incentives, and he was not prepared to slash welfare, health or education expenditure. Devaluation would impact on his wage and price freeze and anti-deflationary strategy. Obviously he would have to borrow to cover the deficit but that would also cost the Government dearly because of high interest rates, which were kept high partly because of competition for funds from the fourteen private finance houses that together made up the New Zealand Finance Houses Association.[34]

The deregulation and institutional development of finance markets overseas was well known to Muldoon and from 1975 he had allowed some such development alongside the traditional banking system in New Zealand. The result was a growth in finance houses, which borrowed from and then re-lent to the public. The Prime Minister was reluctant, however, to allow a completely free financial market and at first restricted the rates of growth of borrowing and later regulated the rates and growth of lending. Effectively all the finance houses could do to make profits was to maximise their efficiency and their margins between borrowing and lending. The market was so tightly regulated that it effectively prevented competition, which might have led to reduced margins and lending rates, though Muldoon was undoubtedly worried that freeing up the market would lead to a competition for funds from investors that would raise the whole interest rate structure. He also always believed that the finance houses were diverting money away from productive investment into consumer spending and speculation on capital gains from property investment, thus fuelling inflation. Attacking banks and finance houses enabled Muldoon to assure the trade unions, with whom he was negotiating wage restraint, that he was prepared to take on wealthy businessmen and attack inflation through lower interest rates and profits and not simply through holding wages. The finance companies, from their perspectives, became scapegoats for Muldoon's inability to accept the monetary consequences of his huge fiscal deficit and the Government's resulting need to borrow heavily to balance its Budget.[35]

On Wednesday 27 July 1983 Muldoon slashed interest rates on government loans from 14 to 8 per cent and on 91-day and 182-day Treasury bills from 12 and 12.5 per cent respectively to 7.8 and 7.9 per cent.[36] Inflation was by that time below 10 per cent per annum and trending quickly down. Muldoon's action lowered the floor provided by government interest rates and he expected market interest rates to follow. He warned the financial community that if it did not follow suit and lower interest rates he would 'legislate or tax accordingly'.[37] His announcement came in a speech to the Bankers' Association annual dinner at the Le Normandie Restaurant the night before the Budget and most stockbrokers present immediately left, anticipating the major rise in the stock market which took place the following morning.

A fortnight later in another speech, this time at the opening of NZI Finance House in Auckland, Muldoon announced plans to fund his $3.169 million budget deficit which, although much larger than he liked, was necessary 'to maintain economic activity at a tolerable level'.[38] He saw 'no contradiction between a heavy borrowing requirement and the aim of reducing nominal interest rates'.[39] He also cut annual interest rates on local body stock by 4 and 4.5 per cent, which many observers believed would stop people lending to local government.[40]

Muldoon's dictatorial and economically unorthodox action to cut interest rates was taken against the advice of Treasury and the Reserve Bank, who argued that interest rates were steadily declining anyway; that cheaper money could refuel inflation; and that the drop in interest rates would shift income from savers to borrowers, and investment funds from banks and finance houses to the stock market. Indeed, the Deputy Governor of the Reserve Bank, Dr Rod Deane, who had opposed government intervention and distortions in the financial sector, complained publicly that Muldoon sometimes acted without the Bank even being aware of what changes he was making: 'On some occasions we've only had a day or two's notice ourselves and at times haven't had a chance to discuss them until after the event.'[41] Muldoon countered that high interest rates were themselves an inflationary factor and that they were also an impediment to growth and increased employment. Faced with Muldoon's threat to regulate if voluntary reductions were not made, banks and finance houses all dropped their interest rates by up to 4 per cent.

The drop in interest rates helped home owners with mortgages and commercial property investors but cut the incomes of the 750,000 people with money deposited in the companies that made up the New Zealand Finance Houses Association.[42] Many of these people were traditional supporters of the National Party and made no secret of their annoyance with Muldoon's intervention in the market, which was clearly detrimental to their financial interests.

According to some of the bankers and financiers with whom Muldoon found himself in dispute, he regarded them as 'evil, as moneylenders in the temple' exploiting the poor.[43] Muldoon made it plain to them that 'I'm elected to make the best deal for the shareholders of New Zealand and that is the ordinary New Zealander' not for 'the executives of the finance companies who say, "my goodness, you're squeezing my profit."'[44] On another occasion Muldoon stated that he was 'responsible to the community at large, not to the business community or finance houses . . . Who are the financial community when all is said and done?'[45] Although by September–October 1983 interest rates had come down generally 4–6 per cent from the levels earlier in the year, Muldoon still believed that they could come down 'a little' more and he was also concerned at the rates being charged by some solicitors and some members of the Finance Houses Association.[46] He seemed unwilling to accept that private sector finance companies, with less security than the state, had to pay more than the state to attract funds and that, therefore, their rates would of necessity be several percentage points higher.

Because the finance industry was so competitive and interest rates so unstable many investors were lending for shorter and shorter periods in order to maximise their return from interest. As a result, although the stronger finance companies continued to make healthy profits,[47] a number of the weaker finance houses came close to collapse and had to be rescued by others in the sector.[48] That prospect of some finance houses collapsing did not seem to trouble Muldoon, despite the disaster it would have been for small investors, and on one occasion Wells recalled Muldoon in private, responding 'I don't care if you go broke. It doesn't worry me.'[49] Publicly, Muldoon admitted that in his dealings with the financial institutions, 'I don't pretend to be a gentleman.'[50]

Relations between Muldoon and the Finance Houses Association, never particularly warm, deteriorated drastically during the latter part of 1983 and early 1984 as Muldoon became more and more frustrated by what he regarded as still excessive interest rates when compared to the rate of inflation. Some companies, such as General Finance, were still lending at an interest rate of 22.5 per cent for second mortgages.[51] While the financial community argued that high interest rates were beyond their control because of the tight liquidity in the community caused at least partly by the Government's excessive borrowing to fund its Budget deficit and the 'think big' projects, Muldoon countered that a major factor in keeping interest rates high was the fierce competition for finite public savings from an increasing number of new, private, non-bank finance companies, whose re-lending at usurious rates, often to people speculating for capital gains, was fuelling inflation. Although initial meetings between Muldoon and executives of the Finance Houses Association were reasonably pleasant, as time went on Muldoon often lost his temper and would 'launch off, rage, become flushed, would get up and stomp round, and get it out of his system'.[52] When told by Wells that he could not regulate to control interest rates and the financial markets, Muldoon on one occasion exploded, 'Mr Wells, I can do anything in this country – anything at all. Only one thing I can't do – I can't make men women.'[53]

The Government could freeze wages and prices through regulation because it was empowered to do so under existing legislation, the 1948 Economic Stabilisation Act. It did not have similar authority to freeze interest rates and new legislation, the Finance Bill 1983, was therefore required and introduced into Parliament. Three National MPs – Quigley, Richardson and Dail Jones – crossed the floor and voted against the Government, which should have seen the legislation defeated. Muldoon, however, who had persuaded several other sceptical National MPs to vote against their personal dislike of the legislation, was also able, by threatening to call an early election, to persuade the two dissident Labour MPs – Kirk and MacDonell – to vote for the legislation, which also had the support of the two Social Credit MPs, who despised moneylenders and high interest rates.[54]

On 9 November 1983 regulations were announced to bring down mortgage interest rates to a maximum of 11 per cent for first mortgages and 14 per cent for subsequent mortgages, and all property transactions including commercial ones were covered. The regulations would stay in force until the expiry of the wage and price freeze in March 1984.[55] Because of confusion over whether the regulations applied only to new mortgages, lending dried up until the Government clarified its intentions; the banks were more affected than the finance houses, whose loans were often personal rather than for buildings. In order to stop a diversion of funds into the finance houses and out into consumer spending, Muldoon in December raised the ratio of their funds which had to be held in Government securities from 20 to 25 per cent, and increased the ratio further to 30 per cent in March the following year.[56] This forced the finance houses to borrow at 14 per cent but lend almost a third of what they borrowed to the Government at 11 per cent.

To many observers Muldoon's attempts to control interest rates appeared ludicrous, with money simply moving from banks, to finance houses, to solicitors and finally offshore. High interest rates on such credit as was available fuelled speculation and inflation. The extension of controls and regulation into more and more areas angered people and in time became unsustainable as those people lost their respect for the law and increasingly sought ways of avoiding it.

On Monday 19 March 1984 Muldoon met representatives of the various financial institutions. After a brief introductory statement Muldoon asked why interest rates were still too high. According to one detailed report on the meeting prepared by J. A. Anderson, chairman of the Merchant Banks Association and chief executive of South Pacific Merchant Finance Ltd, a National Bank subsidiary which was offering rates significantly higher than most of its competitors, within '45 seconds' of the chairman of the New Zealand Bankers' Association starting his prepared statement 'Mr Muldoon interrupted him . . . The meeting then changed from an "off the record free interchange of ideas" to cut and thrust operation.'[57] Muldoon attacked specifically BNZ Finance before turning his attention generally to the finance houses and merchant banks. At the end of the exchange, 'The Prime Minister then stated he believed that we had got absolutely nowhere', though he subsequently added that 'he found it very productive and that it would help him in formalising policy in the next two weeks'.[58]

Some members of the Finance Houses Association wanted a more dramatic showdown with Muldoon than their association as a whole was prepared to countenance. Allan Hawkins, for example, the managing director of CBA Finance, which was dominated by Westpac Bank, wanted to expand beyond Muldoon's voluntary guideline of 1 per cent per month lending growth for finance houses and merchant banks. The CBA Board disagreed and Hawkins subsequently left CBA and set up Equiticorp Holdings, taking with him a number of CBA and Marac managers.[59] By April 1984 it was reported that eight of the association's fourteen members and many of the twelve other finance companies who were not members were prepared to break the agreement and pay more than 11 per cent for funds. Muldoon announced that he had no option but to bring in further regulations, which he did after a long debate in National's caucus, where Quigley accused the Prime Minister of being responsible for the 'gross disarray' in Government financial management.[60] Muldoon announced that from 1 June finance companies who had exceeded the 1 per cent a month growth since the end of 1983 would be required to buy additional government stock equal to 100 per cent of the excess in growth.[61] Interest rates were restricted to 15 and 17 per cent respectively for banks and finance companies. The new regulations were to last until the end of August but if necessary would be reimposed.[62] Despite Muldoon's actions some finance houses continued to flout his guidelines. Broadbank and Equiticorp, for example, in June 1984 were still borrowing at rates above the Government's 11 per cent maximum and, according to some observers such as Lange, lending at up to 22.58 per cent.[63]

Hawkins, Michael Fay, and others were very keen to take advantage of deregulated capital markets but became convinced that this was dependent on the defeat of Muldoon and a change of government. Discussions with key Labour politicians had reassured them that many in the Opposition were 'ready and willing to listen' and to free up the finance sector.[64] Shortly before the 1984 election, Lange announced that a Labour Government would deregulate interest rates, much to the delight of finance house executives, many of whom changed from National to Labour supporters as a result of Labour's promise and their experience with Muldoon.[65] At the start of the 1984 election campaign, Wells publicly declared the agreement over the 11 per cent guideline 'null and void' and accused Muldoon of 'totalitarianism'.[66] A furious Prime Minister subsequently told Wells, 'I will get you if it's the last thing I do.'[67]

During his last term in office Muldoon found himself arguing not only with bankers, financiers, farmers, businessmen, trade unionists, the media, the Labour Opposition, and free marketeers and liberals in his own party but also with many of the Government's official advisers. One well-published row was with the Auditor-General, Fred Shailes. In 1982 Shailes, in his annual report to Parliament, reported that in the previous four years the Government had borrowed some $2000 million which had been used to meet daily state expenses.[68] While Shailes admitted that this had been lawful, and defensible during an economic downturn, he questioned whether it was responsible and prudent. This was the fourth year in succession Shailes, a former Treasury assistant secretary for finance, had criticised

Muldoon's borrowing to cover a budget current account deficit and had suggested ways in which borrowed money to cover government operating expenses could be limited and controlled. Muldoon retaliated by publicly attacking Shailes on Radio New Zealand's *Morning Report* and in newspaper interviews, arguing that Shailes had gone beyond examining the probity, effectiveness and efficiency of the administration of financial policy in terms of the resources used and had criticised the policy itself. Shailes agreed that in future he would confine his remarks to official reports and would not comment to the media, but rejected the suggestion that he had exceeded his authority.

Muldoon was 'always happy to have the Planning Council from time to time brief both the Government and Opposition caucuses even when the Council was critical of the Government.'[69] Birch, as the minister responsible for the Planning Council, always warned the council if he foresaw any problems with the Prime Minister. But Muldoon became increasingly reluctant to take its advice. Finally Muldoon told the council's chairman, Frank Holmes, 'I don't think your reports are helpful. I have decided to abolish the Council.' Holmes challenged Muldoon's decision and stressed the advantages of the Government continuing to have advice on the economy independent of Treasury and the Reserve Bank. Muldoon agreed to ask a working party of Merv Probine, chairman of the State Services Commission, Hensley and Galvin to reconsider the matter. On their recommendation Muldoon changed his mind and agreed that the Planning Council should continue in a slightly modified form.

The Prime Minister's tolerance of the Planning Council chairman's independent views, however, was then tested severely when Sir Frank Holmes addressed the New Zealand Finance Houses Association annual dinner in August 1983. Holmes offered 'a toast to 1984. May it take us well away from the nightmare society which George Orwell envisaged in his novel. May it set us more firmly on a path of freer choice and of recovery from stagnation and unemployment, towards better living for all New Zealanders.' Holmes then went on to deal critically with the freeze, using the metaphor of a passenger plane whose pilot had decided that 'an accelerated, near-vertical descent will be good for the passengers'. Holmes concluded that the National Party said it favoured 'freedom of enterprise' but its Government put 'excessive reliance on protection and regulation . . . a major cause of our relatively poor record of slow growth and instability in recent years . . . we do not accept, like the brainwashed people of Orwell's *1984*, that 'freedom is slavery", "ignorance is strength", and "two plus two equals five" because the Leader says so.'[70] Muldoon remembered the speech, which was widely publicised, some months later when Holmes accepted an invitation from the Minister of Education to become the new chairman of the University Grants Committee. Although Holmes had the support of the minister, the outgoing chairman, Dr Alan Johns, and the chancellors and vice-chancellors of all seven universities, when the appointment went to cabinet for confirmation it was decided that the process of finding a new chairman of the UGC should be recommenced and alternative names to Holmes produced by the minister. Holmes believed that Muldoon had persuaded cabinet not to accept his nomination and subsequently withdrew from further consideration.[71]

Another official who sometimes challenged Muldoon's policies and actions was Ray White, the Governor of the Reserve Bank. White, who was Governor for five years from 1977 to 1982 and before that Deputy Governor for ten years, was a man of considerable courage and integrity who always told Muldoon the truth and was quite prepared to argue with him even when Muldoon was at his most difficult and intimidating. By 1982, although Muldoon was prepared to reappoint him to a further term as Governor, White had, in one close colleague's words, 'had a gutsful of Muldoon', especially because of the reintroduction of arbitrary controls on interest rates in late 1981, and chose to retire.[72]

The Bank's board unanimously recommended as White's successor the Bank's chief economist, Dr Roderick Deane. Muldoon rang Deane, told him of the recommendation, and then said that he intended instead to appoint Dick Wilks, the Deputy Governor, to succeed White. Deane would be appointed the new Deputy Governor. Muldoon then asked Deane if he knew why he was not being appointed the new Governor and Deane, certain that it was because of his persistent opposition as the Reserve Bank's economist to Muldoon's policies over the previous seven years, said, 'Yes'. Muldoon later stated publicly that his major concern about Deane was not his advocacy of Friedmanite monetarist views and policies but that, in Muldoon's opinion, 'in the years in which I worked with him I never detected any real understanding of the way economic policy impacts on the ordinary New Zealander and that, indeed, is what is wrong with monetarism'.[73] Even in the most difficult and stressful of circumstances and with Deane clearly identified as one of Muldoon's major public sector critics and opponents, however, Deane recalled that Muldoon always treated him courteously and politely.[74] He believed Muldoon respected him because Deane was not frightened of him and always prepared himself as if for an exam before going to see the Prime Minister. Those who made suggestions to Muldoon without evidence and substantiating argument would invariably be demolished by him. In 1984, when the position of Governor again became vacant, Muldoon for a second time overrode the Bank board's recommendation of Deane and appointed Spencer Russell, who had been chief executive of the National Bank and president of the Bankers' Association.

Treasury officials also became increasingly concerned at aspects of Muldoon's policies and told him so through a series of secret reports. Between 4 March 1983 and 30 May 1984 Galvin, as Secretary of the Treasury, reported confidentially to Muldoon through a new series of Treasury reports known as the P series. Only three copies of such reports were produced and were for the Prime Minister's eye only. In all, forty-four such reports on unusually sensitive economic material were sent to Muldoon during those fifteen months.[75] The P reports covered a range of topics such as the restructuring of the domestic tyre industry;[76] the rationalisation of the woollen textile industry;[77] the transition from the wage and price freeze;[78] the New Zealand Steel expansion;[79] and Standard and Poor's concern at the Government deficit and its dropping of New Zealand's credit rating from AAA to AA+.[80] In one of its earliest P reports, Treasury, which was worried by the Government Budget deficit and the rising cost of social welfare payments, suggested to Muldoon that he should reduce the net cost of National Superannuation by imposing a surtax of 10 per cent on all income in excess of either $100 per week or $70 per week.[81]

Not coincidentally, the P reports commenced two days after an IMF Executive Board meeting on 2 March 1983 discussed a staff report on the New Zealand economy. The authors of that IMF report expressed concern at New Zealand's external debt; the deterioration in its Budget deficit; the 16 per cent inflation rate; the protection enjoyed by New Zealand manufacturers; and the possible overvaluation of the New Zealand currency.[82] They also doubted whether the freeze on prices, wages and interest rates as a means of breaking inflationary expectations would succeed in the light of the record of such measures previously in other countries. Treasury, loyally defending government policies with which they disagreed, responded that there was heavy and systematic discrimination against New Zealand's exports internationally; that there was 'insufficient recognition of the growth attained in recent years and relatively low unemployment rate by international standards despite falls in the terms of trade'; that 'the freeze has been received well by the people' of New Zealand and 'has also provided a breathing space to put in place sound monetary and fiscal policy'; and that a significant proportion of debt had been used to finance capital-intensive projects in the energy field which were 'expected to yield high pay-offs in the future'.[83]

Although he was not always impressed with the advice he was receiving, Muldoon did not need convincing that New Zealand's economy was in a mess. By late 1982 he was very pessimistic about New Zealand's economy in the short term. He felt that 'the recession was going to last for a long time' and that indeed 'there could be a financial collapse within twelve months'.[84] He told his party's Executive that he would have to continue to subsidise farmers to keep them in business until export prices went up and inflation was brought under control. He also intended to crack down on tax avoidance and increase the tax paid by two-income families. Although the party president, Sue Wood, warned Muldoon that 'there was no way the Party could sustain another year like 1982', Muldoon responded that the economy in 1983 would probably be worse and he would have difficulties with the Budget deficit.[85] Although the IMF had said that government expenditure should be cut more, in Muldoon's judgment 'there was very little room for cutting Government spending' and he believed 'acceptance of their advice would put the Government out of office'.[86]

Muldoon never forgot where he had come from, and with his genuine concern for the poor and the powerless was instinctively unable to accept policies that would hurt lower-income people. Unlike the Labour politicians who succeeded him, Muldoon never believed that economic and social policies could be dealt with separately. To him it was inconceivable that consideration of economic policies could be divorced from their social contexts and consequences. Although undoubtedly always aware of the electoral results of unpopular policies, Muldoon was not (as his critics asserted) motivated entirely by the thought of winning the next election. He genuinely hated the idea that people might be impoverished by his Government's actions and was determined, as far as possible, to protect paternalistically the living standards of the less fortunate in society. As a result he scrawled across the bottom of documents from Treasury advocating radical policies comments such as 'I will not do this. It would raise unemployment and hurt those least able to protect themselves' or 'What do you mean there is no alternative? There are always alternatives.'

Even the Treasury and Reserve Bank officials who disagreed with and fought Muldoon most over economic policy found him always proper, formal and courteous.[87] He rarely attacked officials personally over their advice but he kept Treasury as a whole in its place as advisers not decision-makers. He was discreet in keeping his own counsel and only told people what he wanted to. He was very loyal and supportive of his staff and although he rarely thanked or praised them personally would comment on them favourably to other people. All commented on his wicked sense of humour and his enjoyment of a good joke. Graham Scott described Muldoon in retrospect as 'one of the most profoundly intelligent men I ever met – not a formally educated brain but sheer, native cleverness.' He had a 'head full of facts, an indelible memory, could always see a weakness in any argument, and understood a complex problem or briefing'.[88] But because his 'belief system' was dominant Muldoon found himself increasingly opposed to 'modern corporate management practices in the public sector' and his 'instinctive sympathy for those not his equal and care for the little people' had him 'constantly asking how it would affect the ordinary bloke'.[89]

Muldoon was not usually as dictatorial as his critics alleged and on most occasions would discuss matters fully, especially with people whose judgement he respected and trusted, before making up his mind. Nor was he opposed to Treasury or to lobby groups such as the Business Roundtable per se, but he disliked their unwillingness to consider alternatives, the effect of their policies on people, and their attempt not simply to influence government and public opinion but to capture and dictate to them. Muldoon's deputy, MacIntyre, was not alone in agreeing with him that most New Zealanders did not want the country to be run by Treasury, whose staff were 'young, bright, and had magnificent academic credentials but who did not have to deal with people', or by those politicians like Douglas and Richardson who, as Muldoon and MacIntyre later came to believe, simply followed the Treasury line.[90]

Although Muldoon on balance defended the Keynesian economy and welfare state against the New Right monetarists, he was not committed dogmatically to any model and on occasion did accept advice from advisers such as Deane and Scott. He certainly 'watched the money supply like a hawk', for example, and 'was a monetarist in trying to control the growth of the aggregate money supply'.[91] Only during the period 1982–84 did Muldoon start to see the choice between the two positions as a stark choice between good and evil and as a result, in the opinion of some senior advisers, committed himself totally to an anti-New Right position.[92]

Both Deane and Scott, who became major critics and opponents of Muldoon's policies and actions during the 1980s, had earlier admired him as an intelligent Minister of Finance in the 1960s and 1970s, attentive to advice and with instincts to be a liberal and orthodox Minister of Finance. Scott, indeed, worked for three years in Muldoon's 'think tank'. Deane believed that Muldoon was 'first class administratively and in a management sense but lost his way in policy strategy'.[93] He was always willing, except during the 1984 election campaign, to give his advisers a good hearing even when he disagreed with them, but whereas, in Deane's opinion, in the early days of his prime-ministership Muldoon could distinguish between economic and political arguments, towards the end he came to confuse the two.

Another who believed Muldoon had changed for the worse was his loyal secretary Margaret Mouat. In 1981 Mouat, who had been on a working trip overseas since 1979, returned at Muldoon's request to join his private secretarial staff for the 1981 election. She found Muldoon very tired and more ruthless. His friends were going, his enemies increasing and 'like dogs were baying at his back'. Never one for confiding in or trusting others, he now seemed even less so and 'he appeared to have lost sight of himself and his ideals'. Mouat sadly recalled, in hindsight, that she 'didn't like what Muldoon had become'.[94] She also was worried about his drinking, which she thought had started to become a problem first in about 1974. Shortly after returning to his office in 1981 Mouat gave Muldoon a whisky at an office party. Muldoon said it was not strong enough and asked for another. When Mouat refused on the grounds that Muldoon had to go back into the House he got someone else to refill his glass.[95] In August 1982, not enjoying being back in Muldoon's office, Mouat left and joined the National Research Unit where she stayed until rejoining Muldoon when he became Leader of the Opposition in July 1984.

Throughout the early part of 1983 the Labour Opposition, despite its own divisions between the Rowling-Anderton and Lange-Douglas factions, maintained constant pressure on the National Government. Lange, who replaced Rowling as Leader of the Opposition in February 1983, launched savage and effective attacks on Muldoon personally and his policies. Lange rejected the price, wage and rent freeze; criticised the record of overseas and internal debt and Muldoon's pressure on the financial institutions; lamented the fact that, by mid-August 1983, Parliament had met for only 17 of 208 days; and condemned Muldoon as a man who 'thrives on confrontation, division, bullying and fear'.[96] According to Lange, under Muldoon New Zealand was rapidly becoming comparable to an East European Communist state. In September 1983, however, Lange and Labour at a caucus retreat decided that thenceforth they would ignore Muldoon inside and outside Parliament and would attack him only during major set debates. Instead Labour would 'assume the mantle of government without being elected' and create a positive and confident image leading up to the 1984 election campaign.[97] That strategy of treating Muldoon largely as an irrelevancy to the future continued up to and throughout the 1984 election campaign.

Muldoon was like a battle-scarred ageing boxer. When he came up against Lange he was past his best, and although he had the skills and knowledge was unable to defeat a younger rival who was not as well-informed but who had great natural ability, good instincts, and passion. As a speaker in Parliament Muldoon was nearly always effective but, although when he spoke there was sometimes considerable drama because of the situation, he was not a great orator capable of giving a theatrical dramatic performance like Talboys or Lange. Muldoon's strength as a debater was in his content and his precise, sometimes repetitive, prose, not in his oratorical use of poetic language or dramatic appeal to conscience or ideal. While Muldoon could get laughs and cheers from his own supporters when making points or jokes in the House, he could not, as Lange did so effectively, entertain MPs of every persuasion with his incredible quick wit and exceptional turn of phrase. It was obvious even to Muldoon's admirers such as the chief whip, McKinnon, that Lange was 'awesomely more powerful' and 'absolutely devastating' in debate.[98] On one occasion Lange landed verbal blow after verbal blow on Muldoon while National MPs 'sat rigid in their seats paralysed by Lange's attack'. Amidst the 'longest and loudest applause' McKinnon had ever heard from Labour MPs in the House, Muldoon turned to MacIntyre and McKinnon and remarked, 'That wasn't a bad speech.' Increasingly, Lange established an edge in Parliament over the still formidable but tired, battered and isolated Muldoon. The Prime Minister's harsh, heavy, sometimes sarcastic point-scoring contrasted with his younger opponent's jovial, light, humorous rejoinders, which often had a majority of National's MPs laughing with the Labour leader, much to Muldoon's chagrin. It hurt Muldoon that he was clearly being beaten by a man who was his opposite in so many ways and whom he despised.

Lange quickly became the favourite of the fifty members of the parliamentary Press Gallery while Muldoon continued to regard many journalists with reciprocated hostility and contempt. Muldoon banned Tom Scott of the *Listener* from his press conferences and refused to be interviewed on television by Simon Walker or Ian Fraser. He ordered a *NZ Herald* journalist out of his office after alleging bias by that newspaper, and complained to the Speaker of Parliament that a private radio reporter, Barry Soper, had been persistent to the point of rudeness at one press conference.[99] The Prime Minister's most serious breach with the press occurred in September 1983 when he and cabinet decided that ministers would refuse to give interviews or official Government material to Wellington's *Dominion* newspaper.

On Friday 9 September the *Dominion* published on its front page selected details from a confidential document on the tripartite long-term wage-fixing negotiations. The document was not only leaked but, as the Press Council later found, was written in a misleading way and was less than accurate.[100] The following Monday, at a post-cabinet press conference, Muldoon announced the ban on the *Dominion*.[101] He was supported in his condemnation of the newspaper by the FOL president, Knox, who claimed that the article might well prevent agreement being reached on the wage talks.[102] Although Muldoon continued to attack the *Dominion* and defend his actions over the following seven weeks,[103] he finally lifted the ban after 48 days when the Press Council, in condemning the article, also found that the Government's retaliation constituted a clear attack on the freedom of the press.[104] Even before the ban was lifted it had had little effect on the *Dominion* because most other newspapers and Press Gallery journalists simply shared with the *Dominion* documents they had received or interviews they had conducted with ministers. The incident, however, did nothing to enhance Muldoon's reputation or relations with the press.

Muldoon sold his Tamaki home at 290 Kohimarama Road in September 1983 and subsequently bought a house at Homewood Place in McLay's Birkenhead electorate on the other side of Auckland's harbour so that Thea could be closer to her daughters and grandchildren. He still found time, however, to deal personally with local constituents' problems and continued as he had for the previous twenty-three years to meet voters in his electorate on Saturday mornings. For example, on Saturday 10 September he met and dealt sequentially with a deserted wife about Social Welfare assistance to her young family; a Maori woman seeking backing for a scheme to help unemployed youths in Glen Innes; a man with an invalid benefit problem; a Vietnamese migrant seeking to bring his family to New Zealand; a woman whose son had committed suicide; a man complaining about being kept awake at night by the howling of his neighbour's tethered dog; a couple worried by the rent freeze on two rental units they owned; another man concerned about the rent freeze; and a teacher who wanted to discuss secondary teacher gradings.[105]

On 4 November 1983 the Governor-General, Sir David Beattie, wrote to Muldoon asking him if he would accept the submission of his name to the Queen for the honour of Knight Grand Cross of the Most Distinguished Order of St Michael and St George (GCMG) in the 1984 New Year's Honour List.[106] This was the same knighthood that had some years before been awarded to Holyoake, and Muldoon had earlier suggested to Patrick Millen, the secretary to the Executive Council, that perhaps it was time that he also received a GCMC.[107] Millen, who thought that the timing was premature and that the knighthood should wait until Muldoon retired, did not put in the nomination which others such as MacIntyre, however, thought was justly deserved and did.[108] Muldoon's critics, led by Lange, who commented that 'a very long year had ended with a very short knight', derided the knighthood.[109]

On 8 December 1983 Holyoake died. Muldoon was visibly upset by the passing of his mentor and model and his staff watched aghast as he broke down and cried at the news.[110] In his obituary to Holyoake, Muldoon told the House that he 'loved' Holyoake who had been 'the greatest political figure of our time'.[111] He found little consolation in Norma Holyoake's recollection after the funeral that 'Keith . . . was so fond of you . . . and as he sat, most of his time, the last two years watching TV he always exclaimed his admiration for your utterances and decisions. I can hear him now saying, "Isn't he marvellous."'[112] Holyoake's continued admiration and support for Muldoon up to the time of his death was not only recorded by Holyoake's wife. Days before Holyoake died, Wood and Leay visited their ailing former leader, who went out of his way to praise Muldoon.[113]

On Sunday 18 December, Muldoon attended the Black Power children's Christmas party in Wellington before heading north to Hatfields Beach. He remained there or cruising on *Sirdar* in the Bay of Islands until 23 January when he returned to Wellington. Despite the many unresolved problems facing him, however, Muldoon gave no indication during the first few months of 1984 that he believed a Labour victory was inevitable later that year. Nor did he become preoccupied with electioneering. On the contrary, he continued to be extremely busy on day-to-day administration and on an amazing number and variety of domestic and overseas matters. In addition to Parliament, cabinet meetings, caucus, National Party meetings and public functions, Muldoon was almost overwhelmed with a mass of paper and people trooping in and out of his office. His appointments book, for example, reveals that day after day he was seeing ministers, officials, businessmen and others scheduled in at fifteen- or thirty-minute intervals between 9 a.m. and 5.30.[114] He spent long hours earlier in the morning and later at night clearing the paper.

Nevertheless, there were signs that Muldoon was losing touch with the political mood of the country and was finding it more difficult than in the past to enthuse his own supporters. On 2 May 1984, for example, a few days before he left for a fortnight overseas to attend an OECD meeting in Paris and during which he missed his party's Auckland, Waikato and Otago-Southland divisional conferences, Muldoon delivered an unusual address to an augmented meeting of the Auckland Divisional Executive of the National Party.[115] The Prime Minister said somewhat surprisingly and certainly incorrectly that the public was not concerned with the nuclear issue or South African rugby tours. Most New Zealanders, he believed, were concerned much more with lower interest rates, National Superannuation, personal taxation, violence, and glue-sniffing young people. Muldoon pleaded with party members to tell National's 'good and positive story' and suggested 'don't knock Labour, forget Social Credit, don't remember Jones'.[116] As a rallying address prior to a critical election it was less than convincing or inspiring.

CHAPTER 21

The 1984 Election

B Y 1984 MULDOON WAS CLEARLY A MAN ALONE AND HIS isolation was largely of his own making. He had few close friends either inside or outside Parliament. The world around Muldoon, politically and economically, was changing dramatically but he did not. As a result more and more of his colleagues and advisers moved away from him. Muldoon's preoccupation with solving short-term problems, rather than with devising longer-term solutions to remove the causes of the problems, became even more marked as he grappled with ways of reducing the Budget deficit, unemployment, the unfavourable balance of trade, government debt, interest rates, wage increases and inflation. He was resisting advice to devalue, to dismantle import protection, and to introduce indirect taxation. He was frustrated by the difficulties in finding a way out of the freeze and establishing a new long-term process of fixing wages, including wage–tax trade-offs, and in freeing up the finance market without fringe financial institutions bidding up interest rates and diverting capital away from productive investment into inflationary speculation. Muldoon tried to preserve the old order but everything seemed to be crumbling about him and the tide of public opinion was running strongly against his policies and his personal style. He was increasingly a figure under siege and the stress showed.

Muldoon had always exhibited extraordinary vitality but during late 1983 and 1984 he became physically and mentally deeply tired and that undoubtedly affected his judgement and his temper. Chronic fatigue was worsened by his neither walking nor exercising, by an awful diet, by the onset of diabetes, and by heavy drinking, especially in the evening. A visit to Professor John Scott in Auckland on 10 February 1984 confirmed the diabetes, raised questions about his heart, and led to a serious warning to lose weight and cut down on alcohol. Muldoon still, however, had tremendous physical strength and stamina. He could work incredibly long hours, appear frequently in the House, speak often, hold numerous press conferences, and appear at functions around the country. This was one advantage he had over Lange who was nowhere near as energetic. But then Lange did not have to be, because unlike Muldoon he was not a one-man band.

By 1984 Labour believed that they had Muldoon beaten. In the set debates in the House they employed what one Labour MP called 'the tactics of a wolf pack'.[1] One Labour MP would get a tired Muldoon's attention 'and then another attacked from behind and then more MPs in different parts of the House interjected in a way he couldn't reply to'. In the words of Prebble, Muldoon was 'a brilliant debater with the memory of a bloody elephant'. He 'just played with Bill Rowling, a plucky sort of guy who stood up to Muldoon though never an even match'.[2] Like a former Labour leader, Nordmeyer, Muldoon was the master of the succinct, repetitive speech. He knew exactly what to say and how to say it. But although formidable, Muldoon was slow and ponderous by comparison with Lange's nimble intelligence, superb turn of phrase and quick wit, and increasingly Lange gained the ascendancy in the House. Not since Kirk had Labour had such a superb debater in the House and one who could not only rise to oratorical heights but could also respond devastatingly to interjections before the interjector had even finished.

The election year commenced with Muldoon giving his annual address, the eighteenth, to the Orewa Rotary Club on 18 January 1984. Somewhat surprisingly, considering it was an election year and in light of all the domestic problems occupying his every working hour, he largely ignored both and spoke mainly about the reform of the international economic system.[3] He did spend some time defending his Government's overseas borrowing, first for investment and then to maintain consumption until the terms of trade improved in New Zealand's favour. He argued that to do otherwise would result in higher unemployment, more bankrupt businessmen and farmers, and more damage to both the domestic economy and New Zealand's standard of living.

In February 1984 Muldoon visited the United States and had talks with nearly all the top political figures: President Reagan; Secretary of State Schulz; Secretary of Defence Caspar Weinberger; and Secretary of the Treasury Regan. He returned to New Zealand to the task of replacing his deputy prime minister.

In April 1982 MacIntyre, who not only was one of Muldoon's major supporters but also a critical link between the Prime Minister and Wood and Leay, had suffered a rupture of the aorta in a car on his way to Auckland airport. He was rushed to hospital where his life was saved by open-heart surgery. Although he recovered and there appeared to be no permanent damage, MacIntyre decided that he did not want to continue the frantic life of being a senior cabinet minister and the MP for a sprawling rural electorate. Muldoon tried to persuade him to stay on but MacIntyre early in 1984 announced that he would retire from Parliament at the election later that year.

Gair reserved the right to contest the leadership at some future time but he realised that his relationship with Muldoon prevented him serving as his deputy. Muldoon made it plain that not only Gair but also Quigley, who was thinking of retiring from politics for personal as well as political reasons, was totally unacceptable to him.

Muldoon made no secret of the fact that he preferred Birch, his Minister of Energy and National Development, to either McLay or Bolger as his new deputy and at the caucus meeting on 15 March he nominated him for the position. An incredibly hard worker with tremendous stamina and drive, a one-time surveyor from Pukekohe, Birch had been an MP since 1972 and had served Muldoon loyally as a whip and minister. He had rallied Muldoon's supporters during the Colonels' Coup and had carried with conviction, determination and energy the planning and construction of the 'Think Big' strategy. Unfortunately Birch, although a superb administrator, enthusiastic builder, and effective technocrat, was seen as being too much Muldoon's man and he lacked charisma as a speaker and campaigner able to retain National's dwindling urban liberal support.

McLay, the 39-year-old Attorney-General, had impressed many in the party with a brilliant speech to the 1983 party conference in Dunedin in which he emphasised free market economics and the freedom of the individual. A lawyer before he entered Parliament as MP for Birkenhead in 1975, McLay had been active since 1963 at almost every level of the party organisation, including being deputy chairman of the Auckland Division and a member of the Dominion Council. As Attorney-General since 1978 he had become valued by Muldoon for his political-legal advice, though regarded with some suspicion by the Prime Minister because of his leading role in the 1980 Colonels' Coup, his very close personal friendship with Quigley, and his economic views, which he shared not only with Quigley but with Richardson, Cox and McLean, none of whom Muldoon liked.

Bolger, a 48-year-old King Country farmer, had been Minister of Labour since 1978. An MP since 1972, Bolger's popularity in the party had been boosted in 1983 by his introduction of voluntary unionism and he had also been instrumental in freeing up New Zealand's very restrictive shopping hours and in deregulating freezing works. A blunter and more pragmatic politician than McLay, Bolger was a methodical and effective speaker who was rarely flustered. He was self-confident, naturally charming and had a droll sense of humour. Socially, the Catholic Bolger was very conservative on issues such as abortion and traditional family values and economically he wanted to combine the best features of Muldoon's interventionist and Quigley's free market approaches in a mixed economy which recognised legitimate roles for both the public and private sectors.

Although Bolger appeared to be a better balance to Muldoon than McLay in both occupation and geographic location, the balance National required was not so much geographical or sectional as attitudinal. National had been losing its younger, educated, liberal urban vote even before the advent of Bob Jones's New Zealand Party, and a majority of National's caucus and its organisational leaders such as Wood and Leay hoped that McLay could reverse the exodus. McLay was elected deputy leader on the first ballot, a decision apparently accepted quite gracefully by Muldoon.

Muldoon should have taken the opportunity provided by the change of deputy leader to rejuvenate his cabinet and his front bench, but he did not. MacIntyre and Thomson had decided to retire from Parliament at the 1984 election. Highet was seriously ill in hospital and Gair and Cooper both had bowel surgery in April and May respectively. Wellington, who told Muldoon that he 'could not continue the strength of mainstream education if cuts went further', and who was under considerable personal pressure from the various and vocal education lobbies, had notified Muldoon several times in 1983 that he wished to resign from cabinet and also, at the 1984 election, from Parliament, though he subsequently changed his mind.[4] Another loyal minister, Malcolm, had also given Muldoon two letters of resignation which the Prime Minister had refused to accept. Muldoon had disagreed publicly with Malcolm's decision, following a Privy Council judgment, to put an immediate stop to action against Samoans accused of overstaying. After consideration, Malcolm presented the Prime Minister with a letter resigning from the immigration portfolio. Muldoon responded, 'You can't resign a portfolio. If you're a minister I decide what portfolios you have.'[5] Malcolm went away and typed up another letter resigning from cabinet and took it back to Muldoon. Muldoon read it and said 'I don't accept it'. Malcolm returned to his office uncertain as to what to do next. After about twenty minutes a staff member told Malcolm that Muldoon was on the radio making another statement on the Samoan overstayers' issue. To Malcolm's astonishment Muldoon was making 'a public u-turn on the issue' although he never apologised to Malcolm or mentioned the matter again.

Keith Allen, like Muldoon a diabetic who still unwisely drank alcohol, also found being a minister very onerous and had decided to retire at the end of the session. The morning after the selection of McLay as deputy leader, Allen rang the police and complained that he had been attacked by three men while walking home from Parliament about 9.40 p.m. the previous evening. As Muldoon was later to admit, 'the story was probably a figment of his imagination, arising from his medical condition, but the news media wrote every story as though he had been plain drunk'.[6] The police quickly came to the conclusion that Allen's injuries and the damage to his clothes, together with his somewhat incoherent account of the incident, raised grave doubts about whether he had been assaulted and told the Minister of Police (Couch) so.[7]

Muldoon at first, however, accepted without question that Allen had been assaulted, a conclusion which he reached not only after talking with Allen as the two men flew together to Tauranga the day after the alleged incident but after also receiving a letter from Allen's doctor saying that 'As a result of my examination of Mr. Allen I believe his injuries were consistent with his description of an assault with a broken bottle'.[8] The Prime Minister expressed publicly his outrage but, when a police report was leaked to the news media and a television crew then followed an apparently inebriated Allen home and showed the film to the nation, Muldoon reluctantly had to conclude that Allen had been deluded.[9] Intensely loyal to Allen, however, Muldoon did not blame his ill colleague but attacked both the press for humiliating a sick man and the Labour Opposition which would not let the matter rest but taunted Allen as a drunkard and the 'minister of funny walks'.[10] Muldoon was so enraged, for example, at Barry Soper's questions about Allen that he threatened to raise with the Speaker the possibility of Soper being barred from the Press Gallery, though nothing came of the threat.[11] Allen did not stand again at the 1984 election but died a week after it. Delivering the eulogy at a memorial service Muldoon accused the press of murdering Allen, although Templeton believed that it was the pressure Muldoon put on Allen which led to their mutual friend's death.[12]

Muldoon's general thinking about the New Zealand economy in early 1984 was revealed in a lengthy letter he wrote to McLay, who had earlier raised with him a number of questions on New Zealand's recent economic performance.[13] Muldoon admitted that 'there is no question that New Zealand's recent performance does not compare favourably with the experience of the 1950s and 1960s' but blamed this on 'the successive oil shocks of 1973 and 1979' and the 'large consequent drop in our terms of trade', which not only led to 'a significant loss in national income' but also 'exposed certain structural rigidities which have seriously impeded the adjustment ability of our economy'. His response had been to steer a course between 'avoiding the potentially severe social consequences of the decline in our terms of trade, and improving the flexibility of the economy to enable a more rapid movement of resources to better uses'. This had 'involved judgements about the costs and, hence, the appropriate speed of adjustment'. Muldoon noted that he could have moved faster and more radically but was not prepared to accept harsh social consequences and as a result had inevitably had to run large fiscal deficits, which admittedly could not be sustained indefinitely.

Although Muldoon spent a fortnight overseas during May in the United States, Britain, France and Canada, and also briefly flew to Melbourne in June to address the Chamber of Commerce and give the annual Sir Robert Menzies Memorial Lecture, most of his energy in early 1984 was spent either trying to find a way out of the freeze or preparing the 1984 Budget. Preparation for that Budget was very difficult, not least because he wanted to remove the wages, prices and interest freeze, terminate SMPs, and liberalise import controls without unduly damaging farmers, businessmen, workers, consumers or beneficiaries. Under pressure also from the United States to reduce export subsidies, Muldoon asked the assistant secretary of the Treasury in charge of economic policy to find a way of doing it so that manufacturers who lost the subsidies would get back through tax changes and deductions for research and development exactly the same amount as they lost.[14]

The Long Term Wage Reform Committee met on 28 May and 6 June to discuss comments from the Federation of Labour and the Employers' Federation on legislation which the Government was proposing to introduce into Parliament in early July to reform the wage bargaining system and allow the end of the wage and price freeze. The committee agreed that industry or enterprise bargaining through a single agent, rather than by individual unions, should be encouraged. The FOL was concerned, however, about the implications of that reform on the national award system and also on the status of independent unions, whose members might lose their rights to be represented in negotiations or to influence an overall agreement because of their relatively small numbers across a particular site, enterprise or industry. Both the FOL and the Employers' Federation expressed their opposition to Government intervention in the future, as there had been in the past, 'in settlements that are freely reached between unions and employers'.[15] The FOL also rejected the proposal to allow by majority vote in any industry or enterprise the formation of new unions based on that particular industry or enterprise, which would clearly damage national awards and existing craft-based or occupational unions. Muldoon was adamant that any final solution should include agreement that, while the reforms would make it less likely that the Government would intervene in wage settlements in the future, the Government had a responsibility to the rest of the community to intervene 'if the health of the economy is at risk or monopoly power on either side of a dispute is being used unreasonably to the detriment of the public'.[16]

Trade unions were also causing Muldoon and his Government considerable concern at Marsden Point, where two separate industrial disputes had closed down the refinery. One involved maintenance workers on the existing refinery, the other a union ban on scaffolders employed by subcontractors on the refinery extension. The shutting-down of the refinery meant that reserves of refined petrol would be exhausted by 22 June if the refinery failed to reopen or if alternative imports could not be brought in from overseas, and delays in the extension would delay its completion date beyond the target of April 1986 and make the extension more costly. This led Muldoon to seek advice on the courses of action, particularly through regulation or legislation, that he could use to deal with the disputes, get the refinery reopened and avoid a petrol shortage.[17]

Throughout May and early June, Muldoon was also deluged with letters, documents and reports from Treasury on the economic problems facing his Government. On 9 May, for example, he received Treasury's comments on Federated Farmers' Budget submission; on 25 May, comments on the effect of inflation on farming incomes; on the 29 May papers on the balance of payments and wage talks; and on 6 June a further paper on wage reform.[18] Federated Farmers, for example, were pushing for a devaluation of the New Zealand dollar followed by a floating exchange rate but accompanied by lower inflation; a tighter monetary policy but lower interest rates; and a reduction in the fiscal deficit but tax reductions instead of wage increases. There was obviously some difficulty in delivering these contradictory expectations. Although the Ministry of Agriculture wanted SMPs kept in place for 1984–85, Muldoon accepted Treasury arguments that SMPs should be terminated at the end of the 1983–84 production season. SMPs for dairy products were to be terminated by 30 May 1984, for wool by 30 June 1984, and for meat by 30 September 1984.[19]

At the time Muldoon called an early election, the 1984 Budget was well advanced although not in its final form. On 8 June he received a 28-page draft text from Treasury, but the sections on transport, energy, tourism, taxation and the conclusion were still being compiled. Scott, Treasury's assistant secretary, told Muldoon that the remainder of the text would be forwarded to him the following week. Muldoon immediately corrected the draft, which commenced with his statement that his major objectives were 'sustained, non-inflationary expansion', monetary policies that would keep the external deficit, inflation and government demand for funds under control, and the reduction of interest rates. He was concerned, however, that 'the restraint imposed on the heavily indebted countries will damage the process of recovering while at the same time producing social, political and in some cases strategic instability' internationally and that this would impact negatively on New Zealand's domestic economy.[20] Later in 1984, after the election, there was considerable public debate between Muldoon and various Labour MPs, notably Douglas, Prebble and de Cleene as to whether Muldoon's draft 1984 Budget even existed.[21]

Public opinion polls during the early months of 1984 suggested that the 1984 election would be close and National might win for a fourth time. In February the Heylen Poll showed National support at 40 per cent; Labour at 38; the New Zealand Party at 15; Social Credit at 7; and the undecided at 11. Muldoon was preferred as prime minister by 34 per cent compared to Lange, 14; Jones, 7; and Beetham, 2. By the start of the election campaign in June, however, Labour with 46 per cent had replaced National, with 39 per cent, as the preferred Government. The New Zealand Party was down to 9 per cent and Social Credit and undecided voters were unchanged on 7 and 11 respectively. Muldoon was still preferred as prime minister by 33 per cent to Lange at 18 per cent.[22]

National's Policy Committee met in Muldoon's office on 28 March 1984 to consider strategy for the election later that year. They believed that the pattern of a substantial National Party lead in public opinion polls evaporating during the 1975, 1978 and 1981 election campaigns would be repeated in 1984.[23] Polling revealed that 85 per cent of voters believed New Zealand had a 'bright future' and a majority approved of the 'Think Big' projects, voluntary unionism and the wage and price freeze. However, 89 per cent mentioned unemployment as one of New Zealand's most urgent problems and more than twice as many voters (58.8 per cent to 25.3 per cent) thought Labour rather than National was the most capable of reducing it. Labour was also seen as more caring for people (59.5 per cent to 16.1 per cent). On leadership, which 93 per cent of voters saw as being a very important influence on their vote, Muldoon was seen as the strongest and most intelligent but Lange was regarded as the most caring leader.

At its April meeting the National Party's Dominion Council was told by Muldoon that, while the freeze had held prices and wages, there would be some price rises when it ended and there was need for a new system of long-term wage-fixing. He believed that 'a significant number of National supporters were uneasy about the nuclear issue but did not think that the Party would change its policy for the election'.[24] He was concerned that the parliamentary Press Gallery was 'bitterly antagonistic to the Government' and that the New Zealand Party had not yet peaked, although he believed that 'Bob Jones was finding it difficult to maintain his personal enthusiasm'.[25] The party president, Wood, assured the Prime Minister that party membership and finances were very good and, with polls still putting National marginally ahead, the election later that year would be a close contest.

Despite the assurances given to Wood by dissident MPs the previous year, the whips, McKinnon and Cox, had to go to Muldoon seven times during the early part of 1984 and tell him that they could not deliver a majority in the House.[26] On a number of those occasions Muldoon was able to persuade Kirk, MacDonell, Beetham and Knapp to support the Government. At the end of May, however, a frustrated Muldoon asked Hensley to prepare a paper on the law relating to the minimum time between dissolving Parliament and an early election and on the processes involved.[27] Concerned that trying to prolong the Government's life if he lost his guaranteed majority would result in various dissident MPs holding him to ransom, he had reached the end of his patience with Waring, Minogue, Dail Jones, Quigley, Richardson, Upton, Beetham, Knapp, Kirk and MacDonell. Unlike the end of 1983 and earlier in 1984, when he was openly considering an early election, Muldoon appears in May and early June 1984 to have discussed the possibility of an early election with few (and perhaps even with none) other than Hensley.

Muldoon addressed a meeting of his Tamaki electorate committee on 8 June. In an overview of the economy he was comprehensively optimistic about business, unemployment, inflation, interest rates and overseas developments. He said that he was particularly pleased with the major energy projects and believed that the situation would be even better by the time of the election in November. Although he noted that all National's candidates had been chosen there was no suggestion that before the week was out he would be calling an early election.[28]

Nor was a snap election discussed at the party's Dominion Executive meeting on Wednesday 13 June. Wood opened that meeting by observing that the 'Government was fighting for its political life' and that the organisation in some crucial seats was bad and the National vote collapsing. She added that 'the next twelve weeks would determine whether the Party won or lost' the next election.[29] Leay then outlined the party's 'well advanced' preparations for the election campaign which would open on 29 October with election day being 24 November. Muldoon gave a more optimistic assessment than the party president, admitting that younger voters were more volatile and moving against the Government and noting that the party's membership was too low, but asserting that he was starting to get results in the battles against inflation and unemployment, had dealt firmly with militant unionists at Marsden Point, and was confident of winning Rangitikei and East Coast Bays back from Social Credit. He believed that the election would be won or lost in about fifteen seats where organisation would be vital. Wood, supported by the Auckland and Waikato divisional chairmen, responded by informing Muldoon that the seats of Ohariu, Eden, West Auckland, Gisborne, Hamilton West, Hamilton East and Awarua would be very difficult to retain, and Leay listed the marginals on a board and tagged with a skull and crossbones those he thought would be lost.[30]

Certainly, the president of the party, Wood, and the director-general, Leay, were opposed to a snap election. They had seen Fraser defeated in 1983 when he had called an early election in Australia, and they believed that the timing was not right in New Zealand in mid-1984. By November, they hoped, with some justification, that Jones would have given the New Zealand Party away, frustrated by the cost in time and money and the lack of personal satisfaction he was getting from his involvement. They also believed Labour, divided by ongoing resentment at the replacement of Rowling and deadlocked in its policy committee between the Anderton and Douglas factions over economic policy, might well be in a weaker position later in the year. Wood and Leay were confident that their own party would be better organised by November than it was in June, and Muldoon, at least until 13 June, appeared to share their assessment.

After lunch Muldoon left the Executive meeting and returned to Parliament for the debate on a Nuclear Free New Zealand Bill moved by Prebble. Passage of that Bill would have banned US nuclear ships from New Zealand waters and, as US officials had made plain, would have effectively withdrawn New Zealand from the ANZUS alliance. Muldoon had warned his caucus that he regarded the vote as a matter of confidence and that defeat for the Government could well lead to a snap election, because it would reinforce his growing belief that he could no longer rely on a majority in Parliament.[31] He had already been able to pass legislation on the Clyde dam, a freeze on interest rates, and voluntary unionism only with the help of the two disaffected Labour MPs and the Social Crediters. Prebble's Bill was defeated 40–39 with Waring, Minogue and the two Social Credit MPs voting with Labour and Kirk and MacDonell voting with National, the latter only after a personal conversation with Muldoon.

Since 1981 Waring in her own words had been 'driven by the nuclear free issue'.[32] To Muldoon, who was preoccupied with the difficulties of inflation, unemployment, fostering economic growth, balance of payments difficulties, and coming out of the wage and price freeze with a sustainable agreement with the unions on income policy, the nuclear issue was an unwelcome distraction which had the potential to cause a serious rift with one of New Zealand's major allies and trading partners. While Muldoon could not stop Waring crossing the floor, he saw no reason to allow her one of the Government's speaking slots to give her reasons and, even when Labour offered her an Opposition call, National did all it could to cut her out of the debate. Waring was further incensed when Thomson suggested that even if the Bill was passed the Government might not send it to the Governor General for his signature. After discussing the matter with Charles Littlejohn, the Clerk of the House, Waring decided to leave the National caucus and to do so in such a way as to enrage Muldoon and hopefully provoke him into calling a snap election on the nuclear issue as he had threatened to do.[33]

At breakfast on Thursday 14 June Waring told the chief whip, McKinnon, that she would not be attending caucus that day and was 'rethinking her position and her involvement in the Government Caucus.'[34] She then went off to a violin master class and spent the rest of the morning at a gymnasium before returning to Parliament Buildings and writing a short memo formally outlining her intentions. That letter, marked 'Confidential and Personal', was delivered to McKinnon in the House at about 3 p.m. during question time. It read, 'Dear Don, I have to advise you that I will no longer be available to attend any Select Committee or Government Caucus meetings for the remainder of the parliamentary term. Yours sincerely, Marilyn Waring, MP Waipa.'[35]

After Muldoon finished answering questions and went to leave the House, McKinnon showed him the letter. Muldoon responded, 'Well, what the hell does she mean by that?' and the chief whip said he would talk with Waring and find out. McKinnon invited Waring to meet him in his office where she told him that her letter was clear and that the last straw had been his decision to refuse her permission to speak during the debate on Prebble's Nuclear Free Bill. Not only would she not attend caucus but she would no longer attend select committee meetings or be in Parliament Buildings except during sitting hours of the House. Waring assured McKinnon that 'she would always be prepared to vote with the Government' and 'be the kind of lobby fodder that most everyone else is here, anyway' but reserved her position to vote independently on 'nuclear issues, disarmament issues, and rape'. Muldoon was informed of the discussions in a written memo about 4.30 that afternoon. Shortly afterwards he went home for dinner. At 7.25 p.m. Muldoon summoned McKinnon to his office.

According to McKinnon, 'The PM looked a little weary, looked as though he might have had a couple of drinks to freshen up before dinner, but was acutely aware of the impact of her letter'. Muldoon commenced by telling the chief whip that he was bothered by Waring's actions and that 'when I left home tonight, I said to my wife, I may well be announcing a General Election tonight.' The two then discussed the matter, with McKinnon noting that Waring had 'taken a beating on the nuclear issue . . . is obviously tired . . . and seems somewhat distraught'. Muldoon replied that he had given a 'considerable amount of support' to Waring 'from time to time' but felt that on occasions she got herself 'unhinged mentally and emotionally' and that 'I don't know really how I can go on governing the country with a girl like this . . . we've really got to consider whether we can survive any longer with Marilyn, 'cause I just don't trust her.'

Muldoon asked McKinnon how many National MPs would favour an early election if one of their number effectively became an Independent MP, and McKinnon responded, 'about 90 per cent'. Muldoon then asked the chief whip to check by asking especially the MPs in marginal seats. McKinnon returned to the House where the Address in Reply debate was in full swing and moved from MP to MP. Opinions varied though the consensus was clearly in favour of an early election. Cox, Gray, Thompson, Burdon, Wellington and Dail Jones, for example, all thought the Government should 'fight the election now' and 'the sooner we go the better'. Others such as East, Shearer and Bell were 'distinctly nervous about the proposition of an early election' but on reflection agreed that there was probably no alternative. Birch 'analysed the situation very carefully' and though 'not worried himself was concerned for marginal MPs'.

Waring had waited in her office for several hours for Muldoon's reaction but finally, concluding that the Prime Minister had decided to ignore her action, went out to dinner with some women friends. When she returned to her office at 7.30 p.m. she found half a dozen messages including requests to ring Wood and Leay, but still no contact from Muldoon. Wood had arrived back in Auckland at about 5 p.m. after flying from Wellington and had just got home when Muldoon rang to tell her of Waring's decision. Wood was surprised because Waring had assured her at the end of 1983 that while she reserved the right to vote independently on nuclear and women's issues she would do nothing else to embarrass the Government during the election year.[36] Realising the seriousness of the situation Wood, although not requested to by Muldoon, decided to return immediately to Wellington and rang McKinnon to arrange a meeting with Waring in his office.

At 9.15 p.m. Wood and Leay met with McKinnon in his office and the chief whip brought them up to date on the situation. He explained that most National MPs were very angry with Waring and that feeling was building up in favour of a snap election. Wood and Leay were horrified and Leay suggested Muldoon might be bluffing. McKinnon's response was, 'I have never seen him more serious or more determined to resolve this issue of Marilyn once and for all.'[37] McKinnon then rang and asked Waring to come to his office, which she did after changing into tracksuit and trackshoes, grabbing an apple, and asking her dinner guests to stay in her office and wait for her return no matter how late it might be.[38]

Before Waring arrived, Muldoon, who had been told earlier by the chief whip of Wood's return to Wellington, walked into McKinnon's office. When Waring arrived, Muldoon, with personal abuse quite uncharacteristic of their relationship over the previous eight and a half years, greeted her with something like, 'You perverted little liar. What the fuck do you think you're up to now?'[39] Waring responded, 'Those words leave your lips again and I'll sue the shit out of you!' It was not the way to start a rational discussion.

Muldoon, who usually drank whisky, was drinking brandy and ginger ale. Waring took off her trackshoes and put her feet on the coffee table in front of Muldoon and started to crunch her apple. As she intended, this enraged Muldoon further and for a time there was an almost vindictive monologue from the Prime Minister, fuelled deliberately from time to time by provocative replies from Waring.[40] Wood, Leay and McKinnon were at first a stunned, even horrified, audience rather than participants in the discussion. Eventually, however, Wood told Muldoon that she wanted to talk to Waring on her own and the two women went into the deputy whip Cox's vacant office. During the fifteen minutes they were away, Leay and McKinnon tried to calm Muldoon and make him more conciliatory. When Wood and Waring returned, Wood argued that Waring could be trusted and that there was no need for an early election.

According to McKinnon's 'Notes', generally confirmed by the others present, Muldoon, responding to Wood, stated, '"I do not trust her, I cannot govern with a member whom I do not know where she is from day to day". Marilyn laughed and said "well, that's your business".' Muldoon agreed and then observed that at times he thought Waring was 'emotionally unhinged' and not very stable. Waring, according to McKinnon, 'let out a roar of laughter and said, "say that outside and I'll sue you," and laughed again. The PM said, "that's exactly what I mean".' Muldoon then asked Waring if she would support his forthcoming Budget, to which the Waipa MP responded, 'Prime Minister, I have always supported your budgets, I've been one of the great champions of your budgets in the past', but added that on this occasion he would just have to trust her. Muldoon replied that because she had let him down in the past he no longer could. Wood and Leay interjected that they trusted Waring, that she was being consistent with the assurances given the previous year, and that there was no need for an election which Leay for one 'wouldn't like to go into'.

By 10 p.m. the discussion was getting more heated. Waring clearly was not going to change her position and as McKinnon recorded, 'We went through tears, we went through defiance, we went through conciliation. She smoked her three cigarettes, I gave her some fruit juice, I offered her a handkerchief to wipe her eyes.' And then Muldoon attacked Waring personally and bitterly. He told her, 'Marilyn . . . you have paraded out there as a saint, you're on a pinnacle, you look clean, and I know you're not.' By contrast 'we are looked upon as dishonest, the grubby, the play-by-the-party-rules all the time, and you're the one that benefits out of it, we suffer.' He reminded her of all the times she had been helped by him and other MPs and how others, some in marginal seats, would have loved to vote against the Government on some issues but had not because they were not prepared to see it defeated. He then accused her of telling lies in public but when he or others tried to correct what she had said, 'then we are seen to be belting you, we are seen to be demeaning you as a person'. He concluded, 'If we go out of here tonight into a General Election, I know you're likely to be held up as a saint . . . as a woman in white.'

Towards the end of the meeting, Paul East arrived with the news that a quick poll of MPs in marginal seats had revealed an overwhelming majority in favour of an early election. By then Waring was crying again and Wood appealed to her to 'bend one little bit and think of what the National Party meant to her'. Waring replied that in future 'the only thing that means anything to me are the people of Waipa'. As far as Muldoon was concerned that was a clear indication that Waring had declared her intention of becoming an Independent MP. Waring then left the room.

After a moment's ominous silence, Muldoon said, 'Well, that's it, we're going to the country. I want to talk to the Caucus. We'll have a Caucus at half past 10.' All sat silent again for a few minutes, then Muldoon laughed and said, 'Well, Madam President, what do you think of a General Election?' Wood replied that 'she was not entirely happy' but accepted there was no alternative. Leay observed that National would lose the election by eight seats.[41] Another round of drinks was poured and Muldoon, Wood and Leay started to discuss the impending campaign while McKinnon and Cox arranged the caucus meeting and contacted the deputy prime minister, McLay, who with Labour's deputy leader, Palmer, was attending a dinner largely for journalists at Government House. McLay was at first dismayed by news of a possible snap election when called to the phone, but after rushing back to Parliament was convinced by McKinnon that there was really no alternative. To limp on uncertainly from day to day until the end of the year would be painful and debilitating. In hindsight the death of Allen a few weeks later would probably have precipitated an early election anyway.[42]

Caucus was without a large number of its senior MPs. Cooper, Gair, Highet, Allen, Austin and MacIntyre were all away ill; Bolger was on his way back from Geneva; Friedlander was in Canberra; Templeton was in Hobart; and Kidd was in Blenheim. Muldoon gave a summary of the situation and in passing snapped at Minogue, 'This is partially your fault', to which Minogue replied, 'Balls!'[43] In Minogue's view neither he nor Waring was going to bring the Government down on a confidence motion, Muldoon knew it, and therefore there was no need for a snap election. Minogue did not, however, dissent from the decision to hold one. Although Muldoon had clearly been drinking, he was, in the words of one caucus opponent, 'lucid and precise and put the matter to caucus very fairly. He ended by saying he intended recommending an election to the Governor-General. Then he said, "Is there any member of caucus who would counsel against this?" He paused for about fifteen seconds. There was dead silence. No one spoke against.'[44] Wood then expressed surprise that no one had spoken against.[45] There was still no dissent. Finally, Muldoon said, 'Then that's what we'll do', announced that he would go and see the Governor-General and thanked his caucus colleagues, who 'rose and gave him a round of polite applause'.[46] Muldoon walked out of the caucus room into a battery of journalists and made a brief general statement to them.

Following the Prime Minister's bombshell, the Press Gallery journalists stampeded to Waring's office. A woman at the door told them that Waring was not there and that no one could come in. Waring was actually hiding in a cupboard and after the journalists left was smuggled out of the building by one of her friends, Barbara Goodman, a one-time mayoress of Auckland, and then flew to Australia where she remained throughout the election campaign.[47] Muldoon and Waring never met again after their confrontation that night, though, in his post-election report to the National Party's Dominion Council, Muldoon did note that 'Miss Waring to her credit' said little to cause problems for the National Party during the election campaign itself.[48]

While Muldoon was at Government House, McLay, McKinnon, Wood and Leay waited for him in his Beehive office. They were joined there by Birch and Thomson. While waiting they rang Friedlander, Templeton and Bolger, the latter two finding the decision to call the snap election incredible. One of Muldoon's private secretaries, Malcolm Fearn, who had remained on duty, also rang several of Muldoon's other personal staff, notably Jenny Officer and Lesley Miller, and got them to come into the office. The secretary to cabinet and the Executive Council, Millen, also received a call at about 10 p.m. to go to Government House to advise Muldoon and the Governor-General, Sir David Beattie, on the statement being prepared calling the snap election. Millen raised a problem, namely that the Prime Minister claimed, on the one hand, that he had a majority in Parliament and therefore had the right to advise the Governor General to dissolve Parliament and call an election, but that, on the other hand, his reason for doing so was that Waring had defected and he might not have a majority in the future when the House met.[49] Muldoon, however, was insistent that, at the worst there would be a tied vote, not a Labour–Social Credit–Waring majority, and that the statement calling the election should be issued that night. Because no typist was available the formal press statement was typed up by David Beatson, one of the journalists at the Government House media dinner.

The Social Credit leader, Beetham, argued in retrospect that the Governor-General should not have agreed to Muldoon's recommendation that, because of Waring's defection, he no longer had a majority in Parliament and that an early election should be called. Beetham believed that further anti-nuclear legislation moved by him, which was due to be reported back to Parliament from the Disarmament and Arms Control Committee, could have been delayed until after the election later in 1984. Even had the Government suffered a defeat on the Nuclear Free Bill that would not have constituted the loss of a majority to govern. At the very least Beetham believed that the Governor-General should have waited until the Government was actually defeated in the House.[50]

Muldoon arrived back from Government House at about 11.15 p.m. and flanked by McLay, Wood, Leay and McKinnon announced the election day, 14 July, to the excited journalists. One observed that it did not leave Muldoon much time, to which he responded, 'It doesn't leave my opponents much time, does it?' Muldoon's general demeanour and slurred speech revealed to television viewers throughout New Zealand that in addition to the half-dozen whiskies and brandies he had drunk earlier in the evening he had consumed several more at Government House. In Leay's opinion, Muldoon was 'in a very bad shape by 8 p.m.' and in his confrontation with Waring verged on 'drunken megalomania'.[51] Others who were close to Muldoon during the evening, such as McKinnon and Fearn, dispute that and argue that, while he was undoubtedly drunk later in the evening, during the meeting with Waring and when he decided to call the snap election he was, despite having had a number of drinks, still quite sober and rational.[52] McKinnon, for example, recalled that, 'At times the PM, whom I'd given a couples of whiskies to, was sober, at times he was furious, but I always felt he was controlled, he can be very cool, calm, cold and very calculating. He could raise his voice, glare at her, shout at her and then sit back and speak to her very softly.'[53] The chief whip was in no doubt that had Waring agreed to tear up the letter, stay in the caucus, and attend select committees, Muldoon would have accepted that and not contemplated a snap election.

Muldoon's calling of the snap selection was out of character. He had battled on and survived for two and a half years with a fragile majority of one and yet finally appeared to give up power and fight an election he admitted he probably could not win when only threatened with the loss of his majority, not defeated in the House. It would have been much more in keeping for Muldoon to have defied Waring and Minogue to cross the floor and be responsible for bringing the Government down rather than give in to the threat.

While the amount Muldoon drank earlier in the evening may have distorted his judgement and made his personality more belligerent, it is more likely that his abnormal behaviour on the night of 14 June was a combination of tiredness, frustration, alcohol and, not least, diabetes. Muldoon had been monitored throughout 1982 for sugar levels and by 1983 had been put on medication. At the time he called the snap election he was taking three different tablets at the same time: one for diabetes, one for high blood pressure, and one to relax the muscles in a bad back.[54] He should not have been drinking alcohol at all, let alone the amount he consumed that day.

After Muldoon returned from Government House and had announced the date of the election he went back to his office and commented generally to those with him, 'Well, I'm not going to drink coffee at this time of night', got himself another scotch, and started to plan the election campaign. He commented that, 'I think I'd be more confident of winning in November. I think I can win now, but I can't be totally sure we can win it.'[55] About midnight an Australian journalist got through on the telephone to Muldoon's office. He asked the Prime Minister, 'Isn't it bloody stupid calling a snap election?' Muldoon responded, 'You're bloody stupid too!' and put down the phone.[56]

Elsewhere in Parliament buildings there was turmoil throughout much of the night. Labour was celebrating and could not believe that Muldoon had exposed himself to an early election. Because they could not accept that he was not prepared to ignore Waring and continue governing, Labour MPs started to speculate that she was simply an excuse for a much more serious problem, perhaps the inability of Muldoon to bring together a credible 1984 Budget in the current economic circumstances.

National's backbench MPs and Kirk and MacDonell were 'drinking copious amounts' in Bell's room.[57] According to another observer everyone drank too much and by 2 a.m. Muldoon was not the only one drunk.[58] Some National MPs started to have second thoughts and East, Cox and Gray reported to McKinnon that some of their colleagues were saying that Muldoon 'had obviously had more than one or two drinks and was he, in fact, making a rational decision'.[59] Kidd, who chaired the select committee considering the proposed nuclear legislation, was unimpressed by Muldoon's argument that Waring's defection was justification for an early election. By reasonable management it would have been easy to prevent the issue coming back into the House during 1984.[60] Cox suggested that Muldoon call another caucus meeting next morning to clear the matter up. McKinnon 'got the clear impression that some were getting cold feet about the whole thing' and he agreed with Birch, who did not like the idea of another meeting now that the decision had been made and announced publicly. As far as they were concerned MPs had had their chance to oppose the proposal. Muldoon, however, even though he was on a 10.40 a.m. flight to Auckland the next morning, agreed to have another caucus at 9 a.m.

Muldoon 'had a couple of more drinks and was looking a little bit hazy' and those with him decided that 'the sooner we got out of the place the sooner he would go home.'[61] After he left Muldoon, McKinnon went to his own office and then decided to have a last drink with East in East's office. To his surprise he found Muldoon on his own in the bottom foyer of the Beehive. By then it was 2 a.m. and, according to McKinnon, Muldoon 'was swaying, his eyes were looking glazed, he saw me and the funny grin slipped in, and he said "Where's all the Caucus?"' McKinnon did not want the crowd drinking in Bell's office to see Muldoon in that condition. He bundled the Prime Minister into East's office and 'promptly locked the door'. Shortly afterwards they were joined by Birch. Muldoon 'was absolutely beat, he really slumped into a chair and had a scotch'. He was 'drifting off to sleep and then suddenly coming wide awake, made a pertinent comment, then dropped off to sleep again'.[62] McKinnon decided to walk Muldoon to the basement car park and put him in a chauffeured car but when they got there Muldoon insisted that he wanted to drive his own car. Foreseeing this, McKinnon had arranged for one of Muldoon's secretaries, Fearn, to let down a tyre on Muldoon's car. When told he had a flat tyre, Muldoon asked to see it and only then allowed himself to be driven home.

The next day, Muldoon flew to Auckland where he fulfilled a number of prior commitments: lunch with the Auckland Harbour Board, a ceremony at the Regent Hotel, and cocktails with the National Party's Auckland Divisional Finance Committee at the Northern Club. He made a television broadcast at 7.30 p.m. explaining his reasons for calling the election and then dined with the executive of the Wine Institute. In the broadcast, Muldoon did not communicate clearly or convincingly his reasons for calling the snap election or why voters should continue to support him and the National Government. Instead he simply challenged the electorate to choose 'my lot or the other lot'.

National's published manifesto for the 1984 election was the briefest and most bland in the party's history, indicative of the fact that its policy had not been finally developed when the election was called. As a result, Government candidates had to fight largely a defensive campaign on their record over the previous eight and a half years and respond to the much larger number of specific proposals being put forward by Labour and the New Zealand Party.[63]

The Government's advertising campaign was also appalling, not only because of a shortage of funds, and Muldoon's subsequent condemnation of it was quite understandable.[64] It was typified by full-page newspaper advertisements which consisted of an unflattering photo of Muldoon with the caption, 'Who needs this man?' Allegedly, when Lange first saw this advertisement he rang Simon Walker, who was helping to run Labour's campaign, and chided him for wasting money in the last week of the campaign when Labour was clearly going to win but was seriously in overdraft and did not need such expensive, unnecessary negative advertising against Muldoon. Walker gleefully pointed out that the advertisement was not a Labour one but had been paid for by National.[65] Muldoon was angry at what he regarded as either gross incompetence or sabotage by the party organisation. Nor was National helped by the lacklustre slogan 'We're winning' or by a final television broadcast in which the visibly gloomy and ill-at-ease McLay, Bolger and Wood read unconvincing prepared scripts. The absence of Muldoon from National's key television advertisements in the last week of the campaign indicated to many observers that the Prime Minister was regarded by those organising the campaign as a liability whose impact had to be minimised.

Muldoon had for a long time regarded the media as adversaries and had made many enemies of interviewers, producers, reporters, editors and commentators. By 1984 the press was almost universally anti-Muldoon and highlighted his policy failures and the less likeable aspects of his personality. Muldoon was not alone in believing that in 1984, as far as the majority of the media was concerned, he and National could do no right and Lange, Jones, Labour and the New Zealand Party could do no wrong.

By 1984 Muldoon had come to typify for many traditional National voters what the founders of the National Party had criticised the first Labour Government of Savage and Fraser for – an almost totalitarian form of economic management, overlaid with a political style which could be portrayed by its opponents as neo-fascism or neo-socialism. Muldoon appeared to believe that he understood more than anyone else about the economy, about what the people of New Zealand wanted, and about how he could use economic levers to achieve the best possible outcomes in extremely difficult circumstances.

Muldoon had developed an image, which had considerable substance, of an able, tenacious and blunt political giant who overshadowed all his colleagues and opponents. But because he constantly used his pungent wit to demean critics, opponents and scapegoats he was regarded by many as an often petty, abrasive and vindictive man who degraded the office of prime minister. Many people also tired of his arrogant overconfidence and the 'I'm always right' and 'one-man band' images. The economic credibility which he had enjoyed for most of his nearly fourteen years as Minister of Finance was by 1984 considerably tarnished, not only by the country's many ongoing economic problems and Muldoon's inability to resolve them but also by the growing number of professional economists and business, banking and farming leaders who were criticising him, if not always to his face then at least in day-to-day public comment and general conversation. Muldoon had offended many conservative voters who looked back with nostalgia to the New Zealand of the prosperous and relatively unfractious 1950s and 1960s, which ironically Muldoon was trying to defend, but he had antagonised also those who realised New Zealand needed to reform more radically and more quickly than he was prepared to do and those who had adapted to the more unstable, inflation-ary environment and were profiting from it. There is no doubt that interest rate controls, rent controls and the Land and Income Tax Amendment No. 2 Bill and other measures to counter tax avoidance hurt the pockets and angered politically many people who usually voted National. Retrospective legislation, overuse of orders in council, the greater involvement of regulations and bureaucracy in constraining the lives of citizens, and the fast-tracking of bills, all damaged National's reputation for respecting the rule of law and made more tenable and widespread the criticisms that Muldoon and his Government were increasing to dangerous levels the power of the state and were eroding the rights of individuals.

Muldoon's election addresses centred on half a dozen main points which he first used in his campaign opening speech.[66] He started by declaring that the election was about leadership. Then he pointed out that New Zealand had come through a ten-year recession with its standard of living and employment levels maintained better than in many countries with stronger economies. Intervention had been a temporary necessity to hold inflation, wages and interest rates, and had succeeded in reducing inflationary expectations and giving producers a year of stability to plan with some certainty what their costs would be. On this he received some support from the influential *Financial Times*, the British newspaper, which in a New Zealand supplement on 20 June 1984 observed that 'The government's main success in recent months has been its wages and price freeze . . . Which has lowered inflation from an annual rate of 16 per cent in the year March 1982 to what is expected to be 5 per cent in calendar year 1984.'[67] Muldoon also boasted about New Zealand's growth in exports since 1975: in volume terms 53 per cent overall; fishing 266 per cent; manufactured goods 146 per cent; forestry 76 per cent; and grasslands agriculture 34 per cent.[68] Horticulture was a particular success story and Muldoon was to claim in 1984 and subsequently that horticultural production had grown as a result of his Government's policies from about $250 million in 1975 to about $2500 million in 1984.[69] Imports overall had gone up only 5 per cent while costly oil imports had dropped 25 per cent.[70] While the 1981–84 National Government had not gone down the path of radical free market reform, as some (such as Quigley and Richardson) would have liked, Muldoon pointed out in his opening address that transport had been delicensed; voluntary unionism had been introduced; shops were opened on Saturdays; Air New Zealand was reformed; and a start had been made on modernising the railways, rationalising industry, removing farm subsidies, lowering import controls, freeing up the financial sector, creating a new system of setting wages, overhauling the taxation system, and establishing through CER free trade with Australia. He defended 'Think Big', before taking a token, verbal swing at communists and left-wing unionists and stressing the danger of a Labour victory to the continuation of ANZUS. He concluded abruptly with a reference to Lange not being able to find his seat at a rugby game at Eden Park.

During the four-week campaign Muldoon tried hard to raise concerns about divisions within the Labour Party and about what Labour's real post-election intentions were. He noted that Lange had contradicted Douglas on devaluation, O'Flynn on leaving ANZUS, Prebble on increasing Pacific Island immigration, and Hercus on a superannuation 'clawback' for those with other income and on the removal of tax deductibility for medical insurance. He predicted, correctly, that despite Lange's assurances Labour would implement all those policies after the election.[71] While Muldoon was also right in believing that voters would punish disunited parties, Labour was clearly, however, not the only party open to that criticism. At least six National MPs – Quigley, Waring, Minogue, Richardson, Upton and Dail Jones – had constantly talked about their consciences and their adherence to free market, or liberal, or true National principles. That highlighted National's divisions and seemed to confirm the Labour, New Zealand Party and Social Credit criticism of the ethics as well as the actions of Muldoon and his Government.

Lange retaliated by claiming that inflation, which had become Muldoon's 'only obsession', was 'not the number one objective of a government in New Zealand'; unemployment was a much more critical matter.[72] Muldoon's defence was that he had controlled inflation and fostered economic growth. New Zealand had 'come through ten years of recession with our living standards intact, certainly higher unemployment, but unemployment at a level lower than any other country in the OECD apart from Japan and about half the level of Socialist Australia'.[73]

Unlike the previous three elections, Muldoon's meetings were not packed out and his major rivals enjoyed larger and much more enthusiastic rallies. One of Muldoon's meetings, in Rotorua, was a particular disaster. Although told that he would have a full house and that there was a waiting list of 200 for tickets, Muldoon found himself addressing a half-empty hall, with the numerous empty seats even more obvious to the television viewers because they were coloured orange. Almost as if realising that this half-empty hall foretold the defeat of his Government, Muldoon told his audience a strange story from his childhood which seemed related to nothing. He recalled that when he was eight years old he was sent on his own for a holiday in Rotorua. He was to be met on arrival but when he stepped down from the train there was no one there and he took a wrong turning and ended up alone staring at the drifting steam vapours of Lake Rotorua.[74] At another meeting, in Wellington, Muldoon delayed his entry to suit television only to find that Templeton had raised the crowd's enthusiasm and the Prime Minister had not then appeared as expected. In Auckland the local divisional organisation had not been told that the meeting time had been changed by the Dominion organisation from 7 p.m. to 7.45 p.m. At Christchurch the Town Hall was only about three-quarters full and then only after allowing in a large number of Labour hecklers.

Muldoon not only lost the campaign on the hustings. Unlike previous campaigns he was beaten on television by an increasingly confident and impressive Lange. Nowhere was Lange's dominance more evident than in the final televised leaders' debate on Sunday 8 July. It was chaired by the veteran broadcaster Ian Johnstone, who records in his summary of that event that Muldoon and Lange 'behaved themselves, thank God, and stuck to the rules' and at first Muldoon held his own. 'But then the spark of energy which triggered his fearsome gall and gunfire seemed to sputter and fade, and Lange forged ahead . . . I knew Lange had won and that, barring a miracle, he would be our next Prime Minister. David Lange must have realised it too. He used his closing ninety-second statement to compliment Muldoon, patronise him, overwhelm him.'[75] As the cameras concentrated on Lange, viewers heard the invisible Muldoon end with the cryptic and perhaps sarcastic comment, 'I love you too, Mr Lange'.

In hindsight, Muldoon readily admitted that from the time he announced the reasons for calling the election he and National had a bad campaign, though he put more of the blame on the party organisation than on himself.[76] Muldoon, however, was a shadow of the campaigner of earlier elections and to many observers seemed tired and resigned to defeat. Muldoon was like a battered boxer in the final round, no longer boxing to a conscious plan but surviving by instinct and sheer courage while looking desperately for a last unexpected knockout punch that would save an otherwise clearly lost fight. He even admitted candidly to his press secretary, 'I'm getting tired of speaking in election campaigns; I almost go to sleep during my own speeches.'[77] After his last election meeting in Auckland's St James Theatre on Thursday night 12 July, he sat chatting and drinking red wine with two journalists, Barry Soper and Mark Scott, in the South Pacific Hotel. Soper eventually asked, 'Do you think you've won the election?' to which Muldoon replied, 'No.' Scott did not think it fair to broadcast Muldoon's response, given off the record in a social setting, the day before the election, but Soper did so.[78]

Although he defended his record and made obligatory attacks on his opponents, Muldoon significantly and perhaps prophetically chose to use the last minute of his final television broadcast on the eve of the election attacking the IMF and its policies. In his opinion the IMF's 'remedy is a rapid turnabout accompanied by massive unemployment, business failures and in many cases social chaos and political destabilisation leading, indeed, to strategic destabilisation. My campaign in world forums, which started as long ago as 1976, has been to get the IMF to recognise these results of its hard-line attitude . . . The IMF solution of making the rich richer and the poor poorer is not an answer for New Zealand'.[79]

In contrast, the Labour Party, led by the ebullient and confident Lange, was more outwardly united and better prepared for an election than probably at any previous time in its history. There is no doubt that Lange completely upstaged an almost fatalistic Muldoon. The Labour Party, well-organised by its energetic president, Jim Anderton, himself a candidate for the Labour stronghold of Sydenham, previously held by Norman Kirk and his son John, had more active members, funds, organisational expertise, determination and enthusiasm than in any election over the previous forty years. The trade unions and the anti-nuclear, anti-apartheid, feminist, civil liberties, environmental and educational lobbies all threw their full weight behind Labour. Most of these groups had favoured it prior to 1984 but they were now joined in opposing Muldoon's Government by interest groups such as financiers, speculators, kiwifruit farmers, women's groups and church people, many of whom had traditionally supported National.

Those who disliked Muldoon and his interventionist policies, but who in 1984 could still not bring themselves to vote Labour, found in Jones's New Zealand Party an acceptable, even exciting, alternative to National. While Jones did find support among those who resented Muldoon's controls on interest rates, inflation, rents, speculation, and tax loopholes, the New Zealand Party leader went beyond that to provide much of the vision, optimism and enthusiasm lacking elsewhere in New Zealand politics during 1983 and 1984. Jones, whom one observer described accurately as 'a fascinating and remarkable political personality, mercurial, egotistic, boundlessly confident and very able',[80] captured the imagination of many voters with his uncompromising but forward-looking and quite radical economic, social, educational, foreign and defence politics. Jones and the New Zealand Party appealed particularly to middle-class professionals and managers and some farmers with their promises to float the New Zealand dollar; radically reform the taxation system; liberalise economic regulation; increase spending on education and tourism; cut spending on defence; withdraw from ANZUS; and replace the unemployment benefit with public works programmes. In some ways it can be argued that Labour did not win the 1984 election: Muldoon lost it. It was a National defeat rather than a Labour victory, and the votes cast for National and the New Zealand Party combined outnumbered those cast for Labour.

The guillotine fell on Muldoon and his Government on Bastille Day, 14 July 1984. National slumped to the lowest vote it had received since its foundation, 36 per cent compared to Labour's 43 per cent, the New Zealand Party's 12 and Social Credit's 8. National retained only 37 seats to Labour's 56 and Social Credit's 2 and lost all its seats in the four main cities except for one in Christchurch and five in Auckland. Wellington was a disaster area. In the urban area National polled only 28 per cent of the vote and lost all ten seats to Labour. Six of the eight largest drops in National electorate votes in percentage terms were in Wellington, with the largest loss of 13.8 per cent occurring in Ohariu, where Jones did extremely well. Although Jones's New Zealand Party took only 12 per cent of the vote nationwide and won no seats, their intervention undoubtedly turned a National defeat into a débâcle by splitting the vote and adding significantly to the size of the Labour's parliamentary majority. Although, because of a controversial boundary change, National won back Rangitikei from the Social Credit leader Beetham, it failed to regain East Coast Bays from Knapp and also surprisingly lost its one-time stronghold of Pakuranga to Social Credit's Neil Morrison.

In Tamaki, where Muldoon had the third-largest party membership, 2691, in the Auckland Division, the National vote dropped by 7 per cent, the thirteenth-largest decline in a National vote in the country. Muldoon's own electorate executive at its post-election meeting recorded its 'continued loyalty' to Muldoon and its 'confidence in his leadership of the National Party', deploring 'the spectacle of the National Party tearing itself apart in a post-election witch hunt' led by some MPs and Dominion Councillors.[81] Subsequently the Tamaki executive in a lengthy post-election analysis told a committee reviewing the National Party's organisation that there were a number of weaknesses in the National Government which had recently been defeated.[82] Cabinet had been 'aging, unduly compliant to the leadership, and containing a fair number of Ministers . . . palpably less competent than some of their back-bench colleagues.' Muldoon at his press conferences had had to 'shoulder the bulk of the "bad news" so that the electorate came to accept that the Government was led and controlled completely by one all-powerful person.' The policy committee had not operated independently of cabinet, and conference remits were disregarded. Ministers were often unprincipled, curt and 'quite insulting' in replying to correspondence. There had been inadequate progress on deregulation, privatisation and generally reducing the role of the state. The National Government had 'overspent seriously, run up unacceptable budget deficits, and not reduced personal taxes enough or spread taxation more through indirect taxation'. The 1984 election campaign had been a disaster in terms of advertising and public relations as well as results. And 'progressively in the late 1970s the National Party . . . drifted into a state of subjugation to its Government.'

In a frank, thoughtful and revealing hour-long interview with Sharon Crosbie on Radio New Zealand ten days after the election, Muldoon compared his 1984 election defeat with National's 1972 defeat. He then discussed his ongoing attempts since 1968 to maintain minimal unemployment in New Zealand and to broaden and balance New Zealand's economy.[83] He claimed the energy projects, National Superannuation and CER as major achievements of his Government and regretted that his Bretton Woods campaign overseas had not been reported well by the New Zealand media. He stressed the broad-based nature of the National Party, which would be endangered by a radical movement to the right. He defended his opposition to devaluation following the election. He explained why it was the politician who had to put the social content into the hard economic advice of Treasury, not just to cushion the effect on the poor but also to maintain the country's social fabric. Muldoon accepted that he would not remain National's leader indefinitely and when Crosbie suggested that 'History will judge you harshly', Muldoon responded, 'I couldn't comment on that'. He added that he saw the attempt to blame him for everything as 'scapegoating . . . the ancient rite of putting all of the sins of the people on a poor old goat. Well I'm not a poor old goat.' Crosbie then concluded the interview by asking, 'And if the party abandon you, your own party?' to which Muldoon interjected firmly, 'They won't!'

CHAPTER 22

The Post-Election Currency Crisis

THE DRAMA AND EXCITEMENT OF THE ELECTION RESULT ON Saturday was almost overshadowed by a currency crisis the following Monday and Tuesday. New Zealand at that time had a fixed exchange rate, with the Reserve Bank buying and selling its own currency at a rate fixed and guaranteed by the Government. Until June 1979 the New Zealand dollar was pegged to a weighted average basket of foreign currencies and adjusted very occasionally, usually in a downward depreciation, the devaluation reflecting the higher rate of domestic inflation compared to New Zealand's trading partners.[1] Throughout his life Muldoon was very reluctant to make such changes. In his 1979 Budget he announced that in future the peg would 'crawl' and as a result after June 1979 the rate was changed by smaller amounts and at more frequent intervals, thus preventing larger, more traumatic devaluations or revaluations. Exchange rates again became fixed in June 1982 as part of the overall freeze on incomes, prices, interest rates and the exchange rate.

The Reserve Bank and the trading banks were traditionally the only institutions authorised to undertake a full range of foreign exchange dealings but in June 1979 a liberalised forward exchange scheme was introduced which enabled both New Zealanders and overseas people to enter into forward exchange contracts with a trading bank. The Reserve Bank effectively underwrote the trading banks' contracts by reinsurance. There was concurrently a great expansion in the brokerage activities of merchant banks, who negotiated between customers and trading banks. In effect the merchant banks became foreign exchange dealers but were not subject to the reporting and supervisory requirements of the trading banks. In January 1983, concerned at 'the potential that this unsupervised situation gave for unauthorised capital outflows', the Reserve Bank and the Government moved to limit the activities of the merchant banks.[2] Those who favoured deregulation of the financial sector were disappointed at the restraint on competition and the apparent re-establishment of the trading banks' traditional monopoly position. As a result in April 1983 the Government agreed 'to extend new foreign exchange dealing authorities to suitably qualified applicants . . . to encourage the further development of competition and expertise.'³ It also made it much more difficult for a government to control the inflow and outflow of foreign exchange.

The Reserve Bank and Treasury from December 1982 had been recommending a devaluation of 'at least 15 per cent, and probably more'.⁴ Muldoon just as steadfastly refused to do it except for a 6 per cent adjustment in March 1983 in response to a 10 per cent devaluation of the Australian dollar. He believed that to devalue further would signal a failure of his policies and would put considerable upward pressure on prices, interest rates, costs, debt servicing, and eventually wages, especially during a freeze.

In February 1984 the Secretary to the Treasury and the Governor of the Reserve Bank again submitted a lengthy recommendation to Muldoon advocating a significant devaluation of the exchange rate, though this time instead of a minimum 15 per cent devaluation they preferred 'a crawling peg option' which would not preserve the existing exchange rate but over the following 'two or three years' would 'achieve a durable reduction in the real exchange rate to promote growth'.⁵

To senior Reserve Bank and Treasury officials and many observers it was obvious, however, that as soon as an election was called there would be a run on the New Zealand dollar. In anticipation of a substantial devaluation after the election, many people started converting their New Zealand dollar holdings into foreign currencies from the day after Muldoon called the early election. Many undoubtedly intended reconverting after the devaluation, thus making hopefully a tidy profit at the expense of the Reserve Bank and ultimately the taxpayer, while others were bringing forward payments which would have to be made after the election and the predicted devaluation, thus seeking to reduce their costs. If, for example, the devaluation was, as it turned out to be, 20 per cent, the dealers would make a 20 per cent profit on their funds over a four-week period. Within twenty-four hours of Muldoon calling the snap election the Reserve Bank had sold $256 million of foreign exchange and was left with only $240 million of liquid reserves for when trading recommenced after the weekend.⁶

At midnight on 14 June, the night the election was called, Deane, the deputy governor of the Reserve Bank, rang the Governor, Spencer Russell, in London. Russell, who had been the chief executive of the National Bank from 1976 to 1984, had only recently in May been appointed Governor of the Reserve Bank and was seen at that time by Lange and some journalists as a political appointment designed to muzzle the Muldoon critics such as Deane within the Reserve Bank. Deane told Russell that the election would precipitate an exchange rate crisis and suggested Russell return to New Zealand. Russell declined but agreed to go to Basel, Switzerland, to arrange loans to support the New Zealand dollar if necessary.

Deane then contacted Galvin on Friday 15 June and asked Treasury to access other foreign reserves and lines of credit. Because there was usually a run on the New Zealand dollar before an election, Treasury invariably set up lines of credit to cover the demand for foreign currency. Of some $1.2 billion in foreign reserves supposedly available in 1984 about half was in Japanese long-term bonds. During 1983 Deane had become concerned about their availability in the event of a sudden balance of payment crisis and repeatedly had suggested to Treasury that the bonds should be sold so that liquid reserves would be readily on hand. Deane was apoplectic when he was informed by Galvin that the funds were still unavailable to cover the huge amounts of foreign exchange being sold. Treasury had been working on the assumption that the election would be in November and as a result their foreign exchange resources were not structured to meet the pressures that came in June and July. Following a tense discussion, Deane ordered Galvin and other senior Treasury officials out of the Reserve Bank building and said that the Bank would handle the crisis on its own over the weekend and would try to borrow overseas to cover the sales during the following week. The Reserve Bank also found, however, that it could not access all its credit lines with overseas banks. None of those banks said they would not lend but some who were not committed to do so imposed unacceptable interest rates, which effectively meant the Reserve Bank could not use those loans.

The heavy sales of foreign currency in obvious anticipation of a substantial devaluation following a Labour victory at the forthcoming election led Deane to ring Muldoon about 2 p.m. on the Friday with details of the sales. Deane advanced a number of possible actions, and strongly recommended an immediate devaluation. Muldoon refused and told Deane that he was neither to recommend devaluation in writing nor to raise the matter again during the four weeks of the election campaign. The Prime Minister suggested that instead the Reserve Bank should continue to use its existing reserves, borrow more, and charge a higher premium on forward exchange transactions.

Contrary to Muldoon's warning, Deane and other Reserve Bank staff over the weekend prepared a confidential memorandum. It was agreed to and signed by Galvin before being sent to Muldoon late on Sunday afternoon. The Prime Minister was told that, 'a major exchange crisis has emerged as a result of speculation against the New Zealand dollar'.[7] Six responses were suggested in order of preference: devalue; support the forward market; tighten exchange controls; tighten domestic credit; tighten import controls; decontrol short-term interest rates.[8] The officials strongly favoured a devaluation of 15 per cent. Only if a devaluation was rejected did the officials reluctantly recommend supporting the forward market.

Muldoon, who had resisted attempts by the Reserve Bank to devalue earlier in 1984 and who suspected that they were seizing the opportunity provided by the pre-election run on the dollar to resubmit their advice, again rejected devaluation. Instead he instructed that the forward exchange market should be supported by the use of reserves and the drawing of credit standbys. He believed that many of those buying foreign currency, particularly in the forward market where they did not have to pay immediately the full amount in New Zealand currency, would reconvert that foreign currency back into New Zealand currency either following a devaluation or once it became clear that there would be no devaluation. Muldoon also believed that overseas payments were being made early in fear of devaluation and that receipts were being held outside New Zealand in anticipation of devaluation but would have to be brought into New Zealand by firms running short of cash to meet their domestic commitments.[9] Deane received his memorandum back with 'no' written in Muldoon's scrawl on the bottom.

On Monday the premium on forward sales of foreign exchange was raised from 12 to 20 per cent for terms of up to three months and the forward market was closed to non-residents and Government-owned corporations. This led to a sharp drop in the demand for both forward and spot funds and an immediate crisis was averted. Over the next few days the market appeared to be returning to normal but neither the Reserve Bank nor Treasury doubted that the currency would again come under pressure as the election drew nearer.

The situation was worsened by a lengthy paper advocating devaluation which Douglas, Labour's finance spokesman, had prepared in October 1983 but which he circulated publicly at a meeting in his Manurewa electorate on 18 June at the start of the 1984 election campaign.[10] Labour's Policy Council was divided over Douglas's proposal and Lange also realised that Labour could not go into an election campaign openly advocating a massive devaluation without a crippling run on the New Zealand dollar, so at its November 1983 meeting the Policy Council had decided that devaluation would not be included in Labour's published economic policy at the 1984 election.[11]

Although Douglas subsequently claimed that the paper had been issued by accident and was not official Labour Party policy, his and Lange's denial that 'Devaluation does not feature in Labour's economic policy'[12] had little effect on the widely held perception that Labour, if it won the election, would devalue by 15 or 20 per cent. Only three days after Lange's and Douglas's denials, Labour's spokesman on agriculture, Moyle, told the Dairy Board that 'he would not rule out a devaluation if Labour won the election'.[13] Consultants were advising business firms throughout the election campaign that Labour would win and would devalue[14] and as it became more obvious that Labour was winning so speculation on the foreign exchange markets increased dramatically.

As in most currency exchange crises, devaluation becomes much more difficult, if not impossible, to resist when people believe that it is about to happen and there is a sudden, speculative shift into harder currencies. The widespread belief that there is going to be a devaluation drives the reality. That drastic deterioration can only be resisted if a government or central bank has available reserves or credit lines clearly greater than the critical level of investor flight. That was not the case in New Zealand in July 1984. Reserves were drawn down quickly and, because there was a strong possibility of devaluation, overseas banks were reluctant to lend without extremely high interest rates. The clear unwillingness of the incoming Labour Government to defend the currency also led to devaluation becoming a self-fulfilling expectation.

Although Muldoon had told Treasury and the Reserve Bank not to raise the matter of devaluation with him during the election campaign, Hensley, the head of the Prime Minister's Department, and Dr Don Abel, one of the Advisory Group, at the end of each day and using material provided by the Reserve Bank and Treasury, did prepare a report on the monetary situation and send it to Muldoon.[15] It was clear that the situation was steadily deteriorating but Muldoon made it plain to Hensley, as he had to Russell, Deane and Galvin, that he believed the crisis was temporary, caused by speculation, and that devaluation would simply and unnecessarily reward the speculators. Muldoon again rejected formal advice from Russell and Galvin on 28 June to announce an 'immediate and sizeable' devaluation, writing on the memorandum that 'There is an element of panic in this which is totally unwarranted' and returning it to the senders.[16] Although the outflow of funds slowed during the two middle weeks of the campaign, it rose sharply during the last week to about $100 million a day and to $180 million on the Friday before polling.

Russell and Deane had only one meeting with Muldoon during the four-week election campaign. On 5 July they told him that the Reserve Bank anticipated a steep increase in forward sales of foreign exchange during the last week of the campaign, but Muldoon believed that the worst was over.[17] He was wrong. During the final week spot sales greatly increased and total sales of foreign exchange from 14 June until 13 July reached $1,391 million, leaving liquid reserves at what was described as a 'precarious' level of $929 million.[18] Those reserves did not cover foreign exchange forward commitments to the end of August which totalled $1,477 million. Although in addition to its liquid reserves the Reserve Bank had available another $537 million of standby loans, some of that, according to officials, 'would have been injudicious to seek to activate'.[19]

On 11 July, three days before the election, Russell and Galvin again wrote jointly to Muldoon observing that 'Clearly, so long as there is widespread public expectation of devaluation, we will continue to be subjected to these strong outflows. In that regard, it matters little whether those expectations are well founded or not. Our problem is that we will not be able to sustain the resultant outflows much beyond the end of next week . . . In our view, devaluation is the only effective option open to us and is indeed now inevitable. The timing question is only a matter of days.'[20]

On the Sunday morning after the election, 15 July, Russell, Deane, Galvin and Hensley met in Russell's office and agreed that the foreign exchange market could not open the following Monday without a devaluation.[21] Hensley suggested that Galvin, as the Secretary of the Treasury, should ring Muldoon but the other three preferred that Hensley should do so. When Hensley rang, Muldoon was quite 'gruff' and when Hensley proposed a meeting at 3 p.m. on the Sunday afternoon Muldoon replied, 'No'. This was the first time in four years that Muldoon had refused a request by Hensley to see him and a disconcerted Hensley queried, 'What do you mean by "No"?' Muldoon responded, 'I mean no.' Hensley then asked what Russell, Deane, Galvin and Hensley should do about the foreign exchange crisis, specifically the opening or closing of the markets on Monday. Hensley added that Russell wanted to close the foreign exchange market but was uncertain whether, under the Reserve Bank Act, he could do that as Governor without the approval of the Minister of Finance.[22] Muldoon responded, 'Whatever you like' and 'That's his business' and ended the conversation by agreeing to meet the advisers in his office at 8.30 a.m. the next day. The group took Muldoon's comments to mean that they could close the market if they wished but that Muldoon had no intention of discussing devaluation until after the weekend. On Sunday evening Russell closed the market. Deane then drafted a letter to Lange, and Russell and Galvin signed it. That night also a senior Treasury officer gave Douglas a preliminary unofficial briefing on the crisis.

Russell's, Galvin's, and Deane's main purpose for meeting Muldoon early on Monday morning was to go through the protocol for them to brief the incoming Labour Government on the exchange crisis. Muldoon had no problem with that, but commented that he knew Russell and Galvin would recommend devaluation and said that he would oppose it as unnecessary and excessive. He suggested that Lange should be offered the option of making a joint statement with Muldoon that there would be no devaluation. He believed that such a statement would see the situation return to normal as it had after the 1981 election when there had been a similar speculative run on the New Zealand dollar.

Muldoon clearly found it difficult to come to terms with the fact that the decision was no longer his to make and continued to argue vigorously with Russell and Galvin against devaluation on the ground that it was largely a temporary crisis caused by the early payment of bills, delayed repatriation of overseas funds, and short-term speculation, all fuelled by the expectation of a devaluation. Muldoon was also aware that devaluation would have to be accompanied by the abolition of interest rate controls and by upward pressure on prices and could well commence another round of inflation which he believed would double as a result. He lamented 'the social consequences of devaluation' which he claimed Labour's leaders and the advisers 'had not taken into consideration'.[23] He believed that the speculators would cave in if the Government indicated that it would not devalue. Russell and Galvin responded that this was an unrealistic and untenable position and that by election day the situation had deteriorated past the point at which the risk of weathering the crisis through without a devaluation could be maintained. They added that in their opinion the currency had been overvalued for some time before the crisis.

Muldoon's approach to defending the value of New Zealand's currency was old-fashioned and in the circumstances probably unrealistic but it came from an honourable tradition. While his advisers understood why Muldoon was so reluctant to devalue during the election campaign they believed that, especially after the huge run on the dollar on the Friday before the election, Muldoon would have no option but to agree to devalue after it. The trading banks had been hit very hard by the outflow of funds and the slowdown of incoming receipts from overseas during the election. But, as Muldoon argued, clients had used overdraft facilities either to move funds temporarily offshore, in anticipation of a short-term profit when they repaid the overdrafts after the devaluation, or used an overdraft facility rather than bring onshore payments which they had received in overseas funds and which it was generally accepted would convert at a much more favourable rate following the devaluation. Much of the money could not be kept offshore indefinitely and certainly some of the $800 million which flowed back into New Zealand in the two days after the devaluation would have had to be repatriated anyway.[24]

In response to a question from Muldoon concerning the possible cost of devaluation to the Reserve Bank through its honouring forward exchange contracts, Russell used a hypothetical illustration saying that a 10 per cent devaluation would cost the Reserve Bank about $120 million. Deane observed correctly to Russell after the meeting that Muldoon had been left with the impression that his advisers were recommending a 10 per cent devaluation. As a result Muldoon subsequently was to have a public dispute with Russell when ordered by Lange to devalue by 20 per cent.[25] In fact the Reserve Bank had been advocating a 15 per cent devaluation up until the Friday before the election, but the massive drain on the Friday persuaded them that a more decisive devaluation was necessary to reassure the market and prevent further speculation. Both Deane and Hensley, in retrospect, believed that there was a genuine misunderstanding between Muldoon and Russell over this matter, although Russell and Galvin in a 'Secret' document detailing the foreign exchange position written on Tuesday 17 July recorded that 'on 16 July we recommended to the Minister of Finance an immediate devaluation of 20 percent'.[26]

After Russell and Galvin flew out of Wellington to meet Lange in Auckland, Deane was invited to brief Labour's deputy leader, Geoffrey Palmer, who was meeting in his office with Henry Lang, the former Secretary of the Treasury. At first, Deane refused to go but finally was persuaded to do so when Lange by phone from Auckland authorised the briefing.[27] Although journalists found out Deane was with Palmer he managed to avoid them by escaping out through a back door of Parliament.

Muldoon at about 10.30 a.m. rang Lange, told him about both the crisis and the advice he would be getting from the officials, and suggested that Muldoon and Lange make a joint statement that New Zealand would not devalue. Lange replied that he would give Muldoon an answer later in the day after Lange had been fully briefed by Russell and Galvin. Muldoon was not convinced that he would necessarily accept the advice to devalue although he was in no doubt that Douglas wanted to do so. Muldoon knew that devaluation would make it almost impossible for the new Labour Government to deliver most of its election promises on matters of economic and social policy. That would disappoint Labour voters, and Muldoon was determined that it must be clear to the electorate that he had opposed the devaluation as unnecessary. He also believed that the FOL and many Labour supporters would be devastated if Roger Douglas's policy views prevailed in the new cabinet. The FOL was aware of Douglas's economic agenda, including the proposed devaluation, and in March 1984 had raised their concern at a meeting of the Joint Council of Labour at which leaders of the FOL and the Labour Party met periodically to discuss matters of mutual interest. Lange and Palmer at that time had totally rejected any suggestion that Douglas's views would be the policy of a new Labour Government.[28] Muldoon predicted correctly that the devaluation, coupled with the end of the freeze and the concurrent deregulation of financial markets which Labour allowed, would lead to much higher inflation and interest rates. In Muldoon's view devaluation meant the loss of all the anti-inflationary benefits that had been hard-earned by two years of wage and price freezes.[29]

Galvin and Russell briefed Lange, who was accompanied by Douglas and David Caygill, in the VIP lounge at Auckland airport and recommended a 20 per cent devaluation. They also told Lange, in response to his questioning, that a joint statement along the lines suggested by Muldoon would not be sufficient, and Lange then told Galvin and Russell to inform Muldoon that there would be no joint statement. Lange and his advisers also seriously considered inviting the IMF to oversee the response to the crisis as 'an externalising and legitimising agent'.[30] The two officials on their return to Wellington decided that it was not appropriate for them to convey Lange's views to Muldoon but that the Prime Minister-elect should contact the Prime Minister directly.[31] Lange in the meantime had flown to Ohakea to meet the US Secretary of State, George Shultz, and then on to Wellington to greet the Australian Foreign Minister, Bill Hayden, both of whom were visiting New Zealand for an ANZUS meeting.[32] Lange then returned to Auckland.

Muldoon sat waiting all afternoon for Russell and Galvin to report back but there was a long and mysterious silence. He kept coming out of his office to ask his staff whether there were any messages from Lange or if they knew whether Russell and Galvin were back from Auckland. Finally, at about 3.30 p.m. Hensley rang Galvin who had returned to Wellington and asked where they were and why they had not reported back to Muldoon after talking with Lange. Galvin and Russell replied that they had gone to Lange as advisers to the new Government, not as emissaries from Muldoon, and had no intention of reporting back to Muldoon. He would hear directly from Lange what the new Labour administration required from the outgoing National Government. Because Hensley was told this in strictest confidence, he chose not to convey this conversation to Muldoon although he did ring Galvin back and hour or so later to plead with Galvin and Russell to tell Muldoon what had transpired between them and Lange and Douglas in Auckland earlier that day. Galvin, after discussing the matter with Russell, rang back about 5 p.m. He told Hensley that Lange had rejected Muldoon's suggestion of a joint statement saying that there would be no devaluation, but again refused to contact Muldoon saying that it was up to Lange to do so. Hensley told Ken Richardson that Russell and Galvin were back but would not speak to Muldoon and Richardson told Fearn and Officer. All agreed that Muldoon should be told but none thought it was his or her place to do so.[33] Fearn contacted Doug Kerr, Muldoon's principal private secretary, who rang Galvin again to argue that it was Galvin's and Russell's responsibility to inform the Prime Minister.

Later in the week, Fearn told Muldoon that Hensley had deliberately withheld from Muldoon information that Galvin and Russell were back in Wellington but did not intend seeing him or reporting on their discussions with Lange and Douglas. Muldoon was hurt and commented that although Hensley's sympathies were probably with Labour he had been an impartial civil servant who only once in four years as head of the Prime Minister's Department had held back information from Muldoon. On hearing of this comment, Hensley rang Muldoon and threatened to sue if Muldoon repeated it. Muldoon claimed that he had been actually defending Hensley and that he regarded him as a friend as well as a civil servant. Although the two men did not speak to each other for six months after the change of government, Hensley finally approached Muldoon at a function and friendly relations were restored.

At about 5 p.m. on the Monday night, a weary and baffled Muldoon returned to Vogel House. His wife told him to have a rest and, unknown to Muldoon, took the phone off the hook so that he would not be disturbed. Deane had been annoyed with the lack of communication with Muldoon during the afternoon and insisted to Russell and Galvin that Muldoon had to be told what was going on. When he was unable to contact Muldoon on the phone, Deane 'sent a Reserve Bank official out to Vogel House with a handwritten note bringing Muldoon up to date on the state of play.'[34] Unfortunately, the letter arrived shortly after Muldoon had heard Radio New Zealand's parliamentary reporter, Dick Griffin, saying on the 6.30 television news that Lange had imposed a twenty-four hour news blackout on the currency problem and that Muldoon was 'refusing his advice on the matter'.[35] Griffin had earlier that evening been briefed by Lange himself.

Muldoon, who had still not heard from Lange or anyone else, with the help of his press secretary, Lesley Miller, immediately issued a press statement that Lange's claim was 'untrue'. Shortly afterwards, at about 7.15 p.m., a letter from Lange did arrive at Vogel House. Lange, after noting Muldoon's views, summarised the advice he had received from Russell and Galvin and concluded with an assurance that Lange would take responsibility for any decision he might ask Muldoon to implement. No exact percentage in regard to devaluation was mentioned. By that time, however, Muldoon had already given an interview for a television news broadcast later that night.

Intrigued by Griffin's comments, TV's Richard Harman had asked for a pre-recorded interview with Muldoon for its later *Eye Witness News* programme at 9.30 p.m. and Muldoon agreed. He recounted briefly the events of the day as he knew them and what his advice to Lange had been. He regretted that Lange had still not responded, although conceding that Lange would make the decision. When asked again if he saw any need to devalue, Muldoon replied that he did not and ended, 'I am not going to devalue, so long as I'm Minister of Finance. I hope that tomorrow Mr. Lange can get someone to explain it to him sufficiently so that he says – "We will not devalue either."'[36] Muldoon had a good command of the English language and used it precisely and simply on most occasions. It was not surprising that Lange, Muldoon's colleagues, and others thought there was nothing ambiguous and little room for interpretation in his statement that 'I am not going to devalue'.

Lange then went on television, accusing Muldoon of being a 'King Canute' who was committing economic sabotage and putting the country at risk. Lange suggested that Muldoon should either implement the incoming Government's instructions or resign and let another member of the National Cabinet take over as caretaker Prime Minister for a week until Labour took office.[37]

The deputy prime minister, McLay, was aware of the massive outflow of funds during the election campaign and speculation about a large devaluation after it. He was, therefore, not surprised when the foreign exchange markets were closed on the Sunday after the election. In a brief discussion with Muldoon on Monday, McLay mentioned the exchange crisis, but Muldoon responded that it was no longer the National Government's business and that Russell and Galvin would be briefing Lange later that day.[38] About 9.30 p.m. McLay's wife rang him in his office to tell him Muldoon was on television saying that Lange did not understand basic economics and that Muldoon would not devalue. McLay then sent for Bolger, Birch and Templeton, who all agreed the matter was serious, though Birch took the view that Muldoon had simply been expressing his own view of what should be done, not necessarily refusing to do it.[39] McLay tried about six times to phone Muldoon at home but could not get through because the phone was off the hook. Phone calls to Russell and Galvin revealed that they were both at the annual bankers' dinner at Le Normandie restaurant, as was Hensley and the Governor-General, Sir David Beattie. When Russell and Galvin came to the phone they told the ministers gathered in McLay's office that New Zealand was within twenty-four hours of defaulting on overseas payments and that it would be very serious if Muldoon refused to take action. Deane also rang Russell with news of the broadcast.

Throughout the latter part of the evening the Government's chief economic advisers held a number of meetings in the bar and toilets of the restaurant, out of sight of others at the dinner. Beattie, who was the guest speaker, asked that he be kept informed. It was generally agreed, in consultation with the group of ministers in McLay's office, that until the writs were returned the newly elected MPs could not change the Government so Labour could not take office immediately. If Muldoon, as he seemed to have implied, would not devalue as instructed by Lange, then the existing National cabinet and caucus would have to replace Muldoon and appoint a caretaker Prime Minister and Minister of Finance who would carry out Labour's instructions. McLay undertook to confront Muldoon first thing Tuesday morning.

At midnight Hensley met the Governor-General, who agreed to help in any way necessary. If Muldoon persisted then Beattie agreed that, on the advice of the deputy prime minister that Muldoon no longer enjoyed the confidence of the National cabinet and caucus, he would dismiss Muldoon and appoint McLay as temporary Prime Minister to effect the devaluation. Hensley remained awake all night, and early the next morning went to see the Solicitor-General about the matter. The Solicitor-General told Hensley that he had already discussed the matter with McLay who was with the Prime Minister.

In the meantime, Falloon, the Associate Minister of Finance, had heard on the 6 a.m. radio news on Tuesday 17 July that Muldoon was allegedly refusing to devalue. Falloon rang Russell and after expressing the view that there had to be co-operation with the newly elected Government was given the relevant documents by Russell.[40] Falloon then contacted McLay, who told him that there was no crisis because Muldoon, whom McLay had already seen, would carry out Labour's instructions and devalue.

McLay, after ringing the Governor-General's secretary, had gone to see Muldoon at about 9 a.m. As soon as he entered Muldoon's office and before McLay had a chance to say anything, Muldoon said that his deputy should not worry about the issue.[41] Lange by his public statements had made devaluation inevitable, although Muldoon added that he still thought that it had been unnecessary before. Muldoon would do what was required but wanted it clearly on the record that it had been against his advice. McLay was relieved that the apparent constitutional crisis that he and others had feared had been averted, and indeed Muldoon later argued it had never arisen. Muldoon claimed that he had never said that he would not carry out a clear, written instruction from Lange to devalue. He simply wanted it made plain that he would not have made such a decision himself and that the devaluation was done against his advice. As one non-partisan expert observer commented retrospectively, there was never a constitutional crisis as some people feared because after an 'emotional hiccup' brought about by Muldoon's understandable frustration on the Monday, once Lange told him what to do Muldoon did it albeit reluctantly and gracelessly.[42]

At the start of the Cabinet meeting at 11 a.m. on the Tuesday, Muldoon told his colleagues that Lange the previous night had 'refused to make a joint statement on devaluation and that at that point it had become obvious that the Government would have to devalue'.[43] As a result, Muldoon had that morning written to Lange agreeing to devalue when he was told the percentage required, although he still believed Lange was wrong. Muldoon explained rather misleadingly that Treasury and the Reserve Bank had not recommended devaluation several weeks before but had warned that, because the public believed Labour would devalue if it won the election, considerable pressure had been placed on the New Zealand dollar. Muldoon still believed that there were alternative options to devaluation, which might be preferable because 'devaluation will destroy the low inflation level and will cost in forward exchange to the Reserve Bank'. Lange's reply to Muldoon's letter agreeing to devalue had been received at 10.30 a.m., half an hour before the cabinet meeting, and Lange had requested not only a 20 per cent devaluation but also an assurance that the outgoing National Cabinet would undertake to implement other measures the incoming Labour Prime Minister deemed necessary.[44]

McLay commented that because the National cabinet was now only a 'caretaker' it had 'little alternative other than to give what DRL [Lange] proposes' and the incoming Government would take the responsibility for the actions. Muldoon agreed with this assessment. Birch observed that he 'would have expected DRL [Lange] to have taken advice and asked the PM [Muldoon] to agree and implement' but Falloon interjected that Muldoon had 'pre-empted that by saying [he] wouldn't do [it] while Minister of Finance'. McLay added that now Lange 'has made [a] specific request . . . [the] Government must agree' and Gair concurred that the outgoing cabinet 'must take [the] whole package'. Birch then questioned whether 'the Treasury options have equal weight' to the devaluation option, which was clearly favoured by the Reserve Bank. Muldoon replied that that was a 'difficult question to answer' because it was a 'series of options rather than a preferred option' but the question was now 'do we agree or not' to devaluation and one should concentrate on that 'rather than the consequences.' Templeton commented that the 'Reserve Bank should deal with devaluation and Treasury with the consequences'. Muldoon concluded that 'We must tell DRL [Lange] that his analysis is wrong but we will act as your agent. Tell us what you want done because he has the responsibility and as the outgoing government we must defend what we might have done had we the power to do it.' On Wednesday morning 18 July Muldoon implemented a Labour economic package which included not only a 20 per cent devaluation and the withdrawal of the Reserve Bank from the forward exchange market but the removal of all controls on interest rates and a new three-month wage and price freeze.

There is no doubt that the exchange rate crisis was unnecessarily prolonged because of Muldoon's refusal to see anyone on the Sunday and then by Russell and Galvin not getting back to Muldoon after they had seen Lange on Monday. Once Muldoon knew Lange had been briefed, that Lange was not prepared to resist the officials' advice to devalue, and Lange had informed him in writing to do so, Muldoon acted without further hesitation even though he thought the decision was wrong. He was not concerned that the devaluation crisis revealed his reluctance to devalue, because he believed it was unnecessary, but he was annoyed that he was seen to be acting unconstitutionally out of pique. He was also furious that the devaluation, combined with the concurrent removal of interest rate restrictions, would fuel inflation back up to double figures, thus increasing pressures to raise wages also.[45]

On Friday 27 July at 9.50 a.m. Muldoon left his Beehive office for the last time and went to the opening of the National Party's annual conference at the Michael Fowler Centre. When he returned to Parliament Buildings later that day it was to a new office in the Opposition wing. Ironically, his address at the 'Leader's Rally' at 8 p.m. that night marked the formal end of his eight and a half years as prime minister. A new Government and a new approach to the New Zealand economy would soon sweep away many of the policies and processes that had been advanced or defended by Muldoon.

After the 1984 election everyone was astonished at the speed with which Labour moved away from its interventionist economic management and universal social welfare traditions. There had been little sign prior to the election that they intended to do so. The raft of controls and regulations which marked the latter stages of the Muldoon Government, together with the exchange rate crisis following the 1984 election, bequeathed to the incoming Labour Government a legacy which made it much easier than it would otherwise have been for Douglas to unleash his radical free market revolution.

The Labour Government's immediate economic package following the 1984 election, involving a 20 per cent devaluation, a three-month freeze on wages and prices, and the abolition of interest rate controls, was put together largely by Douglas and Caygill and followed closely the advice they were given by Russell and Deane of the Reserve Bank and Galvin, Scott and Paul Carpinter of Treasury.[46]

Following the abolition of interest rate controls, the finance houses immediately raised their lending rates by between 1 and 10 per cent.[47] In the year after the 1984 election the finance houses greatly increased their combined assets and deposits by 31.7 per cent and 26.9 per cent respectively and NZI Finance, for example, lifted its after-tax profit by 66 per cent compared to the last year of the Muldoon Government. By May 1985 NZI Finance's interest rates were 22 per cent per annum for two years and 17 per cent per annum on call.[48]

Roger Douglas's first major speaking engagement as Minister of Finance was to the New Zealand Finance Houses Association annual general meeting on 1 August 1984. The chairman, Wells, in introducing Douglas, referred to the Association's relationship with Muldoon as having been similar to 'sleeping with an elephant . . . [who] kept taking more room in the bed and hogging all the blankets leaving the industry squeezed and chilled'.[49] The finance houses 'warmly applauded' the devaluation and deregulation of financial markets for which the new Labour Government was responsible but looked forward to even greater deregulation in the future. In response Douglas largely traversed the devaluation crisis and the structural problems facing the New Zealand economy. He expressed some concern at the initial results of deregulating the finance sector and complained that 'in the year to May 1984 private sector credit grew by 20 per cent, a level that is clearly unsustainable'. He warned that he intended to run a firm monetary policy that would curtail such growth in the future.[50] Aggressively confident finance houses such as Hawkins's new merchant bank Equiticorp Holdings were unimpressed and almost immediately announced new peak interest rates of 16.5 per cent for six month debentures.[51] Muldoon's fears of soaring interest rates and rising inflation were being quickly realised.

Subsequently, when later in 1984 the Public Expenditure Committee of Parliament set up a subcommittee chaired by Labour's Jim Anderton to investigate the devaluation, Russell immediately told Douglas that such an inquiry would destroy New Zealand's credibility in the currency markets.[52] His concern was heightened by the presence of Muldoon on the committee as chief protagonist and chief prosecutor and Russell and Galvin both told the committee that they intended to be present when anyone from the Reserve Bank or Treasury was summoned to appear before the committee. Muldoon stated that the committee would call whom it wished and that Russell and Galvin had no right to be present, a stance adopted by the rest of the committee. At its first meeting on 13 September the subcommittee called Deane and Scott as its first witnesses. Only Deane was heard before the Labour Government aborted the committee and its investigation on the grounds that Muldoon's presence on the committee clearly showed that it was not an impartial forum.[53] Muldoon had started to cross-examine Deane about the advice Muldoon had received at the time and had stated that he was prepared to table all the papers on the subject in his possession. Because such a hearing might also have revealed the very deep division within the Labour Party over Douglas's economic and financial policies, Muldoon tried to persuade the National caucus to make a major public issue out of the decision to abort the committee.

McLay, Richardson and others, however, took the view that the Muldoon period of government should be rejected and forgotten as quickly and as completely as possible. Although Muldoon might want to defend his past actions, his younger colleagues were determined to start afresh with new faces and new ideas, even if Muldoon felt denigrated and betrayed by that strategy.[54]

CHAPTER 23

The Leadership Transition:
Muldoon, McLay, Bolger 1984–86

IN THE WEEK AFTER THE 1984 ELECTION THERE WAS A MEETING in McLay's office nearly every night which went on until the early hours of the morning and where people discussed what should be done about the leadership of the National Party. Many agreed with the *Dominion*'s editorial writer that at the caucus meeting on Thursday 19 July Muldoon, 'a man who won't concede when he is beaten, and misuses the power he holds in trust', should be replaced.[1] While nearly everyone in caucus hoped Muldoon would retire gracefully, as Fraser had done in Australia, and become an elder statesmen in the party, it soon became clear that that was not Muldoon's intention and his opponents started to organise his removal.

There were at least three groups in caucus immediately following the 1984 election: a remnant of Muldoon loyalists such as Wellington, Talbot, Friedlander and Norman Jones; a group including Bolger and Gair, who thought Muldoon should be replaced immediately; and a significant faction including McLay, Birch, Peters and Burdon, who believed Muldoon should go before the 1987 election but should be given time to go decently and after taking the initial onslaught as Opposition Leader from the rampant new Labour Government. Gair and Bolger were supported by the party president, Wood, and all five divisional chairmen, who contacted each of the MPs in their division. By the day prior to the caucus meeting they believed that they had sufficient support to oust Muldoon if he would not step down gracefully. Richardson and the new MP for Remuera, Doug Graham, announced publicly that they would raise the leadership issue and Gair stated that he would be a candidate.[2]

Muldoon was also busy speaking with most MPs individually and soon realised that he would not survive if there was an immediate vote for the leadership. The chief whip, McKinnon, after talking with all caucus members, also reported to Muldoon that when faced with three options – an immediate leadership vote, a vote before Christmas, or a vote at the end of February 1985 – the majority preferred one of the last two. If Muldoon said he would accept a leadership vote at the second caucus of 1985, McKinnon believed most MPs would agree; if he did not and gave the impression he intended to remain leader, then McKinnon thought that Muldoon would be 'rolled' immediately. To Muldoon's comment that if he survived to March 1985 'I'll be all right', McKinnon responded that he thought Muldoon could not remain leader later than February 1985.[3] It was clear also from Muldoon's and McKinnon's discussions that there was no consensus as to who should succeed Muldoon.

There were four possibilities: McLay, Gair, Bolger and Birch, with various combinations of leader and deputy leader depending on who won the leadership. Muldoon was later to claim that he had become uncertain about McLay's leadership ability and emotional response to pressure during the last week of the 1984 election campaign. McLay, according to Muldoon, had become worried not only that National was losing the election but that he might not even hold his own Birkenhead seat and wanted to cancel his speaking engagements during the last week of the campaign in order to concentrate on holding it. Muldoon also thought that McLay, who had never been in Opposition, needed until 1985 to build up experience in that role. One further reservation which Muldoon had about his deputy was that, while he admired his intelligence and energy, he thought he was too cautious, perhaps because he lacked confidence. Whereas Muldoon's attitude was 'when in doubt, do, and hope that two-thirds of the time things will come right', McLay seemed to have the attitude 'when in doubt, don't' and as a result did not act intuitively and decisively.[4]

At the start of the caucus meeting on 19 July Muldoon seized the initiative and suggested that the leadership should be reviewed at the first caucus meeting in February 1985, adding that it was unlikely he would be a candidate. The delay would allow the party to settle down after the election catastrophe and give the new caucus six months in which to consider the alternatives for leader and how they coped in Opposition. Bolger and Gair opposed any delay and pressed for an immediate vote. Bolger attacked Muldoon for 'talking like a man who had won an election rather than lost it'.[5] McLay, to the consternation of Muldoon's opponents, did not lend his support to an early vote on the leadership. Prior to the caucus he had observed that because Fraser had resigned as Australia's Liberal Party leader on election night, his successor, Andrew Peacock, had been forced to try to establish his leadership credentials and image in the worst possible circumstances. He noted that Muldoon still had very substantial support, which would be offended by treating him as a scapegoat, and that if by chance Muldoon won a majority in caucus that would also be very damaging at that time.[6] McLay thought it would be better for Muldoon to take the pressure of being Leader of the Opposition for the next difficult six months and hoped that he would then relinquish the post gracefully, support an orderly succession to McLay, and retire with dignity. Birch also argued that Muldoon had to be treated decently and not made a scapegoat and that the wishes of the large segment of Muldoon supporters within the party and electorate had to be respected.[7]

A majority of caucus decided to delay the leadership change in the hope of an orderly succession in early 1985 rather than have a bitter and divisive battle in the wake of the election débâcle.[8] There was also a feeling that Muldoon should be given the opportunity to make a dignified departure. An argument put forward by Muldoon's supporters was also persuasive: that the eight new MPs had not had time to get to know McLay, Bolger, Gair and Birch sufficiently well as colleagues to choose a new leader from among them and that six months would enable them to make a more informed choice.

Although most of those who heard Muldoon speak in caucus thought he intended to continue for six months only in a caretaker leadership role while the succession was worked through, Muldoon himself within a day was denying publicly that he would definitely step down the following February.[9] One of Muldoon's major critics within the National Party, Julian Watts, a former chairman of the Wellington Division, labelled the caucus a bunch of 'gutless wonders' for not removing Muldoon; and two Auckland Dominion Councillors, John Peebles and Peter Kiely, called on the Dominion Council to reject the caucus decision and not confirm Muldoon as the party's leader.[10] It became clear to many of Muldoon's critics that they might well have lost their best chance of removing him at a time when he was being widely condemned for calling the snap election and then losing it so disastrously and also for his handling of the devaluation problem after the election, which was judged to be, at the best, an error of judgement and, at the worst, a constitutional crisis and an economic disaster provoked by his own intransigence and arrogance. Now there was a real danger that Muldoon could rebuild his not inconsiderable support within the party and the wider electorate over the following six months. As time went on, it appeared obvious that he was indeed positioning himself to try to retain the leadership the following February.

Until September Muldoon remained subdued and, by his standards, relatively inactive. Part of the time was spent collecting and writing up material for a personal history of the New Zealand economy since the 1960s which would record his version of events over the previous twenty-five years. It was finally finished in March 1985 and published in July as *The New Zealand Economy: A Personal View*. In September 1984, however, Muldoon started to hit back at his critics both in the Labour Government and within his own party. He gave a fifteen-page memo on the 1984 election defeat to Dominion Councillors on 12 September and discussed his views the same day with television and newspaper reporters. Needless to say, Muldoon took no personal responsibility for the party's staggering defeat, blaming instead caucus dissidents, the long economic downturn, the party's organisation at the national and divisional but not the electorate levels, the party's advertising, (which was 'a mess'), and the media (which was 'uniformly hostile'). He also summarised his version of the devaluation crisis.[11]

Muldoon came under strong attack at the special Dominion Council meeting on 11 and 12 September. Wood told the councillors that she had called the meeting not to review the election campaign or the state of the party's organisation but 'to address the question of leadership'.[12] The tone of the meeting was set by a tabled report from the Canterbury-Westland Division, which cited what it called a random sample of voters. Typical of the opinions expressed were 'Come back and see me when you have a new leader'; 'Muldoon was the most socialist leader this country has ever had'; 'People want to see a united National Party with a new leader'. The Division concluded that 'leadership . . . was the key issue upon which National lost the election'.[13]

Wood introduced the leadership issue and then her predecessor as president, Chapman, spoke, saying that it was 'inevitable' that leadership should be discussed though he believed that Muldoon was genuine in saying that he would not be a candidate if the leadership election was held in February 1985.[14] Birch immediately responded that caucus chose the leader and the party then approved that choice. He opposed any 'precipitous decision to dump Rob Muldoon . . . Those who worship the ground Rob Muldoon walks on would not understand.' His advice to leave the matter until a caucus meeting in February 1985 was supported by Pat Baker, Graham Latimer, Murray Reeves and Clem Simich, though Reeves added that 'there is an expectation of a change in leadership' at that time. Michelle Boag disagreed strongly that the matter should be decided only by the caucus, arguing that many electorates 'want the Leader's head on a plate', and Julian Watts said that a decision was needed before the party's forthcoming conference. Other members, including some very antagonistic to Muldoon, were prepared to allow him to retire with dignity from the leadership but wanted a clear indication from him that he would go by February 1985 at the latest.

Muldoon then replied, saying that time was important because, although 'I have no wish to be Leader of this Party at the next election', he was not sure who his successor would be and he also needed time to convince his supporters to support that person when he did become leader. Muldoon pointed out that McLay had no experience of being in Opposition and that leaving himself as leader for a time would help in a smooth transition.

After Talboys had remarked that 'It would be a grave error of judgement for the Leader to signal that he would definitely not be there in six months' time', Chapman moved a motion that the council endorse the caucus decision to postpone any vote on the leadership until February 1985. That was carried after the defeat of an amendment moved by Watts, which stated that, 'for the well-being of the Party, Dominion Council expects the present Leader, in line with his public statements, not to be a contender at the said election'. Watts, who was chairman of the party's Rules Committee, made it plain that if the council withdrew its approval of a leader then caucus was obliged to confirm or change the leader.

Following the September Dominion Council meeting, Muldoon became busier, giving addresses, issuing press statements and creating every impression that he intended to remain leader if he could. His opponents within the party started to criticise him more openly and call for his resignation or removal, but Muldoon still according to the polls enjoyed more support than any other National Party politician, and his enthusiastic admirers, who continued to send him telegrams and letters and pack his public meetings, encouraged him to remain as leader.

In early October 1984 Muldoon took a strong public stance against the Adult Adoption Information Bill. The Bill, originally moved unsuccessfully in 1982 and

1983 by Labour's Jonathan Hunt, had been taken over by Fran Wilde and was very controversial. Muldoon's views on the Bill were influenced by a Rakaia nurse and National Party member, Margaret Quin, who lobbied Muldoon on the matter and also by the correspondence he received on the issue. Although 276 of the 344 letters he received personally supported the Bill, as did over three-quarters of the 118 submissions to the Statutes Revision Committee, Muldoon found the 68 letters against the Bill more compelling.[15] Most of the letters in favour were from people who had been adopted or from birth mothers who wished to be available if their child ever wanted to find them, although one suggested that birth mothers were immoral or dishonest and should be punished and that Muldoon's protection of such women raised questions as to whether he was a father who did not wish his adopted child or children to find him. Muldoon tersely replied to that correspondent, 'I acknowledge your unpleasant little letter. Your lack of compassion does you no credit.'

The 68 letters from those opposed, however, were much more heart-rending. Nearly every one was from a birth mother and some told Muldoon horrific stories of, for example, a 14-year-old raped by two men or 16-year-olds who had conceived children to fathers or stepfathers. Many were now older women, who had kept the truth from later husbands and children, who were living in constant terror of their past returning, and who felt they could not cope if their adopted child turned up. As a result Muldoon made his own submission to the Statutes Revision Committee, arguing that his 'principal concern and reason for opposing the bill relates to its impact on elderly women who have given a child for what was believed to be a secret adoption many years ago. In their case this is retrospective legislation of a most cruel kind . . . I cannot recall ever having seen a piece of legislation that inflicts such mental anguish and cruelty on such a large number of women whose only offence was a very common form of human frailty.'[16] He also believed that such legislation would make abortion rather than adoption a more likely choice for many women. Muldoon attached to his submission extracts from letters he had received. Despite Muldoon's opposition the Bill was passed.

On 24 October Muldoon came back from a brief visit to Niue and on his return found considerable speculation about a possible change in National's leadership. The speculation had been fuelled by a weekend seminar held by the Wellington Division of the National Party on 22 and 23 October. The seminar had debated the party's principles and policies and what kind of party it was and should be. Most of the speakers, who included Watts, John Isles, Max Bradford, Rosemary Young-Rouse and Roy Johnston, were critics of Muldoon. Johnston, for example, referred to 'the megalomaniac politician' who could not accept he was in Opposition, before going on to assert that Muldoon had ignored the party between 1981 and 1984 while 'the unaccountable caucus' had indulged in 'calculated nonsense'.[17]

Over the next few days Muldoon talked with nearly every member of the parliamentary Press Gallery on a one-to-one basis about the leadership situation.[18] Although he realised that an overwhelming majority of his colleagues wanted a change in leader, Muldoon was encouraged by the warm reception he received at large meetings at Nelson (5 November), Papatoetoe (9 November), West Auckland (10 November) and Tamaki (20 November). His chief whip, McKinnon, however, sounded out twenty-seven MPs, excluding those known to be totally hostile to Muldoon. Only four said without qualification that they wanted Muldoon to lead the party into the 1987 election; six wanted the leadership reviewed before February 1985; ten before the party's conference in mid-1985; and seven before the next election.[19]

In early November, the Wellington Division sent a strong message to the caucus that it wanted the leadership question resolved and Muldoon replaced before Christmas. It believed that Muldoon had made it clear by his statements and his campaigning throughout New Zealand that he would be a candidate for the leadership against the four possible successors: McLay, Bolger, Gair and Birch. Muldoon's intransigence upset many party officials who thought he should retire gracefully, a view put forcefully in a press release by six Wellington electorate chairpersons led by Pencarrow's Roger Sowry.[20] While Birch and Gair said that they anticipated Muldoon would retire from Parliament if he lost the leadership and that, therefore, the question of his becoming a minister in the future was 'academic', Bolger differed and said that Muldoon would have 'a very responsible role to play' in any future Bolger-led cabinet.[21]

Rather than have a drawn-out leadership contest early in the new year, at a time when branch and electorate annual meetings were being held, caucus at its meeting on 22 November decided to advance the leadership vote from February to 2 December, the last caucus meeting before Christmas. Muldoon was annoyed at this change and at a post-caucus press conference announced that, although he had genuinely indicated in July that he would probably not stand again for leader, he had now changed his mind because not 'one of the declared candidates is as capable of turning this Government out as I am'.[22] As a result he would be a candidate. He did not expect to win but preferred to go down fighting.

Following Muldoon's announcement he received over the following week some 4000 telegrams and letters, overwhelmingly in support of his decision, and newspaper advertisements paid for by a Christchurch man called on 'all thinking New Zealanders' to back Muldoon.

An *Eyewitness News*-Heylen poll a few days later showed that the public generally preferred McLay to Muldoon and that McLay was also considered most likely to be able to lead National to a handsome victory over the new Labour Government.[23] McLay polled 39 per cent to Muldoon's 23 per cent, Gair's 19, Bolger's 8 and Birch's 4. Significantly, among National supporters Muldoon still outpolled McLay by 43 to 39 per cent, but the poll indicated that led by Muldoon National would lose an election to Labour by 2 per cent but would win under McLay by 23 per cent. Muldoon interpreted the poll as showing that 'The National people put me ahead and my enemies . . . don't want me. That means that I'm the leader that my enemies fear doesn't it?'[24] He added that if caucus 'want someone else, okay I'll lose, but I'll go down with my flag flying', and if McLay became 'the leader, okay, that's it.'[25]

Gair had been campaigning openly and actively since July and had gained the support of Sir John Marshall and many in the party organisation. He made it plain that he did not see himself as a long-term leader but one who could oversee the rejuvenation of the party and allow younger alternative leaders more time to establish themselves. Bolger had announced his candidacy for the leadership early in October and McLay declared his intention to stand on 29 October. [26] Muldoon commented that a McLay-Birch leadership might be able to lead National to victory at the next election but that Gair was totally unacceptable to him as a successor.[27]

Birch was in an interesting position. Long one of Muldoon's most faithful defenders, he had decided that neither Muldoon nor he himself were serious contenders for the leadership whenever it was resolved. Birch accepted that he had lost any real chance of the succession when he had polled only 7 votes to McLay's 25 and Bolger's 15 for the deputy-leadership earlier in the year.[28] In early November, therefore, Birch and Falloon over drinks with Muldoon told their 'far from impressed' leader that it was time for him to go.[29] Birch then approached McLay and told him that he was prepared to stand for deputy on a McLay-Birch ticket. He pointed out that even if McLay defeated Bolger for the leadership Bolger would remain the real alternative to McLay, who would need a strong loyal deputy like Birch to reinforce his leadership. Bolger, with his ambition to be leader, would not be able to fill that role. McLay rejected Birch's offer.[30] Nevertheless, Birch continued to support McLay because he believed that McLay had proved himself as deputy leader and deserved a chance at the top position.[31] Birch also, however, decided to stand himself for the leadership, not because he expected to win, and indeed he did not actively lobby, but because he believed that the new deputy leader would come from among the unsuccessful contenders for leader. When the Dominion Executive met on 28 November and Wood announced that she expected caucus to choose a new leader the following day, Birch told the Executive that 'he believed McLay would be elected leader'.[32]

Wanting to avoid further rancorous division, and believing that most MPs had had ample time to consider their options, Winston Peters and Philip Burdon, who also believed that delay and dispute would further weaken Muldoon's effectiveness as Leader of the Opposition, moved at the caucus meeting on 29 November that the leadership vote should not even be delayed three weeks until Christmas but should be taken immediately.[33] Caucus agreed, though some such as Birch and McKinnon still wanted to wait until February as earlier decided.

The caucus meeting at which the vote was taken was chaired by Venn Young, the most senior MP not involved as a candidate. The five candidates were Muldoon; his deputy McLay, an articulate crusader for free enterprise and the rights of the individual; Gair, an older, diplomatic, skilful and energetic liberal; Bolger, bluff, amiable, moderate but with definite views on what needed to be done; and Birch the very able organiser and administrator. The choice was perceived as being really between McLay and Bolger, and a number of liberal MPs, who personally preferred Gair to anyone else, felt that they had to give their votes to McLay to ensure his victory over the more pragmatic Bolger. In the event McLay won on the first ballot, according to his own account obtaining 22 of the 37 votes cast. Bolger received 9 and Muldoon 5, reportedly his own and those cast by Friedlander, Wellington, Talbot and Norman Jones.[34] The change of leadership occurred exactly nine years to the day that Muldoon had first been elected Prime Minister. Bolger then won the deputy leadership, also on the first ballot, from Gair, Birch and Richardson. Subsequently, the National Party's Dominion Council confirmed the new leadership, with only one Muldoon loyalist dissenting.

Muldoon stood sad and alone in the background of the post-caucus press conference at which McLay, Wood and Leay were obviously and understandably jubilant. He quickly excused himself afterwards and, after joking with the press that he hoped to be remembered as an 'elderly backbencher – not an elder states-man', left the House and was mobbed by sympathetic superannuitants protesting in the grounds outside against Labour's superannuation surtax. Returning to his office for a press conference, Muldoon sat silently at his desk shuffling messages before, his eyes filling with tears, he removed a television microphone, excused himself and left the room. As one not usually sympathetic journalist noted, 'the man who for 24 years maintained the impression, at least for public consumption, that he was constructed of granite with a surface coating of rhino hide, abandoned all pretence and wept openly, burying his face in a white hanky. Most who bore witness to these rare, unprecedented scenes, could not help but be shocked and affected by it all.'[35] When Muldoon returned five minutes later he struggled throughout the conference to control his emotions but finally lashed out at party officials, especially from the Wellington Division, who 'night after night' had lobbied MPs and tried to persuade them that Muldoon had to be removed.[36] After inviting four colleagues, East, McKinnon, Burdon and Peters, to join him for drinks in his office, Muldoon then started clearing out his office, farewelling his staff, and dispatching his collection of eighty-four model aircraft to the Auckland Museum of Transport and Technology.

McLay realised that Muldoon had been bitterly hurt: first by the election defeat; then by the denigration he had been subjected to by the new Labour Government, the media, officials, various farming, business and financial leaders, and even many within the National Party itself; and finally by being dumped as leader before he was prepared to hand over to a successor. McLay hoped that given some time to get over his hurt and disappointment, he would relent, accept seat number 10 and a spokesmanship on either overseas trade or foreign affairs, and play a positive role as a mentor to new MPs and an effective Opposition voice in Parliament. When McLay refused, however, to give Muldoon one of the eight seats on the Opposition front bench, the former leader chose to become a backbencher without specific responsibilities.

The new leadership's apparent unwillingness to defend the policies and actions of the 1975–84 National Government and the change of direction towards free market economic and anti-welfare-state policies, which McLay and other members of the self-styled 'new generation' now pursued, worsened Muldoon's resentment and disaffection. After the 1984 election Muldoon desperately wanted to show that he had been right. He found it impossible to admit publicly that any of his decisions or actions had been wrong or that times were changing so that even where his policies had been right in the past they were now no longer so. Muldoon's annoyance at his replacement by McLay as leader of the party was further aggravated by the pleasure it gave to Sir John Marshall, who predicted 'a reaffirmation of our principles and policies, a good relationship with the party organisation and a new style of leadership with emphasis on the party working as a team', which meant that 'many former National supporters would return to the fold'.[37] Sir Wallace Rowling also observed that the change 'should help focus the political scene on to the issues rather than personalities'.[38]

Typical of the many letters Muldoon received, even from those who had had reservations about his leadership, was one from the Auckland divisional chairman, Pat Baker, who noted that 'over the last ten years there may well have been differing opinions about style or some individual policies, but we are also conscious of the many things that we in the National Party have to thank you for. We all remember the excitement of 1975 and the fact that, in spite of difficult economic conditions, we won the next two elections. Nor in the future should we forget that the major developments in the fields of energy and horticulture had their genesis in the Muldoon administration of 1975 to 1984.'[39]

Muldoon had accepted an invitation to address an augmented Auckland Divisional Executive meeting on 3 December, and the invitation was confirmed after he lost the leadership. Muldoon surveyed the eleven years of recession in New Zealand starting in 1973 with the first oil shock and the drop in the terms of trade. He predicted prophetically that those economic difficulties would culminate with a further downturn in the American economy which he expected to occur about August 1987. New Zealand could not insulate itself from the world economy and as a result would continue to suffer from high inflation, high interest rates and the problem of markets for products such as lamb.[40]

In retrospect Muldoon admitted that he became rather 'grizzly' following his removal as National's leader.[41] He claimed that he was not really hurt because he had been in politics a long time and accepted that these things happened 'to oneself as well as others'. But he became increasingly angry at National's inability to fight back effectively against the Labour Government or to defend itself against Labour's total condemnation of National's administration between 1975 and 1984.

During the first six months of 1985 Muldoon kept a very low profile. He spent Christmas and New Year at Hatfields Beach, cruised on the *Sirdar* from 7 to 13 January, and gave his annual speech to the Orewa Rotary Club on 15 January. During the first half of that year, he had few meetings with other MPs or party members, gave few interviews to journalists, and largely confined himself to parliamentary and constituency matters. He rarely attended formal functions and restricted himself to a couple of dinners with personal friends. In declining many invitations to speak at National Party meetings throughout the early part of 1985

Muldoon usually gave as a reason that 'I want Jim McLay and the new team to have the opportunity of settling down in their relationship to the Party outside the House'.[42] He told his correspondents to approach McLay instead. With time on his hands he commenced a fifth book, his fourth autobiography, which was published the following year under the title *Number 38*. A disjointed and anecdotal collection of memories and observations, which originated in a set of poorly edited tape recordings, it made no pretence to be balanced or seriously analytical. It was almost universally described by reviewers as superficial, self-serving and disappointing.[43]

Muldoon could not understand or reconcile himself to the concept of retirement. To him life was going to work and when there was no more work there was no more life. Work, in other words, was not a means to an end but very much an end in itself to which Muldoon was totally committed. After he lost the leadership at the end of 1984 Muldoon may well at first have seen himself as a Churchillian figure, who in time would be rehabilitated and called back to office, but there is little evidence of this before about April 1985. He had, however, a sense of history and knew that not only Churchill but other political figures such as Gladstone and Nash had become prime minister at ages considerably older than he was and after apparently having been rejected by their parties and electorates.

Muldoon was convinced that there was a constant battle in the House to assert dominance over the other side. If the morale of one party went up, that of the other went down. Throughout 1984 and 1985 Labour was definitely on top. They had excellent debaters, were prepared to break the rules to gain competitive advantage, and realised the importance of ridicule. Lange, in particular, Muldoon believed, even when totally out of order, could be devastating and could get his side laughing at his furious but hapless targets on the National side of the House.[44] Labour MPs generally between 1984 and 1986 were very tough on both Muldoon and McLay and ridiculed them constantly and cruelly. Although a 'sad and bitter figure', Muldoon, according to one Labour MP, 'continued to fight back but McLay, an intelligent, liberal and decent man, was eventually undermined and then destroyed by the combination of Muldoon's criticism, Labour's ridicule and Bolger's ambition'.[45]

McLay, however, enjoyed a brief honeymoon period as Leader of the Opposition and by May 1985 National was, for a short time, actually ahead of Labour in the polls. In June National somewhat surprisingly won the relatively safe Labour seat of Timaru in a by-election following the death of its long-time incumbent Sir Basil Arthur. A *Herald*-NRB poll published on 25 June showed that Lange had dropped to 26 per cent as preferred prime minister, down from 36 per cent the previous October. McLay had also dropped from 6 to 4 per cent but Muldoon, despite his relatively low profile, had risen from 11 to 26 per cent.[46]

The growing influence of New Right MPs like Richardson and Cox continued to anger Muldoon, for they rejected and vilified not only him personally but his policies and achievements. He was also saddened that many people he had worked with, chosen for cabinet posts, and supported when they personally had been under attack now denigrated him or tried to distance themselves from him. Muldoon was not the only one surprised at the way some of his colleagues recalled recent history. The secretary to the cabinet, Millen, was also astonished in the years after 1984 to hear former cabinet ministers and senior officials say how much they had disagreed with what Muldoon had done. He could not recall most of them saying anything at all at cabinet and cabinet committee meetings he attended and recorded between 1975 and 1984. In charity he suggested that perhaps people in hindsight subsequently recognised as wrong things that were not evidently so at the time but 'among the first to kick Muldoon when he was down on his knees after 1984 were certainly some who had been quite happy to hang uncritically on his coat-tails for many years before his defeat'.[47] Muldoon felt he had much to offer the National Opposition but found himself constantly having to defend himself rather than being allowed to attack the Labour Government, which was actually doing things which Quigley, Richardson, Cox and others had wanted to do prior to 1984 but which Muldoon had prevented. As a result from mid-1985 he took every opportunity admirers gave him to speak at public meetings.

The pressure to change the leadership earlier than originally agreed generated considerable sympathy for Muldoon and provided him with a platform from which to express resentment at his treatment. A number of National Party members were annoyed at the rush by senior members of the caucus and party organisation to attack him personally and to reject his legacy following the 1984 election and particularly after McLay became leader. Many of Muldoon's supporters realised that they would not get him back as leader, but as one admirer, Bill Matthewson, observed, they were determined to show their support for him and try 'to give Rob back his dignity' and reprimand those in the party's hierarchy who had treated him, in their opinion, so shamefully.[48] Another Muldoon supporter, Suzanne Mackay, argued that 'Sir Robert was a "one man band" purely because he was surrounded by a bunch of incompetent, disloyal cabinet members and party members' who 'were obviously also "yes men" as they are claiming now not to have agreed with his ideas at the time but they are not on record as having spoken out against him'.[49] Bert Walker criticised the party's organisational leadership for 'public disloyalty and backstabbing' and 'criticising the most effective member we have in opposition, Sir Robert'.[50] The Tamaki electorate executive observed: 'Failings and shortcomings, where they have occurred, are attributable to Cabinet, Caucus and the National Party at large, and not merely to one man.'[51]

The Sunday Club was started in Christchurch on Sunday night, 10 February 1985, when a small group of twelve National Party members were having coffee in Walker's lounge and chatting about Muldoon's apparent rejection by the party's hierarchy.[52] When one woman suggested forming a ginger group such as the British Conservatives' Monday Club to support Muldoon, the idea appealed. A committee consisting of Walker and five other active National Party members was established: Richard Whitehouse, who had been chairman of the Papanui and St Albans electorates; Ken Gough, a former electorate chairman, who had also chaired the party's Rules Committee in Canterbury; Helen Garrett, a former National candidate and electorate chairperson; Valerie Miller, who had been a naval commander and also an electorate chairperson; and John Curtis, who was on the executive of the Fendalton electorate.

When the Sunday Club was announced publicly, the organisers were overwhelmed by the response. Some 20,000 people eventually joined or sent donations, and Walker estimated that at least that number again actively supported the Sunday Club by attending its meetings.[53] Some twenty branches of the Sunday Club were quickly formed in Wellington, Auckland, New Plymouth, Timaru, Westport, and elsewhere throughout New Zealand, not counting similar groups such as the 'Blue Ribbon Association' or 'True Blues' set up by Win Cozens in West Auckland. Margaret Mouat, in Muldoon's Wellington office, brought together various Muldoon supporters such as McKay in Wellington, Cozens in Auckland, and Matthewson in Hastings, people who had not previously known each other.[54]

A larger steering committee of the Sunday Club was formed in March 1985 consisting of twenty-six people, all but one of whom were current members of the National Party. Most had held office in the National Party, some over many years. The attitude of most Sunday Club members was that the hierarchy of the National Party's organisation only wanted the rank and file to raise money and door-knock and were not prepared to listen to their views, especially about Muldoon.[55] Although the Sunday Club's aim was officially 'to reform and revitalise the National Party', it was apparent from the first that Sunday Club members believed that this could best be done by providing a platform and support base for Muldoon, even if he did not return as leader, though that was not excluded as a possibility. Spokespeople for the club also deplored the treatment of Muldoon by senior figures in the party; were not impressed by McLay as leader; wanted Wood and Leay replaced; detested Lange and the new Labour Government; and were opposed to the New Right direction in which both Labour under Douglas and National under McLay appeared to be going. Some of the Sunday Club founders certainly displayed a simple and total faith in Muldoon, as expressed by one in a letter to Muldoon's secretary: 'If we can get him back as Leader of the Opposition and then Prime Minister, all other problems will resolve themselves.'[56]

At first Muldoon's critics and enemies ridiculed the Sunday Club and believed that it could be easily dismissed. Minogue, for example, publicly labelled the club 'a pathetic joke . . . ex-Muldoonists hoping for a second coming, but that corpse has been well and truly laid to rest'.[57] McLay derided the club's members as 'a sort of Famous Five that might get up to a secret seven'.[58] Others of Muldoon's critics were more concerned, Simon Upton arguing that the Sunday Club was 'a trogan [sic] horse for the politics and personalities of the past. And they pose a serious threat to the rejuvenation of the National Party.' Such 'simmering factionalism' would result in 'demoralising consequences'.[59] A meeting of electorate chairmen from the Canterbury-Westland Division unanimously resolved to ask the party's Dominion Council to expel Walker.[60] That threat was dropped after Walker's solicitor, another senior National Party official, told the divisional chairman, Neville Young, that Walker would take out an injunction against the party's Executive.[61]

A public meeting in Timaru on 10 May 1985, which attracted 650 people to hear Muldoon, was followed on 15 May by another at the Christchurch Town Hall, where people had to pick up tickets in advance to get in. That attracted some 3000 Muldoon supporters from as far north as Nelson and as far south as Central Otago and a collection for expenses totalled over $7000. The meeting overflowed into an adjoining building, where people watched Muldoon on closed-circuit television. Muldoon defended his 1975–84 Government; slammed into the new Labour Government's 'extreme right-wing' agenda and actions; and generally entertained and enthused his admiring audience. As one journalist recorded, the crowd of Muldoon supporters had gathered 'on a bleak Wednesday night' to 'cheer him, chuckle with him, be comforted with him, remind ourselves what it was like and tempt ourselves with thoughts that it could be that again.'[62] James observed that Muldoon 'really knows how to make a speech easy to listen to. Full of facts. But full of fun too.' Less funny to McLay was Muldoon's public reference to him as 'McClaytons – the Opposition Leader you have when you're not having an Opposition leader'.[63]

In the same month 1000 tickets were sold to a Muldoon rally in Hamilton and 2300 people paid $4 each to attend a public meeting in the Wellington Town Hall at 8 p.m. on 3 July. The Hamilton meeting was held at the same time as the Waikato Division's annual conference, a clash which concerned McLay and the Waikato divisional chairman Murray Reeves, who sought to have Muldoon cancel or change the date of his meeting. Muldoon replied that he 'did not realise that it coincided with the Divisional Annual Meetings' but could not change the date because hundreds of tickets had been sold, most of those attending would not be at the conference anyway, and he did not intend saying anything which would embarrass the National Party.[64] The Wellington meeting, organised by Sue Mackay, commenced with entertainment by Suzanne Prentice and concluded with a supper for 134 invited guests believed to be Muldoon supporters, including Merv Wellington, Keitha Holyoake, Des Dalgety, and Lance Adams-Schneider. Some journalists were also present, including 2ZB's Paul Holmes who the following morning conducted a live interview with Muldoon. Some of Muldoon's former cabinet colleagues, notably Walker, Wellington, Shearer and Friedlander, associated themselves with him at Sunday Club rallies. Successful Sunday Club meetings continued to be held throughout 1985 despite divisions and disputes among both the Auckland and Christchurch committees. Muldoon spoke at Hawera in July, Paraparaumu and New Plymouth in August, West Auckland in September, and Papakura, Invercargill and Tamaki in October.

McLay accepted that Muldoon was aggrieved both by McLay's refusal to defend the 1975–84 National Government's record and by McLay's speeches on the need for a different style of economic management in the future, but he also had no doubts that the Sunday Club was a calculated attempt to return Muldoon to the leadership of the National Party. Muldoon's consistent failure to disown the group, and indeed his active co-operation with it, convinced McLay that Muldoon was setting out deliberately to destabilise him and recover the leadership. Muldoon's attitude and opposition to both Labour and McLay was not just hurt personal pride or thwarted ambition but did reflect a deeply rooted belief that their policies were wrong. Nevertheless, personalities became increasingly important in the dispute. On one occasion Muldoon told McLay, 'You will not become Prime Minister by climbing over my dead body', and said that he personally and deeply resented any suggestion that the change in National's leadership meant a rejection of his policies and style.[65] As a result relations between the two men deteriorated drastically.

Considerable concern about the activities of both Muldoon and the Sunday Club had been expressed at the April 1985 meeting of the Dominion Executive where the Canterbury-Westland delegates had argued than there was clearly 'an open attack on the leader in an endeavour to supplant him with the former leader'.[66] Wood agreed and reported that 'The division within the Party was having a negative effect on the Party's ability to raise membership and money' and 'the organisation was being de-stabilised by the activities of the dissident group within the Party and MPs who were identifying with the group.'[67] McLay then observed that Muldoon had 'dominated the party and the political scene' for ten years and that understandably 'it was difficult for any other politician in the National Party to achieve any degree of public profile'.[68] Birch argued that while 'Muldoon was a deposed leader and felt wounded' and that had to be appreciated, 'Caucus was totally in support of Mr McLay', a sentiment echoed by Bolger, who added, however, that while 'he was 100 per cent behind the Leader', he did not believe it was possible to blame Muldoon alone for National's 1984 defeat.[69]

After Ross Armstrong of Auckland and Murray Reeves of Waikato had also attacked the Sunday Club, Hamish Kynoch of the Wellington Division and Duncan Taylor of Otago-Southland moved a motion expressing the Executive's 'grave concern' at the 'association of Caucus members with public meetings sponsored by the Sunday Club or other groups whose aims include the defeat of the present leadership of the Organisational and Parliamentary wings of the National Party'.[70] While most of those who spoke supported the motion, McLay warned that such an action 'would set the Party on a course where it may be expelling the man who had led the Party for ten years, who was Prime Minister for eight years, and who enjoyed support in the electorate'. While he knew the Executive would not 'shrink from the task' he moved that the resolution should lie on the table.[71] Bolger supported McLay's suggestion, arguing that Muldoon was 'a person of standing in the Party's history' and that Bolger had 'absolute confidence' in McLay's ability to deal with the problem.[72] Reluctantly a majority of the Executive agreed that the motion should lie on the table.

A few days before the National Party conference, McLay's first as leader, at the end of July 1985, McLay publicly reprimanded his press secretary, Wendy Mehaney, for checking with Australian journalists a rumour that Lange had gone to Australia for health tests. Mehaney, who had been previously Muldoon's press secretary, resigned and Muldoon, who had received a copy of her letter of resignation, publicly defended her and said that she was being made a scapegoat and that McLay had been aware of her inquiries in advance.[73] McLay was furious and declared on television that 'For six months, I have ignored publicly everything that Sir Robert Muldoon has said about me – and I've done so because I believe that to be in the interests of the National Party.' The public, however, McLay said, like the party, wanted a different style of leadership from that provided by Muldoon.[74]

The National Party conference was overshadowed by the McLay–Muldoon dispute. As one commentator noted, the conference was designed for 'exorcising Sir Robert Muldoon', who was being publicly condemned for deviating from the free enterprise principles of the National Party and for being responsible for National's disastrous 1984 election defeat, especially in urban New Zealand.[75] As the same commentator noted, however, McLay at his first leader's rally on the Saturday night of the conference spoke to 700 delegates and party members in the Christchurch Town Hall which 'was only half full', when not long before Muldoon had spoken at a Sunday Club rally which had 'that hall packed to the gunwales and people overflowing in the James Hay [theatre]'.[76] Despite his popularity elsewhere, however, Muldoon, according to reporters, 'hardly featured as even a discussion point over the three days' of the conference, and the delegates 'buried the policies of Rob Muldoon' and adopted McLay's 'new agenda of right wing political policy, less government, less government spending and therefore lower taxes . . . the individual must reign supreme'.[77]

Muldoon did not attend the National Party conference during the last weekend in July, instead chairing a BNZ–TVNZ Festival Debate in Dunedin on Saturday 27 July and returning to Auckland to host his Radio Pacific programme on Sunday 28 when his special topic was not politics but fuchsia flowers and bulbs.

The carefully stage-managed image of unity and a new direction for the National Party was marred when Shearer questioned whether party funds had been lent to Jim Gerard, a former divisional chairman and new member of Parliament for Rangiora.[78] Shearer, who after losing his Hamilton East seat in 1984 had become chairman of Muldoon's Tamaki electorate committee early in 1985, had (like Muldoon) blamed Wood and Leay for what he argued had been the disastrous state of the party's organisation, membership and funds prior to the 1984 election and for the debt incurred in building the party's new Wellington headquarters. From May 1985 Shearer had been questioning the party's financial situation and management. He had also challenged Wood for the Auckland Division's nomination as president and polled a significant 63 votes to the incumbent's 141. This was an indication not so much of support for Shearer personally as a reflection of the core pro-Muldoon bloc and an element of male chauvinism among leading National Party electorate and branch office-holders in the Auckland Division. Shearer's persistent questioning about the loan infuriated Wood, Leay and McLay. When Shearer threatened to reveal other controversial matters regarding National's finances and administration, Wood admitted that the loan had been made but attacked Shearer and other dissident National Party members, notably Sue Mackay of Wellington and Margaret Quin of Methven.

In April 1985 Muldoon had received a copy of a long letter from Quin, the deputy chairperson of the Methven Branch of the National Party, to Wood.[79] Quin complained that at the Ashburton electorate's AGM she had raised her concern at a rumour that a personal loan had been made out of party funds to a senior party officer at a time when the party was having difficulty meeting its financial commitments. Quin claimed that Young, the Canterbury divisional chairman, had then attacked her motives and integrity, accused her of 'muck-raking', and asserted that there was nothing 'out of the ordinary' in the party giving financial help to MPs and other members. Quin disagreed and proceeded to ask Wood in writing a series of questions about the matter.

Shearer and Quin had not only been campaigning privately for some months prior to the July conference to force the National Party's Dominion Executive to investigate their allegations about financial mismanagement but were also publicly identified as leading supporters of Muldoon and the Sunday Club. When Quin stated that Muldoon, as leader at the time, and Bruce Cathie, the party's treasurer, had known nothing of the loan, and copies of Quin's correspondence over a four-month period with Wood, Cathie, McLay and the chairpersons of the Canterbury Division and the Ashburton electorate were released to the media, suggestions were made that Muldoon was responsible for leaking details of the secret loan to his supporters.[80] Muldoon rejected the allegations, though he admitted he had been aware of Shearer's and the others' concerns, which he also shared, and that many of the details they had made public he had first learnt from Gerard and Cathie almost twelve months previously.[81] Tamaki's other delegates were appalled at Shearer's clash with Wood at the conference and disassociated their electorate from its chairman's comments 'because the Press would link Tamaki's position with Sir Robert and the Sunday Club as a conspiracy'.[82] Quin also after the conference, in a lengthy letter to Muldoon detailing her involvement, wrote that she had 'no idea that Dr Shearer would move so quickly' in bringing the matter out in to the open and she regretted that people were claiming Muldoon was behind the campaign. Such claims were 'false. I acted independently; as did Dr Shearer . . . Being a "Muldoon supporter" does not invalidate my concern.'[83]

At the end of the conference in July, Muldoon's strongest parliamentary supporter, Wellington, sent McLay a twelve-page letter strongly advocating Muldoon's return to National's front bench.[84] He blamed Muldoon's alienation primarily on 'actions and statements made at the time of the leadership change [which] were profoundly humiliating to Sir Robert' and went on to argue that the 'sizeable portion of the electorate' to which Muldoon still appealed were concerned by McLay's moving the National Party 'very close to merely following the economic policies espoused by Bob Jones and practised by Roger Douglas' and becoming 'a pale . . . replica of Labour'.[85] In Wellington's opinion, National Party 'policies should be designed to ensure "the greatest good for the greatest number" not to advance the fortunes of the wealthy few. This was the essence of the Holyoake–Muldoon era.'[86] He predicted that many of National's traditional voters would not accept a party that 'follows an unholy alliance of liberalism in social issues and hard right wing economic and fiscal policies' and which 'can't employ its most able politician in a constructive way'.[87] McLay was unimpressed and unconvinced.

In August McLay met the party's National Executive and shared with them his vision of a market economy. He distinguished his approach from that of Roger Douglas by pointing out that 'Douglas's attitude to monetary policy was abandoned in the United States four years ago'.[88] He also asserted that 'Treasury's projections were completely wrong' and that 'Labour did not understand the implications of the policies they were implementing'.

Most of the meeting, however, was spent discussing Muldoon's continued popularity and Shearer's criticisms of the party's internal financial management. Simich, a Muldoon loyalist, suggested that Muldoon had to be treated with respect if McLay wanted 'to win over the section who solidly support the former leader' and Latimer said that 'people had a dual loyalty . . . to Sir Robert and Mr McLay'.[89] Others argued that Muldoon had to be persuaded to state clearly that the leadership struggle was over. In regard to Shearer, Simich claimed that Muldoon was not supportive of his electorate chairman's and former cabinet colleague's public campaign against the party hierarchy, but Bolger took the view that irrespective of where Muldoon stood on that issue Shearer had to be dealt with quickly and eliminated as an ongoing embarrassment to the party.[90]

McLay was overseas for the September meeting of the National Executive and Bolger took the opportunity to give a strong address arguing that the party 'would not survive and win if it could not leave behind the arguments . . . as to who was to blame for the defeat' in 1984.[91] Bolger was clearly by this time impatient with those who were still constantly attacking Muldoon.

On Thursday 26 September 1985 Colin McLachlan died. He had been Muldoon's close friend, arguably his closest. Although Muldoon was speaking at a dinner in Sydney at 8 p.m. that night on the topic 'The Crisis of Democracy' and was in a caucus meeting in the morning, he left the caucus after an hour and flew to Christchurch to visit McLachlan's family before flying on to Sydney later in the day. He returned home from Australia on Saturday 28th to speak at the Ponsonby Rugby Club's 'Player of the Year' dinner and on Monday 30th flew from Auckland to Christchurch for McLachlan's funeral and then at 4 p.m. back to Auckland to catch a 6.50 flight to Honolulu.

McLay had tried several times informally during the early part of 1985, once it became clear that Muldoon had no intention of retiring, to involve Muldoon as a spokesman for a non-economic portfolio. McLay certainly did not want Muldoon upstaging the new economic spokesmen: Birch, Cox, Falloon and McLean. But Muldoon, who might have accepted overseas trade or foreign affairs, was not interested in any offer which did not involve one of the eight seats on National's front bench.

On Sunday 13 October, McLay, in a discussion with Muldoon's friend Harry Julian at the Remuera Golf Club, said that he would again have a discussion with Muldoon about a worthwhile shadow portfolio and a seat on the front bench.[92] It was probably not a coincidence that the following day Muldoon's Tamaki electorate committee sent a resolution to McLay, Wood and the divisional chairman Ross Armstrong expressing the electorate's 'widespread concern about the performance of National as an Opposition' and asking that 'Sir Robert should be promoted to the front bench'.[93]

In a forty-minute discussion on Thursday 17 October an agreement was reached between McLay and Muldoon that Muldoon would take up a spokesman's role, though specifics would not be finalised until after McLay had talked with several senior colleagues. Muldoon rang McLay the next day but the leader had not completed his consultations and told Muldoon that the matter would not be finalised until the following Monday. When Muldoon then talked to the media and intimated that he would be taking a frontbench seat and a major responsibility, McLay reacted angrily and immediately contradicted Muldoon, said he had not been promised a frontbench seat, and decided not to give him a spokesman's role after all.[94]

Following Muldoon's comments on the Friday night, Gair, Cox, Kidd, Richardson and Graham publicly opposed Muldoon's return to the front bench and the party president, Wood, stated that 'it's time former party leader, Sir Robert Muldoon, either joined the National Caucus team or got out'.[95] While the former president, Chapman, said Muldoon should be promoted to 'somewhere in the top 10 of the party',[96] other senior party figures such as the Auckland, Wellington, Canterbury-Westland and Waikato divisional chairpersons supported McLay and Wood and said Muldoon should be left on the backbench.[97] Sir John Marshall also met with McLay to offer advice and support and suggested publicly that Muldoon should retire.[98] Even Muldoon's old friend Peter Gordon told the press that Muldoon had been 'so disloyal' that his demotion was justified and Muldoon would never again lead the National Party.[99]

In the following *Sunday* current affairs programme on TV1 Muldoon, when asked if he would resign from National, responded 'No. Never . . . I've been active in the National Party since 1947 . . . I'm not going to give away all those years of effort and endeavour . . . The National Party's part of me and I'm part of the National Party and some of those who are criticising me I think weren't even born when I was first active in the National Party.'[100] In a radio interview the same day Muldoon suggested McLay, Wood and Leay might be in collusion to silence him and stated that he believed he was only 'the off-course substitute' as an alternative to McLay as leader but that Bolger was the 'obvious choice'.[101]

On the *Sunday* programme and again on a *Morning Report* interview on radio, McLay refused to rule out the possibility that Muldoon might be expelled from the National Party.[102] The controversy continued throughout the following week. Minogue launched an attack on Muldoon, reminding the former prime minister that he had asked Minogue to resign and sit as an Independent for opposing the SIS Bill in 1977.[103] He accused Muldoon of having over the years 'intimidated all his colleagues and caucus' into 'total subservience which he called loyalty' and said that Muldoon's current actions were motivated not by policy or principle but by an obsession for personal power.

The discussion of the issue by the National Party's Dominion Executive on Wednesday 23 October and by the caucus on Thursday 24 October was over-shadowed by the release of an *Eyewitness News*-Heylen poll on television which revealed that McLay's rating as preferred prime minister had dropped to a dismal 2.6 per cent, down from 4.3 in August which had been the lowest ever received by any Leader of the Opposition.[104] Muldoon was on 20 per cent, Lange on 32 per cent and Bolger on 5.7 per cent. Labour led National as the preferred party by 51 to 39 per cent. The poll had been taken on 19 October at the height of the row between McLay and Muldoon. The gap between the two parties, coming only months after National had won the Timaru by-election from Labour, reflected the public's perception that National was ripping itself apart and that McLay was too weak to deal with Muldoon. Muldoon described the poll figures as 'a disaster for the National Party'[105] and Wellington declared that McLay was 'political history'.[106]

Following a lengthy caucus meeting on 24 October at which 28 of the MPs present spoke, the caucus reaffirmed its loyalty to McLay but decided not to discipline Muldoon for criticising the leader. Muldoon made it clear that 'he would not be muzzled' and that it would be 'ridiculous' to try because 'I have a three hour radio programme every Sunday'.[107] McLay, who was suffering from legionnaires' disease, then decided to make one last attempt at reconciliation with Muldoon. He offered him the spokesmanship on transport, held at that time by Winston Peters, and again seat number 10 on National's second bench. This was the same seat which Muldoon had rejected earlier in the year when McLay had offered him overseas trade. McLay also told Muldoon that he would never put him back on the front bench. In an unpleasant meeting with McLay on Thursday 31 October, Muldoon rejected the offer and added that in his opinion McLay was not performing well as leader and that he had 'the weakest front bench that we've had in my 25 years in the House'.[108] When Muldoon repeated these remarks publicly on Friday, McLay summoned journalists to his office and within half an hour had demoted him from seat number 17 to seat 38, and also demoted Wellington to seat 37. Wellington's offence was that he had met with McLay, Bolger and McKinnon and told them that they were perceived as condemning Muldoon personally and all that the National Government had done collectively between 1975 and 1984, and that he had threatened to resign and fight a by-election in his seat of Papakura as a pro-Muldoon Independent.[109] McLay indicated by his removal of Muldoon and Wellington to the last two seats on the Opposition benches that he regarded both men as already having become independent MPs in all but name.

Muldoon then called a press conference and attacked McLay's actions as 'totally irrational' and suggested that McLay was 'a panic-stricken leader who has reached the stage where it is not just a question of whether he goes, but when'.[110] He called on the grass roots of the National Party to rise up 'against Jim McLay's leadership and the party hierarchy' because 'there's no alternative but that he has to go'.[111] Muldoon repeated the call a week later.[112] For the next four months virtual civil war broke out in both the National Party caucus and its organisation at all levels throughout New Zealand. One of McLay's supporters, Ruth Richardson, called publicly for Muldoon to be expelled from the party while another, Ian McLean, suggested he consider resigning. A former minister, Talbot, responded that if Muldoon was 'pushed aside, that will certainly be a dividing factor as far as the National Party is concerned'.[113]

The outbreak of public hostility between McLay and Muldoon was followed by a marked increase in Sunday Club activity. Muldoon addressed meetings at Westport, Papakura and Mount Roskill in November, and at Masterton, Dunedin and Tauranga in December. The meeting at Rosehill College in Papakura on 8 November, for example, which was addressed by both Muldoon and Wellington, attracted over 800 people who paid $5 a head to attend. Among the audience there to support Muldoon was the former Speaker of Parliament, Alf Allen, the former mayors of Auckland and Papakura, Sir Dove-Myer Robinson and Jack Farrell, and Shearer.[114] Walker started to suggest that because of the 'chaos within the National Party caucus' the Sunday Club might put up its own candidates at the next election under the label 'National Conservative Group'.[115] He told critics that 'Public opinion polls taken among National Party people consistently give Sir Robert Muldoon more than twice the popular support than for any other member as the most preferred Parliamentary Leader, yet the Dominion Executive argue about the merits of two others who are almost off the bottom of the list.'[116] Walker's observation was confirmed by a NZ Herald-NRB poll in early November which showed that among National voters Muldoon was preferred as prime minister by 42 per cent to McLay's 10 and Bolger's 14.[117]

During October–November 1985 Muldoon received 277 letters supporting him and criticising McLay, Wood and Leay. Many wanted Muldoon back as leader. The Nelson electorate committee, for example, sent Muldoon its 'unanimous support' and said that, 'having lost confidence in the present leadership', it was 'desirous of an immediate change of Leader'.[118] A large number of the correspondents were prominent electorate officials from throughout New Zealand and one letter was signed by a group from within McLay's own Birkenhead organisation.

Muldoon also received during the same period 71 letters from electorate committees and National Party members criticising his disloyalty to McLay. Some asked him to give McLay the loyalty he had himself expected as leader. Others suggested he retire gracefully. Many said that they had been admirers and strong supporters of Muldoon but were disappointed with his current criticism of McLay and the National Party. Among the critics were party officials and members of his own Tamaki electorate, who told him that they had been 'proud of you as our Prime Minister' and pleaded with him 'do not spoil that image'. Others attacked him as 'foolish', 'acting like a child', being a 'Samson' bringing down the National Party and concurrently destroying himself, 'doing your best to destroy the National Party', doing 'dreadful harm' to National, and 'the reason for the National Party's problem'. Among the electorate committees that wrote censuring him were Tarawera, Gisborne, Horowhenua, Rangitikei, Miramar, Wellington Central and Waipa. In replying to the Waipa electorate, Muldoon wrote, 'Of all the electorates in New Zealand yours should be the last that should write to me in that manner. Your former Member of Parliament, Miss Waring, was totally disloyal to me, her colleagues and the National Party whenever it suited her and my understanding was that she retained the overwhelming support of her electorate committee . . . You are quite wrong in parroting this cry that I always demanded loyalty from Caucus. The best examples are your own former member and Minogue, neither of whom was brought to heel by me, nor indeed did I at any time attempt to do so.'[119] One 'former admirer' from Masterton wrote that, 'you will be remembered in the future as "the ex-Prime Minister who didn't know how to let go" – and that would be a great shame for *in your time* you *were* a great man'. That view was shared by other correspondents. Others were less complimentary, one from Remuera stating bluntly, 'You are the reason for the National Party's problem. Keep quiet or get out.'

One of the most telling letters was from Ken Comber, Holyoake's son-in-law and the former MP for Wellington Central. Comber told Muldoon that at lunch with eleven other former National MPs he had found all twelve upset by the clash between Muldoon and McLay. 'I merely ask', Comber wrote, 'what would you, as Leader, have done if a member of your Caucus had acted as you did on Friday night?' He went on, 'Both of us shared a deep and abiding admiration for K.J. [Holyoake]. As the split opened up in recent days I asked myself what wise counsel would he be giving us now? I have a pretty good idea – and so have you. He once told me that on occasions I would have to exercise a degree of "blind loyalty" to the Party. I would ask this of you now in spite of the hurt and disappointment you may feel – for K.J.'s memory . . . Rob, I beg you, consider the lasting damage that is done to the Party by such public spectacles.'[120] Comber pleaded with Muldoon to support, not criticise, McLay.

Muldoon replied personally and sometimes at length to all the people who wrote criticising or supporting him. The tenor of those replies is given in one to a very strong critic, Muldoon concluding, 'We will differ on McLay's actions and mine over the past year, although it is true that I have deplored the manner in which he and some of his close friends have tried to distance themselves from the policies of the Governments in which he was a senior Minister and Deputy Prime Minister, and in the framing of which he played a full and active part.'[121]

The National Executive at its meeting of 23 October had again discussed Muldoon's activities and statements. McLay said that he did not believe that 'he had to defend or justify' the recent action he had taken against Muldoon.[122] He was supported by several other members, with Geoff Thompson observing that 'the former leader, by his recent behaviour, had created confusion and deep concern'.[123] A Muldoon supporter, Simich, who came from Muldoon's Tamaki electorate, then argued that 'the Party had taken the wrong direction and offered no alternative to Labour . . . The Party had lost . . . ground because our people chose to disown the past.'[124] Muldoon represented many people who were hurting. Three MPs present, Bolger, Birch and East, then opposed those on the Executive who believed that the Executive should 'be seen to be strong on a rebuttal of the things that Sir Robert was saying and attempting to do' and recommended instead that the Executive should leave it to the caucus to resolve the matter. Bolger accused the Executive of being 'too pessimistic' but agreed that 'the complex personalities involved' in the controversy would need careful handling in the future.[125] After discussing Shearer's and Quin's connection with Muldoon it was decided, with McLay's support, but against Bolger's reservations, to suspend them from party membership, a move resisted also by Simich and East. Muldoon's fate was left to caucus.

As soon as she received her telegram from Leay suspending her, Quin rang Muldoon, who after discussing the matter with her made a statement that he was 'astonished' and that if the Dominion Executive 'suspended every member of the party who's made a statement in public that's prejudicial to the National Party we'd lose thousands of people at the present time'.[126] He also gave individual interviews to four influential journalists: Dick Griffin, Oliver Riddell, Bill Ralston and Richard Harman. In a subsequent public comment Muldoon added that, while he found the suspension of Shearer 'understandable', he found that of Quin 'quite incredible' because she had done 'nothing to warrant suspension'.[127]

When the National Executive met next on 27 November, it was informed that Shearer and Quin were taking legal action against the party, and the lawyer Julian Watts advised the Executive that it should not proceed any further in moving against the two critics.[128] Bolger, Birch and East also questioned the suspensions and argued that the matter should be settled quickly and preferably out of court. The suspensions of Shearer and Quin were lifted.[129] At the meeting, McLay and Bolger disagreed as to what information Shearer should be given. McLay's view was that not only Shearer but members of the National Executive did not need to know financial details because the Finance Committee should be trusted as a 'body in which we reposed the responsibility to deal with these matters appropriately and decide what information if any should be made available'.[130] Bolger, on the other hand, referred to 'the modern practice of freedom of information' and argued that the Executive had a right to know what its committees were doing and that information previously regarded as confidential should now be shared. Birch added that such information should be given not only to the Executive and to Shearer but should be released more generally.

The National Executive was dismayed at its December meeting when Shearer notified it that he would not appear as arranged to discuss his previous suspension because his lawyer, Kevin Ryan, was involved in a murder trial in Auckland and could not be present. Although McLay wished to proceed without Shearer's presence, the majority of the Executive decided on the advice of Watts and Ted Thomas QC not to proceed or make any decision against Shearer without his being given a hearing and the matter was deferred until after Christmas.

At its meeting on 29 January 1986, although Shearer again did not attend, this time because National Executive would not pay his and his lawyer's airfares, the Executive decided to resolve the matter. Wood and Leay left the room and the Canterbury-Westland divisional chairman, Neville Young, took the chair. After McLay had attacked Shearer, who had taken 'rumour and innuendo' and turned them into 'public allegation against the party', which was definitely 'prejudicial to the interest of the Party', a motion was passed to that effect.[131] Bolger, who had again stressed the principle of 'freedom of information in modern society' and spoken against the motion, then strongly opposed a subsequent motion to cancel Shearer's party membership. Bolger argued that it was not a 'sign of strength . . . to expel a dissident member' but simply indicated an inability to take criticism, which one would always find and should always accept in a political organisation.[132] The motion was lost 8–13 but it was then agreed unanimously at McLay's insistence that Shearer should be 'severely censured'. The division between the party's leader and deputy leader over this issue was very marked. By this time Shearer had resigned as chairman of the Tamaki electorate and largely withdrawn from activity within the National Party. Quin continued with her legal action, which was resolved in March 1986 when the Executive apologised to her and paid her $35,000 damages and $5000 costs.[133]

The open conflict between Muldoon and McLay provided the opportunity for Bolger to reassert his claim to the leadership. Numerous press reports suggested that McLay would be replaced at a caucus meeting on 5 December.[134] McLay's lieutenants, Cox and McLean, believed that his support at that time never dropped below 24 of the 38 MPs in the caucus.[135] Bolger certainly had a hard core of 10, organised by Townshend and Muldoon's former supporter Friedlander, but some were not prepared to pay the cost required to persuade Muldoon's small group of four MPs to support Bolger.[136] Although worried about McLay's public image, his inability to counter Lange in the House, and his low ratings in opinion polls, the majority of MPs remained loyal to their leader. At the caucus meeting on 5 December, McLay asked three times if anyone wanted leadership added to the agenda and when no one spoke reprimanded the dissidents.[137] Muldoon, however, the same day called publicly for rank-and-file party members to make their views known; a week later claimed that National could never win under McLay; and a fortnight later stated that Bolger was the only National MP, apart from Muldoon himself, who could lead National to victory in 1987.[138] Muldoon might not have many supporters left in caucus, but the public opinion polls showed that he still had more influence than any other National MP with tens of thousands of voters throughout New Zealand, and his seal of approval or disapproval on a leader such as McLay was still very significant.

Muldoon's open condemnation of McLay and public endorsement of Bolger led to the Sunday Club throwing its support behind McLay's deputy. McKinnon, who was not only chief whip but chairman of National's caucus strategy committee, had attended a meeting of the Sunday Club in Christchurch where he had been told that the Club's two main aims were to remove McLay as leader and return Muldoon to the front bench, though not necessarily as leader.[139] In January 1986, the Sunday Club wrote to McKinnon stating that they would welcome Bolger's election as leader and expected him to put Muldoon back on the front bench. They believed the two could work well together.[140]

McLay's easy victory at the December caucus meeting might have made him overconfident. As he had become more influenced by supporters such as Richardson and Cox and appeared to be renouncing almost everything National had done between 1975 and 1984, Gair and Birch had become concerned and argued that doing so was a major tactical error.[141] It would make opposition to the Labour Government much more difficult and would enrage Muldoon, who would be provoked even more into defending his record and criticising not only Labour but also opponents within his own party. Like Muldoon, Birch also wanted to defend 'Think Big', but the free marketeers in National's caucus disapproved of the growth strategy and the liquid fuels import substitution policy and, like Labour, argued that the projects had been unnecessary, too costly and too closely tied to New Zealand's accumulated and arguably unsustainable level of public debt.

McLay made three critical decisions which destroyed his caucus majority. First by refusing to put Muldoon back on the front bench he guaranteed that Muldoon would continue to attack him publicly and that the four or five votes in the Muldoon faction would be cast for Bolger, who had given such an assurance. The ongoing public feud with Muldoon also continued to damage National's unity and McLay's poll ratings, further destabilising his position. Secondly, McLay and his key supporters seemed to be moving too fast down the same policy reform paths as the Labour Government, apparently endorsing rather than opposing and providing a clear alternative to that Government. Thirdly, in McLay's opinion, Birch could not stop defending 'Think Big' and Gair was not performing well in Opposition, and so in February he demoted both from his front bench.[142] Birch and Gair immediately became part of a conspiracy to win back their seats by replacing McLay with Bolger. As Friedlander later recalled, although he and Townshend had been working hard organising support in caucus for Bolger, they had not been able to get anywhere near the numbers until joined by Birch and Gair.[143]

Muldoon might have undermined McLay's leadership but he was not a leading figure in the coup which replaced McLay with Bolger at a caucus meeting on 26 March 1986. He did, however, give it his blessing in advance. Invited by Birch and Gair to join them in Bolger's office, Muldoon was asked for his views. He said he would support Bolger but wanted to be moved to the front bench with a reasonable portfolio. In response to a query from Bolger, Muldoon suggested Foreign Affairs. Bolger agreed.[144]

Birch, with some help from Gair, then persuaded 26 of the 38 MPs to sign a letter requesting a caucus vote on the leadership.[145] McLay had an inkling a week before the coup that his opponents were organising again and rang Birch forty-eight hours before it happened. Birch denied that a coup was imminent.[146] McLean then checked with twelve other MPs, all of whom said that they had no intention of voting for a leadership change. Checks with key senior officials in the organisation, most of whom were loyal to McLay, also revealed that there had been no consultation with them about a possible leadership challenge. McLay accepted all these assurances and was absolutely devastated when told the night before the caucus meeting that Bolger had the numbers and would challenge McLay for the leadership the following morning.[147] Although one MP who signed the letter voted for McLay, another who did not voted for Bolger, who won by 26 votes to 11, with

Upton, a McLay supporter, absent.[148] Gair overwhelmed Richardson for the deputy's position. Gair's promotion reassured some of Bolger's supporters, who had voted for him only after being told that the leadership change would not mark a surrender to Muldoon.[149]

CHAPTER 24

Court Cases, Radio Pacific and the 1987 Election

OLLOWING THE REMOVAL OF MCLAY, BOLGER APPOINTED Muldoon spokesman on Foreign Affairs and promoted him from seat 38 to seat number 8 on the front bench. Muldoon was delighted and immediately re-established links with the American ambassador, Paul Cleveland, with whom he lunched at the Wellington Club three days later. He also threw himself over the following months into a round of large public meetings in Lower Hutt, Hamilton, Opotiki, Levin, Taradale, Richmond, Albany, Mount Albert, Papatoetoe and Franklin, attacking with vigour the Lange-Douglas Government.

At Bolger's first National Executive meeting as leader he notified the Executive that the Sunday Club had handed over its proposed Christchurch meeting to the National Party and that Bolger had replaced Muldoon as the guest speaker.[1] Thereafter, there was very little attention paid at National Executive meetings to Muldoon, Shearer, or the Sunday Club.

At Wood's last Executive meeting as president, in June 1986, Leay announced his retirement as secretary-general of the party.[2] Leay's relationship with Muldoon, which from 1974 to 1984 had been largely cordial and productive, had deteriorated badly after the 1984 election defeat. Leay was later to recall that he always admired Muldoon's 'brilliant mind, fantastic recall, and genius for simplifying and concentrating on issues' and that on a one-to-one basis Muldoon could be 'gentle, likeable and sensitive' and 'a delightful person to work with'.[3] In political skills Leay respected Muldoon as 'the master'. But Leay also believed that Muldoon was 'a brilliant tactician and a disastrous strategist who could not see the big issues but was superb on little issues'. Muldoon's excessive caution was accompanied by his self-centredness and an intense competitiveness, which could make him 'waspish and mean-spirited' and, especially when he had been drinking, 'arrogant, unnecessarily offensive and even vicious'. Leay made no secret of the fact after 1984 that he regarded Muldoon's treatment of McLay as unforgivable.

Within the space of three months Muldoon's and the Sunday Club's major targets, McLay, Wood and Leay, had been removed from their positions and the club's major objective, to get Muldoon back on National's front bench, had been achieved. The mainly elderly organisers decided that the personal cost in time, money and stress in maintaining the Sunday Club was too great and a decision was made to cease its activities and return cheques to those who continued to send them.[4]

Throughout the latter part of 1985, Muldoon had been distracted from his battle with McLay by libel cases which he had brought against Bob Jones and Jones had brought against him. Muldoon over the previous two and a half years had found himself frequently engaged in litigation over alleged defamation, both as a plaintiff and a defendant.[5] In July 1983, for example, he and Tama Te Kapua Poata settled out of court an action Poata had brought after Muldoon in August 1981 had released an SIS list of radical Springbok tour protesters. Muldoon admitted that Poata was not one of those he had in mind when referring to violent and dangerous terrorists. In July 1984 the BCNZ paid Muldoon $30,000 in damages and costs to settle a statement on 2YA's *Sunday Supplement*, which had suggested incorrectly that taxpayer funds had been used to settle previous defamation claims against the Prime Minister. In June 1985 Muldoon and Des Monaghan, the director of programming for TVNZ, decided to stop litigation and pay their own costs with Muldoon accepting that Monaghan had taken no part in deciding to show a contentious programme *Death of a Princess*, which Muldoon believed was factually incorrect and would harm New Zealand's relations and trade with Saudi Arabia, from whom New Zealand was importing about 50 per cent of its crude oil.

Muldoon v. Jones originated in Jones's suspicions late in 1983 that the Security Intelligence Service, possibly at Muldoon's instigation, had bugged his telephone and also the offices of the New Zealand Party. Over a four-week period Jones and the director of the SIS, Brigadier John Smith, whom Muldoon had reluctantly appointed to the post in 1983, exchanged eleven letters on the matter, with Smith assuring Jones that 'the Security Intelligence Service . . . has taken no interest in the New Zealand Party or in you as spokesman for the party at all.'[6] There the matter should probably have ended.

In March 1984, however, the *Sunday News* reported that the New Zealand Party's offices had been bugged, a claim Muldoon as minister in charge of the SIS angrily refuted after seeking a report from the SIS.[7] Various journalists raised the matter with Jones, who allegedly told two of them that Muldoon was 'power mad', that the Prime Minister's 'gross misuse of the SIS would eventually be revealed when the New Zealand Party became the Government', and that Jones looked forward 'to the pleasure of stripping him of his knighthood for his quite loathsome behaviour'.[8] Although Jones immediately denied making some of the comments and claimed that others were hypothetical responses to journalists' questions and had commenced, 'If Muldoon was involved then . . .', Muldoon refused to believe Jones's denial and subsequently sued Jones for $600,000 damages for defamation. Muldoon claimed that he was defending not only his own reputation as Prime Minister but also the reputation of the SIS. Jones, for his part, continued to believe that the SIS had bugged his office and was hurt by Muldoon's refusal to believe that he had never said that Muldoon had told them to do it.[9]

The dispute between the two men was aggravated in July when Muldoon in a television interview suggested that 'Jones objected to my bringing the rate of inflation down because he's made his money out of inflation' and that this had been Jones's motivation in forming the New Zealand Party, splitting the National vote, and thus removing Muldoon as Prime Minister.[10] Jones then sued Muldoon for $500,000 for his alleged defamation.

The libel trial over Jones's alleged comments about Muldoon was heard before Justice Jeffries and a jury in late November and early December 1985. Jeffries was a former Citizen for Rowling but that did not concern Muldoon, who had on a number of occasions praised Jeffries as a man of integrity. Muldoon might well have been more concerned had he known that at least ten members of the twelve-person jury were, as Jones subsequently asserted, people who had voted in 1984 for Jones's New Zealand Party.[11] Muldoon was, as usual in his court cases, represented by Des Dalgety and Jones by Mike Camp. In the end the jury found that Jones had either not said the words complained of or that, while the statement that he was 'power mad' had been made and was defamatory, it was fair comment and had been made without malice. Justice Jeffries ordered costs against Muldoon.

Muldoon was shaken by the verdict. He considered appealing but was concerned that the appeal could go as far as the Privy Council with crippling costs and no guarantee of vindication. He also questioned whether he could afford to defend himself against Jones in the second case which was still to be heard. Dalgety advised him: 'The problem in all of this is costs, and I am sure you see the implications of your getting on an on-going merry-go-round of litigation with multi-millionaire Jones . . . he doesn't have to care about mounting costs and the risks of unfavourable verdicts.'[12] Muldoon had never been a materialist who used his position to accumulate wealth and possessions, although he was comfortably off, his total assets including his Chatswood home, his Hatfields Beach bach, his shares in the accounting firm, and his savings totalling some $543,000 at that time.[13] But his access to ready cash was finite and considerably less than the resources available to Jones. Nor had Muldoon set aside damages he had been awarded in his previous defamation cases. Unlike most other politicians, Muldoon had always chosen to meet his own costs rather than ask for the Crown to pay them. When, as infrequently happened, he lost, he paid all the damages and costs personally. When, as usual, he won, he donated the balance after deducting legal fees to charity. For example, in 1979 he claimed $40,000 against the *Listener* for a Tom Scott article blaming Muldoon for the collapse of the Public Service Investment Society and, after settling out of court for an apology, correction and $12,000, Muldoon had paid $3500 of that amount to his lawyers and gave the remaining $8500 to the Salvation Army for work with needy children.[14]

Shortly before Christmas, Dalgety advised Camp that, although Dalgety believed that there were reasonable grounds for moving to set aside the jury's verdict, 'Sir Robert does not wish to proceed further. He has had his day in Court, and he accepts that . . . it is unrealistic to contemplate a further action.'[15] Muldoon chose not only to abandon an appeal against the decision in his case against Jones but also publicly accepted in the second pending case that 'Jones was motivated by genuine concern in respect of the issues he raised in forming and leading the New Zealand Party', and as a result Jones withdrew his defamation case against him. Muldoon and Jones agreed to pay their own costs in the second defamation action, but Muldoon was left with both sets of costs in regard to the first. Although friends donated $42,000 towards those costs and Dalgety gave Muldoon a 25 per cent deduction on legal charges and wrote off other costs totalling some $20,000, Muldoon was still left to pay almost $85,000 of his own legal expenses and a further $37,000 of Jones's costs.[16] Those amounts were not finally cleared until late 1986 and only after Muldoon had taken on a number of activities to raise the money.

Muldoon took on some extra work to help pay his legal fees though most of his numerous activities remained voluntary. He prepared, as a consultant, annual and long-range forecasts of the New Zealand economy for his friend Fred Dobbs. He received $20,000 for making television commercials for Countrywide Bank and also made television advertisements for Vogel's bread and Sabco garden hoses and tools.[17] The garden shed shown on television was in Christchurch, not as stated at the back of his and Thea's new home at Chatswood, somewhat ironically in McLay's Birkenhead electorate. Nor incidentally was it Muldoon who mowed the lawns and looked after the impressive garden. Both were done by Thea. After writing a weekly column, 'Rob Says' in *Truth*, since 1974 Muldoon started writing another column, 'Rob's View', each Saturday in the *Auckland Star*. He visited schools throughout New Zealand, talking about his childhood and reading favourite children's stories, and he gave frank and very entertaining guest lectures to Stage I Political Studies students at Auckland and Wellington Universities. He was guest conductor at a Continental Airlines brass band Christmas concert in Auckland's Queen Elizabeth II Square. He collected and dispatched thousands of new and second-hand books to a high school in the Samoan village of Siumu after a visit to it. He shared the stage with Diamond Lil, Max Cryer, Gary McCormick and others at a 'Rain Aid Concert' in the Auckland Town Hall which raised $7000 for victims of an East Coast storm. He was Santa Claus at both the children's party at Auckland's Mercy Hospital and Wellington's Black Power marae. Until his death Muldoon retained a close connection with Wellington's Black Power gang, acting as patron and adviser, particularly encouraging their work schemes and better care of women and children associated with gang members.

Most surprising to many people was Muldoon agreeing to do ten performances in July 1986 as the narrator in the raunchy *Rocky Horror Show*, dancing the 'Time Warp' with seductively underdressed girls and transvestites. The 13,000 people who saw Muldoon perform at His Majesty's Theatre in Auckland found him a little unsure of his lines and movements at first, but by the last night he had gained in confidence, was enjoying the humour of the occasion, and was getting thunderous ovations for his attempts at a pelvic thrust. He also enjoyed a small cameo role in

1986 as 'Groves', the sinister head of a secret service organisation in the TV children's series *Terry and the Gun Runners*. Such activities undoubtedly contributed to Muldoon's being voted by *Truth* readers as New Zealand's 'most lovable politician' ahead of Tim Shadbolt, Cath Tizard, Mike Moore and David Lange.[18] His rating was also undoubtedly assisted by his weekly talk-show on radio.

On 16 December 1984 Muldoon commenced broadcasting weekly for three hours from 3 p.m. to 6 p.m. on Sundays over Radio Pacific. His talk-show was called 'Lilies and other things' and, while most of Muldoon's guests and callers discussed politics and the economy, he also dealt regularly with gardening and various social topics. Muldoon usually had a guest for the middle hour. Each year, with the help of his grandchildren he posted out free lily seeds to over a thousand listeners who sent him stamped, addressed envelopes. Six months after he started the programme, an audience survey found that on one particular Sunday he had 74,500 listeners, of whom 71,200 were over 40 years of age.[19] While many of Muldoon's listeners were older members of 'Rob's Mob', others were former opponents who either responded favourably to his criticism of Rogernomics or found themselves reassessing their opinion of Muldoon because he seemed more tolerant, patient, kindly and humorous in dealing with callers than they had expected him to be. As one listener wrote to Derek Lowe, the managing director of Radio Pacific, after Muldoon's first broadcast, 'I am not a Muldoon fan – In fact I detest him, BUT I am prepared to congratulate him through you. I had no idea he could be human and I enjoyed the other side of his character very much. If he keeps on like this I think I will listen every Sunday.'[20] Not everyone approved, however, and the Labour cabinet minister, Richard Prebble, wrote privately to Muldoon observing that, 'You are a politician campaigning for leadership with the assistance of a private radio station . . . Radio Pacific has clearly decided that even though Labour supporters are switching off Radio Pacific that there are enough Sunday Club National people in Auckland to make a viable radio station. Their action may make commercial sense . . . I do not see how you, Sir Robert, can claim to be serving your constituency while accepting a contract to be a radio performer.'[21]

Muldoon continued broadcasting every Sunday for almost eight years until the Sunday before he died. He twice won the Australasian Academy of Broadcast Arts and Sciences Pater Award for the best regular consultant on radio, the first time at the end of 1985 and his first year on the air. When asked by the Pater organisers what he liked and disliked about broadcasting, Muldoon replied that he liked 'to communicate with people' in a 'relaxed atmosphere' where 'we just talk to each other on important subjects', but he disliked 'the regular commitment' of four hours every Sunday afternoon.[22]

Although Muldoon would not praise an opponent publicly, privately he admired some Labour politicians even if he did not like them. Lange proved to be a totally different prime minister to Muldoon. The Labour leader resembled the chairman of a board of directors rather than a managing director responsible for the day-to-day operation of the whole firm, as Muldoon had been. In Muldoon's mind, the managing director's role in the Labour Government elected in 1984 went to

Roger Douglas, whom Muldoon saw as 'not an original thinker' but a man who 'had grasped the essentials of the New Right ideology to which he had been converted' by Treasury and self-interested businessmen.[23] Douglas was also an able strategist in implementing his policies speedily, before his opponents – inside as well as outside the Labour Party – had a chance to mount an effective defence.

For a time Muldoon believed, and perhaps hoped, that Lange, with his exceptional intellect and impressive speaking ability, might be able to impose his values and will on the new Government. Lange appeared to think laterally and had a core of genuine humanitarian values but, in Muldoon's view, his attention span appeared somewhat limited, he was 'an economic ignoramus' and he lacked the steely strength and persistency required for long-term successful leadership.[24] Above all else, however, Muldoon admired Lange's ability to raise Labour's morale and devastate National's in the House. Muldoon had always believed that the Government or the Opposition dominated each other not just through voting numbers or strength of logical and incisive debate but significantly through the use of humour and sarcasm. For many years Muldoon had been unequalled in ridiculing Labour but even before the 1984 election, and certainly after it, he had to concede that Lange was pre-eminent.[25] Muldoon at his best could still sometimes counter Lange but McLay, although an intelligent and effective debater, was not a witty one and also took more personally the contemptuous jibes that Lange threw at him.

Even after he lost the leadership and retreated to the backbench, Muldoon was still National's most effective critic of what he termed 'the dry sterile free market monetarist policies of the present Government which had squeezed out every human aspect.'[26] He tried to win back rural support by attacking the 'essentially city-based' Labour Government which was blindly implementing the 'mad-scientist approach' of young, inexperienced Treasury and Reserve Bank officials who 'with soft hands and hard heads' totally failed to understand the reality of the effect of 'free-running interest rates and tight money' on an economy.[27] That theme of high interest rates, coupled with speculative rather than productive investment, dominated his speeches during the period 1984–1987. In his own electorate newsletter, for example, he advocated controls on interest rates which, at 20 per cent and coupled with inflation rates of 15 per cent and considerably higher than New Zealand's major trading partners, would damage 'farmers, home owners and small businessmen'. Many of those, he predicted, 'will lose the whole equity in the farm, home or business as capital values drop' when the speculative boom inevitably ended.[28] As a result of Labour's policies unemployment would also increase and real wages for those still with jobs would decrease. Muldoon was particularly worried by the fact, as he noted in September 1985, that 'the Financial Sector in New Zealand is not equipped by either experience or personnel to cope with the totally unregulated position that now exists and I have serious fears that we will see one or more collapses before too long'.[29] Muldoon, of course was not only attacking Labour but still defending his own reputation and administration, which were being widely condemned.

In an article written for the Christmas 1985 issue of the Tamaki National Party's electorate newsletter *Communique*, Muldoon looked back on his twenty-five years as the local MP.[30] He reminisced that, in the late 1970s and early 1980s at a time when the terms of trade had dropped savagely against New Zealand, his aim had been 'to keep the farmers on their farms, the businessmen in business, and the maximum possible number of New Zealanders in jobs . . . to keep the economy on an even keel while we built up the "think big" projects to assist our farming industry in earning and saving the overseas funds upon which we are so dependent'. That was all now being undermined and he predicted that 1986 might well 'see the worst economic calamity since World War II' as the result of the Fourth Labour Government's reckless economic policies.

Muldoon's political-economic forecasts for both 1986 and for the five-year period 1986–90 were recorded in two lengthy documents he prepared in February and May 1986 as a consultant for Fred Dobbs.[31] Internationally Muldoon predicted a downturn in the US economy during 1986 which would be reflected in the rest of the world, putting pressure particularly on debt-crisis countries, US and other western banks, and exchange rates. While he did not believe it would be as bad as the 1930s, in Muldoon's assessment there would be another economic depression both worldwide and within New Zealand before the end of the 1980s and, with a major downturn in the sharemarket, 'some of the high flying investment companies will crash' in New Zealand.[32] Because the 'National Party . . . is in such disarray' and because 'factors such as the visits of nuclear ships and the Rainbow Warrior Affair, both of which have been skilfully used as exercises in xenophobia, give the Government a substantial lead over a disorganised Opposition', Muldoon stated that the Labour Government would probably be returned at 1987 election, possibly but not certainly with a reduced majority. It would then be faced with some horrendous economic problems partly but not totally of its own making.[33]

Labour's decision to introduce a surtax on superannuation payments enraged Muldoon. He did not accept Treasury advice that the National Superannuation scheme he had introduced after the 1975 election had been proved to be unsustainable. It was already taxed together with other income so that the net cost above means-tested old age benefits was, in his view, considerably less than the scheme's critics contended. He saw National Superannuation not as a charitable payment but as a retirement insurance paid for by taxpayers throughout their working life. The surtax was 'vicious' and discriminated against some taxpayers on the basis of their age, not their income. In articles and speeches Muldoon launched repeated attacks on the superannuation surtax, receiving warm applause from elderly audiences throughout the country.[34]

While most of Muldoon's attention was directed at the economy and, to a lesser extent, to the breach with the United States over the nuclear ship ban and its effect on the ANZUS Treaty, two other long-standing divisive issues reappeared in 1985: sporting contacts with South Africa and homosexual law reform. Late in 1984 the New Zealand Rugby Union decided to send an All Black team to South Africa in 1985. Muldoon, who was still Leader of the Opposition, wrote a brief, formal, not very persuasive letter to Blazey stating that, 'I was one of those involved in the drafting of the Gleneagles agreement. It is my duty to put it to you that the All Blacks should not tour South Africa next year.'[35] He added that, 'the decision is one for the Rugby Union and the Rugby Union alone to make' and promised that 'the National Party Caucus and I will strenuously oppose any action by the Government or any other group to prevent by act or omission the Tour taking place if it is the decision of the Rugby Union to proceed'. This was clearly not a letter calculated to help in the cancellation of the tour and that was recognised by Blazey, who replied that he was pleased to note Muldoon's assurance if the Union decided to accept the South African invitation.

Although in March 1985 Parliament voted unanimously to call on the Rugby Union to decline the invitation to tour South Africa, the union's council in April announced that an All Black team would be sent. Shortly before the tour in July, two Auckland lawyers and rugby players, Philip Recordon and Patrick Finnegan, backed financially by a large number of other people and represented by Ted Thomas QC, took out an injunction against the NZRFU. At Blazey's suggestion the Rugby Union's counsel, Kit Toogood, subpoenaed Muldoon to give evidence 'that you and the National Party Caucus gave your support to the Rugby Union'.[36] When Recordon and Finnegan were granted an interim injunction, however, the tour was subsequently cancelled by the Rugby Union. It was clear, however, where Muldoon's sympathies were.

In March 1985 the Labour MP Fran Wilde introduced into Parliament a Homosexual Law Reform Bill, which was designed first to decriminalise consensual homosexual acts by males over the age of 16 and secondly to outlaw discrimination on the ground of sexual orientation. By June and July 1986 when Parliament in debate and votes split almost equally over the legislation, the Justice and Law Reform Committee of the House, on which Muldoon sat, had considered 1096 submissions and 1138 letters on the Bill. A petition signed by some 835,000 people opposed to the Bill had also been presented to Parliament. Muldoon, because of his previous support of homosexual law reform, was one of the MPs who came under particular pressure. Of 729 letters in his correspondence on the topic, 452 were in favour of the Bill and 277 against. The three main arguments used by the majority of correspondents both for and against were religious considerations, fear of AIDS, and the danger of young people being put under pressure.

While Muldoon was prepared to vote for decriminalisation, he was opposed to the age of 16. He voted for amendments by Gair to raise the age to 18 and by Labour's Stan Rodger to raise it to 20, but when both amendments were defeated he decided he could not support the bill if it included the lower age. He therefore voted against the Bill at both its second reading and in the critical committee stage in Parliament where it was passed by a majority of five votes, 41 to 36, with 18 MPs absent and not voting.[37] Muldoon subsequently voted against the second part of the Bill, prohibiting discrimination against homosexuals, arguing that this infringed the rights of those who did not wish to employ or be associated with them. That brought him, among other correspondence, an abusive letter from the

National Affairs Officer of the Auckland University Students' Association accusing Muldoon of discriminating against and not being representative of his constituents and of reflecting instead the views of Queen Victoria, whose 'moral values should have died with her'. Muldoon responded, 'I acknowledge your insulting letter. Your arrogance is matched only by your ignorance.'[38]

Dismayed at the Labour Government's rush to free up the financial sector of the economy, Muldoon claimed that the deregulation of the banking system was particularly dangerous in the light of lack of protection for depositors and the shortage of competent, trained and experienced personnel to handle the more sophisticated and experienced financial environment. While his major concern was about the new merchant banks and fringe financial institutions, he was also worried about the traditional trading banks, the trustee savings banks which had existed since 1847, and the Post Office Savings Bank which had been established in 1867. He believed that the changes would destroy depositors' security and open up the danger of some savings banks collapsing as they did from time to time in the United States. He predicted that the banking changes generally would raise the risk of some major banks and financial institutions crashing 'in the not-too-distant future' and for that reason believed that government-guaranteed trustee savings banks should be retained to protect the savings of small, conservative depositors.[39]

His repeated attacks in 1985 and 1986 on Labour's amalgamation and transformation of local trustee savings banks, whose deposits were government-guaranteed, into full trading banks, without government guarantees, upset even some of his closest and most loyal supporters in the National Party organisation.[40] In a long letter to Muldoon, the Auckland divisional director, Tremewan, who was a long-time trustee of the Auckland Savings Bank, told him bluntly that he was wrong both in opposing the evolution of the trustee savings banks and in blaming the Labour Government for the changes, which had been initiated by and had the full support of, among others, the ASB trustees, who had been 'appointed overwhelmingly by the National Party', not the new Labour Government.[41] He criticised particularly Muldoon's ill-informed comment first to a meeting of the Mount Roskill Kiwanis and then on Radio Pacific about 'not keeping $5.00 in the ASB' and noted that immediately 'people started phoning to see if their money was safe'.[42]

According to the president of the bank, 'these remarks caused a number of customers to close their accounts' and on 17 July the bank's solicitors contacted Muldoon advising him that his statements about the bank were 'incorrect and defamatory statements'.[43] The executive director of the bank, Dennis Ferrier, then closed Muldoon's 60-year-old savings account which contained $169.19 and had not been used since 1981. Ferrier observed that, as Muldoon had no confidence in the bank, he would not want his money left there.[44] The president of the bank later told Muldoon: 'It only needed a public statement from you that you had closed your account with us for a run on the bank to have probably eventuated. This could have been infinitely more damaging than that which has resulted from you advising the world at large that the bank has closed your account.'[45]

Furious with Ferrier's action, Muldoon wrote a letter to Terry Harris, the president of the ASB trustees, noting that, although the account had 'not been active for some seven or eight years', he had opened it as a child and 'kept it open for sentimental reasons'.⁴⁶ He detailed his involvement as Minister of Finance with the trustee bank movement and the differences he saw between trustee and trading banks. He attacked as 'legal thuggery' threats made by the ASB in the wake of his comments; accused Ferrier of 'a lack of sensitivity' not only to Muldoon but also to 'thousands of little old ladies who have their life savings in the Auckland Savings Bank'; and noted that 'it is clear that I have made some errors of judgement in the past' as Minister of Finance in appointing trustees to the ASB and that if Harris will 'identify those who support you in your action I will endeavour to ensure that the next National Government rectifies those errors'.⁴⁷ He also threatened to raise matters prejudicial to the ASB under privilege in Parliament if the ASB and its solicitors proceeded against him.⁴⁸

Muldoon continued his vendetta against the ASB and Ferrier in particular later in 1986 when he wrote to the Chairman of the Higher Salaries Commission and the Secretary of Labour complaining that Ferrier was receiving a salary of $150,000 and had the use of a BMW car and the option to borrow $400,000 from the bank at an interest rate of 4 per cent.⁴⁹ The HSC Chairman replied curtly that the Secretary of Labour would look into the matter and the following day Muldoon was informed that the Department of Labour would not 'verify or otherwise the information you put forward' and 'can take your complaint no further'.⁵⁰ Muldoon was not satisfied and continued to raise the matter publicly to no avail throughout November and December.⁵¹

The controversy over reforms in the finance and banking sector also allowed Muldoon to express concern about changes in the accounting profession. He noted that he was 'deeply disturbed at the current practice of the listed so-called investment companies which take into account unrealised capital profits, including revaluations of buildings and, of course, the relatively new equity accounting approach to the affairs of their subsidiaries'.⁵² As a result he believed book assets and loans were being inflated well beyond the real value of the securities involved. Muldoon made it plain that he had nothing but contempt for many of his fellow accountants, arguing that the term 'creative accounting' was in his opinion simply a euphemism for 'fiddling the books'.⁵³ Such accountants and also lawyers broke the spirit, even if most only bent the letter, of the law as they prostituted themselves to the rogue businessmen whom Muldoon equally despised and criticised.

Muldoon's obvious unpopularity in caucus and among senior figures in the National Party organisation led Tom Fletcher, one of his deputy chairmen in Tamaki, to announce in March 1986 that he would challenge Muldoon for the party's nomination for the seat.⁵⁴ Muldoon was unimpressed and his supporters were enraged. At the electorate AGM shortly afterwards, Fletcher was defeated both for his deputy-chairmanship and as an electorate delegate to the party's annual conference. Subsequently, he decided not to continue with his challenge and Muldoon was reselected unopposed.

Shortly before Christmas 1986 Muldoon entered North Shore hospital where surgeons removed 30 centimetres of his intestine and rectum. An earlier operation to remove a growth in the colon three weeks before had revealed that Muldoon was suffering from bowel cancer. The operation went well and although he spent Christmas Day in hospital Muldoon returned home six days after it. The 66-year-old Muldoon made it plain that he had no thoughts of retiring from Parliament but intended to campaign actively during 1987 not only to help defeat the Labour Government but also to keep a close eye on National MPs such as Richardson who wanted National to outflank Labour by adopting the policies of the New Right. He was determined to stop that.

Labour's rapid dismantling of the protection given for so many years to New Zealand's manufacturing industry and the consequences for employment genuinely concerned Muldoon. In speeches leading up to the 1987 election he argued that, if a manufacturer 'closes down his . . . factories and moves them offshore making a good profit out of importing the articles that were previously made in New Zealand what are we going to produce to pay for those imports and will that production provide jobs for his former employees who are now on the dole?' He concluded: 'You must add to lower price [of imports] the cost of the dole for the workers previously employed in that factory because that, too, will be paid out of taxes by the consumers of those goods.'[55]

During the early part of 1987 Muldoon tried hard in caucus and elsewhere to influence policy and prevent the New Right seizing control. This brought him into conflict not only with Richardson, Cox, McLay and McLean but also with the party's finance spokesman and deputy leader, Gair. In March, for example, Muldoon and Gair had a public debate over whether National would or would not move to a managed float of the New Zealand dollar.[56] Muldoon argued that caucus had resolved the matter, but Gair backed by Cox said that the party's policy did not include the word 'managed' even though caucus at a previous meeting had reached a consensus on an interim policy paper that had contained the phrase. Muldoon and Gair also clashed on whether a National Government would try to control the outflow of capital overseas and whether the New Zealand dollar should be devalued to make exporters more competitive.[57]

Throughout 1987 Muldoon campaigned almost entirely in electorates where the National Party organisation or its candidate was well disposed towards him: Manurewa, Kaipara, Ashburton, New Plymouth, Napier, Waitotara, Te Atatu, Miramar, Taupo, Bay of Islands, West Auckland, Hobson, Yaldhurst, Christchurch North and his own seat of Tamaki. This was not simply Muldoon's preference. He was prepared to go elsewhere but many free-market MPs, candidates and party officials were as critical of their former leader as they were of the Labour Government, some more so, and refused to have Muldoon associated in any way with their local campaigns.

The result of the election was a disaster for National. In 1987 Labour's victory was achieved by a temporary alliance of usually irreconcilable sections of the electorate, the very rich and the very poor. The former approved of Roger Douglas's deregulation and other economic policies and made a rational business decision to support them. The poor were persuaded that, despite the negative effects of Labour's actions on them, a National Government would probably not only continue economically in that direction but would also slash welfare spending, thus reducing further what little the unemployed and beneficiaries had. Labour held all its seats, though later losing one, Wairarapa, after two judicial recounts and a High Court petition. National lost three of its remaining seats: Cox's Manawatu, Friedlander's New Plymouth, and Birkenhead, from which McLay had retired and where National's new candidate was a former senior Labour Party official.[58] The New Zealand Party and Democrat votes collapsed, with National benefiting in rural areas but Labour gaining overwhelmingly in the urban areas. Such was the swing of New Zealand Party voters to Labour in the wealthiest urban seats that the National strongholds of Fendalton, North Shore and Remuera were only just held with shockingly small majorities, and among National's urban MPs only Muldoon, with a much depressed majority of 1947 votes, had a reasonably safe margin. Muldoon polled 52.03 per cent of the votes cast in the Tamaki electorate compared to the 62 per cent he had gained in 1975 when his popularity was at its height and the 46.35 per cent in 1984 when it was at its nadir. In 1987 no other National MP in an urban seat received over half the votes cast.[59]

The election loss devastated National Party morale, and pressure came on Bolger to revitalise his front bench. Richardson decided to challenge Gair for the deputy-leadership but when it became obvious that Gair would not win and he decided to step down, Bolger threw his support behind McKinnon, who defeated Richardson by one vote.[60] Impressed, and probably worried, by Richardson's strong showing, Bolger later the same day appointed Richardson to be the new Opposition spokesperson on finance, a position she accepted with the proviso that Bolger remove Muldoon from the front two benches of the Opposition. After considering her condition Bolger, according to Richardson, agreed to demote Muldoon.[61] The condition was unnecessary. There was no way Muldoon was going to stay on the front bench and support even by silence the economic policies Richardson espoused.

Immediately after the selection of McKinnon and Richardson, Muldoon wrote to Bolger reminding him that when Bolger became leader and put Muldoon back on the front bench, 'I gave you my assurance that I would support your leadership.'[62] Muldoon went on to add: 'At no time since then have I ever criticised you as Leader, not even when you made certain derogatory comments in public during the election campaign following distortions by the news media of things that I have said.' He argued that he had resisted news media attempts to make him disagree with National Party policy and that his support for Bolger had been 'clear and unequivocal'. He welcomed 'the right choice of McKinnon' as the new deputy leader replacing Gair, but believed Bolger had 'made the wrong choice in appointing Miss Richardson as spokesman on Finance. She will not rest until she has your job and in the meantime she will pursue an extreme right wing attitude to the economic policy which will only alienate the vast majority of National members.' While Muldoon admitted Richardson had 'a keen mind', he attacked her as one who 'speaks and thinks in cliches', was 'completely impervious to any views that do not coincide with her own current opinion', and 'advocated . . . the half digested views of the latest academic or businessman that she has spoken to'. Muldoon went on to express his concern that Bolger had 'fallen into the trap of thinking that in order to get financial support from the business community principally those in the financial sector we must publicly advocate views which they support and which to a very considerable extent are being implemented by the Labour Party'.[63] He argued that those policies were wrong and would eventually fail and that by trying to copy them National would alienate its 'core middle of the road supporters and be seen as nothing more than a party of right wing opportunists'.

Because he could not support Richardson and her right-wing economic policies, Muldoon warned Bolger that 'I am already under pressure to lead a new political party of the Centre but after 40 years in the National Party that prospect does not appeal'. Instead, 'during the next three years I intend to advocate policies that will regain for the National Party that middle ground' and oppose 'certain loud mouthed extremists mainly in the Wellington Division'.[64] Bolger was also told that 'whether you permit, support, or oppose my efforts will to some considerable extent determine your future in politics. The same comment applies to those in the upper echelons of the National Party.' Muldoon ended his letter by stating that he no longer felt constrained to refrain from public criticism of Bolger; did not want to cross the floor as Richardson and others had done but was only required as a National MP to support the Party on a vote of confidence; and that any attempt to gag or discipline him would damage the party more than him. Personally, Muldoon told Bolger, he had no political ambitions other that to see Labour defeated and a moderate, not right-wing, National Government returned to office.

CHAPTER 25

The Global Economic Action
Institute and the 1990 Election

URING THE 1987 ELECTION MULDOON HAD PREDICTED, AS
he had been predicting on Radio Pacific for some time before, that
Labour's policies, and especially deregulation of the finance markets and a
totally unrealistic rise in the sharemarket, would probably result in a crash
comparable to that almost sixty years before at the start of the Great Depression. In
October 1987, a few months after the election, the sharemarket slumped and over
the following weeks more than half its value disappeared. In all some $20 billion
was lost off the value of quoted shares, much of which was being used as security
for unwise loans from financial institutions.[1] The drop in the New Zealand
sharemarket was the greatest in the Western world and was the slowest to recover.
The inflated property market collapsed shortly after and credit tightened as over-
extended banks and finance houses rushed to reduce their exposure. Bankruptcies,
unemployment and interest rates rose. The Labour Government became increasingly divided, directionless and discredited.

Muldoon repeatedly argued thereafter that the crash of October 1987 'showed
that the policies of the present Government were fatally flawed . . . destroyed the
savings of many thousands of good New Zealanders, and showed that many people
in commerce and industry who previously were seen as respectable members of
society, were in fact common criminals.'[2] He lashed out at the speculative entrepreneurs, who 'believe in the law of the jungle . . . the cleverest and indeed the most
unscrupulous at the expense of the ordinary bloke . . . becomes a millionaire, one
thousand others are one thousand the poorer. If one man can avoid tax on a massive
income, one thousand ordinary blokes share the extra that has to be made up.'[3] In
later years he was to argue that 'I am in favour of privatisation if it is done properly
but the private sector did not show up all that well following the 1987 sharemarket crash, did it? If we say that . . . the private sector always does it better one
should have a look at some of the white collar criminals who live in the Tamaki
electorate. They did not do it better. The high-flyers . . . I hope . . . are heading for
jail today.'[4]

The 1987 crash not only intensified Muldoon's opposition to Rogernomics, it also made him even more determined to stop National going down the same path. He reasserted the need for New Zealand to move back towards a more interventionist and protectionist economic policy. As the guest speaker at the Auckland Division's pre-Christmas meeting in December 1987, he regretted that National was divided into factions and was still operating as if it were the Government instead of an Opposition before devoting the remainder of his address to attacking what he described as 'the simplistic economic theories of the past three years'. He compared New Zealand with other countries such as Japan and Taiwan, which had 'hands-on economic management', and argued that New Zealand was facing unfair competition in products 'where we are clearly internationally efficient' because none of New Zealand's trading partners and competitors had abolished all their protection and subsidies. As a result, 'if we free up our own market we receive products that are subsidised, not simply by breadline wages but by other artificial forms of assistance, such as tax holidays, bounties and the like.'[5]

Aghast at what he claimed was the cost of Rogernomics, Muldoon savaged the need to provide more than $1 billion for the dole in the 1988 Budget when 113,753 New Zealanders were registered as unemployed.[6] He challenged the Labour Government in Parliament by asking:

> Do you ever give a thought to what it is like to be unemployed in this country? Do you ever give it a thought? Do you ever give a thought to a man in his forties . . . with a family and with a house with a mortgage on it, who thought that he was in a job – not a high-paid job, but a job that he did to the best of his ability and took home his pay at the end of a week with a feeling of satisfaction; an ordinary New Zealander, who went to the football and occasionally had a small bet on a racehorse – and then suddenly in the last few months found that his job had disappeared . . . [and that he and many others were] condemned for the rest of their lives to be beneficiaries of the State.[7]

As a backbench MP Muldoon had much more time for reading. An avid user of the Parliamentary Library, he worked systematically through the new books on economics as they were accessioned. As soon as one was read he exchanged it for another. At any given time, there were on a small table next to his favourite armchair in the lounge of his Chatswood home several books, together with the most recent issue of the *Economist* and a pile of copied articles, many chosen from the monthly *Spotlight* summaries provided by the United States Information Service. He was also often the first to order new books from the USIS Library.

Although his favourite reading matter related to economics, Muldoon also read more widely about education, health and international affairs, at least partially as background to his weekly programme on Radio Pacific. He also read and answered all his mail and objected to any attempt by his secretaries to lighten his load. On one occasion, after a Black Power member mentioned that he had sent Muldoon some cartoons which Muldoon had not seen, Muldoon challenged a secretary. She recalled some crude and rude drawings which she had thrown into the wastepaper basket. Muldoon told her off for censoring his mail and, thereafter, because he insisted on seeing everything, she presented his mail in a tray with unimportant matters on the bottom, important matters in the middle, and anything unusual or bizarre on top. Muldoon was usually heard chuckling before he got out of her office.

Muldoon continued to be a conscientious constituency MP and also relished the opportunity to speak in the House, even though he was often ridiculed by the Labour MPs present and ignored by many of the National members. On one occasion when he was speaking there was hardly anyone in the debating chamber. The Labour MP Jack Elder, from behind a newspaper he was reading, interjected, 'Oh shut up, you old, little, pear-shaped man.' Muldoon stopped speaking, fixed his gaze on Elder, and retorted, 'The Right Honourable old, little, pear-shaped man to you, sonny.'[8]

He also served on a number of parliamentary committees, one of which was examining whether New Zealand should purchase Australian, Dutch or Danish frigates. He listened carefully while an Australian admiral and various officials explained the reasons for buying Australian. Then Muldoon mentioned that he had studied the matter carefully and thought that the European ships were better and cheaper than the Australian. The admiral replied that, even if they were, northern hemisphere ships were not made for southern hemisphere conditions where the seas had longer waves. After a moment's consideration Muldoon asked, 'Are you saying that Captain Cook came here in an unsuitable ship?'[9] When the laughter died away the Australians had considerable difficulty regaining the initiative.

Muldoon's humour, however, continued to get him into trouble on occasions. Katherine O'Regan, for example, had a poster on her office door: 'Women can do anything'. Muldoon teased O'Regan by observing, 'No, Kathy. You wouldn't be able to prop for the Auckland rugby team.' O'Regan was annoyed at Muldoon's flippancy but was even more incensed when he compounded his misdemeanour by adding that on reflection he thought she was right after all. O'Regan couldn't prop the scrum but Jenny Shipley could. Neither O'Regan nor Shipley was amused.[10]

Freely admitting that he did not 'make personal friends very easily', Muldoon after 1987 had few friends left in Parliament.[11] The closest both personally and politically was Wellington, with whom Muldoon would occasionally have a drink in the evenings. He was also still on reasonably good terms with McKinnon, Birch, Banks and Peters, although they did not agree on all policy matters and socially had little to do with each other.

Outside Parliament Muldoon was involved in a range of activities: the weekly Sunday afternoon broadcast on Radio Pacific; a weekly column in the *Sunday Star*; periodic lectures to Political Studies students at Auckland and Victoria Universities, where in addition to speaking from his own experience he expounded on the views of Edmund Burke on the role of the state and the duties of MPs; free cruises through the Pacific in 1987 and 1988 on the cruise ship *Royal Viking* in return for giving four addresses to passengers on New Zealand and the Pacific; and his role as Count Robula, the ghoulish vampire who fronted the 'Friday Frights' late-night horror movie slot on TVNZ's Channel Two. In his Count Robula role, which was

Right: Rob and Thea in front of their Chatswood home, 1987. *AUCKLAND STAR*/NEWS MEDIA

Below: Muldoon could not bring himself to vote with the Labour Opposition against National welfare cuts in November 1991 but his expression showed his feelings and he abstained from voting. *NZ HERALD.*

Above: Although not solely responsible for McLay's demise as leader, Muldoon certainly made a major contribution.
J. VAN DER VOO/*NZ HERALD*.

Left: A mischievous photograph taken during *The Rocky Horror Show* in which Muldoon was the narrator.
PETER PAYNE/*DOMINION*.

Top right: Bert Walker chairs a Sunday Club meeting for Muldoon in New Plymouth, 1985. TARANAKI NEWSPAPERS LTD.

Centre right: Muldoon and his supporters in the Sunday Club targeted new party leader McLay, party president Sue Wood, and party director general Barrie Leay and by 1986 all three had gone and Bolger had become leader. *PRESS.*

Below: Ian Shearer (left) and Merv Wellington (right) were two of Muldoon's former ministerial colleagues who strongly supported Muldoon and the Sunday Club. MULDOON PAPERS.

Above: Muldoon at the Hastings
Centennial Celebrations at the
Tomoana Showgrounds.
Mayor Jim O'Connor holds his
coat while Bill Matthewson
(grey-haired man in football
jersey), Duncan MacIntyre's
longtime organisational right
hand and later a Sunday
Club leader, looks on.
BILL MATTHEWSON.

Left: Rob and Thea with
daughter Barbara and
grandchildren Dylan and baby
Emma at Vogel House, 1983.
MULDOON PAPERS.

Above: Rob titled his talkback programme on Radio Pacific after his favourite flower, 'Lilies and Other Things'. *NZ HERALD.*

Left: Muldoon wipes a tear away after announcing on Radio Pacific his decision to retire from Parliament, Sunday 17 November 1991. GLEN JEFFIE/*NZ HERALD.*

Left: The cartoon by Murray Webb presented to Muldoon at the 1992 valedictory dinner. MURRAY WEBB.

Below: Bob Jones, Thea, Muldoon and Wyatt Creech, the minister Muldoon regarded as the best of the Bolger cabinet, at the 1992 dinner organised by Jones. *EVENING POST.*

Below: Four past and present prime ministers at the 1992 valedictory dinner: Lange, Bolger, Muldoon and Moore. PETER BUSH.

Left: A yellow lily placed on the desk in front of Muldoon's empty seat in Parliament the day after his death. *NZ Herald.*

Below: A haka of respect by 100 Black Power members as Muldoon's hearse leaves the funeral service at the Auckland Town Hall, Friday 7 August 1992. *Dominion.*

Sir Robert Muldoon. NEALE MCMILLAN/SOPACNEWS.

suggested by Neil Roberts of Communicado, Muldoon, black-cloaked, pale-faced and red-eyed, introduced various horror films, but admitted in an interview that he was not really a fan of them. He added facetiously that the producers obviously thought that 'I was the most horrible creature in Parliament', although he person-ally thought that 'Nothing in the movies is as awful as the people I see across the floor of the House'.[12]

Throughout the late 1980s, Muldoon was still working very hard. For example, a typical week from his appointments diary shows that on Monday 7 August 1989, the day Lange resigned as Labour's leader, Muldoon was in Christchurch where he met a group of businessmen; addressed a full hall of superannuitants and housewives; spoke to two hundred students at St Bede's School; talked about super-annuation at an insurance company; and addressed a large public meeting in the evening in the Christchurch North electorate. He was in Parliament Tuesday, Wednesday and Thursday, discussing with colleagues until after midnight each night the dramatic political developments in the wake of Lange's departure from the prime-ministership. On Friday, he attended the National Party conference, fitting in an address at a testimonial dinner to the cricketer Stephen Boock. He spent Saturday morning at the conference in Wellington before flying to Christ-church and then driving to Culverton as guest speaker at a fund-raising function for the local football club. On Sunday morning, he returned to Auckland for his weekly programme on Radio Pacific.

Even as Prime Minister, a significant proportion of Muldoon's interest and energy had been directed into research and analysis of the international economy rather than into domestic politics. Muldoon, who had been a governor of the International Monetary Fund, World Bank and Asian Development Bank in 1967–72 and 1975–84 and who had chaired both the IMF and the World Bank in 1978–79 and the Organisation for Economic Co-operation and Development in 1982, retained especially his interest in the reform of the international monetary system after he returned to the Opposition benches in 1984.

In September 1984 he accepted an invitation to address a forum organised by the American Bankers' Association in conjunction with the bankers' associations of fourteen other industrialised countries. The forum, entitled 'Maintaining the Fragile Balance', was held in Washington DC to coincide with the annual meeting of the IMF and World Bank, and the impressive list of speakers included leading bankers from the United States, Europe and South America.[13] Muldoon gave the final address on external factors affecting the need to balance trade and financial payments. He emphasised the danger of socio-political instability if the living standards of the poor were lowered too much as the result of excessive debt repay-ment and resulting austerity programs in countries such as Mexico. At the confer-ence he met Janos Fekete, the first deputy president of the National Bank of Hungary and the Hungarian director of the IMF, who expressed almost identical views to Muldoon.[14]

After he lost the National Party's leadership at the end of 1984 Muldoon was able to spend much more time reading and thinking about the global economy. In

April 1985 he sent to the publishers Reed Methuen a synopsis and chapter outline for a proposed book entitled *The Precipice: 1929 Re-visited – The Reform of the International Trade and Payment System*.[15] The book was intended to be a history of the world financial system since World War II, stressing its interdependence and the fact 'that a collapse in the economy of one country is capable of starting a process that will bring the whole edifice tumbling down . . . A 1929 type collapse is a distinct possibility.'[16] The resulting depression and destabilised strategic situation, Muldoon wrote, 'are fearful to contemplate'. He continued to believe that 'some of the policies of the International Monetary Fund have in recent years exacerbated the problem'. As a result, 'the rich become richer and the poor become poorer' because the IMF had cemented in a 'process of impoverishment by requiring massive devaluation of the currencies of the poorer countries'. He blamed the United States for preventing reform of the IMF but hoped that the USA might well in the future co-operate in finding an international solution. Although noting that such a book might be of interest to an overseas publisher, Reed Methuen declined to publish it and Muldoon did not get round either to finishing the book or seeking another publisher.

Muldoon believed that Lange was sympathetic to his views and speeches on the world debt problem. Shortly after the 1984 election, elaborating on comments which he had made on television just before polling day in which Lange had indicated that there could be a role for Muldoon to play in the future, Lange stated that Muldoon's views on Third World debt were 'extraordinarily accurate and perceptive'.[17] Had Muldoon been prepared to retire from Parliament and as Leader of the Opposition he might well, Lange observed, have become 'some sort of roving ambassador for Bretton Woods' because his 'acute' analysis did represent a 'view which the Commonwealth is going to come up with'.[18] Although Lange was still prepared to consider such a position, he believed Muldoon by his aggressive partisanship after the election had spurned any such offer. Despite some such conciliatory public comments, Lange detested Muldoon personally and shortly before the 1984 election had written to a bank manager that Muldoon was 'a mere toad in slime of the lowest order', a 'vindictive dishonourable shyster' whose mind was unbalanced.[19] Muldoon had apparently questioned and delayed the reimbursement of some of Lange's expenses incurred during the Labour leader's visit to the United States shortly before.

It is understandable, therefore, why Lange reacted negatively to a request from Muldoon in August 1985 for the Government to meet his expenses to attend an international conference on exchange rates and trade reform.[20] Two prominent US congressmen, Jack Kemp and Bill Bradley, had invited Muldoon to attend the Congressional Summit in Washington DC and he was flattered to be included among the select guest list.[21] Lange replied to Muldoon by return mail, stating curtly that, 'Being aware of your New Zealand record in the area of exchange rates, I am not surprised that the Summit organisers consider you will have something to offer, even if it is only in the form of warning them on how to avoid the pitfalls . . . But I am not convinced it would be an appropriate use of taxpayers' funds for the

Government to meet your expenses as requested.'[22] Muldoon immediately issued a press statement accusing Lange of 'blatant hypocrisy' for promising on television to assist Muldoon's work but refusing now to authorise the expenses.[23] The $3000 was paid by a friend, Bob Owens, and Muldoon was able to attend the Washington forum.[24] Muldoon's expenses for a subsequent seminar in Zurich in 1986 were paid by another admirer, Jim Sprott.[25]

The Washington Conference was held on 12 and 13 November 1985 at the National Academy of Sciences and included a reception at the Federal Reserve Bank. The 'Summit Core Group' included, besides Muldoon, Alan Greenspan, Paul Volcker, Helmut Schmidt, Kiichi Miyazawa, Neil Kinnock, Donald Regan, Valéry Giscard d'Estaing, and James Baker. Muldoon, whose campaign for a new international monetary order had earned him considerable attention and respect among small nations and especially Third World debtor states, may well have speculated that he had an outside chance of being considered as a possible replacement for A. W. Claussen, the World Bank president, who was retiring the following year.[26] Such an appointment, however, never appears to have been considered seriously either by Muldoon or others.

In June 1986, shortly after returning to Bolger's front bench, Muldoon travelled to Zurich to address an international parliamentary forum on exchange rates.[27] While there he came into contact with the Global Economic Action Institute, an organisation formed following a world conference on economic and social order held in Geneva on 22–26 August 1983 and attended by a number of leading monetarists including Friedrich Hayek, Allan Meltzer and Fritz Leutwiler, chairman of the Bank for International Settlements and president of the Swiss National Bank. GEAI was designed to provide international, private sector support for the G7's attempts to maintain and co-ordinate international economic stability, especially monetary stability.[28] A diverse participatory network of public and private sector leaders was set up to try 'to help strengthen the global economy while maintaining the underlying tenets of pluralistic democracy, free enterprise, and a reliance on moral and ethical principles.'[29] GEAI was also committed to free trade and opposed to the fragmentation of the world into hostile trading blocs. Various private donors, including American and Japanese banks and corporations and the Unification Church,[30] set up an investment fund with a target of US$21 million to meet the cost of GEAI offices in New York and Washington DC and to provide an income flow for GEAI's research and conferences. GEAI's first two chairmen were from 1983 to 1986 Robert Anderson, a former Secretary of the US Treasury, and from 1986 to 1988 Eugene McCarthy, the one-time US presidential candidate and Democrat senator.

At the Zurich conference, GEAI's leaders invited Muldoon to attend another forthcoming conference in Jakarta in September 1986 as GEAI's guest and subsequently, in 1987, also asked him to attend the Rondini Conference on monetary reform which GEAI was organising in Rome. Muldoon responded that while he was able to get a 90 per cent discount on his overseas airfares he was 'unable to regularly supplement this from my own resources' in order to keep attending international conferences. If GEAI could assist, however, he would attend.[31] McCarthy immediately confirmed that GEAI would meet all the additional costs and Muldoon attended.[32] It was to be the start of a close relationship between Muldoon and GEAI.

Following National's second loss at the 1987 election and his own return to the backbench, Muldoon prepared several confidential reports for GEAI. These reports built on the Rondini Conference and suggested ways in which there could be international co-operation to prevent excessive exchange rate volatility, to attack Third World debt, and to use the Uruguay Round of GATT to remove barriers to agricultural trade.[33]

Muldoon flew to Washington DC to participate in a GEAI meeting in late September 1987 and also to attend as a guest the annual meeting of the governors of the IMF and World Bank. He addressed about a hundred people at a luncheon organised by GEAI and had more than twenty private meetings with prominent US, Japanese, European and Third World bankers, politicians and officials. Muldoon was pessimistic and expressed the view that there was 'only slightly less than an even chance that within the next two years we will see a major depression of the 1930s type'.[34] He admitted that his views were influenced by two recent books, *The Great Depression of 1990* by Ravi Bahtra and *Apocalypse 2000* by Peter Jay and Michael Stewart. Perhaps not coincidentally, Muldoon and Jim Anderton had been the first two borrowers of those books from the Parliamentary Library.[35]

In April 1988 Muldoon succeeded McCarthy as the chairman of GEAI's four-person policy-making board of directors. The other three were McCarthy, Thomas Bolan, a lawyer and co-founder of the New York State Conservative Party, and Dr Mose Durst, president of the Unification Church of America. Muldoon's leadership of GEAI was shared with its president, Dr Lev Dobriansky, a former US ambassador to the Bahamas who was director of the Institute for Comparative Economic and Political Systems at Georgetown University in Washington DC. Dobriansky also served as chairman of GEAI's executive committee and official representative to the fifteen national divisions elsewhere in the world. By 1988 GEAI also had five standing committees, 1400 corporate and individual members from 75 countries, and was organising internationally a number of conferences and working parties.

Muldoon's role as chairman involved at least one annual meeting of the board each year, visits to various countries as GEAI's representative, and chairing and speaking at conferences and smaller functions. In April 1988, for example, he travelled to New York where he lunched with Peter Drucker, met UN Secretary-General Pérez de Cuellar, talked with numerous prominent diplomats, officials, bankers, businessmen and academics, and was the guest of honour at six dinners and luncheons over three days hosted by GEIA supporters. After another round of functions and meetings in Washington DC Muldoon departed for London where he spent two days calling on bankers before returning to Auckland.[36]

He also travelled to Africa to chair a GEIA conference, held at Abidjan, the Ivory Coast, 29–31 August 1988. The conference, co-sponsored by the African

Development Bank, looked particularly at foreign investment and development financing to increase both production and productivity in both rural and urban, public and private enterprises in Africa.[37]

In October Muldoon chaired and spoke at another conference in New York co-sponsored by GEAI and the Japanese Chamber of Commerce of New York on Japanese investment in the United States.[38] He then spent four days meeting GEAI supporters and potential supporters in Washington DC and New York including the international financier George Soros for breakfast at Soros's home; Paul Volcker, formerly chairman of the Federal Reserve; Harold McGraw III, president of McGraw-Hill Financial Services; Caspar Weinberger, former Secretary of Defence; Robert Heller of the Federal Reserve; Michel Camdessus, director of the IMF; and Jeane Kirkpatrick for a private dinner.

In November 1988 Muldoon travelled overseas again, this time to chair a conference in Taipei, Taiwan. The conference examined particularly the rapid economic development of Taiwan, Japan, Singapore, Hong Kong and South Korea and the lessons that could be learnt from those policies and experiences. Most speakers were from Asia though a number of Americans also participated.[39]

One of Muldoon's first tasks as chairman was to bring together, with Jeremiah Schnee, GEAI's special adviser to the chairman, a report based on the work of three subcommittees chaired by Americans: Joe Greenwald (former US ambassador to the EC and OECD) on trade; William Dale (deputy managing director of the IMF) on finance; and John Holdridge (one-time US ambassador to Indonesia) on Third World debt and international burden-sharing.[40] Preparation of the report led to Muldoon making fact-finding visits to Germany and Japan in September and November of 1988 respectively. The release of the report early in 1989 was accompanied by seminars in Washington, New York, Frankfurt and Tokyo to encourage dialogue between public and private sector opinion leaders on the issues raised. Over the following months further seminars were held in Africa, Taiwan, Chile, China and Russia with Muldoon meeting as GEAI's chairman some people he had had difficulty meeting when he had been Prime Minister.[41] In Tokyo, in 1988, for example he had about forty meetings with former prime ministers, the current foreign minister, and the chairmen of the Bank of Japan, the Japanese Stock Exchange, and the Mitsubishi Corporation.[42]

In March 1989 Muldoon was again in Washington DC for meetings of the GEAI board and to chair and speak at a GEIA-sponsored Congressional Seminar on 'Economic Co-operation or Confrontation: The Challenge of the 1990s' and then at a GEAI Seminar at Pace University, New York, on 'Europe after 1992: How it will effect international business —Perspectives from the US, Japan and the EC'.[43]

GEIA also hosted annually the Pinehurst International Seminar for members of its GEAI Global Club, i.e. those who paid US$10,000 for membership. The conference was held at a luxurious conference and recreational center, the Pinehurst Hotel in North Carolina. In May 1989 Muldoon chaired the Pinehurst Seminar over four days with speakers such as Frans Andriessen, deputy chairman of the European Community's Commission; Ambassador Kenneth Adelman, former director of the US Arms Control and Disarmament Agency; John Block, former US Secretary of Agriculture; Kiyoaki Kikuchi, former president of the UN Security Council and recently retired Japanese ambassador to the US; and Jeane Kirkpatrick, former US ambassador to the UN. The topics discussed included US–Soviet relations; the global financial market; 'Europe 1992'; managing the US Budget; and international trade.[44] According to Muldoon, those who attended were charged US$25,000 for registration and accommodation.[45] Following the Pinehurst Seminar, Muldoon and Kikuchi spent four days in Washington DC and in New York meeting politicians, diplomats and businessmen, including the media magnate Rupert Murdoch, on GEAI's behalf. The visits ended with a dinner in honour of Muldoon and Kikuchi hosted by Makoto Taniguchi, the Japanese ambassador to the United States. While in New York Muldoon also chaired another GEAI Seminar on increasing US exports to Japan.[46]

One of the highlights for Muldoon in 1989 was a conference organised by GEAI and the National Bank of Hungary in Budapest from 9 to 11 November. The political and economic face of Eastern Europe was changing rapidly and dramatically as communism collapsed. Hungary was in the forefront of the economic changes and Muldoon and Ferenc Bartha, the president of the National Bank of Hungary, co-chaired the conference which included addresses from speakers not only from Eastern Europe but also from the Soviet Union, Japan, the United States and Western Europe. On the first day the conference was devoted to the topic 'Creating the Environment for change'. On the second day the speakers addressed 'Growth through Trade and Investment'. The final day involved papers on 'Eastern Europe: Looking to the Future'.[47]

Although Muldoon's ailing health hindered his activities in late 1989 and early 1990, he recovered sufficiently to chair a further GEAI conference, 'Paving the Way to the Market Economy', at the Academy of National Economy, Moscow, on 17, 18 and 19 September 1990. Some seven hundred Soviet politicians, officials and economists and eighty participants from foreign countries took part in the conference. The Moscow conference was one of a triad of conferences organised by Muldoon and GEAI in communist countries which were moving towards a market economy and was designed to expose senior figures in the Soviet Union to western business interests and free-market thinking and to reinforce the Soviet Union's progress along the path of economic and political liberalisation. The first of the three conferences had been the Budapest conference in November 1989, the second the Moscow conference in September 1990, and the third a conference planned for Shanghai in May 1991 but delayed until May 1992 and eventually cancelled because of difficulties in finding both funding and a national co-sponsor.[48] In opening the Moscow conference, Muldoon 'stressed that foreign participants had not come to present simplistic formulae for change . . . economics is about people. And people are a diverse lot. This means we can't take a successful blueprint for economic reform in one country and plant it down whole in another.'[49]

Muldoon thoroughly enjoyed his visit to the Soviet Union and his meetings with such leading reformers as Alexander Yakovlev, Stanislav Shatalin, Leonid

Abalkin, Abel Aganbegyan, Nikolai Shmelyev and Nikolai Ryzhkov. The meeting with Yakovlev, Gorbachev's main foreign policy adviser and the leading defender of the reform policies of perestroika (economic restructuring), glasnost (openness), and democratisation, was held in the Kremlin and lasted for an hour and a half. Later, as Muldoon sat chairing the conference in the auditorium of the Academy of National Economy with a large bust of Lenin above him, he kept thinking as speakers made repeated statements critical of communism and in praise of the tenets of private enterprise and pluralistic democracy that Lenin's bust would fall off the wall and crush him.[50] Buoyed by 'one of the most extraordinary experiences' of his life, Muldoon returned to New Zealand but was astonished that the New Zealand media appeared uninterested in his impressions of the situation in the Soviet Union.

Early in 1991 Muldoon accepted a visit to South Africa sponsored by the South African Information Department. He found the visit very tiring and rather depressing. Ill and not fit, Muldoon was easily fatigued by the relatively long distances he had to walk in the thin air. He claimed that he had always found apartheid abhorrent and had 'not been impressed by bullying Afrikaaners I met during World War II.'[51] His negative impressions were confirmed by the widespread violence in the black townships, the ultra-extremist whites, the failure to educate everyone in a common language, English, and the obvious difficulties in fostering economic growth to provide employment. He was heartened by movement towards the integration of sports bodies and by the possibility of an economic region encompassing South Africa and neighbouring states. He believed McKinnon had been wrongly advised by officials when he had recently refused Piet Botha, the former South African Foreign Minister, a visitor's visa for New Zealand, and thought New Zealand should join the British, Australians and Europeans in supporting South Africa's return to international sport.

As Muldoon's health deteriorated during late 1989 and 1990 he and GEAI, which was starting to rupture acrimoniously at the top level over the continued involvement of the Unification Church as a supporter and funder, started to search for a successor as chairman. Muldoon's unpleasant experience travelling in Africa made him even more determined in 1991 to hand over the position. Muldoon's and GEAI's first choices were former US Secretary of State George Shultz, former US Secretary of Commerce William Verity, former chairman of the US Federal Reserve Paul Volcker, or former World Bank president Tom Claussen, but all four declined. GEAI was by early 1991 in considerable financial difficulties. During 1990 its total income had been US$962,700 but US$600,000 of that had come from the Unification Church. GEAI's expenses for the year had been US$1,001,176.[52] Finally, in November 1991, even though his replacement had not been found, Muldoon resigned as chairman of GEAI at the same time as he resigned from Parliament.

Apart from the onset of diabetes in the early 1980s and the bowel cancer operation in December 1986, Muldoon had enjoyed remarkably good health throughout his life. He had dismissed the cancer operation as an unpleasant incident on which he did not intend dwelling further. 'They opened me up, chopped out the bit of thing and that was it . . . As far as I'm concerned, what was there is gone. Clearly. Finished. There is no point worrying.'[53] He admitted that he might be concerned if it reappeared within the following five years. The cancer might not have been a worry but almost exactly three years later other health problems did cause Muldoon considerable concern.

Throughout 1989 Muldoon was taking medication for a variety of ailments: diabetes, a heart valve problem, and a persistent rash on the legs. Muldoon believed that the drugs he took for about a year for the last of those problems may have 'killed the healthy bacteria and destroyed my immune system'.[54] Towards the end of 1989 Muldoon cut his heel and the resulting bacterial blood infection did not respond to antibiotics. Muldoon suffered serious damage to the heart as the infection spread, bacterial endocarditis was diagnosed, and an operation to replace a damaged aortic valve became necessary. During the operation in Green Lane Hospital, Muldoon's kidneys stopped functioning and, on the Sunday night, it was thought likely that he would die.

Muldoon, who was unconscious for eight days after the operation, recovered but December, January and February were in his own words 'the worst couple of months of my life'.[55] For the first of those months he lost track of time and was completely unaware of what was going on and was astonished to hear of the dramatic collapse of communism in Eastern Europe while he was unconscious. Later he was to joke that he had spent the time 'attached to drips . . . worse than some of the bad drips I've been attached to in Parliament over the years'.[56]

Some of the drugs used had unpleasant side effects and required further drugs to combat them. One drug permanently damaged Muldoon's hearing, necessitating the fitting of a hearing aid. Thereafter, even with the aid, he had difficulty listening to debates and particularly in hearing interjections in Parliament. Another drug, to get his kidneys working and to stimulate the flow of urine, dried out his skin and caused a new rash which had to be treated with an antibiotic cream. His heart drug caused chronic nausea. The drugs worsened gout in his big toe, which caused persistent pain, upset his balance and forced him to walk with a stick. A drug to minimise the gout caused diarrhoea and further drugs to halt that resulted in constipation. In mid-April, four months after entering hospital, Muldoon was still taking ten different drugs.[57]

During his illness, Muldoon shed a great deal of weight, some 20 kilograms, much of it in muscle loss. This made him tire easily and prevented him climbing even the back stairs at home or walking with his grandchildren slowly more than fifty yards to the end of the street. He returned home from hospital with a stick, a hearing aid, and impaired memory, and was at first unable to read, concentrate or even attempt normal work. At the end of February, he started reading and answering correspondence, including the 2000 cards and get-well messages he had received while in hospital. One was from Queen Elizabeth and Prince Philip. Others came from a wide range of people, not only from the National Party and personal friends but also from many admirers in the general public, from acquaintances overseas, and from some long-time opponents. Mike Moore assured

Muldoon that he was praying for his recovery; Jim Anderton, who also offered his prayers and good wishes, added that he had 'a good deal of respect for the strength, honesty and principles of the economic policy ground on which you have stood so firmly'; and a trade union secretary writing on behalf of many concerned members of his union referred to 'the measure of goodwill and affection working people of New Zealand bear to you and your efforts on their behalf over so many years'.[58] Muldoon also started to take phone calls and read books. He went to Hatfields Beach for a swim. He attended the opening of Parliament by the Queen and a Royal garden party the following day. In April he compered a Senior Citizens' Free Variety Concert at Wanganui. He insisted that Thea, who was exhausted after caring for her husband over the previous three months, should go to a hotel for a week's rest and promised to take her for a holiday in the Cook Islands later in the year as soon as he felt strong enough.

It took Muldoon six months to recover sufficiently to return to work and even then he found it difficult to work in the evenings. By the end of 1990, however, his new heart valve was working well, he no longer needed a walking stick, and he had cut back his drugs to three: to keep the heart beating regularly, to stop the build-up of body fluid, and to replace potassium. Although frustrated at being unable to hear interjections in the House, his hearing with an aid was adequate for him to follow normal conversations and debate. According to Mike Moore, in 1990 the Labour Government was still 'more afraid of Muldoon in an oxygen tent in hospital than they were of Bolger aided by forty researchers'.[59] Indeed when Muldoon came out of hospital he immediately attacked the Government over the rundown in the health services.

Muldoon while recuperating had been determined to return to Parliament by the beginning of March so that he could participate in the Address in Reply debate and attend caucus, where National's financial policy for the 1990 election was being finalised prior to its public launch by Bolger and Richardson in Auckland on 2 March. Although he was reasonably happy with that policy, he was concerned that the inflation and growth targets should be goals, not firm promises, which might come back to haunt the party if they could not be achieved by the 1993 election. While he felt a second paper by Simon Upton on social policy was 'more moderate and humane than Upton would have written before he went to Oxford', Muldoon was disturbed by a group in caucus, which included 'Richardson, Shipley, et al.', who 'were giving the impression by attacking women on the DPB and the unemployed that National was anti-welfare and callous towards those in real need. Only a small proportion were ripping the system off and that should be addressed without giving the impression that National was hostile to the overwhelming majority of honest beneficiaries.'[60] The parlous state of Muldoon's health, however, and the fact that by 1990 he lacked any reliable allies in caucus meant that he had little influence on the determination of National's policy.

That did not stop him from trying to do what he could to prevent Richardson and her allies from getting their way in the preparation of both economic and social policy. One of his major unexpected defeats, however, was not in those policy areas but in foreign and defence policy. National in March 1990 decided to adopt Labour's anti-nuclear ship policy. The National Party's Policy Advisory Committee had been considering recommending such a move for several months but had deferred a formal recommendation in February in order to allow caucus to discuss the matter and express its opinion first. On Thursday 8 March, the day before the Policy Advisory Committee reconvened, caucus not only discussed the matter but announced immediately that, by a margin of more than two to one, it had been resolved that a National Government after the 1990 election would continue to ban nuclear warship visits and thus, by implication, would continue to accept New Zealand's exclusion from the ANZUS Alliance. Kidd and others in caucus had been trying to change National's nuclear ships policy since 1984.[61]

McKinnon, National's deputy leader and defence spokesman, immediately announced his resignation from the latter role in protest, and Merv Wellington launched a bitter public attack on Bolger for permitting such a reversal of traditional policy. Muldoon, who had been absent from caucus, was equally outspoken. He told the press that he was totally opposed to the decision and claimed that the caucus majority had been motivated not by principle but by a misguided desire to win over younger, anti-nuclear voters. He concluded: 'I never thought I would ever be ashamed to be a part of the National Party caucus. But I am today.'[62]

Despite his illness and slow, only partial, recovery, Muldoon rejected any suggestion that he might not contest his Tamaki seat at the 1990 election. Indeed, polls still showed that he was the preferred prime minister of some 11 per cent of New Zealand voters, and in March Muldoon stated publicly that he hoped that after the election Bolger as Prime Minister would appoint him to cabinet as Minister of State, thus repeating the precedent Muldoon set with his appointment of Holyoake to the same position in 1975.[63] As he became stronger later in the year, Muldoon's ambitions increased and by August he was telling reporters that, following the election, Bolger should appoint him Minister of Foreign Affairs and that he also should give him a seat on the new Government's front bench.[64] It was clear to almost everyone except Muldoon, however, that Bolger would not appoint him to his cabinet after the election in any capacity.

By the 1990 election Muldoon was visibly older, thinner, and spoke more hesitantly. His thoughts, however, when he expressed them were still ordered, clear and factually accurate. He rarely reminisced or became nostalgic about the past but would defend his previous actions if provoked and continued to attack not only the Labour Government but also the right wing of the National Party. In his speeches and pamphlets he compared New Zealand's economic growth rate of 8.5 per cent in the June 1984 year to the 0.8 per cent in 1990. He claimed Government spending as a proportion of GDP had risen from 39 per cent under his Government in 1984 to 43 per cent by 1989–90 and that the public debt had doubled from $21.8 billion in 1984 to $42.4 billion in 1987 and was only by 1990 being somewhat reduced through the sale of state assets. He deplored the rise in inflation and unemployment and the severe damage he contended had been done to export industries, especially farming, and to domestic manufacturing. The aim of government should be to foster 'more growth, more production, more workers paying income tax instead of receiving the dole'.[65]

Muldoon believed National would have an easy election victory in 1990 and that belief strengthened during the campaign. He sensed, however, that while people were determined to vote out the Labour Government, many of those voters were suspicious of and reluctant to support National. A large proportion of those who finally chose National as the lesser of two evils did so with little enthusiasm.

Throughout the campaign, Muldoon maintained his weekly Radio Pacific programme, teasing Labour's leader Mike Moore with the slogan, 'Four weeks, Moore', 'Three weeks, Moore', 'Two weeks, Moore', 'One week, Moore', 'No Moore'. He was interviewed on television by Lindsay Perigo and took part in four relatively good-natured and humorous television debates with Labour's Richard Prebble on the Paul Holmes programme. He also addressed public meetings in Dunedin, on the West Coast, in Pencarrow, Horowhenua, Nelson, Whakatane, Taneatua, Opotiki, Birkenhead, Waiheke, Glenfield and Howick as well as four in his own electorate of Tamaki.

Prior to the election Muldoon listed thirty seats he thought National would win, although he later deleted one, West Auckland, because he believed, correctly as it transpired, that deep and public divisions within the local National Party would cost it the victory there. When the votes were counted on Saturday 27 October 1990, of those thirty only Papatoetoe, Yaldhurst, Palmerston North, and Wellington Central, in addition to West Auckland, were still held by Labour. National won 67 seats, Labour 29, and Labour's former president, NewLabour's leader Jim Anderton, held the once Labour stronghold of Sydenham.

In Tamaki, partly because the Labour vote not only collapsed but was divided, Muldoon recorded his largest-ever majority. With 59 per cent of the total votes cast he gained a majority of 7592 votes.[66] He felt that his 1990 majority reflected the fact that by then fewer people were saying unkind things about him than in 1984 or 1987, possibly because 'they don't fear me any longer.'[67]

Muldoon might no longer be feared as much but he was still disliked by many people in his own caucus and party and there was no way in which Bolger was going to appoint him to the new National cabinet, although for a time there was a suggestion that he might be offered a minor portfolio outside cabinet. It was clear, however, that Muldoon would not accept. Indeed, Bolger and nearly all the National party hierarchy would have been delighted to have seen him retire at the 1990 election. Most, however, appreciated that Muldoon had been determined to remain in Parliament until the Labour Government, which had so decisively replaced his six years before, was itself defeated. Once that was accomplished it was hoped that he would be satisfied; would accept a role as an 'elder statesman' on the backbenches mentoring new MPs; and then perhaps because of his obviously deteriorating health would choose to retire gracefully in 1993 if he not die in office before then. For his part, Muldoon during the 1990 election campaign had told inquirers that he had no thought of retirement and expected to die an MP.

CHAPTER 26

'Mr Speaker, I Say Goodbye'

WHAT MANY OVERLOOKED WAS THE FACT THAT MULDOON not only was bitterly and personally opposed to the members of the Labour Government from 1984 to 1990 but that he was also opposed, if anything more vehemently, to their policies. He saw himself not only as the defender of the reputation of his own Government between 1975 and 1984 but also as the conscience of the new Bolger ministry. He was determined to prevent Richardson and her allies from consolidating and extending Labour's New Right legacy. As a result, from the first, Muldoon, although a shadow of his earlier formidable self, became a one-man third force in Parliament, critical not only of the Labour Opposition but also of the economic policy direction and, as he saw it, the lack of social compassion shown by the new National Government. Muldoon particularly hoped that he could persuade his colleagues on National's Caucus Economic Committee, of which he became a member, to 'water down the stupid and extreme policies of the Treasury and the Reserve Bank'.[1]

Muldoon was contemptuous of the decimated Labour Opposition after the 1990 election. While Moore was struggling to disassociate himself from the unpopular actions of the fourth Labour Government, much of his energy had to go not into attacking the new National Government but into holding together the demoralised and deeply divided Labour Party. Labour was factionalised into the remnants of the right-wing Douglas supporters now led by Prebble, the more radical left of caucus who had rallied around Clark, and Lange who tended to become something of a maverick MP. According to Muldoon it was obvious to him that 'Prebble hated Clark, Clark hated Lange, and Lange hated Prebble'.[2] Muldoon was typically dismissive of Labour's other leading MPs: Wetere was 'all Maori'; Tapsell was 'half-Maori, half-National'; Caygill lacked strength; and Cullen was 'too clever for his own good'.[3] Nevertheless, as early as April 1991, Muldoon was stating that despite Labour's 'poor shape' there was a distinct possibility that it would win the 1993 election. He predicted that National, as a result of its betrayal of election promises, flawed economic policies, lack of compassion, and internal divisions which matched Labour's, would lose up to 32 of its seats in Parliament and that any National MP with a majority less than 5000 votes could be in danger.[4]

Critical also of the leadership, competence and policy direction of the National Government after 1990, Muldoon believed that it 'created uncertainty and insecurity in every walk of life'.[5] Although he admired Bolger's political instincts, he regretted the Prime Minister's lack of confidence in following them. Instead, Muldoon asserted, the Prime Minister after the 1990 election had supported Richardson and her policy initiatives even though he apparently recognised and was disturbed by their social impact and their political implications. Confident in public, Bolger's ambivalence was, according to Muldoon, much more evident in caucus throughout 1990 and 1991. So also was the concern of the deputy prime minister, McKinnon, who Muldoon wished would play a much stronger role in cabinet and caucus than he did. By early 1991 Muldoon saw at least four broad groups within National's caucus, ranging through ideologically driven certainty that the Government's policies were economically rational and morally desirable, a fatalistic acceptance that there was no alternative to policies whose results caused serious concern, pragmatic alarm about the political consequences and a search for alternatives, to total opposition to the New Right's principles and policies, which Muldoon blamed for the increase in those on the unemployment benefit from 38,419 in 1985 to 146,812 in 1991.[6]

The minister whose personality and policies Muldoon most detested was Richardson. He believed that she had 'a very limited vision' and was obsessed with cutting the internal deficit irrespective of the human cost or the political consequences. His growing frustration exploded publicly when he described how, because Richardson was 'totally inexperienced' in economic and financial matters, it had been 'very easy for Treasury and the Reserve Bank to capture their new Minister'. As a result, 'all over the country, people are now saying that they did not throw out the previous Government so that a new Government could simply continue with the same policies with merely the addition of the deregulation of the labour market'.[7] A fortnight later, Muldoon lambasted one of Richardson's major speeches on the economy as 'the usual claptrap of cliches and slogans' and added, 'I am sick and tired of the cliches and slogans put out so smugly by our Minister of Finance'.[8]

Throughout 1991 Muldoon, in his speeches outside Parliament, continued his trenchant attack on Richardson's policies and personality. On 20 September 1991, for example, in an address to the New Zealand Bakers Association Conference in Christchurch, he asserted Richardson 'has been a prisoner of Treasury since long before the change of Government and 'reiterates . . . simplistic ideas'.[9] On 27 September, he told the Auckland Textile Care Association that 'Our Minister of Finance . . . finds it difficult to grasp complex subjects because of her lack of any background in economic training or experience.'[10] Three days later, in a speech to the Association of International Economic and Commerce Students, he referred to his 'amusement' at 'the peregrinations of our Minister of Finance' and 'the clutch of cliches and slogans in a typical address' from her.[11] In other speeches he described

Richardson as 'arrogant, inflexible and economically illiterate', as having 'a tiny mind set in concrete', and as being 'a prisoner of right-wing businessmen pushing for privatisation'.[12] He criticised her also for treating National's 1990 election manifesto as 'targets' rather than 'promises' which she had no compunction about changing after the election.

New Zealand's businessmen and women did not agree with Muldoon's denigration of Richardson. In a survey conducted by the business journal *The Examiner*, Muldoon in 1991 was rated the politician who would be worst for business, scoring 137 votes from business respondents who were asked to name the three politicians they rated worst for business and the three they rated best. Lange was rated second-worst with 113 votes, while Richardson on 223 easily polled the best with Moore second-best on 88 and Douglas third with 81.[13] This poll indicated the extent to which Muldoon was now alienated from the business community, with which National Party politicians had traditionally shared such a close relationship.

During the 1990 election Muldoon had campaigned aggressively against what he termed the indirect government of New Zealand by the Treasury and the Business Roundtable. By early 1991, with the new Government apparently adhering slavishly to Treasury's 1990 *Briefing to the Incoming Government*, he had concluded that 'they are still governing the country'.[14] He repeatedly expressed his contempt for the 'theoretical idiots in Treasury'[15] who enthusiastically and uncritically embraced and advocated New Right economic policies. These 'Treasury babes' were 'straight out of university, knowing everything in the latest textbook but nothing about what happens in the real world'[16] but those 'young kids . . . are governing New Zealand'.[17] In an article written for the backbench MPs in the National caucus, Muldoon stated that he had 'no difficulty with the National Party's election policy of 1990' but 'inexperienced ministers . . . were subverted, principally by Treasury, which sold to them the faulty economic policies which they had sold to the previous Labour government in 1984' and National's ministers, like Labour's before them, were also in his view impressed by 'outside advice . . . based on self-interest rather than a detailed appreciation of what is good for the country'.[18]

Richardson was blind, so Muldoon argued, to the failure of similar policies when applied by Thatcher in Britain and Reagan in the United States a decade before. In an effort to influence National caucus thinking against New Right monetarism, he had distributed to all National MPs and candidates prior to the 1990 election an article by a key Reagan economic adviser stressing the importance of the velocity rather than the quantity of money in circulation.[19]

He was particularly sceptical of the practical application of many Friedmanite theories because of the imperfections and the altruism in both individual human nature and collective society. In an ideal world of logical and rationally motivated people such theories might work. In reality, however, there would always in any society, Muldoon believed, be many citizens who wanted or needed decisions made for them by teachers, doctors, employers and politicians whom they trusted.[20] For example, not all parents would be able to use educational vouchers or pay for private health insurance in the best interests of their children.

The New Right's 'hidden hand' theory (originally formulated by Adam Smith), that individual people make their decisions solely on the basis of self-interest and greed in an automatically operating market, was totally rejected by Muldoon. In a speech to the Wellington North Rotary Club, he commented:

> I am the chairman of a trust on the North Shore which runs a home care and a day care service for the terminally ill and we are busily raising money for a live-in hospice. There is no hidden hand motivating the nurses who spend their days, their nights and their weekends smoothing the way for the terminally ill, counselling and consoling the relatives and inevitably losing all of their patients sooner or later.[21]

Too many of National's ministers had been captured not only by Treasury but also by their departmental officials or by interest groups, according to Muldoon. As an example, he believed that there was, as a result, a 'terrible mess' in education. Muldoon did not blame the education débâcle entirely on the minister, Lockwood Smith, whom he judged to have inherited many of his problems – mainstreaming; 'white flight'; the movement from state to private schools; the increasing diversion of resources into teaching non-native English speakers at the expense of children born in New Zealand; and the finding of suitable trustees for the boards of many schools in lower socio-economic areas.[22] But Smith's deference to official advice was not helping to resolve these problems.

One right-wing minister whom Muldoon respected for his 'intelligence, flexibility, willingness to do his sums, and ability to change his mind' was Upton, the Minister of Health.[23] Upton had come back to New Zealand from Oxford having modified his previous New Right stance by accepting the importance of a social contract between a government and the people and the necessity of collective action in social policy such as health. Muldoon had discussed with Upton his own experiences in the public health system during the year before the 1990 election. He pointed out the cost of his treatment and stressed that even people on good incomes would not wish to face the uncertainty and costs of a user-pays health scheme. More importantly, there were many people who could not pay for health insurance or who, as they became older, were uninsurable. According to Muldoon, one sure way of alienating the vast majority of New Zealanders and of guaranteeing National's defeat in 1993 would be to privatise health and introduce a user-pays system.

The 'intense jealousy' shown by many in the National cabinet and caucus towards Winston Peters worried Muldoon. He believed that for a long time some of National's more 'mediocre' MPs had been developing an antagonism towards Peters because of his superior political instincts and ability to command media attention.[24] That jealousy and hostility increased after the 1990 election and according to Muldoon even Bolger became involved and regarded Peters as a potential threat to his leadership. When Bolger 'excessively' criticised Peters's Maori policy programme, *Ka Awatea*, however, Muldoon declared that it 'made sense' and associated himself with Peters by going to its launch. Although, perhaps with an element of wishful thinking, he speculated that Peters or Philip Burdon were 'two people who could be in line one day to be leaders of the National Party' and Peters 'could be our first Maori Prime Minister', on reflection he concluded that the jealousy of colleagues, the opposition of the New Right, and an element of racism in the National Party would prevent Peters from ever becoming National's leader. Instead Peters could become to the National Party what John A. Lee had been to the first Labour Government.[25]

The cabinet minister whom Muldoon particularly admired by 1991 was not Birch, McKinnon, Banks, Burdon or Peters, with all of whom he had some sympathy, but Wyatt Creech, who had become Richardson's major opponent in cabinet.[26] Muldoon was attracted to Creech, a relatively recent convert to National from the Labour Party, not only because of Creech's ongoing battle with Richardson but also because he saw him as a hard-working administrator and a very good 'details man' who also had an apparent concern for the elderly and the unemployed. Creech, like Muldoon, was adamant that the majority of the unemployed should not suffer because there were a few among them who did not want to work.

Muldoon was enraged that National had 'failed to enunciate any credible policy to deal with unemployment' but instead tried to 'deal with it by cutting back on welfare and saying that it was doing it for people to get jobs that do not exist'.[27] He believed (rightly) that the overall effect of the benefit cuts Bolger, Richardson and Shipley imposed in late 1990 would not only hurt the poorest and most vulnerable members of society but would also further deflate the economy and increase unemployment.

Although after the 1990 election Muldoon was a lone figure in the National caucus and became neither leader nor member of a caucus faction, he did find himself acting informally as a self-described 'father figure' for a number of back-bench MPs. Most of these were critics of Richardson and sought Muldoon's advice on policy, press releases, caucus tactics and whether or not they should publicly oppose some of the Government's actions, even to the extent of crossing the floor of the House and voting against the Government. Among those who frequently sought out Muldoon were Ross Meurant, Grant Thomas, Hamish MacIntyre, Cam Campion, Michael Laws and Gilbert Myles. On one occasion Muldoon persuaded Thomas not to move in caucus a vote of no confidence in Richardson as Minister of Finance but subsequently when Myles, whom Muldoon saw as 'a sincere and determined man', agonised with Muldoon over whether he could continue to support National, Muldoon advised him to do what he believed in.

By April 1991 Muldoon's anger with National's 'patently ridiculous' actions was not only leading him to oppose them in caucus but was also making him reassess his public support for the Government. His intense opposition to the Government's dishonouring of its election promises on the superannuation surtax, its dishonesty of using the one-off cost of bailing out the Bank of New Zealand to excuse both that betrayal and also welfare cuts, and its commitment to 'job creation – or lack of it', all brought Muldoon 'near the point where I will have to say so publicly'. His 'role in life' by April 1991 was to get National's policies changed, especially so that the priority was on getting 'people into jobs not just to win elections but people in jobs per se'.[28]

New Zealand's overseas debt, Muldoon accepted, had become over the previous fifteen years an appalling problem, but it could only be remedied by a greater range and quantity of exports, both agricultural and manufactured. Economic growth was necessary to strengthen the economy and reduce debt, the Budget deficit and unemployment. The way to reduce the budget deficit was not by slashing health expenditure and welfare benefits, although Muldoon accepted that some other Government expenditure cuts could bring about economies and efficiencies. Reducing unemployment would greatly increase the Government's tax income and reduce its expenditure in the longer term. In the short term he still believed that widely spread tax increases were infinitely preferable to cuts in health, social welfare and superannuation.

Prior to the 1990 election Muldoon had forcefully led the opposition in National's caucus to Richardson's wish to endorse Labour's Reserve Bank Act with its single goal of restricting inflation to under two per cent per annum. Richardson had won a majority for her position, by one report by as little a margin as twelve to eleven, so Muldoon after the election again tried to widen the Reserve Bank Governor's concerns to include growth and employment as well as inflation.[29] He was again unsuccessful as indeed he was in most other battles he fought in caucus against the cabinet during 1991.

As leader Muldoon had always stressed loyalty to himself and to the National Party but after he lost the leadership in 1984 he found loyalty to his successors, first McLay and then Bolger, often difficult. While he had never approved of MPs crossing the floor, he had accepted that it was a National MP's right to do so and during 1975–84 a number of his colleagues including some who became senior ministers after 1990 did so. Muldoon in 1991 was tempted to emulate their example. A leader who had frustrated many of his colleagues by his use of power between 1975 and 1984, he now suffered deep frustration at his own powerlessness to affect the outcomes as he desired in what was to be the final year of his long parliamentary career. Although he had the limited consolation of being able to speak out in caucus, party gatherings, public meetings, to the media generally, and each Sunday afternoon on Radio Pacific, he increasingly agonised over whether he should cross the floor or even leave the National Party altogether.

Persistently ill, easily tired, and deeply disheartened by the attitudes and actions of the Richardson-driven National Government, Muldoon was frequently absent from Parliament during 1991. When he was there he rarely contributed to the debate and when he did it was usually as a critic not a supporter of the Government. Because he could not bring himself to associate with the Labour Opposition, however, he continued to attack it also and as a result his isolation in Parliament became very obvious.

During the course of 1991 Muldoon made only five speeches of any length on the floor of the House and three shorter, more specific comments on Bills. These contributions ranged from vintage Muldoon to almost the ridiculous. The first of the five speeches was in January in support of New Zealand's involvement in the United Nations' military action against Iraq following Saddam Hussein's invasion of Kuwait. He compared Saddam to Hitler, praised the precedent of Michael Joseph Savage's stand against appeasement and fascism, and suggested that while oil was a factor in the West's response there was a higher principle involved.[30]

During debate on the Appropriations Bill (No. 3) in March, Muldoon seized the opportunity to attack both the previous Labour Government's and the current National Government's 'simplistic, free-market monetarism . . . tried ten years ago in 1979 in Britain and in the United States in 1981. It failed in both countries.'[31]

In March Muldoon also made two apparently off-the-cuff comments on Bills before the House. He opposed the introduction of Instant Kiwi tickets in the Gaming and Lotteries Amendment Bill on the grounds that there were already ample opportunities for gambling and that this would encourage further gambling by people who could not afford it.[32] As far as he was concerned gamblers were more than adequately catered for by Lotto and racehorses. He also spoke on the Rodney District Council Sewerage Charges and Empowering Bill, referring to his bach at Hatfields Beach as his reason for speaking but not, as an affected ratepayer, voting on the Bill. He joked about the relative contributions of urinals and 'arsenals' (as he called them) to the sewerage problem; praised the Rodney District Council Chairman and abused the Council's manager; in passing called a fellow National MP, Roger Sowry, 'simple' and 'stupid'; and ended by criticising the Rodney Council's poor administration for 'murdering' retired people with excessive rates.[33]

Muldoon's speech in the General Debate in June was a curious mixture. He commenced by commenting about the ferocity of the Labour women MPs' attacks on the three National women ministers: Richardson (Finance), Shipley (Social Welfare), and O'Regan (Consumer Affairs). He added that, although he came 'from a family of women achievers', he personally was scared of women MPs when they attacked.[34] He then devoted the rest of his speech to his concern at the growth of trading blocs and bilateral agreements and stressed the importance of keeping international trade open, especially for agricultural products. He concluded with a brief reference to the end of the cold war and his fear that ethnic conflict would now emerge in the former Soviet Union and in Eastern Europe.

Considering his objections to the retention of the superannuation surtax, to the welfare cuts, and to the general direction of the Government's economic and social policies, and his strident criticism of them inside caucus and outside Parliament, Muldoon was remarkably restrained in his comments and voting in the House. Unlike MacIntyre, Myles, Campion, Laws, McCardle and Winston Peters, who crossed the floor and voted against some of those measures, Muldoon could not bring himself to vote with Labour and chose instead to abstain by leaving the House before the votes were taken. Nor like MacIntyre and Myles was he prepared finally to leave the National caucus and try to form a new party.

In September, speaking towards the end of the Budget debate, Muldoon made his sole attempt in the House to explain his position. He commented that, despite his criticisms and reservations, 'When divisions were held on the Budget material I did not vote against any of it, although I abstained once. I was not prepared to cross the floor and stand alongside members of the failed Labour Government.'[35] Muldoon went on to demand that cabinet's policies should not be set by the Business Roundtable; suggested that the Reserve Bank of New Zealand Act should be amended so that the Government could use monetary policy to encourage economic growth and employment and not just attack inflation; and advocated increasing, not reducing, the Budget deficit to foster growth and job creation. Failure to do these things, he predicted, would make National 'a one-term Government'.[36]

Until November 1991 Muldoon retained some hope that the tide could be turned against Richardson within the caucus and in the National Party outside Parliament. Banks and Burdon both told him privately that Richardson and her allies were starting to lose battles in cabinet and Muldoon had a lot of faith in the ability, common sense and compassion of the 'two outstanding new MPs', Bruce Cliffe and John Robertson, who were 'beginning to assert themselves in caucus and in dealing with officials'.[37] Muldoon concluded, however, that this was probably 'too little too late' and that the public did not see any great improvement. Unemployment would also continue to plague National at the 1993 election.[38] Indeed, so pessimistic was he by the end of 1991 that, whereas earlier in the year he had identified 32 National seats at risk, by the end of the year he was listing 42, including Richardson's Selwyn electorate. In his opinion the only thing that might prevent a National rout was the splitting of the overwhelming anti-National majority of voters between Labour and the Alliance.

Muldoon's detestation of the members of the Business Roundtable was as virulent as ever at the time he decided to retire. He believed their influence was secured not by the strength of their ideas but by their large political donations, which had made some ministers in both the Labour Government after 1984 and the National Government after 1990 the Roundtable's 'direct personal prisoners'.[39] He compared that with his and Holyoake's governments and recounted an occasion when he found Holyoake fuming after a prominent businessman had left his office. When Holyoake had refused a favour the businessman had requested, the businessman had reminded Holyoake that he was the largest donor to National Party funds. Holyoake had responded furiously, 'Get out of my office, you bastard.' Muldoon believed that unfortunately not all members of recent governments had reacted the same way.

In Muldoon's opinion, the 1991 Budget was 'appalling' and the subsequent debate and legislation taken under urgency created an 'embarrassing mess'.[40] His growing and by then almost complete alienation from the Bolger Government culminated at a full-day caucus meeting on Thursday, 7 November.[41] Cabinet, which had considered the superannuation issue the previous day, brought three options to caucus. The 'softest and least expensive one' involved a new 25 cents in the dollar surtax on income above $80 per week for single superannuitants and above $120 per week for married superannuitants. About twenty MPs, including Muldoon and Peters, were opposed to all three options but a majority went with the softest. Muldoon claimed that as he sat listening to the caucus debate and realised that only a third of the caucus was prepared to challenge cabinet on the issue, he also realised that the chances of successfully changing policy not only on that issue but on other economic and social directions in the future were almost non-existent.

At about 3.45 in the afternoon Muldoon rose. After commenting that it was clear no one and no argument could change cabinet's collective mind he delivered a tirade at his colleagues.[42] He told Bolger that he was presiding over a Government that had broken more promises than any other he could remember. He denounced the majority of his fellow MPs as 'spineless' for not being prepared to honour election promises and force ministers to do so. He admitted that he 'had had enough' and was so disappointed and depressed that he was seriously considering resigning from Parliament and forcing a by-election in Tamaki to bring the message home. National might hold the seat but it would do so with such a drastically reduced majority that, faced with their own likely extinction at the next election, more MPs might reconsider the Government's direction and assert themselves against the ministers who were implementing Roundtable policies that were totally unacceptable to a majority of New Zealanders. Muldoon added that the only thing that had kept him from crossing the floor was his reluctance to be seen to be voting with Labour. He concluded by challenging Bolger or anyone else to debate with him on a public platform what Muldoon believed was wrong with the Government and its policies. Five of Muldoon's angry opponents, Lockwood Smith, Nick Smith, John Luxton, Max Bradford and Peter Gresham, immediately indicated that they would be happy to do so but Muldoon's real targets – Bolger, Richardson and Shipley – treated his challenge with silent contempt.

Having vented his feelings, Muldoon left the caucus meeting and caught a 4.40 p.m. flight to Auckland. On arrival at Auckland airport at 5.40 p.m. he was met by a *New Zealand Herald* reporter and photographer. They knew exactly what he had said in caucus less than two hours before. Clearly breaching caucus confidentiality, at least one of Muldoon's opponents had immediately rung the paper or spoken to the paper's reporter in the parliamentary Press Gallery in an attempt to force Muldoon's hand. Although Muldoon had threatened to resign he had not finally made up his mind but he now felt pressured to do so.

A number of other considerations also inclined him towards retirement. One relatively minor incident had confirmed Muldoon's feeling that he no longer had any significant influence in National's caucus. Muldoon was a trustee of the National Library and had become increasingly concerned at the way in which it was being run by its chief librarian and the chairperson of the Trustees. When Jim Traue, whom Muldoon respected and had supported, retired as the librarian of the Alexander Turnbull Library, Muldoon nominated him for a vacancy on the National Library Board of Trustees. At first the two ministers concerned, Roger McClay and Lockwood Smith, supported Traue's appointment, but according to Muldoon it was vigorously opposed by the National Librarian and the chairperson of the Trustees. After discussing the matter with Don Hunn, the chairman of the

State Services Commission, Lockwood Smith changed his mind and Traue was not appointed. The following day a furious Muldoon resigned in protest from the Board of Trustees.

Further pressure on Muldoon to resign from Parliament came from his wife. Thea had become depressed by the constant stream of sad and frightened people who rang the Muldoon home seeking advice and reassurance and she was also concerned that her husband's health was not being helped by his continued life as an MP. While Muldoon was concerned at the effect on his wife, Thea was equally worried at the way her husband was becoming tearful and depressed at his inability to change things and help those who daily sought his assistance.

On the evening of Monday 11 November, Muldoon met his Tamaki electorate committee. About twenty people were present. Muldoon chose not to share with them either his health problems or the likelihood of his resignation as their MP. His trusted long-time lieutenant, Tremewan, the Auckland Division's director, guessed, however, that Muldoon had decided to go and the following day not only shared that belief with others but started to prepare for the selection of a new candidate and a by-election in Tamaki.[43]

Muldoon himself had decided to think through the situation during a short visit to Fiji where, on Wednesday 13 November, he gave a speech to a Fiji Investment and Trade Forum at the Sheraton Fiji Resort. The address was a very general one on 'Changing International Trade and Finance – Its Implications for the Pacific'.[44] Muldoon's logic told him that the time had come for him to retire even though he found it emotionally a difficult decision to make. The stress on himself and Thea; the alienation from most of his colleagues; his opposition to major Government policies and the Government's overall direction; the thought of another two frustrating and exhausting years in Parliament with no sense of influence or achievement and only a disastrous election defeat for National to look forward to at the end of it; and his health – all led to the conclusion that it would be nonsense for him to carry on until 1993. Muldoon was concerned that his ill health, and certainly his possible death, would cheat him of time to spend at last with his family, especially his grandchildren, and to do other things he had not had time for while he was in Parliament. Although x-rays taken a few days before he went to Fiji revealed that his heart was slightly enlarged and he had some congestion on the lungs, the heart valve appeared to be working reasonably well. His cardiologist had pointed out to Muldoon, however, that most people his age and with his recent medical record would have retired and the doctors were also concerned that Muldoon's chronic and evident frustration and depression were putting unnecessary pressure on the heart which was having to pump harder than normal to keep the circulation going.

On Saturday 16 November Muldoon returned from Fiji. Met again by reporters at Auckland airport, he refused to say what he had decided to do but told the press, 'I do not like being part of a party that's broken so many very explicit promises and not done things it said it would do about changing the direction of economic policy.'[45] He advised people to listen to his Radio Pacific programme the next day.

When he got home Muldoon rang the deputy chairman of the Auckland Division of the National Party, Clem Simich. Simich had been also an official in Muldoon's Tamaki electorate organisation for seventeen years. Muldoon told Simich he was on the point of resigning and asked Simich if he would be prepared to seek the Tamaki nomination. Muldoon was determined that there would be at least one person acceptable to him and around whom his local supporters could rally in the contest for National's new candidate. Simich, a former policeman of Dalmatian-Maori descent who had become a commercial property manager after completing degrees in law and political studies as a mature student, agreed to seek the nomination. The National MP Christine Fletcher also contacted Muldoon to say that Aussie Malcolm, a former cabinet minister, who was very critical of Bolger and Richardson, would seek the nomination if no other candidate acceptable to Muldoon was forthcoming.[46] Satisfied that suitable potential successors were available, Muldoon decided to announce his retirement. He did not forewarn Bolger or anyone else in the party hierarchy.

Muldoon was still somewhat ambivalent and later admitted that he had not finally made his decision until about 2 p.m. on Sunday 17 November, one hour before he broadcast. He started his programme on Radio Pacific by reading a letter from the Minister of Energy, Luxton, declining Muldoon's challenge to debate with him on radio National's broken election promises. Then he read a series of other letters, the first urging Muldoon to resign, the rest pleading with him to stay. He admitted that ten days before in caucus he had threatened to go. Finally, an hour into the programme Muldoon, in a weary voice, told his listeners: 'I am going and I don't want to make a big emotional thing about it.'[47] His health was a factor, but not the major one, and he was not certain whether his depression over the previous few months 'is a health thing or a psychological thing'. What he was certain of was that 'I have come to the end of the time when I have any confidence that what I think and believe is having any influence on Government policy'. He referred to his conversation with Simich and without naming his preferred successor observed that he would be able to 'do the job better than I am doing at this moment'. He predicted that National would hold Tamaki in the by-election but with a slashed majority. Muldoon then fielded over a hundred calls from listeners, nearly all praising him, thanking him and wishing him well. He was offered a cat, a poodle pup, a holiday in California and the suggestion that he should take up bowls to help occupy himself in his retirement.[48]

The way the media subsequently handled the announcement of Muldoon's retirement, resurrecting many of his negative comments and quips about other politicians and, in his opinion, not giving a balanced picture or assessment of his long career, did not please him.[49] Nor did most of his National Party colleagues make any secret of their relief that their former leader would at last be no longer in caucus or Parliament. Muldoon was consoled and touched, however, by the hundreds of letters, cards and phone calls he received, thanking him or pleading with him not to retire. Only three of the many letters were nasty. A few were from parliamentary colleagues: Gandar, Bill Young, Roger McClay, Comber, Shearer, and Anderton, the latter writing, 'I wanted to thank you for your outstanding contribution to New Zealand over the past three decades . . . I do hope you will continue to lend your voice to the cause of ordinary New Zealanders in the months and years ahead.'[50] Others were from businessmen such as Sir Robertson Stewart, John Ingram, Peter Martin, and Harry Julian. Most were from ordinary voters, superannuitants, solo mothers and others Muldoon had helped personally. G. T. Drain, president of the New Zealand Superannuitants Federation, thanked Muldoon for his 'wonderful service' to the people of New Zealand generally and the elderly in particular and observed: 'You will long be remembered as a man who did not break his promises.'[51] Tofilau Eti Alesana, Prime Minister of Western Samoa, recorded that his country's 'relationship with New Zealand . . . owes much to your personal involvement during your years as Prime Minister'.[52] The Dunedin Mongrel Mob sent Muldoon a collection of James K. Baxter's poems as a token of their regard and affection.[53] Many of those who wrote mentioned that they had always been National supporters but would not vote for that party again. Muldoon's invariable response in his replies was that they needed to make their views known if they wished to influence the National caucus and he also added in some letters sentiments such as, 'I cannot readily forgive some of my Parliamentary colleagues and those who have advised them, both inside and outside the State Services, for what they have done to so many people in recent times.'[54]

Having announced his retirement, Muldoon took little part in the House over the passage of the National Superannuation Bill, the Social Welfare (Transitional Provisions) Amendment Bill (No. 3), the Social Security Amendment Bill (No. 4), and the Income Tax Amendment Bill (No. 7), all of which passed their third readings on 4 December. Although Muldoon was in the House that day he deliberately missed all the votes.[55] Peters and Campion joined the two former National MPs Myles and McIntyre in voting against some of these measures.

Muldoon appeared in the House on that day only to speak on the Orakei Bill, which amended the settlement his Government had made with the Ngati Whatua of Orakei over Bastion Point in 1977 and 1978. Although he stated, after briefly recounting the history, that he would not vote against the new settlement, he warned against growing racial division and concluded that unless 'we can say to each other that we are all New Zealanders the future for the country is bleak'.[56] Apart from his valedictory speech it was Muldoon's last contribution in the House.

The week after he announced his retirement Muldoon returned to Wellington to discuss the impending Tamaki by-election with the Auckland divisional chairman, John Slater, the deputy chairperson, Cheryl Parsons, and the Auckland MPs. The National Government's electoral support by that time according to the polls had slumped from 48 per cent at the 1990 election to 26 per cent.[57] Muldoon was incensed, though not surprised, when nearly all his Auckland colleagues chose to miss the meeting and go instead to a reception hosted by the Business Roundtable. To Muldoon this was symbolic of what had happened to his party.[58] It also confirmed his opposition to a New Right supporter taking his place as MP for Tamaki, an opposition he had declared publicly earlier in the month when he told the *Herald* that he 'did not want to see someone with some of the policies of the present cabinet standing in his place'.[59]

On 17 December 1991 Parliament adjourned for the year following a number of valedictory speeches. Bolger outlined Muldoon's 31-year career in Parliament and the many changes that had taken place in the world, in New Zealand and in Parliament over that time. In particular he referred to the way Muldoon had dominated the controversial years of conflict between 1975 and 1984 but emphasised that by 1984 'the New Zealand that he had represented was already changing'. Bolger ended with a somewhat ambiguous compliment, noting that Muldoon had been 'a tough and bruising debater' who 'never sacrificed his judgment to the opinion of others'.[60] The Leader of the Opposition, Moore, while recalling the great differences between himself and Muldoon, notably the Springbok tour and the Moyle affair, warmly and humorously farewelled Labour's greatest foe. Muldoon, Moore lamented, had been one of Parliament's most successful members who 'kept me and people like me from office'. Moore said:

> We had different ambitions: I only wanted to be the Prime Minister; he wanted to be the Government – and he was, for 9 years. He is the most dynamic and dominating political figure in the lifetime of my generation. His power, alas, his success, his strengths, his talents, his temper, and his temperament, imposed themselves on this country for more than a decade . . . Let not my respect and admiration for his political skills be misunderstood. For all of the Opposition's attacks on him, it did not ever claim that he was out of step with the average bloke. Frequently he was in step – we just wished that he had marched the country in a different direction.[61]

Finally, Muldoon rose. He started with a heartfelt tribute to his wife, then talked about the grassroots membership of the National Party, before identifying himself as a '"Liberal" in the old political style of the Liberal Party of 100 years ago in this country'. Such people were 'individualistic in outlook' but 'at the same time . . . deeply compassionate . . . for the unfortunates and misfits of the community'.[62] Although he had come into Parliament 'to help people not to hurt people' he had found that 'it has not been possible for me this year to stop too many people being hurt'. He again reflected on women MPs in the House, praising some elected in 1990 and by implication noting that he was not impressed with National's senior women MPs, Richardson and Shipley. He paid tribute to a number of civil servants, notably Galvin, members of the parliamentary staff, and friends, such as Gordon, MacIntyre and Sloane, before identifying the three politicians he admired most during his time in Parliament. Surprisingly two were Labour: Kirk, 'a remarkable man' of 'incredible' mental energy and intelligence; and Nordmeyer, 'a remarkable politician and parliamentarian, as straight as they come' and with 'probably the most brilliant mind of any politician in my time'.[63] The third, more predictably, was 'the greatest of them all, in my view, Keith Holyoake – my mentor in politics' and, although 'underestimated by the public', in Muldoon's opinion 'the greatest parliamentarian that I know of'.[64] After a couple of reminiscences and a joke at

Australia's expense, Muldoon appealed for growth in the economy as the only way to produce jobs and reduce unemployment. He ended with a quip at his own expense. A nurse from Tauranga walking down Pitt Street in Auckland met Muldoon and thought she knew him. Muldoon doubted it but said, 'My name's Muldoon'. She had replied, 'You're not related to that bastard in Parliament are you?' As the listening MPs laughed, Muldoon said, 'And on that salutary note, Mr Speaker, I say goodbye', and sat down.

The week before Christmas, on 19 December, National chose its candidate to contest the Tamaki by-election. From nineteen original nominations, five nominees, three men and two women, faced eighty-four voting delegates and a packed hall of observers from the party and the press. It was obvious that the final choice would be between Simich and a former All Black captain and Rhodes Scholar Dr David Kirk, who had flown from London for the selection.[65] Kirk, an exciting prospect for the National Party's future, had the open support of the party's parliamentary and organisational leadership, the business community, and younger, free-market members of the National Party in Tamaki. He was, however, seen by Muldoon and many of his older electorate stalwarts as having no history of commitment to or activity in the party and as being in his views and personal support too close to the Richardson faction. At least one senior journalist believed that the selection of anyone other than Simich as the new candidate could split the National Party. Dick Griffin, in an interview with Maggie Barry on National Radio, stated, 'I know that Clem Simich has been telling the National Party hierarchy that if he doesn't get the nod he'll stand as Independent National . . . I don't think a Muldoon person is going to get it and so Clem Simich may well stand as Independent National.'[66]

Muldoon sent a very clear message to his local supporters, many of whom were voting delegates at the candidate selection meeting. On Radio Pacific, for example, a caller to Muldoon's programme commended Kirk. Muldoon responded that he did not support Kirk for the candidacy and indeed would not support him if he was selected as National's new candidate.[67] When the caller observed that Kirk had studied politics at university, Muldoon replied that it was 'impossible to learn politics from books. Politics is not a science but an art. It is concerned with understanding people.' After asserting that 'no political science graduate has ever made a successful politician', Muldoon compared such people with Norman Kirk who had 'never been near a university but was a good politician because he understood people'. Muldoon concluded by saying that the decision on his successor, however, was not his but 'the people of Tamaki will decide'.

Again in his valedictory address in Parliament, a few days before the selection, Muldoon observed that there were two All Blacks already in Parliament, both backs.[68] Muldoon suggested that if there was to be another it should not be Kirk but a forward, and mischievously proposed among other possibilities Colin Meads in Bolger's King Country electorate.[69] Even better, went on Muldoon, would be for National to select two women athletes, the Baker sisters, to contest Richardson's Selwyn and Shipley's Ashburton seats at the next election.

While Muldoon was less critical of the two women seeking the Tamaki nomination, there was no question in anyone's mind that Simich had his blessing and indeed he conveyed that message personally to a number of the voting delegates over the telephone and by the comments he made on Radio Pacific. Although at the selection meeting Muldoon and Simich could not muster a majority on the first ballot, Simich eventually received sufficient preferences to take the nomination narrowly from Kirk and Langley on the third ballot, after Greer and Eardley-Wilmot had been eliminated. Muldoon was delighted.[70]

The by-election, fought throughout January and early February 1992 when many voters and party activists were absent from the electorate on holiday, turned quickly into a potential disaster for National. Muldoon and Simich stated publicly that they wished to send a message to the Government. The by-election became a referendum on National Government policies, especially those of Finance Minister Richardson, and not just about finding a successor in Parliament for Muldoon. But both wanted Simich to be the MP who took the message to Wellington. For a time, however, it looked as if the voters would send such a decisive message that it would be conveyed by an Opposition MP.

In the 1990 election Muldoon had polled 12,191 votes; the Labour candidate, Malcolm Johnston, 4599; the Green candidate, the aptly named Richard Green, 2633; the NewLabour candidate B. Logue 789; and the Democrat candidate, C. D. Thomas, 134.[71] The last three parties, together with Matiu Rata's Mana Motuhake Party and eventually the Liberal Party, formed by the defecting National MPs MacIntyre and Myles, on 1 December 1991 launched an Alliance under the leadership of NewLabour's Jim Anderton. The Alliance decided to put forward a single candidate for the Tamaki by-election and a twelve-person selection committee finally and somewhat unexpectedly chose Chris Leitch, the president of the Democrat Party, in preference to Green, who seemed the more logical choice. Labour also chose a new candidate, Verna Smith, who worked for the Foundation for the Blind.

Muldoon's contribution to the opening of the by-election campaign was not helpful. In his annual speech, the twenty-third, to the Orewa Rotary Club at the start of 1992, he lashed out at length at National's 'incompetent cabinet', most of whom were 'prisoners of Treasury'.[72] They had to be sacked and replaced. He went on to savage the majority of National's caucus, Treasury, the Reserve Bank and most political journalists. Muldoon told the Rotarians that he had 'quit politics after increasing depression brought on by being unable to persuade his colleagues Government policies were wrong and must be changed'. He concluded that 'I reached the point where I felt that I had to give the people the opportunity to send their message directly to the Government through a by-election' and if that failed he would, nearer the 1993 election, indicate publicly which National MPs should be challenged and removed as National's candidates.

Bolger opened National's official campaign a few days later on 20 January at a picnic in the Tamaki electorate attended by several hundred National supporters. The launch was marred by bad weather and dozens of vocal protesters. As National's campaign progressed it deteriorated further and by the beginning of

February Bolger was publicly admitting that he would not be surprised if National lost the Tamaki seat in the by-election, Muldoon, although himself later predicting a majority of 'something under 500', immediately called Bolger's remarks 'stupid' while Simich suggested that they were 'unwise'.[73] By that time, however, Simich was distancing himself from the Government by listing policies, especially Upton's health policies, with which he personally disagreed and polling was showing not Labour but the Alliance starting to challenge National for top place. Many National voters were confused. Those who supported the Government, Bolger and Richardson, and who had preferred Kirk to Simich as National's candidate, were reluctant to vote for a candidate supported by Muldoon. Others who were admirers of Muldoon were reluctant to vote even for Simich if National took the retention of the seat as endorsement of its policies. Simich was in a difficult situation appealing to Muldoon's loyal supporters while trying not to be too critical of Bolger and the Government.

It was obvious to pollsters and canvassers of all persuasions that the electorate was polarising into National and anti-National positions and that the candidate increasingly seen as having the best chance of defeating Simich was not Labour's Smith but the Alliance's Leitch. An Alliance victory, however, was in neither National's nor Labour's interests and during the final week of the campaign National made its canvassing records available to Labour so that Labour could target its core remaining vote and prevent it slipping further. Muldoon also started to campaign even more openly and actively for Simich, asking his supporters to vote for the man even if they could no longer with any enthusiasm vote for the National Party. If they could not do that then they should stay at home and protest by not voting rather than by supporting Labour or the Alliance.

On election night, a seemingly relaxed Muldoon joined Bill Ralston on a TV3 election report entitled 'On Trial in Tamaki'. While Muldoon was present through-out the TV3 coverage he also found time to comment on TV1's 'One Network News By-election Special' and was described by one TV critic as 'the star of each . . . His words, his posture, his gestures and his chuckle all made one thing very clear . . . It was yet another chapter in the Robert Muldoon story.'[74] The result of the by-election gave Muldoon exactly what he wanted: a successor of his choosing; Tamaki remaining National; and a majority slashed so drastically that no one could be left in any doubt that the Government as a result of its attitudes and actions was in serious electoral difficulty even in its true-blue heartland.[75]

The vote in the by-election on Saturday 15 February was a reasonably high one, 17,383 people voting compared to 20,689 in the previous general election. The National vote dropped from 12,191 to 7901; the Alliance vote rose from 3556 (the combined votes for Green, NewLabour and Democrat in 1990) to 6649; and the Labour vote collapsed from 4599 to 2121.[76] Instead of Muldoon's 7592 majority, Simich retained the seat by 1252 votes. Whereas Muldoon had taken 58.92 per cent of the vote in the electorate in 1990, an increase of 6.89 per cent on his 1987 share, at the 1992 by-election Simich dropped 13.5 per cent to 45.42 per cent of the total vote. It was the biggest swing in a by-election in over sixty years. The message had been sent, though Muldoon throughout the following months doubted that it had been received by National's leadership.

One would have expected the National Party at the end of 1991 to have farewelled Muldoon from Parliament with a function befitting a former leader and Prime Minister and an MP of 31 years. It was not to be. Instead, television viewers watching the news saw Muldoon, following his valedictory address, being ushered into a empty room where he expected there would be a surprise farewell party. 'It looks like no one has come, Sir Robert', said the reporter, and a dejected Muldoon turned and slowly walked away. Among those furious with both television news and the National Party for their treatment of Muldoon were Bob Jones and the former Governor-General, Sir David Beattie. The two men organised a bipartisan surprise dinner for Muldoon in Wellington on 28 January 1992.[77] A large number of Labour and National politicians, including McLay and Lange, attended, as did various journalists and others who had been associated with Muldoon over the years. Tom Scott organised a number of cartoons signed by the cartoonists for presentation to Muldoon and greetings letters were obtained from President Reagan and from Lee Kuan Yew. One highlight was a video from Margaret Thatcher, arranged through the former television interviewer Simon Walker, who had clashed so dramatically with Muldoon years before. A dozen people, Jones, Beattie, Bolger, Lange, Moore, Ken Douglas, Venn Young, Sir Ronald Davison, Ben Couch, Ian Fraser, Tom Scott and Sharon Crosbie, spoke briefly during the course of the evening and, at Thea's suggestion, the keynote address was delivered by Trevor De Cleene. Muldoon, who had no prior warning until he came face to face with Jones and Beattie at the door of the Wellington Club, was delighted and grateful and became very emotional as the evening went on. When it came time for Muldoon to speak, he could not, however, refrain from making a political point, namely that he had lived to see the maxim that politics should never be about anything but people mocked and ridiculed.

In the months after he left Parliament Muldoon continued to deal with correspondence and phone calls from numerous people. He chaired the North Shore Hospice; broadcast nationwide each Sunday on Radio Pacific; with the help of his granddaughter Emma sent out 2600 envelopes containing lily seeds to listeners; made about two speeches a week to various groups around the country;[78] spent more time with his grandchildren; watched television; and continued to read, being particularly impressed by Lester Thurow's *Head to Head: The Coming Economic Battle Among Japan, Europe and America*. He also was tempted by an invitation from a group of people in the Rodney District north of Auckland, where Muldoon had his holiday bach, to stand for the mayoralty.[79] Muldoon had been a strong public critic of the Rodney District Council. He realised, however, that his poor health made an active role in local politics impossible.

From Christmas 1991 and throughout the first half of 1992, Muldoon was troubled with recurrent stomach pains and diarrhoea. As the year went on he weakened physically so that even with Thea's help it was a struggle to walk across the road. Despite taking sleeping drugs he only dozed for a short while at night and became very tired.[80] He continued to read, talk to visitors, host with some physical difficulty his Radio Pacific programme,[81] and watch with continued sadness and despair what was happening politically and socially. He empathised with those who were suffering, especially the unemployed, the sick, and the lonely and frightened aged. When asked by a local official of the party in July 1992 if he wanted to renew his National Party membership, Muldoon thought for a brief moment and then said, 'No. I will wait until an ordinary National Party member comes canvassing and knocks on my door. Then I will ask him to give me one good reason why I should support this Government and if he can I'll think about renewing.'[82]

Suffering from nausea and unable to sleep, Muldoon was admitted to North Shore Hospital for tests in mid-June and on 5 and 6 July spent two days in Green Lane Hospital having further tests and a scan. Although publicly Muldoon kept saying that his condition was caused by the side effects of the drugs he was taking, privately he was concerned that something was seriously wrong. He was right. Although tests showed that there was no recurrence of his earlier bowel cancer, they also now indicated that cancer had probably occurred elsewhere. If that was confirmed, the doctors told Muldoon and his wife, the prognosis was not good. Because of Muldoon's heart condition and generally weak state of health it would not be possible to operate. Chemotherapy could be tried but it would be very unpleasant and probably unlikely to delay death long. The most likely scenario was that Muldoon would become even weaker, suffer some pain, and would probably die before the end of the year.

By mid-July Muldoon was so ill that he was unable to attend the opening on Saturday 18 July of the North Shore Hospice, of which he was trust board chairman, or to host his Radio Pacific programme the following day. He phoned his biographer to call and see him and handed over a file of selected documents which he had extracted from his personal files and which he wanted to be sure the biographer had seen. With his arm around his wife's shoulder Muldoon also told the biographer to be sure that he noted that the best thing he had done during his lifetime 'was to marry Tam'.[83]

On Sunday 2 August, although very weak, Muldoon broadcast on Radio Pacific but became so exhausted that he finished the programme early. He told his listeners, 'Well that's it for tonight. I'm finishing a little earlier than usual because, as you know I haven't been 100 per cent fit recently and although I've enjoyed it thoroughly today being back with you, I shall be a tired little boy when I'm finished. Cheerio. Goodnight.'[84]

The next morning, Monday 3 August, Muldoon rang the talkback host on Radio Pacific's all-night programme. It was 5 a.m. and Muldoon, who could not sleep, had been listening to the radio. As the host recalled later in the week, 'He wasn't happy with the way things were going in the country, particularly the health system, and he really sounded down'.[85] After complaining about his lack of sleep and the particular combination of drugs he was taking, Muldoon told Radio Pacific that 'there are so many things that are amiss with the current medical system and nothing that this Government is doing at this moment is making it any better; they're making it worse. They've got four ministers of health which is a joke in itself and between them they can't get it right.'[86] He then went on to abuse Upton, Williamson, O'Regan and East before inviting listeners to call into his programme the following Sunday when they could give the 'mess' and 'chaos' in health a wider audience. He would have 'one of the new Members of Parliament with me, a very good one, called Michael Laws and he's not afraid of officialdom'. After discussing the privatisation of electric power and housing, both of which Muldoon said he opposed, and lamenting that profit was replacing public service as a guiding principle, Muldoon ended his phone call by responding to the host's best wishes for his health by commenting, 'I'm far too fit for the comfort of my enemies. They haven't got me down yet.'

The next day Muldoon again entered North Shore Hospital preparatory to having a biopsy the following morning. Thea believed that only her husband's very strong will had kept him going over the previous months. He now realised, however, that his symptoms and condition were not simply the side effects of drugs he had been taking.[87] He did not really want to know the result of the biopsy the next day or to face becoming gradually more dependent than he already was. Early on the morning of Wednesday 5 August he died in his sleep. He was seventy years of age. Muldoon's death certificate recorded that he had died within ten minutes of an 'acute left ventricular failure' of his heart following some ten years of 'ischaemic heart disease and aortic incompetence'.[88]

The news of Muldoon's not unexpected death was recorded in Parliament that afternoon.[89] Eight National MPs, three Labour and Anderton, the Alliance Leader, took the opportunity to speak.[90] The first and longest contribution came from the Prime Minister. Bolger detailed Muldoon's life and noted that he was farewelling 'a legend' but added perceptively that 'the private Muldoon . . . was seldom seen in public. He was an intensely private person.'[91] Perhaps significantly, of the three party leaders who spoke, the Prime Minister's contribution, accurate and gracious though it was, was a more formal and less warmly affectionate tribute than those of the Labour and Alliance leaders. Both Moore and Anderton also somewhat surprisingly assessed Muldoon to have been the major political figure of the previous half-century.

In a shrewd, humorous and partisan speech, which Muldoon would have appreciated, Moore summed up the essence of Muldoon the person and the politician. Irrespective of whether history judged Muldoon's policies as right or wrong, no one could ignore the fact that this 'man of demonic and ferocious energy, and awesome intelligence, with an enormous capacity for paperwork and for sheer hard work', had 'dominated part of the sixties, all of the seventies, and some of the eighties'.[92] He had not just been in or even led the Government between 1975 and 1984 but 'he was the Government'. Muldoon had been also 'a most successful broadcaster and author'; 'a counter-puncher [who] always got the first punch in'; a politician who successfully imposed his will, vision and ideas on New Zealand through 'the power of his personality and the genius of his ability to communicate, especially on television', where 'he mesmerised the cameraman, he hypnotised the audience, and with one chuckle could demolish the most logical argument'; an advocate for 'the ordinary blokes' fears as well as their aspirations'; a 'committed' and 'unforgiving' party politician; and a leader who was loyal to and in return received back the intense loyalty of 'Rob's Mob'. Moore spoke for most New Zealanders when he ended, 'Like him, love him, hate him, or despise him – one knew him, and he was part of our life and part of our country. He was many things but he was not bland.'[93]

That assessment was endorsed by Anderton who, while conceding that he had for most of his political career been an opponent of the 'fiercely aggressive' Muldoon, praised Muldoon's honesty, courage, and 'personal vision for New Zealand. He wanted to see ordinary people prosper and he was genuinely concerned for them and their children.'[94] In Anderton's opinion, Muldoon had been 'the most formidable politician in nearly 50 years of New Zealand history'. He 'always had my respect . . . and in later years I must admit even a deal of affection for his warmth towards me personally, and his courage in reflecting the truth as he saw it about New Zealand's plight – even at great cost, I imagine, to his sense of loyalty to his own party'.[95] It was somewhat ironic, an irony that Muldoon had himself recognised for some time before his death, that Anderton more than most other MPs shared his misgivings about New Zealand's economic and social policies and direction since 1984 and, like Muldoon, had been prepared to alienate himself from his party by having the courage to speak out publicly in opposition to them.

Outside Parliament, among the thousands of communications Thea received on her husband's death, one from Merle Bell, the electorate chairperson of Tamaki, summed up the feelings of Rob's Mob. In Bell's words, Muldoon 'was sincere, he was loyal, and he was industrious. He tried so hard to interpret the wishes of the people he led and served . . . this splendid man of great intellect and big heart. He was our friend.'[96] Radio Pacific marked Muldoon's death with a fascinating three-hour 'Tribute to Sir Robert Muldoon' put together by Derek Lowe and broadcast in Muldoon's 3–6 p.m. slot on Sunday 9 August. Transcriptions of the programme were later sold to listeners.[97]

Thea and her children wanted a church funeral for their husband and father.[98] They realised that St Thomas's Church in the Tamaki electorate would be too small so they arranged with John Rymer, the former Dean of Auckland, to have the service in St Mary's Cathedral. Dean Rymer had been asked by Muldoon in 1991 to conduct the service when it was required, and Muldoon had told Rymer then that he 'knew he was living on borrowed time'.[99] On the Wednesday afternoon, in an effort to escape the onslaught of visitors and telephone calls at the house, Thea and her daughters went for a walk along Milford Beach. They returned home at 3.15 p.m. for an appointment with Dean Rymer at 3.30 p.m. to finalise the funeral service. The house was packed with friends, politicians and bureaucrats, the phone was ringing, television and other reporters were encamped on the street outside. When the family entered the house they found McKinnon and officials finalising the arrangements with Rymer. The funeral would be a large public one in the

Auckland Town Hall and even a separate, small, private service for family and a few close friends to be held earlier at St Thomas's Church had been extended to include virtually everyone associated with the Tamaki National Party, a fact that the family was unaware of until they entered the church.

The 11 a.m. public service on Friday 7 August was held on the opening day of the National Party's annual conference in Auckland's Downtown Convention Centre.[100] The party's National Executive and councillors from its five divisions met earlier in the morning before adjourning, so that most, though not all, could walk up Queen Street and join other mourners in the packed Town Hall. As Muldoon's body was carried in the power failed, blacking out the Town Hall and forcing the choir and congregation to sing without the organ's accompaniment. After his daughter Barbara had read the lesson (1 Corinthians 13 on the primacy of love) and Sir Graham Latimer and Prime Minister Bolger had spoken, Dean Rymer in his eulogy emphasised Muldoon's Christian compassion for the poor, the weak, the powerless and the marginalised. That message was emphasised by the thousands of mourners, many of them elderly, who crowded in the back of the Town Hall or waited silently in the streets outside, and by the ferocious Black Power haka which erupted in Queen Street as Muldoon's coffin left for the cemetery at Remuera on the boundary of his Tamaki electorate. The haka had been organised by Denis O'Reilly, who borrowed the airfare to fly back to attend the funeral from Melbourne where he was an MBA student. Over a hundred Black Power gang members representing every chapter in New Zealand took part in the haka.[101] Among the floral tributes at the graveside was one 'From your sister Dame Whina Cooper', which read, 'Farewell, farewell, farewell, farewell the ocean rock. You have been pounded by the great wave. Sleep your long sleep, you have arrived before our Father in heaven.'[102] The inscription carved on the tombstone read simply, 'He loved his country.'

Survivors write, and often rewrite, history. Sometimes they are neither balanced nor fair. They seek to maximise their own role and justify their actions. Often they blame, misrepresent and even demonise those who are no longer able to answer, let alone fight, back. Since his death Muldoon has been denounced not only by opponents, most of whom were no match for him when he was alive, but also by many in his own party who found they disagreed with him only after he fell from office in 1984, or even not until after his death in 1992. Books, newspaper articles, television documentaries, numerous speeches in Parliament and on the hustings have blamed most of New Zealand's problems on this one man and tried to persuade New Zealanders that all the reforms, the radical restructuring, the social dislocation, and the individual human pain that took place after 1984 under the Lange–Douglas Labour Government and after 1990 under the Bolger–Richardson administration resulted from either Muldoon's actions or his equally reprehensible inactions. Not only his policies and actions but also his personality and character have been systematically and comprehensively denigrated.

Muldoon was no saint; he never pretended to be one. A competitive and combative man, he could be brutal to those with whom he disagreed, including many in his own party; he baited and ridiculed intellectuals and some dissident minorities; and he did not conceal his contempt for many of those who regarded themselves as New Zealand's commercial, social or bureaucratic elite. But he was also an intelligent and complex man with the courage to take a stand and accept that not all would agree with him, a sincere belief in New Zealand nationalism and a deep concern for the underdog. One of the reasons Labour disliked him so much was that he more than any other leader in National's history was able to reach across and articulate the views and appeal to the emotions of some traditional Labour voters. He was a compassionate not a callous conservative and a man who believed not only in the importance of the individual but also recognised the significance of maintaining a sense of community in any healthy civil society. He tried to conserve values, a system and a way of life which he believed had been good for New Zealand.

It must always be remembered that Muldoon viewed New Zealand and the world very much from the perspective of his generation, the generation of the Great Depression of the 1930s and of World War II in the 1940s. Politicians of all persuasions in New Zealand during that generation, not only Muldoon, believed in interventionist government, the Keynesian economy, the welfare state, collective security and the balancing of individual rights with communal responsibilities. Full employment; equality of opportunity through a free state education system; a taxpayer funded, universally available public health system; reasonable welfare benefits in times of misfortune; decent superannuation based on the right of citizenship not charity; and a future in which New Zealanders were not divided by ethnic origin – all these together comprised the New Zealand he sought to defend. It was a New Zealand that still existed to a large extent when he became Prime Minister but it was a reality increasingly difficult to maintain in a rapidly and markedly changing world. Muldoon tried but in the end watched impotently from the sideline of politics as nearly everything he valued and which he had devoted his life to preserving was swept away. Frustrated and depressed he may have been during the last years of his life, but his spirit flared to the end. Although he loved winning, to Muldoon it was better to have fought for the things he valued and believed in and to have lost than never to have fought at all. By 1992 New Zealand had not become what Muldoon or many other New Zealanders wanted it to be but he was not prepared to take the blame for that. Muldoon died unrepentant and still convinced that his way, even if never perfect, had been a better way.

Notes

Introduction

1   Ruth Richardson–BSG, 21 March 1990.

2   For concise and excellent analyses of
     Richard Nixon see the obituaries by John
     Herbers, Tom Wicker, and Garry Wills in
     the *New York Times*, 24 April 1994.

3   James McGregor Burns, *Leadership*. Another
     useful introduction to visionary leadership
     is James M. Kouzes and Barry Z. Posner,
     The Leadership Challenge. See also John
     Gardner, *On Leadership*. For my discussion of
     Burns's views on leadership and Savage see
     my *From the Cradle to the Grave: A Biography
     of Michael Joseph Savage*, Reed Methuen,
     Auckland, 1986, pp 2–3.

4   Doug Kidd–BSG, 1 March 1990.

5   *Otago Daily Times*, 3 August 1984.

6   *Auckland Star*, 16 July 1984.

7   For a very interesting discussion of Muldoon
     and the National Party's populist tradition
     see David Orwin, 'Conservatism in New
     Zealand', 1999, pp 189–209. See also the
     discussion of populism and New Zealand
     politics in my 'Regeneration, Rejection or
     Realignment: New Zealand Political Parties
     in the 1990s', in G. R. Hawke (ed),
     *Changing Politics? The Electoral Referendum
     1993*, esp. pp 82–5. For populism generally
     see Ghita Ionescu and Ernst Gellner (eds),
     *Populism: Its Meaning and National
     Characteristics*; Michael Kazin, *The Populist
     Persuasion: An American History*; and
     Margaret Canovan, 'People, Politicians and
     Populism'.

8   cit. *Sunday Star*, 8 March 1987.

9   Oliver Riddell, *Press*, 21 October 1985.
     One of the best short analytical essays on
     Muldoon is Warwick Roger, 'The Real
     Muldoon'.

10   *Dominion* editorial, 18 November 1991.

11   Robert Dilenschneider, *On Power*, pp 2–3.
     See also Jeffrey Pfeffer, *Managing With
     Power: Politics and Influence in Organisations*.

12   Gardner, *On Leadership*, p 24.

13   Roy Johnston, paper delivered to Wellington
     Divisional Seminar, 22 and 23 October
     1984, NPP A 89/75 MSC 145/2325.

14   Pfeffer, *op cit.*, p 304.

15   John Henderson, 'Muldoon and Rowling:

A Preliminary Analysis of Contrasting
Personalities'. See also James Barber,
The Presidential Character.

16   Jock Phillips (ed), *Biography in New Zealand*.

17   J. C. Davis, 'Clio's Lost Sheep', in Phillips
     (ed), *Biography in New Zealand*, pp 7–18, p 8.

18   Ben Pimlott, review of *Macmillan: Volume 2,
     1957–1986*, in *New Statesman and Society*,
     23 June 1989, pp 35–36, p 35.

19   Jock Phillips, 'Introduction', in Phillips
     (ed), *Biography in New Zealand*, pp 1–6, p 1.

20   Keith Sinclair, 'Political Biography in
     New Zealand', in Phillips (ed), *Biography
     in New Zealand*, pp 30–36.

21   Ibid., p 30.

22   Antony Alpers, 'Literary Biography (in
     New Zealand)', in Phillips (ed), *Biography
     in New Zealand*, pp 19–29, p 27.

23   Robert Muldoon, *The Rise and Fall of a
     Young Turk*; *Muldoon*; *My Way*; *The New
     Zealand Economy: A Personal View*; *Number
     38*; 'The Precipice – 1929 Revisited',
     unpublished typescript of book dated
     25 September 1985 and in Muldoon Papers.

24   Spiro Zavos, *The Real Muldoon*.

25   Hugh Templeton, *All Honourable Men:
     Inside the Muldoon Cabinet 1975–1984*,
     and Bob Jones, *Memories of Muldoon*.

26   Margaret Clark, 'Clash of the Titans'.

27   Erik Olssen, 'Political Biography:
     A Commentary', in Phillips (ed), *Biography
     in New Zealand*, pp 39–41.

28   Michael King discusses this problem in an
     article, 'Tread Softly For You Tread On My
     Life: Biography and Compassionate Truth'.

29   Murray McCully–BSG, 21 March 1990.

1   Family and Childhood

1   The information in this chapter came largely
     from the author's interviews with Muldoon
     22 April 1985, 24 February, 7 and 15 July
     1989; Lawrence Browne, 15 July 1989;
     Richard Fickling, 2 June 1989; Jack Ryder,
     1 June 1989; Lady Thea Muldoon,
     10 August 1992 and 12 August 1994;
     Bert Stokes, 24 April 1990; and Joe Jones,
     22 April 1998. See also Muldoon's first three
     autobiographies, *The Rise and Fall of a Young*

Turk, Muldoon, and *My Way*. The Muldoon Papers include birth, death and marriage certificates; photocopies of the monthly *Helping Hand*, January-October 1893; Wes Muldoon's and Jim Muldoon's war service records; Wes Muldoon's war diary; and Church of Jesus Christ of Latter-Day Saints Research Report 20 November 1979. The Wederell Papers include Muldoon's war service records and correspondence with some of Muldoon's contemporaries. Muldoon also discussed his family and early life with Jim Sullivan, Oral History Centre, National Library of New Zealand, 3 March 1992.

2   *The Rise and Fall of a Young Turk*, p 2, and *The Helping Hand*, September 1893.

3   Frank Adams to Wederell 31/1/69 WP 1655 1/1.

4   Interview Bert Stokes, 24 April 1990. Also NZEF conduct sheet. The entry was subsequently cancelled as was the punishment of 96 hours' detention and reversion from the rank of corporal to gunner. Also RDM-BSG 24 February 1989.

5   Wes Muldoon's diary, 30 April 1915, MP. See also *Rise and Fall of a Young Turk*, p 3.

6   Ibid, 24 June – 4 July 1915. MP.

7   RDM–BSG, 24 February 1989, and Lawrence Browne–BSG, 15 July 1989. See also marriage certificate of Amie Rusha Browne and James Henry Muldoon, 29 October 1919, and birth certificate of Robert David Muldoon, 25 September 1921.

8   Lawrence Browne–BSG, 15 July 1989.

9   Undated Greymouth newspaper clipping, MP, and RDM–BSG, 24 February 1989. Muldoon at the launch of his book *The Rise and Fall of a Young Turk* dedicated the book to 'his boyhood hero – Dick Seddon . . . the greatest politician New Zealand has ever known'. *Cit. NZ Herald*, 11 July 1974.

10 Lawrence Browne–BSG, 15 July 1989, and Colin Busfield–BSG, 7 June 1989.

11 *Rise and Fall of a Young Turk*, pp 6–7.

12 RDM article in *NZ Truth*, 18 September 1973, and RDM–BSG, 24 February 1989.

13 Lawrence Browne–BSG, 15 July 1989, and RDM–BSG 22 April 1985.

14 Ibid.

15 RDM-BSG, 24 February 1989. See also *The Rise and Fall of a Young Turk*, p 8. A copy of Jim Muldoon's death certificate giving syphilis as the primary cause of death is in the Muldoon Papers. Dr Pat Savage, one-time Superintendent of the hospital, in an interview with the author on 1 March 1993, said that the disease took about seven years to come and took up to twenty years to affect seriously the brain or heart. During

World War I without penicillin it could not be cured even if caught in its early stages, but attempts were made to treat it by brushing on mercury externally and dosing with intravenous arsenic. Dr Ronald Barker, a one-time Director-General of Health, also discussed this matter with the author and questioned because of the time factor whether Jim Muldoon was initially in the asylum because of syphilis or because of some other reason. See also Allan M. Brandt, *No Magic Bullet: A Social History of Venereal Disease in the United States Since 1880*, Oxford University Press, New York, 1985, and Roy Statham, *V.D. Explained*, Priory Press, London, 1972.

16 Lawrence Browne–BSG, 15 July 1989.

17 Richard Fickling–BSG, 2 June 1989, and Lawrence Browne–BSG, 15 July 1989.

18 Ibid and RDM–BSG, 15 July 1989.

19 RDM–BSG, 7 July 1989, Thea Muldoon BSG, 10 August 1992 and 12 August 1994.

20 RDM–BSG, 7 July 1989.

21 Thea Muldoon–BSG, 10 August 1992 and 12 August 1994.

22 *Muldoon*, p 3.

23 Jack Ryder, 1 June 1989.

24 *My Way*, p 2.

25 Fickling-BSG, 2 June 1989.

26 G. W. Adam (YMCA) to Wederell, 7 August 1969, WP 1655, 1/13; George Adair to Wederell, 24 December 1968, WP 1655, 1/1; Lawrence Browne–BSG, 15 July 1989; Bill Adair–BSG, 31 May 1989.

27 Lawrence Browne–BSG, 15 July 1989.

28 Ibid.

29 Frank Adams to Wederell, 31 January 1969, WP 1655 1/1.

30 Jack Ryder–BSG, 1 June 1989, and Dave Fickling–BSG, 2 June 1989. Most of the following information comes from Ryder, Fickling and Muldoon. Muldoon recalls the Auckland of his childhood in a 1988 article in the *NZ Listener*, 'My Place: The Big City'.

31 Joe Jones–BSG, 22 April 1998.

32 *Muldoon*, p 5.

33 RDM interview with Robert Gilmour, *Auckland Star*, 14 December 1968, and RDM–BSG, 24 February 1989.

2   *School and Church*

1   Muldoon recalls his primary schooling in 'Memories' in *Mount Albert School Centenary*, 1969, p 34.

2   *The Rise and Fall of a Young Turk*, p 10. Muldoon summarises his education on pages 10–12 of this book.

3   Report of Ministry of Education, Year to December 1933, WP 1655 4/2.
4   Kathleen Currie to RDM, 2 November 1960, MP. Details on the Rawlings Scholarship provided by Swann, Faucett and Partners, Public Accountants and trustees of the Rawlings Scholarship, to Wederell, 8 October 1969, WP 1655, 1/11. See also Ronald Barker to BSG, [nd] 1990. Barker, who became Director-General of Health, was also a Rawlings Scholar, winning the scholarship for 1934, the year after Muldoon.
5   Barker–BSG, [nd] 1990.
6   RDM–BSG, 24 February 1989.
7   Bill Adair–BSG, 31 May 1989.
8   RDM–BSG, 7 July 1989.
9   Lawrence Browne–BSG, 15 July 1989; Bill Adair–BSG, 31 May 1989; and RDM–BSG, 7 July 1989.
10   *The Albertian*, No. 15, November 1936.
11   George W. Adair to Wederell, 24 December 1968, WP 1655, 1/1.
12   Bill Adair–BSG, 31 May 1989, and RDM–BSG, 24 February 1989.
13   Dick Fickling–BSG, 2 June 1989.
14   Murray Nairn, Headmaster MAGS, to Wederell, 14 April 1969, WP 1655 1/10.
15   RDM interview with Wederell, nd [1968–69], WP 1655, 2/1.
16   Ibid and Harvey Blanks to Wederell, 21 February 1970, WP 1655, 1/2; RDM–BSG, 15 July 1989.
17   *The Albertian*, No. 15, November 1936.
18   Mount Albert Grammar School Record Card for RDM and University Entrance results, WP 1655, 4/2.
19   RDM–BSG, 24 February 1989.
20   Mount Albert Grammar School records on RDM, WP 1655, 1/1.
21   RDM interview with Wederell, nd [1968–69], WP 1655, 2/1.
22   RDM–BSG, 24 February 1989 and *The Rise and Fall of a Young Turk*, p 14.
23   RDM interview with Wederell, nd [1968–69], WP 1655, 2/1.
24   AEPB staff file on R. D. Muldoon, WP 1655, 1/1.
25   RDM–BSG, 7 July 1989.
26   A. S. Don, AEPB General Manager, to Wederell, 8 August 1969, WP 1655, 1/1.
27   AEPB staff file on R. D. Muldoon, WP 1655, 1/1.
28   Information on Muldoon and Mount Albert Baptist Church came from interviews by the author with RDM, 24 February 1989; Lawrence Browne, 15 July 1989; Alan Busfield, 17 March 1995; Colin Busfield 7 and 13 June 1989; Rev. Hayes Lloyd, 6 June 1989; Jack Turner, 1 June 1990; Alan Jenkins 10 May 1990. See also A. V.

Windsor, Assistant to the Minister, Mount Albert Baptist Church, to Wederell, nd [1969], WP 1655, 1/8. Muldoon devotes only one paragraph in *The Rise and Fall of a Young Turk*, p 12, to the part Mount Albert Baptist played in his early life, and almost completely ignores it in his later books.
29   Colin Busfield–BSG, 7 June 1989. Among the young men were many who became very prominent in Auckland business and/or Baptist circles in later years, for example, Lawrence, Warwick and Graham Browne; Jack, David and Graham Turner and their cousins such as Arnold Turner; Colin, Rawden and Alan Busfield; Graham Glaister; Stan Walker; Merv Probine; Owen and Spencer Stevens; Shelford Penman; Alan Jenkin; and Owen Cobb.
30   Ibid.
31   Lawrence Browne–BSG, 15 July 1989; RDM–BSG, 24 February 1989; Rev. Lloyd–BSG, 6 June 1989; Colin Busfield–BSG 7 ad 13 June 1989; Alan Busfield–BSG, 17 March 1995.
32   Hayes Lloyd–BSG, 6 June 1989.
33   RDM–BSG, 24 February 1989.
34   Ibid.
35   Lawrence Browne–BSG, 15 July 1989.
36   Alan Busfield–BSG, 17 March 1995. Also RDM–BSG, 24 February 1989 and Hayes Lloyd–BSG, 6 June 1989.
37   A. V. Windsor, Assistant to the Minister, Mount Albert Baptist Church, to Wederell, WP 1655, 1/8.
38   *NZ Baptist*, 3 April 1996.
39   G. Campbell, 'Robert Muldoon: politics of survival', pp 18–21 and 42.

3   *War and Work*

1   Ministry of Defence, Robert David Muldoon's Record of Service, WP 1655, 4/2, from which much of the detail of Muldoon's war service in this chapter comes. See also RDM–BSG, 7 July 1989, and *The Rise and Fall of a Young Turk*, pp 14–19.
2   RDM–BSG, 7 July 1989.
3   *The Rise and Fall of a Young Turk*, pp 14–15. In a later book *Muldoon*, p 7, he repeated these sentiments noting: 'I was never a keen soldier . . . I was much more concerned with enjoying the novelty of life in the forces and preparing myself to return to civilian life than in seeking what I saw as temporary promotion . . . In the event I was lucky and had a good war. I was mainly in jobs where a certain amount of skill, training and experience kept me interested and with just

enough rank to avoid the more menial tasks.' In an article in the *Sunday Star*, 10 September 1989, he recalled, 'I was one of the lucky ones . . . [and] to a very large extent by fortunate postings, did not sustain more than a scratch.'

4   Bill Adair–BSG, 31 May 1989.
5   *The Rise and Fall of a Young Turk*, p 17, and RDM–BSG, 7 July 1989.
6   *The Rise and Fall of a Young Turk*, p 18.
7   Ibid, p 17.
8   Vic Stace–BSG, 9 May 1990, and RDM–BSG, 7 July 1989. Stace provided initially much of the information about Muldoon in the Pacific. This was later confirmed in discussions with RDM. See also for added details *The Rise and Fall of a Young Turk*, pp 15–16, and *Muldoon*, p 8.
9   *The Rise and Fall of a Young Turk*, p 16.
10   RDM–BSG, 7 July 1989.
11   D. MacIntyre–BSG, 10 July 1991.
12   RDM–BSG, 7 July 1989.
13   Ibid; *The Rise and Fall of a Young Turk*, p 17, where he says there were 30 soldiers in the troop; and *Muldoon*, p 9.
14   RDM–BSG, 7 July 1989.
15   Ibid.
16   J. R. Marshall to Wederell, 26 January 19969, WP 1655, 1/9. Muldoon's version is in *The Rise and Fall of a Young Turk*, p 19.
17   RDM–BSG, See also *The Rise and Fall of a Young Turk*, pp 19–20, and *Muldoon*, p 9.
18   *Muldoon*, p 9.
19   Lawrence W. Robson to Wederell, 26 February 1969, WP 1655 1/11.
20   T. B. Degenhardt, Deputy Secretary, Institute of Cost and Works Accountants, London, to Wederell 17 January and 11 February 1969, WP 1655, 1/7.
21   K. R. Macdonald, Secretary NZ Society of Accountants, to Wederell, 15 August 1969, WP 1655, 1/1.
22   Resolution of AEPB Board, 3 March 1947, *cit.* A. S. Don, AEPB General Manager, to Wederell, 8 August 1969, WP 1655, 1/1.
23   RDM–BSG, 15 July 1989, and Muldoon's AEPB staff file, WP 1655, 1/1.
24   N. M. Speer, Secretary AEPB, 1 July 1947, WP 1655, 1/1.
25   Much of the information in this section came from interviews: RDM–BSG, 22 September 1989; Fred Mills–BSG 13 September 1989; Harry Julian–BSG, 28 May 1990. Mills also made available to the author the records of the firm.
26   Account Books of Kendon Mills for 1950–51, shown to the author by Fred Mills, 13 September 1989.
27   Fred Mills–BSG, 13 September 1989.
28   Ibid. Some of the detail also comes from

RDM–Wederell, nd [1969], WP 1655, 2/1; RDM–BSG, 22 September 1989; and Colin Busfield–BSG, 13 June 1989.
29   Fred Mills–BSG, 13 September 1989.
30   Ibid.
31   RDM–BSG, 22 September 1989, and Fred Mills–BSG 13 September 1989.
32   Ibid.
33   RDM–BSG, 22 September 1989.
34   Harry Julian–BSG, 28 May 1990.
35   RDM–BSG, 22 September 1989.
36   K. R. Macdonald, Secretary, NZ Society of Accountants, to Wederell, 15 August 1969, WP 1655 1/1.
37   Fred Mills–BSG, 13 September 1989.

4   *The Junior Nationals and Marriage*

1   Alex McKenzie, cit. Minutes of the Auckland Divisional Committee, 29 May 1945. Much of the information on Muldoon and the Junior Nationals came from the author's interviews with RDM, 22 April 1985, 24 February and 15 July 1989; Thea Muldoon (née Flyger), 10 August 1992; Alan Busfield, 17 March 1995; Colin Busfield, 7 and 13 June 1989; Peter Dempsey, 27 September 1989; Thea Frogley (née McKinstry), 29 May 1990; Alan Jenkin and Geraldine Jenkin (née Byrne), 10 May 1990; Sir Alex McKenzie, 21 December 1984; and Merv Probine, 6 March 1990. See also *The Rise and Fall of a Young Turk*, pp 20–22, and *Muldoon*, pp 16–17, although in his books Muldoon says little about his Junior National activities. The Wederell Papers contain, inter alia, an interview with RDM, nd [1969], including recollections of the Junior Nationals; copies of *Junior News*, August 1947–May 1951; Auckland Junior National Party Annual Reports, 1945–49; and correspondence including letters regarding the Junior Nationals to Wederell from L. E. Adams, 30 December 1968; W. J. Allingham, 28 August 1969; Colin Busfield, 17 July 1969; K. C. Ewington, 2 February 1970; and Marjorie Prince (née Gadsby), 14 January and 17 May 1969. Wederell also met and interviewed Mrs Prince in early 1969 [nd]. See WP 1655, 1/1, 1/2, 1/5, 1/9, 1/10, 5/3, 6/1. The sixth Annual Report of the Auckland Junior Nationals for the year ended 15 March 1950, during which Muldoon was chairman, is in the Auckland Division records. See also minutes of the Auckland Divisional Committee and Executive 1944–51. See also Barry Gustafson, *The First 50 Years: A History of*

the New Zealand National Party,
pp 255–259, for the early history of the
Junior Nationals.

2   See Annual Reports, 1946 and 1947,
WP 1655, 5/3.

3   *Junior News*, October–December 1947,
WP 1655, 6/1.

4   Peter Dempsey was a particularly
interesting Junior National leader in the
later 1940s and at that time was seen as a
much more likely future possibility for a
prominent position in the National caucus
than Muldoon. The nephew of Willis Airey,
the very left-wing Rhodes Scholar and
Auckland University historian, Dempsey
was one of two Auckland MA students in
History in 1944. The other was E. J. (Ted)
Keating, who later became Labour MP for
Hastings. Dempsey was recruited into the
Junior Nationals at their inception by
Professor Rutherford. He stood for National
in Ponsonby in 1946 and was Junior
President from 1947 until October 1948
when he took up a Rotary scholarship to
study diplomatic history at the London
School of Economics. Returning to New
Zealand Dempsey missed nomination for
Tamaki in 1949, being defeated by three
votes by Eric Halstead. In 1954 he defeated
Muldoon and others for the Waitemata
nomination but subsequently withdrew
shortly before the election. Although active
for many years in the party organisation, he
never again stood for Parliament.

5   *Junior News*, October 1948, WP 1655, 6/1.

6   RDM–BSG, 15 July 1989.

7   Colin Busfield–BSG, 7 June 1989.

8   Ibid.

9   Alan Busfield–BSG, 17 March 1995.

10   *Junior News*, April–May 1949.

11   Minutes of the Auckland Divisional
Committee, 7 June 1950. See also K. C.
Ewington to Wederell, 2 February 1970,
WP 1655, 1/5. By February 1949 Muldoon
was able to report that only two electorates
in the Division did not have Junior sections.
Minutes of the Auckland Divisional
Executive, 4 April 1949.

12   Sixth Annual Report of the Auckland
Junior Nationals for the year ended
15 March 1950, *Junior News*, April–May
1949, and Marjorie Prince to Wederell,
17 May 1969, WP 1655, 1/10.

13   *Junior News*, April–May 1949.

14   Muldoon to Wederell, nd [1969], WP
1655, 2/1.

15   Thea Frogley–BSG 29 May 1990; Thea
Muldoon–BSG, 10 August 1992; and
Geraldine Jenkin–BSG, 10 May 1990.

16   *Junior News*, October–December 1949.

17   Thea Frogley–BSG, 29 May 1990.

18   Among them were Colin and Alan Busfield,
Peter Dempsey, Vaughan Mountjoy, Alan
Jenkin, Fred Brittain, Alistair Martin, Vic
Percival, Squire Speedy, Bill Twentyman,
Geoff Taylor, Ferguson Prince, Danny
Kerruish and Gainor Jackson.

19   Thea Frogley–BSG, 29 May 1990, and
Colin Busfield–BSG, 13 June 1989.

20   E.g. Rob and Thea Muldoon, Peter and
Beverly Dempsey, Colin and Ailse Busfield,
John and Thea Frogley, Alan and Geraldine
Jenkin, Marjorie and Ferguson Prince, Fred
and Freda (and later Ann) Brittain.

21   E.g. Colin Busfield–BSG, 7 June 1989;
Alan Busfield–BSG, 17 March 1995; Thea
Frogley–BSG, 27 May 1990; Alan and
Geraldine Jenkin–BSG, 10 May 1990; Peter
Dempsey–BSG, 27 September 1989.

22   Thea Frogley–BSG, 27 May 1990, and
Peter Dempsey–BSG, 27 September 1989.

23   Colin Busfield–BSG, 7 June 1989.

24   RDM–BSG, 15 July 1989.

25   Sixth Annual Report of the Auckland
Junior Section for year ended 15 March
1950, in Auckland Division records.

26   Colin Busfield–BSG, 7 June 1989. Busfield
was best man at Muldoon's wedding and
Gadsby was godmother to Muldoon's
younger daughter Jennifer.

27   Thea Frogley (née McKinstry)–BSG,
29 May 1990.

28   Information in this section comes from
RDM–BSG, 15 July 1989; Thea
Muldoon–BSG, 10 August 1992; Alan and
Geraldine Jenkin–BSG, 10 May 1990;
Colin Busfield–BSG, 7 and 13 June 1989;
and Thea Frogley–BSG, 29 May 1990. Thea
Muldoon also gave an interview on her life,
times and relationship with and opinions on
her husband to Jim Sullivan, Oral History
Centre, National Library of New Zealand,
on 7 May 1992.

29   RDM–BSG, 15 July 1989, and Alan
Jenkin–BSG 10 May 1990.

30   Colin Busfield–BSG, 7 June 1989.

31   RDM–BSG, 24 July 1989, and Thea
Muldoon–BSG, 19 February 1992.

32   Thea Frogley–BSG, 29 May 1990.

33   Thea Muldoon–BSG, 19 February 1992,
and Barbara Williams–BSG, 19 June 1999

34   RDM–BSG, 24 July 1989.

35   Mrs E. L. Dowding to Wederell, 4 February
1969, WP 1655, 1/4. Mrs Dowding was
secretary of the Auckland Horticultural
Council at the time Muldoon was first
treasurer and then president. See also *The
Rise and Fall of a Young Turk*, pp 21–22.

36   Gordon Nicholl to Wederell, February
1968, WP 1655, 1/10.

37 Mrs E. L. Dowding to Wederell, 4 February 1969, WP 1655, 1/4.

38 RDM–BSG, 24 July 1989 and Then Muldoon–BSG, 19 February 1992.

5 Three Times Lucky

1 L. E. Adams to Wederell, 30 December 1968, WP 1655, 1/1.

2 RDM–BSG, 24 July 1989. Much of the information in this chapter came from the author's interviews with Muldoon, 22 April 1985 and 24 July 1989; Eric Halstead, 19 July 1985; Sir Alex McKenzie, 21 December 1984; interviews with Muldoon in 1969 and correspondence with various people in the Wederell Papers; the 1954, 1957 and 1960 Election Files and the Divisional Committee and Divisional Executive Minutes in the Auckland Division of the National Party's Records; 1954, 1957 and 1960 Election Files in the Muldoon Papers, including newspaper clippings from NZ Herald and Auckland Star and Muldoon's and National Party's pamphlets; The Rise and Fall of a Young Turk, pp 24–42, and Muldoon, pp 20–27. As president of the Auckland Junior Labour Party the author worked for Bob Tizard when he won the Tamaki seat from Halstead in 1957 and was the Labour candidate in the adjoining seat of Remuera when Muldoon won Tamaki from Tizard in 1960.

3 Divisional Executive Minutes, 2 December 1952.

4 Ibid, 7 April 1953.

5 Ibid, 3 August 1954.

6 1954 Election File, Auckland Division Records.

7 Charles Mills to Secretary Auckland Division, 2 April 1954.

8 See RDM–BSG 24 July 1989; 1954 Election File, Auckland Division Records; 1954 Mt Albert Campaign Clippings, Muldoon Papers; The Rise and Fall of a Young Turk, pp 24–26; and Muldoon, pp 20–21.

9 NZ Herald, 20 October 1954. See also Auckland Star, 30 October 1954, and NZ Herald, 4 November 1954.

10 NZ Herald, 4 November 1954.

11 RDM–Wederell, nd [1969] WP 1655, and Muldoon, p 21.

12 Muldoon reproduced this list twenty years later in The Rise and Fall of Young Turk, p 28, and noted 'I would not change a word of it today'.

13 RDM in Mt Albert Enterprise, November 1954, MP

14 Divisional Executive Minutes, 2 November 1954.

15 Divisional Executive Minutes, 7 December 1954 and 1 March 1955.

16 Ibid, 7 June 1955.

17 Ibid, 4 October 1955.

18 Ibid, 13 March 1956.

19 Ibid.

20 Ibid, 3 July 1956.

21 Ibid, 4 September 1956.

22 Ibid, 5 March 1957.

23 1957 Election File, Auckland Division Records. See also RDM–BSG, 24 July 1989. The Rise and Fall of a Young Turk, pp 33–34, and Muldoon, pp 22–23.

24 1957 Election File, Auckland Division Records.

25 Muldoon to Divisional Secretary, 7 January 1957, 1957 Election File, Auckland Division Records.

26 Divisional Executive minutes, 6 August 1957.

27 W. J. A. Stewart to all branch chairmen, 20 November 1957, 1957 Election File, Auckland Division Records.

28 RDM–Wederell, nd [1969], WP 1655, 2/1.

29 RDM–BSG, 24 July 1989.

30 Ibid. In the Muldoon Papers there is a briefcase full of pamphlets, clippings and notes on Social Credit, largely collected during the 1954–58 period but added to throughout the sixties. While mainly concerned with the financial theories, Muldoon paid also critical attention to the anti-Semitic writing of some Social Crediters such as Wing Commander Leonard Young, some of whose virulent comments in his pamphlet Deadlier than the H Bomb, Britons Publishing Society, London, 1956, Muldoon annotated. Among the material in the briefcase were copies of New Zealand Social Credit News and the New Zealand Social Crediter 1955 and 1956; C. Barclay-Smith, It's Time They Knew, Monetary Research Group, Sydney, 1967; W. D. Brockie, Local Body Loans, NZ Social Credit Association, Wellington, 1967; W. D. Brockie, Not for Old Clay Bottles, typescript, Nelson, 1970; A. J. Danks, What Everyone Should Know About Social Credit, Caxton Press, Christchurch, 1955; A. N. Field, The Bretton Woods Plot, self-published, Nelson, 1957; H. J. Kelliher, Why Your Pound Buys Less and Less, Dawson Printing, Auckland, 1954; G. Hinton Knowles and F. D. Danks, Social Credit Is the Key, Scott Printing, Auckland, nd; D. S. Milne, Social Credit Is the Answer, Hartleys, Lower Hutt, nd; M. J. S. Nestor, Monetary Reform and the Reformers,

Whitcombe and Tombs, Wellington, 1956;
W. B. Owen, *Social Credit's Solution,*
Whitcombe and Tombs, Wellington, nd;
W. B. Owen, *Let Us Be Positive,* Dunford,
Christchurch, 1963; W. B. Owen, *How
Social Credit Works,* Pegasus, Christchurch,
1954; and R. G. Young, *The Key to
Prosperity,* NZ Social Credit Political
League, Hamilton, nd [1954].

31 *NZ Herald,* 6 and 14 November 1957.
32 *Auckland Star,* 23 November 1957.
33 *NZ Herald,* 17 October 1957.
34 Divisional Executive Minutes, 3 December
1957.
35 Eric Halstead–BSG, 19 July 1985.
36 RDM–BSG, 24 July 1989.
37 W. M. Wilson to Secretary, Auckland
Division, 29 April 1960. See also reply,
11 May 1960. Auckland Division Records.
38 The eight candidates were J. R. Firth,
W. H. Fortune, R. C. Haszard, H. V. Long,
R. D. Muldoon, P. B. Phillips, I. T. T.
Rendle, and G. G. P. Taylor. The seven
branches with their memberships in
brackets were: Glendowie (498), Glen Innes
(200), Kohimarama (1127), Mission Bay
(951), Orakei (496), Pt England (64), and
St Heliers (1011). 1960 Election File,
Auckland Division Records.
39 *Glen Innes Gazette,* 22 June 1960, in 1960
Election File, Auckland Division.
40 Sir Alex McKenzie–BSG, 21 December
1984. See also Sir Alex McKenzie to
Wederell, 22 January 1969.
41 Ibid.
42 Eric Halstead to Wederell, 14 August 1969,
WP 1655, 1/7.
43 Eric Halstead–BSG, 19 July 1985.
44 Ibid.
45 *The Rise and Fall of a Young Turk,* pp 38–39;
RDM–BSG, 22 April 1985 and 24 July
1989; Sir Alex McKenzie–BSG,
21 December 1984; and Jolyon Firth to
Wederell, 25 August 1969, WP 1655, 1/6.
Firth was one of the eight nominees for
Tamaki.
46 RDM–BSG, 22 April 1985.
47 Jolyon Firth to Wederell, 25 August 1969,
WP 1655, 1/6.
48 Ibid.
49 RDM–Wederell, nd [1969], WP 1655, 2/1.
50 Divisional Committee Minutes, 30 May
1961. Other figures taken from B. S.
Gustafson, 'Continuing Transformation: The
Structure, Composition, and Functioning of
the New Zealand Labour Party in the
Auckland Region, 1949–70' (unpublished
PhD thesis, University of Auckland, 1974),
Vol II, Table 4.2, and Barry Gustafson, *The
First 50 Years: A History of the New Zealand*

National Party, p 83.

51 RDM–Wederell, nd [1969], WP 1655, 2/1.
In *The Rise and Fall of a Young Turk,* p 41,
Muldoon says it was the doorbell not the
handle that came off.
52 RDM–BSG, 1 August 1989.
53 Ibid.
54 Father P. O'Reilly to the *Listener,* 9
September 1978, p 10.
55 R. M. Chapman, W. K. Jackson, A. V.
Mitchell, *New Zealand Politics in Action: The
1960 General Election,* pp 290–1.

6   *The MP for Tamaki 1960–63*

1   Gavin Muldoon discusses some of the
problems of being the young son of such a
controversial politician in an interview with
Joanna Wane in *Sunday,* 2 September 1990,
pp 26–27. This chapter is based particularly
on the author's interviews with Muldoon,
22 April 1985, 24 February, 1 August and
2 October 1989; Lance Adams-Schneider,
21 August 1985; Colin Brenton-Rule,
4 July 1985; Bevan Burgess, 5 March 1990;
Peter Gordon, 12 March 1990; Duncan
MacIntyre, 10 July 1991; John Marshall,
9 July 1985; Thea Muldoon, 10 August
1992; John Tremewan, 29 September 1989;
and Barbara Williams, 19 June 1999. Also
Peter Gordon to BSG, 20 February 1990.
The Wederell Papers contain, inter alia,
correspondence with L. E. Adams,
30 December 1968; R. M. Algie, 23 July
1969; Bevan Burgess, 4 August 1969;
G. Caldwell, 6 September 1969;
H. M. Davies, 21 February 1970; C. R. Day,
15 May 1969, 28 July 1969 and 9 December
1969; J. R. Hanan, 19 February 1969;
J. Harris, 10 August 1969; J. Rendle,
15 January 1969; H. F. Waugh, 7 August
1969; and transcripts of interviews with
Muldoon nd [1969]. There are also various
files and clippings in the Muldoon Papers,
including ten newspaper scrapbooks covering
the period from 1961 until 1975. See also
minutes of the Auckland Division, National
Executive and Caucus of the National Party.
Unfortunately the records of the Tamaki
Electorate prior to April 1967 could not be
found. Muldoon discusses the 1960–63
period in *The Rise and Fall of a Young Turk,*
pp 43–64.
2   RDM–BSG, 1 August 1989.
3   'Bob Muldoon' 1963 election pamphlet.
4   Graham Caldwell, President Glen Innes
Residents and Ratepayers Association, to
Wederell, 6 September 1969, WP 1655,
1/3.

5   L. E. Adams to Wederell, 30 December 1968, WP 1655, 1/1.

6   John Harris, former editor, *Eastern Suburbs Courier*, to Wederell, 10 August 1969, WP 1655, 1/3.

7   Henry F. Waugh, President Glen Innes Senior Citizens Club, to Wederell, 7 August 1969, WP 1655, 1/13.

8   *The Rise and Fall of a Young Turk*, pp 62–63.

9   RDM–BSG, 24 February 1989, and address to Auckland Creditmen's Club cit. *Auckland Star*, 22 November 1961.

10   Rendell, Tremewan and Matthews, three of the most prominent, were all schoolteachers, and Rendell had been one of the unsuccessful nominees when Muldoon won the Tamaki nomination in 1960. Others also worked for Muldoon and the party in Tamaki over a long period of time, for example, Doug Tillyshort, Terry Sanders, Cliff Holt, Charles Leach, Mavis Finlayson, Ed Smallwood, David Bagley, Lois and David Morris, Clem Simich, Tom Kincaid, Jeanette Fromm, Ann Miller, Brian Grigg, Warwick Watts, and Ian Revell. Four of those key activists, Wilkinson, Downie, Simich and Revell went on to become MPs, Shearer had been an MP and a number of the others stood as National Party candidates. Most of these people enjoyed each other's company and not only worked for Muldoon but dined, partied and even holidayed together.

11   RDM–BSG, 21 August 1989, and John Tremewan–BSG, 29 September 1989.

12   RDM–Wederell, nd [1969], WP 1655, 2/1. Holyoake meant that each new MP should listen and not talk too much at first. They should choose the areas in which they wished in the future to become the caucus expert and thus the logical choice for cabinet minister and having become a minister a possible contender for the prime-ministership, and in other areas where there was insufficient time to become well informed an MP should rely on the expertise of trusted colleagues and use their views and judgements in speaking and voting in the House.

13   Peter Gordon to BSG, 20 February 1990, and Gordon–BSG, 12 March 1990.

14   Peter Gordon to BSG, 20 February 1990.

15   Ibid.

16   Duncan MacIntyre to Wederell, 30 August 1969, WP 1655, 1/9. See also *The Rise and Fall of a Young Turk*, pp 44–45.

17   RDM–Wederell, nd [1969], WP 1655, 2/1. See also RDM article on Lee in *NZ Truth*, 11 December 1973.

18   *The Rise and Fall of a Young Turk*, p 27.

19   John A. Lee to Wederell, 6 May [1969], in which he quotes from an article Lee wrote for *NZ Truth* in 1963, WP 1655, 1/8. See also John A. Lee to RDM, 6 January and 26 May 1982, and RDM to Lee, 29 January and 3 June 1982, MP.

20   A. D. Mackie, Collins Publishers, to Wederell, 8 August 1969, WP 1655, 1/3.

21   RDM–BSG, 1 August 1989.

22   *The Rise and Fall of a Young Turk*, p 47, and RDM–Wederell, nd [1969], WP 1655, 2/1.

23   cit. *Evening Post*, 23 June 1961.

24   *ODT*, 29 June 1961.

25   *Dominion*, 28 June 1961.

26   RDM–Wederell, nd [1969], WP 1655, 2/1.

27   R. M. Algie to Wederell, 28 July 1969, WP 1655, 1/1.

28   George Burns to Wederell, 29 July 1969, WP 1655, 1/2.

29   Bevan Burgess–BSG, 5 March 1990.

30   RDM–BSG, 2 October 1989, and Peter Gordon–BSG, 12 March 1990.

31   *The Rise and Fall of a Young Turk*, pp 53–55. Also RDM–Wederell, nd [1969], WP 1655, 2/1.

32   J. R. Hanan to Wederell, 19 February 1969, WP 1655, 1/7.

33   Muldoon's speech notes, 12 October 1961, are in the Muldoon Papers. See also *The Rise and Fall of a Young Turk*, pp 48–51, *NZ Herald*, 13 October 1961, and *Evening Post*, 13 October 1961.

34   *Auckland Star*, 13 October 1961.

35   RDM–BSG, 2 October 1989.

36   Caucus Minutes, 14 July and 25 August 1960.

37   RDM–BSG, 22 April 1985, and RDM–Wederell, nd [1969], WP 1655, 2/1.

38   Peter Gordon–BSG, 12 March 1990, and RDM–BSG, 22 April 1985.

39   RDM's address to NZ Society of Accountants, nd [1961], WP 1655, 5/6. See also *Dominion*, 6 October 1961.

40   Martin Nestor to Wederell, 13 February 1969, WP 1655, 1/10, and notes in WP 1655, 5/1. For Blanchfield's comments see *Dominion*, 13 July 1962. Holyoake reference in Caucus Minutes, 18 May 1967.

41   See David Mitchell, 'The Nelson Cotton Mill', and *The Rise and Fall of a Young Turk*, pp 56–59.

42   RDM–BSG, 1 August 1989.

43   cit. *Dominion*, 17 August 1961.

44   *NZPD*, v 327, p 1524.

45   RDM–Wederell, nd [1969], WP 1655, 2/1.

46   Ibid.

47   *NZPD*, v 328, p 2724.

48   Ibid, p 2748.

49   Mitchell, 'The Nelson Cotton Mill', p 111.

50   *The Rise and Fall of a Young Turk*, p 58, and

Mitchell, pp 138–9. A very good summary of the dispute is also given by Marshall in his *Memoirs: Volume II*, pp 14–18.

51 *The Rise and Fall of a Young Turk*, p 62.
52 RDM–BSG, 1 August 1989; Peter Gordon to BSG, 20 February 1990; and *The Rise and Fall of a Young Turk*, pp 62–63.
53 RDM–BSG, 1 August 1989.
54 Ibid and Duncan MacIntyre–BSG, 10 July 1991, and Peter Gordon–BSG, 12 March 1990. See also Duncan MacIntyre to Wederell, 30 August 1969, WP 1655, 1/9.
55 Gordon to BSG, 20 February 1990.
56 RDM–BSG, 1 August 1989, and Peter Gordon–BSG, 12 March 1990. See also RDM–Wederell, nd [1969], WP 1655, 2/1.
57 Caucus Minutes 1963.
58 RDM to Holyoake, 10 April 1962, MP.
59 Caucus Minutes, 15 October 1963.
60 Ibid.
61 *The Rise and Fall of a Young Turk*, pp 59–62.
62 Ibid.
63 Ibid.
64 R. Hunter Wade to BSG, 5 August 1992. Wade, who was NZ Commissioner to Singapore 1962–63, was later NZ Ambassador to Japan, South Korea, Germany and Switzerland and Deputy Secretary-General of the Commonwealth.
65 Alan Jenkin–BSG, 10 May 1990, and Alan Jenkin to Wederell, 9 February 1970, WP 1655, 1/7.
66 *Auckland Star*, nd [1963], clipping in MP.

7 *The Under-Secretary 1963–66*

1 Ed. Buckton–BSG, 22 August 1989.
2 Ibid.
3 Ibid.
4 RDM–BSG, 2 October 1989.
5 RDM–BSG, 1 August 1989.
6 RDM–BSG, 2 October 1989.
7 RDM–Wederell, nd [1969], WP 1655, 2/1.
8 Ibid.
9 Ibid.
10 Bernard Galvin–BSG, 25 October 1989.
11 *Auckland Star*, 5 December 1964.
12 *Evening Post*, 5 December 1964.
13 Caucus Minutes, 2 July 1964.
14 Ibid, 13 February, 1964.
15 Ibid, 19 March 1964.
16 Ibid, 29 April 1964.
17 Colin Busfield–BSG, 13 June 1989.
18 Caucus Minutes, 15 October 1964.
19 RDM–BSG, 2 October 1989, and RDM–Wederell, nd [1969], WP 1655, 2/1. See also *The Rise and Fall of a Young Turk*, pp 74–80.
20 RDM–Wederell, nd [1969], WP 1655, 2/1.
21 Ibid.
22 *The Rise and Fall of a Young Turk*, p 77.
23 Ibid.
24 Ibid.
25 The tape of Bick's conversation with Reid was made by another member of the *Compass* team, Ian Johnstone, who describes the incident in *Stand and Deliver*, pp 84–7. See also Muldoon, *The Rise and Fall of a Young Turk*, pp 78–80, and Gordon Bick, *The Compass File*, pp 103–17.
26 Caucus Minutes, 15 September 1966.
27 Ibid, 22 September 1966. The 'pirates' referred to were the first private radio station, Radio Hauraki, which broadcast from a ship just outside New Zealand's three-mile coastal jurisdiction.
28 *The Rise and Fall of a Young Turk*, pp 68–71. See also the detailed programme prepared for RDM by the US Governmental Affairs Institute and RDM's report on the trip, MP. Muldoon kept a detailed diary in his own handwriting which is also in the MP.
29 Fred Shailes–BSG, 19 August 1994.
30 *The Rise and Fall of a Young Turk*, pp 68–71. See also RDM–Wederell, nd [1969], WP 1655, 2/1.
31 RDM–Wederell, nd [1969], WP 1655, 2/1.
32 Caucus Minutes, 20 May 1965.
33 Ibid, 21 May 1965.
34 *New Echo Courier*, 21 September 1966. In the Muldoon Papers there is a file of telegrams from various people including National Party divisional and electorate chairmen, the chairman of the Stock Exchange, and a former mayor of Auckland (Sir John Allum), congratulating Muldoon on his performance against Watt in this programme.
35 Caucus Minutes, 22 September 1966.
36 Ibid, 21 May 1965.
37 Ibid, 12 February 1965.
38 Ibid, 8 April 1965.
39 Ibid, 12 February 1965.
40 For example, D. W. Baker, Secretary to the Treasury, to Lake, 12 May 1966; G. Wilson, Governor of the Reserve Bank, to Lake, 24 May 1966; S. A. McLeod, for Secretary to the Treasury, to Lake, 21 September 1966, MP.
41 Baker to Lake, 12 May 1966, MP.
42 Lake, 'New Zealand's Balance of Payments and Economic Outlook', 9 September 1966.
43 RDM–BSG, 2 October 1989.
44 Kevin Ryan to Wederell, 8 August 1969, WP 1655, 1/11.
45 *Evening Post*, 26 June 1965.
46 Caucus Minutes, 1 December 1966.
47 *The Rise and Fall of a Young Turk*, p 82.
48 Muldoon–Sullivan interview, 31 March 1992.

49   *Sunday Times*, 18 December, 1966.

50   Holyoake interview with W. J. Gardner, 20 March 1970, *cit*. W. J. Gardner, *The Farmer Politician in New Zealand History*, p 18.

51   Duncan MacIntyre–BSG, 10 July 1991, and Peter Gordon–BSG, 12 March 1990. See also *The Rise and Fall of a Young Turk*, pp 81–83, and RDM–BSG, 2 October 1989.

52   Caucus Minutes, 10 February 1967.

53   John Marshall, *Memoirs, Volume II: 1960 to 1988*, p 5.

54   *The Rise and Fall of a Young Turk*, p 85.

8   Minister of Finance 1967–69

1   Tamaki Electorate Minutes, AGM 4 April 1967.

2   The World Bank, *Report on the New Zealand Economy 1968*, esp pp 13–31, pp 13–14.

3   Caucus Minutes, 2 March 1967.

4   Ibid. 3 March 1967.

5   Ibid. 6, 7 and 26 April 1967.

6   *The Rise and Fall of a Young Turk*, p 86.

7   Resolution moved by Pakuranga Electorate and carried after considerable debate at Auckland Divisional Executive meeting, 10 June 1968.

8   Sir Frank Holmes–BSG, 12 March 1990.

9   Caucus Minutes, 8 June 1967.

10   Henry Lang–BSG, 5 March 1990. Muldoon discusses this overseas trip and the devaluation issue in *The Rise and Fall of a Young Turk*, pp 90–96.

11   Caucus Minutes, 23 November 1967.

12   Lang–BSG, 5 March 1990.

13   Caucus Minutes, 23 November 1967.

14   Muldoon to P. Schweitzer, Managing Director IMF, 13 October 1967, MP.

15   McNamara was president of the World Bank from 1968 to 1981 and during that time the World Bank reoriented its focus towards development projects to counter poverty. See M. Gavin and D. Rodrik, 'The World Bank in Historical Perspective', *American Economic Review*, May 1995, pp 329–34.

16   Ed Buckton–BSG, 22 August 1989, and John Martin–BSG, 12 December 1990. Muldoon also discusses 'the toughest personal confrontation of my political career' in *The Rise and Fall of a Young Turk*, pp 116–19.

17   Buckton–BSG, 22 August 1989.

18   *NZPD*, v 361, 8 July 1969, pp 1266–9.

19   Buckton–BSG, 22 August 1989.

20   George Burns to Wederell, 29 July 1969, WP 1655, 1/2.

21   Lang–BSG, 5 March 1990.

22   Ibid.

23   Fred Shailes–BSG, 19 August 1994. Shailes, who was later Auditor-General, was while in Treasury in charge of the coin sets.

24   See summary of the economy during 1968 in *NZ Herald*, 26 December 1968.

25   Caucus Minutes, 16 February and 21 March 1968.

26   *Timaru Herald*, 3 April 1967.

27   *Weekly News*, 3 April 1967.

28   RDM–BSG, 27 September 1989.

29   Lang–BSG, 5 March 1990.

30   *Cit*. Tony Reid, "He puts efficiency ahead of public image', *NZ Weekly News*, 24 March 1969. This was one of two particularly revealing, though as usual self-serving, interviews Muldoon gave in 1968 and 1969. The other was with Robert Gilmore, 'Q and A with Mr Muldoon', *Auckland Star*, 14 December 1968.

31   Ibid.

32   Ibid.

33   Ibid.

34   Jack Shallcrass, to Wederell, 17 February 1969, WP 1655, 1/11.

35   Jack Shallcrass, *The Control of Power*, Perspective 3, Paper published by Farm Road (Wellington) branch of the Labour Party, nd {1987], in which Shallcrass develops his argument. There is a copy of this in the Wederell Papers annotated by Shallcrass with reference to Muldoon in the margins, WP 1655, 1/11.

36   O. S. Hintz to Wederell, 21 July 1969, WP 1655, 1/7.

37   George Burns to Wederell, 29 July 1969, WP 1655, 1/7.

38   Ibid.

39   Norman Shelton–Wederell, 16 August 1969, WP 1655, 4/2.

40   *Australian Financial Review*, 25 November 1969.

41   John Martin–BSG, 12 December 1990. The group of businessmen included Clifford Plimmer, chairman and managing director of Challenge Corporation from 1953 to 1970, and John Meadowcroft, managing director of Ackmead Holdings and President of the National Party 1962–6.

42   Lawrence Browne–BSG, 15 July 1989.

43   C. G. Prebble, Secretary Hatfields Bay Ratepayers' and Residents' Association, to Wederell, 5 September 1969, WP 1655, 1/7.

44   Gordon–BSG, 12 March 1990.

45   Gordon McLauchlan, 'In a Way I Suppose I'm Ruthless', *NZ Weekly News*, 3 April 1967.

46   Jack Shallcrass, 17 February 1969, WP 1655, 1/11.

47   For example, see the assessment of

Muldoon's personality by Brian Edwards, *The Public Eye*, pp 250–258. For a more sympathetic analysis see John Kennedy, *Straight from the Shoulder*, pp 90–102. Kennedy, the editor of the Catholic newspaper *NZ Tablet*, devotes two chapters specifically to Muldoon: Chapter 7, 'The Muldoon Years', pp 79–92, and Chapter 8, 'Muldoon and the Media', pp 93–102. Muldoon also occupies a large part of Chapter 11, 'The Terror of Television', pp 121–32.

48 *NZ Tablet*, 9 August 1967. See also Kennedy, *Straight from the Shoulder*, pp 79–102.

49 *Auckland Star*, nd [December 1968], MP. Also see Dai Hayward to Wederell, 17 January 1969, WP 1655, 1/12; *The Rise and Fall of a Young Turk*, pp 110–111.

50 *Taranaki Herald*, 11 March 1967.

51 John Luxton, statement to conference on Sir Keith Holyoake, Wellington, 20 February 1996.

52 Caucus Minutes, 4 May 1967.

53 Muldoon's version is given in *The Rise and Fall of a Young Turk*, pp 96–99.

54 Caucus Minutes, 3 July 1968. See also 8, 9 and 10 July 1968.

55 Ibid.

56 *The Rise and Fall of a Young Turk*, p 98.

57 Caucus Minutes, 31 October and 14 November 1968.

58 Gordon–BSG, 20 February and 12 March 1990.

59 Treasury Report to RDM, 10 May 1968, MP.

60 L. E. Adams, Principal of Glendowie College and President NZPPTA 1964, to Wederell, 30 December 1968, WP 1655, 1/1.

61 'School and University Enrolment Projections for the Years 1967–80', E2, 1967. See also reports on inflow and outflow of graduates provided by Department of Statistics, 21 February 1968, MP. The New Zealand Department of Scientific and Industrial Research published in 1964 'Scientific Research in New Zealand. Expenditure and Manpower 1953–62'. This was compiled by Conor P. McBride, who also authored with Christine de Joux in 1966 a similar report covering the period 1926–66 for the National Research Advisory Council. In 1967, for the same Council, McBride wrote a 'Report on University Entrance Scholars', which overlapped with a similar report by G. W. Parkyn, 'The Problem of Failure' for the New Zealand Council for Educational Research. For a discussion of Muldoon's attempts to hold expenditure on buildings

in the tertiary sector 1967–69 see also John Gould, *The University Grants Committee 1961–1986: A History*, pp 48–49.

62 Treasury to Minister of Finance, 19 April and 10 May 1968, MP. Current expenditure was projected to rise from $19.2 million to $30.4 million and capital expenditure on new buildings from $13.2 million to $30.1 million.

63 Buckton to Muldoon, 20 December 1968. See also H. G. Lang, Secretary to the Treasury, to Chairman, Cabinet Economic Committee, 10 February 1969. MP.

64 *NZ Weekly News*, 24 March 1969.

65 For Muldoon's version see *Rise and Fall of a Young Turk*, pp 102–105. Also RDM–BSG, 22 September 1989.

66 Copies of all these speeches are found in the Muldoon Papers in a file entitled 'Education File 1968–69'. The file also includes Treasury reports, various other reports, press statements, and newspaper clippings. See also RDM–BSG, 24 February 1989. The speech was published with others under the title 'Education and the New Zealand Economy' in Michael Volkerling (ed), *The Politics of Education*, pp 10–27.

67 *Craccum*, 13 March 1969. Ruth Butterworth and Nicholas Tarling, *A Shakeup Anyway: Government and the Universities in New Zealand in a Decade of Reform*, pp 38–40, note that in his Curious Cove address 'Muldoon in fact made it clear that he wished to avoid a clash between government and universities. He believed that the rapid increase in expenditure on universities . . . would reach a point when "some Minister of Finance will say 'stop, I cannot finance this'.". . . . what he had pressed for was "an examination . . . by the appropriate authorities so that this head-on collision may be avoided."'

68 Interview with Llewellyn published in the *Christchurch Star*, 9 August 1968.

69 *Press*, 3 February 1969.

70 *Waikato Times*, 13 March 1969.

71 Ibid.

72 Ibid.

73 Caucus Minutes, 16 October 1969.

74 Ibid.

75 Ibid.

76 MacIntyre–BSG, 10 July 1991.

77 RDM–BSG, 2 October 1989.

78 *Auckland Star*, 14 December 1968.

79 *NZ Herald*, 3 May 1969.

80 Gordon–BSG, 12 March 1990, and MacIntyre–BSG, 10 July 1991.

81 Caucus Minutes, 1 May 1969.

82 Ibid. 24 and 31 July 1969.

83 Transcript and comment in Brian Edwards,

The Public Eye, pp 152–154. For Muldoon's version see Rise and Fall of a Young Turk, pp 113–114. Muldoon also debated on radio with Hugh Watt, Bob Tizard and Mrs Whetu Tirikatene-Sullivan.

84 Australian Financial Review, 25 November 1969.

85 W. F. Massey, the Reform Party leader and also a farmer, arguably won in 1911, 1914, 1919 and 1922 but his party never had an absolute majority of seats in Parliament and he became Prime Minister in 1912 only because six Liberal MPs changed parties.

86 Gordon–BSG, 12 March 1990. Holyoake also admitted in his retirement address to the National Party caucus that he 'expected defeat' in 1969. Caucus Minutes, 28 April 1977.

9   The End of the Holyoake Era 1969–72

1 Marshall deals with this topic fully in his Memoirs, Volume II, particularly Chapter 8 which he entitled revealingly 'A sentence of hard Labour', pp 115–32.

2 Ibid, p 115.

3 MacIntyre–BSG, 10 July 1991. See also Gordon–BSG, 12 March 1990.

4 RDM–BSG, 2 October 1989. See also Muldoon, The Rise and Fall of a Young Turk, pp 124–44, and Muldoon, pp 66–7.

5 Auckland Divisional Executive Minutes, 6 March 1972.

6 RDM interview with Ian Fraser, Seven Days, 27 July 1975, and Muldoon, Muldoon, op cit., p 153.

7 Muldoon, The New Zealand Economy, p 77, and Jim Eagles and Colin James, The Making of a New Zealand Prime Minister, p 72.

8 Muldoon The Rise and Fall of a Young Turk, pp 124–5.

9 Ibid, p 125.

10 The Todd family is New Zealand's richest family and controls New Zealand's largest privately owned company, the Wellington-based Todd Corporation. The company was started as a wool scouring and gold and coal mining company in 1885. It subsequently moved into automobile importing and motor assembly (Todd Motors); oil importing and marketing (Europa); petrochemicals, notably Maui and Kapuni gas; telecommunications (Clear and Sky TV); forestry (Baigent); casinos (Harrah's Sky City); and property (Shortland Properties). The family also funds two major charitable trusts, the Todd Foundation and the Todd Charitable Trust, which support medicine, the humanities and the arts.

11 A. R. Low, Governor, Reserve Bank of New Zealand, to RDM, 4 July 1969; D. A. Stevens, Commissioner, Inland Revenue Department, to RDM, 18 February and 22 October 1970 and 11 April 1972, MP.

12 See Gilbey's Gin File, 1971, MP. Muldoon discusses the incident in The Rise and Fall of a Young Turk, pp 131–3. For a copy of the Gilbey's advertisement see Auckland Star, 13 May 1971.

13 David Exel with Rudd Hughes, Gallery interview, 27 July 1971.

14 David Exel with RDM and Bill Andersen, Gallery, 29 July 1971.

15 I. G. Lythgoe to RDM, 11 August 1971, in which Lythgoe informed Muldoon that he would be making this statement at the PSA's annual conference, MP.

16 Muldoon's File on 'Extremists 1948–75', MP. The file included a large collection of pamphlets, press clippings, statements and minutes on or by communists. One of Muldoon's informants on the Communist International and the way it worked was the former Auckland Labour MP (1946–69), Ritchie MacDonald.

17 Andersen, Gallery, 29 July 1971.

18 H. E. Gilbert, Director of the SIS, to RDM, 4 August 1971, MP.

19 For Muldoon's version see The Rise and Fall of a Young Turk, pp 134–6. For Marshall's see Memoirs, Volume II, pp 118–19. See Gallery, 7 September 1971, Sunday News, 5 September 1971, and Auckland Star, 7 September 1971. Also NZ Herald, 18 and 19 May 1972, and Auckland Star, 18 and 23 May 1972.

20 Brooks v Muldoon [1973] 1 NZLR 1.

21 NZBC 'Lobby Report', 11 September 1971.

22 Gallery, 7 and 9 September 1971.

23 Ian Templeton, Auckland Star, 11 September 1971.

24 Cit. Keith Hancox in article sent to the Age, Melbourne, on 26 January 1972. Typescript in MP. See also Marshall, Memoirs, Volume II, p 159.

25 Gordon–BSG, 12 March 1990, and MacIntyre–BSG, 10 July 1991.

26 NZ Herald, 20 November 1971, refers to the Chapman faction campaign to replace Holyoake with Marshall. See also for a full discussion of both the 1972 and 1974 leadership contests between Marshall and Muldoon, Keith Jackson, 'Political Leadership and Succession in the New Zealand National Party'.

27 Stuart Masters–BSG, 31 August 1993. See also Muldoon, review of volume 2 of Sir

John Marshall's *Memoirs* in *Press*, 7 October 1989. Muldoon also claimed to have been shown the letter by Holyoake who had ripped the letter up on receiving it but had subsequently stuck it together with sellotape and put it in his safe. The letter claimed that Holyoake was too old and was making mistakes and should retire in Marshall's favour.

28 Masters–BSG, 31 August 1993, and George Chapman, comment at Conference on Sir Keith Holyoake 1996.

29 Gordon–BSG, 12 March 1990.

30 For a fuller discussion see Robert Rabel, 'The Dovish Hawk: Keith Holyoake and the Vietnam War' in Margaret Clark (ed), *Sir Keith Holyoake: Towards a Political Biography*, pp 173–93.

31 Gordon–BSG, 12 March 1990.

32 NZBC 'Lobby Report', 11 September 1971.

33 Ibid.

34 Robert Gilmore interview with RDM, *Auckland Star*, 17 September 1971.

35 RDM–BSG, 2 October 1989.

36 Alf Allen–BSG, 4 August 1985.

37 Caucus Minutes, 2 February 1972.

38 *Press*, 3 July 1972.

39 Caucus Minutes, 2 February 1972. For Muldoon's version of the changes of leadership in 1972 see *The Rise and Fall of a Young Turk*, pp 125–9 and 136–8, and *Muldoon*, pp 69–70; for Marshall's version see *Memoirs, Volume II*, pp 157–60. A close participant-observer was Templeton; see *All Honourable Men*, pp 22–23.

40 Marshall to Keith Jackson, 7 April 1975; Caucus Minutes, 2 February 1972; and Gordon–BSG, 12 March 1990.

41 *NZ Herald*, 18 March 1972. This margin was never denied though Muldoon found it difficult to accept.

42 MacIntyre–BSG, 10 July 1991.

43 Gordon–BSG, 12 March 1990.

44 Caucus Minutes, 3 February 1972.

45 Marshall, *Memoirs, Volume II*, pp 162–3.

46 Caucus Minutes, 11 May 1972.

47 Ibid, 29 June 1972.

48 Ibid, 15 June 1972.

49 *NZ Herald*, 26 May 1972. For Muldoon's version of events see *The Rise and Fall of a Young Turk*, pp 146–8.

50 RDM to R. J. Birchfield, Managing Editor, *NBR*, 29 August 1972.

51 Bell, Gully and Co. for ANZ Bank to RDM, 14 June 1972, MP.

52 Muldoon, *The Rise and Fall of a Young Turk*, p 148.

53 David Inglis of Radio New Zealand *cit.* Kennedy, *Straight from the Shoulder*, p 93.

54 Muldoon, *The Rise and Fall of a Young Turk*,

p 148. See Chapter 10, pp 143–60, 'The Media'.

55 David Beatson–BSG, 5 April 1990.

56 Muldoon, 'We'll be back', in Edwards, *Right Out: Labour Victory 1972*, p 63.

57 Edwards, *Right Out*, p 9.

58 Brian Edwards, *The Public Eye*, esp pp 150–4 and 250–73.

59 Muldoon, *The Rise and Fall of a Young Turk*, p 150.

60 Edwards, *Public Eye*, pp 254–73. For Muldoon's version see *The Rise and Fall of a Young Turk*, pp 154–6.

61 Edwards, *The Public Eye*, pp 257–8.

62 Ibid, pp 261 and 264.

63 *The Rise and Fall of a Young Turk*, pp 155–7.

64 *Gallery*, 19 May 1972. Marshall was active in the Presbyterian Church and Adams-Schneider had been a member of the Open Brethren and later a Baptist lay preacher.

65 *Dominion*, 12 June 1972.

66 *NZ Law Journal*, 18 July 1972.

67 *Dominion*, 3 August 1972.

68 A very good summary of the Manapouri issue is Wayne Thompson, 'Legacy of the Lake', *NZ Herald*, 30 December 1992.

69 For Muldoon's version of the 1972 election campaign see *The Rise and Fall of a Young Turk*, pp 140–3, and Muldoon, 'We'll be back', in Brian Edwards, *Right Out: Labour Victory 1972*, pp 59–71. For Marshall's version see *Memoirs, Volume II*, pp 171–81, and Marshall, 'And that was it' in Edwards, *Right Out*, pp 39–58. In addition to Edwards's book there were four others on the 1972 election: Robert Chapman, *Marginals '72*; Eagles and James, *The Making of a New Zealand Prime Minister*; Warren Page and Brian Lockstone, *Landslide '72*; and Ian Templeton and Keith Eunson, *In the Balance: Election '72*.

70 Marshall, *Memoirs, Volume II*, p 178.

71 Edwards, *Right Out*, p 4.

72 Ibid. pp 4–5.

73 Eagles and James, *The Making of a New Zealand Prime Minister*, pp 219–20.

74 Muldoon, 'We'll be back', in Edwards, *Right Out*, p 70.

75 Chapman, *Marginals '72*, discusses these seats in detail and in Table 1, p 42, lists the twelve most likely to fall to Labour: Awarua, Taupo, Hastings, East Coast Bays, Whangarei, Gisborne, Wanganui, Oamaru, Hamilton West, Invercargill, Otago Central and Eden. All except East Coast Bays were lost. Of Chapman's seven long shots Kapiti, Hamilton East, and Rangiora also fell.

76 Marshall, *Memoirs, Volume II*, p 178, and Muldoon, 'We'll be back', in Edwards, *Right Out: Labour Victory 1972*, p 59.

77 Eagles and James, *The Making of a New Zealand Prime Minister*, pp 212–13.

10 In Opposition 1972–75

1 Caucus Minutes, 7 December 1972 and 30 August 1973. *NZ Herald*, 4 February 1973, identified three groups in the party: old-style conservatives, a conservative-liberal element, and young liberals.

2 Caucus Minutes, 7 December 1972. See also 30 August 1973.

3 Ibid, 30 August 1973.

4 Ibid, 1 March 1973.

5 Ibid, 1 February 1973.

6 For a detailed history from Meates' point of view see *Meates v Attorney-General* [1979] 1 NZLR 415; [1983] NZLR 308.

7 E.g., Kirk's private secretary Margaret Hayward records in *Diary of the Kirk Years*, p 117, that on 5 March 1973 Meates contacted Kirk seeking assistance and claiming Freer and Rowling were not very supportive but that Kirk, 'as far as I know, has not replied to Kevin. He seems to be keeping well out of it.' Again on 7 May 1973, p 131, she notes that 'Meates has gone ahead with establishing Matai Industries on the Coast, though he knows the boss [Kirk] wants no involvement in the project'.

8 J. R. Marshall to K. F. Meates, 30 April 1973, MP, and *Christchurch Star*, 24 March 1973.

9 *Meates v Attorney-General* [1979] 1 NZLR 415; [1983] NZLR 308.

10 Hayward, *Diary of the Kirk Years*, p 179, 15 November 1973.

11 RDM to Freer, 9 February 1974, MP, details these approaches and Muldoon's views on the situation.

12 Henry Lang, Secretary of the Treasury, to W. E. Rowling, Minister of Finance, 24 December 1973, MP.

13 Kevin Meates to Norman Kirk, 8 August 1973, MP.

14 Ibid.

15 See detailed minutes of the meeting on 15 February 1974, MP. There are 31 typed pages of transcript of the meeting.

16 Ibid. Other references to the assurances given can be found in correspondence such as R. Thompson to W. E. Rowling, 14 December 1973, and Thompson to Kirk, 16 July 1973 and 14 January 1974, MP.

17 Ibid.

18 Ibid.

19 E.g. Freer in Parliament, *NZPD*, v 417, 2 June 1978, pp 595–8. See also *Press*, 3 June 1978.

20 *Meates v Attorney-General* [1979] 1 NZLR 415; [1983] NZLR 308.

21 See RDM reply to question for oral answer by L. Schultz, *NZPD*, v 420, 7 September 1978, p 3259. Also Muldoon press statement re Matai Industries, 15 December 1978, MP.

22 E.g. *cit. Auckland Star*, 18 April 1974.

23 Auckland Divisional Executive Minutes, 11 March 1974.

24 The author discussed the 1974 leadership change with Baker, Bray, Brenton-Rule, Dempsey, McLay, Masters, and Tremewan.

25 Tamaki Electorate Minutes, 2 and 30 November, 1973.

26 Auckland Divisional Executive Minutes, 11 February 1974.

27 Ibid, 17 February 1974.

28 Caucus Minutes, 19 July 1973.

29 Ibid.

30 RDM–BSG, 2 October 1989, and Ken Comber–BSG, 7 March 1990.

31 Marshall to Keith Jackson, 7 April 1975. See also Keith Jackson, 'Political Leadership and Succession in the New Zealand National Party', p 13. The article deals in detail with Muldoon's accession to the leadership in 1974. Professor Jackson also in August 1993 discussed the matter with me and gave me access to his research material, including letters to him commenting on a draft of the article from Muldoon, 29 December 1974, and Marshall, 7 April 1975. In his letter Muldoon wrote that the article was 'close to the mark'. See also a revised version of the article in Stephen Levine (ed.), *Politics in New Zealand*, pp 161–81.

32 Ibid.

33 Ibid.

34 Caucus Minutes, 31 May 1973.

35 Ibid., 17 May 1973.

36 Ibid., 21 July 1972 and 1 March 1973.

37 Ibid., 1 November 1973.

38 RDM–BSG, 24 July 1989. Muldoon discusses this trip and his impressions in *The Rise and Fall of a Young Turk*, pp 190–4.

39 Gair–BSG, 14 July 1985.

40 Marshall, *Memoirs, Volume II,* pp 196–7.

41 J. B. Gordon to BSG, 12 March 1990.

42 Muldoon to Jackson, nd [1975]. For Muldoon's version of the leadership change see Muldoon, *Muldoon*, pp 84–85 and 87–90. For Marshall's version see his *Memoirs, Volume II*, pp 213–24. See also Templeton, *All Honourable Men*, pp 29–33, and Zavos, *The Real Muldoon*, pp 130–8. Templeton, although not an MP at that time, was Marshall's personal assistant and as secretary of caucus kept the caucus minutes.

43 Margaret Hayward, *Diary of the Kirk Years*, p 154, which is a Labour version of the event. Also discussion between the author and Margaret Hayward, 8 December 1997. For Muldoon's version see *The Rise and Fall of a Young Turk*, pp 186–9. Also *NZPD*, v 384, 27 July 1973, pp 2781–2 and 31 July 1973, pp 2815–20. See also Caucus Minutes, 2 August 1973.

44 Hayward, *Diary of the Kirk Years*, p 154.

45 Public Expenditure Committee and Department of Statistics File, 1973, MP. Muldoon discusses this incident in *The Rise and Fall of a Young Turk*, pp 189–90.

46 Marshall to Jackson, 7 April 1975. Also Marshall–BSG, 9 July 1985.

47 Brian Talboys–BSG, 20 April 1990. Even in retrospect Talboys believed caucus had made the correct choice in 1974. See also Templeton–BSG, 9 July 1985, and Gordon–BSG, 12 March 1990. Templeton gives a very interesting comparison of Marshall and Muldoon as leaders and deals with the 1974 leadership change in *All Honourable Men*, pp 28–33. He agrees with Talboys by noting, p 31, that 'Members . . . liked Marshall but resented his amateur approach to their war . . . in Muldoon they had a ready-made answer to their hopes.' Chapman, *The Years of Lightning*, p 86, observed in hindsight that 'the choice being made by the Parliamentary section was not so much between Jack Marshall and Rob Muldoon, but between Jack Marshall and the prospects of a National victory in 1975.'

48 J. B. Gordon to Keith Jackson, 17 October 1974. In possession of Professor Jackson.

49 Ibid. See also Gordon–BSG, 12 March 1990, and Templeton, in *All Honourable Men*, pp 30–31.

50 Muldoon to Jackson, nd [1975].

51 *Sunday News*, 10 March 1974.

52 *NZ Truth*, 1 October 1974.

53 *The Rise and Fall of a Young Turk*, p 194.

54 Notice of Seminar on Saturday 2 19 June 1974.

55 Chapman–BSG, 9 July 1985, and Gair–BSG, 14 July 1985. See also Chapman–BSG, 6 March 1990 and Gair–BSG, 8 March 1990.

56 Marshall, *Memoirs, Volume II*, p 203, and Margaret Hayward, *Diary of the Kirk Years*, pp 265 and 267. Hayward records that Kirk 'is delighted [at the prospect of Muldoon replacing Marshall]. He dislikes everything Mr Muldoon stands for, and relishes the thought of showing him up.'

57 RDM–BSG, 2 October 1989. Muldoon's version of the campaign to make him leader in 1974 is found in his second

autobiography *Muldoon*, pp 82–90. Marshall's version is found in his *Memoirs, Volume II*, pp 213–24.

58 RDM–BSG, 2 October 1989.

59 Gordon to Jackson, 17 October 1974.

60 Gair–BSG, 14 July 1985.

61 Jackson, 'Political Leadership and Succession in the New Zealand National Party', *op cit.*, p 13.

62 Symmans–BSG, 19 February 1993. For Marshall's version of the 1974 leadership change see his *Memoirs, Volume II*, pp 213–23.

63 Although recorded as a unanimous resolution, two pro-Muldoon members of the Executive abstained rather than suggest disloyalty to the existing leader by voting against the motion. Gordon to Jackson, 17 October 1974. For Chapman's version of the leadership battle, the Executive meeting of 11–12 June 1974, and Chapman's own role in the situation see Chapman, *The Years of Lightning*, pp 82–87. The author discussed this meeting with eleven of the people present.

64 RDM to Jackson, 29 December 1974. Muldoon did at the conference oppose challenges to sitting MPs provoking some hostility from delegates who felt his own challenge to Marshall revealed a double standard.

65 Gordon to Jackson, 17 October 1974. See also Marshall, *Memoirs, Volume II*, p 220, writing that Talboys and Gordon 'reported that opinion was divided.'

66 Marshall to all National MPs including 'Dear Rob', 2 July 1974, MP, and RDM to all caucus members, 2 July 1974, MP.

67 Muldoon–BSG, 2 October 1989.

68 Marshall, *Memoirs, Volume II*, p 221. Muldoon, *Muldoon*, p 88 claimed 28 out of 32 MPs supported a change.

69 Gair–BSG, 14 July 1985

70 *Cit.* Marshall, *Memoirs, Volume II*, pp 222–3. Unfortunately, the minutes for this particular meeting of caucus have gone missing from the caucus minutes deposited in the Turnbull or kept by the Parliamentary caucus. Marshall, in his *Memoirs, Volume II*, quotes at some length from them.

71 Gerald Hensley–BSG, 19 August 1994. See also RDM–BSG, 22 April 1985. For Marshall's version of his discussions with Holyoake about the latter's retirement see Marshall, *Memoirs, Volume II*, pp 157–9. For Marshall's discussion with Holyoake in 1974 see *Memoirs, Volume II*, p 220. Templeton, *All Honourable Men*, p 32, describes a meeting between Holyoake and

Marshall about the time of the leadership change and gives his opinion of the reasons for Holyoake's antipathy towards Marshall.

72   RDM to Jackson, 29 December 1974. See also Zavos, *The Real Muldoon,* p 137.

73   *Press,* 6 July 1974. See also Chapman, *The Years of Lightning,* p 83.

74   Ibid., p 85.

75   Stuart Masters–BSG, 31 August 1993.

76   Auckland Division Executive Minutes, 2 August 1974.

77   Waikato Division Sub-Executive Minutes, 7 May 1974.

78   Ibid., 9 July 1974.

79   Irene Hanan to RDM, 25 July 1974, MP.

80   *NZ Herald,* 4 February 1973. See also *NZ Herald,* 28 February 1973, and *Auckland Star,* 20 March 1973, for a fuller discussion of Pol-Link's intentions.

81   E.g. *Auckland Star,* 21 September 1974.

82   RDM–BSG, 22 September 1989.

83   RDM–BSG, 14 December 1991.

84   Ian Fraser interview with Muldoon, *Seven Days,* 27 July 1975.

85   Ibid.

86   *NZ Truth,* 6 May 1975, and Muldoon, Submission to the Privileges Committee, 25 June 1975, MP.

87   *Auckland Star,* 24 July 1974. He subsequently repeated such sentiments, e.g. *South Auckland Courier,* 1 June 1975.

88   *Sunday News,* 15 June 1975.

89   E.g. David Beatson interview with Muldoon and Bill Andersen, *Nationwide,* 6 August 1974, and *Sunday Times,* 11 August 1974.

90   See Tony Neary and Jack Kelleher, *Neary: The Price of Principle,* pp 124–5, for Neary's recollections of this programme; T. Skinner and J. Berry, *Man to Man,* pp 142–5 for Skinner's; and Muldoon, *Muldoon,* pp 101–2, for Muldoon's.

91   John Tremewan–BSG, 29 September 1989.

92   Audio-recording of the programme in the Robert and Noeline Chapman Audio-Visual Archive, Political Studies Department, The University of Auckland.

93   E.g. Skinner, *Man to Man,* p 142, and Neary, *Neary: The Price of Principle,* p 124.

94   The material is still extant in MP.

95   For Muldoon's version of this incident see Muldoon, *Muldoon,* pp 101–4.

96   For Jones' version of this incident see Jones, *Memories of Muldoon,* pp 27–32. See also Zavos, *The Real Muldoon,* pp 151–4, *NZ Herald,* 26, 27 and 28 August 1974, and *Auckland Star,* 26 August 1974.

97   Jones, *Memories of Muldoon,* p 28.

98   W. H. A. Sharp, Commissioner of Police to Minister of Police, 3 September, 1974, MP.

99   Sharp to Minister of Police, 3 September

1974, *op cit.*

100 John Tremewan–BSG, 29 September 1989.

101 *Auckland Star,* 26 August 1974.

102 Ibid.

103 Muldoon, *Muldoon,* p 103.

104 *NZ Herald,* 27 August 1974.

105 Ibid.

106 Jones, *Memories of Muldoon,* p 32.

107 Eg. *Evening Post,* 21 September 1974.

108 Ibid.

109 *Auckland Star,* 21 September 1974.

110 *Dominion,* 19 September 1974.

111 File of material on Muldoon's public image 1974 and 1975, MP.

112 *Auckland Star,* 14 September 1974. See also 11 and 12 September 1974.

113 *Auckland Star,* 21 September 1974.

114 E.g. motion passed to that effect, Auckland Divisional Executive Minutes, 2 December 1974.

115 Highet *cit.* Auckland Divisional Executive Minutes, 2 December 1974.

116 Sloane *cit.* Auckland Divisional Council Minutes, 3 March 1975.

117 Report to Auckland Divisional Executive, 2 September 1974.

118 Ibid. Semple had been a fiery and controversial 'Red Fed' union leader and Labour MP during the first half of the twentieth century.

119 RDM article in *Dominion,* 21 December 1974.

120 *Levin Weekly News,* 11 June, 1975.

121 Ibid.

122 Mrs Alice Wylie–BSG, 13 September 1985.

123 Tamaki Electorate Chairman's Memorandum, 13 June 1978.

124 'Muldoon *cit. NZ Truth,* 1 October 1974.

11   *The 1975 Election*

1   David Elworthy to RDM, 1 December 1972, MP.

2   *The Rise and Fall of a Young Turk* was first published on 11 July 1974 with a print of 9982. The first reprint was on 30 July (5060 copies); the second on 20 August (9845 copies); the third on 1 November (7649 copies). By 12 November, i.e. almost exactly 4 months after first publication, 28,415 of the 32,536 copies had already been sold and by 1 April 1975 Muldoon had been paid $24,839.06 in royalties. See Royalty Statement, 7 December 1975, MP.

3   Ray Richards to RDM, 7 February 1974, MP, and David Elworthy to RDM, 7 February 1974, MP.

4   David Elworthy to RDM, 16 July 1974, MP.

5   RDM–BSG, 14 August 1989.

6 An interesting and perceptive review of the first two of Muldoon's books is Keith Sinclair, 'The Red Hand of Tamaki'.

7 Fred Davies, General Manager, Reeds, to RDM, 3 July 1978, MP.

8 Paul Bradwell to RDM, 15 July 1982, MP.

9 Bradwell to RDM, 30 September and 2 October 1986, MP.

10 Denis Wederell to RDM, 14 October 1969. See also Wederell to RDM, 31 July 1971, WP 1655, 1/9, and G. C. A. Wall, Editor, A. H. and A. W. Reed, to Wederell, 13 August and 3 September 1969, WP 1655, 1/13. Wall had been overruled about publishing by three other readers (Ray Richards, A. W. Reed and David Elworthy) who believed that Muldoon 'needs more crises and victories before the time is right' and might fade between 1969–72, would not become leader in 1972, and might also be eclipsed by Labour.

11 Wall to Wederell, 3 September 1969, WP 1655, 1/13.

12 Wederell to RDM, 10 December 1972, WP 1655, 1/9.

13 Spiro Zavos, interview with Robert Gilmore, *Auckland Star*, 16 August 1978.

14 Ibid.

15 Ibid.

16 Ibid.

17 Lawrence Browne–BSG, 15 July 1989. See also *Prime Time*, TV1, 18 August 1978, audio-tape in the Robert and Noeline Chapman Audio-Visual Archive, The University of Auckland.

18 Muldoon, *My Way*, p 125.

19 RDM to *Listener*, 2 September 1978, p 6. Zavos replied *Listener*, 9 September 1978, p 10, sourcing the assertion to Freer.

20 Muldoon, *My Way*, pp 125–7.

21 *Cit.* Ian Fraser interview with RDM, *Seven Days*, 27 July 1975.

22 Jonathan Hunt–BSG, 13 March 1990.

23 RDM to W. E. Rowling, 10 September 1974, MP. See also Tony Potter, 'First lady from old school', obituary of Dame Ruth Kirk, *Sunday Star-Times*, 26 March 2000.

24 RDM to R. G. Collins, Chairman, Board of TV1, 21 October and 30 October 1975, MP.

25 Chapman *cit.* Auckland Divisional Executive Minutes, 3 March 1975.

26 Caucus minutes, 31 January 1975.

27 *NZPD*, v 331, 2 August 1962, p 1204.

28 Caucus minutes, 31 January and 3 April 1975.

29 Caucus minutes, 8 May 1975.

30 Hunt–BSG, 13 March 1990.

31 *Cit.* Ian Fraser and agreed to by RDM, *Seven Days*, 29 July 1975.

32 For a sympathetic biography of Rowling see John Henderson, *Rowling: The Man and the Myth*. Among the obituaries that by Tony Verdon, *NZ Herald*, 1 November 1995, is a good short assessment.

33 Trip Book in possession of Gray Nelson.

34 Caucus minutes, 21 March 1975.

35 Tamaki Electorate chairman's Memorandum, 16 February 1976.

36 The branches were Glendowie, St. Heliers, Achilles Point, Kohimarama, Mission Bay, St. Thomas, Orakei and Glen Taylor.

37 See Confidential Memorandum by John Tremewan, Tamaki Electorate Chairman, 14 June 1974.

38 *Sunday News*, 8 June 1975. Other meetings were at Wanganui (9 April), Hastings (14 April), Lower Hutt (17 April), Invercargill (19 April), Birkenhead (7 May), Greymouth (12 May), Gisborne (19 May), Tasman (25 June), Te Awamutu (30 June), Napier (9 July), Whakatane (6 August), Tokoroa (12 August), Palmerston North (20 August), Whangarei (1 September), Dunedin (5 September), Eden (8 September), Blenheim (24 September), and East Coast Bays (4 October).

39 Stuart Masters–BSG, 31 August 1993.

40 H. J. Mackley, Colenso, to Chapman and Leay, 29 July 1975, NPP 89/75, 79/4.

41 Caucus Minutes, 29 May and 5 June 1975.

42 Ian Fraser interview with RDM, *Seven Days*, 27 July 1975.

43 Ibid.

44 Muldoon, *Sunday Times*, 7 December 1975. In a subsequent speech to a Canadian audience in 1982 Muldoon also observed in regard to the comment about wishing to leave New Zealand 'no worse than I found it': 'Had I been a politician from some great continental power, perhaps I would have subscribed to a rather grander vision. In fact, given the external shocks we have had to cope with, even the modest goal of mine has proved difficult enough.' Muldoon address to the Canadian Club, Ottawa, 10 September 1982, in *NZ Foreign Affairs Review*, v 32 no 3, July–September 1982, p 13.

45 E.g. RDM memo to all candidates, 19 November 1975, and Chapman to RDM, 13 November 1975, MP.

46 See Templeton to RDM, 24 September and 13 November 1975; Young to RDM, 10 and 14 November 1975; Mark to RDM, 21 August, 22 September, 7, 13, 20 October and 7 November 1975; and RDM to Mark, 24 and 30 September, 7, 14, 31 October and 19 November 1975, MP.

47 RDM memo to all candidates, 19 November 1975.

48 Caucus Minutes, 18 September 1975.

49 RDM–BSG, 27 September 1989.

50 Caucus Minutes, 8 May 1975. See also National Party 1975 General Election Policy, Number 8, Immigration.

51 Frank Gill cit. Auckland Divisional Executive Minutes, 2 September 1974

52 Muldoon's Abortion file 1974–75, MP. For a detailed discussion of this issue see Raewyn Stone, 'The Political Response to the Question of Abortion in New Zealand from 1970–1975'.

53 Muldoon's Homosexual Law Reform File 1974, MP.

54 Caucus Minutes, 16 August 1973.

55 Ibid. 22 March 1973.

56 RDM articles in Truth, 4 September 1973.

57 Tamaki Electorate Minutes, 11 October 1974.

58 Auckland Divisional Executive Minutes, 2 September 1974.

59 Rowling interview, cit. Stone, 'The Political Response to the Question of Abortion in New Zealand from 1970–75', p 340.

60 RDM article in NZ Truth, 11 September 1973.

61 Caucus Minutes, 26 March 1975.

62 Ibid., 23 April 1975. SPUC was the anti-abortion Society for the Protection of the Unborn Child.

63 Ibid.

64 Ibid., 18 September 1975.

65 Ibid., 25 September 1975.

66 Ibid., 18 September 1975.

67 Waring–BSG, 24 February 1993, Wood–BSG, 17 April 1985 and Caucus Minutes, 18 September 1975.

68 Caucus Minutes, 26 March 1975.

69 Waring–BSG, 24 February 1993.

70 H. J. Mackley, Colenso, to Chapman and Leay, 29 July 1975, NPP.

71 Caucus Minutes, 9 October 1975.

72 Cameron was National's candidate for Heretaunga in 1975 and woman vice-president of the National Party 1976–77. Young and Templeton were the wives of the National MPs Venn Young and Hugh Templeton. All three women were intelligent, independent, vigorous and socially liberal.

73 Ibid., 18 September 1975.

74 RDM–BSG 22 September 1989.

75 Caucus Minutes, 13 September 1973. For Muldoon's criticism of Labour's superannuation scheme see Muldoon, The Rise and Fall of a Young Turk, pp 180–1. For other contemporary analyses see Barry Gustafson, 'Social Democracy in New Zealand'; Barry Gustafson, 'Education, Health and Social Welfare', in Ray Goldstein and Rod Alley, Labour in Power. Promise and Performance, pp 61–80; and

Michael Bassett, The Third Labour Government, pp 81–91.

76 M. A. Wall, Colenso, advertising proposal, 11 September 1975.

77 RDM interviewed by Ian Fraser, Seven Days, 27 July 1975.

78 National Party Policy Statement on Superannuation, 24 June 1975. Also National Party 1975 General Election Policy, Number 6, Superannuation.

79 Caucus Minutes, 9 October 1975.

80 John Tremewan, Tamaki Electorate Chairman, Memorandum, 14 June 1975.

81 Bob Harvey, 'Labour Pains', p 63, details his and Exel's setting up of the campaign.

82 Sympathetic descriptions of the Citizens for Rowling campaign are found in John Henderson, Rowling: The Man and the Myth, pp 136–8, and Neary: The Price of Principle, pp 125–7. Unsympathetic analyses are found in Muldoon, Muldoon, pp 114–16; Chapman, The Years of Lightning, pp 110–12, and Jones, Memories of Muldoon, pp 58–61.

83 Muldoon, Muldoon, p 115.

84 Neary, Neary: The Price of Principle, p 126, Bob Jones–BSG, 23 April 1990, and Jones, Memories of Muldoon, pp 33–42.

85 Neary, op cit., p 126.

86 Exel to members of Victoria University of Wellington staff, November 1975. The most detailed account of the Citizens for Rowling Campaign is Kevin P. Clements, 'The Citizens for Rowling Campaign: An Insider's View'. The intellectual community generally came to loathe Muldoon as indicated by how writers used him negatively in New Zealand literature, e.g. see Brian Easton, 'Muldoon, Robert', in The Oxford Companion to New Zealand Literature, pp 383–4.

87 Press, 24 October 1975.

88 National Research Bureau Poll taken 13 November 1975 in NZ Herald, 26 November 1975.

89 A. C. A. McDonald to RDM, 18 November 1975. A large number of such letters are found in the Muldoon Papers.

90 Rev. John Drew to RDM, 17 November 1975, MP.

91 Douglas Smith to RDM, 18 November 1975, MP.

92 Henderson, Rowling, pp 137–8.

93 Evening Post, 18 November 1975. See also NZ Herald, 18 November 1975.

94 Ibid.

95 The telegrams are in two large boxes in MP.

96 See Jones, Memoirs of Muldoon, pp 60–61, for an interesting account of how Jarden's name came to be on the list.

97 Tremewan–BSG, 29 September 1989.

98 Caucus Minutes, 11 September 1975.

99 Detailed Project List and Budget Breakdown prepared for the National Party by Colenso, nd [1975] and Andrew Mazey, Colenso, to Leay, 1 August 1975, NPP 89/75, 79/4.

100 Ibid.

101 Caucus Minutes, 19 May 1977.

102 Alan Blackburn, 'Political Symbols and Propaganda': The New Zealand National Party and the 1975 Election', p 144.

103 For a detailed analysis see D. A. Pankhurst, 'Political Advertising in New Zealand Elections, 1957–75'. See also David J. Strachan, 'Press Coverage of the 1975 and 1978 New Zealand Election Campaigns', and Blackburn, 'Political Symbols and Propaganda: The New Zealand National Party and the 1975 Election'. For general studies of the 1975 election see S. Levine and J. Lodge, *The New Zealand General Election of 1975*; G. A. Wood, *Why National Won*; R. Chapman's series of articles, 'The Politics of Change'; K. Jackson, 'The 1975 New Zealand General Election'; S. Levine and J. Lodge, 'The New Zealand General Election of 1975'; N. S. Roberts, 'The New Zealand General Election of 1975'; and J. Rowe, 'Swings in the 1975 General Election'.

104 For a description and report of the speech see *ODT*, 5 November 1975. The full text of the speech in Muldoon's own speech notes, 4 November 1975, is in MP.

105 Sir John Grace, who was at the time the administrator of the Tuwharetoa Trust Board, had from 1959 to 1967 been Maori vice-president of the National Party, and from 1947 to 1958 had served both Labour and National ministers of Maori Affairs as their private secretary.

106 Sir Jack Butland was chairman of Butland Industries, an Auckland firm prominent in the processed and packaged food industry, and also a director of the Rothman's tobacco company.

107 1975 Election File, MP.

108 RDM's 1975 Appointments Book, MP.

109 Peter Acland–BSG, 28 February 1990.

110 Caucus Minutes, 16 October 1975.

111 See John Tremewan, election analysis, 23 January 1976. Also Tamaki Electorate Chairman's Memorandum, 25 February 1978.

12 Power, Personality and Political Process

1 1975 Cabinet Selection File, MP. Muldoon's comments on his 1975 cabinet selection and cabinet colleagues come from interviews with the author on 22 and 27 September 1989.

2 MacIntyre–BSG, 10 July 1991.

3 Highet–BSG, 12 March 1990.

4 Millen–BSG, 29 March 1990.

5 RDM–BSG, 22 September 1989.

6 Stuart Masters–BSG, 31 August 1993.

7 Gordon–BSG, 12 March 1990.

8 Bill Renwick–BSG, 15 March 1990.

9 Robin Williams–BSG, 1 March 1990.

10 MacIntyre–BSG, 10 July 1991.

11 RDM–BSG, 2 October 1989.

12 Gordon to BSG, 20 February 1990, and Gordon–BSG, 12 March 1990.

13 Gordon–BSG, 12 March 1990.

14 Ibid.

15 MacIntyre–BSG, 10 July 1991, and Gordon–BSG, 12 March 1990.

16 Renwick–BSG, 15 March 1990.

17 Cabinet Minutes (75) 49, 12 December 1975, MP.

18 Gray Nelson–BSG, 3 April 1990.

19 Buckton–BSG, 22 August 1989, and Galvin–BSG, 25 October 1989.

20 RDM–BSG, 22 September 1989.

21 Galvin–BSG, 25 October 1989.

22 RDM–BSG, 22 September 1989. See also Muldoon's Press Statement on Lang's retirement, 2 August 1976, MP. The author also discussed Lang's relationship with Muldoon with Galvin, 25 October 1989; Lang, 5 March 1990; and Max Bradford, 26 March 1990. Two interesting articles, which discuss Muldoon's relationship with Treasury and which draw on interviews with four Treasury Secretaries, Henry Lang (1968–77), Noel Lough (1977–80), Bernard Galvin (1980–86), and Dr Graham Scott (from 1986), were written by Alastair Morrison and published in the *Dominion*, 9 and 10 November 1987.

23 Frank Corner–BSG, 16 June 1999.

24 Margaret Mouat–BSG, 8 March 1990.

25 Ibid.

26 Muldoon, 'To whom it may concern', 16 July 1984, MP.

27 RDM–BSG, 19 April, 1990.

28 RDM–BSG, 22 September 1989; Galvin–BSG, 25 October 1989; Symmans–BSG, 19 February 1993; *Auckland Star*, 18 December 1975; *NZ Herald*, 17 April 1976; Muldoon, *Muldoon*, p 167; Jonathan Boston, 'High Level Advisory Groups in Central Government: A Comparative Study of the Origins, Structures and Activities of the Australian Priorities Review Staff and the New Zealand Prime Minister's Department'. A detailed analysis of the role and success of Muldoon's Think Tank between 1975 and 1982 is found in *NZ Herald*, 17 February 1982.

29 RDM–BSG, 22 September 1989.

30 Hensley–BSG, 19 August 1994.

31 Galvin–BSG, 25 October 1989.

32 E.g. cit. *NZ Herald* 15 January 1976, and *Auckland Star*, 28 February 1976.

33 Gordon–BSG, 12 March 1990. Information on Muldoon's chairing of cabinet and caucus comes from interviews with Bill Birch, 1 March 1990; Warren Cooper, 22 March 1990; John Falloon, 8 March 1990; Tony Friedlander, 27 March 1990; George Gair, 8 March 1990; Peter Gordon, 12 March 1990; Alan Highet, 12 March 1990; Duncan MacIntyre, 10 July 1991; Aussie Malcolm, 3 December 1991; Jim McLay, 12 July 1993; Patrick Millen, 29 March 1990; Robert Talbot, 2 April 1990; Sir Brian Talboys, 20 April 1990; Venn Young, 28 February 1990; Bert Walker, 22 June 1989; and Merv Wellington, 23 August 1989. Also RDM–BSG, 16 December 1990.

34 Mervyn Probine to author, 6 March 1990, and Probine–BSG, 6 March 1990. This description of the policy process under Muldoon was confirmed in interviews with other senior civil servants and cabinet ministers during the period 1975–84.

35 Rob Talbot–BSG, 2 April 1990.

36 Millen–BSG, 29 March 1990.

37 Waring–BSG, 24 February 1993. Significantly among other MPs whom Waring identified as 'good friends' were other Muldoon supporters: Tony Friedlander, Aussie Malcolm and Norman Jones.

38 E.g. Buckton–BSG, 22 August 1989, and Gordon–BSG, 12 March 1990.

39 RDM–BSG, 16 December 1990.

40 Buckton–BSG, 22 August 1989, and Millen–BSG, 29 March 1990.

41 RDM–BSG, 1 August 1989.

42 Robin Williams–BSG, 1 March 1990. Another former chairman of the SSC, Dr Mervyn Probine, in an interview on 6 March 1990, endorsed this observation.

43 Hensley–BSG, 19 August 1994.

44 Galvin–BSG, 25 October 1989.

45 E.g. Lang–BSG, 5 March 1994, Shailes–BSG, 19 August 1994, Galvin–BSG, 25 October 1989, and Scott–BSG, 18 August 1994.

46 Hensley–BSG, 19 August 1994.

47 Malcolm–BSG, 3 December 1991.

48 Chapman–BSG, 6 March 1990.

49 Mary Millen–BSG, 29 March 1990.

50 Stuart Masters–BSG, 31 August 1993.

51 Millen–BSG, 29 March 1990.

52 Hensley–BSG, 19 August 1994.

53 Colin James, *Sunday Times*, 9 August 1992.

54 Sharon Crosbie, speech notes at farewell dinner for Muldoon, 28 January 1992, MP.

55 Ian Fraser–BSG, 23 April 1990.

56 Ibid.

57 Johnstone, *Stand and Deliver,* pp 93–94.

13 Turbulent Times

1 He also served on the staff of the Labour Minister of Finance Walter Nash after 1935, was Secretary-General of the New Zealand Delegation to the United Nations 1947–50, and after his return to New Zealand became Assistant Secretary of Industries and Commerce. For admiring obituaries of Sutch, who died in September shortly before the 1975 election, almost exactly a year after being apprehended by the SIS, see Jack Lewin, 'Bill Sutch', and Alister Taylor, 'Prophet Rejected', in *NZ Monthly Review,* XVI:172, November 1975, pp 1–3.

2 H. E. Gilbert, Director of Security, to RDM, 27 May 1976, MP.

3 Corner–BSG, 16 June 1999. Corner was with Kirk when the Prime Minister was briefed by Gilbert. A summary of the Sutch affair was given in National Party Caucus Minutes, 25 August 1977. Muldoon discusses the Sutch case and the SIS more generally in *Muldoon*, pp 169–74. See also Sir Guy Powles to B. V. Galvin, 4 February 1980, and 'The Sutch Case', Annex A, from Powles' report on the Security Intelligence Service of May 1976, both in MP. Alexei Makarov, the counsellor and acting ambassador at the USSR Embassy, subsequently wrote a detailed account of the incident which was published in the *Sunday Star,* 10 October 1993.

4 See Minutes of Special Cabinet Committee on Security, 25 August 1977, MP, and Muldoon, Press Statement on 'Completion of Action on Sir Guy Powles' Report', 13 July 1978, MP.

5 Galvin–BSG, 25 October 1989, and Millen–BSG, 29 March 1990.

6 J. B. Stevenson, Izard Weston and Co., Barristers and Solicitors, to RDM, 9 December 1975 and 14 May 1976, and to Director SIS, 20 October 1975; and H. E. Gilbert to RDM, 4 December 1979, MP.

7 E.g. TV *News at Nine* transcript, 22 August 1975, MP; *Evening Post,* 22 and 23 August 1975.

8 Commissioner K. B. Burnside to the Minister of Police, 8 March, MP.

9 P. L. Molineaux, Director NZSIS, to RDM, 26 August 1976, MP.

10 *Sunday Times*, 11 July 1976.

11 *NZ Herald*, 24 July and 27 September 1976.

12 *NZ Herald*, 29 September and 2 October 1976.

13   *Auckland Star*, 3 August and 13 September
      1977.
14   Caucus Minutes, 25 August and 27 October
      1977, and Minogue–BSG, 23 August 1991.
15   *Auckland Star*, 15 September 1977.
16   Caucus Minutes, 15 September 1977, for
      full summary of Minogue's explanation,
      Muldoon's reaction and subsequent debate.
      Also *NZ Herald*, 14 September 1977, and
      Minogue–BSG, 23 August 1991.
17   *Auckland Star*, 15 September 1977.
18   Caucus Minutes, 11 October 1977. See also
      a lengthy interview of Muldoon on the SIS
      by Ian Fraser, *Prime Time*, 13 October 1977,
      transcript, MP. A detailed summary of this
      affair is found in a nineteen-page typescript
      of the minutes of the Broadcasting
      Corporation of New Zealand's Complaints
      Investigation Committee, 15 and 20
      September and 6 October 1977, MP.
19   Minogue–BSG, 23 August 1991.
20   *NZ Truth*, 24 August 1976, pp 1 and 5.
21   Waring–BSG, 24 February 1993.
22   Ibid.
23   Peter Hamilton, *cit. Sunday Times*,
      5 September 1976.
24   *Auckland Star*, 27 September 1976, and
      Sunday Times, 24 October 1976.
25   Caucus Minutes, 16 May 1977.
26   Caucus Minutes, 8 June and 27 July 1978.
27   Muldoon's appointments diary for 1977, MP.
28   Caucus Minutes, 18 August 1977.
29   McLay–BSG, 12 July 1993, and Caucus
      Minutes, 18 August 1977.
30   Auckland Divisional Executive Minutes,
      1 February 1978.
31   Tremewan to Muldoon, 27 March 1978, MP.
32   Waring–BSG, 24 February 1993,
      Leay–BSG, 17 October 1985, and
      Wood–BSG, 17 April 1985. By 'he made
      up for himself', Waring meant his abuse
      was prolonged and severe, contrasting with
      his earlier restraint.
33   *NZPD* v 414, 11 October 1977, p 3520.
      Also Gair–BSG, 14 July 1985, and
      RDM–BSG, 22 April 1985.
34   *NZPD*, v 405, 4 November 1976,
      pp 3645–80. The exchange between Moyle
      and Muldoon is on p 3677.
35   Beetham–BSG, 11 July 1991. Russell
      Marshall, at a conference in Wellington on
      24 April 1999, admitted in an address that
      the strategy was to prevent Muldoon
      speaking until Parliament stopped
      broadcasting and that Marshall had made a
      'not very kind speech' to annoy the
      frustrated Prime Minister.
36   A very full and fair record of the Moyle
      Affair by a National MP can be found in
      Templeton, *All Honourable Men*, pp 81–88.

      An anti-Moyle version by another National
      MP is Barry Brill, 'The Moyle Affair',
      Listener, 22 July 1978.
37   Fred Mills, interview with BSG,
      13 September 1989. Mills also pointed out
      that, while theoretically it was an advantage
      for a firm of accountants to have the
      Minister of Finance or Prime Minister as a
      partner, in practice it was often an
      embarrassment because the firm's clients
      came from a range of political views and
      some clearly disliked Muldoon, especially as
      he became more controversial.
38   Moyle to Kendon, Mills, Muldoon and
      Browne, 16 November 1976, MP.
39   The police reports of 18, 19 and 20 June
      1975 and 10 November 1976 are attached
      to the North Report, MP.
40   File note attached to report of Walton's
      interview with Moyle on that date.
41   Muldoon, Press Conference transcript,
      8 November 1976, MP. Inglis, who worked
      in Parliament for fifteen years for the Press
      Association, *Truth* and the NZBC, often
      enjoyed a drink and a chat with Muldoon.
      He died in early December 1977. The
      television interviewer Ian Johnstone, in his
      memoirs *Stand and Deliver*, p 92, also recalls
      that the Press Gallery knew of the Moyle
      incident a year before Muldoon mentioned
      it in the House.
42   Templeton, *All Honourable Men*, p 84.
43   Minogue–BSG, 23 August 1991.
44   McLay–BSG, 12 July 1993, and Merv.
      Wellington–BSG, 23 August 1989.
45   Gordon–BSG, 12 March 1990.
46   *NZPD*, v 407, 5 November 1976,
      pp 3681–2 for Moyle's statement; pp
      3695–6 for Muldoon's response; and p 3696
      for Rowling's reply to Muldoon.
47   Burnside *cit.* File Note, Meeting at 0810
      hours: Wednesday, 10 November 1976,
      Alfred North, 'Report of a Commission of
      Enquiry into an Alleged Breach of
      Confidentiality of the Police File on the
      Honourable Colin James Moyle, MP',
      21 December 1976, Appendix, p 44, MP.
48   Rowling to RDM, 12 and 22 November
      1976, MP. See also Muldoon Press
      Conference transcripts, 10 and 11
      November 1976, MP.
49   North Report, pp 39 and 41–42.
50   Ibid., pp 40–41.
51   Ibid., pp 42–43.
52   Moyle, *cit. Auckland Star*, 12 February 1977.
53   RDM–BSG, 2 October 1989. The author,
      who was at the time the chairman of the
      Labour Party's Auckland Regional Council,
      and Arthur Faulkner, MP for Roskill, who
      was party president, were Moyle's strongest

defenders on the party's Executive although the author, unlike Faulkner, was a supporter of Rowling's leadership.

54   Templeton, *All Honourable Men*, p 87.

55   Caucus Minutes, 30 March 1978, and Muldoon Press Statement, 12 April 1978, MP. Moyle used the term 'intracranial condition' in a letter to the *Northern Advocate*, 18 March 1978, following his selection as Labour's candidate for Whangarei at the 1978 election. Although defeated at that election, Moyle returned to Parliament as MP for Hunua in 1981 and was Minister of Agriculture in the Labour Government of 1984–90.

56   *NZ Herald*, 8 November 1976.

57   The letters and petitions are filed in MP.

58   Venn Young, speech notes for meeting of invited organisations to discuss Crown proposals for Bastion Point, 17 February 1977, MP.

59   Cabinet Paper 77 (1236), 5 December 1977, MP.

60   *Auckland Star*, 27 February 1978 and *NZ Herald*, 28 February 1978. A retrospective summary of the Bastion Point occupation is found in *NZ Herald*, 16 May 1998.

61   RDM to D. F. Quigley, Minister of Housing, 16 November 1979, MP. See also Quigley to RDM, 14 November 1979, MP.

62   RDM *cit. NZ Herald*, 5 May 1981, and *Press*, 6 May 1981.

63   Caucus Minutes, 18 May 1981.

64   Muldoon discusses this incident in *Muldoon*, pp 187–8. Also Galvin–BSG, 25 October 1989, and Denis O'Reilly–BSG, 21 January 2000.

65   Muldoon, *Muldoon*, p 187. Also O'Reilly–BSG, 21 January 2000.

66   Muldoon to O'Reilly, 10 April 1978, O'Reilly Papers.

67   Caucus Minutes, 16 May 1977.

68   Muldoon, Press Statement, 7 March 1977, MP.

69   Millen–BSG, 29 March 1990.

70   Ibid.

71   Muldoon, Press Statement, 11 March 1977.

72   Talboys–BSG, 20 April 1990.

73   Caucus Minutes, 17 March 1977.

74   Millen–BSG, 29 March 1990.

75   Ibid. Symmans–BSG, 19 February 1993, also commented on Holyoake regarding the appointment' as 'the cream on the cake' of his career.

76   Caucus Minutes, 28 April 1977.

77   Muldoon, Press Statement, nd [1978], MP.

78   Moore–BSG, 14 March 1990.

79   John Tremewan, Tamaki Electorate Chairman's Memorandum, 15 November 1976.

80   Sarah Campion, letter in the *Listener*, 23 September 1978.

81   Tom Scott, *Listener*, 25 March 1978, p 13.

82   K. O. Thompson, Deputy Commissioner of Police, to Minister of Police, 23 August 1978, MP, and *NZ Herald*, 27 July 1978.

83   Minogue–BSG, 23 August 1991.

84   Of 47 posters between September 1978 and May 1985, 20 referred specifically to the Prime Minister. Mr Jim Traue, the former Chief Librarian if the Alexander Turnbull Library, obtained for the author a full list of the posters from one of the women who produced them and who had retained copies.

85   RDM–BSG, 27 September 1989; Helen and Fritz Eisenhofer, 7 March 1990; and Jenny Officer, 28 August 1992.

86   *Auckland Star*, 27 July 1976.

87   Rob Talbot–BSG, 2 April 1990.

88   Jones *cit. NZ Herald*, 6 September 1976.

89   Auckland Divisional Executive Minutes, 31 May 1976.

90   *Auckland Star*, 11 July 1976, and *Nelson Evening Mail*, 14 December 1976.

91   Dominion Executive Minutes, 19 October 1977.

92   Caucus Minutes, 11 May 1978.

93   Caucus Minutes, 28 April 1977.

94   Douglas J. (Bandy) Ewert to RDM, 10 July and 28 August 1978, MP. The National Party at election times always has a 'central business house committee' which approaches the major New Zealand companies for donations to fund the party's nationally organised election campaign. Each of the party's five divisions also have divisional business house committees which approach second level regional or smaller businesses in their divisional area for campaign funds which are usually spent locally.

95   G. A. Chapman and P. B. Leay to RDM, 3 May 1978, MP.

96   Ibid.

97   Ibid.

14   *Foreign Policy and Overseas Trade 1975–78*

1   Muldoon, 'An Exclusive Interview with the Prime Minister', p 6. This was the first of several interviews on Muldoon's foreign policy in *NZ International Review*, 1977–81. For other summaries of his views on foreign policy and foreign leaders see also Muldoon, *Muldoon*, pp 128–43 and 192–208; *My Way*, pp 87–124 and 135–58; and *Number 38*, pp 76–116 and 183–8. This chapter draws on a number of interviews by the author, especially RDM–BSG,

27 September 1989; Talbots–BSG, 20 April
1990; Galvin–BSG, 25 October 1989;
F. Corner–BSG, 16 June 1999;
D. McLean–BSG, 27 March 1990;
M. Norrish–BSG, 23 March 1990; and
Cooper–BSG, 22 March 1990. Very
perceptive contemporary analyses of
Muldoon's foreign policy views and style are
three articles by John Henderson:
'Muldoon, New Zealand and the World';
'The "Operational Code" of Robert David
Muldoon'; and 'Leadership, Personality and
Foreign Policy: The Case of Prime Minister
R.D. Muldoon', the last appearing in John
Henderson et al., *Beyond New Zealand. The
Foreign Policy of a Small State*, pp 230–7.

2   Henderson, 'Leadership, Personality and
Foreign Policy', p 231.

3   Muldoon, *NZ Foreign Affairs Review*,
January–March 1977, p 8. See also
Muldoon, 'Our foreign policy is trade'. That
view was shared by his Labour opponents
although they also added secondary moral
aspirations such as a nuclear-free South
Pacific, e.g. interviews with Rowling in
NZ International Review, September–October
1978, pp 4–7; September–October 1978,
pp 6–7; and September–October 1981,
pp 16–18. See also Lange, 'Trade and
Foreign Policy: A Labour Perspective', in
which he stresses that 'Trade must be the
first object of New Zealand diplomacy'.

4   Muldoon *cit*. Henderson, 'The "Operational
Code" of Robert David Muldoon', p 369.

5   RDM–BSG, 27 September 1989.

6   Corner–BSG, 16 June 1999. The Advisory
Group has been discussed earlier. The
Intelligence Council comprised the
Permanent Head of the Prime Minister's
Department (Chair), the Secretaries of
Foreign Affairs and Defence, the Chief of
Defence Staff, and the Directors of the
Security Intelligence Service and the
External Intelligence Bureau. The roles of
and relationships among the Ministry of
Foreign Affairs, The Department of Trade
and Industry, Treasury, The Intelligence
Council, and the Prime Minister's
Department including the Advisory Group
are described in J. Henderson, 'PM Power'.

7   RDM–BSG, 27 September 1989.

8   *NZ Foreign Affairs Review*, July–September
1977, p 41. See also Galvin–BSG,
25 October 1989, and Tim Groser–BSG,
19 November 1997.

9   Galvin–BSG, 25 October 1989.
Norrish–BSG, 23 March 1990, and
Corner–BSG, 16 June 1999, both
mentioned Muldoon's deep dislike of India.

10 Galvin–BSG, 25 October 1989, and

11 Norrish–BSG, 23 March 1990.

E.g. Thatcher in Muldoon, *My Way*,
pp 89–92, and *Number 38*, pp 99–100; Lee
and Schmidt, *My Way*, p 88; Lee, *Number
38*, p 115; Reagan, *Number 38*, pp 99–100.

12 Corner–BSG, 16 June 1999.

13 Muldoon, *My Way*, p 102. See also *Press*,
18 March 1977.

14 cit. *NZ Herald*, 9 April 1977.

15 RDM–BSG, 27 September 1989;
Galvin–BSG, 25 October 1989; Muldoon,
My Way, p 103. Corner's first-hand
recollection of this incident and its
subsequent consequences are in typescript
recollections written in 1992, a copy of
which is in the possession of the author.
Also Corner–BSG, 16 June 1999,
Norrish–BSG, 23 March 1990, and John
Martin–BSG, 12 December 1990

16 Muldoon's visit to the USA was marked by
his photo on the cover of *Time* magazine,
21 November 1977, accompanied by a
seven-page article on Muldoon and New
Zealand, pp 14–20, and interviews with
Muldoon and Rowling.

17 Muldoon, article on Ramphal in the *Sunday
Star*, 6 May 1990.

18 *NZ Foreign Affairs Review*, July–September
1976, p 7. See also John Henderson, 'New
Zealand in a Changing World: The Talboys'
Speeches'; and Talboys–BSG, 9 July 1985
and 20 April 1990, and Norrish–BSG,
23 March 1990.

19 RDM–BSG, 27 September 1989. Muldoon
made this assessment after Marshall's death
and only two days after the publication of
the second volume of Marshall's *Memoirs*,
which were highly critical of Muldoon.

20 Corner–BSG, 16 June 1999.

21 Ron MacIntyre, 'New Zealand and the
Middle East', and Ted Woodfield,
'Marketing in the Middle East'.

22 RDM–BSG, 27 September 1989. Also
'Bahrain Port Facility', Muldoon Press
Statement, 15 August 1978, MP.

23 See Michael Hobby, 'The Bahrain–New
Zealand Cold Storage and Warehouse
Company (BANZ): Political and Economic
Considerations in Policy Making. A Case
Study'.

24 Boston, 'High Level Advisory Groups in
Central Government', p 309.

25 Muldoon discusses his views on South
Pacific countries and leaders, as well as the
Forum, in *My Way*, pp 110–20 and 152–3,
and *Number 38*, pp 49–52.

26 cit. *NZ Foreign Affairs Review*,
July–September 1976, p 41.

27 Muldoon, *Number 38*, p 49.

28 RDM–BSG, 22 September 1989.

29   T. Nightingale, *The Pacific Forum Line: A Commitment to Regional Shipping*, p 28. Muldoon discusses the Pacific Forum Line in *My Way*, pp 152–3.

30   Nightingale, *The Pacific Forum Line*, pp 28, 53–4, 58–62 and 66–7, and Harry Julian–BSG, 28 May 1990. Julian, who was elected chairman of directors of the Forum Line at his first meeting, was also deputy chairman and soon became chairman of the New Zealand Shipping Corporation.

31   Muldoon *cit.* Nightingale, *The Pacific Forum Line*, p 67.

32   Norrish–BSG, 23 March 1990.

33   Muldoon, *My Way*, p 114.

34   Muldoon, *Number 38*, p 49, and RDM–BSG, 27 September 1989.

35   Muldoon, *My Way*, p 116.

36   In 1974 imports from Japan to New Zealand at NZ$248.0 million were almost exactly the same as New Zealand's exports to Japan at NZ$248.3 million. The comparable figures for the 1975 year were NZ$335.6 million and NZ$185.9 million. See Steve Hoadley, *Negotiating with Japan: Lessons from the Fish-for-Beef Dispute 1976–1978*, p 9. For a full discussion of this dispute see Hoadley and also Malcolm McKinnon, *Independence and Foreign Policy: New Zealand in the World since 1935*, pp 216–17; Bruce Wallace, 'What Now Brown Cow? The Impasse in New Zealand Japan Trade Relations'; Bruce Wallace, 'The Right to Fish Lottery' in Henderson, et al., *Beyond New Zealand*, p 85; and Muldoon, *My Way*, pp 122–3.

37   *Cit. NZ Foreign Affairs Review*, April–June 1977, p 11.

38   *Cit.* Wallace, 'What Now Brown Cow', p 13, and Hoadley *Negotiating with Japan*, p 25. See also *NZ Herald*, 14 November 1977, and Muldoon, 'Speech to National Party Conference', Christchurch, 11 March 1978, MP.

39   *NZ Foreign Affairs Review*, April–June 1978, pp 12–13, and July–December 1978, pp 20, 39–42, for texts of the agreement, and Muldoon, *NZ International Review*, September–October 1978, p 5, and *My Way*, p 123, where he claims success.

40   Corner–BSG, 16 June 1999. For his own impressions of this trip see Muldoon, *Muldoon*, pp 128–35, in which Muldoon significantly discusses the countries he visited in inverse order so that he starts with China. Other recollections of this trip come from Galvin–BSG, 25 October 1989, and Corner–BSG, 16 June 1999. Muldoon's overseas trips as Prime Minister are recorded in detail in individually bound Overseas Trip Books, copies of which were in both Muldoon's possession and also in the possession of Gray Nelson, the private secretary who helped organise many of Muldoon's trips, accompanied him on most of them, and compiled the books as a permanent record.

41   Denis McLean–BSG, 27 March 1990. Muldoon discusses this topic briefly in *My Way*, p 108.

42   Ibid.

43   Gray Nelson–BSG, 3 April 1990, and Galvin–BSG, 25 October 1989.

44   Galvin–BSG, 25 October 1989, and Corner–BSG, 16 June 1999. Muldoon mentions the incident in *Muldoon*, p 133, and identifies one woman who suffered 'mild distress' at the revelation that he understood French as Madame Chirac.

45   Transcript of meeting between Muldoon and Mao, 30 April 1976, MP. The transcript was typed up after the meeting by Corner, who was also present.

46   Frank Corner, Secretary of Foreign Affairs, to Muldoon, 28 and 30 April 1976, MP. See also Corner to Muldoon, 7 April 1976, for an earlier, more general briefing paper, MP. Also transcript of meetings between Muldoon and Hua, MP. The visit was covered extensively in *Peking Review*, No 19, 7 May 1976, pp 5–6 and 11–13.

47   Corner to Muldoon, 28 April 1976, MP.

48   RDM speech notes for 29 April 1976, MP.

49   Hua Guofeng, transcript of speech, 29 April 1976, MP. See also transcript of his second speech, 30 April 1976, MP, in which Hua elaborated on China's relations with the Soviet Union and went on to discuss China's views on Asia and the Pacific.

50   Hua Guofeng speech transcript, 30 April 1976, MP.

51   Muldoon, transcript of speech, 30 April 1976, MP.

52   *Cit. Christchurch Star*, 7 May 1976.

53   Darryl Walker and John Henderson, 'China: A study in Changed Perceptions', in Henderson et al. *Beyond New Zealand*, pp 195–8, p 197.

54   Briefing paper by J. W. H. Clark to Muldoon, 22 April 1976, MP.

55   For descriptions of Muldoon's 1980 visit to China see Margaret Clark, 'The Prime Minister and the Premier', and Richard Griffin, 'China Lurches to the Right'.

56   Galvin–BSG, 25 October 1989.

57   Ibid. Also Norrish–BSG, 23 March 1990.

58   Muldoon, 'Visits to New Zealand by Nuclear-Powered Warships – and the rules', Press Statement, 28 June 1976, MP, and *NZ Foreign Affairs Review*, January 1976, p 40.

For a fuller discussion of ANZUS, nuclear ship visits, and the nuclear-free zone issues during Muldoon's Government 1975–78 see McKinnon, *Independence and Foreign Policy*, pp 189–200. For a summary of documents relating to negotiations between the United States and the Labour Government during 1975 see *Christchurch Star*, 13 March 1976. Corner–BSG, 16 June 1999, discussed with the author the meeting of ANZUS in 1975 before Labour lost the election at which Labour's Minister of Defence, Arthur Faulkner, gave the impression that Congress's assurance opened the way for a US ship visit if the US wanted one.

59 *NZ Foreign Affairs Review*, April–June 1976, p 11.

60 Corner, typescript of recollections, 1992, and Corner–BSG, 16 June 1999.

61 *NZ Foreign Affairs Review*, April–June 1976, pp 10 and 25.

62 Stephen Levine, et al., 'Public Opinion, Political Parties, and Foreign Policy', in Henderson, *Beyond New Zealand*, pp 242–58.

63 Ibid., pp 253–4 and pp 253–4.

64 Ibid., p 255. The three academics were Stephen Levine, John Henderson and Paul Spoonley.

65 Norman Kirk to NZRFU, 23 January and 6 April 1973, MP. The January letter noted that 'it would be in the larger interests of New Zealand that the tour should not take place' while the April letter directed the NZRFU to defer the invitation until the South Africans picked a team through mixed trials. Kirk would 'welcome' such a team. For a full discussion of the apartheid and sporting contact issue see Malcolm Templeton, *Human Rights and Sporting Contacts: New Zealand Attitudes to Race Relations in South Africa 1921–94*, and Trevor Richards, *Dancing on our Bones: New Zealand, South Africa, Rugby and Racism*.

66 Kirk statement to Labour Party Conference, 1972, MP.

67 NZNP, *1975 General Election Policy*, 'Policy No. 18, Sport and Recreation', p 1. For Muldoon's personal history of this issue from 1972 to 1977 see Muldoon, *Muldoon*, pp 192–208.

68 *Auckland Star*, 16 October 1975.

69 Ibid., 28 April 1976. See also Templeton, *Human Rights and Sporting Contacts*, p 122.

70 E.g. *NZ Herald*, 19 June 1976. Between May and September 1976 there was a dramatic turnaround in the polls, the percentage supporting a further All Black tour of South Africa dropping from 61 to 31 percent and of those opposing a future tour increasing from 22 to 62. A majority also

emerged opposed to a Springbok tour of New Zealand, by September 1976 35 percent in favour and 56 percent opposed. See Templeton, *Human Rights and Sporting Contacts*, pp 135–6.

71 E.g. *Auckland Star*, 23 June 1976, and *NZPD*, v. 404, pp 872–5, 22 July 1976.

72 *Cit.* transcript of *Brian Edwards Show*, 17 July 1976, MP.

73 For a full discussion see Luke Trainor, 'Race, Sport, Gleneagles', in Henderson et al., *Beyond New Zealand*, pp 134–41, and Richards, *Dancing on our Bones*, pp 152–65.

74 Muldoon, transcript of interview on the *Brian Edwards Show*, 17 July 1976, MP.

75 Ibid.

76 Holyoake, Press Statement, 16 October 1976, MP. Richards, *Dancing on our Bones*, pp 168–9, discusses Holyoake's UN speech.

77 Muldoon, Press Statement, 10 November 1976, MP.

78 Caucus minutes, 26 May 1977.

79 Denis McLean–BSG, 27 March 1990.

80 Muldoon, speech notes for address to Petone Association Football Club, 2 June 1989, MP.

81 Corner, typescript of recollections, 1992. Also Norrish–BSG, 23 March 1990, and Symmans–BSG, 19 February 1993.

82 *Commonwealth Statement on Apartheid in Sport* (Gleneagles Agreement), London 15 June 1977, MP. For a full discussion of Gleneagles see Templeton, *Human Rights and Sporting Contacts*, pp 141–60, and Richards, *Dancing on our Bones*, pp 189–202, 216–22, and 255–6.

83 Caucus minutes, 14 July 1977.

84 Ibid. Also Muldoon, *Muldoon*, p 205, where he notes that he vetoed Fraser as a member of the drafting committee because 'I was not prepared to take the chance that someone would subsequently say that in fact Malcolm Fraser had straightened Muldoon out'.

85 RDM Press Statement, 14 July 1977, MP.

86 Caucus Minutes, 8 December 1977.

87 Ibid.

88 Shridath S. Ramphal, Commonwealth Secretary General, to Muldoon, 26 June 1978, MP.

89 Muldoon, Press Statements, 28 July 1978 and 15 August 1978, MP.

90 Corner, typescript of recollections, 1992.

91 Denis McLean–BSG, 27 March 1990.

15 *National Superannuation and 'Restoring New Zealand's Shattered Economy'*

1 *1975 General Election Policy*, No. 20, Economic Policy.

2   Shailes–BSG, 19 August 1994. For a fuller
    discussion of the superannuation debate see
    Gustafson, 'Education, Health and Social
    Welfare' in Goldstein, *Labour in Power*,
    pp 61–80, and D. B. Collins, 'Formulating
    Superannuation Policy: The Labour Party
    Approach', and C. J. Booth, 'The National
    Party's Superannuation Policy', both in
    Geoffrey Palmer (ed), *The Welfare State
    Today*. Also Brian Easton, *Social Policy and
    the Welfare State in New Zealand* and Brian
    Easton, *Pragmatism and Progress: Social
    Security in the Seventies*. David Orwin, 'The
    National Government, 1975–78', deals in
    detail with all aspects of the first three years
    of Muldoon's Government.

3   Cabinet Minutes, (75) 50, 15 December
    1975, and notes to the Prime Minister on
    superannuation from R. C. Savage, Solicitor-
    General, which were tabled at the meeting.

4   For Muldoon's version of the controversy
    over this action see Muldoon, *My Way*,
    pp 76–77. Muldoon deals in retrospect
    more generally with National
    Superannuation in *The New Zealand
    Economy: A Personal View*, pp 91–94, and
    Number 38, pp 178–9, where he defends the
    cost sustainability of the scheme.

5   *Fitzgerald v Muldoon and Others* (1976) 2
    NZLR 615.

6   Walker, *NZPD*, v 415, 27 October 1977,
    p 4005.

7   E.g. Muldoon, *No 38*, pp 178–9.

8   Walker, *NZPD*, v 415, 27 October 1977,
    p 4005.

9   Brian Easton, *Pragmatism and Progress,* p 88.

10 NZ Planning Council, *Planning Perspectives
    1978–83*, p 41.

11 Ibid.

12 In 1975–76 Health was 12.09 per cent as a
    percentage of public expenditure and 4.79
    as a percentage of GDP; Education 11.31
    and 4.48 respectively; Housing 2.02 and
    0.80; and Social Security transfers 19.16
    and 7.59. Three years later, in 1978–79, the
    comparable percentages were Health 12.20
    and 5.25; Education 11.30 and 4.86;
    Housing 0.76 and 0.33; and Social Security
    transfers 24.88 and 10.77. See NZ Planning
    Council, *Public Expenditure and its Financing,
    1950–79*, Table 5.

13 E.g. NZ Planning Council, *Planning
    Perspectives 1978–83*, and *The Welfare State?
    Social Policy in the 1980s*; and Harvey
    Franklin, *Trade, Growth and Anxiety: New
    Zealand Beyond the Welfare State*.

14 E.g. in the 1977 Budget he raised and
    distributed $18 million this way.

15 Les Gandar, *cit.* NZPPTA *Journal*,
    September 1976, p 25, and NZ Planning

16 Muldoon, *cit.* NZEI, *National Education*,
    3 July 1978, p 92.

17 At that time secondary school students in
    the sixth and seventh forms competed in
    national examinations at the end of each
    year for a finite number of scholarships and
    A and B grade bursaries to help fund their
    study at university.

18 Muldoon, *cit.* NZEI, *National Education*,
    3 July 1978, p 92.

19 Department of Education, *Growing, Sharing,
    Learning*.

20 Muldoon, *My Way*, p 68, discusses his views
    on social welfare.

21 *1976 Budget*, p 28.

22 *1977 Budget*, p 39.

23 RDM–BSG, 27 September 1989.

24 *1975 General Election Policy*, No. 22.

25 Walker, *NZPD*, v 415, 9 June 1977, p 523.

26 Derek Quigley, *cit.* NZPD, 27 October
    1977, p 4001.

27 Muldoon, interview with Ian Fraser, *Seven
    Days*, 27 July 1975.

28 RDM–BSG, 22 September 1989.
    Surprisingly, Muldoon devotes almost no
    attention to the economy during the
    1975–78 period in either his second or
    third autobiographies, *Muldoon* and *My
    Way*. His major retrospective account of
    economic problems and management
    1975–78 is Chapter 9, 'Picking Up The
    Pieces', in Muldoon, *The NZ Economy: A
    Personal View*, pp 97–107.

29 See New Zealand Planning Council,
    Planning Perspectives 1978–83, p 30, and
    R. S. Deane et al., *External Economic Structure
    and Policy*, p 556.

30 John Gould, *The Rake's Progress*, p 149.

31 Cabinet Minutes (75), 49, 50 and 51, 12,
    15 and 18 December 1975, and 'Current
    Economic Situation' CP (75) 918, 'Overseas
    Exchange Transactions' CP (75) 926, and
    'Overseas Borrowing', CP (75) 914, all
    12 December 1975. The Cabinet Papers in
    Muldoon's possession covered the entire
    period of his prime-ministership 1975–84.
    They included, inter alia, Agendas,
    Supplementary Agendas, Reports of Cabinet
    Committees, other Reports and
    Memoranda, copies of Regulations, Orders
    in Council, Executive Council matters,
    Bills, copies of letters from the Secretary of
    the Cabinet to various ministers noting
    cabinet decisions. Attached to each meeting
    file were handwritten notes taken during
    the meeting by Patrick Millen, the
    Secretary to the Cabinet. These were never
    typed up and because they were very

abbreviated and cryptic and Millen's handwriting was almost illegible, he had to decipher some for the author. In footnoting I have identified Cabinet Minutes as CM; then the year (75), (76), (etc); the number of the meeting that year, e.g. 45, 46, 47, etc; and then the date, e.g. 15 December 1975. Cabinet Papers are footnoted as CP plus year e.g. (81), plus the number of the paper during that year, e.g. 1169.

32   CP (75) 918.

33   *Cit.* Muldoon, Press Conference transcript, 12 December 1975, MP.

34   CP (75) 926.

35   CM (75) 50, 15 December 1975, and R. J. Tizard to RDM, 9 December 1975, CP (75) 913.

36   CM (75) 51, 18 December 1975.

37   Ibid.

38   *Cit. Evening Post*, 13 December 1975.

39   'Current Economic Situation', Treasury document, CP (78) 1149, prepared for Cabinet Meeting (78) 46, 18 December 1978.

40   *1976 Budget*, p 41.

41   RDM–BSG, 27 September 1989. Also Sir Frank Holmes–BSG, 12 March 1990.

42   'How New Zealand's Financial Sector Grew Up', *Euromoney*, September 1980, p 23.

43   Securitibank Ltd was a merchant bank formed in 1971 by changing the name of a company originally set up in 1962 as Short Term Deposits Ltd. Securitibank dealt in commercial bills, government and local authority stock, contributory mortgages, property investment and the short-term money market.

44   RDM to R. W. R. White, Governor of the Reserve Bank, 1 March 1977. See also J. W. B. Hardie, Managing Director, McBreen Jenkins Construction Ltd, to RDM, 23 February 1977, and RDM to Hardie, 1 March 197, MP.

45   Report by Governor of Reserve Bank to Minister of Finance, 11 March 1977, MP.

46   *NZ Herald*, 9 February 1977, notes that farmers' share of national income had fallen from 12 per cent in 1967–68 to 7.2 per cent in 1975–76. See also, Ministry of Agriculture and Fisheries, *The State of the Livestock Industry.*

47   *Budget 1976*, p 10.

48   Chapman to RDM, 3 June 1976, NPP 89/75, 79/4.

49   Ibid.

50   Sir Laurence Stevens and Sir Earle Richardson were both Auckland manufacturers and presidents of the NZ Manufacturers Federation, Richardson succeeding Stevens in 1983. Stevens had known Muldoon since he had tutored him

in cost accounting in Italy where, Stevens later recalled, Muldoon had been his 'star student' in terms of ability (Stevens-BSG, 11 April 2000). Stevens, who was also for a time president of the NZ Institute of Cost Accountants and a director of the Reserve Bank 1977–86, was managing director of Auckland Knitting Mills Ltd 1962–80 and from 1969 to 1983 a director of Lane Walker Rudkin Industries Ltd after the Auckland Knitting Mills became part of that company. He was friendly with Muldoon and the National Party and generally supportive of their policies. Richardson, who was the chief executive of the clothing manufacturer Holeproof Ltd, was more critical of Muldoon and after 1984 became a leading business supporter of Roger Douglas and his economic policies.

51   Muldoon speech notes for address to Gisborne/Wairoa Federated Farmers, 4 May 1989, MP.

52   Max Bradford–BSG, 26 March 1990. Bradford was at that time Treasury's Budget co-ordinator.

53   Sir Roderick Weir–BSG, 4 April 1990. Sir Roderick Weir was managing director of Rod Weir and Co., which was a stock and station and land agents company and later became the Crown Corporation and then Dalgety NZ Ltd. He was an influential member of the National Party's fundraising network.

54   Muldoon *cit.* J. G. Pryde, 'The New Zealand Economy'.

55   E.g. Colin James, *National Business Review*, 29 March and 19 April 1978.

56   *Budget 1976*, p 19.

57   *Budget 1977*, p 21.

58   Muldoon, *The New Zealand Economy*, p ii.

59   Muldoon, *The Rise and Fall of a Young Turk*, p 195.

60   RDM–BSG, 2 October 1989.

61   Gordon–BSG, 12 March 1990.

62   Muldoon and Gordon *cit.* Caucus Minutes, 2 February 1978.

63   Gordon–BSG, 12 March 1990.

64   CP (78) 1149. This was the total of registered unemployed (6416) and people on subsidised employment (4201).

65   Ibid. 5275 registered unemployed and 6001 on subsidised work in January 1977; 8121 and 17,155 in October 1977; and 26,307 and 20,587 in July 1978.

66   *Cit. NZ Foreign Affairs Review*, April–June 1976, p 56.

67   *NZ Herald*, 15 May 1976. See also Muldoon, Press Statement, 14 May 1976, MP.

68   See Jonathan Boston, *Incomes Policy in New Zealand: 1968–84*, pp 171 ff.

69   Muldoon, *Muldoon*, p 177.
70   *Cit.* John Deeks, 'Chronicle', p 36.
71   *Cit. Dominion*, 29 July 1977.
72   Ibid.
73   Boston, *Incomes Policy in New Zealand*, p 179, and Deeks, 'Chronicle', p 70. See also Muldoon, Press statement, 9 May 1977, MP.
74   Caucus Minutes, 4 August 1977.
75   Caucus Minutes, 10 November 1977.
76   Muldoon, Memorandum for Cabinet, 20 March 1978, MP. See Muldoon, *My Way*, pp 123–5, and Skinner, *Man to Man*, pp 146–9.
77   Ibid. and RDM, Memorandum for Cabinet, 28 March 1978, MP.
78   *National Business Review*, 29 March 1978. See also Muldoon, Press Statements, 17 and 28 March 1978.
79   Muldoon, Press Statement, 28 March 1978, MP. Also John Falloon–BSG, 8 March 1990, and Ken Douglas–BSG, 9 August 1992.
80   RDM–BSG, 27 September 1989.
81   Caucus Minutes, 30 March 1978.
82   Ibid., 8 June 1978.
83   Ken Douglas–BSG, 9 August 1992.
84   Caucus Minutes, 31 August 1978.
85   Ibid., 21 September 1978.
86   Ibid., 3 October 1978.
87   Ibid., 4 May 1978. The construction of the BNZ building in Willis Street, Wellington, was plagued by industrial disputes involving the Boilermakers Union.
88   *1977 Budget*, p 43, and OECD, *Economic Survey*, January 1979, p 22.
89   *Cit. Dominion*, 13 October 1977.
90   Caucus Minutes, 11 October 1977.
91   'Economic Measures', *Reserve Bank Bulletin*, December 1977, p 451, and Muldoon, Press statement on 'October 1977 Economic Policy Package – Implementation', 12 December 1977, MP.
92   Caucus Minutes, 11 October 1977.
93   Caucus Minutes, 8 September 1977.
94   National Research Bureau poll *cit.* transcript of *Dateline* programme, TVNZ, 28 November 1977, MP.
95   Muldoon, Press statement, 14 August 1978, MP. See also D. L. Wilks, Deputy Governor of the Reserve Bank, Press Statement, 14 August 1978, MP.
96   Caucus Minutes, 1 December 1977.
97   Muldoon, *My Way*, p 81, devotes only fifteen lines to the Rangitikei by-election. George Chapman, *The Years of Lightning*, pp 159–64, gives a more detailed analysis. Gandar did not stand in the by-election but was defeated subsequently by Beetham at the 1978 general election.
98   Caucus Minutes, 30 March 1978.
99   Caucus Minutes, 4 May 1978.
100 *NZ Herald*, 29 May 1978.
101 *cit.*, *National Business Review*, 7 June 1978.
102 *NZ Herald*, 22 March 1978.
103 *Budget 1978*, p 21.
104 Reserve Bank of New Zealand, 'Reserve Bank Annual Report', in *Bulletin*, October 1979, p 375, *cit.* Jane Birdsall, 'The Economic Policies of the National Government: 1978 to 1981', p 22.
105 OECD, *Economic Outlook*, July 1984, p 161.
106 OECD, *Economic Surveys*, January 1979, p 22.
107 Ibid, March 1980, p 59.
108 Ibid.
109 *NZ Herald*, 18 November 1978.
110 CP (78) 1149.
111 Ibid.
112 Economic Monitoring Group, *Economic Trends and Policies*, New Zealand Planning Council, 1978, pp 32–33.
113 Caucus Minutes, 28 July 1977.
114 *Cit.* Transcript of *Dateline* programme, TVNZ, 28 November 1977, MP.
115 *Christchurch Star*, 27 March 1978, *cit.* Chapman, *The Years of Lightning*, p 165.
116 Rowling interviewed by Ian Fraser on 'Dateline', transcript 28 November 1977, MP.
117 Ibid.
118 Cabinet Minutes (78) 46, 18 December 1978.
119 For the 1978 election see Robert Chapman, 'The Case of the Pulled Punch. The 1978 Election'; Alan McRobie and Nigel S. Roberts, *Election '78*; and Howard R. Penniman, *New Zealand At the Polls: The General Election of 1978*. Muldoon deals briefly with the election in *My Way*, pp 128–9, and George Chapman, *The Years of Lightning*, pp 165–83, gives a fuller account. The seats National lost in 1978 were Taupo, Palmerston North, Lyttelton, Papanui, Dunedin North, Western Hutt and Hastings.
120 Heylen Poll *cit.* Nigel Roberts, 'The Outcome' in Penniman, *New Zealand at the Polls*, pp 241–2.
121 Caucus Minutes, 30 November 1978.
122 Ibid.
123 The ten were Michael Cox, Paul East, Robert Gray, Pat Hunt, Doug Kidd, Don McKinnon, Ian McLean, Winston Peters, Geoff Thompson and Bruce Townshend.
124 Kidd–BSG, 1 March 1990, Michael Cox–BSG, 2 March 1990, and Ian McLean–BSG, 6 March 1990.
125 Caucus Minutes, 30 November 1978.
126 Ibid.
127 Dominion Executive Minutes, 6 December 1978.

128   Summary of meeting in Mount Eden
      Memorial Hall, 4 December 1978, in
      Auckland Divisional Executive Minutes.
129   Masters *cit.* Auckland Divisional Executive
      Minutes, 5 March 1979.
130   Auckland Divisional Executive Minutes,
      7 May 1979.

16   *Economic Restructuring and 'Think Big' after 1978*

1   *NZ Herald*, 29 October 1977.
2   1978 Cabinet Selection File, MP. Muldoon
      discusses his 1978 cabinet selection in
      Muldoon, *My Way*, pp 133-5, and *Number
      38*, pp 27-29.
3   *NZ Herald*, 14 December 1978.
4   RDM–BSG, 2 October 1989.
5   Hunter–BSG, 26 August 1993, and Jim
      Gerard–BSG, 28 February 1990.
6   Highet–BSG, 12 March 1990.
7   Ibid.
8   Waring–BSG, 24 February 1993.
9   Jenny Officer (née Edwards)–BSG, 28
      August 1992.
10   *NZ Herald*, 19 December 1978.
11   Neale McMillan–BSG, 2 April 1990.
12   *Sunday News*, 25 February 1979.
13   Marshall, *cit. Auckland Star*, 14 April 1978.
14   *cit.* Marshall, *Memoirs, Volume II*, pp 226-7.
      Marshall notes that in 1984 Muldoon led
      National to an even worse defeat than he
      had in 1972.
15   Ralph Thompson to Sir John Marshall,
      15 December 1978, MP.
16   Sir John Marshall to Ralph Thompson,
      20 December 1978, MP.
17   Marshall *cit. Auckland Star*, 28 November
      1978, and *NZ Herald*, 22 December 1978.
18   E.g. *Auckland Star* 10 January, 7 March, and
      5 July 1979.
19   Peter Gordon to RDM, 21 March 1979, MP.
20   Marshall to RDM, 23 July 1979, MP.
21   RDM to Marshall, 26 July 1979, MP.
22   Marshall to RDM, 21 December 1979, MP.
23   RDM to Sir John Marshall, 5 March 1980,
      MP.
24   *Auckland Star*, 10 February 1978. Chapman
      elaborates on the economic miracle on
      pp 144-5 of *The Years of Lightning*.
25   *Auckland Star*, 3 April 1979.
26   *Auckland Star*, 25 June 1979.
27   *NZ Herald*, 24 October 1979.
28   *Auckland Star*, 19 and 20 October 1979.
29   E.g. *NZ Herald*, 15 and 27 September 1979.
30   Economic Monitoring Group to the NZ
      Planning Council, Report No. 1, September
      1978, p 4.
31   New Zealand Planning Council, *Economic

      Strategy: 1979*, p 2.
32   Colin James, *National Business Review*,
      31 January 1979.
33   Richard Yates, 'Memorandum', 18 June
      1979.
34   IMF Mission Statement, 15 March 1979,
      and covering letter from Secretary of the
      Treasury to RDM, 19 March 1979, MP.
35   Ibid.
36   Ibid.
37   Ibid.
38   Muldoon, *Financial Statement*, 1979, p 32.
39   Muldoon, *cit. Auckland Star*, 3 March 1979.
40   Dominion Executive Minutes, 24 October
      1979.
41   Ibid., 13 February 1980.
42   RDM–BSG, 22 September 1989.
43   *cit. NZ Herald*, 3 May 1979.
44   J. Birdsall, 'The Economic Policies of the
      National Government: 1978 to 1981', gives
      a detailed description.
45   *NZ Herald*, 5 March 1979.
46   'COPE Report', CP (78) 1169; 'Treasury
      Report on COPE Report', T 3/4/79; 'State
      Services Staffing Policy and Ceilings', CP
      (78), 1177; and Cabinet Minutes CP (78)
      46, 18 December 1978.
47   *NZ Herald*, 10 January 1981.
48   RDM–BSG, 27 September 1989. For
      Talboys' account of the Nareen Declaration
      see Brian Talboys, 'Australia and New
      Zealand: A Ministerial View' in Ralph
      Hayburn (ed.), *Australia and New Zealand
      Relations*, p 11.
49   Ibid.
50   Galvin–BSG, 25 October 1989. For a
      detailed account of the CER negotiations
      see Templeton, *All Honourable Men*, pp 128-
      38, 177-83, 191-200, and S. Hoadley, *New
      Zealand and Australia. Negotiating Closer
      Economic Relations*, esp pp 34-57. See also
      Talboys–BSG, 9 July 1985 and 20 April
      1990; Norrish–BSG, 23 March 1990;
      Adams-Schneider–BSG, 21 August 1985;
      and Templeton–BSG, 9 July 1985.
51   E.g. *Auckland Star*, 31 January 1980, and
      NZ Herald, 28 July, 19 August,
      9 September, 30 December 1980.
52   *Cit. Auckland Star*, 15 September 1979.
53   *Financial Statement*, 1980, p 7.
54   *Auckland Star*, 21 April 1981.
55   E.g. *NZ Herald* and *Auckland Star*, 10 July
      1981.
56   John Gould, *The Muldoon Years*, p 73.
57   Jonathan Boston, in Jonathan Boston and
      Martin Holland (eds.), *The Fourth Labour
      Government*, p 152.
58   *NZ Herald*, 10 September 1979.
59   *Sunday News*, 30 September 1979.
60   *NZ Herald*, 1 March 1980.

61   *Evening Post*, 18 March 1980.
62   E.g. *NZ Herald*, 31 October 1980, and *Auckland Star*, 14 January 1981.
63   *Auckland Star*, 20 May 1981, and *NZ Herald*, 21 May 1981.
64   *Cit. Auckland Star*, 21 July 1980.
65   *NZ Herald*, 22 July 1980.
66   For Muldoon's retrospective account of 'Think Big' see Muldoon, *The New Zealand Economy: A Personal View*, pp 109–18, and Muldoon, *Number 38*, pp 32–34. Also Templeton, *All Honourable Men*, pp 115–27. Information and insight into 'Think Big' reflected in this chapter also came particularly from interviews the author conducted with RDM, 27 September 1989; Birch, 1 March 1990; Sir Roger Douglas, 29 March 1990; Gair, 8 March 1990; Galvin, 25 October 1989; Sir Frank Holmes, 12 March 1990; Sir John Ingram, 11 June 1996; Doug Kidd, 1 March 1990; Sir Colin Maiden, 22 June 1999; Professor Ray Meyer, 11 June 1996; and Winston Peters, 27 February 1990. A very useful short description and assessment of Muldoon's import substitution and energy and export based industrialisation policies is Brian Easton, *In Stormy Seas: The Post-War New Zealand Economy*, Chapter 11, 'Industry and Energy'. Also Brian Easton, 'Development Strategies for the Eighties' See also a series of studies on the energy crisis, including Bill Birch, "Maui offers one way out', and Muldoon, Press Statement on "Utilisation of Maui Gas' and accompanying background notes, 1 September 1978, MP. Michael Bassett, *The State in New Zealand 1840–1984*, pp 359–67, gives a critical summary of 'Think Big'. Sir Colin Maiden deposited all his papers on the synthetic fuel project in the Library of the Engineering School of the University of Auckland.
67   W. W. Freer, Development of the Maui Gas Field, AJHR 1973, v 2, section D5A.
68   Report of Officials' Economic Committee to Cabinet Economic Committee, E(81) 208, 8 December 1981. For earlier reports on the importance of energy development in New Zealand see G. S. Harris, et al., *Energy Scenarios for New Zealand*; G. F. Gair, *Goals and Guidelines: An Energy Strategy for New Zealand*; W. F. Birch, *Energy Strategy '79*; and Liquid Fuels Trust Board, Development of an Initial Strategy for Transport Fuels Supply and Gas Utilisation in New Zealand, two reports, August and October 1979. For a comparative overview see Wilfrid L. Kohl, *After the Second Oil Crisis: Energy Policies in Europe, America and Japan*.

69   E.g. *Economist*, 11 August and 3 November 1979.
70   Kidd–BSG, 1 March 1990.
71   *cit.*, *NZ Herald*, 4 July 1978.
72   *Implications of New Energy Developments*, NZPC, No. 13, October 1979, Birch Papers. Also Holmes–BSG, 12 March 1990, and Maiden–BSG, 22 June 1999.
73   Ibid.
74   Roger Douglas *cit.* NZPD, v 469, 12 March 1986, p 233.
75   Meyer–BSG, 11 June 1996, and Maiden–BSG, 22 June 1999.
76   Birch–BSG, 1 March 1990.
77   Birch–BSG, 1 March 1990, and Maiden–BSG, 22 June 1999.
78   Ibid. See also *Auckland Star*, 29 March 1980, which has Birch incorrectly listed as a Petrocorp supporter.
79   CM (81), 38, 28 September 1981. See also CM (81), 36, 14 September 1981.
80   Shane Cave, 'Think Debt'.
81   Ibid. and *NZ Herald*, 28 November 1979, and *Auckland Star*, 23 December 1981. For a comprehensive analysis of the Marsden Point development see Mike Paterson, *The Point at Issue: Petroleum Energy Politics in New Zealand, 1955–90*, where on p 190 he estimates the finished cost of the job as only $1848 million.
82   Peters–BSG, 27 February 1990. Chapman and Leay, on behalf of the party, told Muldoon in a letter, 3 October 1980, that he should 'embody National's Growth Strategy and Economic Policy into a total package', and Fred Dobbs, the chairman of the National Party's publicity advisers Dobbs-Wiggins-McCann-Erikson, also pressed his friend Muldoon in a letter, 15 July 1981, to sell the projects as a 'growth philosophy' through a determined media campaign. Both letters in MP.
83   Birch–BSG, 1 March 1990.
84   Birch's response to question for oral answer in Parliament, 14 June 1984, Birch Papers.
85   Synfuels 314 directly and 785 indirectly; Petrocorp 153 and 382; NZ Steel 2200 and 5500; Refinery 534 and 1335; third potline at Bluff smelter 400 and 1000. See Appendix A of 'Think Big Revisited', report prepared by John Benn, Opposition Research Unit economist, June 1989, Birch Papers.
86   *NZ Herald* 7 March 1979.
87   G. Bertram and C. Dunn, *Comalco: The First Ten Years*, p 4.
88   E.g. *NZ Herald*, 23 February 1980, and *Auckland Star*, 24 March 1980.
89   Galvin–BSG, 25 October 1989, and *NZ Herald*, 29 September and 2 October 1981. See also Birch–BSG, 1 March 1990.

90 John Ingram–BSG, 11 June 1996.
91 *NZ Herald*, 15 and 25 August 1980.
92 *NZ Herald*, 28 October 1981.
93 Galvin–BSG, 25 October 1989.
94 Ingram–BSG, 11 June 1996.
95 New Zealand Steel Ltd, Plan of Reconstruction, February 1986.
96 F. R. A. Hellaby, Chairman of Directors, Board of New Zealand Steel Ltd, to all shareholders, 23 December 1985, Birch Papers.
97 R. O. Douglas, 'Government Decision-Making on Think Big Projects', Memorandum to Cabinet, 16 December 1986, CS (86) 748. See also Treasury, Review of the Major Projects, Wellington, 1984; Treasury, Review of electricity planning and electricity generation costs, Wellington, 1985; Government Audit Office, Refinancing of Major Projects, Producer Boards and State Corporations, Wellington, 1987; and Ministerial Review Committee, Report to Cabinet on *Clyde Dam Project Decision Making*, Wellington, 1990.
98 B. Jamieson, 'The result of Government intervention in major capital projects in New Zealand in the 1970s and 1980s'. In Chapter 13 and the Conclusion of his thesis, Jamieson identifies the major write-offs as NZ Steel $2.508 billion, NZ Refining (Marsden Point) $2.502 billion, and NZ Synthetic Fuels (Syngas) $2.255 billion, with some $3 billion being the additional cost of inefficiencies and overruns in the electricity sector.
99 For a detailed discussion of these concerns see Birdsall, 'The Economic Policies of the National Government: 1978 to 1981', pp 537–52.
100 Ken Douglas–BSG, 9 August 1992.
101 Auckland Divisional Executive Minutes, 3 November 1980.
102 Ibid., 6 April 1981. Another way of looking at the exports needed to pay for oil imports is that one barrel cost two kilos of exported butter in 1968, eleven kilos in 1978, and nineteen kilos in 1984. *Cit. Financial Times*, 20 June 1984.
103 Ibid., 4 May 1981.
104 *Auckland Star*, 5 December 1980.
105 Shearer–BSG, 15 December 1993.
106 Minogue–BSG, 23 August 1991; Shearer–BSG, 4 December 1985; Waring–BSG, 24 February 1993.

17 *The Colonels' Coup 1980*

1 Ambassador of the USA to Minister of Foreign Affairs, 4 December 1978, MP.

2 Brian Talboys to RDM, 7 December 1978, MP.
3 See Arthur Allan Thomas File, MP. By April 1973 he was writing to people that 'I can tell you I am most uneasy about the verdict'.
4 Muldoon's Appointments Diary 1976, MP.
5 MacIntyre to RDM, 15 July 1977.
6 David Yallop, *No Reasonable Doubt?* Hodder and Stoughton, London, 1979.
7 McLay–BSG, 12 July 1993.
8 D. J. Payne, Chairman of the Thomas Retrial Committee, to author, 26 August 1992.
9 Article by Muldoon in *NZ Truth*, 12 January 1982.
10 Hensley–BSG, 19 August 1994.
11 RDM to Board of Air New Zealand, 4 May 1981, and C. W. Mace, chairman of Air New Zealand, to RDM 3 June 1981, MP. Mace's letter is 17 pages of typescript.
12 *NZ Herald*, 1 May 1981.
13 Muldoon addressing Hutt Rotary Club, *Evening Post*, 7 May 1981.
14 RDM Press Release, 14 January 1982, MP. See also Air New Zealand Ltd and Others v Peter Thomas Mahon and Others CA 95/81 22 December 1981. Three of the five Justices ruled that while there was 'the probability that false evidence was given' Mahon should not have made such a finding in his Report without the persons concerned being warned of his intention. The other two Justices totally exonerated Air New Zealand. See also *Evening Post* and *Auckland Star*, 22 December 1981, *Dominion*, 23 December 1981, and *NZ Herald*, 31 December 1981.
15 Mahon to Secretary for Justice, 23 December 1981, MP.
16 Mahon to the Secretary of Justice, 23 January 1982, MP.
17 Sir Duncan McMullin to BSG, 7 October 1999, and McMullin–BSG, 9 October 1999.
18 Galvin–BSG, 25 October 1989. Further details of the incident came from Ken Douglas–BSG, 9 August 1992, and Corner–BSG, 16 June 1999. See also Muldoon, *My Way*, pp 136–7. Both the Soviet invasion of Afghanistan and the expulsion of Ambassador Sofinsky are discussed in Barry Gustafson, 'The Kiwi and the Bear' in *NZ International Review*, September–October 1980, pp 14–17. See also Government Research Unit, 'New Zealand/Soviet Relations', typescript reference note 80/5, 13 February 1980, which summarises from the news media, but not official sources, the response to Afghanistan, the Sofinsky expulsion, and

19 the FOL–SUP relationship, MP.
    Ken Douglas–BSG, 9 August 1992.
20 Aide-memoire of 25 March 1980 from US
    Embassy *cit.* Templeton, *Human Rights and
    Sporting Contacts*, p 175.
21 Brian Easton–BSG, 3 February 1993.
22 'Rob Says' article, *NZ Truth*, 31 July 1979.
23 Detailed record of meeting between RDM
    and Thatcher, 1 August 1979, MP.
24 Foreign Affairs report from Lusaka to
    Wellington, 5 August 1979, MP.
25 *NZ Foreign Affairs Review*, vol. 29, nos 3 and
    4, July–December 1979, pp 50–1.
26 Frank Corner to RDM, 15 August 1979,
    MP.
27 E.g. *Sunday Times*, 22 July 1979, and
    Auckland Star, 12 September 1980. See
    detailed trip book for itinerary, MP.
28 Gill to RDM, nd, 1978 Cabinet Selection
    File MP.
29 Muldoon, *My Way*, p 161. He learnt of this
    the day after he called the by-election when
    Leay showed him a report on the result in
    the seat at the 1978 election and told
    Muldoon that on current indications the
    seat could be lost. Leay–BSG, 2 March
    1990.
30 Alan and Geraldine Jenkin–BSG, 10 May
    1990.
31 Chapman–BSG, 6 March 1990.
32 Leay–BSG, 2 March 1990.
33 John Tremewan to RDM, Divisional
    Chairman, Dominion President, and
    General Director, 18 August 1980, MP.
34 Auckland Divisional Executive minutes,
    1 September 1979.
35 Ibid.
36 Beetham–BSG, 11 July 1991.
37 E.g. Chapman in *Auckland Star*, 8 and 12
    September 1980; Bob Browne, East Coast
    Bays Electorate Chairman, *Auckland Star*,
    8 September 1980 and *NZ Herald*,
    9 September 1980; Baker, Auckland
    Divisional Chairman, *NZ Herald*,
    10 September 1980; Dail Jones, MP, and
    other unnamed MPs, *Auckland Star*,
    9 September 1980; Quigley, *NZ Herald*,
    10 September 1980.
38 *NZ Herald*, 10 September 1980. See also
    Muldoon, *My Way*, p 162.
39 Auckland Divisional Executive minutes,
    6 October 1980.
40 This passage is based largely on interviews
    with Birch, 1 March 1990; Bolger,
    21 August and 25 September 1985;
    Chapman, 9 July 1985 and 6 March 1990;
    Cox, 2 March 1990; Falloon, 8 March 1990;
    Friedlander, 27 March 1990; Gair, 14 and
    20 July 1985 and 6 March 1990; Leay,
    2 March 1990; MacIntyre, 10 July 1991;

    McKinnon, 17 January 1986 and 7 March
    1990; McLay, 20 April and 14 December
    1985 and 12 July 1993; McLean, 6 March
    1990; Malcolm, 3 December 1991;
    Muldoon, 22 and 29 April 1985; and
    Talboys, 9 July 1985 and 24 April 1990.
41 *Auckland Star*, 26 September 1980, and
    NZ Herald, 27 September 1980.
42 Renwick–BSG, 15 March 1990.
43 Gordon–BSG, 12 March 1990.
44 Peters–BSG, 27 February 1990.
45 Canvassing lists compiled by Malcolm and
    Birch now in possession of author.
46 Richard Yates to RDM, 9 October 1980,
    MP.
47 G. A. Chapman and P. B. Leay to RDM,
    3 October 1980.
48 Ibid. The 'Fitzgerald affair' referred to the
    Marginal Lands Board loans controversy
    involving MacIntyre, his daughter and son-
    in-law, and Venn Young.
49 Ibid.
50 RDM Press Conference, 15 October 1980,
    transcript MP. Also *Auckland Star*,
    15 October 1980.
51 Dominion Executive minutes, 15 October
    1980.
52 Ibid.
53 Waring–BSG, 24 February 1993.
54 Kidd–BSG, 1 March 1990.
55 Birch to Thomson, nd, MP.
56 Ibid.
57 Thomson to Muldoon and MacIntyre,
    16 October 1980, MP.
58 Ibid. 'Thomson agreed that the caucus
    should 'stick with' Muldoon and ventured
    the opinion that National would win the
    next election with Muldoon as leader.
59 *NZ Herald*, 17 October 1980.
60 Thomson's notes for the call with Muldoon's
    addition, MP.
61 Muldoon's 1980 Appointment Book.
62 RDM Press Conference, 20 October 1980,
    transcript, MP.
63 Ibid.
64 Thomson to Muldoon, 21 October 1980,
    MP.
65 Talboys–BSG, 20 April 1990.
66 Hensley–BSG, 19 August 1994. Also
    Symmans–BSG, 19 February 1993.
67 *NZ Herald*, 8 November 1980.
68 *Auckland Star*, 20 December 1980, and *NZ
    Herald*, 22 December 1980. Muldoon deals
    with MacIntyre's election as deputy in
    Number 38, p 54.
69 *Auckland Star*, 20 December 1980, and *NZ
    Herald*, 22 December 1980.
70 *NZ Herald*, 10 and 19 December 1980.
    Also Muldoon, Press Conference transcript,
    11 December 1980.

71 McLay–BSG, 12 July 1993.
72 *NZ Herald*, 15 January 1981.
73 *Auckland Star*, 23 January 1981.
74 *Auckland Star*, 27 January 1981.
75 *Auckland Star*, 6 February 1981.
76 *NZ Herald*, 5 February 1981.
77 McKinnon–BSG, 7 March 1990.
78 *Auckland Star*, 14 February 1981.

18 *The Springbok Tour and the 1981 Election*

1 Statement by United Nations' Special Committee Against Apartheid, 4 December 1980, MP.
2 Brian Talboys to Ces Blazey, 9 April 1980 MP. See also Talboys' statement to parliament and a subsequent press release, both 12 September 1980, MP. The Leader of the Opposition and former Prime Minister, W. E. Rowling, also wrote to the NZRFU on 7 April 1980 arguing that 'an invitation . . . would be a blow to New Zealand's integrity abroad, and a source of division and bitterness at home'. *Cit*. Statement by B. Akporode Clark, Chairman United Nations Special Committee Against Apartheid, 4 December 1980, MP. Templeton, *Human Rights and Sporting Contacts*, gives a detailed account of negotiations concerning the 1981 Tour in Chapter 10, pp 178–203. Richards, *Dancing on our Bones*, pp 186–245, deals with the 1981 tour and its aftermath.
3 Statement from the NZRFU, 15 September 1980, MP.
4 Statement by the Commonwealth Secretary-General, 16 September 1980, MP. For a detailed summary of opposition within New Zealand, including opposition from churches, newspapers and current and former All Blacks, see Richards, *Dancing on our Bones*, pp 206–9.
5 Talboys statement, 17 September 1980, MP.
6 Talboys to Commonwealth Secretary-General, 19 September 1980, MP.
7 Talboys to Blazey, 30 September 1980, MP.
8 Statement by Supreme Council of Sport in Africa, 27 November 1980, MP.
9 Statement by Minister of Foreign Affairs, 27 November 1980, MP.
10 Talboys to Blazey, 3 December 1980, MP.
11 Marshall *cit*. *Kapiti Observer*, 21 September 1981. In the article Marshall explains why he had opposed the tour before it took place and adds in retrospect that he believed it had divided and disrupted New Zealand and disastrously damaged its reputation overseas. See also Auckland Divisional

Executive minutes, 3 November 1980.
12 Hensley–BSG, 19 August 1994.
13 RDM to President Shagani of Nigeria, 27 June 1981, MP.
14 E.g. RDM to President Kenneth Kaunda of Zambia, 3 July 1981, MP; RDM to President Julius Nyerere of Tanzania, 16 June 1981, MP; RDM to Robert Mugabe of Zimbabwe, 24 June 1981, MP. A number of letters from African leaders and Muldoon's responses, including these, are also found in *NZ Foreign Affairs Review*, vol. 31, no. 2, April–June 1981, pp 46–57.
15 *Auckland Star*, 7 July 1981. Transcript of Muldoon's broadcast, 6 July 1981, MP. Richards, *Dancing on our Bones*, p 219, gives his negative reaction to this broadcast.
16 Talboys–BSG, 20 April 1990.
17 Richards, *Dancing on our Bones*, p 244. Richards, pp 241–5, discusses more fully and very perceptively the generational, sectional and attitudinal divisions within New Zealand society over the tour.
18 Richards, *Dancing on our Bones*, pp 219–25, summarises the tour, the protests, and the emotions engendered by both.
19 Hensley–BSG, 19 August 1994.
20 Record of Meeting, on Springbok Tour, 4 August 1981, MP. Consists of seven pages of typescript detail of the discussion.
21 Minutes, Ad Hoc Cabinet Committee meeting, 6 August 1981, MP. See also minutes of meeting, 10 August 1981, and R. J. Walton, Commissioner of Police, memorandum to Minister of Police, 10 August 1981, MP.
22 Walton to Minister of Police, 10 August 1981, MP.
23 Muldoon's Draft Brief of Evidence 1985, MP.
24 Waring–BSG, 24 February 1993, and 24 June 1991 for her identification of the three anti-tour MPs.
25 Leay–BSG, 2 March 1990.
26 Beetham–BSG, 11 July 1991, and Minogue–BSG, 23 August 1991.
27 RDM Press Conference transcript, 10 March 1981, MP.
28 Ibid.
29 Dominion Executive minutes, 10 June 1981.
30 John Tremewan to Muldoon, 8 October 1981, MP.
31 Fred Dobbs to Muldoon, 15 July 1981, MP.
32 Press conference transcript, London, 28 July 1981, MP.
33 *NZ Truth*, 22 September 1981.
34 *Auckland Star*, 9 September 1981.
35 RDM writing in *NZ Times*, 20 September 1981.

36   *Christchurch Star*, 11 August 1981.
37   MacIntyre statement, 27 July 1981, MP.
38   RDM statement, 25 August 1981, MP. See also for a discussion of police and SIS analysis and advice, Templeton, *Human Rights and Sporting Contacts*, pp 181 and 195–6. The police and SIS suggested that the Auckland protest group was much more radical and potentially much more violent than the Wellington protest leaders who were having difficulty restraining some of the Aucklanders. For the division in the protest movement especially over tactics see Richards, *Dancing on our Bones*, pp 209–12.
39   P. L. Molineaux, Director NZSIS to RDM, 24 August 1981, MP.
40   Record of Post-Rugby Tour Meeting, 23 September 1981, MP.
41   Hensley–BSG, 19 August 1994.
42   *NZ Herald*, 11 October 1981, and *Auckland Star*, 14 October 1981. For a full discussion of the 1981 tour and its effects, including a discussion of the Melbourne CHOGM, see Richard Thompson, 'An Unhealed Wound' in *NZ International Review*, July–August 1983, pp 2–5; Angus Ross, 'New Zealand and the Commonwealth' in *NZ International Review*, November–December 1981, pp 8–12; Tom Newnham, *By Batons and Barbed Wire*, Real Pictures Ltd, Auckland, 1981; and Geoff Walker et al (eds), *56 Days: A history of the Anti-Tour Movement in Wellington*, Citizens Opposed to the Springbok Tour, Wellington, nd [1981]. For Mugabe's comment see Templeton, *Human Rights and Sporting Contacts*, p 201.
43   RDM CHOGM notes, October 1981, MP. See also *NZ Herald*, 8 October 1981. Norrish–BSG, 23 March 1990, said that Muldoon's apology was delivered 'in a flat voice while Muldoon looked at the desk' but Mugabe accepted it.
44   RDM statement to Commonwealth Committee on South Africa in London, 21 July 1981, MP.
45   Hensley–BSG, 19 August 1994. Templeton, *Human Rights and Sporting Contacts*, p 200, also deals with this incident.
46   See Muldoon, *My Way*, p 146.
47   Millen–BSG, 29 March 1990.
48   Waring–BSG, 24 February 1993.
49   Tony Garnier and Stephen Levine, *Election '81: An End to Muldoonism?* The best analysis of the 1981 election is Robert Chapman, 'New Zealand Defers Decision'.
50   Muldoon, 'Opening Address', speech notes, 2 November 1981, MP.
51   Hensley–BSG, 19 August 1994.
52   Leay to RDM, 26 November 1981, MP.
53   John Banks–BSG, 7 March 1990, and Paul Goldsmith, *John Banks: A Biography*, pp 71–85. Also Leay–BSG, 2 March 1990.
54   Dominion Executive minutes, 9 December 1981.
55   Millen–BSG, 29 March 1990.
56   Beetham–BSG, 11 July 1991.
57   RDM's Appointments Diary 1981, MP; Bill Young to RDM, 30 November 1981; Comber–BSG, 7 March 1990.

19   Third World Debt, the Clyde Dam, the Quigley Affair, and Bob Jones's New Zealand Party

1   RDM–BSG, 27 September 1989.
2   Cooper–BSG, 22 March 1990.
3   CM (81), 45, 14 December 1981.
4   Communique of Meeting in Wellington between Muldoon and Fraser, 20–21 March 1980.
5   CM (81) 45, 14 December 1981.
6   Ibid.
7   Report of Officials' Economic Committee, E (81) 208, 8 December 1981.
8   CM (81), 45, 14 December 1981.
9   Ibid.
10   Task Force on Tax Reform, Interim Report, December 1981, CP (81), 1293.
11   CM (81), 45, 14 December 1981. Unfortunately Millen's notes are too cryptic to reconstruct the exact nature of the disagreement.
12   Hensley–BSG, 19 August 1994, Corner–BSG, 16 June 1999, Norrish–BSG, 23 March 1990 and Denis McLean–BSG, 27 March 1990. Muldoon discusses New Zealand and the Falklands War in *Number 38*, pp 108–9. See also McKinnon, *Independence and Foreign Policy*, pp 206–8. One of Muldoon's ministers, Venn Young, in retrospect differed from the version of Muldoon as the driving force over New Zealand's response on the Falklands and told the author that although Muldoon ultimately got the credit for New Zealand's support of Britain in the Falklands dispute, the initiative in cabinet came from McLay and other ministers, not Muldoon who was far less willing to become involved. Venn Young–BSG, 28 February 1990.
13   Hensley–BSG, 19 August 1994.
14   Muldoon discusses the problem and his views on it in *The New Zealand Economy*, pp 69–76 and 145–53.
15   RDM–BSG, 27 September 1989. Muldoon discusses his early concerns about the IMF and his long-time interest in reform of the world monetary system in R. D. Muldoon,

The Art of Political Economy, NZ Institute of Economic Research, Wellington, 1983, pp 2–4.

16   RDM–BSG, 27 September 1989.

17   Muldoon, press conference transcript, 14 October 1982, MP.

18   D. R. Lange, 'Bretton Woods – Can we see the wood for the trees', typescript speech notes of address to Massey University Business Faculty Winter Lecture Series, 1 July 1983, MP.

19   Copies of all these speeches are in 'Muldoon's Speeches on Bretton Woods, 1982–4', typescripts, MP. One of the most important speeches on this topic, to the IMF and IBRD, is found in *NZ Foreign Affairs Review*, vol. 32, no. 3, July–September 1982, pp 3–5.

20   Margaret Thatcher to Muldoon, 1 December 1982, MP.

21   Galvin–BSG, 25 October 1989, Deane–BSG, 18 August 1994, Groser–BSG, 19 November 1997, and Norrish–BSG, 23 March 1990. Muldoon was also at this time and over the following years reading, page marking and using in his speeches a number of contemporary publications on the topic, e.g. W. Brandt et al., *Common Crisis: North South Co-operation for World Recovery*, Pan, London, 1983; Commission on Critical Choices for Americans, *Trade, Inflation and Ethics*, Lexington Books, Lexington, 1976; Commonwealth Study Group, *Towards a New Bretton Woods: Challenges for the World Financial and Trading System*, Commonwealth Secretariat, London 1983; and K. Haq (ed), *Crisis of the '80s: World Monetary, Financial and Human Resource Development Issues*, North South Roundtable, Washington DC, 1984. These books are in MP.

22   E.g. see Toronto *Sunday Sun*, 19 September 1982, and *Washington Post*, 26 February 1984. Clippings in MP.

23   Address to European Management Forum, Davos, Switzerland, 27 January 1983, typescript, MP.

24   The correspondence is in the 'Davos 1983' file, MP.

25   'Muldoon's Speeches on Bretton Woods 1982–4', typescripts, MP.

26   R. D. Muldoon, 'Rethinking the Ground Rules for an Open World Economy', *Foreign Affairs*, Summer, June 1983, 1078–98, p 1080.

27   Address to Reform Club, London, 17 May 1983, typescript, MP.

28   Commonwealth Study group, *Towards a New Bretton Woods: Challenges for the World Financial and Trading System*, Commonwealth Secretariat, 1983. See also

Muldoon, speech notes for Commonwealth Finance Minister's meeting, 22 September 1983, typescript, MP.

29   Renwick–BSG, 15 March 1990.

30   Government Research Unit, 'Update on Social Credit's voting record in the House', 12 November 1980, MP.

31   Beetham–BSG, 11 July 1991.

32   Ibid.

33   Muldoon press conference transcript, 27 May 1982, MP.

34   Minogue–BSG, 23 August 1991.

35   Dominion Executive Minutes, 9 June 1982.

36   Muldoon press conference transcript, 28 June 1982, MP.

37   Beetham *cit. Auckland Star*, 2 July 1982.

38   Press conference by Birch, Friedlander and McLay, transcript, 9 July 1982, MP. For Labour's position on the Clyde dam and MacDonell's support for the high dam see *Auckland Star*, 29 May 1982, *Evening Post*, 2 July 1982, and *NZ Herald*, 4 June and 10 July 1982.

39   Beetham–BSG, 11 July 1991; Beetham to author, 18 November 1993; 'Bruce Beetham's Case Over the Clyde Dam', typescript nd, copy given to author by Beetham, 18 November 1993; and *ODT*, 23 July 1982.

40   *Dominion* and *Evening Post*, 13 July 1982.

41   Muldoon press conference transcript, 13 July 1982, MP. See also *NZ Times*, 18 July 1982, which also concludes that National had already agreed to most of the things Social Credit listed as concessions.

42   Muldoon press conference, 15 July 1982, MP.

43   Beetham–BSG, 11 July 1991. See also *Evening Post*, 19 July 1982.

44   *Dominion* and *Evening Post*, 14 July 1982. The full text of the agreement between National and Social Credit is in the *NZ Herald*, 16 July 1982.

45   E.g. Lange *cit. Dominion*, 6 January 1983.

46   Shailes–BSG, 19 August 1994. See also *Evening Post*, 15 July 1982.

47   Muldoon press conference transcript 23 August 1982, MP.

48   See Richardson, *Making a Difference*, pp 25–27.

49   Beetham and Knapp, press release, 4 November 1982, MP, *Evening Post* and *ODT*, 8 November 1982.

50   See papers prepared by Barrie Leay, Dorothy McNab, Julian Watts, Murray McCully and Ian McLean for meeting of the Dominion Council, 21–22 September 1982, MP.

51   Barrie Leay, 'A Philosophical View of the Achievements of the Past Ten Years and the Challenges of the Next Ten', typescript,

52   E.g. Falloon–BSG, 8 March 1990, and
      Birch–BSG, 1 March 1990.
53   Falloon–BSG, 8 March 1990.
54   The Task Force on Taxation Reform
      1981–82 was chaired by Malcolm McCaw, a
      Wellington accountant and company
      director.
55   Muldoon, *The New Zealand Economy*, p 142.
56   Falloon–BSG, 13 March 1990.
57   See D. R. Henry, Regional Controller, and
      J. D. Nash, Inspector, to Deputy
      Commissioner of Inland Revenue, 'Farm
      Tax Shelters Report', 18 June 1982. A copy
      of this 15-page report was given to the
      author by John Falloon, 13 March 1990.
58   See Muldoon, *The New Zealand Economy*,
      pp 121–2, and *Number 38*, pp 61–3, and
      Templeton, *All Honourable Men*, p 173.
59   Cooper–BSG, 22 March 1990.
60   Friedlander–BSG, 27 March 1990.
61   Ibid.
62   Falloon–BSG, 13 March 1990.
63   Templeton, *All Honourable Men*, p 173.
64   E.g. see Dominion, 6 January 1983,
      Auckland Star, 8 and 23 December 1982,
      and *NZ Herald*, 9 December 1982, and
      Doug Graham, report, 'The Income Tax No.
      2 Bill', to the Finance Caucus Committee,
      12 September 1984, MP.
65   Dominion Executive Minutes, 8 December
      1982.
66   Auckland Divisional Executive Minutes,
      6 December 1982.
67   A. L. Gardner, Chairman, Auckland Central
      Electorate Executive, to Chairman,
      Auckland Division, 22 April 1983.
68   MacIntyre–BSG, 10 July 1991.
69   *NZ Herald*, 13 February 1982.
70   Banks–BSG, 7 March 1990. For other
      accounts of this incident see Richardson,
      Making a Difference, pp 51–2, and Banks,
      John Banks, pp 88–9.
71   Baker–BSG, 17 March 1996.
72   *Sunday Times*, 20 June 1982, and *NZ
      Herald*, 15 November 1982. The 'Quigley
      Affair' is discussed by Muldoon, *Number 38*,
      pp 146–7, and Templeton, *All Honourable
      Men*, pp 174–7. Quigley's speech is found in
      full in *Auckland Star*, 15 June 1982.
73   *Auckland Star*, 8 June 1982.
74   Muldoon press conference transcript, 8 June
      1982, MP.
75   RDM–BSG, 22 September 1989, and
      Birch–BSG, 1 March 1990.
76   Malcolm Fearn–BSG, 29 August 1994.
      Fearn was Quigley's secretary at that time.
77   Muldoon press conference 14 June 1982,
      MP. See also *Auckland Star*, 14 June 1982,
      and *NZ Herald*, 15 June 1982; Muldoon

      interviewed by David Beatson, 'Eyewitness'
      14 June 1982; and Muldoon interviewed by
      Lindsay Perigo, 'Morning Report', 16 June
      1982.
78   Muldoon to Beatson, *op cit.*, 14 June 1982.
79   *NZ Herald*, 15 June 1982.
80   *Auckland Star*, editorial, 15 June 1982.
81   *NZ Herald*, editorial, 15 June 1982.
82   *Cit.* Auckland Divisional Executive
      Minutes, 7 February 1983.
83   Muldoon interviewed by Perigo, *op cit.*,
      16 June 1982.
84   *Auckland Star*, 30 March and 4 April 1983,
      and *NZ Herald*, 7 April 1983.
85   *Cit.* Auckland Divisional Executive
      Minutes, 7 March, 11 April and 2 May
      1983.
86   Ibid., 3 October 1983.
87   *Auckland Star*, 9, 14 and 30 May 1983.
88   Auckland Divisional Executive Minutes,
      30 May, 4 July, 8 August and 5 September
      1983.
89   Fred Dobbs to RDM, 21 September 1983.
90   Ibid.
91   Ibid.
92   *Cit. Auckland Star*, 7 October 1983.
93   Ibid.
94   Dail Jones *cit.* Muldoon, *Number 38*, p 148.
95   *NZ Herald*, 7 December 1983. For
      recollections of this incident see Muldoon,
      Number 38, pp 148–9; and Richardson,
      Making a Difference, p 31.
96   *Cit. NZ Herald*, 7 December 1983.
97   Wood–BSG, 17 April 1985, and Muldoon,
      Number 38, p 149.
98   Dominion Executive Minutes, 14 December
      1983.
99   Ibid.
100   Ibid.
101   Wood to Muldoon, 13 October 1983, MP.
102   Wood to members of the Government
      Caucus, 13 October 1983, MP.
103   Jones–BSG, 23 April 1990, and Muldoon,
      affidavit presented during the
      Muldoon–Jones libel trial, November 1985,
      MP.
104   Jones, *Memories of Muldoon*, pp 126–7.
105   Ibid. Also Jones–BSG, 23 April 1990.
106   Jones, *cit. NZ Herald*, 21 January and
      16 April 1983.
107   Dominion Executive Minutes, 8 December
      1982.
108   Jones, *Memories of Muldoon*, pp 140–1, and
      Jones–BSG, 23 April 1990.
109   *NZ Herald*, 21 January 1983. For Jones's
      view of this decision and the subsequent
      formation of the New Zealand Party see
      Jones, *Memories of Muldoon*, p 144 ff, and for
      Templeton's see his *All Honourable Men*,
      pp 207–8 Surprisingly, Muldoon ignores

completely both Jones and the New Zealand
Party in his autobiographical account of this
period, *Number 38*.

110 *NZ Times*, 27 February 1983.
111 For a description and analysis of the New
Zealand Party see Peter Aimer, 'The New
Zealand Party', in Hyam Gold ed, *New
Zealand Politics in Perspective*, Longman Paul,
Auckland, 1985, pp 189–203. On
pp 197–9, Aimer details the social
composition and the attitudes of New
Zealand Party voters at the 1984 election,
revealing that they were disproportionately
young, well-off, well-educated, white-collar
urban workers and farmers with a belief in
private enterprise and antagonistic to
Muldoon and what he represented. Most
were former National voters.
112 Jones to author, 27 August 1999.
113 *Auckland Star*, 23 August 1983.
114 See The New Zealand Party Manifesto,
Freedom and Prosperity, for the party's
principles, policies and photos and short
biographies of its candidates.
115 Jones–BSG, 23 April 1990.
116 Dominion Executive Minutes, 2 February
1984.
117 Jones–BSG, 23 April 1990. See also Jones,
Memoirs of Muldoon, p 149.
118 Storey–BSG, 21 March 1990.
119 Ibid.
120 Peters–BSG, 27 February 1990.

20 *The Freeze: Unions, Consumers and
    Finance Houses*

1   Bradford–BSG, 26 March 1990.
2   Rowe–BSG, 4 April 1990.
3   Ibid.
4   For Muldoon's views on Knox see *Number
    38*, pp 117–45.
5   Ken Douglas–BSG, 9 August 1992.
6   Ibid.
7   Bradford–BSG, 26 March 1990, and Rowe–
    BSG, 4 April 1990.
8   Ken Douglas–BSG, 9 August 1992.
9   Ibid.
10 Ibid.
11 Hensley–BSG, 19 August 1994.
12 P010, 13 April 1983 MP. (See later
    discussion in this chapter about the
    'P series' of reports.)
13 P029, 7 October 1983, MP.
14 RDM–BSG, 2 October 1989.
15 Muldoon press conference transcript,
    27 May 1982, MP. Muldoon discusses the
    dispute and the freeze in Muldoon, *The New
    Zealand Economy*, pp 119–23.
16 Galvin–BSG, 25 October 1989; Scott–BSG,

17 Galvin–BSG, 25 October 1989.
18 Hensley–BSG, 19 August 1994.
19 Muldoon typescript of address, 22 June
    1982, MP, and also D. L. Wilks, Governor
    Reserve Bank, to the Chairman of the New
    Zealand Finance Houses Association,
    22 June 1982. Wells Papers.
20 Ken Douglas–BSG, 9 August 1992.
21 Ibid.
22 'Wages Policy Talks' typescript of tape-
    recording of meeting, 23 February 1983,
    21 pp, MP. These verbatim minutes were
    reproduced in total as Chapter 9 of
    Muldoon's book *Number 38*, pp 117–45.
23 Falloon–BSG, 13 March 1990, and
    Rowe–BSG, 4 April 1990.
24 K. G. Douglas, Secretary NZFOL, and
    W. E. B. Tucker, Secretary CSU, to the
    Prime Minister, 14 December 1983, MP.
25 J. W. Rowe, Executive Director, NZ
    Employers' Federation to Muldoon,
    14 December 1983, MP. Also Rowe–BSG,
    4 April 1990.
26 C. J. McKenzie for Secretary of Treasury, to
    Minister of Finance, 15 December 1983, MP.
27 Galvin, 'Report to Plenary Session',
    14 March 1984, MP. See also D. B. Abel to
    Muldoon, 30 January 1984, and Abel to
    Hensley, 23 and 28 February 1984;
    K. G. Douglas, Secretary FOL, to Muldoon,
    3 March 1984; P. S. Carpinter, Treasury, to
    Minister of Finance, 13 March 1984; and
    M. C. Probine, Chairman of the State
    Services Commission, to Minister of State
    Services, 22 March 1984, MP.
28 Muldoon summarised his attitude in his
    weekly 'Rob Says' column in *NZ Truth*,
    29 February 1984. See also Muldoon, *The
    New Zealand Economy*, pp 124–5.
29 E.g. Radio NZ, 'Midday Report', 23 March
    1984.
30 The author discussed interest rate
    regulation among others with Deane,
    18 August 1994, Spencer Russell, 8 March
    1990, and John Wells, 5 July 1994.
    Russell, who was chief executive of the
    National Bank and chairman of the Bankers'
    Association, before in 1984 becoming
    Governor of the Reserve Bank, was told by
    Muldoon just prior to the 1981 election
    that 'if bankers could not get interest rates
    down to a reasonable level then he would',
    Russell–BSG, 8 March 1990.
31 Muldoon, typescript address to Federated
    Farmers, 19 July 1983, Wells Papers.
32 Muldoon Press Statement, 19 August 1983,
    Wells Papers.
33 *Dominion*, 1 August 1983.

34 The New Zealand Finance Houses
    Association included such companies as
    AGC, Broadbank, National Mutual
    Finance, Nathan Finance, NZI Finance,
    Marac, CBA Finance. Natwest Finance,
    Allied Mortgage Guarantee, and Fisher and
    Paykel Finance. Twelve other finance houses
    reporting monthly to the Reserve Bank
    were not members of the association.

35 Wells, cit. Evening Post, 19 October 1984.

36 Dominion, 28 July 1983.

37 Ibid. See also Dominion, 29 July 1983;
    NZ Herald, 28 July 1983; Press, 28 July
    1983; ODT, 28 July 1983. The full text of
    his address is found in both the Muldoon
    Papers and the Wells Papers.

38 Dominion, 13 August 1983.

39 Ibid.

40 Dominion, 12 August 1983.

41 Cit. Evening Post, 24 August 1983. See also
    R. S. Deane, ''Private Sector Investment:
    Some Fundamental Issues', typescript
    address to Assembly of Business, New
    Zealand Chambers of Commerce,
    Wellington, 22–24 August 1983. Deane's
    comments were later simplified and
    summarised in an attack on Muldoon by
    M. J. Wells addressing the Auckland
    Branch of the Society of Accountants on
    9 March 1984. See typescript, Wells Papers.

42 'Financier John Wells', in Management,
    September 1984, pp 49–52. Wells was
    general manager of NZI Finance and from
    August 1982–August 1984 chairman of the
    New Zealand Finance Houses Association.

43 John Wells–BSG, 5 July 1994. See also
    'Financier John Wells', Management, op cit.,
    p 50.

44 Muldoon, cit. Evening Post, 24 August 1983.

45 Cit. NZ Herald, 4 February 1984.

46 Muldoon cit. NZ Herald, 14 October 1983,
    and Evening Post, 18 October 1983

47 For example, Wells's own NZI Finance
    lifted their tax-paid earnings by 35.9 per
    cent to a record $4,738,248 in the year
    ending 31 March 1984 and declared a total
    dividend of over 56 per cent to shareholders.
    Wanganui Herald, 31 May 1984, and Evening
    Post, 24 July 1984. As another example,
    Marac's after-tax profit for the year ending
    30 June 1984 was up 29 per cent to
    $11,549,000 and it declared a tax-free
    dividend of 36.5 per cent. Auckland Star,
    9 August 1984.

48 Wells–BSG, 5 July 1994.

49 Ibid.

50 Interview on Sunday TV programme,
    10 June 1984, cit. NBR, 18 June 1984.

51 D. R. Abel to Muldoon, 19 October 1983,
    MP.

52 Wells–BSG, 5 July 1994.

53 Ibid.

54 For Muldoon's version see Number 38,
    p 148, and for Richardson's see Making a
    Difference, pp 31–32.

55 NZ Herald, 10 November 1983. See also
    NZ Herald, 12 November, 3 and
    17 December 1983, and Dominion, 14 and
    16 November 1983. See transcript of
    Muldoon Press Conference, 9 November
    1983, and New Zealand Finance Houses
    Association, 'Memorandum to Members',
    15 December 1983, both Wells Papers.
    Muldoon also discusses these events briefly
    in The New Zealand Economy, p 123.

56 Muldoon, Press Release, 27 January 1984,
    Wells Papers.

57 J. A. Anderson, 'Meeting with R.D.
    Muldoon and the Finance Industry',
    typescript report, 19 March 1984, Wells
    Papers.

58 Ibid.

59 Auckland Star, 29 February 1984.

60 Radio NZ, 'Midday Report' transcript,
    19 April 1984, Auckland Star, 19 April
    1984, and Dominion, 4 May 1984.

61 Dominion, 8 May 1984. See also 'The
    Finance Companies (Investment)
    Regulations 1983 Amendment No 4 1984,
    7 May 1984, Wells Papers. Also Muldoon,
    Press Statement, 7 May 1984, MP, and
    Weekend Australian, 16–17 June 1984.

62 Auckland Star, 29 May 1984.

63 Auckland Star, 6 and 7 June 1984.

64 Auckland Star, 2 June 1984.

65 See 'Financier John Wells', Management,
    op cit., pp 49 and 51.

66 Cit. NZ Herald and Dominion, 6 June 1984.

67 Wells–BSG, 5 July 1994.

68 See 'Editorial', The Accountants Journal,
    September 1982, p 299, and Shailes–BSG,
    19 August 1994.

69 Holmes–BSG, 12 March 1990.

70 'A Toast to 1984', typescript of address by
    Sir Frank Holmes to NZFHA Annual
    Dinner, 8 August 1983, in possession of
    author.

71 Frank Holmes to Merv Wellington, 9 May
    1984. Copy in possession of author. Also
    Holmes–BSG, 12 March 1990.

72 Deane–BSG, 18 August 1994.

73 Muldoon, speech notes for address to Orewa
    Business Association, 27 April 1987.

74 Ibid.

75 P001, 4 March 1983, to P044, 30 May
    1984. Copies of all these reports are in MP.

76 P001, 4 March 1983.

77 P026, 31 April 1983.

78 P008, 29 March 1983; P010, 13 April
    1983; P011, 16 April 1983; P013, 21 April

1983; P029, 7 October 1982.
79 P027, 9 September 1983.
80 P007, 28 March 1983, and P016, 29 April 1983.
81 P005, 18 March 1983.
82 Summary of IMF Executive Board meeting, 2 March 1983, and G .C. Scott, assistant secretary to the Treasury, to Muldoon, 4 March 1983, P002.
83 Ibid.
84 Dominion Executive minutes, 20 October 1982.
85 Dominion Executive minutes, 8 December 1982.
86 Ibid.
87 E.g. Scott–BSG, 18 August 1994, and Deane–BSG, 18 August 1994.
88 Scott–BSG, 18 August 1994.
89 Ibid.
90 MacIntyre–BSG, 10 July 1991.
91 Scott–BSG, 18 August 1994.
92 Ibid. Deane and Galvin made similar comments.
93 Deane–BSG, 18 August 1994.
94 Mouat–BSG, 8 March 1990.
95 Ibid
96 Cit. Christchurch Star, 16 August 1983.
97 David Lange–BSG, 26 August 1999.
98 McKinnon–BSG, 7 March 1990.
99 Dominion, 26 October 1983, and Press, 23 April 1984.
100 Dominion, 9 September 1983.
101 Evening Post, 12 September 1983.
102 Evening Post, 14 September 1983.
103 E.g. 'Rob Says', NZ Truth, 21 September 1983.
104 Dominion, Press and NZ Herald, 26 October 1983, and editorial, Dominion, 1 November 1983.
105 Appointments Summary for 10 September 1983, and Tamaki Electorate Records.
106 David Beattie, Governor-General, to Muldoon, 4 November 1983, and again on 15 December 1983 when Beattie notified Muldoon of the Queen's formal approval, MP.
107 Millen–BSG, 29 March 1990.
108 Ibid and MacIntyre–BSG, 10 July 1991.
109 See Muldoon, Number 38, pp 73–74, for Muldoon's recollection of the knighthood and Lange's attack on it. Also Lange–BSG, 26 August 1999.
110 Lesley Miller–BSG, 5 April 1990.
111 Muldoon, NZPD, 8 December 1983, pp 4718–19. For other obituaries and comments on Holyoake see Auckland Star, 8,9,12 and 13 December 1983; NZ Herald, 9 December 1983 (by Sir John Marshall); and NZ Times, 11 December 1983 (by Muldoon).

112 Norma Holyoake to Muldoon, 12 January 1984.
113 Leay–BSG, 2 March 1990.
114 Muldoon's 1984 Appointments Book, MP.
115 Auckland Division Executive Minutes, 2 May 1984.
116 Ibid.

21 The 1984 Election

1 Prebble–BSG, 13 March 1990.
2 Ibid.
3 Auckland Star, 18 January 1984.
4 Wellington to Muldoon, 5 May, 30 June, and 18 July 1983, MP. Also Wellington–BSG, 23 August 1989.
5 Malcolm–BSG, 3 December 1991.
6 Muldoon, Number 38, pp 154–6, deals with the Allen affair, as do Jones, Memories of Muldoon, pp 133–5, and Templeton, All Honourable Men, pp 216–7 and 222.
7 K. O. Thompson, Commissioner of Police, to Minister of Police, 19 and 21 March 1984, MP.
8 Dr A. G. Singh to Muldoon, 22 March 1984, MP.
9 RDM–BSG, 14 August 1989.
10 E.g. Prebble to McLay, 16 May 1984, MP.
11 Barry Soper–BSG, 22 March 1990.
12 Templeton, All Honourable Men, p 222.
13 Muldoon to McLay, 7 June 1984, MP.
14 Scott–BSG, 18 August 1994.
15 'Long Tern Wage Reform: Summary of Meeting on 6 June 1984', op cit.
16 Ibid.
17 Attorney General to Prime Minister, 5 June 1984, MP. The memorandum was prepared after consultation with the Secretaries of Labour and Energy, the Solicitor General, and the Acting Minister of Labour.
18 Secretary of Treasury, 'Comments on Federated Farmers of NZ Budget Submission' T 835 KS:NK, 9 May 1984; 'Effect of Inflation on Farming Incomes', IF:JTD, 25 May 1984; 'Balance of Payments Projections', T 61/1, IF:JTD, 29 May 1984; 'Wage Talks – Outcome of Meeting on 28 May' T 61/1/22/10/1, PC:NK, 29 May 1984; and 'Long Term Wage Reform : Summary of Meeting on 6 June 1984', T 61/1/22/10/1, PSC:JTD, 11 June 1984, MP.
19 Draft Budget Text, 8 June 1984. Also Treasury Papers No. 6, 2 April 1984; No. 7, 12 April 1984; and No. 8, 12 April 1984; and Ministry of Agriculture, 'SMPs and Stabilisation Schemes', 10 April 1984. All these and 70 other Treasury Papers on the 1984 Budget are in MP. See also Muldoon,

Press Statement on ending of SMPs, 26 June 1984, typescript MP.

20 Draft Budget Text and Budget Report, No. 70, 8 June 1984, MP.

21 Prebble Press Statement, 30 August 1984, MP; Douglas *cit. Evening Post*, 11 October 1984; de Cleene *cit. NZ Herald*, 5 September 1984.

22 Heylen Polls, 4 February and 16 June 1984, NZNP 115/5.

23 Policy Committee minutes, 28 March 1984, NZNP 115/12.

24 Dominion Council minutes, 3 April 1984, NZNP 117/1.

25 Ibid.

26 Cox–BSG, 2 March 1990.

27 Hensley–BSG, 19 August 1994.

28 Tamaki electorate committee minutes, 8 June 1984.

29 Dominion Executive minutes, 13 June 1984, NZNP 115/3.

30 Ibid. and Leay–BSG, 2 March 1990.

31 For Muldoon's version see *Number 38*, pp 156–7. Also Waring–BSG, 24 February 1994, and Minogue–BSG, 23 August 1991.

32 Waring–BSG, 24 February 1994.

33 Ibid.

34 McKinnon, 'Notes on background to snap election', 15 June 1984. The day after the snap election was called, McKinnon dictated his recollections of the previous day on to a tape which was then typed up into 28 pages. The tape and the transcript are in McKinnon's possession. Muldoon's detailed account of events leading up to the election, the election campaign, and its results and aftermath is found in a 15-page confidential 'Report by the Leader, Right Hon. Sir Robert Muldoon on the 1984 General Election' to the National Party's Dominion Council, [nd], which was distributed subsequently to National MPs on 15 April 1985, MP. Muldoon deals very briefly with the topic in *Number 38*, pp 157–9. This section on the events surrounding the calling of the 1984 election also draws on the author's interviews with Malcolm Fearn, 29 August 1994; Barrie Leay, 17 October 1985 and 2 March 1990; Don McKinnon, 17 January 1986 and 7 March 1990; Jim McLay, 20 April 1985 and 12 July 1993; Mike Minogue, 23 August 1991; Muldoon, 22 and 29 April 1985; Marilyn Waring 24 February 1993; and Sue Wood, 17 April 1985.

35 Here and for the next three paragraphs my authority is McKinnon's 'Notes' and also McKinnon to Muldoon, 14 June 1984, MP.

36 Ibid. Also Muldoon's 'Report . . . on the 1984 election', *op cit.*, p 1, and Wood–BSG, 17 April 1985.

37 McKinnon, 'Notes', *op cit.*

38 Waring–BSG, 24 February 1993.

39 Ibid.

40 Ibid. In this interview Waring emphasised her intent to provoke Muldoon and push him into an early election.

41 Leay–BSG, 2 March 1990.

42 McLay–BSG, 20 April 1985.

43 Minogue–BSG, 23 August 1991.

44 McLean–BSG, 6 March 1990.

45 McKinnon 'Notes'. The minutes of the caucus meeting included with McKinnon's 'Notes' were taken by East.

46 Ibid. and McLean–BSG, 6 March 1990.

47 Waring–BSG, 24 February 1993.

48 Muldoon, 'Report . . . on the 1984 General Election', *op cit.*, p 3.

49 Millen–BSG, 29 March 1990.

50 Beetham–BSG, 11 July 1991, and Beetham to Sir Paul Reeves, Governor General, 21 June 1988, copy given by Beetham to author, 11 July 1991.

51 Leay–BSG, 2 March 1990.

52 McKinnon, 'Notes', and Fearn–BSG, 29 August 1994.

53 McKinnon, 'Notes'.

54 Thea Muldoon–BSG, 12 August 1994, Officer–BSG, 8 August 1994, Leay–BSG, 2 March 1990, and RDM–BSG, 22 April 1985.

55 McKinnon, 'Notes'.

56 Fearn–BSG, 29 August 1994.

57 McKinnon, 'Notes'.

58 Fearn–BSG, 29 August 1994.

59 McKinnon, 'Notes'.

60 Doug Kidd–BSG, 1 March 1990.

61 McKinnon, 'Notes'.

62 Ibid.

63 For Muldoon's recollections of the 1984 election campaign see Muldoon, *Number 38*, pp 162–9; for a Labour point of view, Roger Douglas and Louise Callan, *Toward Prosperity*, pp 39–50; for a New Zealand Party viewpoint, Jones, *Memories of Muldoon*, pp 150–3; and for a non-partisan account, Colin James, *The Quiet Revolution*, pp 102–10. See also J. Fyfe and H. Hanson, *The Gamble: Snap Election '84: The Campaign Diaries of the Challengers*, and K. Jackson, 'The New Zealand General Election of 1984'. A very comprehensive and informative unpublished study of the 1984 election is N. W. Walker, 'The 1984 Election Defeat', a 99-page unpublished typescript in the National Party Papers deposited in the Alexander Turnbull Library, NPP, A89/75, 148/2. Also Beetham–BSG, 11 July 1991; Douglas–BSG, 29 March 1990; Jones–BSG, 23 April 1990; Leay–BSG, 2 March 1990; and RDM–BSG, 22 and 29 April 1985.

64 Muldoon, 'Report . . . on the 1984 General

Election', *op cit.*, pp 6–8. Leay–BSG,
2 March 1990, claimed that the National
Party had very limited funds in 1984 and,
anticipating that income would dry up after
the election, the party's finance committee
was reluctant to go into debt.

65 Jones–BSG, 23 April 1990. Jones was told
this story by Walker. The story was
confirmed by Lange, 26 August 1999. A
devastating critique of National's 1984
election advertising is found in an article by
Belinda Gillespie in the *National Business
Review*, 23 July 1984, pp 33 and 35.

66 Muldoon's opening address speech notes, MP
and also NPP A 89/75, 81/3. The policies of
the four main parties at the 1984 election are
well summarised in 'Election 84', a *Listener*
Special Edition, 14–20 July 1984.

67 *Financial Times*, 20 June 1984, 'New
Zealand', p III.

68 Muldoon's opening address speech notes,
MP.

69 Muldoon *cit.* Auckland Divisional minutes,
7 December 1987.

70 Muldoon's opening address speech notes,
MP.

71 Muldoon, 'Speech notes', 13 July 1984, MP.

72 Lange, *Sunday*, 29 July 1984.

73 Muldoon, 'Speech notes', 13 July 1984, MP.

74 *Cit. Sunday Star*, 9 August 1992. Muldoon
also later told the story in an address to the
Rotorua and District JPs Association, see
Muldoon, speech notes, 15 February 1991.
MP.

75 Ian Johnstone, *Stand and Deliver*, pp 163–6,
p166. There is a full transcript of the TV1
Lange–Muldoon Debate of Sunday 8 July
1984 in the MP.

76 E.g. Muldoon *Number 38*, pp 162–72, and
Muldoon, 'Report . . . on the 1984 General
Election', *op cit.*

77 Lesley Miller–BSG, 5 April 1990.

78 Soper–BSG, 22 March 1990 and
29 November 1999.

79 Muldoon, 'Speech notes', 13 July 1984, MP.

80 Walker, 'The 1984 Election Defeat', *op cit.*,
p 93.

81 Tamaki electorate committee minutes,
23 July 1984.

82 Tamaki electorate executive, submission to
Organisation Review Committee,
30 October 1984, copy MP.

83 Muldoon interviewed by Sharon Crosbie,
Radio NZ, 24 July 1985.

22 *The Post-Election Currency Crisis*

1 For a description of the New Zealand
foreign exchange market during the

1979–83 period see R. S. Deane, 'Recent
Developments in the New Zealand Foreign
Exchange Market', typescript of address at
Macquarie University, 7 July 1983, Wells
Papers.

2 Ibid.

3 Ibid.

4 Secretary to the Treasury and Governor of the
Reserve Bank to the Minister of Finance,
23 December 1982, pp 1–2, T61/1/24 Vol.
9, *cit.* Treasury document of the 1984 events
in the author's possession. A copy of the
original document is in the MP and the
specific recommendation 'of at least 15
percent, and probably more' is on p 5.

5 Secretary to the Treasury and Governor of
the Reserve Bank to the Minister of
Finance, 8 February 1984, MP.

6 Information on the post-election
devaluation crisis in 1984 comes from the
author's interviews with Roderick Deane,
18 August 1994; Roger Douglas, 29 March
1990; John Falloon, 8 and 13 March 1990;
Bernard Galvin, 25 October 1989; Gerald
Hensley, 19 August 1994; David Lange,
26 August 1999; Jim McLay, 14 December
1985 and 12 July 1993; Muldoon, 22 and
29 April 1985; Spencer Russell, 8 March
1990; Graham Scott, 18 August 1994; and
Henry Lang, 5 March 1990. Lang was
acting as adviser to the Labour Opposition
during the interregnum. Other major
sources were a detailed 44-page Treasury
document on the crisis [nd]; Cabinet
Minutes (84) 26, 17 July 1984;
Government Research Unit, 'The
Devaluation Argument', 26 June 1984;
Deane to Muldoon, 'Forward Exchange
Market/Overseas Reserves', 15 June 1984;
Galvin and Deane to Muldoon, 'Foreign
Exchange Situation', 17 June 1984; Deane
to Muldoon, 'Foreign Exchange Situation',
18 June 1984; Russell and Galvin to
Muldoon, 'Foreign Exchange Position',
28 June 1984; Russell to Muldoon ,
'Liquidity Conditions', 3 July 1984; Russell
to Muldoon, 4 July 1984; Russell and
Galvin to Muldoon, 11 July 1984; Russell
and Galvin to Muldoon and Lange, 17 July
1984; McLay, 'Press Statement', 17 July
1984; Muldoon to Lange, 17 July 1984;
Lange to Muldoon, 17 July 1984; Russell to
Muldoon, 18 July 1984; Muldoon to
Russell, 18 July 1984; R. O. Douglas, 'The
Consequences of High Overseas Debt and
Low Overseas Reserves', paper distributed at
meeting, Methodist Church Hall,
Manurewa, 18 June 1984; all MP. Many of
the documents relating to the devaluation
are found in Public Expenditure

Committee, *Report on Inquiry into Devaluation*, I.12c, Government Printer, Wellington, 1984, 148 pp See also Roger Douglas and Louise Callen, *Toward Prosperity*, pp 51–62; Brian Easton, 'From Run to Float: the Making of the Rogernomics Exchange Rate Policy'; Muldoon, *Number 38*, pp 172–4; Muldoon, *The New Zealand Economy*, pp 127–35; Geoffrey Palmer and Matthew Palmer, *Bridled Power*, pp 33–34; and Templeton, *All Honourable Men*, p 221. See also 'Fallout', a two-part television dramatisation of the events surrounding the 1984 election and the subsequent devaluation, written by Tom Scott and Greg McGee and broadcast in July 1994.

7   Treasury document of the 1984 events, p 11. See also Galvin and Deane to Muldoon, 17 June 1984, MP esp. pp 3–5. On Muldoon's copy he has written that he approved only the immediate re-entry of the Reserve Bank into the forward market and the liquefying of existing reserves and drawing of credit standbys.

8   Ibid., p 8.

9   Muldoon, 'Report . . . on the 1984 General Election', *op cit.*, p 11.

10 Douglas, 'The Consequences of High Overseas Debt and Low Overseas Reserves', nd, distributed 18 June 1984, and Douglas, 'Speech notes', Methodist Church Hall Manurewa, 18 June 1984, MP. One of Muldoon's staff, who was with Muldoon when he first heard of the release of the Douglas paper, recalled that 'he was very upset' and 'knew money would disappear overseas' as a result. Officer–BSG, 28 August 1992.

11 Douglas and Callan, *Toward Prosperity*, p 38.

12 *Dominion*, 20 June 1984.

13 *Dominion*, 23 June 1984.

14 The author, acting as a part of a HUGO Consultants' team, was present at a luncheon for chief executives from a number of large corporates in Auckland during the first week of the campaign during which Frank Holmes and Len Bayliss made such predictions.

15 Hensley–BSG, 19 August 1994, and Treasury document on the 1984 events, p 16.

16 Galvin and Russell to Muldoon, 28 June 1984, T61/1/24 Vol. 9, *cit.* Treasury document on the 1984 events, p 17.

17 Minutes of meeting 5 July 1984, *cit.* Treasury document on 1984 events, pp 18–19.

18 Reserve Bank Memorandum, 16 July 1984, MP.

19 According to the Treasury document on the 1984 events, Appendix 3, p 36, foreign exchange commitments to the end of August totalled $1477 million and total reserves $1466 million including the $537 million of standby loans.

20 Russell and Galvin to Muldoon, 'External Reserves Position', 11 July 1984, p 2, MP.

21 Hensley–BSG, 19 August 1994.

22 Ibid. and Russell–BSG, 8 March 1990.

23 Muldoon *cit.* Tamaki Electorate Committee Minutes, 17 August 1984. Some of the points Muldoon made to his officials repeated observations which had earlier been made to Muldoon by Russell in a memorandum, 3 July 1984, MP.

24 *Press*, 20 July 1984.

25 Russell–BSG, 8 March 1990, and Muldoon to Lange, 17 July 1984, and Muldoon to Russell, 18 July 1984, MP.

26 Deane–BSG, 18 August 1994, and Hensley–BSG, 19 August 1994.

27 Deane–BSG, 18 August 1994.

28 Ken Douglas–BSG, 9 August 1992.

29 Muldoon, address to Wellington Branch of the Accountants' Society, *cit. Hawke's Bay Herald Tribune*, 19 July 1984.

30 Lange–BSG, 26 August 1999.

31 Details of this meeting were first revealed by Galvin in an interview on July 9 1985 *cit.* Treasury document on 1984 events, p 24, and confirmed subsequently by the author's interviews with Galvin, 25 October 1989, Russell, 8 March 1990, Douglas, 29 March 1990, and Lange, 26 August 1999.

32 Lange–BSG, 26 August 1999. Muldoon discusses this ANZUS meeting in *Number 38*, pp 184–5.

33 Fearn–BSG, 29 August 1994, and Officer–BSG, 28 August 1992.

34 Deane–BSG, 18 August 1994.

35 Muldoon, 'Report . . . on the 1984 General Election', *op cit.*, p 12, and Treasury document of the 1984 events, *op cit.*, p 25.

36 Muldoon, *Eye Witness News*, 16 July 1984, *cit.* Treasury document on the 1984 events, *op cit.*, p 28. Also Lesley Miller–BSG, 5 April 1990. As Muldoon's press secretary, Miller helped prepare the 6.45 press release and also contacted Muldoon on Harman's behalf to arrange the subsequent recorded interview.

37 Ibid.

38 McLay–BSG, 12 July 1993.

39 Ibid. and Templeton, *All Honourable Men*, p 221.

40 Falloon–BSG, 13 March 1990.

41 McLay–BSG, 12 July 1993. See also Muldoon, *Number 38*, p 173, and McLay, Press Statement, 17 July 1984, in which he

gave an account of this meeting with Muldoon and McLay's interpretation of the constitutional position.

42   Millen–BSG, 29 March 1990. Oliver Riddell from the Press Galley, in a lengthy, informed article on the crisis, *Press*, 18 July 1984, wrote that the clash over devaluation between Lange and Muldoon 'was not a constitutional crisis but a jockeying for future political advantage'.

43   CM (84) 26, 17 July 1984. The discussion was summarised as it occurred by Patrick Millen, the Secretary to the Cabinet, and his handwritten notes were deciphered by Mr Millen for the author on 21 April 1990.

44   Muldoon to Lange, 17 July 1984, and Lange to Muldoon, 17 July 1984, MP, and also *cit.* Treasury document on the 1984 events, p 31.

45   Muldoon, 'Report . . . on the 1984 General Election', *op cit.*, p 13.

46   *Auckland Star*, 18 July 1984. Also Douglas–BSG, 29 March 1990; Russell–BSG, 8 March 1990; Deane–BSG, 18 August 1994; Galvin–BSG, 25 October 1989; and Scott–BSG, 18 August 1994. For a description and analysis of Labour's economic changes immediately after coming to office in 1984 and an interview with Roger Douglas on his economic outlook and programme see *Asiabanking*, September 1984, pp 56–59.

47   E.g. *Dominion*, 20 July 1984, which gives the increases for General Finance, Broadbank, UDC, AGC, and Marac, the last of which was borrowing at 13–15 per cent and lending at 20–21 per cent. Also *NZ Herald*, 20 July 1984, which reported that Allied Finance had increased its lending rate by 10 percentage points to 24 per cent.

48   *NZ Herald*, 17 August 1985.
49   Wells address typescript, 1 August 1984, Wells Papers.
50   Douglas, address typescript, Finance Houses Association AGM, 1 August 1984, Wells Papers. Also *cit. Auckland Star*, 1 August 1984.
51   *Auckland Star*, 6 August 1984.
52   Russell–BSG, 8 March 1990. See also Agenda and papers prepared for meeting of Public Expenditure Committee's Subcommittee on Devaluation, 13 September 1984. The subcommittee comprised Anderton (chair), two other Labour MPs, Peter Neilson and Peter Dunne, and two National MPs, Muldoon and Falloon.
53   The Public Expenditure Committee at a meeting on 26 September 1984 disbanded the subcommittee on the motion of Labour's

Fran Wilde who claimed that Muldoon's presence and statements 'left the integrity of the subcommittee somewhat in doubt' and as a result 'Witnesses would be unhappy and reluctant to appear and the subcommittee would get very little out of its inquiry.' Minutes of the Public Expenditure Committee 26 September 1984, MP. After the motion was carried on a party vote, Muldoon and the other National MPs present withdrew from the Public Expenditure Committee in protest.

54   RDM–BSG, 14 August 1989.

23   The Leadership Transition

1   *Dominion*, 18 July 1984.
2   *ODT*, 19 July 1984, *Auckland Star*, 16 July 1984, and *Evening Post*, 17 July 1984.
3   McKinnon–BSG, 7 March 1990.
4   RDM–BSG, 14 August 1989, and Muldoon, *Number 38*, p 93. McLay reacted strongly to Muldoon's suggestion in *Number 38* that McLay wanted to cancel his speaking engagements around the country during the last week of the election campaign. See McLay's denial in 'Press Statement', 17 November 1986. Copy in author's possession from McLay.
5   *cit. Dominion*, 20 July 1984.
6   McLay–BSG, 13 May 1995.
7   *NZ Herald*, 21 July 1984.
8   *Press*, 20 and 21 July 1984; *ODT*, 21 July 1984; and *Dominion*, 23 July 1984.
9   *Dominion*, 21 July 1984.
10   *Auckland Star*, 23 July 1984, *NZ Herald*, 24 July 1984, and *Dominion*, 23 July 1984.
11   Muldoon, 'Report by the Leader . . . on the 1984 General Election', 12 September 1984, MP.
12   Dominion Council Meeting Minutes, 11–12 September 1984, NZNP 117/1.
13   Ibid.
14   Chapman–BSG, 6 March 1990.
15   Adult Adoption Information Bill File, 1983–5, MP.
16   R. D. Muldoon, Submissions to the Statutes Revision Committee. Adult Adoption Information Bill, 11 October 1984.
17   The papers and typed addresses from the seminar are in the National Party Papers deposited in the Alexander Turnbull Library, A 89/75 MSC 145/2325.
18   E.g. Tuesday 30 October 1984 at 11.45 Brian Woodley; 12.25 Barry Soper; 2.30 Ewart Barnsley; 3.15 Ian Higgins; 4.00 Richard Harman; 4.30 Neale McMillan; and Wednesday 31 October at 10.00 Fran

O'Sullivan; 11.00 Brian Woodley; 2.15 Roger Foley; 4.00 Anthony Hubbard. See RDM s 1984 Appointments Book, MP.

19 McKinnon to Muldoon, nd, MP.

20 *Evening Post*, 2 November 1984.

21 *Auckland Star*, 6 November 1984.

22 *Dominion*, 18 November 1984, and *Press*, 22 and 23 November 1984.

23 *NZ Herald*, 29 November 1984, and TV2 *Eyewitness News*, 28 November 1984. Among National voters only, Gair polled 7 per cent, Bolger 6 per cent, and Birch 2 per cent.

24 Muldoon, TV2 *Eyewitness News*, 28 November 1984.

25 Ibid.

26 Radio New Zealand 'Midday Report', 30 October 1984.

27 Ibid.

28 Birch *cit. Press*, 14 November 1984.

29 Falloon–BSG, 13 March 1990.

30 McLay–BSG, 12 July 1993.

31 Birch–BSG, 1 March 1990.

32 Dominion Executive Minutes, 28 November 1984, NZNP 115/3.

33 Peters–BSG, 27 February 1990. Peters could not understand McLay and Bolger wanting to remove Muldoon before early 1987. It was obvious that an orderly succession with Muldoon endorsing the new leader would be much better than Muldoon being dumped unceremoniously. A bitter and frustrated Muldoon would clearly be a destabilising influence.

34 McLay–BSG, 12 July 1993. There is some doubt about these figures. If Birch and Gair voted for themselves, even if no one else did, the total of votes would have been 38 if McLay was correct about the votes received by Bolger, Muldoon and himself, i.e. one more than the number of MPs voting. It is of course possible that Birch received no votes because he did tell the author that he supported McLay for the leadership. Birch–BSG, 1 March 1990.

35 Tom Scott, *Evening Post*, 1 December 1984.

36 *Dominion*, 30 November 1984.

37 Ibid.

38 *ODT*, 30 November 1984.

39 Baker to RDM, 1 December 1984, MP.

40 *Cit.* Auckland Divisional Executive Minutes, 3 December 1984.

41 RDM–BSG, 14 August 1989.

42 E.g. Muldoon to Robyn Leeming, East Cape electorate, 13 February 1985, MP.

43 E.g. Tim Grafton, *Evening Post*, 29 November 1986; Anon, *Bay of Plenty Times*, 27 December 1986; Lynn McConnell, *Southland Times*, 3 January 1987; and Bernard Lagan, *Dominion*, 10 January 1987.

44 RDM–BSG, 1 August 1989.

45 Clark–BSG, 10 June 1991.

46 *NZ Herald*, 26 June 1985. For an interesting analysis of McLay at this time see N.Legat, 'Has Jim McLay Got the Right Stuff', *Metro*, July 1985, pp 42–66.

47 Millen–BSG, 29 March 1990.

48 Bill Matthewson–BSG, 12 August 1989.

49 Suzanne Mackay to Bryan Madden, Wellington Division, 26 October 1984, copy MP.

50 Bert Walker to Organisation Review Committee, 31 October 1984, copy MP.

51 Tamaki Electorate Executive submission to Organisation Review Committee, 30 October 1984, copy MP.

52 Walker–BSG, 22 June 1989. See also minutes of 'meeting of National Party people held at home of Hon H. J. and Mrs Walker, 10 February 1985, MP. Besides Mr and Mrs Walker, those present who formally and unanimously passed a resolution to 'form a group to be known, in the meantime, as the "Sunday Club", were K. A. Gough, H. Garrett, R. Whitehouse, J. Curtis, L. Martin, Mr and Mrs L. R. Wilkinson, V. Miller, E. Sutherland and A. Hoggen.

53 Ibid.

54 Matthewson–BSG, 12 August 1989.

55 Ibid.

56 Sybil Gunson, New Plymouth member of Sunday Club's inaugural national steering committee, to Margaret Mouat, 17 March 1985, MP.

57 Minogue, *cit. Sunday News*, 17 March 1985.

58 McLay, *cit. Press*, 15 March 1985.

59 Upton, 'A Message from Simon Upton, National Party newsletter of the combined electorates of Waikato, Raglan, Hamilton East and Hamilton West, nd [May 1985].

60 Margaret Quin to Muldoon, 17 March 1985, MP.

61 Walker–BSG, 22 June 1989.

62 Colin James, *NBR*, 20 May 1985.

63 *Cit Brisbane Courier Mail*, 21 May 1985. Muldoon used the term originally in a *NZ Truth* article. At the time Claytons was being widely advertised as a non-alcoholic alternative to alcoholic spirits, a non-potent substitute for the real thing.

64 Muldoon to Murray Reeves, 17 May 1985, MP.

65 McLay–BSG, 12 July 1993.

66 A. Willy of the Canterbury-Westland Division, Dominion Executive Minutes, 30 April 1985.

67 Wood, ibid.

68 McLay, ibid.

69 Birch and Bolger, ibid.

70 Dominion Executive Minutes, 30 April 1985.
71 McLay, ibid.
72 Bolger, ibid.
73 Wendy Mehaney to McLay, 17 July 1985, MP, and Muldoon, TV2 *Eyewitness News*, 23 July 1985. Also *NZ Truth*, 23 July 1985.
74 TV2 *Eyewitness News*, 23 July 1985.
75 See TV1 National Party conference reports, 27, 28 and 29 July 1985; TV2 *Eyewitness News*, 23 and 29 July 1985; and Radio New Zealand 'Morning Report', 30 July 1985.
76 Keith Jackson, TV1 National Party conference special, 29 July 1985.
77 TV1 *6.30 News*, 30 July 1985.
78 *Auckland Star*, 29 July 1985, and TV1 *6.30 News*, 29 July 1985.
79 Margaret Quin to President, National Party, 14 April 1985, copy in MP.
80 E.g. *Press*, 29 and 30 July 1985; *Dominion*, 1 August 1985; *NZ Herald*, 7 August 1985.
81 *Press*, 29 July 1985.
82 Tamaki Electorate Committee Minutes, 12 August 1985.
83 Margaret Quin to Muldoon, 4 August 1985, MP.
84 Wellington to McLay, 31 July 1985, copy in MP.
85 Ibid.
86 Ibid.
87 Ibid.
88 National Executive Minutes, 14 August 1985.
89 Ibid.
90 Ibid.
91 National Executive Minutes, 18 September 1985.
92 Julian–BSG, 28 May 1990, and McLay–BSG, 12 July 1993.
93 Tamaki Electorate Committee Minutes, 14 October 1985.
94 RDM–BSG, 1 August 1989, McLay–BSG, 12 July 1993 and 13 May 1995, and *Christchurch Star*, 19 October 1985.
95 Wood and Graham *cit.* Radio New Zealand News, midday, 19 October 1985, and Gair, Cox and Wellington *cit.* Radio New Zealand News, 6 p.m., 19 October 1985, Kidd and Richardson, *Press*, 21 October 1985.
96 *Cit. Press*, 21 October 1985.
97 Ibid.
98 *Christchurch Star*, 24 October 1985.
99 *Timaru Herald*, 2 November 1985.
100 TV1, *Sunday*, 20 October 1985, transcript.
101 Muldoon responding to a question from Dick Griffin, Radio New Zealand 'Focus', 20 October 1985.
102 Radio New Zealand 'Morning Report', 21 October 1985. Also *Press*, 21 October 1985.
103 Radio New Zealand 'Checkpoint', 23 October 1985.
104 *Cit. Press*, 24 October 1985.
105 Holmes' Programme, 2ZB, 24 October 1985.
106 *Midday Report*, 24 October 1985.
107 *Cit. Christchurch Star*, 25 October 1985.
108 Muldoon, *Number 38*, p 201, and Radio New Zealand 2 p.m. News, 1 November 1985. McLay explained his version of events in detail to the Auckland Divisional Executive; see detailed summary of his address in the Minutes, 4 November 1985. See also *Christchurch Star*, 31 October 1985.
109 Wellington–BSG, 23 August 1989. The demotions of Muldoon and Wellington were extensively covered on television and radio e.g. TV1 *6.30 News*, TV2 *Eyewitness News* and Radio New Zealand 'Checkpoint', all 31 October 1985, and Radio New Zealand 'Morning Report', 1 November 1985.
110 *Cit. Timaru Herald*, 2 November 1985.
111 Radio New Zealand 'Morning Report', 31 October 1985.
112 *Auckland Star*, 9 December 1985.
113 All three *cit.* Radio New Zealand 'Checkpoint', 6 November 1985.
114 *NZ Herald* and *Auckland Star*, 9 November 1985.
115 Walker, *cit.* Radio New Zealand 'Morning Report', 16 December 1985.
116 Walker to W. M. Bremner, Karori Branch Chairman, who had criticised the Sunday Club, 20 December 1985, MP. The 'two others' were McLay and Bolger.
117 *NZ Herald*, 5 November 1985.
118 J. Baumfield, Secretary, Nelson Electorate Committee, Support Correspondence Folder, October–November 1985, MP. See also Non-support Correspondence Folder, October–November 1985, MP.
119 Muldoon to B. C. Smith, Chairman, Waipa Electorate, 12 December 1985. Also Smith to Muldoon, 6 December 1985, MP.
120 Ken Comber to Muldoon, 24 October 1985, MP.
121 Muldoon to W. Mitchell, 21 October 1985, MP.
122 McLay, National Executive Minutes, 23 October 1985.
123 Thompson, ibid.
124 Simich, ibid.
125 Bolger, ibid.
126 TV1 *6.30 News*, 23 October 1985. See also 'Paul Holmes Show', 2ZB, 24 October 1985, for a long interview with Quin, and Radio New Zealand 'Morning Report', 24 October 1985.
127 *Cit. Press* and *Christchurch Star*, 24 October 1985.

128 National Executive Minutes, 27 November 1985.

129 TV2 *Eyewitness News*, 27 November 1985; Radio New Zealand 'Checkpoint', 27 November 1985, and 'Morning Report', 28 November 1985.

130 National Executive Minutes, 27 November 1985.

131 National Executive Minutes, 29 January 1986.

132 Ibid.

133 Radio New Zealand 'Midday Report', 6 March 1986.

134 *Auckland Star* and *NZ Herald*, 2, 3, 4, 5, 6, 7 and 9 December 1985. The articles include an interesting article on McLay by John Goulter, *Auckland Star*, 9 December 1985, and another on Bolger by Greg Shand, *Auckland Star*, 16 December 1985, both in the context of the abortive December coup.

135 Cox–BSG, 2 March 1990, and McLean–BSG, 6 March 1990.

136 Friedlander–BSG, 27 March 1990.

137 McLay–BSG, 14 December 1985.

138 *Cit. Auckland Star*, 9 December 1985.

139 *Press*, 1 November 1985.

140 Walker to McKinnon, 31 January 1986.

141 Birch–BSG, 1 March 1990.

142 McLay–BSG, 12 July 1993.

143 Friedlander–BSG, 27 March 1990.

144 RDM–BSG, 2 October 1989.

145 Birch–BSG, 1 March 1990.

146 McLay–BSG, 12 July 1993.

147 McLay–BSG, 13 May 1995.

148 Ibid. For further insights into the overthrow of McLay see Goldsmith, *John Banks*, pp 115–18; Hames, *Winston Peters*, pp 39–41; Richardson, *Making a Difference*, p 39.

149 That was also one of the reasons why Muldoon's loyal supporter, Wellington, was left in seat 37, although his decision to retire, announced prior to the leadership change but revoked after it, and his implacable opposition to New Right policies also made his rehabilitation by Bolger difficult. For an astute assessment of both Wellington and of Bolger's reluctance to promote him see an article by Oliver Riddell, *Press*, 15 July 1986.

24 Court Cases, Radio Pacific and the 1987 Election

1 National Executive Minutes, 16 April 1986.

2 National Executive Minutes, 18 June 1986.

3 Leay–BSG, 2 March 1990.

4 Walker–BSG, 22 June 1989.

5 Documents relating to all these and other court cases are found in MP.

6 Brigadier John Smith, Director of the SIS, to Robert Jones, 2 December 1983. Copies of the correspondence between Smith and Jones are found in MP. Smith had become director of the SIS in 1983 after Muldoon had initially rejected his nomination by Hensley, the head of the Prime Minister's Department. Muldoon was very conscious of the need to have an SIS director who was seen to be part of an independent judiciary and wanted a judge or prominent lawyer to replace Paul Molineaux when he retired as director after seven years in the post. Only when Hensley returned and told Muldoon that 'it was impossible to find a suitable judge or lawyer to take on the task and Smith was clearly the best person available' did Muldoon 'reluctantly agree to the appointment'. Hensley–BSG, 19 August 1994.

7 *Sunday News*, 18 March 1984.

8 *Evening Post*, 20 March 1984, and *NZ Herald*, *Dominion* and *Press*, 21 March 1984.

9 Jones, *Memories of Muldoon*, p 172.

10 Muldoon interview with Dairne Shanahan, *Sunday*, 27 July 1984.

11 Jones–BSG 23 April 1990. Jones deals in detail with both the SIS incident and the two libel cases in *Memories of Muldoon*, pp 154–74, and Jones also recalled the matter at length in an interview with the author on 23 April 1990.

12 Dalgety to Muldoon, nd, MP.

13 Summary of Muldoon's total assets in 1983, MP.

14 Dalgety to Commissioner of the Salvation Army, 26 July 1979, and Dalgety to Muldoon, 27 July 1979, MP.

15 Dalgety to Camp, 12 December 1985, MP.

16 Detailed accounts in MP.

17 Correspondence and other documents on all these activities are in the Muldoon Papers, e.g. T. Carboon, National Marketing Manager, Countrywide Banking Corporation Ltd to Muldoon, 29 September 1988, MP.

18 *NZ Truth*, 3 December 1986.

19 Dobbs-Wiggin-McCann-Erikson, memo re survey, 11 June 1985, MP.

20 Elizabeth Morgan to The Manager Radio Pacific, 16 December 1984, MP.

21 Richard Prebble to Muldoon, 18 April 1985, MP.

22 Muldoon to Cheryl Dee, Acting Editor, *Australasian Radio Week*, MP.

23 RDM–BSG, 1 August 1989.

24 *Cit. Daily News*, 6 July 1985. For two similar assessments of Lange by astute

journalists see Bruce Jesson, 'The Tragedy of David Lange', and Warwick Roger, 'The End of a Storyteller'. A political scientist's analysis of the characters and political styles of Rowling, Lange, Palmer and Moore is given by John Henderson, who also worked for Rowling as Head of Labour's Research Unit and for Lange as Director of the Prime Minister's Advisory Group, and is found in his 'Labour's Modern Prime Ministers and the Party: A Study of Contrasting Political Styles'.

25 RDM–BSG, 1 August 1989.

26 Muldoon speech to Otago High School Old Boys Society luncheon, nd, MP.

27 Muldoon speech to 2000 suppliers and staff of Kiwi Co-op Dairies Ltd, Hawera, *Daily News*, 6 July 1985.

28 Muldoon in *Communique*, Tamaki National Party Newsletter, nd [June 1985].

29 Muldoon in *Communique*, nd [September 1985].

30 *Communique*, nd [Christmas 1985].

31 Muldoon, Politico-Economic Forecast for 1986/87, 12 February 1986 with addendum 5 March 1986, and Politico-Economic Forecast for the period 1985–1990, 8 May 1985, MP.

32 Muldoon 'Forecast for 1986/87', p 16.

33 Ibid., pp 7 and 18.

34 E.g. at a meeting organised by the Tauranga Superannuitants Association and attended by six hundred people, *Bay of Plenty Times*, 2 April 1987.

35 Muldoon to The Chairman of NZRFU, 18 October 1984, MP.

36 Kit Toogood, summary of phone call to arrange meeting with Muldoon, 25 June 1985, and Muldoon's Draft of Brief of Evidence, 1985, MP. Templeton, *Human Rights and Sporting Contacts,* pp 222–36, details the positions of the Labour Government and the National Opposition on the proposed 1985 tour and the legal action which stopped it. See also Richards, *Dancing on our Bones*, pp 232–4.

37 The individual voting records for all MPs at each stage of the Bill and on critical amendments is found in *Evening Post*, 26 April 1966.

38 Ray Wheeler to RDM, 17 April 1986, and Muldoon's reply scrawled across the bottom, MP.

39 Muldoon, *Auckland Star*, 18 May 1985.

40 Muldoon continued to raise the issue, e.g. in Press Statements on 1 and 12 September 1985, MP.

41 Tremewan to Muldoon, 18 July 1986, MP. Tremewan noted in the letter that he had discussed the matter with and had the support of Colin Brenton-Rule, his predecessor as director of the Auckland Division, who was also both a long-time ASB trustee and Muldoon supporter. Among the other trustees who unanimously supported the ASB reforms were the former National MP, Alf Allen and Mrs E. A. Wylie, the long-time leader of the National Party in Mount Albert. Both were also generally thought of as being part of 'Rob's Mob'.

42 Muldoon's comments had been reported in the *NZ Herald*, 16 July 1986.

43 T. J. Harris, President, ASB Trust Bank, to Muldoon, 7 August 1986, MP. Also Rudd, Watts and Stone, Barristers and Solicitors, to Muldoon, 17 July 1986, MP.

44 Dennis Ferrier, Executive Director ASB Trust Bank, to Muldoon, 18 July 1986, MP. See also *Sunday News*, 20 July 1986.

45 Harris to Muldoon, 7 August 1986, MP.

46 Muldoon to President, Auckland Savings Bank, 23 July 1986, MP.

47 Ibid.

48 Ibid.

49 Muldoon to Professor John Dunmore, Chairman of the HSC, 17 September 1986, and to C. J. McKenzie, Secretary of Labour, 11 September 1986, MP.

50 Dunmore to Muldoon, 20 October 1986, and McKenzie to Muldoon, 21 October 1986, MP.

51 E.g. Muldoon Press Statements, 26 November and 17 December 1986, MP.

52 Muldoon to T. G. Harris, 23 July 1986.

53 Shailes–BSG, 19 August 1994.

54 *Eastern Courier*, 5 March 1986.

55 Muldoon, typescript of speech notes, Orewa Business Association, 27 April 1987, MP.

56 *Press*, 5 March 1987.

57 Ibid., 31 March 1987.

58 National's candidate in Birkenhead in 1987 was the author, who had previously been Chairman of the Labour Party's Auckland Regional Council, 1973–4 and 1975–79.

59 For a summary of the 1987 election see M. Clark (ed), *The 1987 General Election: What Happened?*; J. Boston and K. Jackson, 'The New Zealand General Election of 1987'; and Stephen Levine and Nigel S. Roberts, 'Parties, leaders, and Issues in the 1987 Election'. The National majorities over Labour in Fendalton, North Shore and Remuera were respectively 311, 920 and 406.

60 For Richardson's version of the deputy-leadership vote and her subsequent selection as finance spokesperson see Richardson, *Making a Difference*, pp 41–3.

61 Ibid, p 42.

62 Muldoon to Bolger, 17 September 1987, MP.
63 Ibid.
64 Ibid.

25 *The Global Economic Action Institute and the 1990 Election*

1 Muldoon, *Sunday Star*, 25 June 1989. For brief but interesting summaries of the 1987 sharemarket crash and some of the entrepreneurs involved in it see Brian Gaynor, 'The boom before the crash', and Ron Taylor, 'Broken Wings'.
2 Muldoon, 1990 election pamphlet in Tamaki.
3 Muldoon, *Sunday Star*, 13 September 1987.
4 *NZPD*, v 512, 6 March 1991, p 659.
5 RDM *cit*. Auckland Divisional Executive Minutes, 7 December 1987.
6 *NZPD*, v 491, 16 August 1988, p 6006.
7 Ibid, p 6007.
8 Maurice Williamson–BSG, 20 April 1996.
9 Ibid.
10 Muldoon–BSG, 1 August 1989.
11 Ibid and Muldoon–Sullivan interview, 31 March 1992.
12 *NZ Herald*, 2 November 1989.
13 Muldoon Press Statement, 18 September 1984, MP.
14 RDM–BSG, 14 August 1989.
15 Paul Bradwell to Muldoon, 2 April 1985, and Muldoon to Bradwell, 17 April 1985, MP.
16 Proposed 'Introduction' to the book, attached to Muldoon to Bradwell, 17 April 1985, MP.
17 Lange *cit. Sunday*, 29 July 1984.
18 Ibid. Lange–BSG, 26 August 1999.
19 Lange to the Manager of the Bank of New Zealand, Onehunga, 5 March 1984. Copy in MP. The copy had been sent to Muldoon by a woman who had found it in a book she bought from a Lange family garage sale. See Muldoon, Press Release, 13 June 1986, MP.
20 Muldoon to Lange, 27 August 1985, MP.
21 Jack Kemp and Bill Bradley to Muldoon, nd. [August 1985], MP.
22 Lange to Muldoon, 28 August 1985, MP. Also Lange–BSG, 26 August 1999.
23 Muldoon, Press Statement 30 August 1985, MP.
24 RDM–BSG, 14 August 1989.
25 Ibid.
26 Hobart Rowen, 'Needed Soon: 1 World Bank President', *Washington Post*, 24 November 1985, clipping in MP.
27 Address notes to Parliamentary Working Round on Exchange Rates and Co-ordination, Zurich, Switzerland, 28 June 1986, MP.

28 RDM–BSG, 14 August 1989, and GEAI, *International Policy Coordination. Economic Cooperation or Confrontation? The Challenge of the '90s*, GEAI, New York, 1989.
29 GEAI, *Improving the Global Economy Through Action Policies and Partnerships*, GEAI, New York, nd [1998].
30 The controversial Family Federation for World Peace and Unification, commonly called the Unification Church or the 'Moonies', was formed in the late 1950s by a Korean religious leader, Rev. Moon Sun-myung. The church, which claims millions of adherents worldwide, has always been interested in and involved in conservative politics and was favoured in some senior political circles in the USA. It also has built up considerable business interests.
31 Muldoon to Eugene McCarthy, 22 May 1987, MP. See also GEIA, *The Rondini Conference on International Monetary Reform*, Rome, Italy, 30 June–3 July 1987, GEAI, New York, 1987.
32 McCarthy to Muldoon, 4 June 1987, MP.
33 Muldoon to Jeremiah Schnee, Special Advisor to the Chairman, GEAI, 18 August 1987 and 1 September 1987, MP.
34 Muldoon, Report on Visit to Washington DC, 27 September–1 October 1987, 14 pp, p 5, MP.
35 RDM–BSG, 14 August 1989.
36 See Itinerary and background papers, 58 pp, in MP.
37 'Stimulating Productivity in Sub-Saharan Africa', conference programme, 29–31 August 1988, MP.
38 'Perceptions Versus Realities of Japanese Investment in the US', Seminar programme, 18 October 1988, MP.
39 'Successful Economic Development Strategies of the Pacific Rim Nations', Conference programme, 14–18 November 1988, MP.
40 GEAI, *International Policy Co-ordination*, *op cit.*, 65 pp with a preface by Muldoon.
41 RDM–BSG, 14 August 1989. Muldoon also spoke frequently to New Zealand audiences about GEAI and his role in it, e.g. typescripts of Muldoon's addresses to Newmarket Rotary Club, 28 March 1988; Market Research Society of New Zealand, 25 October 1988; and Wanganui Club, 31 October 1988, MP.
42 GEAI Report of Meetings in Japan, 7–12 November 1988, MP.
43 GEAI board agenda and minutes and seminar programmes, together with itineraries of visits and meetings 13–17 March 1989, MP.
44 Pinehurst International Seminar programme

and related papers, 17–20 May 1989, MP.
The folder also includes details of the
meetings Muldoon held over the following
four days. Muldoon describes the Pinehurst
Seminar in articles in the *Sunday Star*,
21 May 1989 and 4 June 1989, and in
speech notes for an address to the Waipu
Lions Club, 3 June 1989, MP.

45   RDM–BSG, 14 August 1989.

46   'Restoring Global Equilibrium: Increasing
US Exports to Japan', Seminar Programme,
23 May 1989, MP.

47   'Hungary in the Nineties: Enhancing
Productivity, Competitiveness, and
Economic Growth in Eastern Europe',
Conference programme, 9–11 November,
1989, and file of correspondence about the
conference and related papers, MP.

48   See Ambassador John Holdridge, GEAI
Board, to Muldoon, 29 April 1992, MP.

49   *Cit.* GEAI, *Paving The Way to the Market
Economy*, Moscow, 17–19 September, 1990,
Conference Programme and Report, p 1,
MP. *See also* GEAI, *Global Economic Issues*,
No. 90/8 and 90/9, and Graham Simon,
GEAI Program Director, to Muldoon,
5 June 1990 and 15 October 1990, MP.
There is a folder of material on and from the
Moscow conference in MP.

50   RDM–BSG, 16 December 1990.

51   RDM–BSG, 5 May 1991.

52   GEAI Income Statement for 1990 attached
to Agenda for GEAI Board of Directors and
Board of Advisors Meeting, 27 April 1991,
MP. Apart from the US$50,000 paid to
GEAI each month by the Unification
Church during 1990 GEAI had also
received US$138,000 from foundations,
US$177,950 from companies, US$41,000
from conference fees, and US$5,750 from
individuals.

53   Muldoon *cit. North and South*, September
1989, pp 99–100. Also *NZ Herald*, 24 and
26 December 1987.

54   RDM–BSG, 24 February 1990. Also
RDM–BSG, 1 March 1990, 19 April 1990,
and 16 December 1990. See also *Sunday Star*,
3 December 1989, *Auckland Star*, 12 January
1990, and *Woman's Day*, 21 February 1990.

55   RDM–BSG, 24 February 1990.

56   Ibid.

57   RDM–BSG, 19 April 1990.

58   All this correspondence is in the Muldoon
papers. See Moore to Muldoon, nd.
[December 1983]; Anderton to Muldoon,
7 December 1983; Michael Cullen, National
Secretary NZ Freezing and Related
Industries Clerical Officers' Industrial Union
of Workers, 4 December 1983, MP.

59   Moore–BSG, 14 March 1990.

60   RDM–BSG, 1 March 1990.

61   Kidd–BSG, 1 March 1990.

62   Muldoon, *cit. NZ Herald*, 9 March 1990.

63   Muldoon *cit. NZ Herald*, 27 March 1990.

64   *New Idea*, 11 August 1990.

65   Muldoon, 1990 election pamphlet in Tamaki.

66   *The General Election 1990*, E9. Government
Printer. For a detailed study of the 1990
election generally see J. Vowles and
P. Aimer, *Voters' Vengeance: The 1990 Election
in New Zealand and the Fate of the Fourth
Labour Government*, and E. M. McLeay (ed),
*The 1990 General Election: Perspectives on
Political Change in New Zealand*. Also
H. Catt, 'Landslide by Default: The New
Zealand Election of 1990'; S. Levine and
N. Roberts, 'The New Zealand General
Election of 1990'; and A. McRobie, 'The
New Zealand General Election of 1990'.

67   RDM–BSG, 16 December 1990.

26   *'Mr Speaker, I Say Goodbye'*

1   RDM–BSG, 16 December 1990.

2   RDM–BSG, 3 April 1991. For a general
assessment of the Labour Party following
the 1990 election see Barry Gustafson,
'Coming Home? The Labour Party in 1916
and 1991 Compared'.

3   RDM–BSG, 3 April 1991.

4   Ibid.

5   Ibid. For other conflicting views of the post-
1990 National Government, its leaders,
policies and internal conflicts, see
J. B. Bolger, *Bolger: A View from the Top*;
Paul Goldsmith, *John Banks, A Biography*;
Martin Hames, *Winston First: The
unauthorised account of Winston Peters' career*;
Michael Laws, *The Demon Profession*; and
Ruth Richardson, *Making a Difference*.

6   Social Welfare Annual Reports *cit. Sunday
Star*, 13 September 1992.

7   Muldoon, speech notes of address to
NZ Credit and Finance Institute, 18 March
1991, MP.

8   *Cit. NZ Herald*, 4 April 1991.

9   Muldoon, speech notes, 20 September 1991,
MP.

10   Muldoon, speech notes, 27 September 1991,
MP.

11   Muldoon, speech notes, 30 September 1991,
MP.

12   Muldoon *cit. Dominion* and *NZ Herald*,
18 November 1991.

13   *The Examiner*, 14 March 1991.

14   RDM–BSG, 3 April 1991. See also The
Treasury, *Briefing to the Incoming Government*,
Treasury, Wellington, 1990.

15   Muldoon, *NZ Herald*, 22 August 1991.

16   *NZPD*, v 489, 28 June 1988, p 4860.
17   *NZPD*, v 496, 21 March 1989, p 9868.
18   Muldoon, typescript of article for National Caucus 'Back Bench' publication nd [April 1992], MP.
19   Muldoon to all MPs and candidates, 7 August 1990, enclosing the article 'Monetary Policy' by William A. Niskanen, MP.
20   E.g. Muldoon, *My Way*, p 67.
21   Muldoon, speech notes, 8 March 1991, MP.
22   RDM–BSG, 3 April 1991.
23   Ibid.
24   RDM–BSG, 14 August 1989.
25   RDM–BSG, 3 April 1991. Also Muldoon–Sullivan interviews, 6 and 7 May 1992.
26   RDM–BSG, 3 April 1991. See also Richardson, *Making a Difference*, pp 123–6.
27   RDM–BSG, 16 December 1990 and 3 April 1991.
28   RDM–BSG, 3 April 1991.
29   See Muldoon, question for written answer in Parliament, 6 December 1990, when he asked Richardson, 'Does she propose to introduce any amendments to the Reserve Bank Act and if not, why not?' Also Laws, *The Demon Profession*, pp 144–5, for the reference to the pre-election caucus vote, and Richardson, *Making a Difference*, pp 44–8, esp. p 48 where Richardson admits that the vote in caucus was 'extremely close' and that she failed to convince not only Muldoon but also Bolger and Birch.
30   *NZPD*, v 512, 22 January 1991, pp 31–2.
31   *NZPD*, v 513, 6 March 1991, pp 658–61, p 659.
32   *NZPD*, v 513, 20 March 1991, pp 953–4. For the same reasons he expressed in 1991, Muldoon as Prime Minister had consistently blocked attempts by his Minister of Internal Affairs, Highet, supported by his Under-Secretary, Comber, to introduce Lotto or any form of national lottery between 1975 and 1984. Labour did after it became Government. Highet–BSG, 12 March 1990.
33   *NZPD*, v 513, 13 March 1991, pp 781–2.
34   *NZPD*, v 516, 19 June 1991, pp 2509–11.
35   *NZPD*, v 519, 26 September 1991, pp 4565–9, p 4565.
36   Ibid, p 4567.
37   RDM–BSG, 26 November 1991. Although Cliffe and Robertson both held safe National seats, they subsequently left the National Party to set up the United Party and were defeated at the 1996 election.
38   Ibid.
39   Ibid.
40   Ibid.
41   Ibid. Also *NZ Herald*, 8 and 9 November 1991, and *Auckland Star*, editorial,

10 November 1991.
42   The summary of what Muldoon said at caucus is Muldoon's version as provided some days later to the author in an interview on 26 November 1991. The author confirmed most of it subsequently in confidential discussions with a number of other caucus members.
43   Tremewan–BSG, 12 November 1991. Some journalists also were prepared shortly before Muldoon finally and publicly announced his retirement to predict it and analyse why he was going and what the likely effects would be both on Tamaki and the National Government, e.g. Colin James, *National Business Review*, 15 November 1991, p 9.
44   Muldoon speech notes, 13 November 1991, MP.
45   *Cit. Dominion Sunday Times*, 17 November 1991. See also for Muldoon's comments from Fiji, *Dominion*, *Evening Post* and *NZ Herald*, 16 November 1991.
46   RDM–BSG, 26 November 1991, and Malcolm–BSG, 3 December 1991. See also *Dominion*, 21 December 1991, in which Muldoon admitted getting Simich to stand.
47   *Cit. NZ Herald*, 18 November 1991. Also tape recording of Muldoon, 'Lilies and Other Things', Radio Pacific, 17 November 1991.
48   Ibid. and *Dominion*, 18 November 1991.
49   E.g. Richard Long, 'From Young Turk to wily old warrior', *Dominion*, 18 November 1991. One excellent article assessing Muldoon and published at the time of his retirement was by Colin James, *National Business Review*, 22 November 1991, pp 9 and 30. Another interesting contemporary evaluation is John Roberts, 'Measuring Muldoon', a radio broadcast on Concert FM in November 1991 and subsequently published in M. Clark (ed), *The Roberts Report*, Victoria University Press, Wellington, 1999, pp 101–6.
50   Anderton to Muldoon, 19 December 1991, MP.
51   G. T. Drain to Muldoon, 28 January 1992, MP.
52   Tofilau Eti Alesana to Muldoon, 19 December 1991, MP.
53   *ODT*, 21 December 1991.
54   E.g. Muldoon to Bill Matthewson, 21 November 1991, MP.
55   *NZPD*, v 521, 4 December 1991, pp 5897–5928.
56   *NZPD*, v 521, 4 December 1991, pp 5871–3, p 5873.
57   *NZ Herald*–NRB poll, *NZ Herald*, 9 December 1991.
58   RDM–BSG, 26 November 1991.

59 *NZ Herald*, 9 November 1991.
60 *NZPD*, v 521, 17 December 1999,
pp 6449–52.
61 Ibid, pp 6452–3. Moore had expressed the
same sentiments to the author in an
interview, 14 March 1990.
62 Ibid, pp 6455–8, p 6455.
63 Ibid, p 6457.
64 Ibid.
65 The other three shortlisted candidates were
Maureen Eardley-Wilmot, a businesswoman
and the party's woman vice-president; Ron
Greer, a local businessman and party official
in Tamaki; and Jennie Langley, a public
relations consultant.
66 Dick Griffin interviewed by Maggie Barry,
National Radio, 13 December 1991.
67 Muldoon, 'Lilies and Other Things', Radio
Pacific, 15 December 1991, tape in author's
possession.
68 Tony Steele and Chris Laidlaw.
69 *NZPD*, v 521, pp 6455–8, p 6456.
70 *NZ Herald*, 21 December 1991, for articles
on the candidate selection meeting and
Muldoon's reaction.
71 *The 1990 General Election, 27 October 1990*,
E9, Government Printer.
72 *Dominion*, 12 January 1992. Also
NZ Herald, 12 January 1992. Also
Muldoon, speech notes, 12 January 1992,
(incorrectly dated 21 January) MP.
73 Both cit. *NZ Herald*, 4 February 1992. For
Muldoon's prediction see *NZ Herald*,
14 February 1992.
74 Colleen Reilly in *Dominion Sunday Times*,
23 February 1992.
75 Muldoon expressed his satisfaction with the
by-election result in *NZ Herald*,
17 February 1992.
76 *The Tamaki By-election*, 15 February 1992,
E9, Government Printer. For a detailed
study of the by-election see R. Miller and
H. Catt, *Season of Discontent: By-elections and
the Bolger Government*. Bolger in *Bolger: A
View From The Top*, pp 78–89, also discusses
the Tamaki by-election.
77 The dinner and the events surrounding it
are covered in detail by Jones in *Memories of
Muldoon*, pp 178–93. See also Jones to
author, 21 January 1992, and front-page
reports and photos in the *Dominion*, *Evening
Post*, and *NZ Herald*, 29 January 1992.
78 E.g. to the Lions District Convention at
Gisborne, 20 March 1992, and to the Otago
Chamber of Commerce, 26 March 1992.
79 *NZ Herald*, 7 May 1992.
80 Information on Muldoon's last illness and
death comes largely from an interview with
Dame Thea Muldoon, 10 August 1992, and

conversations the author had with Muldoon
during the first seven months of 1992.
81 Derek Lowe, Managing Director of Radio
Pacific, to author, 11 August 1992.
82 RDM–BSG, 14 July 1992.
83 Ibid.
84 A three-hour audio-tape of Radio Pacific's
'Tribute to Sir Robert Muldoon', Sunday
9 August 1992, includes the ending of his
final broadcast the previous Sunday.
85 *Dominion*, 6 August 1992.
86 Radio Pacific's 'Tribute to Sir Robert
Muldoon' includes that early morning call.
87 Thea Muldoon–BSG, 10 August 1992.
88 Death Certificate, Folio 013898, Entry
2243, Auckland Registry, 12 August 1992.
See also *NZ Herald*, *Press*, *Dominion* and
ODT, 6 August 1992, and *Sunday Star* and
Sunday Times, 9 August 1992. Amidst the
polite or even laudatory obituaries, Geoff
Chapple's 'The Get Real Eulogy', *Sunday
Star*, 9 August 1999, is particularly savage,
referring to Muldoon's deprived childhood
as the psychological foundation of his
unpleasant character and summarising why
people such as Quigley, Moyle, McLay, Spiro
Zavos and others would not necessarily be
saddened by Muldoon's death. One of the
most thoughtful and provocative articles,
which suggests that Muldoon tried to
govern New Zealand as 'Napoleon ran
France 200 years ago' and that his 'attitudes
were socialist – more so even than Michael
Savage's or Peter Fraser's', was by Oliver
Riddell, *Press*, 6 August 1992.
89 *NZPD*, v 528, 5 August 1992,
pp 10323–44.
90 The speakers in order were Jim Bolger,
Mike Moore, Jim Anderton, Bill Birch,
Helen Clark, Paul East, Peter Tapsell, John
Banks, Rob Munro, Clem Simich, Christine
Fletcher, and Jeff Grant.
91 Ibid., p 10326.
92 Ibid., pp 10328–9.
93 Ibid., p 10329.
94 Ibid.
95 Ibid., p 10330.
96 Merle Bell to Thea Muldoon, 23 August
1992, MP.
97 Radio Pacific, 'Tribute to Sir Robert
Muldoon', audio-tape, nd [9 August 1992].
98 Thea Muldoon–BSG, 10 August 1992.
99 Rymer *cit. NZ Herald*, 7 August 1992.
100 For a description of the funeral and
comments by some of those, such as Arthur
Allan Thomas, who attended, see *NZ
Herald*, 8 August 1992
101 O'Reilly–BSG, 21 January 2000.
102 *NZ Herald*, 8 August 1992.

Bibliography

PRIMARY SOURCES

A. INTERVIEWS (all by the author except where indicated otherwise)

Sir Robert Muldoon:
Formal interviews on 24.2.89, 7.7.89, 15.7.89, 24.7.89, 1.8.89, 14.8.89, 22.9.89, 27.9.89, 2.10.89, 24.2.90, 1.4.90, 19.4.90, 16.12.90, 3.4.91, 6.5.91 and 26.11.91, and various informal conversations at other times up to 14.7.92.

Parliamentary colleagues and opponents:

Hon. John Banks, 7.3.90
Hon. Michael Bassett, 30.3.90
Mr Bruce Beetham, 11.7.91
Hon. Max Bradford, 26.3.90 (Earlier
    association as Treasury official, Employers
    and Bankers official, and Director-General of
    the National Party)
Sir William Birch, 1.3.90
Mr John Chewings, 20.5.90
Rt Hon. Helen Clark, 10.6.91
Mr Ken Comber, 7.3.90
Hon. Warren Cooper, 22.3.90
Mr Michael Cox, 2.3.90
Sir Roger Douglas, 29.3.90
Hon. John Falloon, 8.3.90 and 13.3.90
Hon. Tony Friedlander, 27.3.90
Hon. George Gair, 8.3.90
Hon. Jim Gerard, 28.2.90 (Earlier association
    as Chairman, Canterbury-Westland Division
    of the National Party).
Hon. Peter Gordon, 12.3.90
Hon. Alan Highet, 12.3.90
Rt Hon. Jonathan Hunt, 13.3.90

Hon. Doug Kidd, 1.3.90
Rt Hon. David Lange, 26.8.99
Hon. Murray McCully, 21.3.90 (Earlier
    association as party official)
Rt Hon. Duncan MacIntyre, 10.7.91
Rt Hon. Don McKinnon, 7.3.90
Hon. Jim McLay, 12.7.93
Mr Ian McLean, 6.3.90
Hon. Aussie Malcolm, 3.12.91
Mr Mike Minogue, 23.8.91
Rt Hon. Mike Moore, 14.3.90
Hon. Winston Peters, 27.2.90
Hon. Richard Prebble, 13.3.90
Hon. Lockwood Smith, 7.3.90
Hon. Rob Storey, 21.3.90 (Earlier
    association as President of Federated
    Farmers)
Hon. Rob Talbot, 2.4.90
Sir Brian Talboys, 20.4.90
Hon. Bert Walker, 22.6.89
Ms Marilyn Waring, 24.6.91 and 24.2.93
Hon. Merv Wellington, 23.8.89
Hon. Venn Young, 28.2.90

Five MPs and former MPs declined to be interviewed on Muldoon. They were Hon. Colin Moyle, Hon. Derek Quigley, Hon. Ruth Richardson, Sir Wallace Rowling, and Hon. Simon Upton.

Professional Staff

Mr Peter Acland, 28.2.90
Mr Ed Buckton, 22.8.89
Mr Malcolm Fearn, 29.8.94
Mrs Lesley Miller, 5.4.90

Mrs Margaret Mouat, 8.3.90
Mr Gray Nelson, 3.4.90
Mrs Jenny Officer, 28.8.92, 3 and 4.9.92
Mr Gerry Symmans, 19.2.93

Senior Civil Servants

Mr Frank Corner, 16.6.99
Dr Roderick Deane, 18.8.94
Mr Bernard Galvin, 25.10.89
Mr Gerald Hensley, 19.8.94
Mr Henry Lang, 5.3.90

Mr Merwyn Norrish, 23.3.90
Dr Mervyn Probine, 6.3.90
Mr Bill Renwick, 15.3.90
Sir Spencer Russell, 8.3.90
Dr Graham Scott, 18.8.94

Mr Denis McLean, 27.3.90
Mr John Martin, 12.12.90
Mr Patrick Millen, 29.3.90

Mr Fred Shailes, 14.8.94
Dr Robin Williams, 1.3.90

Interest Group and Business Leaders
Mr Ken Douglas, 9.8.92
Sir John Ingram, 11.6.96
Sir Robert Jones, 23.4.90
Sir Colin Maiden, 22.6.99
Professor Ray Meyer, 11.6.96

Denis O'Reilly, 21.1.00
Mr Jim Rowe, 4.4.90
Sir Laurence Stevens, 11.4.00
Sir Roderick Weir, 4.4.90
Mr John Wells, 5.7.94

Journalists, Broadcasters and Academic Observers
Mr David Beatson, 5.4.90
Mr Bevan Burgess, 5.3.90
Mr Max Cryer, 3.2.93
Mr Brian Easton, 13.6.89, 12.2.90, 3.2.93

Mr Ian Fraser, 23.4.90
Sir Frank Holmes 12.3.90
Mr Neale McMillan, 2.4.90
Mr Barrie Soper, 22.3.90

National Party Officials
Mrs Merle Bell, 29.5.90
Sir George Chapman, 6.3.90
Mr Peter Dempsey, 27.9.89
Mr Murray Hunter, 26.8.93 and 27.10.93

Mr Barrie Leay, 2.3.90
Mr Stuart Masters, 31.8.93
Mr John Tremewan, 29.9.89, and 15.3.91

Family, Friends and People Associated with his Earlier Life
Mr Bill Adair, 31.5.89
Mr Lawrence Browne, 15.7.90
Mr Colin Busfield, 7 and 13.6.89
Professor Margaret Clark, 25.10.89
Mr Fritz Eisenhofer, 7.3.90
Mrs Helen Eisenhofer, 7.3.90
Mr Richard Fickling, 2.6.89
Mrs Thea Frogley, 29.5.90
Mr Alan Jenkin, 10.5.90
Mrs Geraldine Jenkin, 10.5.90

Mr Joseph Jones, 22.4.98
Mr Harry Julian, 28.5.90
The Rev Hayes Lloyd, 6.6.89
Mr Fred Mills, 13.9.89
Dame Thea Muldoon, 19.2.92 and 10.8.92
Mr Jack Ryder, 1.6.89
Mr Vic Stace, 9.5.90
Mr Bert Stokes, 24.4.90
Mr Jack Turner, 1.6.90
Mrs Barbara Williams (née Muldoon), 19.6.99

Other
Mr Les Gibson, 13.3.90
Ms Shona MacFarlane, 12.3.90

Sir Duncan McMullin, 7.10.99
Dr Pat Savage, 1.3.93

Interviews conducted by the author during earlier research on the history of the National Party which included considerable material on Sir Robert Muldoon
Sir Robert Muldoon, 22 and 29.4.85
Sir Lancelot Adams-Schneider, 21.8.85
Hon. Alf Allen, 4.8.85
Mr Pat Baker, 4.8.85
Rt Hon. Jim Bolger, 21.8.85 and 25.9.85
Mr Colin Brenton-Rule, 4.7.85
Mr Bruce Cathie, 21.8.85
Sir George Chapman, 9.7.85
Mr Morrie Friedlander, 16.8.85 and 15.11.85
Hon. George Gair, 14 and 20.7.85
Hon. Eric Halstead, 19.7.85
Mr Roy Johnston, 10.7.85
Mr Graham Johnstone, 25 and 26.9.85
Mr Hamish Kynoch, 22.8.85
Sir Graham Latimer, 12.1.86
Mr Barrie Leay, 17.10.85
Mr David Lloyd, 4.11.85

Sir Alex McKenzie, 21.12.84
Rt Hon. Don McKinnon, 17.1.86
Hon. Jim McLay, 20.4.85 and 14.12.85
Mrs Dorothy McNab, 25.9.85
Sir John Marshall, 9.7.85
Mr Peter Paterson, 27.9.85
Mr Murray Reeves, 20.9.85 and 8.1.86
Mr Richard Seddon, 21.8.85
Hon. Dr Ian Shearer, 4.12.85
Sir Brian Talboys, 9.7.85
Hon. Hugh Templeton, 9.7.85
Mr John Tremewan, 17.4.85
Hon. Peter Wilkinson, 31.8.85
Mr Ralph Wilson, 22.8.85
Mrs Sue Wood, 17.4.85
Mrs Alice Wylie, 13.9.85

INTERVIEWS OF SIR ROBERT MULDOON BY DENIS WEDERELL, not dated [1968–69] Wederell Papers.

INTERVIEWS OF SIR ROBERT MULDOON BY JIM SULLIVAN, Oral History Centre, National Library of New Zealand, 3, 4 and 31 March, 1 and 2 April, and 6 and 7 May 1992.

INTERVIEW OF DAME THEA MULDOON BY JIM SULLIVAN, Oral History Centre, National Library of New Zealand, 7 May 1992.

B. MULDOON PAPERS

When I worked through Sir Robert Muldoon's papers they were located in various places: his parliamentary office; a large strong room in the National Party Research Unit's office; a large storeroom in Parliament Buildings; and his office, library, garage and storeroom in his home. Some records had been transferred to the National Archives in December 1985 and May and December 1986. After I had examined the papers in the strong room and storeroom in Parliament Buildings, they were moved to the National Archives in November 1990. After Sir Robert's death I sorted the papers in his home and arranged for their transfer to the National Archives in August 1992. Among the more significant or interesting files were those on:

Abortion 1974–75 (and subsequently)
Activities 1986 and 1987
Adult Adoption Information Bill 1983–84
Prime Minister's Advisory Group
Muldoon's aggressive image clippings 1974
Proposed All Black Rugby Tour of South Africa 1984–85
Appointment Diaries 1974–87
Auckland Airport Assault – 21 March 1975
ASB 1986
Banning of *Dominion* 1983
Bastion Point 1976–77
Bastion Point 1977–81
Bolger-McLay leadership 1986
Breach of Privilege 1975
Brooks Case, 1971–72
1984 Budget
Cabinet Committee Papers
Cabinet Meeting Papers 1975–84
Causes – (including Ecology, Forests, Baby Seals, US Ships, Film Censorship, etc.)
Citizens for Rowling campaign
Clyde Dam
Correspondence
Court Cases
DAVOS 1982–84
Defence of John Kirk, 1975
Devon Investments
Dominion articles by Muldoon, 1974
Dominion/NZ Council and Executive Meetings
Economic Situation 1966
Education especially Universities, 1968–69
1975 election
1978 election
1981 election
1984 election
1984 devaluation crisis
1984 post-election leadership

Erebus 1979–82
Europa Tax Case 1968–72
Extremists 1948–75
Freezing Industry Dispute and Stabilization Regulations, 1978
Gilbey's Gin advertisement 1971
Global Economic Action Institute (GEAI)
Harry Julian, Pacific Forum Line, Shipping Corporation
History
Homosexual law reform 1974
Homosexual law reform 1985–86
Horses
Illness 1989–90
Income Tax Amendment No.2 Bill, 1982–4
'Peter Pan' incident, 25 August 1974
IMF Mission and NZ Economy 1979
Jones Defamation Case 1985
Jones and NZ Party
Labour Party
Lange and Labour Party, 1984–86
Leadership Challenge 1980
List of SUP trade unionists March 1980
Long-term wage policy talks, 1983–84
Lowndes Lambert
Margaret Quin
Manapouri
Matai 1972–78
Mt Albert Campaign 1954
Moyle Incident
Muldoon–McLay leadership 1984–85
Muldoon's speeches
My Way
National Party Policy Papers and minutes
National Superannuation Policy 1973–75
National Superannuation General
Norman Kirk, 1974
Nuclear Ships Policy
Number 38
Politico-Economic Forecasts 1985–90 made in 1986
Press Clippings 1960–84
Press Conferences 1975–84
Press Statements 1974–91
Public Expenditure Committee and the Government Statistician 1973
Radio Pacific
Reserve Bank Papers
Rise and Fall of a Young Turk
Rocky Horror Show 1986
Security File 1966–77
SIS list of 'subversive' elements in rugby protest movement, August 1981
Social Credit (includes large number of issues associated with them)
1981 Springbok Rugby Tour of New Zealand
Sunday Club
Tamaki Campaign 1960
Tamaki electorate
Terry and the Gunrunners, 1985
Thomas (Arthur Allan) 1973–81
Transcripts of radio and television news and interviews
Treasury Papers
Truth articles by Muldoon, 1973
Visit to United States on Foreign Leader Program, 20.2.1965–20.4.1965.
Waitemata Campaign 1957

C. MULDOON'S OVERSEAS TRIP BOOKS
(Copies in the Muldoon and Gray Nelson Papers)

1976	9 April – 6 May	UK, France, Korea, Japan, China
	26–28 July	Nauru, 7th South Pacific Forum
	11–14 October	Fiji Law of Sea – South Pacific Forum
1977	16 March – 8 April	Australia, Singapore, Federal Republic of Germany, Belgium, UK, Egypt, Bahrain
	27 May – 1 July	Rarotonga, W. Samoa, Los Angeles, UK, France, Yugoslavia
	5–12 August	Kuala Lumpur (ASEAN), Thailand
	25 Aug – 2 Sept	Papua New Guinea South Pacific Forum
	18–19 October	Niue
	7–30 November	Washington DC and USA
1978	12–14 February	Sydney CHOGM
	19–20 May	Australia, Sir Robert Menzies funeral
	15 Sept – 2 October	Niue, South Pacific Forum, New York, UN General Assembly, Montreal Commonwealth Finance Ministers
1979	7–17 June	Paris OECD
	6–13 July	Solomon Islands, 10th South Pacific Forum, Kiribati independence celebrations
	28 July – 15 August	Mauritius, Zambia, Western Australia
	17 Sept – 15 Oct	Washington DC, London, Bremen, Malta, Belgrade, Romania, Gulf States
1980	25 May – 11 June	Indonesia, London, Paris, Switzerland, San Francisco
	11–16 July	Fiji, Kiribati, W. Samoa 11th South Pacific Forum
	1 Sept – 15 October	India, China, Bermuda, Washington DC, New York, Mexico
1981	14–16 April	Japan and Korea
	10–28 June	Hobart, Italy, Paris, UK, Federal Republic of Germany
	22–31 July	Washington DC and London. Met President Reagan, Vice-President Bush, Secretary of the Treasury Donald Regan. Private dinner with Margaret Thatcher, supper with Queen, wedding of Prince of Wales and Lady Diana Spencer
	9–12 August	Vanuatu 12th South Pacific Forum
	29 Sept – 7 Oct	Melbourne CHOGM
1982	5–24 May	Los Angeles, Paris, Geisenheim, London, Dublin
	10–11 June	Sydney
	26–16 Sept	Los Angeles, UK, Canada
	7–10 October	Brisbane Commonweath Games
1983	25 Jan – 9 Feb	Los Angeles, Davos (Switzerland), Singapore, Port Moresby, Jakarta
	Thurs 27 Jan 6 p.m.	Address Davos Symposium organised by European Management Forum Foundation. There from 27 to 31 January
	6–20 May	Los Angeles, Paris, Hungary, London
	3–11 June	Los Angeles, Belgrade, Athens
	23–25 June	Canberra
	27–31 August	Canberra South Pacific Forum
	15 Sept – 9 Oct	Los Angeles, St Kitts, Trinidad, Washington DC, New York, Boston
	3–6 November	Perth, Adelaide, Melbourne
	20 Nov – 1 Dec	New Delhi CHOGM
1984	10 Feb – 11 March	Los Angeles, Paris, Dublin, London, Washington DC, New York, New Orleans, Austin, San Antonio, San Francisco, Los Angeles, Honolulu
	22–22 June	Melbourne, Sydney.

D. OTHER PERSONAL PAPERS

(in the possession of the person named unless otherwise indicated)

SIR WILLIAM BIRCH PAPERS: Various documents and papers related to the 'Think Big' economic growth strategy.

HON. JOHN FALLOON PAPERS: Various papers relating to financial and taxation matters 1981–84.

SIR KEITH HOLYOAKE PAPERS: Turnbull Library MS 1814.

PROFESSOR KEITH JACKSON PAPERS: Various letters, including some from Marshall, Muldoon and Gordon, re 1974 leadership change.

RT HON. DON McKINNON PAPERS: Background to 1984 snap election including a detailed tape-recording on the events which Mr McKinnon made the morning after the 1984 election was called.

HON. A. G. (AUSSIE) MALCOLM PAPERS: Material related to the 1980 'Colonels' Coup'.

SIR JOHN MARSHALL PAPERS: Turnbull Library MS 1403.

GRAY NELSON PAPERS: Material relating to Muldoon's overseas trips, which Nelson as one of Muldoon's private secretaries arranged.

MARTIN NESTOR PAPERS: Turnbull Library ACC 82–141 83–88. Nestor was the National Party's Chief Research Officer from 1944 to 1973.

DENIS O'REILLY PAPERS: Correspondence between O'Reilly and Muldoon, particularly in 1977 and 1978, covering a range of topics including Maori gangs; race relations in New Zealand and overseas; Bastion Point; South Africa and Springbok tours.

JOHN WELLS PAPERS: Material related to the New Zealand Finance Houses' Association and the deregulation of the financial sector. Wells was the general manager of NZI Finance and the NZFHA's chairman 1982–84.

DENIS WEDERELL PAPERS: Turnbull Manuscripts 1655.
    Denis Wederell, at the time Editor of the *Manawatu Evening Standard*, collected material and started writing a biography of Sir Robert Muldoon during the period between December 1968 and July 1971 when the project was abandoned. His materials were later used extensively by Spiro Zavos for his book *The Real Muldoon*.

    Series 1 – Correspondence (13 folders – see below)
    Series 2 – Transcripts of tape-recorded interviews with R. D. Muldoon (see below)
    Series 3 – Newspaper clippings (3/1 – 3/8 and 3/10): mainly on 1969 election
    Series 4 – Notes – 2 folders: outline and background notes
    Series 5 – Draft chapters: 14 chapters varying from 500 to 7600 words
    Series 6 – Printed material and photographs: Includes photo of RDM in 5 Special, Mt Albert Grammar School. Also *Junior News* (National Party) 1947–48, 1948–49, 1949, 1951, and Annual Reports, Junior National Party, Auckland 1946–49

    Series 1 – Correspondence (13 folders)
        Letters to Denis Wederell include the following more significant ones:
        Adair, G. W.: Auckland YMCA, 24/12/68. Series 1/Folder 1
        Adam, G. W.: Auckland YMCA, 7/8/69. Series 1/Folder 3
        Adams, F.: Knew Muldoon's father and Muldoon as a young boy, 31/1/69. Series 1/Folder 1
        Adams, L. E.: Principal, Glendowie College; former President, Post Primary Teachers Association, and Mt Albert National Party Branch Chairman, 30/12/68. Series 1/Folder 1.

Algie, R. M.: Former Speaker of Parliament, 23/7/69. Series 1/Folder 1

Allingham, W. J.: Former Secretary National Party Mt Albert electorate, 28/8/69. Series 1/Folder 1

Blanks, H.: Classmate of R.D. Muldoon at Mount Albert Grammar School, 21/2/70. Series 1/Folder 2

Brenton-Rule, C.: Former Auckland Divisional Secretary, 4/8/69. Series 1/Folder 10

Burgess, B.: Journalist, 4/8/69. Series 1/Folder 2

Burns, G.: Editor, *Christchurch Star*, 29/7/69. Series 1/Folder 2

Busfield, C.: Former Junior National, Mt Albert Baptist Church, R.D. Muldoon's best man, 17/7/69. Series 1/Folder 2

Caldwell, G.: President Glen Innes Resident and Ratepayers Association, 6/9/69. Series 1/Folder 3

Davies, H. M.: Chairman National Party Tamaki electorate, 21/2/70. Series 1/Folder 4

Day, C. R.: Auckland Division organiser and Tamaki electorate secretary National Party, 28/7/69. Series 1/Folder 4

Degenhardt, T. B.: Deputy Secretary Institute of Cost and Works Accountants London, to Wederell, 17/1/69 and 11/2/69. Series 1/Folder 7

Don, A. S.: General Manager Auckland Electric Power Board, 8/8/69. Series 1/Folder 1

Dowding, Mrs E. L.: Auckland Horticultural Council and acquaintance of Mr and Mrs J.H. Muldoon Snr, 4/2/69. Series 1/Folder 4

Ewington, K. C.: Auckland Division Young Nationals, 2/2/70. Series 1/Folder 5

Firth, J.: Contested Tamaki selection 1960, 25/8/69. Series 1/Folder 6

Freer, W. W.: Labour MP Mt Albert, 30/5/69. Series 1/Folder 6

Halstead, Hon. E.: former National MP Tamaki, 14/8/69. Series 1/Folder 7

Hanan, Hon. J. .: Cabinet Minister, 19/2/69. Series 1/Folder 7

Harris, J.: Editor, *Eastern Suburbs Courier*, 10/8/69. Series 1/Folder 3

Hayward, D.: Journalist, 17/1/69. Series 1/Folder 7

Hintz, O. S.: Editor, *NZ Herald*, 21/7/69. Series 1/Folder 7

Jenkin, A.: 1940s Junior National and Deputy-Chairman Waitemata electorate 1969, 9/2/60. Series 1/Folder 7

Lee, J. A.: Former Labour MP, 6/5/nd[69]. Series 1/Folder 8

Macdonald, K. R.: Secretary NZ Society of Accountants, 15//8/69. Series 1/Folder 1

MacIntyre, D.: National MP, 30/8/nd[69]. Series 1/Folder 9

McKenzie, Sir Alex: Former National Party President, 22/1/69. Series 1/Folder 9

Marshall, Rt Hon. J. R.: Deputy Prime Minister, 23/1/69. Series 1/Folder 9

Muldoon, Hon. R. D.: 12/12/68 and 10/12/69. Series 1/Folder 9

Nestor, M.: National Party Research Director, 13/2/69. Series 1/Folder 10

Nicholl, G.: Auckland Horticultural Council, -/2/68. Series 1/Folder 10

Prebble, C. G.: Secretary Hatfields Bay Ratepayers and Residents Association, 5/9/69. Series 1/Folder 7

Prince, Mrs M.: Former Secretary Auckland Junior Nationals, 14/1/69 and 17/5/69. Series 1/Folder 10

Rendle, J.: Contested Tamaki selection 1960 and later Tamaki Electorate Chairman, 15/1/69. Series 1/Folder 11

Robson, L. W.: Blackburn, Robson Coates and Co. Chartered Accountants London, 26/2/69, Series 1/Folder 11

Ryan, K.: Labour candidate Tamaki 1966, 8/8/69. Series 1/Folder 11

Searle, J. N.: Secretary Decimal Currency Board, 21/1/69. Series 1/Folder 11

Shallcrass, J.: Senior Lecturer Victoria University of Wellington, 17/2/69. Series 1/Folder 11

Swann, Faucett & Partners: Public Accountants Auckland, 8/10/69. Series 1/Folder 11

Verry, H. L.: Managing Editor NZPA, 8/1/69. Series 1/Folder 12

Wall, G. C. A.: Editorial Editor A.H. and A.W. Reed, 13/8/69 and 3/9/69. Series 1/Folder 13

Waugh, H. F., President Glen Innes Senior Citizens Club, 7/8/69. Series 1/Folder 13

Windsor, A. V.: Mt Albert Baptist Church, 20/1/70. Series 1/Folder 8

Wederell, D. to Robert Gilmore: Journalist, 3/3/69. Series 1/Folder 6

Wederell, D. to Robert Muldoon: 14/10/69, 31/7/71 and 10/12/72. Series 1/Folder 9

Wederell to Murray Nairn: Headmaster, Mount Albert Grammar School, 1/4/69. Series 1/Folder 10

Series 2 – Transcripts of 5 tape-recorded interviews with R. D. Muldoon 1968–69 (undated).

E. NEW ZEALAND NATIONAL PARTY PAPERS
(in various places as indicated)

National Party Head Office
Dominion Executive minutes and other papers 1960–92
National Party Papers deposited in the Alexander Turnbull Library (NZNP T89/75)
Among the most useful were:
Auckland, Waikato, Wellington, Canterbury-Westland, and Otago Southland Division files
Caucus Minutes 1960; 18 July 1963 – 1969; 1972–73; 1975; 1977–78
George Chapman's Correspondence
Confidential report on 1973 membership, 19 March 1974
Dominion Conference Minutes; Dominion Council Minutes; Dominion Executive Minutes, Policy
    Committee Minutes
1966, 1969, 1972, 1975, 1978, 1981 and 1984 General Election files and 1978 Rangitikei by-election
    file
Barrie Leay's Correspondence
David Lloyd's analysis of the 1981 election, 9 December 1981
Polls on the Tamaki electorate and leadership of the National Party 1987
Review Committee's minutes, submissions, report on party structure and organisation, 1984
Wellington Divisional Seminar on the 1984 election and the future of the party, 22 October 1984
Auckland Division Papers (Auckland Office)
Especially Divisional Council and Executive minutes 1945–92; Auckland Divisional election files
    1951–92; correspondence files; and electorate files, notably for Tamaki 1960–92, Mount Albert 1951
    and 1954, and Waitemata 1957
Waikato Division Papers (Hamilton Office)
Wellington Division Papers (Wellington Office)
Canterbury-Westland Division Papers (Christchurch Office)
Otago-Southland Division Papers (Dunedin Office)
Tamaki Electorate Papers (in the hands of the Electorate Secretary and some duplicates in the possession
    of John Tremewan)

F. UNPUBLISHED MSS

Beetham, B., 'Bruce Beetham's Case over the Clyde Dam', typescript, nd, copy given to author 18
    November 1993.
Deane, R. S., 'Private Sector Investment: Some Fundamental Issues', typescript of address to Assembly of
    Business, NZ Chamber of Commerce, Wellington, 22–24 August 1983, in Wells' Papers.
Deane, R. S., 'Recent Developments in the New Zealand Foreign Exchange Market', typescript of address
    at Macquarie University, 7 July 1983, in Wells' Papers.
Double Standard: A series of 47 posters published in Wellington between September 1978 and May 1985.
    The author is indebted to Mr J. Traue, the former Turnbull Librarian, for obtaining these posters.
Douglas, R., Address to the NZ Finance Houses Association AGM, 1 August 1984, typescript in Wells'
    Papers.
Douglas, R., 'Alternative Budget: A Personal View', 30 June 1980, MP.
Douglas, R., 'The Consequences of High Overseas Debt and Low Overseas Reserves', nd, distributed 18
    June 1984, MP.
Douglas, R., 'The Politics of Successful Structural Reform', Paper delivered to Mt Pelerin Society, 28
    November 1989, MP.
Galvin, B. V., 'Australia, New Zealand and the United States: National Evolution and Alliance
    Relations', 14 August 1989, MP.
Holmes, Sir Frank, 'A Toast to 1984', unpublished typescript of address to the NZ Finance Houses
    Association annual dinner, 8 August 1983, copy in possession of author.
Leay, B., 'A Philosophical View of the Achievements of the Past Ten Years and the Challenges of the Next
    Ten', typescript, 1 September 1982, MP.
Martin, John, 'Economic Policymaking in the Early Post-War Years – The Stabilization Era', paper
    delivered to Association of Economists Conference, August, 1990, MP.
Muldoon, R. D., 'Address to European Management Forum on New Dimensions of World Leadership',
    unpublished typescript of address to conference at Davos, Switzerland, 27 January 1983, MP.

Muldoon, R. D., Lecture on the National Government 1975–84, Stage I Political Studies class, University of Auckland, 12 June 1989.
Muldoon, R. D., 'The Precipice – 1929 Revisited', unpublished typescript dated 23 September 1985, MP.
Walker, N. W., 'The 1984 Election Defeat', 99-page unpublished typescript in National Party Papers in the Alexander Turnbull Library, NPP, A89/75, 148/2.

G. OFFICIAL GOVERNMENT PUBLICATIONS AND DOCUMENTS

Appendices to the Journals of the House of Representatives, including General Election Reports, E 9
Budgets and accompanying papers
Cabinet schedules and papers, MP
New Zealand Foreign Affairs Review
New Zealand Official Year Books
New Zealand Parliamentary Debates
Registry of Births, Deaths and Marriages
Treasury and various other government department reports, including those to the incoming governments following an election. Many published and unpublished reports from a range of government departments are found in the Muldoon Papers. Note especially the following:
Birch, W. F., *Energy Strategy '79*, Minister of Energy, Government Printer, Wellington, 1979.
Economic Summit Conference, *A Briefing on the New Zealand Economy*, Government Printer, Wellington, 1984
Gair, G. F., *Goals and Guidelines: An Energy Strategy for New Zealand*, Minister of Energy, Wellington, 1978.
New Zealand Treasury, *Briefing to the Incoming Government 1990*, Treasury, Wellington, 1990
New Zealand Treasury, *Economic Management*, Treasury, Wellington, 1984
New Zealand Treasury, *Government Management: Brief to the Incoming Government 1987*, 2 vols, Treasury, Wellington, 1987
Organisation for Economic Co-operation and Development (OECD), New Zealand annual economic surveys, OECD, Paris.
Reserve Bank, *Post-Election Paper to the Minister of Finance on the Areas of Responsibility of the Reserve Bank*, Reserve Bank of New Zealand, Wellington, 1986.
The World Bank, *Report on the New Zealand Economy*, Government Printer, Wellington, 1968

H. NEWSPAPER AND PERIODICAL FILES AND CLIPPINGS

Extensive clippings covering most of Muldoon's time in Parliament can be found in the following:
Muldoon Papers (systematically clipped and filed from 1960)
National Party Research Unit Clippings
National Party Papers in the Alexander Turnbull Library: these contain extensive newspaper clippings arranged under subject headings and names of individual politicians
Turnbull Library Biographical Clippings
University of Auckland, Political Studies Department: clippings since 1967 in the Robert and Noeline Chapman Print Archive
Certain newspapers and journals were also consulted extensively in addition to the above, notably *Freedom*, *Junior News*, *Nathena*, *National Business Review*, *National Observer*, *New Zealand Herald*, and *New Zealand Truth*

I. TELEVISION AND RADIO BROADCASTS

There are extensive transcripts of television and radio broadcasts covering most of Muldoon's time in Parliament in both the Muldoon Papers and in the National Party Research Unit Records.
In addition there are many audio and video tapes of relevance to Muldoon in the Muldoon Papers and in the possession of the author. A very comprehensive archive of radio and television material relating to

Muldoon can be found in the Robert and Noeline Chapman Audio-Visual Archive of the Political Studies Department at the University of Auckland. The Radio New Zealand and Television New Zealand Archives also contain extensive collections of material on Muldoon.

Among the most interesting and useful radio tapes are the following:

Interview of Muldoon by Jessica Weddell, 19 May 1981 (broadcast by Radio NZ on 25 May 1981).
Interview of Muldoon by Sharon Crosbie, Radio NZ, 24 July 1984.
Interview of Muldoon by John Tindle, 2GB Sydney, 27 September 1985.
Interview of Thea Muldoon by George Balani, Radio NZ, 9 July 1986.
Interview of Muldoon by Mark Bennett and Hamish McKay, Radio 1ZB, 25 May 1987.
Interviews with Rob and Thea Muldoon, Radio Pacific, 9 May 1990.
'Sir Robert Muldoon', Radio New Zealand Replay Radio, 1992. A selection of material from Radio NZ Sound Archives, 1974–91, including his election campaign opening address in 1975 and his farewell speech in Parliament in 1991.
'Tribute to Sir Robert Muldoon', Radio Pacific, 9 August 1992. A three-hour compilation including highlights from 'Lilies and Other Things' 1984–92; Muldoon's retirement broadcast; his final comments on Radio Pacific; comments from those who knew him and from listeners; and Muldoon singing his own version of 'I did it my way'.
Radio NZ, 'Morning Report', 'Mana News' and 'Checkpoint', 5 August 1992.
Radio NZ, Broadcast of funeral service, 7 August 1992.
Radio NZ, 'Sunday Supplement', 9 August 1992.

SECONDARY SOURCES

Aimer, P., 'The New Zealand Party' in H. Gold (ed), *New Zealand Politics in Perspective*, Longman Paul, Auckland, 1985, pp 189–203.
Aimer, P., 'Travelling Together: Party Identification and Vote in the New Zealand General Election of 1987', *Electoral Studies*, v 8, 1989, pp 131–42.
Atkinson, J., 'Mass Communications, Economic Liberalisation and the New Mediators', *Political Science*, v 41, no 2, 1989, pp 85–108.
Barber, J., *The Presidential Character*, Prentice Hall, Englewood Cliffs, 1992.
Barry, N. P., *The New Right*, Croom Helm Methuen, London, 1987.
Bassett, M., *Getting Together*, Peter Harris, Auckland, 1979.
Bassett, M., *The State in New Zealand 1840–1984: Socialism Without Doctrines?* Auckland University Press, Auckland, 1998.
Bassett, M., *The Third Labour Government: A Personal History*, Dunmore, Palmerston North, 1976.
Bean, C., 'From Confusion to Confusion: The 1981 General Election in New Zealand', *Politics*, v 17, 1982, pp 108–20.
Bean, C., 'An Inventory of New Zealand Voting Surveys 1949–84', *Political Science*, v 38, 1986, pp 172–84.
Bean, C., and Mughan, A., 'Leadership Effects in Parliamentary Elections in Australia and Britain', *American Political Science Review*, v 83, December 1989, pp 1165–78.
Bertram, G., and Dunn, C., *Comalco: The First Ten Years – Smelter and Foreign Exchange Returns*, Victoria University of Wellington, Wellington, 1981.
Bick, G., *The Compass File*, Caxton Press, Christchurch, 1968.
Birch, W. F., 'Maui offers one way out', *NZ International Review*, November 1979, pp 11–20.
Birdsall, J., 'The Economic Policies of the National Government: 1978 to 1981', thesis, University of Auckland, 1989.
Blackburn, A., 'Political Symbols and Propaganda: the New Zealand National Party and the 1975 Election', thesis, University of Waikato, 1977.
Blake, Lord, and Patten, J., (eds.), *The Conservative Opportunity*, Macmillan, London, 1976.
Bolger, J., *Bolger: A View From the Top – My Seven Years as Prime Minister*, Viking, Auckland, 1998.
Bollard, A. (ed), *The Influence of United States Economics on New Zealand: The Fulbright Anniversary Seminars 1988*, NZIER, Wellington, 1988.

Booth, G., 'Political Party Image Projection', thesis, University of Canterbury, 1973.

Boston, J., *Incomes Policy in New Zealand 1968–84*, Institute of Policy Studies, Victoria University, Wellington, 1984.

Boston, J., 'High Level Advisory Groups in Central Government: A Comparative Study of the Origins, Structures and Activities of the Australian Priorities Review Staff and the New Zealand Prime Minister's Department', MA thesis, University of Canterbury, 1980.

Boston, J., and Dalziel, P., *The Decent Society? Essays in Response to National's Economic and Social Policies*, Oxford University Press, Auckland, 1992.

Boston, J., and Holland, M., *The Fourth Labour Government*, Oxford University Press, Auckland, 1987.

Boston, J., and Jackson, K., 'The New Zealand General Election of 1987', *Electoral Studies*, v 7, no 1, April 1988, pp 70–75.

Boston, J., et al., *Reshaping the State: New Zealand's Bureaucratic Revolution*, Oxford University Press, Auckland, 1991.

Brandt, W., *Common Crisis: North–South Co-operation for World Recovery – The Brandt Commission 1983*, Pan, London, 1983.

Brill, B., 'The Moyle Affair: Another Perspective'. *NZ Listener*, 22 July 1978, pp 25–27.

Bryant, G., *Beetham*, Dunmore, Palmerston North, 1981.

Bryant, G., *The Sting in the Beehive*, Dunmore, Palmerston North, 1982.

Burns, J. M., *Leadership*, Harper and Row, New York, 1978.

Bush, G., *New Zealand – A Nation Divided?* University of Auckland, Auckland, 1983.

Butterworth, R., and Tarling, N., *A Shakeup Anyway: Government and the Universities in New Zealand in a Decade of Reform*, Auckland University Press, Auckland, 1994.

Campbell, G., 'Robert Muldoon: politics of survival', *NZ Listener*, 30 June 1984, pp 18–21 and 42.

Canovan, M., 'People, Politicians and Populism', *Government and Opposition*, v 19, no 3, 1984, pp 312–27.

Carr, S., *The Dark Art of Politics*, Hodder Moa Beckett, Auckland, 1997.

Castles, F., Gerritsen, R. and Vowles, J., *The Great Experiment: Labour Parties and Public Policy Transformation in Australia and New Zealand*, Auckland University Press, Auckland, 1996.

Catt, H., 'Landslide by Default: the New Zealand Election of 1990', *Parliamentary Affairs*, v 44, no 3, July 1991, pp 325–36.

Cave, S., 'Think Debt', *Listener*, 25 June 1988.

Chapman, G., *The Years of Lightning*, A. H. and A. W. Reed, Wellington, 1980.

Chapman, R., 'The Case of the Pulled Punch: The 1978 Election', *Comment*, February 1979.

Chapman, R., 'Election' 72: Why the Change Came', *NZ Listener*, 18 December 1972.

Chapman, R., 'From Labour to National', in W. H. Oliver (ed), *The Oxford History of New Zealand*, Wellington, 1981, pp 333–68.

Chapman, R., *Marginals '72*, Heinemann, Auckland, 1972.

Chapman, R., 'The Mechanics of Representation', *NZ Listener*, 24 October 1969.

Chapman, R., 'New Zealand Defers Decision', *Comment*, August 1982, pp 11–18.

Chapman, R., *New Zealand Politics and Social Patterns: Selected Works by Robert Chapman*, edited and introduced by Elizabeth McLeay, Victoria University Press, Wellington, 1999.

Chapman, R., 'A Political Culture under Pressure: The Struggle to Preserve a Progressive Tax Base for Welfare and the Positive State', *Political Science*, v 44, no 1, 1992.

Chapman, R., 'The Politics of Change', a series of articles in the *National Business Review*, 4 August–13 October 1976.

Chapman, R. M., Jackson, W. K., and Mitchell, A. V., *New Zealand Politics in Action: The 1960 General Election*, Oxford University Press, Wellington, 1962.

Clark, M. (ed), *The 1987 General Election: What Happened?*, Victoria University of Wellington, Wellington 1987.

Clark, M., 'Clash of the Titans', *NBR*, 15 December 1989.

Clark, M. (ed), *The Labour Party After 75 Years*, Victoria University of Wellington, Wellington, 1992.

Clark, M., 'The Prime Minister and the Premier', *NZ International Review*, November 1980, pp 20–22.

Clark, M. (ed), *The Roberts Report*, Victoria University Press, Wellington, 1999.

Clark, M. (ed), *Sir Keith Holyoake*, Dunmore, Palmerston North, 1997.

Clark, M. (ed), *Three Labour Leaders: Nordmeyer, Rowling and Kirk*, forthcoming.

Clarke, P., *A Question of Leadership: Gladstone to Thatcher*, Hamish Hamilton, 1991.

Clements, K. P., *Back from the Brink: The Creation of a Nuclear-Free New Zealand*, Port Nicholson Press, Wellington, 1988.

Clements, K. P., 'The Citizens for Rowling Campaign: An Insider's View', *Political Science*, v 28, no 2, December 1976, pp 81–93.

Cleveland, L., *The Anatomy of Influence: Pressure Groups and Politics in New Zealand*, Hicks Smith and Sons, Wellington, 1972.

Cleveland, L., *The Politics of Utopia: New Zealand and Its Government*, Methuen, Wellington, 1979.

Commission on Critical Choices for Americans, *Trade, Inflation and Ethics*, Lexington Books, Lexington, 1976.

Commonwealth Group of Experts, *The Debt Crisis and the World Economy*, Commonwealth Secretariat, London, 1984.

Commonwealth Study Group, *Towards a New Bretton Woods: Challenges for the World Financial and Trading System*, Commonwealth Secretariat, London, 1983.

Crawshaw, E. M., 'Rationality in Policy Formation: A Case Study of the National Party in 1972', thesis, University of Canterbury, 1974.

Danks, A. J., *What Everyone Should Know About Social Credit*, Caxton Press, Christchurch, 1955.

Davis, D. R., 'The "Operational Code" of Bruce Craig Beetham', *Political Science*, v 32, no 1, July 1980, pp 1–17.

Davis, P. (ed), *New Zealand Labour Perspectives*, Ross, Auckland, 1981.

Deane, R. S. and Nicholl, P. W. E. (eds.), *Monetary Policy and the New Zealand Financial System*, Reserve Bank of NZ, Wellington, 1979.

Deane, R. S., Nicholl, P. W. E. and Walsh, M. J., *External Economic Structure and Policy*, Reserve Bank of NZ, Wellington, 1981.

Deeks, J., 'Chronicle', *NZ Journal of Industrial Relations*, v 2, no 2, August 1977, pp 35–8.

Dilenschneider, R., *On Power*, Harper Business, New York, 1994.

Doughty, R., *The Holyoake Years*, Ross A. Doughty, Feilding, 1977.

Douglas, R., *There's Got to Be A Better Way!*, Fourth Estate, Wellington, 1980.

Douglas, R., *Unfinished Business*, Random House, Auckland, 1993.

Douglas, R., and Callan, L., *Toward Prosperity*, David Bateman, Auckland, 1987.

Duncan, I., and Bollard, A., *Corporatization and Privatization: Lessons from New Zealand*, Oxford University Press, Auckland, 1992.

Dunmore, J., *Norman Kirk*, New Zealand Books, Palmerston North, 1972.

Eagles, J., and James, C., *The Making of a New Zealand Prime Minister*, Cheshire, Wellington, 1973.

Easton, B., *The Commercialisation of New Zealand*, Auckland University Press, Auckland, 1997.

Easton, B., 'Development Strategies for the Eighties', *NZ Monthly Review*, v 31, no 227, November 1980, pp 3–6.

Easton, B., *In Stormy Seas: The Post-War New Zealand Economy*, University of Otago Press, Dunedin, 1998.

Easton, B., *The Making of Rogernomics*, Auckland University Press, Auckland 1989.

Easton, B., 'Muldoon, Robert' in R. Robinson and N. Wattie (eds), *The Oxford Companion to New Zealand Literature*, Oxford University Press, Auckland, 1998, pp 383–4.

Easton, B., *Pragmatism and Progress: Social Security in the Seventies*, University of Canterbury Press, Christchurch, 1981.

Easton, B., *Social Policy and the Welfare State in New Zealand*, Allen and Unwin, Sydney, 1980.

Easton, B., *Structural Change and Economic Growth in Postwar New Zealand*, Massey Economic Papers, Palmerston North, 1991.

Easton, B., *The Whimpering of the State: Policy after MMP*, Auckland University Press, Auckland, 1999.

Edwards, B., *Right Out: Labour Victory '72*, A. H. and A. W. Reed, Wellington, 1973.

Edwards, B., *The Public Eye*, A. H. and A. W. Reed, Wellington, 1971.

Evans, H., *Case Against Robert Muldoon and his National Party Government*, Christchurch, 1978.

Evans, H., *The National Development Bill 1979: Case Against Fast Footwork*, Christchurch 1979.

Evans, H., *The National Development Bill 1979: Case Against Vice-Regal Assent*, Christchurch 1979.

Franklin, H., *Trade, Growth and Anxiety: New Zealand Beyond the Welfare State*, Methuen, Wellington, 1978.

Friedman, M., *Capitalism and Freedom*, University of Chicago Press, Chicago, 1962.

Friedman, M., and Friedman, R., *Free to Choose*, Harcourt Brace Jovanovich, New York, 1980.

Fyfe, J., and Hanson, H., *The Gamble: Snap Election '84 –The Campaign Diary of the Challengers*, Australian and New Zealand Book Company, Auckland, 1984.

Gardner, J., *On Leadership*, Free Press, New York, 1990.

Gardner, W. J., *The Farmer Politician in New Zealand History*, Massey University, Palmerston North, 1970.

Garnier, T., 'Changes in New Zealand Foreign Policy', *NZ International Review*, September 1976, pp 7–10.

Garnier, T., Kohn, B. and Booth, P., *The Hunter and the Hill: New Zealand Politics in the Kirk Years*, Cassell, Auckland, 1978.

Garnier, T. and Levine, S., *Election '81: An End to Muldoonism*, Methuen, Auckland, 1981.

Gaynor, B., 'The boom before the crash', *NZ Herald,* 11 October 1997.

Gilmore, R., 'Q and A with Mr Muldoon', *Auckland Star*, 14 December 1968; also published as 'I'm just a counter-puncher', *Christchurch Star,* 14 December 1968.

Gold, H., *New Zealand Politics in Perspective*, Longman Paul, Auckland 1985, 1989, 1992.

Goldsmith, P., *John Banks: A Biography*, Penguin, Auckland, 1997.

Goldstein, R. and Alley, R., *Labour in Power: Promise and Performance*, Price Milburn, Wellington, 1975.

Gould, J., *The Muldoon Years: An Essay on New Zealand's Recent Economic Growth*, Hodder and Stoughton, Auckland, 1985.

Gould, J., *The Rake's Progress*, Hodder and Stoughton, Auckland, 1982.

Gould, J., *The University Grants Committee 1961–1986: A History*, University Grants Committee, Wellington, 1988.

Greenaway, T. L., 'Token minorities: A study of National and Labour women candidates contesting the 1975, 1984 and 1990 New Zealand general elections', thesis, University of Auckland, 1994.

Grierson, J., *The Hell of It: Early Days in the New Zealand Party*, Reed Methuen, Auckland, 1985.

Griffin, R., 'China Lurches to the Right', *NZ International Review,* November 1980, pp 22–24.

Gustafson, B., *The First Fifty Years: A History of the New Zealand National Party*, Reed Methuen, Auckland 1986.

Gustafson, B., 'The Kiwi and the Bear', *NZ International Review*, September–October 1980, pp14–17.

Gustafson, B., 'The National Governments and Social Change (1949–72)', in K. Sinclair (ed) *The Oxford Illustrated History of New Zealand*, Auckland, 1990, pp 267–94.

Gustafson, B., 'New Zealand Politics 1945–1984' in R. Miller (ed), *New Zealand Politics in Transition*, Oxford University Press, Auckland, 1997, pp 3–12.

Gustafson, B., 'Regeneration, Rejection or Realignment: New Zealand Political Parties in the 1990s', in G. R. Hawke (ed), *Changing Politics: The Electoral Referendum 1993*, Institute of Policy Studies, Wellington, 1993, pp 68–102.

Gustafson, B., 'Sir Robert Muldoon. A Contradictory Political Figure', *Stout Centre Review,* v 4, no 3, September 1994, pp 9–14.

Gustafson, B., *Social Change and Party Reorganization: The New Zealand Labour Party Since 1945*, Sage, London and Beverly Hills, 1976.

Gustafson, B., 'Social Democracy in New Zealand', *The Round Table*, 255, July 1974, pp 331–46.

Guy, Michael, *The Hansard Papers: Excerpts from Parliament*, Alister Taylor, Waiura, 1978.

Hames, M., *Winston First*, Random House, Auckland, 1995.

Hanson, E., *The Politics of Social Security*, Auckland University Press, Auckland, 1980.

Haq, K. (ed), *Crisis of the '80s: World Monetary, Financial and Human Resource Development Issues*, North South Roundtable, UNDP Development Study Programme, Washington DC, 1984.

Harris, G. S., et al., *Energy Scenarios for New Zealand*, NZ Energy Research and Development Committee, University of Auckland, Auckland, 1977.

Harvey, B., 'Labour Pains', *Metro,* March 1992, pp 58–63.

Hawke, G. R., *The Making of New Zealand: An Economic History*, Cambridge University Press, Cambridge, 1985.

Hawkins, A., and McLaughlan, G., *The Hawk*, Four Star Books, Auckland, 1989.

Hawkins, W. R., 'The Hon. Duncan MacIntyre as Minister of Maori Affairs', thesis, University of Auckland, 1975.

Hayburn, R. (ed), *Australian and New Zealand Relations*, University of Otago, Dunedin, 1978.

Hayek, F. A., *The Road to Serfdom*, Routledge and Kegan Paul, London, 1944.

Hayward, M., *Diary of the Kirk Years*, Reed, Wellington; Cape Catley, Queen Charlotte Sound, NZ, 1981.

Henderson, J., 'Labour's Modern Prime Ministers and the Party: A Study of Contrasting Political Styles', in M. Clark (ed), *The Labour Party After 75 Years*, Victoria University of Wellington, Wellington, 1992, pp 98–117.

Henderson, J., 'Leadership, Personality and Foreign Policy: The Case of Prime Minister R. D. Muldoon', in J. Henderson et al., *Beyond New Zealand: The Foreign Policy of a Small State*, Methuen, Auckland, 1980, pp 230–7.

Henderson, J., 'Muldoon and Kirk: "Active Negative" Prime Ministers', *Political Science*, v 30, no 2, 1978, pp 111–14.

Henderson, J., 'Muldoon and Rowling: A Preliminary Analysis of Contrasting Personalities', *Political Science*, v 32, no 1, 1980, pp 26–46.

Henderson, J., 'Muldoon, New Zealand and the World', *NZ International Review*, May–June, 1977, pp 10–11.

Henderson, J., 'New Zealand in a Changing World: The Talboys' Speeches', *NZ International Review*, January–February 1978.

Henderson, J., 'PM Power', *NZ International Review*, April 1979, pp 11–13.

Henderson, J., *Rowling, The Man and the Myth*, Australian and New Zealand Book Co., Auckland, 1981.

Henderson, J., et al., *Beyond New Zealand: The Foreign Policy of a Small State*, Methuen, Auckland, 1980.

Henderson, J. T., 'The Operational Code of Robert David Muldoon' in S. Levine (ed), *Politics in New Zealand*, Allen and Unwin, Sydney, 1978, pp 367–82.

Hoadley, S., *Negotiating with Japan: Lessons from the Fish-for-Beef Dispute 1976–1978*, Centre for Japanese Studies Massey University, Palmerston North, 1993.

Hoadley, S., *New Zealand and Australia: Negotiating Closer Economic Relations*, New Zealand Institute of International Affairs, Wellington, 1995.

Hobby, M., 'The Bahrain–New Zealand Cold Storage and Warehouse Company (BANZ): Political and Economic Considerations in Policy Making – A Case Study', in R. Macintyre (ed), *New Zealand and the Middle East: Politics, Energy and Trade*, Australasian Middle East Studies Association, Christchurch, 1987.

Hooper, M., 'Sir John Marshall: A Knight to Remember', *Insight*, v 5, no 5, October–November 1985, pp 36–47.

Hubbard, A., 'Right by Ruth', *NZ Listener*, 20 August 1990, p 22.

Ionescu, G., and Gellner, E. (eds.), *Populism: Its Meaning and National Characteristics*, Weidenfeld and Nicolson, 1968.

Jackson, K., 'The 1975 New Zealand General Election', *The Round Table,* no 260, October 1975, pp 379–88.

Jackson, K., 'Comment: 1972 General Election', *Landfall,* v 27, no 1, March 1973, pp 3–12.

Jackson, K., 'The New Zealand General Election of 1984', *Electoral Studies,* v 4, no 1, April 1985, pp 75–79.

Jackson, K., *New Zealand: Politics of Change*, A. H. and A. W. Reed, Wellington, 1973.

Jackson, K., 'Political Leadership and Succession in the New Zealand National Party', *Political Science*, v 27, nos 1 and 2, July and December 1975, pp 1–23.

James, C., 'If he had never existed, perhaps we would have invented him', *National Business Review,* 22 November 1991.

James, C., *New Territory: The Transformation of New Zealand, 1984–92*, Bridget Williams Books, Wellington, 1992.

James, C., *The Quiet Revolution*, Allen and Unwin/Port Nicholson Press, 1986.

James, C., and McRobie, A. *Changes? The 1990 Election*, Allen and Unwin, Wellington, 1990.

James, C., and McRobie, A., *Turning Point: The 1993 Election and Beyond*, Bridget Williams Books, Wellington, 1993.

Jamieson, B. 'The result of Government intervention in major capital projects in New Zealand in the 1970s and 1980s', thesis, University of Auckland, 2000

Jesson, B., *Behind the Mirror Glass*, Penguin, Auckland, 1987.

Jesson, B., *Fragments of Labour*, Penguin, Auckland, 1989.

Jesson, B., *Only Their Purpose Is Mad*, Dunmore, Palmerston North, 1999.

Jesson, B., 'The Tragedy of David Lange', *Metro*, July 1986, pp 156–7.

Jesson, B., Ryan, A., and Spoonley, P., *Revival of the Right: New Zealand Politics in the 1980s*, Heinemann Reed, Auckland, 1988.

Johnstone, I. *Stand and Deliver*, Cape Catley, Whataranga Bay, NZ, 1998.

Jones, R., *Memories of Muldoon*, Canterbury University Press, Christchurch, 1997.

Kazin, M., *The Populist Persuasion: An American History*, Basic Books, New York, 1995.

Kelsey, J., *The New Zealand Experiment*, Auckland University Press/Bridget Williams Books, Auckland, 1995.

Kelsey, J., *Rolling Back the State*, Bridget Williams Books, Wellington, 1993.

Kennedy, J., *Straight from the Shoulder*, Whitcoulls, Christchurch, 1981.

King, M., 'Tread Softly For You Tread On My Life: Biography and Compassionate Truth', *New Zealand Studies*, v 8, no 2, September 1998, pp 3–8.

Kirk, N., *Towards Nationhood*, NZ Books, Palmerston North, 1969.

Kohl, W. L., *After the Second Oil Crisis: Energy Policies in Europe, America and Japan*, Lexington Books, Lexington, Massachusetts, 1982.

Kouzes, J. M., and Posner, B. Z., *The Leadership Challenge*, Jossey-Bass, San Francisco, 1995.

Laidlaw, C., *Rights of Passage: Beyond the New Zealand Identity Crisis*, Hodder Moa Beckett, Auckland, 1999.

Lange, D., 'Trade and Foreign Policy: A Labour Perspective', *NZ International Review*, September–October 1984, pp 2–4.

Laws, M., *The Demon Profession*, Harper Collins, Auckland, 1998.

Legat, N., 'Has Jim McLay Got the Right Stuff?', *Metro,* July 1985, pp 42–66.

Levine, S., *The New Zealand Political System*, Allen and Unwin, Auckland, 1979.

Levine, S., *Politics in New Zealand: A Reader*, Allen and Unwin, Sydney 1978.

Levine, S. and Lodge, J., 'The New Zealand General Election of 1975', *Parliamentary Affairs*, v 29, no 3, Summer 1976, pp 310–26.

Levine, S. and Lodge, J., *The New Zealand General Election of 1975*, Price Milburn for NZ University Press, Wellington, 1976.

Levine, S. and Roberts, N., 'The New Zealand General Election of 1990', *Political Science*, v 43, no 1, July 1991, pp 1–19.

Levine, S. and Robinson, A., *The New Zealand Voter: A Survey of Public Opinion and Electoral Behaviour*, Price Milburn for NZ University Press, Wellington, 1976.

Lewin, J., 'Bill Sutch', *NZ Monthly Review*, v 16, no 172, November 1995, pp 1–3.

Lipscombe, J. A., 'A whole new ball game: Norman Kirk's decision to stop the 1973 Springbok tour', thesis, University of Auckland, 1979.

Lloyd Prichard, M., and Tabb, J. B., *The New Zealand General Election of 1960*, University of Auckland, Auckland, 1961.

McCallum, J. *Women in the House*, Cape Catley, Wellington, 1993.

MacIntyre, R., 'New Zealand and the Middle East', *NZ International Review*, January–February 1978, pp 20–30.

McKinnon, M., *Independence and Foreign Policy: New Zealand in the World since 1935*, Auckland University Press, Auckland, 1993.

McLauchlan, G., 'In a Way I Suppose I'm Ruthless', *New Zealand Weekly News*, 3 April 1967.

McLean, I., *The Future for New Zealand Agriculture*, Fourth Estate, Wellington, 1978.

McLeay, E. M. (ed), *The 1990 General Election: Perspectives on Political Change in New Zealand*, Victoria University, Wellington, 1991.

McLeay, E. M., *The Cabinet and Political Power in New Zealand*, Oxford University Press, Auckland, 1995.

MacLeod, A., 'Sir Keith Holyoake Completes a Decade: Difficulties Ahead', *Round Table*, no 241, January 1971, pp 175–80.

McLoughlin, D., 'The Rise and Stall of Bob Jones', *North and South*, August 1992, pp 40–49.

McLoughlin, D., 'When I was the Government', *North and South*, October 1992, pp 40–41.

McMillan, N., *Top of the Greasy Pole: New Zealand Prime Ministers of Recent Times*, John McIndoe, Dunedin, 1993.

McQueen, H., *The Ninth Floor: Inside the Prime Minister's Office – A Political Experience*, Penguin, Auckland, 1991.

McRobie, A., 'The New Zealand General Election of 1990' *Electoral Studies*, v 10, no 2, June 1991, pp 158–71.

McRobie, A., and Roberts, N. S., *Election '78*, John McIndoe, Dunedin, 1978.

Marshall, J. R., *Memoirs, Volume One: 1912 to 1960*, Collins Auckland, 1983.

Marshall, J. R., *Memoirs, Volume Two: 1960 to 1988*, Collins, Auckland, 1989.

Marshall, J. R., 'The New Zealand Cabinet', *Political Science*, v 7, no 1, March 1955, pp 3–10.

Miller, R. (ed), *New Zealand Politics in Transition*, Oxford University Press, Auckland, 1997.

Miller, R., and Catt, H., *Season of Discontent: By-elections and the Bolger Government*, Dunmore, Palmerston North, 1993.

Miller, R. K., 'Social Credit: An Analysis of New Zealand's Perennial Third Party', thesis, University of Auckland, 1987.

Milne, R. S., *Political Parties in New Zealand*, Clarendon Press, Oxford, 1966.

Mitchell, A., 'The 1966 General Election', *Political Science*, v 21, no 1, September 1969, pp 3–23.

Mitchell, A., *Government by Party*, Whitcombe and Tombs, Christchurch, 1966.

Mitchell, A., *Politics and People in New Zealand*, Whitcombe and Tombs, Christchurch, 1969.

Mitchell, D., 'Nelson Cotton Mill: a case study in the politics of development', thesis, University of Canterbury, 1967.

Morris, C., *That Man Muldoon*, Wellington, 1976.

Muldoon, R.D, *The Art of Political Economy*, NZ Institute of Economic Research, Wellington, 1983.

Muldoon, R. D., 'An Exclusive Interview with the Prime Minister', *NZ International Review*, May–June 1977, pp 6–9.

Muldoon, R. D., 'An Interview', *NZ International Review*, September–October 1978, pp 4–5.

Muldoon, R. D., 'An Interview', *NZ International Review*, September–October 1981, pp 13–15.

Muldoon, R. D., 'Memories', *Mount Albert Primary Centenary*, 1969, p 34.

Muldoon, R. D., *Muldoon*, A.H. and A.W.Reed, Wellington, 1977.

Muldoon, R. D., 'My Place: The Big City', *NZ Listener*, 2 April 1988, pp 22–24.

Muldoon, R. D, *My Way*, A.H. and A.W. Reed, Wellington, 1981.

Muldoon, R. D, *The New Zealand Economy: A Personal View*, Endeavour Press, Auckland, 1985.

Muldoon, R. D, *Number 38*, Reed Methuen, Auckland, 1986.

Muldoon, R. D., 'Our foreign policy is trade', *NZ International Review*, January–February 1980, pp 2–3.

Muldoon, R. D. et al., *The Politics of Education*, Auckland University Students Association, Auckland, 1969.

Muldoon, R. D, *Reform of the International Trade and Payments System* (16 Speeches on the subject 1982–83), Ministry of Foreign Affairs, Wellington, nd [1984].

Muldoon, R. D., 'Rethinking the Ground Rules for an Open World Economy', *Foreign Affairs*, Summer, June 1983, pp 1078–98.

Muldoon, R. D., *The Rise and Fall of a Young Turk*, A. H. and A. W. Reed, Wellington, 1974.

Mulgan, R., *Democracy and Power in New Zealand*, Oxford University Press, Auckland, 1984.

Mulgan, R., *Politics in New Zealand*, Auckland University Press, Auckland, 1997.

Neary, T. and Kelleher, J., *Neary: The Price of Principle*, Harlen Publishing, Auckland, 1986.

New Zealand National Party, *Report of the Review Committee of the National Party Dominion Council*, Wellington, 1985.

New Zealand Planning Council, *Economic Strategy: 1979*, Government Printer, Wellington, 1979.

New Zealand Planning Council, *Economic Trends and Policies*, Government Printer, Wellington, 1978.

New Zealand Planning Council, *The Economy in Transition: Restructuring to 1989*, NZ Planning Council, Wellington, 1989.

New Zealand Planning Council, *Implications of New Energy Developments*, Government Printer, Wellington, 1979.

New Zealand Planning Council, *Planning Perspectives 1978–83*, Government Printer, Wellington, 1978.

New Zealand Planning Council, *Public Expenditure and its Financing, 1950–79*, Government Printer, Wellington, 1979.

New Zealand Planning Council, *The Welfare State? Social Policy in the 1980s*, Government Printer, Wellington, 1979.

Nightingale, T., *The Pacific Forum Line: A Commitment to Regional Shipping*, Clerestory Press, Christchurch, 1998.

Organisation for Economic Co-operation and Development, *External Debt of Developing Countries: 1983 Survey*, OECD, Paris, 1984.

Orwin, D., 'Conservatism in New Zealand', PhD thesis, University of Auckland, 1999.

Orwin, D., 'The National Government, 1975–78', MA thesis, University of Auckland, 1989.

Page, W., and Lockstone, B., *Landslide '72*, John McIndoe, Dunedin, 1973.

Palmer, G. (ed), *The Welfare State Today*, Fourth Estate, Wellington, 1979.

Palmer, G., *Bridled Power: New Zealand Government under MMP*, Oxford University Press, Auckland, 1997.

Palmer, G., *Unbridled Power?: An Interpretation of New Zealand's Constitution and Government*, Oxford University Press, Auckland, 1979.

Palmer, G., *Unbridled Power: An Interpretation of New Zealand's Constitution and Government*, 2nd edn, Oxford University Press, Auckland, 1987.

Pankhurst, D. A., 'Political Advertising in New Zealand Elections 1957–75', thesis, University of Otago, 1978.

Paterson, M., *The Point at Issue: Petroleum Energy Politics in New Zealand, 1955–90*, Collins, Auckland, 1991.

Penniman, H. R., *New Zealand at the Polls: The General Election of 1978*, American Enterprise Institute for Public Policy Research, Washington, DC, 1980.

Perera, R., 'Political Ritual or Political Reality? The Accuracy, Source and Relevance of the Information Communicated to the Electorate by the Media during the New Zealand General Elections: 1987, 1990 and 1993', thesis, University of Auckland, 1996.

Pfeffer, J., *Managing With Power: Politics and Influence in Organisations*, Harvard Business School Press, Boston, 1992.

Phillips J. (ed), *Biography in New Zealand*, Allen and Unwin/Port Nicholson Press, Wellington, 1985.

Powles, G., *Security Intelligence Service: Report by Chief Ombudsman*, Wellington, 1976.

Prebble, R., *I've Been Thinking*, Seaview Publishing, Auckland, 1996.

Pryde, J. G., 'The New Zealand Economy', *Current Affairs Bulletin*, 1 July 1979.

Reid, T., 'Interview with R. D. Muldoon', in *New Zealand Weekly News*, 24 March 1969.

Renwick, B., 'Bill Renwick Interviews Barry Gustafson on Muldoon Biography', *Stout Research Centre Newsletter*, no 21, June 1990, pp 4–6.

Richards, T., *Dancing on Our Bones: New Zealand, South Africa, Rugby and Racism*, Bridget William Books, Wellington, 1999.

Richards, T., 'Thou shalt play! What 60 years of controversy over New Zealand's sporting contacts with South Africa tells us about ourselves', *New Zealand Studies*, v 6, no 2, July 1996, pp 26–32.

Richardson, R., *Making a Difference*, Shoal Bay Press, Christchurch, 1995.

Roberts, J. L., *Politicians, Public Servants and Public Enterprise: Restructuring the New Zealand Government Executive*, Victoria University Press, Wellington, 1986.

Roberts, N. S., 'The New Zealand General Election of 1975', *Australian Quarterly*, v 48, no 1, 1 March 1976, pp 97–114.

Robson, J. L., and Shallcrass, J. (eds.), *Spirit of an Age: New Zealand in the Seventies – Essays in Honour of W. B. Sutch*, A. H. and A. W. Reed, Wellington, 1975.

Roger, W., 'How a Tireless Talker Lives His Politics', *New Zealand Weekly News*, 21 June 1971, pp 2–7.

Roger, W., 'The End of a Storyteller', *Metro*, November 1989, pp 8–14.

Roger, W., 'The Real Muldoon', *Metro*, February 1992, pp 6–8.

Roper, B., and Rudd, C. (eds), *State and Economy in New Zealand*, Oxford University Press, Auckland, 1993.

Rosenberg, W., *Full Employment: Can the New Zealand Economic Miracle Last?*, A. H. and A. W. Reed, Wellington, 1960.

Rowe, J., 'Swings in the 1975 General Election', *Political Science*, v 29, no 1, July 1977, pp 24–28.

Rowe, J. W., and Gillion, C., 'Swings in the 1966 General Election', *Political Science*, v 21, no 1, September 1969, pp 24–30.

Rowling, W., 'An Interview', *NZ International Review*, September 1977, pp 4–7.

Rowling, W., 'An Interview', *NZ International Review*, September–October 1978, pp 4–7.

Rowling, W., 'An Interview', *NZ International Review*, September–October 1981, pp 16–18.

Rudd, C., and Roper, B. (eds.), *The Political Economy of New Zealand*, Oxford University Press, Auckland, 1997.

Schick, A., *The Spirit of Reform: Managing the New Zealand State Sector in a Time of Change*, State Services Commission, Wellington, 1996.

Scott, T., 'Now is the time to say goodbye . . .', *NZ Listener*, 25 March 1978, p 13.

Scott, T., *Ten Years Inside*, Christchurch, 1985.

Shallcrass, J., 'The Control of Power', *Perspective*, v 3, nos 1–2, 1969. [Published by Farm Road Branch NZLP].

Shanahan, F., 'Some Reflections on Cabinet Government in New Zealand', *NZ Journal of Public Administration*, v 17, no 1, September 1954, pp 1–9.

Sharp, A. (ed), *Leap Into The Dark: The Changing Role of the State in New Zealand Since 1984*, Auckland University Press, Auckland, 1994.

Sinclair, K., 'Hard Times (1972–89)' in K. Sinclair (ed), *The Oxford Illustrated History of New Zealand*, Auckland, 1986, pp 353–72.

Sinclair, K., 'The Red Hand of Tamaki', *NZ Listener*, 7 January 1978, pp 10–12.

Sinclair, K., *Walter Nash*, Auckland University Press, Auckland, 1976.

Skinner, T., and Berry, J., *Man to Man*, Whitcoulls, Christchurch, 1980.

Stone, R., 'The Political Response to the Question of Abortion in New Zealand from 1970–75', thesis, University of Auckland, 1977.

Strachan, D. J., 'Press Coverage of the 1975 and 1978 General Election Campaigns', thesis, University of Otago, 1980.

Swift, B., 'Bob Jones', *Jet Set*, August–September, 1980, pp 21–24.

Taylor, A., 'Prophet Rejected', *NZ Monthly Review*, v 16, no 172, November 1975, pp 1–3.

Taylor, R., 'Broken Wings', *NZ Herald*, 11 October 1997.

Templeton, H., *All Honourable Men: Inside the Muldoon Cabinet*, Auckland University Press, Auckland, 1995.

Templeton, I., and Eunson, K., *Election '69: An Independent Survey of the New Zealand Political Scene*, A. H. and A. W. Reed, Wellington, 1969.

Templeton, I., and Eunson, K., *In the Balance: Election '72*, John McIndoe, Dunedin, 1972.

Templeton, M., *Human Rights and Sporting Contacts: New Zealand Attitudes to Race Relations in South Africa 1921–94*, Auckland University Press, Auckland, 1998.

Thakur, R., *In Defence of New Zealand: Foreign Policy Choices in a Nuclear Age*, Westview, Boulder, 1986.

Thorn, S. B., 'Petrocorp', thesis, University of Auckland, 1984.

Trickett, P., 'In Perspective: The Moyle Affair', *NZ Listener*, 27 May 1978, pp 8–10.

Trickett, P., 'Justice is the issue', *NZ Listener*, 29 July 1978, pp 26–7.

Trotter, A. (ed), *Fifty Years of New Zealand Foreign Policy Making*, University of Otago Press, Dunedin, 1993.

Upton, S., *The Withering of the State*, Allen and Unwin/Port Nicholson, Wellington, 1987.

Volkerling, M. (ed), *The Politics of Education*, Auckland University Students Association, Auckland, 1969.

Vowles, J., and Aimer, P., *Voters' Vengeance: The 1990 Election in New Zealand and the Fate of the Fourth Labour Government*, Auckland University Press, Auckland, 1993.

Vowles, J., Aimer, P., et al. *Towards Consensus: The 1993 Election in New Zealand and the Transition to Proportional Representation*, Auckland University Press, Auckland, 1995.

Vowles, J., Aimer, P., et al. *Voters' Victory? New Zealand's First Election Under Proportional Representation*, Auckland University Press, Auckland, 1998.

Walker, R., *Ka Whawhai Tonu Matou – Struggle Without End*, Penguin, Auckland, 1990.

Walker, R., *Nga Tau Tohetohe – Years of Anger*, Penguin, Auckland, 1987.

Walker, S., *Rogernomics: Reshaping New Zealand's Economy*, GP Books, Auckland, 1989.

Wallace, B., 'What Now Brown Cow? The Impasse in New Zealand Japan Trade Relations', *NZ International Review*, May–June 1978, pp 11–13.

Wane, J., 'Still a Wasp in the Beehive', *Sunday,* 24 June 1990.

Waring, M., *Counting for Nothing: What Men Value and What Women Are Worth*, Allen and Unwin, Wellington, 1988.

Wilson, J. O., *New Zealand Parliamentary Record 1940–1984*, Government Printer, Wellington, 1985.

Wilson, R., *From Manapouri to Aramoana: The Battle for New Zealand's Environment*, Earthworks Press, Auckland, 1982.

Wilson-Roberts, G., 'The 1988 CER Review: A Negotiation Analysis', thesis, University of Auckland, 1994.

Wood, G. A., *Governing New Zealand*, Longman Paul, Auckland, 1988.

Wood G. A., *Ministers and Members in the New Zealand Parliament*, Otago University Press, Dunedin, 1996.

Wood, G. A., 'The National Party', in H. Gold (ed), *New Zealand Politics in Perspective*, Longman Paul, Auckland, 1985, pp 172–88.

Wood, G. A., *Why National Won*, John McIndoe, Dunedin, 1975.

Woodbury, A. P., 'Social Credit and the Rangitikei By-election, 1978: An Investigation of the Role of Party Organization', thesis, University of Otago, 1981.

Woodfield, T., 'Marketing in the Middle East', *NZ International Review*, March–April 1983, pp 22–23.

Wright, V., *David Lange, Prime Minister: A Profile*, Allen and Unwin, Port Nicholson Press, Wellington, 1984.

Zavos, S., *The Real Muldoon*, Fourth Estate Books, Wellington, 1978.

Index